# CONTENTS

# Michael H... ...vée

**FOUNDER AND ...**
**THE MESCON ...**
**ATLANTA, GEORGIA**

**REGENTS PROFESSOR OF MANAGEMENT,**
**RAMSEY CHAIR OF PRIVATE ENTERPRISE**
**ANDREW YOUNG SCHOOL**
**OF POLICY STUDIES,**
**GEORGIA STATE UNIVERSITY**

**...SS**

**C. ALLEN PAUL DISTINGUISHED CHAIR**
**GROSSMONT COLLEGE**

# John V. Thill

**CHIEF EXECUTIVE OFFICER**
**COMMUNICATION SPECIALISTS**
**OF AMERICA**

Prentice Hall

Upper Saddle River, New Jersey, 07458

**Acquisitions Editor:** David Parker
**Editor-in-Chief:** Jeff Shelstad
**Director of Development:** Steve Deitmer
**Development Editor:** Audrey Regan
**Development Editor, Active Learning Technologies:** John Reisbord
**Editorial Assistant:** Ashley Keim
**Media Project Manager:** Anthony Palmiotta
**Marketing Manager:** Debbie Clare
**Managing Editor (Production):** Judy Leale
**Production Editor:** Michele Foresta
**Production Assistant:** Dianne Falcone
**Permissions Coordinator:** Suzanne Grappi
**Associate Director, Manufacturing:** Vincent Scelta
**Production Manager:** Arnold Vila
**Design Director, Active Learning Technologies:** Eve Adams
**Design Manager:** Patricia Smythe
**Art Director:** Cheryl Asherman
**Interior/Cover Design:** Cheryl Asherman
**Cover Illustration/Photo:** Cheryl Asherman
**Illustrator (Interior):** Carlisle Communications, Ltd.
**Associate Director, Multimedia Production:** Karen Goldsmith
**Manager, Print Production:** Christy Mahon
**Composition:** Carlisle Communications, Ltd.
**Full-Service Project Management:** Lynn Steines/Carlisle Communications, Ltd.
**Printer/Binder:** Quebecor/World Color

Credits and acknowledgments borrowed from other sources and reproduced, with permission, in this textbook appear on page 355 within text.

Pearson Education LTD.
Pearson Education Australia PTY, Limited
Pearson Education Singapore, Pte. Ltd
Pearson Education North Asia Ltd
Pearson Education, Canada, Ltd
Pearson Educación de Mexico, S.A. de C.V.
Pearson Education–Japan
Pearson Education Malaysia, Pte. Ltd

10 9 8 7 6 5 4 3 2 1
ISBN 0-13-066359-X

## CHAPTER 8

## TECHNOLOGY AND INFORMATION MANAGEMENT   135

## CHAPTER 9

## PRODUCTION OF QUALITY GOODS AND SERVICES   157

*Several features referenced throughout the text are offered on the online version. They include the following:

**Component Chapter A: Fundamentals of the Internet and E-Commerce**

**Component Chapter B: Business Law, Taxes, and the U.S. Legal System**

**Component Chapter C: Risk Management and Insurance**

**Component Chapter D: Careers in Business and the Employment Search**

**Appendix: Your Business Plan**

**Focusing on E-Business Today**

**A Case for Critical Thinking**

**Business Plan Pro**

# activebook™ EXPERIENCE USER GUIDE

## > What Is the activebook™ Experience?

The activebook experience is a new kind of textbook that combines the best elements of print and electronic media. In addition to this print version, you'll have access to an online version of your book that is enhanced by a variety of multimedia elements. These include active exercises, interactive quizzes, and poll questions. These elements give you a chance to explore the text's issues in more depth.

## > How to Redeem Your Access Code

Redeeming your access code is fast and easy. To complete this one-time registration process, go to **www.prenhall.com/myactivebook**. Follow the new user link to register and redeem your access code. Enter the access code bound inside your book, and complete the simple registration form. When you are done, click **submit**. It will take a few minutes to redeem your access code, and then you will be taken to your homepage.

## > The activebook Experience Homepage

In this section you'll become acquainted with the features of the activebook experience. Once you're familiar with them, you'll be on your way.

The Toolbar

The Smart Calendar and Other Resources

Additional Resources

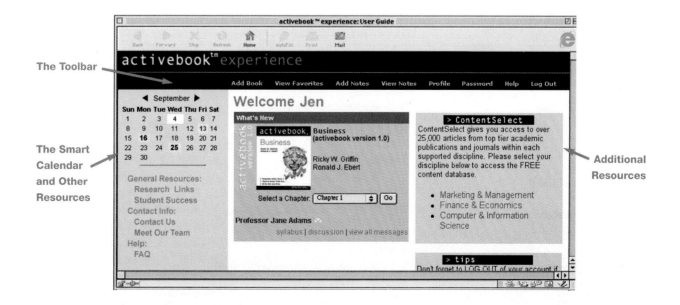

# 1. The Toolbar

Let's begin with the commands in the toolbar near the top of the homepage. This bar features eight commands: **add book**, **view favorites**, **add notes**, **view notes**, **profile**, **password**, **help**, and **log out**.

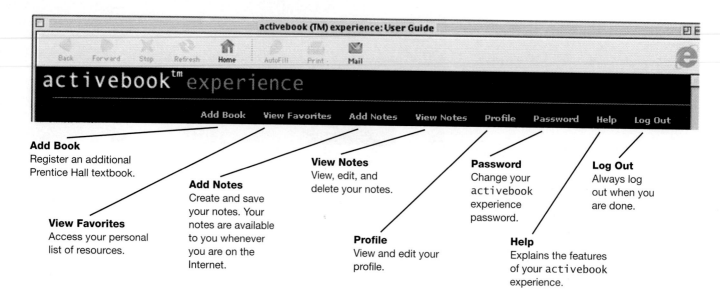

**Add Book**
Register an additional Prentice Hall textbook.

**View Favorites**
Access your personal list of resources.

**Add Notes**
Create and save your notes. Your notes are available to you whenever you are on the Internet.

**View Notes**
View, edit, and delete your notes.

**Profile**
View and edit your profile.

**Password**
Change your activebook experience password.

**Help**
Explains the features of your activebook experience.

**Log Out**
Always log out when you are done.

Now let's take a look at the features presented in the navigation bar on the left side of the screen.

# 2. The Smart Calendar and Other Resources

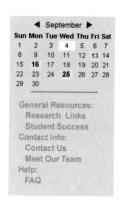

**The Smart Calendar**
Instantly view all the activities for the month by clicking on a date.

**Research Links**
Provides a selection of annotated links to additional resources and search sites.

**Student Success**
Links to Prentice Hall's Student Success Web site. You will find numerous features designed to help you through your educational journey (for example, career paths, money matters, and employment opportunities).

**Contact Us**
Contact Prentice Hall either via telephone or e-mail to share your ideas about your activebook experience or to ask questions.

**FAQ**
Find answers to frequently asked questions about your activebook experience.

# 3. Additional Resources

After redeeming your access code, you can make use of the following resources.

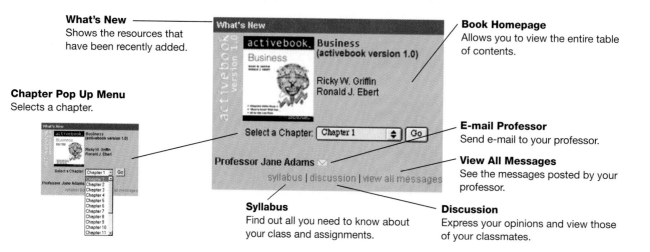

**What's New**
Shows the resources that have been recently added.

**Chapter Pop Up Menu**
Selects a chapter.

**Book Homepage**
Allows you to view the entire table of contents.

**E-mail Professor**
Send e-mail to your professor.

**View All Messages**
See the messages posted by your professor.

**Syllabus**
Find out all you need to know about your class and assignments.

**Discussion**
Express your opinions and view those of your classmates.

## > Finding Your Professor

If your professor has posted course material, you can create a link to him or her on your homepage. Once connected to your professor, you can access the **syllabus**, **view messages** from him or her, and **e-mail** him or her.

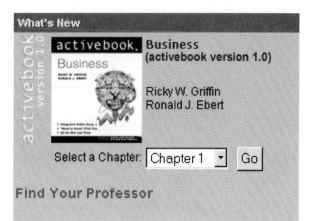

**To Find Your Professor**
- Click on **find your professor**.
- Search for your professor's name (using his or her last name or your school's name). Then select it.
- Click **submit** and you will return to your homepage.

## > Viewing Your Professor's Syllabus

If your professor is using the **syllabus** feature, click the **syllabus** link to check assignments and course announcements.

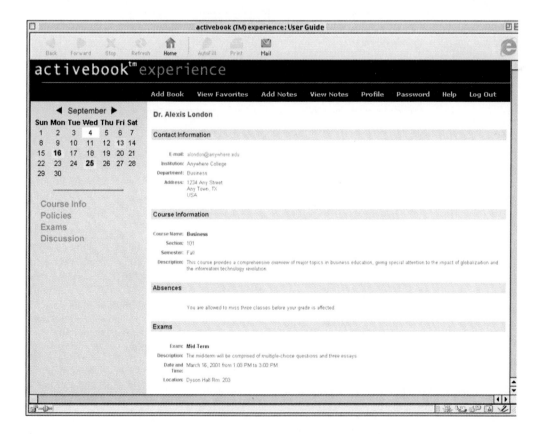

## > Exploring the activebook Experience

When you're ready to begin, select a chapter. In every chapter you will find: the **what's ahead** section, **objectives**, **active concept checks**, **key terms**, and a **chapter wrap-up**. Each chapter may also include a **gearing-up quiz**, **video examples** or **exercises**, **audio examples** or **exercises**, **active polls**, and **active figures**, **maps**, and **graphs**.

Let's take a look at these elements. Every chapter begins with **what's ahead**. This section tells you what material the chapter will cover.

Clicking on any link in the chapter outline takes you to the core text.

The **Book Home** link takes you to the table of contents for the entire book, where the full chapter titles are provided.

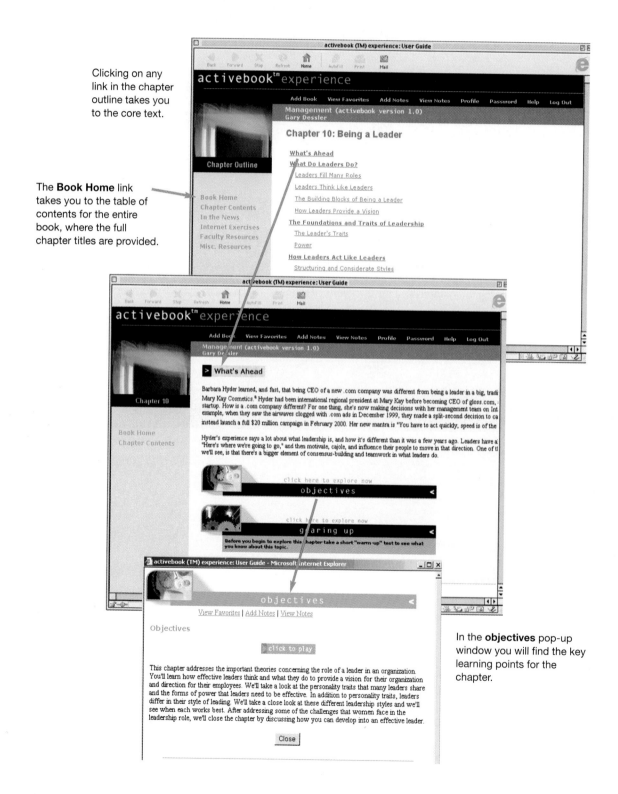

In the **objectives** pop-up window you will find the key learning points for the chapter.

Another element that can appear in the **what's ahead** section is the **gearing up quiz**. This quiz is designed to get you thinking about important topics in the chapter.

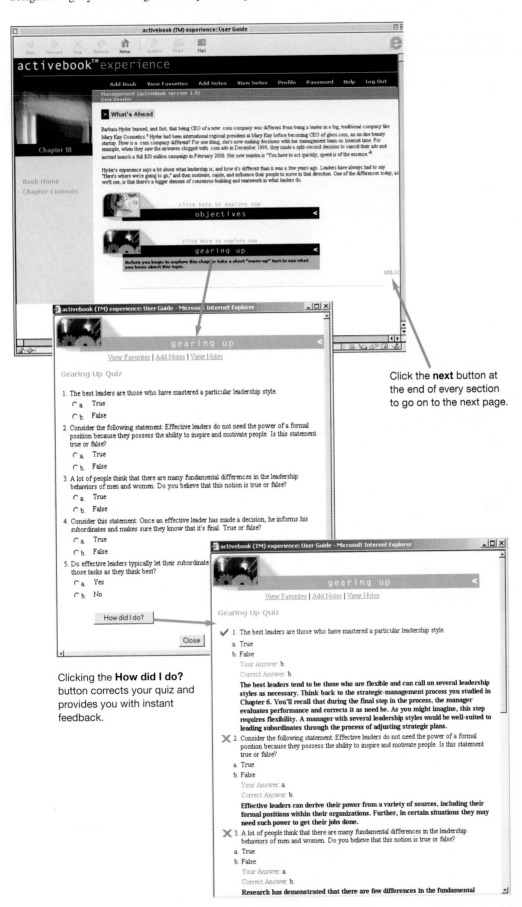

Click the **next** button at the end of every section to go on to the next page.

Clicking the **How did I do?** button corrects your quiz and provides you with instant feedback.

After **gearing up**, you're ready to start reading the chapter. Chapters are divided into major sections.

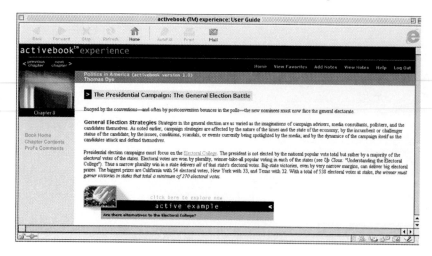

As you read each section, you will encounter the active elements. Let's become acquainted with some of them.

**Professor's Comments** is where you can find your professor's thoughts on a particular topic.

Click on a **key term** to read its definition.

Listen to quotes from key figures by clicking on the **audio example**.

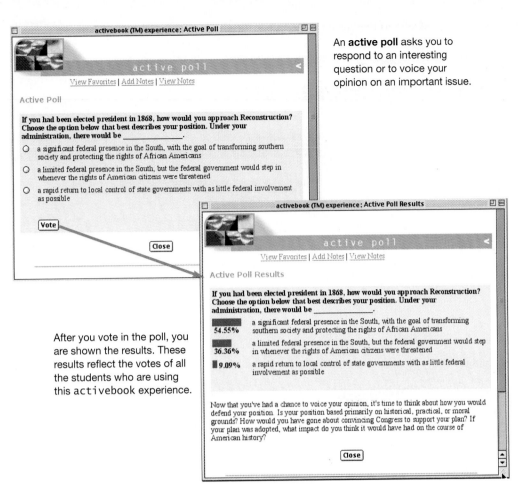

An **active poll** asks you to respond to an interesting question or to voice your opinion on an important issue.

After you vote in the poll, you are shown the results. These results reflect the votes of all the students who are using this activebook experience.

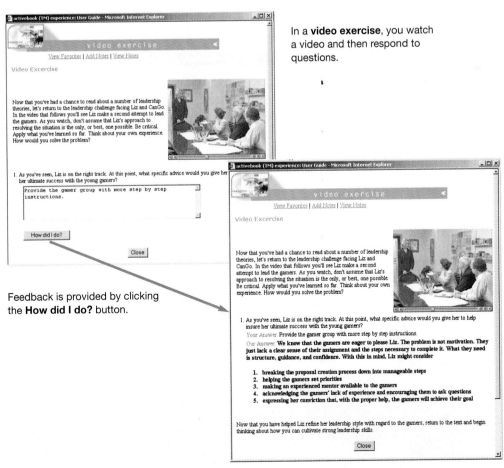

In a **video exercise**, you watch a video and then respond to questions.

Feedback is provided by clicking the **How did I do?** button.

In addition to **video exercises** you might also find an **active exercise** or an **active example**.

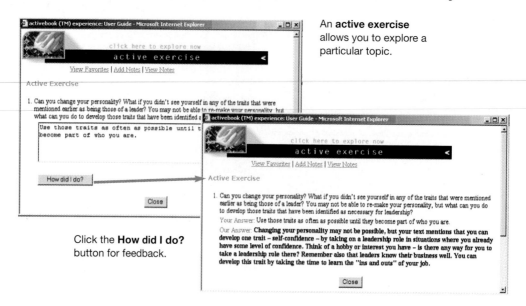

An **active exercise** allows you to explore a particular topic.

Click the **How did I do?** button for feedback.

**Active concept checks** occur at the end of every major section.

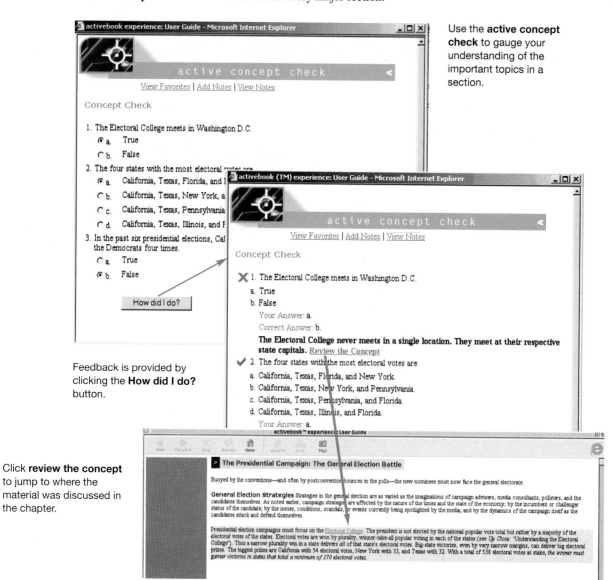

Use the **active concept check** to gauge your understanding of the important topics in a section.

Feedback is provided by clicking the **How did I do?** button.

Click **review the concept** to jump to where the material was discussed in the chapter.

All of your end-of-chapter resources and a practice quiz can be found in the **chapter wrap-up** section.

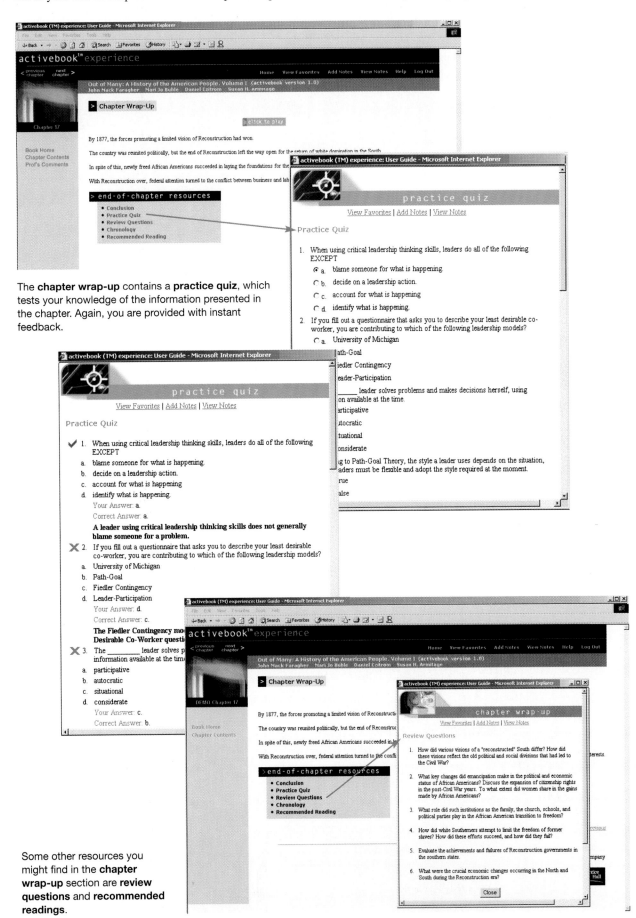

The **chapter wrap-up** contains a **practice quiz**, which tests your knowledge of the information presented in the chapter. Again, you are provided with instant feedback.

Some other resources you might find in the **chapter wrap-up** section are **review questions** and **recommended readings**.

# CHAPTER 1

# Fundamentals of Business and Economics

## > What's Ahead

### INSIDE BUSINESS TODAY
### WEBTIME STORIES: YAHOO!—THE SEARCH ENGINE THAT COULD

Successful entrepreneurs are by definition creative people. They invent new technologies, and they figure out how to open new windows of opportunity in a marketplace. Sometimes they even unleash whole new industries, like Jerry Yang and David Filo did.

Just as Net mania was beginning to flower in 1994, Yang and Filo, two Stanford Ph.D. candidates, noticed that the rich and diverse World Wide Web was becoming increasingly impossible for users to navigate. So for fun they built a straightforward system that sorted and classified their favorite Web sites into categories. Then they posted their lists onto the university's Web site and named their site Yahoo!, an acronym for "Yet Another Hierarchical Officious Oracle."

Working around the clock, the two strained to make sense of the tidal wave of information people were posting online. But they never thought of making a business out of their hobby until university officials asked them to find a company that was willing to host their Web site. That's when Yang and Filo knew they were onto something big. Like most entrepreneurs, they needed money. And they needed people who could help them with the aspects of a business they didn't understand. Yang and Filo found both.

Jerry Yang and David Filo transformed their hobby into a new kind of media company when they developed Yahoo!

With a million dollars and a new CEO, Timothy Koogle, Yahoo! set up shop in Silicon Valley, and recruited a staff to help categorize the Web sites. In 1996 company stock was sold to the investing public. Yahoo! was on the road to billions. Still, Yang and Filo stuck with the fundamentals of business. That is, they listened to customers and gave them abundant reasons to visit the Yahoo! site and to stay for awhile. They also kept the Yahoo! site fast, current, and easy to use. Moreover, Yahoo! set itself apart from competitors by using humans to filter, categorize, and add Web sites to its directory. Excite, Infoseek, and Lycos use computer software programs to catalog Web sites and automate the search process.

Today Yahoo! is much more than a mere directory. Responding to customer requests, Yahoo! has metamorphosed into an interactive information service. Millions of people use Yahoo! every day for e-mail, instant messaging, Web photo albums, personal homepages, shopping, bill paying, games, auctions, news, and much more. In fact, Yahoo! generates more than $1 billion in annual sales and over $60 million in profits by selling absolutely nothing. Instead, Yahoo! charges for advertising on its Web site, providing advertisers with instant feedback on every ad—such as how many people saw the ad, how many clicked futher, and the target group to which they belong. Yahoo! also takes a small percentage of sales earned by featured e-merchants who sign on to hawk their goods and services in one of the largest marketplaces on the Internet. But with 90 percent of its revenue coming from advertising—most of which comes from other Internet companies—Yahoo's stock was clobbered in the early twenty-first century Internet shakeout .

Still, Yang and Filo are confident that Yahoo! will remain profitable and achieve long-term success. After all, with over 166 million registered users, and Web sites in more than 12 languages and 24 countries, Yahoo! is indeed a promising young company. Moreover, Yang and Filo know that to compete in today's economy you must be innovative and fast, and you must anticipate whatever opportunities and challenges the restless Internet may present.[1]

## > objectives

**Take a moment to familiarize yourself with the key objectives of this chapter.**

## > gearing up

**Before you begin reading this chapter, try a short warm-up activity.**

### > Why Study Business?

Business is everywhere. Whether you're logged on to the Yahoo! Web site, flying in an airplane, watching a movie, buying a CD over the Internet, enjoying your favorite coffee drink, or withdrawing money from an ATM machine, you're involved in someone else's business. In fact, you engage in business just about every day of your life. But like many college students, for most of your life you've been observing and enjoying the efforts of others. Now that you're taking an introduction to business course, however, your perspective is about to change.

In this course you'll learn what it takes to run a successful business such as Yahoo! As you progress though this course, you'll begin to look at things from the eyes of an employee or a manager instead of a consumer. You'll develop a fundamental business vocabulary that will help you keep up with the latest news and make more informed decisions. By participating in classroom discussions and completing the chapter exercises you'll gain some valuable critical-thinking, problem-solving, team-building, and communication skills that you can use on the job and throughout your life.

Should you decide to pursue a career in business, this course will introduce you to a variety of jobs that exist in fields such as accounting, economics, human resources, management, finance, marketing, and so on. You'll see how people who work in these business functions contribute to the success of a company as a whole. You'll gain insight into the types of skills and knowledge these jobs require. And most important, you'll discover that a career in business today is fascinating, challenging, and often-times quite rewarding.

## > active poll

**What do you think? Voice your opinion and find out what others have to say.**

### > What Is a Business?

Like David Filo and Jerry Yang, many people start a new **business**—a profit-seeking activity that provides goods and services that satisfy consumers' needs. Businesses play a number of key roles in society and the economy: They provide society with necessities such as housing, clothing, food, transportation, communication, and health care; they provide people with jobs and a means to prosper; they pay taxes that are used to build highways, fund education, and provide grants for scientific research; and they reinvest their profits in the economy, thereby creating a higher standard of living and quality of life for society as a whole.

The driving force behind most businesses is the prospect of earning a **profit**—what remains after all expenses have been deducted from business revenue. Still, not every business exists to earn a profit. Some organizations exist to provide society with a social or educational service instead. Such **not-for-profit organizations** include museums, schools, public universities, symphonies, libraries, and government agencies. Even though these organizations do not have a profit motive, they must still run efficiently and effectively to achieve their goals. Thus, the business principles discussed throughout this textbook—competition, marketing, finance, management, quality, and so on—apply to both profit-seeking and not-for-profit organizations.

## GOODS-PRODUCING BUSINESSES VERSUS SERVICE BUSINESSES

Most businesses can be classified into two broad categories (or industry sectors): goods-producing businesses and service businesses. **Goods-producing businesses** produce tangible goods by engaging in activities such as manufacturing, construction, mining, and agriculture. **Service businesses** produce intangible products (ones that cannot be held in your hand) and include those whose principal product is finance, insurance, transportation, utilities, wholesale and retail trade, banking, entertainment, health care, repairs, and information.

Of course, many companies produce both services and goods. Consider IBM, for example. IBM manufactures computers and other business machines, but at least one-third of IBM's sales come from computer-related services such as systems design, consulting, and product support.[2] Similarly, a manufacturer of industrial and farm equipment such as Caterpillar must provide its customers with services such as product training and technical support. Even though it becomes more and more difficult to classify a company as either a goods-producing business or a service business, such classification is useful for reporting and analysis purposes.

Most service businesses are **labor-intensive businesses;** that is, they rely predominantly on human resources to prosper. A consulting firm is an example of a labor-intensive business because its existence is heavily dependent on the knowledge and skills of its consultants. Even though the firm requires money to operate, a group of consultants can go into business simply by purchasing some computers and some telephones. Businesses that require large amounts of money or equipment to get started and to operate are **capital-intensive businesses.** Airlines, electric utilities, telecommunications companies, and automobile manufacturers are examples of capital-intensive businesses. Although each of these businesses requires a large pool of labor to operate, it would be difficult to start them without substantial investments in buildings, machinery, and equipment.

## GROWTH OF THE SERVICE SECTOR

Services have always played an important role in the U.S. economy. For more than 60 years, they accounted for half of all U.S. employment. In the mid-1980s services became the engine of growth for the U.S. economy (see Exhibit 1.1).[3] In fact, most of the increase in U.S. employment from 1985 to

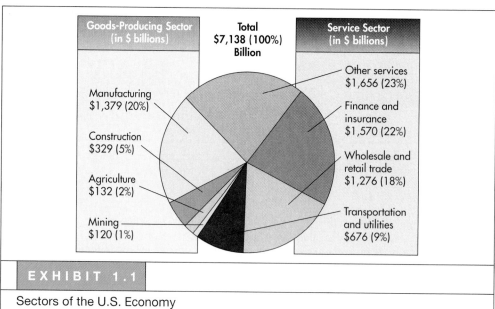

**EXHIBIT 1.1**

Sectors of the U.S. Economy

The service sector accounts for 72 percent of U.S. economic output, and the goods-producing sector accounts for the remaining 28 percent.

the present has been generated by the service sector. Today about half of the 1,000 largest U.S. companies are service-based.[4]

Economists project that the number of service-related jobs will continue to increase—from about 94 million (or 72 percent of the 130 million or so people in today's workforce) to about 112 million by 2006. In contrast, employment growth in the goods-producing sector is projected to remain flat through 2006 (see Exhibit 1.2).[5] The projected growth in the service sector is attributable to several factors:

- *Consumers have more disposable income.* The 76 million baby boomers in the United States (people born between 1946 and 1964) are in their peak earning years. These consumers find themselves with more disposable income and look for services to help them invest, travel, relax, and stay fit.

- *Services target changing demographic patterns and lifestyle trends.* The United States has more elderly people, more single people living alone, more two-career households, and more single parents than ever before. These trends create opportunities for service companies that can help people with all the tasks they no longer have time for, including home maintenance, food service, and child care.[6]

- *Services are needed to support complex goods and new technology.* Computers, home entertainment centers, recreational vehicles, security systems, and automated production equipment are examples of products that require specialized installation, repair, user training, or extensive support services. As new technology is incorporated into more and more products, companies will need to provide more of these types of product-support services to remain competitive.

- *Companies are seeking professional advice to remain competitive.* Many firms turn to consultants to find ways to cut costs, refine business processes, and become more competitive. In addition, the continued growth of global marketing and e-commerce requires more professional support services.

- *Barriers to entry are low for services conducting e-commerce.* Capital-intensive businesses generally have high barriers to entry, which means that conditions exist that make entry into these businesses extremely difficult. Such conditions include significant capital requirements, high learning curves, tightly controlled markets, strict licensing procedures, the need for highly skilled employees or the use of specialized facilities. By contrast, the barriers to entry for most companies transacting electronic commerce are low. Just about any company can build a Web site and enter the electronic marketplace.

- *Internet economy is growing at an unprecedented rate.* Companies or parts of companies that generate revenue from **electronic commerce (e-commerce)**—buying and selling over the Internet—account for more than 2.5 million jobs. Although these jobs employ just a fraction of the 130 million-member U.S. workforce, they are jobs that did not previously exist, and many are service-related.[7]

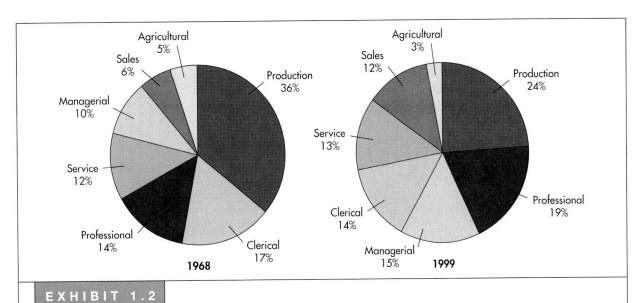

**EXHIBIT 1.2**

The Shifting Economy

Over the past 30 years, workers have moved out of production and into professional jobs.

**active concept check**                                                    **<**

Now let's take a moment to test your knowledge of the concepts you have studied in this section.

## **>** What Is an Economic System?

Whether you're running a service or a goods-producing business, a capital-intensive or a labor-intensive business, world economic situations affect all businesses that compete in the global economy. Thus, running a successful business today requires a firm understanding of basic economic principles, of the different economic systems in the world, and of how businesses compete in the global economy.

**Economics** is the study of how a society uses its scarce resources to produce and distribute goods and services. All societies must deal with the same basic questions: How should limited economic resources be used to satisfy society's needs? What goods and services should be produced? Who should produce them? How should these goods and services be divided among the population? In some countries these decisions are made by individuals (or households) when they decide how to spend or invest their income and by businesses when they decide what kinds of goods and services to produce; in other countries these decisions are made by governments.

Economists call the resources that societies use to produce goods and services *factors of production.* To maximize a company's profit, businesses use five **factors of production** in the most efficient way possible:

- **Natural resources**—things that are useful in their natural state, such as land, forests, minerals, and water

- **Human resources**—anyone (from company presidents to grocery clerks) who works to produce goods and services

- **Capital**—resources (such as money, computers, machines, tools, and buildings) that a business needs to produce goods and services

- **Entrepreneurs**—people such as Jerry Yang and David Filo who are innovative and willing to take risks to create and operate new businesses (see Exhibit 1.3)

- **Knowledge**—the collective intelligence of an organization

Traditionally, a business was considered to have an advantage if it was located in a country with a plentiful supply of natural resources, human resources, capital, and entrepreneurs. But in a global economy, companies can obtain capital from one part of the world, purchase supplies from another, and locate production facilities in still another. Furthermore, companies can relocate their operations to wherever they find a steady supply of affordable workers. Thus, economists no longer point to the proximity of these four factors of production as a requirement for success. Instead, they consider knowledge to be the key economic resource.[8] Today, minds rather than mines are the source of economic prosperity.

How important is knowledge in the global economy? Consider this: Economists agree that the seven key industries of the next few decades will be microelectronics, biotechnology, composite materials, telecommunications, civilian aviation, robotics, and computers.[9] All of these are brainpower industries. Tomorrow's workers will be freelancers, contractors, and analysts-for-hire, and their work will be brain-intensive instead of labor-intensive. Thus, countries with the greatest supply of knowledge workers and ones with economic systems that give workers the freedom to pursue their own economic interests will have the greatest advantage in the global marketplace.

| The Company | Its Start |
|---|---|
| Clorox | In May 1913, five men pooled $100 each and started Clorox. The group had no experience in bleach-making chemistry but suspected that the brine found in salt ponds in San Francisco Bay could be converted into bleach. |
| The Limited | In 1963, 26-year-old Leslie Wexner left his family's retail store after having an argument with his father. He opened one small store in a strip mall in Columbus, Ohio. Today the company operates more than 5,000 stores in the United States. |
| Gateway 2000 | Using $10,000 he borrowed from his grandmother, Ted Waitt started the company in his father's South Dakota barn in 1985. Because a typical computer-industry campaign would have been too costly, Waitt invented its now-famous faux-cowhide boxes. Today Gateway's revenues exceed $5 billion. |
| Coca-Cola | Pharmacist John Pemberton invented a soft drink in his backyard in 1886. Asa Chandler bought the company for $2,300 in 1891. Today it is worth over $170 billion. |
| E & J Gallo Winery | The brothers invested $6,000 but had no wine-making experience when they rented their first warehouse in California. They learned wine making by studying pamphlets at the local library. |
| Marriott | Willard Marriott and his fiancee-partner started a 9-seat A & W soda fountain with $3,000 in 1927. They demonstrated a knack for hospitality and clever marketing from the beginning. |
| Nike | In the early 1960s, Philip Knight and his college track coach sold imported Japanese sneakers from the trunk of a station wagon. Start-up costs totaled $1,000. |
| United Parcel Service | In 1907 two Seattle teenagers pooled their cash, came up with $100, and began a message and parcel delivery service for local merchants. |
| William Wrigley Jr. | In 1891 young Wrigley Jr. started selling baking soda in Chicago. To entice new customers, he threw in two packages of chewing gum with every sale. Guess what the customers were more excited about? |
| Amazon.com | In 1994 Jeff Bezos came across a report projecting annual Web growth at 2,300 percent. So Bezos left his Wall Street job, headed to Seattle in an aging Chevy Blazer, and drafted his business plan enroute. His e-business Amazon.com initially focused on selling books over the Internet, but Bezos later expanded his product offerings to include toys, consumer electronics, software, home improvement products, and more. Today Amazon.com is exploding in size. Although the company is still profitless, it generates over $1.6 billion in annual revenue. |

**EXHIBIT 1.3**

Rags to Riches

Few start-up companies are resource rich. Often they become successful because ingenuity is substituted for capital.

## TYPES OF ECONOMIC SYSTEMS

The role that individuals and government play in allocating a society's resources depend on the society's **economic system,** the basic set of rules for allocating a society's resources to satisfy its citizens' needs. Two main economic systems exist in the world today: *free-market systems* and *planned systems.*

### Free-Market System

In a **free-market system,** individuals are free to decide what products to produce, how to produce them, whom to sell them to, and at what price to sell them. Thus, they have the chance to succeed—or to fail—by their own efforts. **Capitalism** is the term most often used to describe the free-market system, which owes its philosophical origins to eighteenth-century philosophers such as Adam Smith. According to Smith, in the ideal capitalist economy (pure capitalism) the *market* (an arrangement between buyer and seller to trade goods and services) serves as a self-correcting mechanism—an "invisible hand" to ensure the production of the goods that society wants in the quantities that society wants, without regulation of any kind.[10]

Because the market is its own regulator, Smith was opposed to government intervention. He believed that if anyone's prices or wages strayed from acceptable levels that were set for everyone, the force of competition would drive them back. In modern practice, however, the government sometimes intervenes in free-market systems to influence prices and wages or to change the way resources are allocated. This practice of limited intervention is called *mixed capitalism,* which is the economic system of the United States. Other countries with variations of this economic system include Canada, Germany, and Japan. Under mixed capitalism, the pursuit of private gain is regarded as a worthwhile goal that ultimately benefits society as a whole. This is not the case in a planned system.

### Planned System

In a **planned system,** governments control all or part of the allocation of resources and limit the freedom of choice in order to accomplish government goals. Because social equality is a major goal of planned systems, private enterprise and the pursuit of private gain are generally regarded as wasteful and exploitative.

The planned system that allows individuals the least degree of economic freedom is **communism,** which still exists in such countries as North Korea and Cuba. (Keep in mind that even though communism and socialism are discussed here as economic systems, they can be political and social systems as well.) The degree to which communism is actually practiced varies. In its purest form, almost all resources are under government control. Private ownership is restricted largely to personal and household items. Resource allocation is handled through rigid centralized planning by a handful of government officials who decide what goods to produce, how to produce them, and to whom they should be distributed.[11] Although pure communism still has its supporters, the future of communism is dismal. As economists Lester Thurow and Robert Heilbroner put it, "It's a great deal easier to design and assemble the skeleton of a mighty economy than to run it."[12]

Look at Russia. After decades of economic failure and the associated public unrest, the republics that were formerly part of the Soviet Union began restructuring their communist economies. Overnight, the entire Soviet system—its ideology, institutions, and embracing party apparatus—was dismantled. Despite the fervent efforts of Westerners and Russian reformers to shift to a more market-driven system, internal financial and economic turmoil forced the country to throw on the brakes (as Chapter 3 discusses in detail). As a result, Russia moved only partly down the path to a free-market system. Now the country is operating on a system of barters and IOUs fueled by shortages of money and supplies—a system that some economists say grows stranger by the day.[13]

**Socialism,** by contrast, lies somewhere between capitalism and communism in the degree of economic freedom that it permits. Like communism, socialism involves a relatively high degree of government planning and some government ownership of land and capital resources (such as buildings and equipment). However, government involvement is limited to industries considered vital to the common welfare, such as transportation, utilities, medicine, steel, and communications. In these industries, the government owns or controls all the facilities and determines what will be produced and how the output will be distributed. Private ownership is permitted in industries that are not considered vital, and both businesses and individuals are allowed to benefit from their own efforts. However, taxes are high in socialist states because the government absorbs the costs of medical care, education, subsidized housing, and other social services.

### active poll

**What do you think? Voice your opinion and find out what others have to say.**

### THE TREND TOWARD PRIVATIZATION

Although varying degrees of socialism and communism are practiced around the world today, several socialist and communist economies are moving toward free-market economic systems. Anxious to unload unprofitable businesses for badly needed cash and to experiment with free-market capitalism, countries such as Great Britain, Mexico, Argentina, Israel, France, Sweden, and China are **privatizing** some of their government-owned enterprises by selling them to privately held firms. Great Britain, for example, has sold the national phone company, the national steel company, the national sugar company, Heathrow Airport, water suppliers, and the company that makes Rover automobiles. Hopes are high that converting certain industries to private ownership will enable them to compete more effectively in the global marketplace.[14]

Nevertheless, many planned economic systems are discovering that moving toward a free-market system and converting state-owned enterprises into world-class corporations is a formidable task without existing blueprints. Some countries are rushing forward without building effective banking or legal systems to protect their emerging private industries. Others, such as China, are being met with strong resistance from hard-line communists. Still, China expects to privatize more than 60 percent of its state-owned enterprises by 2005. If successful in its privatization attempts, China will indeed serve as a role model.[15]

## > active concept check

**Now let's take a moment to test your knowledge of the concepts you have studied in this section.**

## > How Does a Free-Market Economic System Work?

Earlier in this chapter we noted that in a free-market system the marketplace determines what goods and services get produced. In this section we will discuss the underlying elements or principles that must be present for the free market to work in an orderly fashion. These concepts include the theory of supply and demand, competition, and government intervention.

## THE THEORY OF SUPPLY AND DEMAND IN A FREE-MARKET SYSTEM

The theory of supply and demand is the immediate driving force of the free-market system. It is the basic tool that economists use to describe how the market works in determining prices and the quantity of goods produced. **Demand** refers to the amount of a good or service that consumers will buy at a given time at various prices. **Supply** refers to the quantities of a good or service that producers will provide on a particular date at various prices. Simply put, *demand* refers to the behavior of buyers, whereas *supply* refers to the behavior of sellers. Exhibit 1.4 shows how the two work together to impose a kind of order on the free-market system.

On the surface, the theory of supply and demand seems little more than common sense. Consumers would buy more when the price is low and buy less when the price is high. Producers would offer more when the price is high and offer less when the price is low. In other words, the quantity supplied and the quantity demanded would continuously interact, and the balance between them at any given moment would be reflected by the current price on the open market.

However, a quick look at any real-life market situation shows you that pricing isn't that simple. To a large degree, pricing depends on the type of product being sold. When the price of gasoline goes up, consumers may cut down a little, but most wouldn't stop driving, even if the price were to double. Moreover, a rise in housing prices could set off rumors that prices will rise even more. As a result consumers might rush to buy available homes, forcing the prices to rise higher still.

Nevertheless, in broad terms, the interaction of supply and demand regulates a free-market system by determining what is produced and in what amounts. For example, a movie studio might produce more comedies if ticket sales for similar films are brisk. On the other hand, it might decide to produce fewer comedies and more action-adventure movies if attendance at comedies lags. The result of such decisions—in theory, at least—is that consumers will get what they want and producers will earn a profit by keeping up with public demand.

### Buyer's Perspective

The forces of supply and demand determine the market price for products and services. Say that you're shopping for blue jeans, and the pair you want is priced at $35. This is more than you can afford, so you don't make the purchase. When the store puts them on sale the following week for $18, however, you run right in and buy a pair.

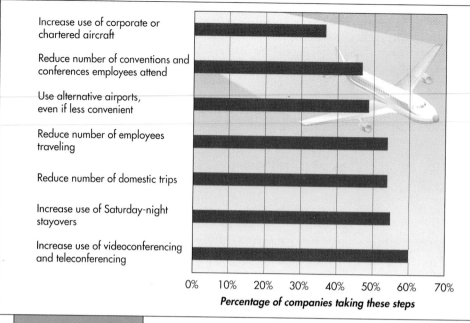

| | | | | | | | |
|---|---|---|---|---|---|---|---|

Increase use of corporate or chartered aircraft

Reduce number of conventions and conferences employees attend

Use alternative airports, even if less convenient

Reduce number of employees traveling

Reduce number of domestic trips

Increase use of Saturday-night stayovers

Increase use of videoconferencing and teleconferencing

0%   10%   20%   30%   40%   50%   60%   70%

*Percentage of companies taking these steps*

**EXHIBIT 1.4**

Effects of Higher Air Fare on Demand for Business Travel

When airlines raise their prices, demand for business travel softens as companies take steps to reduce their travel costs.

But what if the store had to buy the jeans from the manufacturer for $20? It would have made a profit selling them to you for $35, but it would lose money selling them for $18. What if the store asks to buy more from the manufacturer at $10 or $15 but the manufacturer refuses? Is there a price that will make both the supplier and the customer happy? The answer is yes—the price at which the quantity of jeans demanded equals the quantity supplied.

This relationship is shown in Exhibit 1.5. A range of possible prices is listed vertically at the left of the graph, with the lowest at the bottom and the highest at the top. Quantity of blue jeans is represented along the horizontal axis. The points plotted on the curve labeled **D** indicate that on a given day the store would sell 10 pairs of jeans if they were priced at $35, 15 pairs if they were priced at $27, and so on. The curve that describes this relationship between price and quantity demanded is a **demand curve.** (Demand curves are not necessarily curved; they may be straight lines.)

### Seller's Perspective

Now think about the situation from the seller's point of view. In general, the more profit the store can make on a particular item, the more of that item it will want to sell. This relationship can also be depicted graphically. Again, look at Exhibit 1.5. The line labeled **S** shows that the store would be willing to offer 30 pairs of jeans at $35, 25 pairs at $30, and so on. The store's willingness to carry the item increases as the price it can charge and its profit potential per item increase. In other words, as the price goes up, the quantity supplied goes up. The line tracing the relationship between price and quantity supplied is called a **supply curve.**

As much as the store would like to sell 30 pairs of jeans at $35, you and your fellow consumers are likely to want only 10 pairs at that price. If the store offered 30 pairs, therefore, it would probably be stuck with some that it would have to mark down. How does the store avoid this problem? It looks for the point at which the demand curve and the supply curve intersect, the point at which the intentions of buyers and sellers coincide. The point marked **E** in Exhibit 1.5 shows that when jeans are priced at $25, consumers are willing to buy 20 pairs of them and the store is willing to sell 20 pairs. In other words, at the price of $25, the quantity supplied and the quantity demanded are in balance. The price at this point is known as the **equilibrium price.**

Note that this intersection represents both a specific price—$25 in our example—and a specific quantity of goods—here, 20 pairs of jeans. It is also tied to a specific point in time. Note also that it is the mutual interaction between quantity demanded and quantity supplied that determines the equilibrium price.

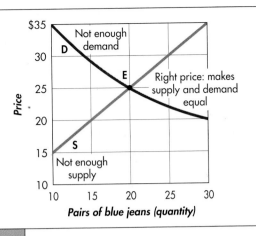

**EXHIBIT 1.5**

The Relationship Between Supply and Demand

In a free-market system, prices aren't set by the government; nor do producers alone have the final say. Instead, prices reflect the interaction of supply **(S)** and demand **(D)**. The equilibrium price **(E)** is established when the amount of a product that producers are willing to sell at a given price equals the amount that consumers are willing to buy at that price.

## COMPETITION IN A FREE-MARKET SYSTEM

In a free-market system, customers are free to buy whatever and wherever they please. Therefore, companies must compete with rivals for potential customers. **Competition** is the situation in which two or more suppliers of a product are rivals in the pursuit of the same customers.

In theory, the ideal type of competition is **pure competition,** which is characterized by marketplace conditions in which multiple buyers and sellers exist; a product or service with nearly identical features such as wheat; and the ability to easily enter and exit the marketplace. Under these conditions no single firm or group of firms in an industry becomes large enough to influence prices and thereby distort the workings of the free-market system. By contrast, a **monopoly** is a scenario in which there is only one producer of a product in a given market, and thus the producer is able to determine the price. A situation in which an industry (such as commercial aircraft manufacturing) is dominated by only a few producers is called an **oligopoly.**

Between pure competition and a monopoly lie a number of firms with varying degrees of competitive power. Most of the competition in advanced free-market economic systems is **monopolistic competition,** in which a large number of sellers (none of which dominates the market) offers products that can be distinguished from competing products in at least some small way. Toothpaste, cosmetics, soft drinks, Internet search engines, and restaurants are examples of products with distinguishable features.

When markets become filled with competitors and products start to look alike, companies use price, speed, quality, service, or innovation to gain a **competitive advantage**—something that sets one company apart from its rivals and makes its products more appealing to consumers. For example, Southwest Airlines competes on price by offering the lowest fares of any of its competitors. And American Airlines sends e-mail listing rock-bottom fares for undersubscribed flights to more than a million Net SAAver subscribers.[16] Competing on price may seem like an obvious and easy choice to make, but the consequences can be devastating to individual companies and to entire industries. During a three-year period in the early 1990s, price wars caused the U.S. airline industry to lose more money than it had made since the Wright brothers' first flight. Unfortunately, the harsh truth of many price wars is that sooner or later everybody sells at a loss. For this reason, companies try to find other ways to compete.

Jiffy Lube, for instance, competes on speed. Mechanics change a car's oil and filter in 15 minutes or less while customers wait. Starbucks competes on quality by delivering a premium product that has changed the definition of "a good cup of coffee." And Enterprise Rent-A-Car blows past its competitors by competing on service. The company establishes convenient rental offices just about everywhere. If your car needs repair service, Enterprise will provide you with a rental car right at the dealer's service center. And the company bets that you won't be in the mood to quibble about prices.[17]

Product innovation is another way that companies compete in the free-market economy. For nearly a century, 3M's management has promoted innovation by giving employees the freedom to take risks and try new ideas. Beginning with the invention of sandpaper in 1904, 3M has produced such staples as masking tape, cellophane tape, magnetic tape, videotape, and Post-it Notes. Sometimes product innovation can revolutionize an entire industry, just as Razor aluminum scooters, Rollerblades, AbFlex, Atomic hour-glass skis, and Burton & Sims snowboards did by creating new market opportunities for the sporting goods industry.[18]

## active exercise  <

**Take a moment to apply what you've learned.**

## GOVERNMENT'S ROLE IN A FREE-MARKET SYSTEM

Although the free-market system generally works well, it's far from perfect. If left unchecked, the economic forces that make capitalism succeed may also create severe problems for some groups or individuals. To correct these types of problems, the government intervenes in free-market systems by enforcing laws and regulations to protect consumers and foster competition, by contributing to economic stability, and by spending for the public good.

### Enforcing Laws and Regulations to Protect Consumers and Foster Competition

The U.S. federal government and state and local governments create thousands of new laws and regulations every year, many of which limit what businesses and consumers can and cannot do. These laws are intended to protect the consumer and foster competition. As a consumer, for example, you can't buy some medications without a doctor's prescription; you can't buy alcoholic beverages without a certificate proving that you're old enough; and you can't buy certain products lacking safety features, such as cars without seatbelts and medication without childproof tops.

Just as governments can create laws, they can also remove or relax existing laws and regulations through a process known as **deregulation.** Industries such as airlines, banking, and telecommunications have been deregulated in order to promote industry competition in hopes of providing consumers with lower prices and improved products or services.

Because competition generally benefits the U.S. economy, the federal government tries to preserve competition and ensure that no single enterprise becomes too powerful. If a company has a monopoly, it can harm consumers by raising prices, cutting output, or stifling innovation. Furthermore, because monopolies have total control over certain products and prices and the total market share for those products, it's extremely difficult for competitors to enter markets where monopolies exist. For these reasons, true monopolies are prohibited by federal antitrust laws. (Some monopolies, such as utilities, are legal but closely regulated.)

**THE UNITED STATES VERSUS MICROSOFT** The government's heavy hand with monopolies has been a subject of continuing concern since the turn of the century. One of the highest-profile antitrust cases of the 1990s involved the software giant Microsoft. Microsoft makes the operating-system software used by 90 percent of personal computers as well as a wide array of application software that runs on those operating systems. In the late 1990s, the U.S. Justice Department accused Microsoft of using its vast clout to give itself an unfair advantage in the application-software business by bundling its popular Internet Explorer Web browser with its Windows operating system. Competitors such as Netscape alleged that Microsoft was willing to use every tool at its disposal to damage competition by forcing or persuading companies to install its Internet Explorer as a condition of licensing the Windows operating system.

Subsequently, in 1998 the U.S. government and 19 states filed lawsuits claiming that Microsoft's practices were in violation of antitrust law. After a much-publicized two-year trial, on June 7, 2000, U.S. District Judge Thomas Jackson ruled that Microsoft had repeatedly and willfully violated antitrust laws and should be broken up to restore competition to the computer software industry. Microsoft, of course, appealed Jackson's ruling and Jackson agreed not to impose any court-ordered restrictions on Microsoft's conduct while the case was under appeal. The final outcome of the Microsoft case will eventually be resolved by the Supreme Court. But until that time, Microsoft is free to forge ahead with major business initiatives and conduct business as usual.[19]

**GOVERNMENT OPPOSITION TO MERGERS** While monopolies are illegal, oligopolies are not. Still, the U.S. government has the power to prevent a combination of firms if it would reduce competition in the marketplace. The $120 billion merger between WorldCom and Sprint was called off because U.S. regulators were concerned that merging the second- and third-biggest long-distance services would stop the decline of long-distance rates.[20] Similarly, bookstore chain Barnes & Noble scrapped its planned $600 million acquisition of Ingram Book Group, the largest book wholesaler in the United States, in the face of regulatory opposition. Regulators alleged that the merger would stifle competition by giving Barnes & Noble an advantage over smaller booksellers.[21]

### Contributing to Economic Stability

Another important role the government assumes in a free-market system is to contribute to the economy's stability. A nation's economy never stays exactly the same size. Instead, it grows and contracts in response to the combined effects of such factors as technological breakthroughs, changes in investment patterns, shifts in consumer attitudes, world events, and basic economic forces. During periods of downward swing, or **recession,** consumers buy less and factories produce less, so companies must lay off workers, who in turn buy less—and so on. During periods of *recovery* companies buy more, factories produce more, employment is high, and workers spend their earnings.

These recurrent up-and-down swings are known as the **business cycle.** Although such swings are natural and to some degree predictable, they cause hardship. In an attempt to avoid such hardship and to foster economic stability, the government can levy new taxes or adjust the current tax rates, raise or lower interest rates, and regulate the total amount of money circulating in our economy. These government actions have two facets: fiscal policy and monetary policy. **Fiscal policy** involves changes in the government's revenues and expenditures to stimulate or dampen the economy. **Monetary policy** involves adjustments to the nation's money supply by increasing or decreasing interest rates to help control inflation. In the United States, monetary policy is controlled primarily by the Federal Reserve Board, a group of appointed government officials who oversee the country's central banking system. (Monetary policy is discussed more fully in Chapter 17.)

### Spending for the Public Good

Although everybody hates to pay taxes, most of us are willing to admit they're a necessary evil. If the government didn't take your tax money and repair our nation's roads, would you be inclined to fix them yourself? Similarly, it might not be practical to rely on individual demand to provide police and fire protection or to launch satellites. Instead, the government steps in and collects a variety of taxes so it can supply such *public goods* (see Exhibit 1.6).

For many years the U.S. government spent more money than it took in, creating annual budget deficits on the order of several hundred billion dollars. The accumulated amount of annual budget deficits (the U.S. national debt) now amounts to almost $6 trillion. As a result, interest payments alone on the national debt cost U.S. taxpayers about $340 billion a year—or $10,000 per second. In 1997 Congress approved a plan to pare down future deficits to balance the budget by 2002.[22] Strong economic growth accompanied by budget modifications put the United States ahead of schedule. For the first time since 1835, the United States is on a path to becoming debt free by 2013.[23]

Although reducing government spending might seem like a practical step, keep in mind that such reduction can have rippling economic consequences. That's because government spending boosts the economy and has a *multiplier effect* as it makes its way through the economy. For example, if the government decides to fund new highway projects, thousands of construction workers will be gainfully employed and earn wages. If some of these workers decide to spend their extra income to buy new cars, car dealers will have more income. The car dealers, in turn, might spend their income on new clothes, and the salesclerks (who earn commissions) might buy compact disks, and so on. This *circular flow* of money through the economic system links all elements of the U.S. economy by exchanging goods and services for money, which is then used to buy more goods and services, and so on.

> ## active poll

**What do you think? Voice your opinion and find out what others have to say.**

## HOW DOES A FREE-MARKET SYSTEM MONITOR ITS ECONOMIC PERFORMANCE?

Each day we are deluged with complex statistical data that depict the current status and past performance of the economy. Sorting, understanding, and interpreting these data are difficult tasks even for professional economists. **Economic indicators** are statistics such as interest rates, unemployment rates,

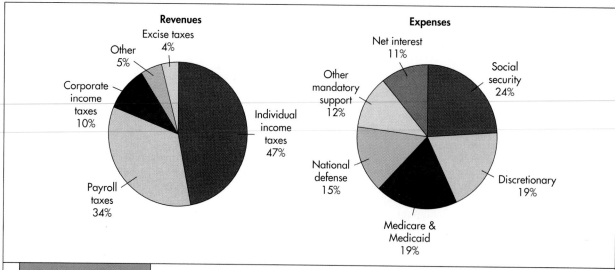

**Revenues**

- Excise taxes 4%
- Other 5%
- Corporate income taxes 10%
- Individual income taxes 47%
- Payroll taxes 34%

**Expenses**

- Net interest 11%
- Social security 24%
- Other mandatory support 12%
- National defense 15%
- Medicare & Medicaid 19%
- Discretionary 19%

---

**EXHIBIT 1.6**

The Federal Dollar

Here's a breakdown of the federal dollar—how it's collected and how it's spent.

and housing data that are used to monitor and measure economic performance. Statistics that point to what may happen to the economy in the future are called *leading indicators;* statistics that signal a swing in the economy after the movement has begun are called *lagging indicators* (see Exhibit 1.7).

Unemployment statistics, for example, are leading economic indicators because they are a signal of future changes in consumer spending. When unemployment rises, people have less money to spend, and the economy suffers. Housing starts are another leading indicator because they show where construction and manufacturing is headed. Housing is very sensitive to interest rate changes. If mortgage rates are high, fewer people can afford to build new homes. When housing starts drop, builders stop hiring, and may even lay off workers. Meanwhile, orders fall for plumbing fixtures, carpets, and appliances, so manufacturers decrease production and workers' hours. These cutbacks ripple through the economy and lead to slower income and job growth, and weaker consumer spending.[24] Besides housing starts and unemployment data, economists closely monitor a nation's output and price changes.

### Measuring a Nation's Output

The broadest measure of an economy's health is the **gross domestic product (GDP).** The GDP measures a country's output—its production, distribution, and use of goods and services—by computing

| Leading Indicators | Lagging Indicators |
|---|---|
| Changes in the money supply in circulation | Changes in the prime rate |
| Number of building permits issued by private housing units | Number of commercial and industrial loans to be repaid |
| New orders for consumer goods | Change in the Consumer Price Index for services |
| Number of contracts and orders for equipment | Size of manufacturing and trade inventories |
| Weekly initial claims for unemployment insurance | Average length of unemployment |
| Average weekly hours for production workers in manufacturing | Labor cost per unit of output in manufacturing |

**EXHIBIT 1.7**

Major Economic Indicators

Businesses and government leaders rely on these major economic indicators to make decisions.

the sum of all goods and services produced for *final* use in a market during a specified period (usually a year). The goods may be produced by either domestic or foreign companies as long as these companies are located within a nation's boundaries. Sales from a Honda assembly plant in California, for instance, would be included in the GDP.

A less popular measure of a country's output is the **gross national product (GNP).** This measure excludes the value of production from foreign-owned businesses within a nation's boundaries (such as Honda U.S.), but it includes receipts from the overseas operations of domestic companies—such as McDonald's in Switzerland. Put another way, GNP considers *who* is responsible for the production; GDP considers *where* the production occurs. Although far from perfect, the GDP enables a nation to evaluate its economic policies and to compare its current performance with prior periods or with the performance of other nations.[25]

### Measuring Price Changes

Price changes, especially price increases, are another important economic indicator. In a period of rising prices, the purchasing power of a dollar erodes, which means that you can purchase fewer things with today's dollar than you could in a prior period. Over time, price increases tend to lead to wage increases, which in turn add pressures for higher prices, setting a vicious cycle in motion.

**INFLATION AND DEFLATION Inflation** is a steady rise in the prices of goods and services throughout the economy. When the inflation rate begins to decline, economists use the term *disinflation.* **Deflation,** on the other hand, is the sustained fall in the general price level for goods and services. It is the opposite of inflation; that is, purchasing power increases because a dollar held today will buy more tomorrow. In a deflationary period, investors postpone major purchases in anticipation of lower prices in the future. Keep in mind that although prices in the overall economy tend to increase year after year, not all industries and product categories necessarily follow this trend. In the electronics industry, for instance, prices tend to drop as technology advances and production becomes more efficient.

**CONSUMER PRICE INDEX** The **consumer price index (CPI)** measures the rate of inflation by comparing the change in prices of a representative basket of goods and services such as clothing, food, housing, and utilities over time. A numerical weight is assigned to each item in the representative basket to adjust for each item's relative importance in the marketplace. As are most economic indicators, the CPI is far from perfect. For one thing, the representative basket of goods may not accurately represent the prices and consumption patterns of the area in which you live. For another, the mix in this basket may not include new innovations, which often play a major role in consumer spending patterns. Nonetheless, many businesses use the CPI to adjust rent increases and to keep employees' wages in line with the pace of inflation.

> ### active exercise

**Take a moment to apply what you've learned.**

> ### active concept check

**Now let's take a moment to test your knowledge of the concepts you have studied in this section.**

> ## Challenges of a Global Economy

Even though economic indicators suggest that the United States is in a period of great economic strength, businesses today are facing a raft of new challenges. Today, financial and product markets are far more interconnected than ever before. **Globalization**—the increasing tendency of the world to act as one market instead of a series of national ones—opens new markets for a company's goods and services while simultaneously producing tougher competition. Thus, doing business in the twenty-first century means working in a world of increasing uncertainty where change is the norm, not the exception. In the coming chapters we will explore each of the challenges that businesses are facing in the global economy and we will provide real-world examples of how companies are tackling and meeting these challenges:

- *Producing quality products and services that satisfy customers' changing needs.* Today's customer is well-informed and has many product choices. For many businesses, such as Yahoo!, competing in the global economy means competing on the basis of *speed* (getting products to market sooner), *quality* (doing a better job of meeting customer expectations), and *customer satisfaction* (making sure buyers are happy with every aspect of the purchase, from the shopping experience until they're through using the product).

- *Starting and managing a small business in today's competitive environment.* Starting a new business or successfully managing a small company in today's global economy requires creativity and a willingness to exploit new opportunities. Small companies often lack the resources to buffer themselves from competition. Furthermore, once a new product or process is brought to the market, competitors need only a short time to be up and running with something similar. Thus, the biggest challenge for small businesses today is to make a product or provide a service that is hard to imitate.

- *Thinking globally and committing to a culturally diverse workforce.* Globalization opens new markets for a company's goods, increases competition, and changes the composition of the workforce into one that is more diverse in race, gender, age, physical and mental abilities, lifestyle, culture, education, ideas, and background. By 2010 minorities will account for 50 percent of the U.S. population, and immigrants will account for half of all new U.S. workers.[26] Thus, to be competitive in the global economy, companies must commit to a culturally diverse workforce, think globally, and adopt global standards of excellence.

- *Behaving in an ethically and socially responsible manner.* As businesses become more complex through global expansion and technological change, they must deal with an increasing number of ethical and social issues. These include the marketing of unhealthful products, the use of questionable accounting practices to compute financial results, and the pollution of the environment (as Chapter 2 discusses). In the future, businesses can expect continued pressure from environmental groups, consumers, employees, and government regulators to act ethically and responsibly.

- *Keeping pace with technology and electronic commerce.* Everywhere we look, technology is reshaping the world (see Exhibit 1.8). The Internet and innovations in computerization, miniaturization, and telecommunication have made it possible for people anywhere in the world to exchange information and goods. Such technologies are collapsing boundaries and changing the way customers, suppliers, and companies interact. Not only are fledgling Internet companies becoming global competitors overnight, but they're changing the way people shop for books, cars, vacations, advice—just about everything. Meanwhile, the Internet is forcing traditional enterprises to explore new ways of doing business—including launching products and services that compete with their existing ones.[27] In short, the Internet has touched every business and industry and is changing all facets of business life.[28] (Consult Component Chapter A for a discussion of Internet fundamentals.)

Customer satisfaction, competition, cultural diversity, ethics, and technology are indeed the key challenges of the twenty-first century. But a closer look at U.S. business history will show that meeting new challenges has been a recurring theme for decades.

## active exercise

**Take a moment to apply what you've learned.**

## > History of U.S. Economic Growth

The first economic base in the United States was the small family farm. People grew enough food for their families and used any surplus to trade for necessary goods provided by independent craftspeople and merchants. Business operated on a small scale, and much of the population was self-employed.

| Year | Event |
|------|-------|
| 1960 | Xerox sells the first convenient office copier using xerography—Greek for "dry writing." |
| 1965 | Gordon Moore predicts exponential growth in chip power. |
| 1969 | Internet started by U.S. Department of Defense. |
| 1971 | Intel produces first microprocessor. |
| 1975 | First commercial personal computers are sold. |
| 1977 | Ken Olsen, founder of Digital Equipment, declares that "there is no reason anyone would want a computer in their home." |
| 1981 | First portable computer introduced. |
| 1983 | Motorola brings out first portable cellular phone system. |
| 1990 | World Wide Web developed; debuts to public two years later. |
| 1991 | IBM reports its first-ever annual loss of $2.8 billion. |
| 1992 | America Online goes public; Microsoft's Bill Gates becomes the richest man in America. |
| 1994 | Jerry Yang and David Filo create Yahoo! |
| 1995 | Netscape goes public. |
| 1997 | More than 50 percent of Schwab's brokerage business is being done online. |
| 1998 | Number of telecommuters in United States reaches 16 million. |
| 1999 | Vodafone acquires AirTouch for $70 billion, creating the world's biggest wireless-communications firm. |
| 2000 | U.S. Justice Department rules that Microsoft is a monopoly and orders it split into two separate and competing companies. |

**EXHIBIT 1.8**

Forty Years of Technological Change

Technological advancement over the last 40 years has been dramatic.

With fertile, flat terrain and adequate rainfall, farmers soon prospered, and their prosperity spread to the townspeople who served them.

In the early nineteenth century, people began making greater use of rivers, harbors, and rich mineral deposits. Excellent natural resources helped businesspeople accumulate the capital they needed to increase production—fueling the transition of the United States from a farm-based economy to an industrial economy.

> **active exercise**

**Take a moment to apply what you've learned.**

## AGE OF INDUSTRIALIZATION: 1900–1944

During the nineteenth century, new technology gave birth to the factory and the industrial revolution. Millions of new workers came to the United States from abroad to work in factories where each person performed one simple task over and over. Separating the manufacturing process into distinct tasks and producing large quantities of similar products allowed businesses to achieve cost and operating efficiencies known as **economies of scale.**

As businesses increased in size, they also became more powerful. In the early 1920s more and more industrial assets were concentrated into fewer and fewer hands, putting smaller competitors, workers, and consumers at a disadvantage. By popular mandate, the government passed laws and regulations to prevent the abuse of power by big business. At the same time, workers began to organize into labor unions to balance the power of their employers. Meanwhile, U.S. businesses enjoyed such an enormously diverse market within the country's borders that they didn't need to trade overseas. But prosperity soon ended. In 1929 the U.S. stock market crashed, ushering in a period of economic collapse known as the Great Depression. Millions of people lost their jobs. By 1941, one in 10 workers remained unemployed, the birthrate was stagnant, and the hand of the U.S. government strengthened as people lost confidence in the power of business to pull the country out of hard times. That same year the United States entered World War II.

## THE POSTWAR GOLDEN ERA: 1945–1969

The postwar reconstruction, which started in 1945, revived the economy and renewed the trend toward large-scale enterprises. The G.I. Bill of Rights opened advanced education to the working classes. The middle class grew and prospered. By 1950 the birthrate had jumped, and the baby boom was on. Accustomed to playing a major role in the war effort, the government continued to exert a large measure of control over business and the economy. President Eisenhower's highway system fueled expansion and the growth of the suburbs. Sales of new homes and U.S.-manufactured automobiles skyrocketed.

Stimulated by a boom in world demand and an expansive political climate, the United States prospered throughout the 1960s. Expanding world trade provided limitless markets for U.S. goods. But once Europe and Japan had recovered from the war, they began challenging U.S. industries—Italy with shoes, Switzerland with watches, and Japan with cameras. By the end of the 1960s, Japanese transistor radios dominated the world market. Still, the more advanced technological industries and their products—televisions, copying machines, and aircraft—remained U.S. preserves.

## THE TURBULENT YEARS: 1970–1979

In the early 1970s, inflation depressed demand and U.S. economic growth began to slump. In 1973 the price of a barrel of oil skyrocketed from $3 to $11, forcing companies to invest in ways to save energy instead of investing in new manufacturing equipment. Meanwhile, with virtually no investment money floating around, and no money for new business start-ups, the U.S. economy wasn't particularly competitive. Companies had no incentive to lower their costs and consumers had fewer product choices, which helped sustain higher prices.

The U.S. economy had barely recovered from the 1973 oil shock when it got hit again in 1979 (oil jumped from $13 to $23 per barrel), resulting in galloping inflation and sky-high interest rates. Exports from Asia began to pour into the United States—some bearing U.S. labels—and the United States entered an era of diminishing growth.[29] Meanwhile, a takeover binge was changing the structure of corporate America. Giant organizations called *conglomerates* emerged as companies acquired strings of unrelated businesses to grow and diversify their enterprises. At the same time, deregulation in several large markets, including transportation and financial services, made it possible for newcomers such as People Express (airline) to enter the marketplace. Even though some of these companies failed, their presence forced significant restructuring in the industries they entered.

## RISE OF GLOBAL COMPETITION: 1980–1989

During the 1980s, global competition slowly crept up on the United States. Since the 1950s, Japanese firms had been refining their manufacturing processes to become more efficient, and by 1980 they had a 30-year head start on the United States. (Ironically, the United States had supplied its foreign competitors with the resources and know-how to stake a claim in the world marketplace.) Sony moved into the fast lane and introduced new product innovations such as the Walkman and the VCR, while pricing them affordably. By the mid-1980s, it became almost impossible to buy a consumer electronic device that was made in the United States.

To regain a competitive edge, many U.S. companies restructured their operations. Some corporations merged with others to produce economies of scale; others splintered into smaller fragments to focus on a single industry or a narrower customer base. The tough times of the 1970s planted the seeds for entrepreneurship of the early 1980s. Little companies such as Staples, Dell, and Home Depot started popping up with founders who said, "We went to work for the safe, big company and it wasn't safe at all."[30] Meanwhile, new technological developments such as the microprocessor and genetic engineering tools were embraced, not by leading companies of the day but by new entrants (such as Microsoft, Cisco, and Oracle) who swiftly attacked the status quo.[31]

## HIGHWAY TO THE NEW ECONOMY: 1990 AND BEYOND

In the early 1990s, U.S. businesses got hit again. The U.S. economy went into full-blown recession, and many companies that had loaded up on debt in the 1980s to expand their operations or to acquire other companies went bankrupt. During this period of upheaval, unemployment soared as hundreds of thousands of jobs were eliminated. General Motors alone laid off 130,000 workers—enough to fill two football stadiums. Had the United States continued in the direction it was headed at the beginning of the 1990s, it might well have experienced the disaster that many economists feared. But it didn't.

Manufacturing improvements helped move the United States from a position of near-terminal decline to renewed world dominance.[32] Managers at IBM and AT&T breathed new life into these two U.S. manufacturing classics. Meanwhile, Motorola struck back with its pagers and cell phones, Hewlett-Packard took over the high-volume market in low-cost computer printers, and once-sleepy Kodak challenged the Japanese with digital and disposable cameras.[33] As more and more U.S. companies reengineered their operations to improve productivity and to focus on product quality, U.S. industries experienced remarkable turnarounds. But it was investments in new technology and the promise of e-commerce that ultimately pushed the U.S. economy into a remarkable period of prosperity. Characterized by faster growth, lower inflation, technology-driven expansion, and thrift, this new era is referred as the *new economy*.

## > active poll

**What do you think? Voice your opinion and find out what others have to say.**

## > active concept check

**Now let's take a moment to test your knowledge of the concepts you have studied in this section.**

## > Chapter Wrap-Up

Now that you've reached the end of the chapter, you may wish to explore the concepts you've been reading about in greater detail, or test yourself to see how well you've comprehended the material. In the box below you'll find a number of links. Click on any one of these links to find additional chapter resources.

## > end-of-chapter resources

- **Summary of Learning Objectives**
- **Practice Quiz**
- **Focusing on E-Business Today**
- **Key Terms**
- **Test Your Knowledge**
- **Practice Your Knowledge**
- **Expand Your Knowledge**
- **A Case for Critical Thinking**

# Ethics and Social Responsibility of Business

## Chapter Outline

## > What's Ahead

### INSIDE BUSINESS TODAY
### BEYOND THE PURSUIT OF PROFITS: PATAGONIA GEARS UP TO SAVE THE ENVIRONMENT

Some business executives believe they have to concentrate on the bottom line before they can turn their attention to worthy causes. But as founder and owner of Patagonia, leading designer and distributor of outdoor gear, Yvon Chouinard sees things differently. A passionate environmentalist, Chouinard believes everyone—from consumers to corporations—should do their part to save the earth's resources. In fact, Chouinard refuses to sacrifice the environment for the sake of his company's profitability. Instead, Chouinard strives for the best of both worlds—profits and environmental responsibility—by making both a key part of his business strategy.

Patagonia works hard to develop production techniques that reduce the environmental impact of the company's operations. Employees also reap the benefits of the company's environmental values. For instance, employees receive full pay for two-month internships at environmental not-for-profit organizations. Moreover, through a self-imposed "earth tax" on annual profits, Patagonia gives environmental groups about $1 million each year—more money than the company allocates for advertising.

Nevertheless, blending profitability with social responsibility isn't always easy. In the 1990s, the company's adherence to rigid environmental standards in the production of its high-priced goods created enormous operating expenses. Faced with sagging sales and a

Environment-friendly products such as those sold by Patagonia give consumers a chance to make a difference while meeting their needs.

severe cash crunch, Patagonia was forced to scale back its operations and lay off one-fifth of its workforce.

Consultants advised Chouinard to sell the company and create a charitable foundation for environmental causes instead of donating a million or so from company profits each year. But Chouinard had established Patagonia to do more than donate money to environmental groups. He wanted to "use the company as a tool for social change" and was convinced that Patagonia could serve as an example for others.

So Chouinard launched an extensive effort to improve Patagonia's bottom line while also focusing on saving the earth's resources. First, he took his case to the public, educating consumers on environmental issues. Lengthy catalog essays by Chouinard explained the company's philosophies about saving the earth's resources and its rationale for developing environmentally sensitive production techniques. Then he refined Patagonia's public image of a "green" business, creating an internal assessment group to evaluate the company's environmental performance. He also constructed a new distribution center with recycled materials and an energy-saving heating system.

Next Chouinard focused on his suppliers. He challenged them to improve their performance and helped them develop techniques for meeting Patagonia's environmental standards. Working with outside contractors, Patagonia developed Synchilla fleece (a fabric made from recycled plastic soda bottles), which now accounts for the recycling of some 8 million plastic bottles each year. Patagonia also worked with farmers to produce organic cotton—grown without artificial pesticides or fertilizers. To offset higher production costs for the cotton, the company split the increased costs with consumers, hoping that they would find value in an environmentally sensitive product. They did. Once the catalogs reached consumers, Patagonia immediately sold out of the new line of all-organic cotton sweaters.

Today, Patagonia is a leader and pioneer of "green" profits. With annual sales exceeding $160 million, Chouinard has proven that Patagonia could achieve success while supporting its environmental values.[1]

> objectives

Take a moment to familiarize yourself with the key objectives of this chapter.

> gearing up

Before you begin reading this chapter, try a short warm-up activity.

## > Ethics in the Workplace

Yvon Chouinard works hard to make sure that Patagonia does the right thing. But as Chouinard knows, a business can't take action or make decisions; only the individuals within a business can do that. From the CEO to the newest entry-level clerk, individuals make decisions every day that affect their company and its **stakeholders**—groups that are affected by (or that affect) a business's operations, including colleagues, employees, supervisors, investors, customers, suppliers, governments, and society at large. These decisions ultimately determine whether the company is recognized as a responsible corporate citizen.

### WHAT IS ETHICAL BEHAVIOR?

Guided by written policies, unwritten standards, and examples set by top managers, every individual in an organization makes choices that have moral implications. We define **ethics** as the principles and standards of moral behavior that are accepted by society as right versus wrong. To make the "right" choice individuals must think through the consequences of their actions. *Business ethics* is the application of moral standards to business situations.

### Ethical Dilemmas versus Ethical Lapses

Ethical decisions can be divided into two general types: ethical dilemmas and ethical lapses. An **ethical dilemma** is a situation in which one must choose between two conflicting but arguably valid sides. For example, Johnson & Johnson (J&J) faced an ethical dilemma when it had to decide how to keep its Tylenol customers well informed without scaring them away altogether. Tylenol is certainly safe enough for all the millions of people who take it each year without ill effects. However, more than 100 deaths per year are caused by acetaminophen, the active ingredient in Tylenol.[2]

Even though J&J strengthened label warnings about not giving Tylenol to children and not taking it in combination with alcohol, the labels did not mention the possibility of death from liver failure when the recommended dose is exceeded. The company believed that such warnings would confuse people and that mentioning the risk of death would promote the use of Tylenol in suicides.[3] Should J&J include organ-specific warnings? Or is it enough to caution users about sticking to the proper dose? J&J decided to clarify the dangers by mentioning that mixing alcohol with painkillers can lead to liver damage and stomach bleeding.[4]

All ethical dilemmas have a common theme: the conflict between the rights of two or more important groups of people. Consumers have the right to be informed about any risks from using over-the-counter medications, and J&J has the right to profit by selling a beneficial medication that is used safely by millions. Similarly, recording artists have the right to earn royalties from the songs they publish, and consumers have the right to copy music for their own enjoyment.

The second type of decision is an **ethical lapse,** in which an individual makes a decision that is clearly wrong, such as divulging trade secrets to a competitor. Be careful not to confuse ethical dilemmas with ethical lapses. A company faces an ethical dilemma when it must decide whether to continue operating a production facility that is suspected, but not proven, to be unsafe. A company makes an ethical lapse when it continues to operate the facility even after the site has been proven unsafe. Other examples of ethical lapses would include inflating prices for certain customers or selling technological secrets to unfriendly foreign governments.

### Cyberethics

The Internet's ability to reach millions of people, combined with its protective cloak of anonymity, makes it a breeding ground for all sorts of ethical lapses. Cyberspace abounds with stories about top company executives who steal one another's intellectual property, auction rip-offs, Internet stock fraud, and e-commerce sites that fail to deliver what they promise. Not long ago Internet scams were rare, but now they are so rampant that regulators are finding themselves blitzed with complaints. The Federal Trade Commission alone identified 18,660 instances of potential Internet fraud in 1999. One-fourth of all its consumer complaints are now about the Internet, up from just 3 percent in 1997.[5] "Never underestimate people's ability to do bad," warns one ethics professional. "Technology is just going to make it easier."[6]

It's not just gullible consumers who are being duped. Businesses of all sizes are becoming targets. The hot Internet business scams include hijacking Web pages and diverting traffic to sites that can charge higher ad fees based on their new audience, fraudulent Internet access offers, and bogus Web page design outfits that prey on small companies. Part of the problem is that ethics "implies periods of contemplation and deliberation, and working through a moral calculus," says one ethics expert. But who has time for this when operating at Internet speed? It seems as if many companies today are created, hyped, and sold with less concern for attracting real customers than for lining one's pockets with investors' money.[7]

## active exercise <

**Take a moment to apply what you've learned.**

## HOW DO BUSINESSES AND EMPLOYEES MAKE ETHICAL CHOICES?

Determining what's right in any given situation can be difficult. One approach is to measure each act against certain absolute standards. In the United States, these standards are often grounded in religious teachings, such as "Do not lie" and "Do not steal." Another place to look for ethical guidance is the law. If saying, writing, or doing something is clearly illegal, you have no decision to make; you obey the law. Nevertheless, telephone companies continually break the law when they switch someone's long distance service without their consent (a practice known as slamming) or slip unauthorized charges into phone bills (a practice known as cramming). Penalties against offenders for such unethical behavior have reached millions of dollars.[8]

Even though legal considerations will resolve some ethical questions, you'll often have to rely on your own judgment and principles. When trying to decide the most ethical course of action, you might apply the Golden Rule: Do unto others as you would have them do unto you. Or you might examine your motives: If your intent is honest, the decision is ethical, even though it may be factually or technically incorrect; however, if your intent is to mislead or manipulate, your decision is unethical, regardless of whether it is factually or technically correct. You might also consider asking yourself a series of questions:

1. Is the decision legal? (Does it break any laws?)
2. Is it balanced? (Is it fair to all concerned?)
3. Can you live with it? (Does it make you feel good about yourself?)
4. Is it feasible? (Will it actually work in the real world?)

When you need to determine the ethics of any situation, these questions will get you started. You may also want to consider the needs of stakeholders, and you may want to investigate one or more philosophical approaches (see Exhibit 2.1).

These approaches are not mutually exclusive alternatives. On the contrary, most businesspeople combine them to reach decisions that will satisfy as many stakeholders as possible without violating anyone's rights or treating anyone unjustly. In any case, wanting to be an ethical corporate citizen isn't enough; people in business must actively practice ethical behavior.

| Is the Decision Ethical? | Does It Respect Stakeholders? | Does It Follow a Philosophical Approach? |
|---|---|---|
| IS IT LEGAL? | WILL OUTSIDERS APPROVE? | IS IT A UTILITARIAN DECISION? |
| ☐ Does it violate civil law? | ☐ Does it benefit customers, suppliers, investors, public officials, media representatives, and community members? | ☐ Does it produce the greatest good for the greatest number of people? |
| ☐ Does it violate company policy? | | |
| IS IT BALANCED? | | DOES IT UPHOLD INDIVIDUAL, LEGAL, AND HUMAN RIGHTS? |
| ☐ Is it fair to all concerned, in both the short and the long term? | WILL SUPERVISORS APPROVE? | ☐ Does it protect people's own interests? |
| CAN YOU LIVE WITH IT? | ☐ Did you provide management with information that is honest and accurate? | ☐ Does it respect the privacy of others and their right to express their opinion? |
| ☐ Does it make you feel good about yourself? | WILL EMPLOYEES APPROVE? | ☐ Does it allow people to act in a way that conforms to their religious or moral beliefs? |
| ☐ Would you feel good reading about it in a newspaper? | ☐ Will it affect employees in a positive way? | |
| IS IT FEASIBLE? | ☐ Does it handle personal information about employees discreetly? | DOES IT UPHOLD THE PRINCIPLES OF JUSTICE? |
| ☐ Does it work in the real world? | ☐ Did you give proper credit for work performed by others? | ☐ Does it treat people fairly and impartially? |
| ☐ Will it improve your competitive position? | | ☐ Does it apply rules consistently? |
| ☐ Is it affordable? | | ☐ Does it ensure that people who harm others are held responsible and make restitution? |
| ☐ Can it be accomplished in the time available? | | |

## EXHIBIT 2.1

Itemized List for Making Ethical Decisions

Companies with the most success in establishing an ethical structure are those that balance their approach to making decisions.

## HOW CAN COMPANIES BECOME MORE ETHICAL?

Many companies are concerned about ethical issues and are trying to develop approaches for improving their ethics. Boeing requires all employees to undergo at least one hour of ethical training a year, and the company's senior managers must undergo five hours. Lockheed Martin has created a newspaper called *Ethics Daily* that runs articles based on ethical problems employees have faced and how they resolved them.[9]

Additionally, more than 80 percent of large companies have adopted a written **code of ethics,** which defines the values and principles that should be used to guide decisions (see Exhibit 2.2). By itself, however, a code of ethics can't accomplish much. "You can have grand motives, but if your employees don't see them, they aren't going to mean anything," says one ethics manager at accounting firm Arthur Andersen.[10] To be effective, a code must be supported by employee communications efforts, a formal training program, employee commitment to follow it, and a system through which employees can get help with ethically difficult situations.[11]

Codes of ethics are so important that according to the Federal Sentencing Guidelines (1991), a company found to be violating federal law might not be prosecuted if it has the proper ethics policies and procedures in place. As one ethics expert explains, "If you have an active ethics program in place ahead of time, then bad things shouldn't happen; but if they do happen, it won't hurt you as badly."[12] Perhaps inspired by these guidelines, some companies have created an official position—the ethics officer—to guard morality. Originally hired to oversee corporate conduct—from pilfering company

We, the members of the IEEE, in recognition of the importance of our technologies affecting the quality of life throughout the world, and in accepting a personal obligation to our profession, its members and the communities we serve, do hereby commit ourselves to the highest ethical and professional conduct and agree:

1. to accept responsibility in making engineering decisions consistent with the safety, health and welfare of the public, and to disclose promptly factors that might endanger the public or the environment;

2. to avoid real or perceived conflicts of interest whenever possible, and to disclose them to affected parties when they do exist;

3. to be honest and realistic in stating claims or estimates based on available data;

4. to reject bribery in all its forms;

5. to improve the understanding of technology, its appropriate application, and potential consequences;

6. to maintain and improve our technical competence and to undertake technological tasks for others only if qualified by training or experience, or after full disclosure of pertinent limitations;

7. to seek, accept, and offer honest criticism of technical work, to acknowledge and correct errors, and to credit properly the contributions of others;

8. to treat fairly all persons regardless of such factors as race, religion, gender, disability, age, or national origin;

9. to avoid injuring others, their property, reputation, or employment by false or malicious action;

10. to assist colleagues and co-workers in their professional development and to support them in following this code of ethics.

**EXHIBIT 2.2**

IEEE Code of Ethics

The Institute of Electrical and Electronics Engineers promotes the public policy interests of its U.S. members. The organization's code of ethics serves as a model for members to adopt.

pens to endangering the environment to selling company secrets—many ethics officers today function as corporate coaches for ethical decision making.

Keep in mind, however, that ethical behavior starts at the top. The CEO and other senior managers must set the tone for people throughout the company. At Aveda, a cosmetics company, the corporate mission is to bring about positive effects through responsible business methods. "We do this, quite frankly, out of self-preservation," says founder and chairman Horst Rechebecher.[13]

Another way companies support ethical behavior is by establishing ethics hot lines that encourage *whistle-blowing*—an employee's disclosure of illegal, unethical, wasteful, or harmful practices by the company. Whistle-blowing can bring with it high costs: Public accusation of wrongdoing hurts the business's reputation, requires attention from managers who must investigate the accusations, and damages employee morale. Moreover, whistle-blowers risk being fired or demoted, and they often suffer career setbacks, financial strain, and emotional stress. The fear of such negative repercussions may allow unethical or illegal practices to go unreported. Still, all things considered, many employees do the right thing.

active poll  <

**What do you think? Voice your opinion and find out what others have to say.**

> ## active concept check

> ## Social Responsibility in Business

In addition to practicing ethics in the workplace, companies such as Patagonia strive to create organizations that encourage social responsibility in their policies and among their employees. Of course, the ideal relationship between business and society is a matter of debate. Supporters of the concept of **social responsibility** argue that a company has an obligation to society beyond the pursuit of profits.

A recent Business Week/Harris poll found that 95 percent of adults reject the notion that a corporation's only role is to make money. In fact, 76 percent of respondents said that if price and quality were equal, they would be likely to switch brands and retailers to support socially responsible companies.[14] Some companies link the pursuit of socially responsible goals with their overall growth strategies, such as Ben & Jerry's, Tom's of Maine (which produces natural personal-care products), and Working Assets (which provides long-distance telephone service).[15] Still, many other managers believe that their primary obligation is to the company's shareholders and that social responsibility is a secondary concern. Finding the right balance is challenging.

### BEN & JERRY'S: SOCIAL RESPONSIBILITY VERSUS PROFITS

Ben & Jerry's founders Ben Cohen and Jerry Greenfield have long struggled to balance the company's social initiative with shareholder demands for better profits. Since its inception in 1978, Ben & Jerry's Homemade Ice Cream has donated 7.5 percent of pretax profits to various causes (including saving the family farm, promoting world peace, saving the world's rain forests, and keeping French nuclear testing out of the South Pacific). Unfortunately, the company fell on hard times in the 1990s, nearly confirming the view that socially responsible companies would ultimately go out of business. But Perry D. Odak became CEO in 1997 and proved the skeptics wrong.[16]

When Odak took over, sales were down, and so was company morale. Employees didn't want to abandon Ben & Jerry's social mission in a search for profits. Many of them regretted the cancellation of efforts such as the Peace Pop program and its "One Percent for Peace." But as colorful as some of those programs were, they had also been inefficient. Nevertheless, things changed under Odak. By focusing on the balance sheet, CEO Odak managed not only to tighten Ben & Jerry's business practices and improve its bottom line but also to enhance its ability to contribute to worthy causes.[17]

In 1999, Ben & Jerry's was sold to Unilever, a $45 billion global giant that owns Breyer's and Good Humor ice cream brands, for $325 million in cash. Protestors were concerned that the new owner would not preserve the company's commitment to social causes. But Unilever assured them that Ben & Jerry's social mission would be encouraged and well-funded. Unilever agreed to donate an initial $5 million and 7.5 percent of Ben & Jerry's annual profits to the Ben & Jerry's Foundation. Moreover, it promised not to reduce jobs or alter the way the ice cream is made. In spite of strong resistance from Vermont residents and loyal customers, some saw the sale as an opportunity to project social consciousness onto a large multinational corporation.[18]

> ## active exercise

### THE EVOLUTION OF SOCIAL RESPONSIBILITY

Social responsibility is a concept with decades-old roots. In the nineteenth and early twentieth centuries, the prevailing view among U.S. industrialists was that business had only one responsibility: to make a profit. "The public be damned," said railroad tycoon William Vanderbilt, "I'm working for the shareholders."[19] *Caveat emptor* was the rule of the day—"Let the buyer beware." If you bought a product, you paid the price and took the consequences. No consumer groups or government agencies would help you if the product was defective or caused harm.

By the early twentieth century, however, reformers were beginning to push politicians and government regulators to protect citizens from the abuses of big business. Their efforts paid off. Laws were passed to ensure the purity of food and drugs, limit the power of monopolies, and prevent unfair business practices, among other reforms. (See Component Chapter B for a list of early government regulations pertaining to business.)

During the Great Depression, which started in 1929, 25 percent of the workforce was unemployed. Many people lost their faith in capitalism, and pressure mounted for government to fix the system. At the urging of President Franklin D. Roosevelt, Congress passed laws in the 1930s and 1940s that established the Social Security system, allowed employees to join unions and bargain collectively, set a minimum hourly wage, and limited the length of the workweek. New laws prevented unfair competition and false advertising and started the Securities and Exchange Commission (SEC) to protect investors.

Public confidence in U.S. business revived during World War II, and throughout the 1950s the relationship between business, government, and society was relatively tranquil. However, the climate shifted in the 1960s, as activism exploded on four fronts: environmental protection, national defense, consumerism, and civil rights. These movements have drastically altered the way business is conducted in the United States. Many of the changes have been made willingly by socially responsible companies such as Patagonia and Ben & Jerry's, others have been forced by government action, and still others have come about because of pressure from citizen groups.

## EFFORTS TO INCREASE SOCIAL RESPONSIBILITY

Today's businesses are about more than just making products or profits. As Ben & Jerry's and Patagonia show, socially responsible businesses can indeed make a difference in the world. *Industry Week*'s 100 Best Managed Companies all actively engage in socially responsible activities. Some work to curb child abuse or domestic violence. Others provide the best benefits packages for employees. Still others have strong recycling programs to keep the environment clean. In the past five years, General Mills has provided some $155 million in donations and contributions to help combat hunger, to provide education to students, and to ensure the safety of the neighborhoods where the company operates.[20] Those that give back to society are finding that their efforts can lead to a more favorable public image and stronger employee morale. Thus, more and more organizations are attempting to be socially responsible citizens by conducting a *social audit,* by engaging in *cause-related marketing,* or by being *philanthropic.*

A **social audit** is a systematic evaluation and reporting of the company's social performance. The report typically includes objective information about how the company's activities affect its various stakeholders. For example, once a year Ben & Jerry's Homemade Ice Cream asks an outsider to conduct a social audit that assesses the impact of the company's operations on its employees, customers, communities, suppliers, and shareholders. The company announces the results of the audit in its annual report to shareholders.

Companies can also engage in *cause-related marketing,* in which a portion of product sales helps support worthy causes. For example, Johnson & Johnson gives the World Wildlife fund a cut from sales of a special line of children's toiletries. Similarly, Peaceworks encourages joint business ventures among people of different backgrounds who live in volatile regions of the world. One of the company's product lines is *sprate,* uniquely flavored spreads produced in Israel by a Jewish-owned company that buys all its ingredients from Israeli Arabs and Palestinians. When consumers buy a jar of spraté, they not only get a tasty spread, but they also support the peace process in the Middle East.[21]

Some companies choose to be socially responsible corporate citizens by being **philanthropic;** that is, they donate money, time, goods, or services to charitable, humanitarian, or educational institutions (see Exhibit 2.3). Corporations such as Microsoft, General Electric, Dell, and Wal-Mart donate billions of dollars in cash and products to charity each year. American Express employees in Phoenix, Arizona, donate time to repair the houses of elderly, disabled, and low-income residents.[22] And Wendy's founder, Dave Thomas, travels around the country urging large companies to help employees with the costs associated with adopting children. "Writing a check is not enough," says Thomas. "You have to let people know that you are putting money where your heart is by giving your time, too."[23]

In short, businesspeople are doing whatever they can—donating computers, taking kids on field trips, supporting basketball teams, building houses for people, or helping people find jobs. "We try to function as though we live next door to everybody in our community," says the director of the Socially Responsible Banking Fund at Vermont National Bank.[24]

David Lubetzky, the founder of Peaceworks, is helping the Middle East peace process on two fronts: by encouraging cooperative business ventures between Jews and Arabs and by increasing awareness among American consumers.

## > video exercise

**Take a moment to apply what you've learned.**

## > active concept check

**Now let's take a moment to test your knowledge of the concepts you have studied in this section.**

## > Business's Response to the Needs of Society

Exactly how much can businesses contribute to social concerns? This is a difficult decision for most companies because they have limited resources. Thus, they must allocate their resources to a number of goals, such as upgrading facilities and equipment, developing new products, marketing existing products, and rewarding employee efforts, in addition to contributing to social causes. This juggling act is a challenge that every business faces. For example, if a company consistently ignores its stakeholders, its business will suffer and eventually fold. If the company disregards society's needs (such as

| Percentage of executives who "strongly agree" or "agree" that companies should: | Percentage |
| --- | --- |
| Be environmentally responsible | 100 |
| Be ethical in operations | 100 |
| Earn profits | 96 |
| Employ local residents | 94 |
| Pay taxes | 94 |
| Encourage and support employee volunteering | 89 |
| Contribute money and leadership to charities | 85 |
| Be involved in economic development | 75 |
| Be involved in public education | 73 |
| Involve community representatives in business decisions that impact community | 62 |
| Target a proportion of purchasing toward local vendors | 61 |
| Help improve quality of life for low-income populations | 54 |

**EXHIBIT 2.3**

Civic Responsibilities

Executives generally support the notion that companies should serve their communities and act in philanthropic ways.

environmental concerns), voters will clamor for laws to limit the offensive business activities, consumers who feel their needs and values are being ignored will spend their money on a competitor's products, investors who are unhappy with the company's performance will invest elsewhere, and employees whose needs are not met will become unproductive or will quit and find other jobs. As Exhibit 2.4 shows, stakeholders' needs sometimes conflict. In such cases, which stakeholders should be served first—society, consumers, investors, or employees?

## RESPONSIBILITY TOWARD SOCIETY AND THE ENVIRONMENT

Environmental issues exemplify the difficulty that businesses encounter when they try to reconcile conflicting interests: Society needs as little pollution as possible from businesses. But producing quality products to satisfy customers' needs can cause pollution to some degree. Business executives such as Patagonia's Yvon Chouinard try to strike a balance by making environmental management a formal part of their business strategy—along with quality, profits, safety, and other daily business operations.[25] Still, merging industrialism with environmentalism is not an easy task, says William Clay Ford Jr., chairman of Ford Motor Company. In an unprecedented step toward that goal, Ford recently admitted that SUVs foul the air more than cars and pledged to engineer breakthroughs to make SUVs cleaner.[26]

### The Pervasiveness of Pollution

Our air, water, and land can easily be tainted by **pollution** (the contamination of the natural environment by the discharge of harmful substances). Moreover, the pollution in any one element can easily taint the others. Environmental pollution pervades industrialized and developing nations alike. The emerging economies of Asia and Latin America have based much of their growth on loose environmental standards. However, Mexico, Malaysia, and other developing countries realize that their prosperity can be sustained only if their citizens can enjoy the quality of life that comes with a clean environment. At the same time, the countries of Eastern Europe are scrambling to reverse the decades of environmental neglect that occurred under communism.[27]

**AIR POLLUTION** The most noticeable form of air pollution is smog, which is produced by the interaction of sunlight and hydrocarbons (gases released when fossil fuels are burned). Another kind of air pollution causes acid rain, which is created when emissions from coal-burning factories and

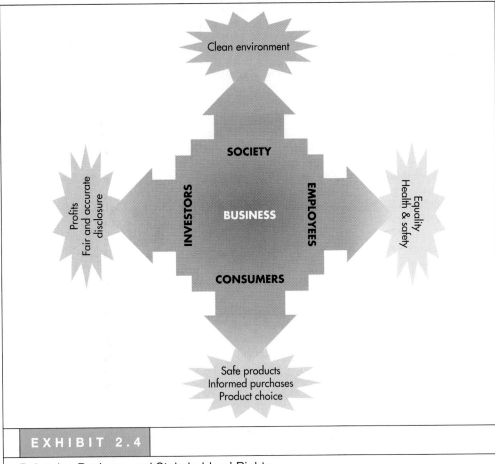

Clean environment

SOCIETY

INVESTORS

Profits
Fair and accurate
disclosure

BUSINESS

EMPLOYEES

Equality
Health & safety

CONSUMERS

Safe products
Informed purchases
Product choice

**EXHIBIT 2.4**

Balancing Business and Stakeholders' Rights

Balancing the individual needs and interests of a company's stakeholders is one of management's most difficult tasks.

electric utility plants react with air. Acid rain has been blamed for damaging lakes and forests in the northeastern United States and southeastern Canada.

Experts also worry about airborne toxins emitted during some manufacturing processes. Large and small companies together release millions of pounds of chemical wastes into the air each year. Although the effects of many of these substances are unknown, some are carcinogenic (cancer-causing).[28] Emissions from factories and cars also contribute to global warming. The greenhouse effect occurs when heated gases form a layer of unusually warm air around the earth, trapping the sun's heat and preventing the earth's surface from cooling. Some scientists estimate that global warming will cause worldwide temperatures to rise by 1 to 3.5 degrees Celsius in the next century. This could lead to increases in both droughts and floods in some regions and raise the sea level about 50 centimeters (20 inches) by 2100.[29]

**WATER POLLUTION** Our air is not the only part of our environment to suffer. Water pollution has damaged many U.S. lakes, rivers, streams, harbors, and coastal waters. Contamination comes from a variety of sources: manufacturing facilities, mining and construction sites, farms, and city sewage systems. Although dramatic accidents are widely publicized (such as the Exxon *Valdez* oil spill in Alaskan waters), the main threat is the careless day-to-day disposal of wastes from thousands of individual sources.

**LAND POLLUTION** Even if all wastewater were purified before being discharged, our groundwater would still be endangered by leakage from the millions of tons of hazardous substances that have been buried underground or dumped in improper storage sites. Much of this pollution was created years ago by companies that carelessly—but legally—disposed of substances (now known to be unhealthy) in landfills, where few (if any) protective barriers could be counted on to prevent dangerous chemicals from leaking into the soil and the water supply. Cleaning up these wastes is extremely difficult and expensive.

In addition, companies and individuals alike generate enormous amounts of solid waste—more than 200 million tons in the United States each year. Much of this waste ends up in landfills. A large part of the landfill problem comes from consumer demands for convenience and fashion. Fortunately, recent efforts to conserve and recycle resources are helping to combat the land pollution problem.[30]

## The Government Effort to Reduce Pollution

Widespread concern for the environment has been growing since the 1960s with the popularization of **ecology,** or the study of the balance of nature. In 1963 federal, state, and local governments began enacting laws and regulations to reduce pollution. (See Component Chapter B for a brief summary of major federal environmental legislation.) In December 1970 the federal government established the Environmental Protection Agency (EPA) to regulate air and water pollution by manufacturers and utilities, supervise the control of automobile pollution, license pesticides, control toxic substances, and safeguard the purity of drinking water. Congress is currently attempting to reform the EPA, because critics contend that the agency's tough restrictions actually prohibit companies from finding the most cost-effective ways to reduce pollution.

Many individual states have also passed their own tough clean air laws. For example, California requires that 10 percent of all new vehicles sold in the state be pollution-free by 2003. In response, both large and small car manufacturers are working to produce electric vehicles. General Motors and Honda have already begun selling their first models.[31]

Progress has also been made in reducing water pollution. Both government and private business have made major expenditures to treat and reuse wastewater, as well as to upgrade sewage systems. Unfortunately, the war on toxic waste has not been quite as successful. Government attempts to force businesses to clean up these sites have yielded many lawsuits and much expense but disappointing results. At some sites, the groundwater may never be restored to drinking-water purity.

Although many companies do a good job of regulating themselves, it is often pressure from the public and the government that causes businesses to clean up their acts. Companies that pollute excessively not only risk being charged with violating federal laws but also risk being sued by private citizens. Of course, such after-the-fact costs are ultimately passed on to consumers. Clearly, society benefits most when companies take it upon themselves to find cost-effective ways of reducing pollution.

3M's decision to discontinue Scotchguard fabric protector is a noteworthy example of company self-regulation. 3M was under no government mandate to stop manufacturing products with perfluorooctane sulfonate (PFOs). Moreover, evidence that PFOs harmed humans did not exist. But when traces of the chemical showed up in humans, 3M decided to pull the plug on the product and not wait until scientific evidence might someday link PFOs to a disease. This decision cost 3M $500 million in annual sales because the company did not have a substitute product to fill Scotchguard's void.[32]

## The Business Effort to Reduce Pollution

Today's managers are learning from the mistakes of their predecessors and are taking steps to reduce and prevent pollution. Some use high-temperature incineration to destroy hazardous wastes, some recycle wastes, some give their wastes to other companies that can use them, some neutralize wastes biologically, and some have redesigned their manufacturing processes so that they don't produce the wastes in the first place. In Kahlundborg, Denmark, some companies practice what they call *industrial symbiosis,* which means that they work together in a mutually advantageous relationship. Manufacturers as diverse as a pharmaceutical company, an oil refinery, a farm, a building materials company, and a power plant are linked via pipes and ground transportation systems so that each can use the waste products from the others as fuel and raw materials for themselves. The idea started among the managers of the companies as a way to lower costs and boost profits. But the reduction of waste and pollution has been so substantial that the EPA has taken notice. It is now supporting the development of similar ecoindustrial parks in the United States.[33]

Another innovative approach to reducing pollution is based on free-market principles. In certain cities, companies can buy and sell pollution rights. Each company is given an allowable "pollution quota" based on such factors as its size and industry. If a company voluntarily reduces pollution below its limit, it can sell its "credits" to another company. This system provides an incentive for companies to find efficient ways of reducing pollution. Evidence so far suggests that the plan is effective in reducing overall levels of pollutants such as sulfur dioxide.[34]

Companies are also reducing the amount of solid waste they send to landfills by implementing companywide recycling programs. The EPA reports that over 20 percent of the solid waste generated in the United States is now recycled.[35] In addition, hundreds of thousands of tons of waste have been eliminated through conservation and more efficient production.[36]

Many businesses such as Patagonia are recognizing the link between environmental performance and financial well-being and are addressing environmental problems by:[37]

- Considering them a part of everyday business and operating decisions
- Accepting environmental staff members as full-fledged partners in improving the company's competitiveness
- Measuring environmental performance
- Tying compensation to environmental performance
- Determining the long-term environmental costs *before* such costs occur
- Considering environmental impact in the product-development process
- Challenging suppliers to improve environmental performance
- Conducting training and awareness programs

More and more companies are discovering that spending now to prevent pollution can end up saving more money down the road (by reducing cleanup costs, litigation expense, and production costs). From building ecoindustrial parks to improving production efficiency, these activities are a part of the *green marketing* movement, in which companies distinguish themselves by using less packaging materials, recycling more waste, and developing new products that are easier on the environment.

> **active poll**

**What do you think? Voice your opinion and find out what others have to say.**

## RESPONSIBILITY TOWARD CONSUMERS

The 1960s activism that awakened business to its environmental responsibilities also gave rise to **consumerism,** a movement that put pressure on businesses to consider consumer needs and interests. Consumerism prompted many businesses to create consumer-affairs departments to handle customer complaints. It also prompted state and local agencies to set up bureaus to offer consumer information and assistance. At the federal level, President John F. Kennedy announced a "bill of rights" for consumers, laying the foundation for a wave of consumer-oriented legislation. (See Component Chapter B for a list of major federal consumer legislation.) These rights include the right to safety, the right to be informed, the right to choose, and the right to be heard.

### The Right to Safe Products

In the 1970s, household clothes irons could overheat into a melted mess, mower blades could continue turning even after users let go of the machine, over-the-counter drugs didn't come in childproof containers, and cars had so many problems that consumers expected to have trouble with them. Of course, today's irons turn off automatically, mowers shut off when the operator lets go, childproof caps are commonplace, and car quality has risen sharply.[38]

The U.S. government imposes many safety standards that are enforced by the Consumer Product Safety Commission (CPSC), as well as by other federal and state agencies. Theoretically, companies that don't comply with these rules are forced to take corrective action. Moreover, the threat of product-liability suits and declining sales motivates many companies to meet safety standards. After all, a poor safety record can damage a company's reputation. But with or without government action, many consumer advocates complain that some unsafe products still slip through the cracks.

Consider Firestone tires, for example. Critics claim that Ford and Firestone didn't act fast enough once they suspected problems with Firestone Wilderness AT and ATX tires. Not only did Ford and Firestone handle the recall of 6.5 million tires poorly, but they waited much too long before they removed the defective tires from the marketplace.[39]

### The Right to Be Informed

Consumers have a right to know what is in a product and how to use it. They also have a right to know the sales price of goods or services and the details of any purchase contracts. The Food and Drug Administration, the Federal Trade Commission, and the Agriculture Department are the federal agencies responsible for regulating product labels to make sure no false claims are made. These agencies are concerned not only with safety but also with accurate information. Research shows that nearly three-quarters of shoppers read labels when deciding whether to buy a food product the first time, so labels are an important element in informing consumers.[40]

If a product is sufficiently dangerous, a warning label is required by law, as in the case of cigarettes. However, warning labels can be a mixed blessing for consumers. To some extent, the presence of a warning protects the manufacturer from product-liability suits, but the label may not deter people from using the product or from using it incorrectly. The billions of dollars a year still spent on cigarettes in the United States illustrate this point. Moreover, as the world economy becomes more and more service-oriented, consumers are buying items that don't necessarily carry a label. Therefore, consumers must take it upon themselves to ensure that they are getting what they pay for.

### The Right to Choose Which Products to Buy

Especially in the United States, the number of products available to consumers is truly amazing. But how far should the right to choose extend? Are we entitled to choose products that are potentially harmful, such as cigarettes, liquor, or guns? To what extent are we entitled to learn about these products? Should beer and wine ads be eliminated from television, just as ads for other types of alcoholic beverages have been? Should advertising aimed at children be banned altogether?

Consumer groups are concerned about these questions, but no clear answers have emerged. In general, however, business is sensitive to these issues. Recent public concern about drunk driving, for example, has led the liquor industry to encourage responsible drinking. Coors now runs advertisements designed to discourage underage drinking and drinking on the job.[41] Similarly, several major broadcast television networks have implemented a rating system to help the public gauge whether a show is appropriate for a young audience. Most U.S. businesspeople prefer to help consumers make informed choices—rather than be told what choices to offer.

Still, some consumer groups say that government does not do enough. For example, when a product has been proven to be dangerous, does the fact that it is legal justify its sale? Should the government take measures to make the product illegal, or should consumers be allowed to decide for themselves what they buy? Consider cigarettes, for example. Scientists determined long ago that the tar and nicotine in tobacco are both harmful and addictive. In 1965 the Federal Cigarette Labeling and Advertising Act was passed, requiring all cigarette packs to carry the now-famous Surgeon General's warnings. Over the years, tobacco companies have spent billions of dollars to defend themselves in lawsuits brought by smokers suffering from cancer and respiratory diseases. As recently as 1996, the Liggett Group (a major U.S. tobacco company) admitted publicly that cigarettes cause cancer, are addictive, and have been promoted to encourage smoking among minors. And in 1997 the tobacco industry agreed to pay $368.5 billion over 25 years and an additional $15 billion per year after that to settle lawsuits brought by smoking victims and 40 state governments. Even so, consumers can still purchase cigarettes in the marketplace. RJR Nabisco chairman Steve Goldstone reminds us that "behind all the allegations . . . is the simple truth that we sell a legal product."[42]

### The Right to Be Heard

Many companies have established toll-free numbers for consumer information and feedback, and these numbers are often printed on product packages. In addition, more and more companies are establishing Web sites that provide product information and access for customer feedback. Of course, businesses benefit from gathering as much information about their customers as possible. Customer information allows companies to make informed decisions about changing current products and offering new ones. However, as this chapter's "Focusing on E-Business Today" highlights, the pursuit of information and the growth of e-commerce have given rise to a new ethical concern—maintaining customer privacy.

The right to be heard also covers a broad range of complaints about discrimination against customers. More than 4,000 African American customers complained to the U.S. Justice Department about racial discrimination by some Denny's restaurants. Among their complaints: They were asked to pay for meals in advance (although other customers weren't asked to do so), and they received slower service than other customers did. Flagstar, the chain's owner, responded by making a public apology and paying $46 million to settle the claims. In addition, the number of African American–owned Denny's franchises has risen from 1 to 27 in three years, and 12 percent of the company's supplies are now purchased from minority-owned vendors.[43]

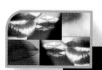

**active poll**  <

**What do you think? Voice your opinion and find out what others have to say.**

## RESPONSIBILITY TOWARD INVESTORS

In addition to their other responsibilities, businesses are responsible to those who have invested in the company. Historically, investors have been primarily interested in a company's financial performance. Clearly, a business can fail its investors by depriving them of their fair share of the profits. But a business can also fail its shareholders by being too concerned about profits. Today a growing number of investors are concerned about the ethics and social responsibility of the companies in which they invest. One study found that 26 percent of investors consider social responsibility to be extremely important.[44]

The job of looking out for a company's investors falls to its board of directors. Lately, more investors are turning up the heat on the individuals who sit on those boards (as discussed in Chapter 5). Concerned investors are targeting board members who fail to attend meetings, who sit on the boards of too many companies, who are underinvested (own very little stock in the companies they direct), and who sit on boards of companies with which their own firms do business. Looking out for investors is no easy task, but investors are finding that holding individual directors more accountable improves overall performance.[45] Of course, any action that cheats the investors out of their rightful profits is unethical.

### Misrepresenting the Investment

Every year tens of thousands of people are the victims of investment scams. Lured by promises of high returns, people sink more than a billion dollars per year into nonexistent oil wells, gold mines, and other fraudulent operations touted by complete strangers over the telephone and the Internet. Shady companies use other types of scams to take people's money, too. For example, con artists can dupe unwary investors by offering shares in start-up companies that don't exist. Investors should be especially careful of opportunities advertised over the Internet because it's so difficult for regulators to control online scams.[46] Other ways of misrepresenting the potential of an investment fall within the law. For example, with a little "creative accounting," a business that is in financial trouble can be made to look reasonably good to all but the most astute investors. Companies have some latitude in their reports to shareholders, and some firms are more conscientious than others in representing their financial performance.

### Diverting Earnings or Assets

Business executives may also take advantage of the investor by using the company's earnings or resources for personal gain. Managers have many opportunities to indirectly take money that rightfully belongs to the shareholders. Perhaps the most common approach is to cheat on expense accounts. Padding invoices and then splitting the overcharge with the supplier is another common ploy. Other tactics include selling company secrets to competitors or using confidential, nonpublic information gained from one's position in a company to benefit from the purchase and sale of stocks. Such **insider trading** is illegal and is closely watched by the Securities and Exchange Commission (SEC).

### Overdoing the Quest for Profits

Even though few companies knowingly break laws in an attempt to gain a competitive advantage, companies have taken questionable steps in their zeal to maximize profits. In order to protect earnings, some companies have used questionable methods to get bankrupt customers to sign repayment agreements. And to get ahead of the competition, some companies have engaged in corporate spying. Although businesses need to gather as much strategic information as they can, ethical companies steer clear of stealing patents, searching rivals' trash bins for sensitive information, accessing telephone records, hiring employees from competitors to gain trade secrets, and electronically eavesdropping.

> **active poll**

**What do you think? Voice your opinion and find out what others have to say.**

## RESPONSIBILITY TOWARD EMPLOYEES

Patagonia's Yvon Chouinard has always emphasized employee relationships that are ethical and supportive. For some companies, the past 30 years have brought dramatic changes in the attitudes and composition of the workforce. These changes have forced businesses to modify their recruiting, training, and promotion practices, as well as their overall corporate values and behaviors. (Consult Chapter 10 for an in-depth discussion of the staffing and demographic challenges employers are facing in today's workplace.)

### The Push for Equality in Employment

The United States has always stood for economic freedom and the individual's right to pursue opportunity. Unfortunately, until the past few decades many people were targets of economic **discrimination,** relegated to low-paying, menial jobs and prevented from taking advantage of many opportunities solely on the basis of their race, gender, disability, or religion.

The Civil Rights Act of 1964 established the Equal Employment Opportunity Commission (EEOC)—the regulatory agency that battles job discrimination. The EEOC is responsible for monitoring the hiring practices of companies and for investigating complaints of job-related discrimination. It has the power to file legal charges against companies that discriminate and to force them to compensate individuals or groups who have been victimized by unfair practices. The Civil Rights Act of 1991 extended the original act by allowing workers to sue companies for discrimination and by granting women powerful legal tools against job bias.

**AFFIRMATIVE ACTION** In the 1960s, **affirmative action** programs were developed to encourage organizations to recruit and promote members of minority groups. Proponents of the programs believe that minorities deserve and require preferential treatment to boost opportunities and to make up for years of discrimination. Opponents of affirmative action believe that creating special opportunities for women and minorities creates a double standard that infringes on the rights of other workers and forces companies to hire, promote, and retain people who are not necessarily the best choice from a business standpoint. Regardless, any company that does business with the federal government must have an affirmative action program.

Still, studies show that affirmative action has not been entirely successful. For one thing, efforts to hire more minorities do not necessarily change negative attitudes about differences among individuals. To combat this problem, about 75 percent of U.S. companies have established **diversity initiatives.** These initiatives often involve increasing minority employment and promotion, contracting with more minority vendors, including more minorities on boards of directors, and targeting a more diverse customer base. In addition, diversity initiatives use diversity training to promote understanding of the unique cultures, customs, and talents of all employees.

**PEOPLE WITH DISABILITIES** In 1990 people with a wide range of physical and mental difficulties got a boost from the passage of the federal Americans with Disabilities Act (ADA), which guarantees equal opportunities for an estimated 50 million to 75 million people who have or have had a condition that might handicap them. As defined by the 1990 law, *disability* is a broad term that protects not only those with obvious physical handicaps but also those with less-visible conditions, such as cancer, heart disease, diabetes, epilepsy, AIDS, drug addiction, alcoholism, and emotional illness. In most situations, employers cannot legally require job applicants to pass a physical examination as a condition of employment. The law also forbids firing people who have serious drinking or drug problems unless their chemical dependency prevents them from performing their essential job functions.

Businesses serving the public are required to make their services and facilities accessible to people with disabilities. This requirement means that restaurants, hotels, stores, airports, buses, taxis, banks, sports stadiums, and so forth must try to accommodate people who have disabilities. A hotel, for example, must equip 5 percent of its rooms with flashing lights or other "visual alarms" for people with hearing impairments.[47]

### Occupational Safety and Health

Each day 17 workers lose their lives on the job while another 24,000 are injured in the workplace (see Exhibit 2.5).[48] During the activist 1960s, mounting concern about workplace hazards resulted in passage of the Occupational Safety and Health Act of 1970, which set mandatory standards for safety and health and which established the Occupational Safety and Health Administration (OSHA) to enforce them.

OSHA's new ergonomic safety regulations, for example, will protect millions of workers from *ergonomic* or repetitive stress injuries such as carpal tunnel syndrome (from repetitive keyboarding) and back injuries (from repetitive lifting). The rules will grant workers up to 90 days of employer-paid sick leave for people injured on the job as a result of repetitive actions. Studies show that about 1.8 million U.S. workers each year suffer musculoskeletal injuries at work from performing repetitive actions, and that about one-third of the cases are serious enough to require time off. Nonetheless, the rules have generated a firestorm of protests from businesses who view them as vague, confusing, onerous, and very expensive.[49]

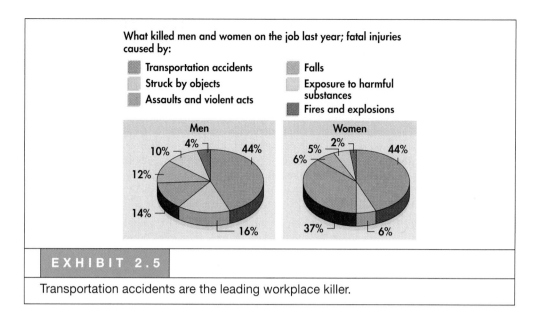

What killed men and women on the job last year; fatal injuries caused by:

- Transportation accidents
- Struck by objects
- Assaults and violent acts
- Falls
- Exposure to harmful substances
- Fires and explosions

**Men**
44%, 16%, 14%, 12%, 10%, 4%

**Women**
44%, 6%, 37%, 6%, 5%, 2%

**EXHIBIT 2.5**

Transportation accidents are the leading workplace killer.

Concerns for employee safety have also been raised by the international expansion of businesses. Many U.S. companies subcontract production to companies in foreign countries, making it more difficult to maintain proper standards of safety and compensation. For example, when a local labor advocacy group inspected a Nike factory in Vietnam, members discovered violations of minimum wage and overtime laws, as well as physical abuse of workers. Nike has been criticized in recent years for similar conditions in its other Southeast Asian and Chinese factories. Many other companies, including the Gap, Guess, and the Body Shop have come under similar criticism. In 1997 a presidential task force composed of apparel industry representatives, labor unions, and human rights groups drafted a code of conduct to uphold the rights of foreign workers of U.S. manufacturing companies. Among the provisions of the code are minimum wage requirements and limits on the number of hours employees work in a week.[50]

## > active concept check

**Now let's take a moment to test your knowledge of the concepts you have studied in this section.**

### > Ethics and Social Responsibility Around the World

As complicated as ethics and social responsibility can be for U.S. businesses, these issues grow even more complex when cultural influences are applied in the global business environment. There, corporate executives may face simple questions regarding the appropriate amount of money to spend on a business gift or the legitimacy of payment to "expedite" business. Or they may encounter out-and-out bribery, environmental abuse, and unscrupulous business practices. What does it mean for a business to do the right thing in Thailand? In Africa? In Norway? What may be considered unethical in the United States may be an accepted practice in another culture. Several areas of corruption are being addressed by international agreements: bribes, air pollution, and corporate behavior.

- *Bribes.* In the United States, bribing officials is illegal, but Kenyans consider paying such bribes a part of life. To get something done right, they pay *kitu kidogo* (or "something small"). In China businesses pay *huilu.* In Russia they pay *vzyatka,* in the Middle East it's *baksheesh,* and in Mexico it's *una mordida* ("a small bite"). The United States has lobbied other nations for 20 years to outlaw bribery, and at last the industrialized nations have signed a treaty that makes payoffs to foreign officials a criminal offense. The ban on bribes came after a string of high-level scandals around the world: Two South Korean presidents went to prison for accepting bribes. French cabinet ministers and mayors resigned during an investigation of kickbacks. The late dictator of Zaire (now Congo) actually merged his family's finances with those of the state. Moreover, corruption is such an obstacle in the Ukraine and Russia that some U.S. companies quit trying to do business there. Of course, bribery won't end just because a treaty has been signed, but supporters are optimistic that countries will ratify the treaty, pass legislation, and enforce the new laws stringently.[51]

- *Air pollution.* In a similar pact, 150 nations recently signed an agreement in Kyoto, Japan, to reduce worldwide emissions of carbon dioxide and other pollutants thought to be contributing to global warming. To comply with the agreement, countries around the world will be turning to energy from renewable sources, such as sun and wind—good news for companies like Houston-based Enron, which markets natural gas and oversees solar and wind projects.[52] The European Union (EU) had proposed a huge 15 percent cut in three of the best-known greenhouse gases by the year 2015, but the Kyoto compromise requires an 8 percent cut in six gases. Will Europe stand by its original offer? Europe would need to drop carbon dioxide emissions by 800 million tons at a cost of $15 billion to $21 billion.[53]

- *Corporate behavior.* Espionage is another issue on the U.S. agenda for global ethics. FBI Director Louis Freeh recently testified that U.S. companies are under economic attack from 23 countries trying to steal trade secrets and other intellectual property in the most severe threat to national security since the Cold War.[54] For instance, when Disney released its animated film *Mulan* in Hong Kong, the city's shopping arcades had already been selling the illegal video compact disc (VCD) for a week—complete with Chinese subtitles. Asian pirates are active not only in Hollywood but also in Silicon Valley and in the music business. In the Philippines, according to the Software Publishers Association, 83 percent of business software is pirated; even government offices openly use illegally copied programs. Laws against such piracy exist, but enforcing them is as difficult for Asian countries as it was for the United States to enforce Prohibition in the 1920s. As soon as one operation is shut down, another pops up in its place.[55] Meanwhile, the Organization for Economic Cooperation and Development (OECD) has drawn up a 22-page world standard for "good corporate behavior." The OECD's 29 members include most of the world's richest countries, and they hope world agencies will get nonmembers to adopt the standards and put them into law.[56]

As you can see, the issue of global business ethics is the ultimate dilemma for many U.S. businesses. As companies do more and more business around the globe, their assumptions about ethical codes of conduct are indeed put to the test.

## active poll    <

**What do you think? Voice your opinion and find out what others have to say.**

## active concept check    <

**Now let's take a moment to test your knowledge of the concepts you have studied in this section.**

 **Chapter Wrap-Up**

Now that you've reached the end of the chapter, you may wish to explore the concepts you've been reading about in greater detail, or test yourself to see how well you've comprehended the material. In the box below you'll find a number of links. Click on any one of these links to find additional chapter resources.

# > end-of-chapter resources

- Summary of Learning Objectives
- Practice Quiz
- Focusing on E-Business Today
- Key Terms
- Test Your Knowledge
- Practice Your Knowledge
- Expand Your Knowledge
- A Case for Critical Thinking

# Global Business

What's Ahead
The Global Business Environment
   Cultural Differences in the Global
   Business Environment
   Legal Differences in the Global
   Business Environment
   Forms of International Business
   Activity
Fundamentals of International Trade
   Why Nations Trade
   How International Trade Is Measured
   Trade Restrictions

Agreements and Organizations
Promoting International Trade
   Trading Blocs
Interdependence of Economies in the
Global Marketplace
   Foreign Exchange Rates and
   Currency Valuations
   The Global Economic Crisis at the
   End of the Twentieth Century
   Effect of the Crisis in the United
   States
Chapter Wrap-Up

## > What's Ahead

### INSIDE BUSINESS TODAY
### TREK BIKES: TREKKING AROUND THE GLOBE

It's a world away from the bright lights of Paris. But the little town of Waterloo, Wisconsin, captured the world's attention during the 1999 Tour de France. When Lance Armstrong zoomed across the finish line on Paris's Champs-Elysées, the American cycler raced to victory on an American bike—a bike made by Trek Bicycle Corporation of Waterloo.

At first glance, Waterloo seems an unlikely place for the headquarters of an international business. Dairy farms dominate the rural landscape. And when Green Bay Packers' fans support their favorite team, they also promote the state's most famous commodity by wearing foam cheese wedges on their heads. Even so, Waterloo is where Trek opened for business in 1976 with five workers assembling bicycle frames by hand in an old wooden barn.

During the company's first few years, Trek sold its bicycles exclusively in the United States. But all that changed in 1985 when Joyce Keehn, now Trek's worldwide sales director, received several inquiries about exporting Treks to Canada. A novice in international trade, Keehn consulted the state's export agency and sought advice from local exporters at state-sponsored trade seminars. After considering Trek's close proximity to Canada, Keehn decided that selling directly to Canadian bicycle shops was the company's best option for international expansion.

As more exporting opportunities opened up, Keehn experimented with other foreign distribution methods. For instance, to minimize cultural and language barriers, she relied on the expertise and knowledge of local distributors instead of approaching retailers directly. In other

Lance Armstrong, winner of the 1999 and 2000 Tour de France, boldly displays his affiliation.

countries, she advised Trek to create wholly owned subsidiaries for handling sales, inventory, warranties, customer service, and direct distribution to retail outlets. Such subsidiary offices allowed Trek to maintain higher profits and more control over its products.

Still, Keehn hit some bumps in the road as she ventured into the global marketplace. For example, customs delays created frequent insurance and financial problems; some shipments even disappeared during customs clearances in Mexico. On one occasion, Trek halted distribution of its catalog after discovering that a featured cartoon character was offensive to Germans. And customizing bikes for the European markets increased Trek's production costs.

Cyberspace presented even more challenges for Keehn. Trek's international dealers must charge higher prices than those charged by U.S. sellers to cover such costs as shipping and tariffs. Moreover, international prices must allow for fluctuating foreign exchange rates. To avoid this confusion and to protect its international sellers, Trek does not sell bicycles or reveal prices on its Web site. Instead, it refers customers to authorized dealers in their area.

Today, whether you're in cyberspace, Cincinnati, or Cyprus, you won't have to travel far to find a Trek. Keehn has established a network of 65 distributors on six continents and seven wholly owned subsidiaries in Europe and Japan. From its humble beginnings in Waterloo, Trek is now the world's largest maker of racing bikes, mountain bikes, and other types of specialty bikes. The company sells more than a half million bikes in more than 70 countries every year. In 10 years, annual revenues have grown from $18 million to over $400 million, of which 40 percent now come from international business.[1]

# objectives <

**Take a moment to familiarize yourself with the key objectives of this chapter.**

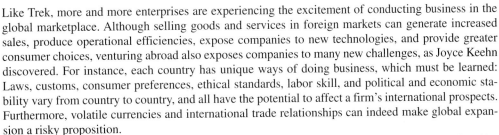

> **gearing up**

Before you begin reading this chapter, try a short warm-up activity.

> **The Global Business Environment**

> **video example**

Take a closer look at the concepts and issues you've been reading about.

Like Trek, more and more enterprises are experiencing the excitement of conducting business in the global marketplace. Although selling goods and services in foreign markets can generate increased sales, produce operational efficiencies, expose companies to new technologies, and provide greater consumer choices, venturing abroad also exposes companies to many new challenges, as Joyce Keehn discovered. For instance, each country has unique ways of doing business, which must be learned: Laws, customs, consumer preferences, ethical standards, labor skill, and political and economic stability vary from country to country, and all have the potential to affect a firm's international prospects. Furthermore, volatile currencies and international trade relationships can indeed make global expansion a risky proposition.

Still, in most cases the opportunities of the global marketplace greatly outweigh the risks. Consider UPS. When this company began its rapid global expansion program in the 1980s, it had to attain air rights into each country, unravel a patchwork of customs laws, learn how to deal with varying work ethics and employment policies, and so on. But the company's efforts paid off. Today UPS delivers over 13 million packages annually in more than 200 countries. Over 13 percent of the company's revenue now comes from international package deliveries.[2]

## CULTURAL DIFFERENCES IN THE GLOBAL BUSINESS ENVIRONMENT

Cultural differences present a number of challenges in the global marketplace, as Joyce Keehn's experience shows. For one thing, companies must recognize and respect differences in social values, ideas of status, decision-making habits, attitudes toward time, use of space, body language, manners, and ethical standards. Otherwise such differences can lead to misunderstandings in international business relationships, particularly if language differences also exist (see Exhibit 3.1). Furthermore, companies that sell their products overseas must often adapt the products to meet the unique needs of international customers, just as Trek does.

The best way to prepare yourself to do business with people from another culture is to study that culture in advance. Learn everything you can about the culture's history, religion, politics, and customs—especially its business customs. Who makes decisions? How are negotiations usually conducted? Is gift giving expected? What is the proper attire for a business meeting? In addition to the suggestion that you learn about the culture, seasoned international businesspeople offer the following tips for improving intercultural communication:

- *Be alert to the other person's customs.* Expect the other person to have values, beliefs, expectations, and mannerisms different from yours. For instance, don't be surprised when businesspeople in Pakistan excuse themselves in the middle of a meeting to conduct prayers. Moslems pray five times a day.

- *Deal with the individual.* Don't stereotype the other person or react with preconceived ideas. Regard the person as an individual first, not as a representative of another culture.

- *Clarify your intent and meaning.* The other person's body language may not mean what you think, and the person may read unintentional meanings into your message. Clarify your true intent by repetition and examples. Ask questions and listen carefully. The Japanese are generally

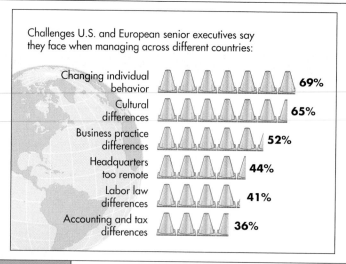

Challenges U.S. and European senior executives say they face when managing across different countries:

| Challenge | Percentage |
|-----------|-----------|
| Changing individual behavior | 69% |
| Cultural differences | 65% |
| Business practice differences | 52% |
| Headquarters too remote | 44% |
| Labor law differences | 41% |
| Accounting and tax differences | 36% |

**EXHIBIT 3.1**

Going Global Has Its Barriers

Learning a country's business customs and cultural differences is the first step in going global.

appreciative when foreigners ask what is proper behavior, because it shows respect for the Japanese way of doing things.[3]

- *Adapt your style to the other person's.* If the other person appears to be direct and straightforward, follow suit. If not, adjust your behavior to match. In many African countries, for example, people are suspicious of others who seem to be in a hurry. Therefore, you should allow plenty of time to get to know the people you are dealing with.

- *Show respect.* Learn how respect is communicated in various cultures—through gestures, eye contact, and so on. For example, in Spain let a handshake last five to seven strokes; pulling away too soon may be interpreted as a rejection. In France, however, the preferred handshake is a single stroke.

## active exercise ◄

**Take a moment to apply what you've learned.**

### LEGAL DIFFERENCES IN THE GLOBAL BUSINESS ENVIRONMENT

All U.S. companies that conduct business in other countries must be familiar with U.S. law, international law, and the laws of the specific countries where they plan to trade or do business. For example, all companies doing international business must comply with the 1978 Foreign Corrupt Practices Act. This U.S. law outlaws actions such as bribing government officials in other nations to approve deals. It does, however, allow certain payments, including small payments to officials for expediting routine government actions.

Critics of this U.S. law complain that payoffs are a routine part of world trade, so forbidding U.S. companies to follow suit cripples their ability to compete. Others counter that U.S. exports haven't been affected by this law and that companies can conduct business abroad without violating antibribery rules. Regardless of whether they agree or disagree with the law, some companies have had to forgo opportunities as a result of it. For example, a U.S. power-generation company recently walked away from a $320 million contract in the Middle East because government officials demanded a $3 million bribe. The contract went to a Japanese company instead.[4]

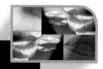

> ## active poll

**What do you think? Voice your opinion and find out what others have to say.**

## FORMS OF INTERNATIONAL BUSINESS ACTIVITY

Once a company decides to operate in the global marketplace, it must decide on the level of involvement it is willing to undertake. Five common forms of international business activities are *importing and exporting, licensing, franchising, strategic alliances and joint ventures,* and *foreign direct investment.* Each has a varying degree of ownership, financial commitment, and risk.

### Importing and Exporting

**Importing,** the buying of goods or services from a supplier in another country, and **exporting,** the selling of products outside the country in which they are produced, have existed for centuries. In the last few decades, however, the increased level of these activities has caused the economies of the world to become tightly linked.

Exporting, one of the least risky forms of international business activity, permits a firm to enter a foreign market gradually, assess local conditions, and then fine tune its product to meet the needs of foreign consumers. In most cases the firm's financial exposure is limited to market research costs, advertising costs, and the costs of either establishing a direct sales and distribution system or hiring intermediaries. Such intermediaries include *export management companies,* domestic firms that specialize in performing international marketing services on a commission basis, and *export trading companies,* general trading firms that will buy your products for resale overseas as well as perform a variety of importing, exporting, and manufacturing functions. Still another alternative is to use foreign distributors.

Working through a foreign distributor with connections in the target country is often helpful to both large and small companies because such intermediaries can provide you with the connections, expertise, and market knowledge you will need to conduct business in a foreign country.[5] In addition, many countries now have foreign trade offices to help importers and exporters interested in doing business within their borders. Other helpful resources include professional agents, local businesspeople, and the International Trade Administration of the U.S. Department of Commerce. This trade organization offers a variety of services, including political and credit risk analysis, advice on entering foreign markets, and financing tips.

### International Licensing

**Licensing** is another popular approach to international business. License agreements entitle one company to use some or all of another firm's intellectual property (patents, trademarks, brand names, copyrights, or trade secrets) in return for a royalty payment. Underwear manufacturer Jockey licenses the rights to use the Jockey name to certain foreign manufacturers of women's active wear, sleepwear, and slippers. Jockey licenses its products in more than 120 countries but is careful that all such arrangements add value to the Jockey name.[6]

Many firms choose licensing as an approach to international markets because it involves little out-of-pocket costs. A firm has already incurred the costs of developing the intellectual property to be licensed. Pharmaceutical firms, for instance, routinely use licensing to enter foreign markets. Once a pharmaceutical firm has developed and patented a new drug, it is often more efficient to grant existing local firms the right to manufacture and distribute the patented drug in return for royalty payments. Israel's Teva Pharmaceutical Industries, for example, has a license to manufacture and market Merck's pharmaceutical products in Israel. This arrangement saves Merck the expense of establishing its own Israeli salesforce.[7] Of course, licensing agreements are not restricted to international business. A company can also license its products or technology to other companies in its domestic market.

### International Franchising

Some companies choose to expand into foreign markets by *franchising* their operation. International franchising is among the fastest-growing forms of international business activity today. Under this arrangement, a franchisor enters into an agreement whereby the franchisee obtains the rights to duplicate a specific product or service—perhaps a restaurant, photocopy shop, or a video rental store—and the franchisor obtains a royalty fee in exchange. Holiday Inn Worldwide has used this approach to reach customers in over 65 countries. Smaller companies have also found that franchising is a good way for them to enter the global marketplace.[8] By franchising its operations, a firm can minimize the costs and risks of global expansion and bypass certain trade restrictions. (The advantages and disadvantages of franchising in general will be discussed in detail in Chapter 4.)

### International Strategic Alliances and Joint Ventures

A **strategic alliance** is a long-term partnership between two or more companies to jointly develop, produce, or sell products in the global marketplace. To reach their individual but complimentary goals, the companies typically share ideas, expertise, resources, technologies, investment costs, risks, management, and profits.

Strategic alliances are a popular way to expand one's business globally. The benefits of this form of international expansion include ease of market entry, shared risk, shared knowledge and expertise, and synergy. In other words, companies that form a strategic alliance with a foreign partner can often compete more effectively than if they entered the foreign market alone. Consider the strategic alliance established by American Airlines, British Airways, Cathay Pacific Airways, Quantas, and others. Named *oneworld,* this partnership makes global travel easier for consumers. Benefits include integrated frequent flyer programs, common airport lounges, and more efficient ticketing among member carriers so that a change of airlines is transparent when booking international flights.[9]

A **joint venture** is a special type of strategic alliance in which two or more firms join together to create a new business entity that is legally separate and distinct from its parents. In some countries, foreign companies are prohibited from owning facilities outright or from investing in local business. Thus, establishing a joint venture with a local partner may be the only way to do business in that country. In other cases, foreigners may be required to move some of their production facilities to the country to earn the right to sell their products there. For instance, the Chinese government would not allow Boeing to sell airplanes in China until the company agreed to move half of the tail-section production for its 737s to Xian.[10]

### Foreign Direct Investment

Exporting, licensing, franchising, and strategic alliances allow a firm to enter the global marketplace without investing in foreign factories or facilities. However, many firms prefer to enter international markets through ownership and control of assets in foreign countries.

The most comprehensive form of international business is a wholly owned operation run in another country, without the financial participation of a local partner. Many U.S. firms conduct business this way, as do companies based in other countries. These operations vary in form, size, and purpose. Some are started from scratch; others are acquired from local owners. Some are small sales offices; others are full-scale manufacturing facilities. Some are set up to exploit the availability of raw materials; others take advantage of low wage rates; still others minimize transportation costs by choosing locations that give them direct access to markets in other countries. In almost all cases, at least part of the workforce is drawn from the local population.

Companies with a physical presence in numerous countries are called **multinational corporations (MNCs).** Because they operate on such a worldwide scale, at times it's difficult to determine exactly where home is (see Exhibit 3.2). Since 1969, the number of multinational corporations in the world's 14 richest countries has more than tripled, from 7,000 to 24,000.[11] Some multinational corporations increase their involvement in foreign countries by establishing **foreign direct investment (FDI).** That is, they either establish production and marketing facilities in the countries where they operate or purchase existing foreign firms, as Wal-Mart did in the late 1990s, when it acquired large retail stores in Germany and Great Britain and later converted them into Wal-Mart supercenters. Such foreign direct investment constitutes the highest level of international involvement. Moreover, it carries much greater economic and political risk and is more complex than any other form of entry in the global marketplace.[12]

The U.S. Commerce Department reports that foreign direct investment in the United States has been rising steadily over the past few years.[13] For example, Daimler-Benz's $40 billion acquisition of Chrysler and British Petroleum's $48 billion acquisition of Amoco propelled Germany and the United Kingdom to the top two foreign countries investing in the United States.[14]

In addition to the United States, areas such as the Chinese Economic Area (China, Hong Kong, and Taiwan), South Korea, Singapore, Thailand, Malaysia, Indonesia, Vietnam, India, South Africa, Turkey, and Brazil are becoming attractive spots for foreign investment. Labeled *big emerging markets,* these countries make up 70 percent of the world's land, 85 percent of the world's population, and 99 percent of the anticipated growth in the world's labor force.[15] As such, they have been identified by the U.S. International Trade Administration as having the greatest potential for large increase in U.S. exports over the next two decades.

| 1999 Rank | Company | Foreign Revenue (in millions) | Total Revenue (in millions) | Foreign as Percent of Total |
|---|---|---|---|---|
| 1 | ExxonMobil | $115,464 | $160,883 | 72 |
| 2 | IBM | 50,377 | 87,548 | 58 |
| 3 | Ford Motor | 50,138 | 162,558 | 31 |
| 4 | General Motors | 46,485 | 176,558 | 26 |
| 5 | General Electric | 35,350 | 111,630 | 31 |
| 6 | Texaco | 32,700 | 42,433 | 77 |
| 7 | Citigroup | 28,749 | 82,005 | 35 |
| 8 | Hewlett-Packard | 23,398 | 42,370 | 55 |
| 9 | Wal-Mart Stores | 22,728 | 165,013 | 14 |
| 10 | Compac Computer | 21,174 | 38,525 | 55 |
| 11 | American Intl Group | 20,311 | 40,656 | 50 |
| 12 | Chevron | 20,020 | 45,198 | 44 |
| 13 | Philip Morris Cos. | 19,670 | 61,751 | 32 |
| 14 | Procter & Gamble | 18,351 | 38,125 | 48 |
| 15 | Motorola | 17,760 | 30,931 | 58 |
| | TOTAL | $522,675 | $1,286,184 | 41 |

## EXHIBIT 3.2

Fifteen Largest U.S. Multinationals

On average, the 15 largest U.S. multinational corporations earn about 41 percent of their revenue from foreign sales.

China is becoming too big a PC market for anyone to ignore. Dell, which recently opened its fourth PC factory in the world on China's southeastern coast, can now deliver PCs to Chinese customers as fast as it does to North American ones.

> active exercise

**Take a moment to apply what you've learned.**

### > Fundamentals of International Trade

The success of U.S. businesses such as Trek, Wal-Mart, UPS, and others that operate in the global marketplace depends, in part, on the international economic relationships the United States maintains with other countries. Basically, the objective of the United States is to devise policies that balance the interests of U.S. companies, U.S. workers, and U.S. consumers. Other countries, of course, are trying to do the same thing. As you might expect, the many players in world trade sometimes have conflicting goals.

### WHY NATIONS TRADE

No single country has the resources to produce everything its citizens want or need. Countries specialize in the production of certain goods and trade with other countries to obtain raw materials and goods that are unavailable to them or too costly for them to produce. Moreover, international trade has many benefits: it increases a country's total output, it offers lower prices and greater variety to consumers, it subjects domestic oligopolies and monopolies to competition, and it allows companies to expand their markets and achieve production and distribution efficiencies.[16]

How does a country know what to produce and what to trade for? In some cases the answer is easy: a nation may have an **absolute advantage,** which means it can produce a particular item more efficiently than *all* other nations, or it is virtually the only country producing that product. Absolute advantages rarely last, however, unless they are based on the availability of natural resources. Saudi Arabia, for example, has an absolute advantage in crude oil production because of its huge, developed reserves. Thus, it makes sense for Saudi Arabia to specialize in providing the world with oil, and to trade for other items its country needs.

In most cases, a country can produce many of the same items that other countries can produce. The **comparative advantage theory** explains how a country chooses which items to produce and which items to trade for. The theory states that a country should produce and sell to other countries those items it produces more efficiently or at a lower cost, and trade for those it can't produce as economically. To see how the theory works, consider the United States and Brazil. Each can produce both steel and coffee, but the United States is more efficient at producing steel than coffee, while Brazil is more efficient at producing coffee than steel. According to the comparative advantage theory, the two countries will be better off if each specializes in the industry where it is more efficient and if the two trade with each other—the United States sells steel to Brazil and Brazil sells coffee to the United States.[17] The basic argument behind the comparative advantage theory is that such specialization and exchange will increase a country's total output and allow both trading partners to enjoy a higher standard of living.

### HOW INTERNATIONAL TRADE IS MEASURED

In Chapter 1 we discussed how economists monitor certain key economic indicators to evaluate how well their country's economic system is performing. One trend that economists watch carefully is the level of a nation's imports and exports. For instance, at any given time, a country may be importing more than it is exporting. As Exhibit 3.3 illustrates, the United States imports more consumer goods than it exports, but it exports more services than it imports. Two key measurements of a nation's level of international trade are the *balance of trade* and the *balance of payments.*

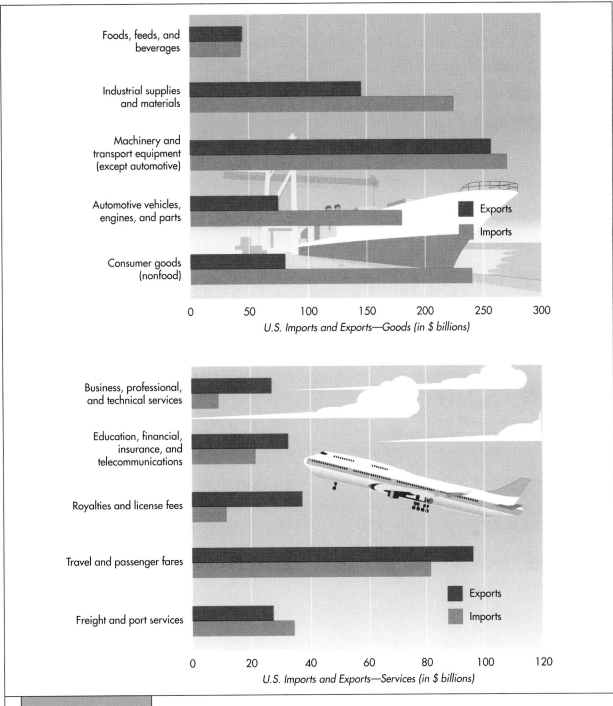

**Foods, feeds, and beverages**

**Industrial supplies and materials**

**Machinery and transport equipment (except automotive)**

**Automotive vehicles, engines, and parts**

**Consumer goods (nonfood)**

Exports
Imports

0    50    100    150    200    250    300

*U.S. Imports and Exports—Goods (in $ billions)*

**Business, professional, and technical services**

**Education, financial, insurance, and telecommunications**

**Royalties and license fees**

**Travel and passenger fares**

**Freight and port services**

Exports
Imports

0    20    40    60    80    100    120

*U.S. Imports and Exports—Services (in $ billions)*

## EXHIBIT 3.3

U.S. Exports and Imports

The United States actively participates in global trade by exporting and importing goods and services.

The total value of a country's exports *minus* the total value of its imports, over some period of time, determines its **balance of trade.** In years when the value of goods and services exported by the United States exceeds the value of goods and services it imports, the U.S. balance of trade is said to be positive: People in other countries buy more goods and services from the United States than the United States buys from them, creating a **trade surplus.** Conversely, when the people of the United States buy more from foreign countries than the foreign countries buy from the United States, the U.S. balance of trade is said to be negative. That is, imports exceed exports, creating a **trade deficit.** As

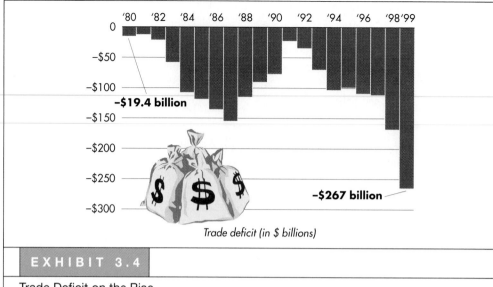

'80 '82 '84 '86 '88 '90 '92 '94 '96 '98'99

−$19.4 billion

−$267 billion

Trade deficit (in $ billions)

EXHIBIT 3.4

Trade Deficit on the Rise

U.S. officials say the exploding trade deficit is evidence that the United States maintains the world's most open markets.

Exhibit 3.4 shows, in 1999 the U.S. trade deficit soared to a record $267 billion (produced by a $347 billion trade deficit in goods and an $80 billion trade surplus in services). Economists attribute this deficit to a falloff in U.S. exports rather than a surge in foreign imports.[18]

Bear in mind that the excess of imports over exports does not necessarily mean that U.S. companies are not competitive in the world market. The balance of trade is obscured by several factors. One such factor is the change in the value of the dollar compared with the value of other currencies. When the dollar is strong, products from other countries seem relatively inexpensive in the United States, and U.S. products seem relatively expensive overseas. As U.S. consumers buy more of the relatively inexpensive imported goods and consumers overseas buy less of the relatively expensive U.S. goods, the U.S. trade deficit grows. When the situation is reversed and U.S. consumers buy fewer imported goods while people in other countries buy more U.S. exports, the U.S. trade deficit narrows and may even turn into a trade surplus. (Currency valuations and their impact on global trade will be discussed later in this chapter.)

Another reason that the balance of trade can be misleading is **intrafirm trade,** which is trade between the various units of a multinational corporation. In fact, intrafirm trade now accounts for one-third of all the goods traded around the world.[19] Multinational corporations such as Whirlpool, AT&T, Texas Instruments, and General Electric set up factories to make components in countries where wage rates are low, then ship the components back to the United States for assembly. These shipments to the United States are counted as imports even though they are used by the same company. By contrast, products produced by subsidiaries of foreign companies in the United States for the U.S. market are not considered imports. As you can see, by itself, the balance of trade does not paint a complete picture of a nation's global competitiveness.

The **balance of payments** is the broadest indicator of international trade. It is the total flow of money into the country *minus* the total flow of money out of the country over some period of time. The balance of payments includes the balance of trade plus the net dollars received and spent on foreign investment, military expenditures, tourism, foreign aid, and other international transactions. For example, when a U.S. company such as Whirlpool buys all or part of a company based in another country, that investment is counted in the balance of payments but not in the balance of trade. Similarly, when a foreign company such as Daimler-Benz buys a U.S. company such as Chrysler or purchases U.S. stocks, bonds, or real estate, those transactions are part of the balance of payments. The U.S. government, like all governments, desires a favorable balance of payments. That means more money is coming into the country than is flowing out. In 1999 the U.S. balance of payments amounted to a deficit of $339 billion, of which 79 percent was attributable to the country's trade deficit.[20]

## TRADE RESTRICTIONS

Even though international trade has many economic advantages, sometimes countries practice **protectionism**; that is, they restrict international trade for one reason or another. Sometimes they restrict trade to shield specific industries from foreign competition and the possible loss of jobs in these industries. Sometimes they try to protect certain industries that are key to their national defense and the health and safety of their citizens. Or, in the case of emerging economies such as China, they engage in protectionist measures to give new or weak industries an opportunity to grow and strengthen.[21]

Are trade restrictions a good idea or a bad idea? Study after study has shown that in the long run, they hurt a country because they remove competition, stifle innovation, and allow domestic producers to charge more for their goods. The most commonly used forms of trade restrictions include:

- *Tariffs.* **Tariffs** are taxes, surcharges, or duties levied against imported goods. Sometimes tariffs are levied to generate revenue for the government, but more often they are imposed to restrict trade or to punish other countries for disobeying international trade laws.

- *Quotas.* **Quotas** limit the amount of a particular good that countries can import during a year. The United States puts ceilings on foreign sugar, peanuts, and dairy products. Limits may be set in quantities, such as pounds of sugar, or in values, such as total dollars' worth of peanuts. In some cases, a product faces stiff tariffs once it reaches its quota. After foreign tobacco products hit their quotas, for example, additional shipments face 350 percent tariffs.[22]

- *Embargoes.* In its most extreme form, a quota becomes an **embargo,** a complete ban on the import or export of certain products. For example, Canada forbids the importation of oleomargarine in order to protect its dairy industry, and the U.S. bans the importation of toys with lead paint because of health concerns.

- *Sanctions.* Sanctions are politically motivated embargoes that revoke a country's normal trade relations status: They are often used as forceful alternatives short of war. Sanctions can include arms embargoes, foreign-assistance reductions and cutoffs, trade limitations, tariff increases, import-quota decreases, visa denials, air-link cancellations, and more. About two dozen countries are now subject to U.S. sanctions, including Iraq (for its invasion of Kuwait) and India (for conducting nuclear tests). Still, most governments today (including the United States) use sanctions sparingly, because studies show that sanctions are ineffective at getting countries to change.[23]

In addition to restricting foreign trade, sometimes governments give their domestic producers a competitive edge by using these protectionist tactics:

- *Restrictive import standards.* Countries can assist their domestic producers by establishing restrictive import standards, such as requiring special licenses for doing certain kinds of business and then making it difficult for foreign companies to obtain such a license. For example, Saudi Arabia restricts import licenses for a variety of products, including chemicals, pasteurized milk, and information technology products.[24] Other countries restrict imports by requiring goods to pass special tests.

- *Subsidies.* Rather than restrict imports, some countries subsidize domestic producers so that their prices can compete favorably in the global marketplace. Airbus, originally an alliance of state companies from Germany, France, England, and Spain, was subsidized for years to help the company compete against rival Boeing. Now that Airbus is a strong competitor the complex alliance has been sold to a joint venture composed of two private companies—the French-German-Spanish European Aeronautic Defense and Space Company NV (EADS), and Britain's BAE Systems PLC.[25]

- *Dumping.* The practice of selling large quantities of a product at a price lower than the cost of production or below what the company would charge in its home market is **dumping.** This tactic is often used to try to win foreign customers or to reduce product surpluses. Most industrialized countries have antidumping regulations. Section 301 of the U.S. Trade Act of 1988, for instance, obligates the U.S. president to retaliate against foreign producers that dump products on the U.S. market. So when reports showed that Japan was dumping coated steel, which is used primarily in metal containers, cans, bakeware, and home builders' hardware, on the U.S. market, the United States imposed a 95 percent antidumping penalty on the coated steel to prevent Japan from materially injuring the U.S. steel industry.[26]

> active poll

**What do you think? Voice your opinion and find out what others have to say.**

## AGREEMENTS AND ORGANIZATIONS PROMOTING INTERNATIONAL TRADE

To prevent trade disputes from escalating into full-blown trade wars, and to ensure that international business is conducted in a fair and orderly fashion, countries worldwide have created trade agreements and organizations. Philosophically, most of these agreements and organizations support the basic principles of **free trade;** that is, each nation will ultimately benefit by freely exchanging the goods and services it produces most efficiently for the goods and services it produces less efficiently. The major trade agreements and organizations include the GATT, the WTO, the APEC, the IMF, and the World Bank.

### The General Agreement on Tariffs and Trade (GATT)

The General Agreement on Tariffs and Trade (GATT) is a worldwide pact that was first established in the aftermath of World War II. The pact's guiding principle—most favored nation (MFN)—is one of nondiscrimination: Any trade advantage a GATT member gives to one country must be given to all GATT members, and no GATT nation can be singled out for punishment. In 1995 GATT established the World Trade Organization (WTO), which has now replaced GATT as the world forum for trade negotiations.

### The World Trade Organization (WTO)

The World Trade Organization (WTO) is a permanent forum for negotiating, implementing, and monitoring international trade procedures and for mediating trade disputes among its 138 member countries. The organization's goals include facilitating free trade, lowering the costs of doing business, enhancing the international investment environment, simplifying customs, and promoting technical and economic cooperation. Experts believe that the WTO should ultimately prove to be more effective than the GATT because the WTO has a formal legal structure for settling disputes.

Admission to the organization is by application process and requires approval by two-thirds of the members. All WTO members enjoy "favored" access to foreign markets in exchange for adhering to a long list of fair-trading rules and laws governing patents, copyrights, and trademarks. China, for example, was required to eliminate many tariffs and quotas on a wide range of products and open its market of 1.4 billion people to foreign goods as conditions to its membership in the WTO. One group that spoke out strongly against China's admission to the WTO was U.S. textile workers, who feared that lifting U.S. quotas on foreign textiles by 2005 would increase textile imports and severely affect the U.S. textile industry.[27]

### The Asia Pacific Economic Cooperation Council (APEC)

The Asia Pacific Economic Cooperation Council (APEC) is an organization of 18 countries that are making efforts to liberalize trade in the Pacific Rim (the land areas that surround the Pacific Ocean). Among the member nations are the United States, Japan, China, Mexico, Australia, South Korea, and Canada. In 1994 the members agreed to eliminate all tariffs and trade barriers among industrialized countries of the Pacific Rim by 2010 and among developing countries by 2020.[28]

### The International Monetary Fund (IMF)

The International Monetary Fund (IMF) was founded in 1945 and is now affiliated with the United Nations. Its primary function is to provide short-term loans to countries that are unable to meet their budgetary expenses. As such, the IMF is often looked upon as a lender of last resort. For example, the IMF has provided well over a combined total of $150 billion in loans to South Korea, Indonesia, Brazil, Thailand, and other countries to help rescue them from a global financial crisis at the end of the twentieth century.[29]

### The World Bank

Officially known as the International Bank for Reconstruction and Development, the World Bank was founded to finance reconstruction after World War II. It now provides low-interest loans to developing nations for the improvement of transportation, telecommunications, health, and education. Currently, the World Bank is focused on bringing the Internet to the less-developed regions of the world, such as Africa. World Bank officials and telecommunication executives hope that Internet connections will attract more companies to the region, and thus lead to more rapid economic development.[30] Both the IMF and the World Bank are funded by deposits from its 182 member nations. The bulk of the funds come from the United States, western Europe, and Japan.

> **active poll**

**What do you think? Voice your opinion and find out what others have to say.**

## TRADING BLOCS

**Trading blocs** are another type of organization that promotes international trade. Generally comprising neighboring countries, trading blocs promote free trade among regional members. Although specific rules vary from group to group, their primary objective is to ensure the economic growth and benefit of members. As such, trading blocs generally promote trade inside the region while creating uniform barriers against goods and services entering the region from nonmember countries. Trading blocs are becoming a significant force in the global marketplace.[31]

Trading blocs can be advantageous or disadvantageous in promoting world trade, depending on one's perspective. Some economists are apprehensive about the growing importance of regional trading blocs. They fear that the world is splitting into three camps, revolving around the Americas, Europe, and Asia. Any nation that does not fall into one of these economic regions could suffer, they say, because members of the trading blocs could place severe restrictions on trade with nonmember countries. The critics fear that overall world trade could decline as members become more protective of their own regions. As a result, consumers could find themselves with fewer choices, and many producers could lose sales in lucrative foreign markets.

Others claim, however, that trading blocs could improve world trade. For one thing, the growth of commerce and the availability of customers and suppliers within a trading bloc could be a boon to smaller or younger nations that are trying to build strong economies. For another, the lack of trade barriers within the bloc could help their industries compete with producers in more developed nations, and, in some cases, member countries could reach a wider market than before.[32] Furthermore, close ties to more stable economies could help shield emerging nations from fluctuations in the global economy and could promote a greater sharing of knowledge and technology; both outcomes could aid future economic development.

The four most powerful trading blocs today are the Association of Southeast Asian Nations (ASEAN), South America's Mercosur, the NAFTA (North American Free Trade Agreement) countries, and the European Union (EU), with the latter two being the largest and most powerful organizations (see Exhibit 3.5). Because many trading nations see Latin America as an area for large-scale economic growth in the future, they are eager to establish ties with Mercosur, which links Argentina, Brazil, Paraguay, and Uruguay, and registers a population of 210 million people that produces more than $1 trillion in goods and services.[33] Like other trading blocks, the Mercosur's objectives include the free movement of goods and services across the borders of its members. Furthermore, the group seeks an economic integration which it hopes will make the four countries more competitive in the global marketplace.[34] Some U.S. officials hope that Mercosur will eventually join the North American Free Trade Agreement (NAFTA) to form a Free Trade Area of the Americas (FTAA).[35]

### NAFTA

In 1994 the United States, Canada, and Mexico formed a powerful trading bloc, the North American Free Trade Agreement (NAFTA). The agreement paves the way for the free flow of goods, services, and capital within the bloc by eliminating all tariffs and quotas on trades between the three nations.[36] Talks are currently under way to expand NAFTA to include Chile. Ultimately, NAFTA's supporters would like to see the agreement expanded to include all of Central and South America by 2005.

NAFTA has always been controversial. Debate still continues about whether the agreement is helping or hurting the U.S. economy. One primary concern is NAFTA's effect on U.S. jobs. Critics contend that many jobs have been lost because U.S. manufacturers have moved production to Mexico and Canada. Supporters, on the other hand, say that U.S. jobs have multiplied as a result of increased exports. Which side is right? It's still too early to tell whether NAFTA's overall impact on the U.S. economy will be positive or negative.[37] Over the coming years, U.S. trade policy and NAFTA will certainly continue to be watched closely.

### The European Union

One of the largest trading blocs is the European Union (EU), which combines 15 countries and more than 370 million people. Talks are under way to admit more countries, including the Czech

| European Union (EU)* | North American Free Trade Agreement (NAFTA) | Association of Southeast Asian Nations (ASEAN) | Mercosur |
|---|---|---|---|
| Austria | Canada | Brunei | Argentina |
| Belgium | Mexico | Indonesia | Brazil |
| Finland | United States | Malaysia | Paraguay |
| France | | Philippines | Uruguay |
| Germany | | Singapore | |
| Ireland | | Thailand | |
| Italy | | | |
| Luxembourg | | | |
| Netherlands | | | |
| Portugal | | | |
| Spain | | | |
| Denmark | | | |
| Great Britain | | | |
| Greece | | | |
| Sweden | | | |

### EXHIBIT 3.5

Members of Major Trade Blocs

As the economies of the world become increasingly linked, many countries have formed powerful regional trade blocs that trade freely with one another and limit foreign competition.

*Boxed countries are members of the Economic and Monetary Union (EMU).

Republic, Estonia, Hungary, Slovenia, and Poland.[38] EU nations are working to eliminate hundreds of local regulations, variations in product standards, and protectionist measures that limit trade between member countries. Eliminating barriers enables the nations of the EU to function as a single market, with trade flowing between member countries as it does between states in the United States.

In 1999, 11 of the 15 countries formed the economic and monetary union (EMU) and turned over control of their individual monetary policies to the newly created European Central Bank. With a combined population of about 300 million people, these 11 countries account for 19.4 percent of the world's gross domestic product (GDP), making them a commanding force in the world economy.[39] The four countries that did not join the EMU are Greece, which did not meet the strict qualification requirements, and Britain, Denmark, and Sweden, which chose not to participate initially.

One of the driving forces behind the decision to join forces was the anticipated advantages these 11 countries would enjoy by creating a unified currency called the **euro.** Officially launched in 1999 (with notes and coins available in 2002), the euro could wipe out some $65 billion annually in currency exchange costs among participants and cut the middleman out of trillions of dollars' worth of foreign exchange transactions. U.S. businesses and travelers alone could save as much as 50 percent of the costs they now pay to convert dollars into multiple European currencies. Moreover, with prices in these 11 nations now in one currency, consumers can compare prices on similar items whether they are sold in Lisbon or Vienna.[40]

Heralded by some as a possible rival to the dollar or yen as the international currency of trade, the euro got off to a rocky start. Confidence in the new currency eroded when its value plunged to 83 U.S. cents—losing more than 28 percent of its original value. Nevertheless, the euro's weak start wasn't all bad for Europe. A decline in the value of the euro lowered the prices of goods sold by the 11 nations and fueled a boom in European exports—a plus for many European manufacturers.[41] In the next section we will discuss how a currency's value affects a country's economy—especially in the global marketplace.

## > Interdependence of Economies in the Global Marketplace

As more and more companies such as Trek seek international markets for their goods and services, or search for the most cost-effective locations to produce their goods or to transact business, they become even more tangled in the global marketplace. The opportunities in the global marketplace are many, but these opportunities are not without risks. A worldwide economic crisis at the end of the twentieth century showed, in dramatic fashion, just how risky the global marketplace could be. In this section, we'll show how one small country's decision to *float* its currency set a spark that ignited a regional economic crisis that sent shock waves throughout the world. But we must first explain some important concepts about foreign exchange rates and currency valuations so that you can understand how the change in value of one country's currency could cause such global economic turmoil.

### FOREIGN EXCHANGE RATES AND CURRENCY VALUATIONS

When companies buy and sell goods and services in the global marketplace, they complete the transaction by exchanging currencies. For instance, if a Japanese company borrows money from a U.S. bank to build a manufacturing plant in Japan, it must repay the loan in U.S. dollars. Or if a South Korean car manufacturer imports engine parts from Japan, it must pay for them in yen (Japan's currency). To do so, companies exchange their currency at any international bank that handles **foreign exchange,** the conversion of one currency into an equivalent amount of another currency. The number of yen, francs, or pounds that must be exchanged for every dollar, mark, or won is known as the **exchange rate** between currencies.

Most international currencies operate under a **floating exchange rate system;** thus, a currency's value or price fluctuates in response to the forces of global supply and demand (as we discussed in Chapter 1). The supply and demand of a country's currency are determined in part by what is happening in the country's own economy (as we we'll see in the next section). Moreover, because supply and demand for a currency are always changing, the rate at which it is exchanged for other currencies may change a little each day. For example, Japanese currency might be trading at 137.6 yen to the dollar on one day and 136.8 on the next.

Even though most governments let the value of their currency respond to the forces of supply and demand, sometimes a government will intervene and adjust the exchange rate of its country's currency. Why would a government do this? One reason is to keep the price of a nation's goods and services more affordable in the global marketplace and to protect the nation's economy against trade imbalances. Another is to boost or slow down the country's economy.

*Devaluation,* or the drop in the value of a nation's currency relative to the value of other currencies, can at times boost a country's economy because it makes the country's products and services more affordable in foreign markets while it increases the price of imports. Because fewer units of foreign currency are required to purchase the devalued currency, such situations tend to raise a country's exports and lower its imports. Conversely, a strong currency boosts imports and dampens exports.

Some countries fix, or peg, the value of their currencies to the value of more stable currencies, such as the dollar or the yen, instead of letting it float freely. Hong Kong, for example, pegs its currency to the U.S. dollar. If a currency is pegged, its value fluctuates proportionately with the value of the foreign currency to which it is linked. So if the U.S. dollar declines, so will the Japanese yen and other currencies that are pegged to it. Of course, this system works well as long as the proportionate relationship between the two currencies remains valid. But if one partner suffers economic hardship, demand for its currency will decline significantly and the exchange rate at which the two are pegged will become unrealistic. Such was the case with many of the Southeast Asian currencies in the late 1990s.

## THE GLOBAL ECONOMIC CRISIS AT THE END OF THE TWENTIETH CENTURY

From the early 1980s until 1997, Southeast Asian countries wooed foreign investment. By the early 1990s, their economies were booming, export sectors were growing, cities were flush with money, and the people enjoyed some of the fastest-rising standards of living in the world. But the Southeast Asian economies soon overheated as consumers spent their newly acquired riches and inflation picked up.[42]

The bubble burst in July 1997 when Thailand unpegged its currency (the baht) from the U.S. dollar to allow the currency to float and gradually seek its true value. Anticipating that its currency would drop somewhat in value, Thailand was caught off guard when the currency went into a free fall. At about the same time, Indonesia unpegged the rupiah from the U.S. dollar to let the currency seek its true value, and the currency fell from 2,500 to 7,900 to the dollar, a devaluation of 300 percent in about 6 months.[43] Subsequent currency devaluations by other countries that felt pressured to keep the price of their exports competitive soon ignited an economic crisis that spread and infected nations as far flung as Guyana, Lebanon, Zimbabwe, Brazil, and Russia.

One by one the crisis struck economies that were already weak as a result of internal economic problems. Currencies plunged, commodity prices fell, stock markets crashed, and investors panicked and fled—taking with them the capital these emerging countries needed to fund their growth.[44] What caused the crisis, and why did the contagion spread? Economists now cite a combination of factors that contributed to the global economic turmoil.

### What Caused the Global Economic Crisis?

As the currencies plunged, foreign investors, who had poured over $100 billion a year into the world's emerging markets, panicked. Overnight, they pulled their money out of these countries, and economic growth hit the brakes. Without this growth, the supply of local currencies exceeded their demand, forcing these currencies to fall even lower.[45]

As currencies devalued, consumers in the Southeast Asian countries were hit hard. Many could not afford to pay back their loans. Others lost their businesses. Still others watched their investments shrink in value overnight. As a result, Southeast Asia's demand for commodities such as oil, copper, aluminum, and gold tailed off, depressing world commodity prices to 10-year lows. This plunge in commodity prices transferred the economic crisis to other emerging markets and to Russia, because a large share of their exports are commodity-based. Meanwhile, to bail these countries out, the IMF and the World Bank lent them large sums of money: $17.2 billion to Thailand, $42 billion to Indonesia, $58.4 billion to South Korea, and $41.5 billion to Brazil.[46]

Although these loans were intended to stabilize the failing economies, some contend that the IMF's strict conditions for loan recipients made matters worse. By imposing tight fiscal and monetary requirements on the recipients, the IMF forced loan recipients to slash budget deficits.[47] To accomplish this goal, governments had to raise taxes and cut government spending; both actions hurt consumers even more. Another condition required recipients to privatize inefficient state-owned industries. This pressure resulted in massive worker layoffs and further depressed economies that were already plagued by internal problems:[48]

- *Excessive amounts of foreign-denominated debt.* Because most emerging nations could not finance their own growth, they had borrowed large sums of money from the United States and Japan to build new roads, dams, and industries. This practice seemed safe as long as the exchange rate for their local currencies remained stable. But once the value of these currencies plummeted, the borrowers could not afford to pay back their dollar- or yen-denominated debts. For example, a $1 million U.S. loan (equivalent to 26 million baht) doubled after the currency's free fall to 52 baht to the dollar. This meant that borrowers would have to exchange 52 million baht to pay back the $1 million loan to U.S. banks.

- *Bad loans.* Many Southeast Asian and Japanese banks worked on a buddy system (called croney capitalism) and made risky loans to friends who were poor credit risks and whose businesses were not financially sound. This practice kept profitless enterprises alive and led to the misallocation of resources. South Korean chaebol (giant family-controlled conglomerates) with the right connections, for example, were granted loans by local banks often in return for under-the-table payoffs.[49]

- *Plunging real estate prices.* Global economic turmoil hit while Japan was experiencing a severe real estate recession. At its peak, the land beneath the Imperial palace in downtown Tokyo was said to be worth as much as all of California, and a parking space in Hong Kong sold for $517,000. Many Japanese banks relied on the overvalued real estate as collateral for loans. When real estate prices plunged—some falling to 10 percent of their peak values—banks were reluctant to call their loans in hopes that real estate values would rebound. With few good lending opportunities at home, Japanese banks began lending elsewhere in Southeast Asia, adding to the banks' own troubles.[50]

### Southeast Asia's Road to Recovery

Today, many Southeast Asian economies have made a significant recovery: Currencies have stabilized; interest rates (which were boosted to attract foreign investors) have declined; and stock markets have recovered to near precrisis levels. Several factors have driven the recovery at a faster pace than originally expected:[51]

- *Increased exports.* Substantial currency devaluations have made the crisis countries more competitive and their exports more attractive. A booming U.S. economy provided a bottomless market for Southeast Asian goods such as semiconductors and telecommunications equipment.

- *Aid from Japan.* Historically the largest investor in the region, Japan slashed its investments in Southeast Asia during the 1990s as its own economy stagnated. But when the crisis hit, Japan offered the region over $35 billion in aid.

- *Rise in oil prices.* A steep rise in oil prices and some of the best weather in the region also helped bail out the crisis-hit economies.

- *Bank and corporate reforms.* The Southeast Asian countries have closed or restructured insolvent banks and removed the corrupt bank officials. Several Southeast Asian countries have passed bankruptcy and foreclosure laws. Meanwhile, many investors have shifted their resources into factories, Internet start-ups, and telecommunications as a source of future prosperity. Such investments will help long-term recovery.

Some experts contend that if these countries continue to restructure their economic systems as a result of the crisis, they could emerge as much stronger nations.[52] Still, recovery is far from assured. Some worry whether recovery is sustainable. Others fear swift recoveries and restored optimism could sideline many of the meaningful reforms that are getting under way and cause Asia to suffer a relapse.[53]

### Recovery in Russia

Foreign direct investment has picked up some in Russia. When the ruble's value plunged against the dollar after the August 1998 crisis, dollar-denominated imports became too expensive for most Russians. So foreign companies concluded that the best way to thrive in Russia was to begin manufacturing there. Nevertheless, big problems loom. Tarnished by scandals and corruption, most of Russia's largest banks have gone bankrupt, defaulting on loans to Western creditors and confiscating the deposits of their domestic clients. Lack of confidence in the Russian economy has prompted Russians to convert their rubles to other stable currencies.[54]

### EFFECT OF THE CRISIS ON THE UNITED STATES

Ironically, the world's financial troubles had little negative impact on the United States economy. Although some businesses such as Boeing faced a slew of cancelled orders from Asian carriers, others prospered.[55] In fact, U.S. businesses thrived during a period of global economic malaise for several reasons: The U.S. government lowered interest rates on several occasions to boost the U.S. economy. (Lower interest rates make it more affordable for companies and consumers to borrow money and purchase more goods.) Plunging commodity prices kept U.S. inflation low and saved U.S. businesses billions of dollars, while the strong dollar made imports cheaper. Meanwhile, U.S. manufacturers found other markets for their goods.[56]

Still, some economists warn that the United States cannot expect to remain "an oasis of prosperity" if global economic turmoil were to reignite.[57] As the Asian crisis demonstrates, in the global marketplace—where economies of the world are entangled—problems in one country can indeed send shock waves around the globe.

## video exercise &lt;

**Take a moment to apply what you've learned.**

## active concept check &lt;

**Now let's take a moment to test your knowledge of the concepts you have studied in this section.**

**> Chapter Wrap-Up**

Now that you've reached the end of the chapter, you may wish to explore the concepts you've been reading about in greater detail, or test yourself to see how well you've comprehended the material. In the box below you'll find a number of links. Click on any one of these links to find additional chapter resources.

## > end-of-chapter resources

- Summary of Learning Objectives
- Practice Quiz
- Focusing on E-Business Today
- Key Terms
- Test Your Knowledge
- Practice Your Knowledge
- Expand Your Knowledge
- A Case for Critical Thinking
- Business Plan Pro: Conducting Business in the Global Economy

# CHAPTER 4

# Small Business, New Ventures, and Franchises

## > What's Ahead

### INSIDE BUSINESS TODAY
### IDEAS BY THE DOZEN: HATCHING INTERNET COMPANIES AT IDEALAB!

Click on Cooking.com, GoTo.com, or Tickets.com, and you've sampled a few of Bill Gross's entrepreneurial ideas. Turning great ideas into Internet companies is Gross's specialty. In fact, he has even created a nurturing environment for giving birth to his ideas: idealab!, a business incubator for Internet start-ups.

Seasoned entrepreneurs like Gross know that starting a business from scratch takes more than a great idea. An entrepreneur since the age of 12, Gross realized that building a successful Internet company required enormous investments of time and resources. Moreover, he knew that Internet ventures needed a jump start on the competition in the vast world of cyberspace. So how could he turn his great ideas into great Internet companies at lightning-fast speeds?

First Gross assessed his own strengths and weaknesses. Although he thrived on creative challenges, Gross disliked the details of managing the daily operations of a business. So he envisioned creating an outlet for his wealth of ideas that would allow his creativity to reign supreme.

Then he assessed ways to speed up the basic steps of starting an e-business. Every Internet start-up required such basic necessities as office space, telephone systems, and computer equipment. But Gross reasoned that start-ups could save valuable time and reduce expenses by pooling resources. If Internet entrepreneurs could draw on a central resource for basic business services, they could devote their time and energy to developing strategies for their new ventures instead of contending with personnel or accounting problems.

Since founding idealab! in 1996, Bill Gross (top) has had a hand in launching CarsDirect.com, Free-PC, GoTo.com, e-Machines, and a number of other ventures.

Confident that he could devise a strategy for streamlining the process of starting Internet companies, Gross focused on creating a model business incubator for Internet start-ups. After rounding up $5 million in initial financing from his own resources and from such notable investors as director Stephen Spielberg and actor Michael Douglas, Gross launched idealab! in 1996. Thirteen months later, Gross's new roost had hatched 23 Internet companies from scratch.

Idealab!'s most recognized e-businesses include CarsDirect.com, Petsmart.com, and CitySearch. But Gross's bright ideas are not always foolproof. Idealab! has canned several start-up ventures, such as the Web broadcast site, EntertainNet.com, and Homelink.com, a search site for real estate, and like other entrepreneurs, Gross got caught up in the early Internet mania and invested in some bad Internet start-ups. Still, Gross contends that the experiences were valuable learning lessons for idealab! "Although the companies failed, we learned a tremendous amount from those experiences, which we now use to benefit our networks of other companies," he insists.

Today Gross's brood of e-commerce chicklings consists of more than 40 Internet businesses, including 7 publicly traded companies. Idealab! supplies the start-ups with ideas, office space, administrative staff and services, and seed money of $250,000 to $500,000 (which Gross obtains from a variety of investors in exchange for a share of ownership in each new venture). In other words, like a busy mother hen, Gross provides his newborns with everything they need to make their way into the world of e-commerce.[1]

## objectives <

Take a moment to familiarize yourself with the key objectives of this chapter.

**Before you begin reading this chapter, try a short warm-up activity.**

## > Understanding the World of Small Business

Small businesses such as idealab! are the cornerstone of the U.S. economic system. The country was originally founded by people involved in small businesses—the family farmer, the shopkeeper, the craftsperson. Successive waves of immigrants carried on the tradition, launching restaurants and laundries, providing repair and delivery services, and opening newsstands and bakeries.

This trend continued for many years, until improvements in transportation and communication enabled large producers to manufacture goods at low costs and pass the savings on to consumers. As a result, many small, independent businesses could not compete. Scores of them closed their doors, and big business emerged as the primary economic force. The trend toward bigness continued for several decades, then it reversed.

The 1990s were a golden decade for entrepreneurship in the United States. Small companies have, in fact, turned the U.S. economy into the growth engine for the world (see Exhibit 4.1). Today, being a small business is equated with being nimble and dynamic.[2] Even so, defining what constitutes a small business is surprisingly tricky, because *small* is a relative term. For example, a manufacturing firm with 500 employees might be considered small if it competes against much larger

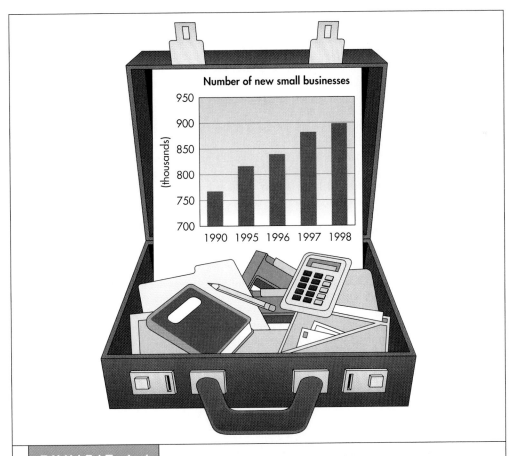

**EXHIBIT 4.1**

New Small Businesses

The growth in the number of small-business start-ups is fueling today's economy.

companies, but a retail establishment with 500 employees might be classified as big when compared with its competitors.

One reliable source of information for small businesses is the Small Business Administration (SBA). This government agency serves as a resource and advocate for small firms, providing them with financial assistance, training, and a variety of helpful programs. The SBA defines a **small business** as a firm that (a) is independently owned and operated, (b) is not dominant in its field, (c) is relatively small in terms of annual sales, and (d) has fewer than 500 employees. According to SBA figures, 80 percent of all U.S. companies have annual sales of less than $1 million.[3]

## active exercise    <

**Take a moment to apply what you've learned.**

## CHARACTERISTICS OF SMALL BUSINESSES

Small businesses are of two distinct types: lifestyle businesses and high-growth ventures. Roughly 80 to 90 percent are modest operations with little growth potential (although some have attractive income potential for the solo businessperson). The self-employed consultant working part-time from a home office, the corner florist, and the neighborhood pizza parlor fall into the category of *lifestyle businesses*—firms built around the personal and financial needs of an individual or a family.[4] Lifestyle businesses aren't designed to grow into large enterprises.

In contrast to lifestyle businesses, some firms are small simply because they are new. Many companies—such as FedEx, Microsoft, and E*Trade—start out as small entrepreneurial firms but quickly outgrow their small-business status. These *high-growth ventures* are usually run by a team rather than by one individual, and they expand rapidly by obtaining a sizable supply of investment capital and by introducing new products or services to a large market. But expanding from a small firm into a large enterprise is no easy task; there's a world of difference between the two.

The typical small business has few products or services, focuses on a narrow group of customers, and remains in close contact with its markets. In addition, small businesses tend to be more open-minded and willing to try new things, whereas big companies tend to say *no* more often than *yes*. Midwest Express, the nation's 17th-largest airline, is a good example of the small-business difference. The airline is reporting high-flying profits in an era when most big airlines are struggling. What's Midwest's secret? The company focuses on serving the growing needs of business travelers. All 34 Midwest routes make direct flights between small cities. Fares match those of the big airlines, but the company offers only business-class service with such amenities as wide leather seats, free coffee and newspapers at terminals, and fresh-baked gooey chocolate chip cookies in flight. Midwest earns high marks from its customers for going that extra mile.[5]

### Innovation in Small Business

Another characteristic of small businesses is that they tend to be more innovative than larger firms. Case studies show that (1) small businesses can make decisions faster, (2) the owners are more accessible, and (3) employees have a greater opportunity for individual expression. Putting an idea into action in big companies often means filing formal proposals, preparing research reports, and attending lots of meetings. This process could kill an idea before it has a chance to take off. Consider Microsoft, for example. One manager quit out of frustration with the company's snail's pace for decision making. It took 10 meetings and three months to act on his suggestion to add a feature to Hot Mail (the company's freebie Internet e-mail service) that would quickly take 40 million users to Microsoft's MSN Web site. In contrast, it took only 30 minutes to write the code for this feature.[6]

To stimulate innovation, many big companies are now dividing their organizations into smaller work units. Xerox, AT&T, du Pont, Motorola, Hewlett-Packard, and others have launched their own small enterprises to keep new ideas from falling through the cracks. Run by *intrapreneurs*— people who create innovation of any kind *within* an organization (not to be confused with *entrepreneurs*—risk takers in the private enterprise system)—these ventures get funding and support from the parent organization. Nevertheless, some intrapreneurial ventures continue to face giant obstacles because the parent corporation burdens them with strict reporting requirements and formal procedures.[7]

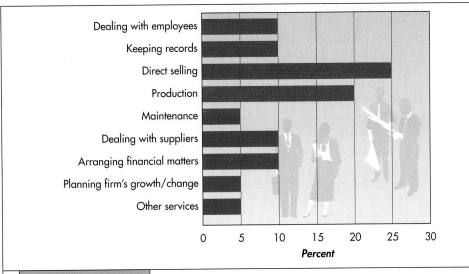

| | | | | | | |
|---|---|---|---|---|---|---|
| Dealing with employees | | | | | | |
| Keeping records | | | | | | |
| Direct selling | | | | | | |
| Production | | | | | | |
| Maintenance | | | | | | |
| Dealing with suppliers | | | | | | |
| Arranging financial matters | | | | | | |
| Planning firm's growth/change | | | | | | |
| Other services | | | | | | |

*Percent*

**EXHIBIT 4.2**

How Entrepreneurs Spend Their Time

The men and women who start their own companies are jacks-of-all-trades, but they devote the lion's share of their time to selling and producing the product.

### Limited Resources and Hard Work

Because most small companies have limited resources, owners and employees must perform a variety of job functions in order to get the work done. Being a jack-of-all-trades, however, is not for everyone (see Exhibit 4.2). Unfortunately, some owners learn this the hard way. They discover that running a small business takes a lot of hard work and that being a successful corporate employee doesn't necessarily translate into being a successful small-business owner.

When Bob Hammer and Sue Crowe purchased Blue Jacket Ship Crafters, a mail-order model-ship-kit manufacturer, they quickly learned that running a small company was not like running Motorola, where the two had been senior managers for the better part of their careers. It took a lot more work and time than they had imagined. Even Crowe admits, "You will put in more money than you thought you would, you will take out a lot less, and you will work harder than you did when you were making a six-figure salary at your large corporation."[8] Many executives who leave the corporate world to start a small business have trouble adjusting to the unglamorous details of daily life in a small business. They miss the support services and fringe benefits they enjoyed in large corporations.[9]

> **active poll**

**What do you think? Voice your opinion and find out what others have to say.**

### ECONOMIC ROLE OF SMALL BUSINESSES

Small businesses play a number of important roles in the economy:

- *They provide jobs.* Small businesses create about 70 percent of new jobs. Moreover, some 24 million small businesses employ 53 percent of the private nonfarm U.S. workforce and generate more than half of the private U.S. gross domestic product.[10]

- *They introduce new products.* The National Science Foundation estimates that 98 percent of the nation's "radical" new-product developments spring from small firms, a staggering percentage given the fact that small companies spend less than 5 percent of the nation's research-and-development money.[11]

- *They supply the needs of large corporations.* Many small businesses act as distributors, servicing agents, and suppliers to large corporations. Consider Parallax. This 160-employee firm inspects nuclear power plants, implements safety procedures, and cleans up hazardous and nuclear waste at power plants and weapons complexes across the nation. Seventy percent of Parallax's business comes from large corporations such as Westinghouse and Lockheed Martin. Not bad for a company launched out of the founder's home with $10,000 in personal savings.[12]

- *They provide specialized goods and services.* When Mike Woods tried to teach his son how to read he couldn't find any toys on the market that helped teach phonics. So he left his job as a partner in a big law firm and started LeapFrog. The company's initial product was the Phonics Disk, a $50 toy that teaches children shapes, sounds, and pronunciation of letters and words. Today LeapFrog, a division of Knowledge Universe, produces 17 toys geared toward teaching children to read and write.[13]

In addition to these roles, small businesses spend $2.2 trillion annually in the U.S. economy, just a bit less than the $2.6 trillion spent by big companies.[14]

## FACTORS CONTRIBUTING TO THE INCREASE IN THE NUMBER OF SMALL BUSINESSES

Three factors are contributing to the increase in the number of small businesses today: technological advances, an increase in the number of women and minority business owners, and corporate downsizing and outsourcing.

### Technology and the Internet

The Internet together with e-commerce has spawned thousands of new business ventures, as this chapter's Focusing on E-Business Today feature shows. Some 548 companies went public in 1999, of which 290 were Internet-related.[15] It is estimated that over 38 percent of small businesses now have a Web site.[16] While the Internet makes it easier to launch or expand your business, there's a twist. If it's so easy for you to start an online business, then it's just as easy for everyone else. No company understands this better than drkoop.com, the Internet-based consumer health care network. Shortly after founder Dr. Everett Koop (former U.S. Surgeon General) launched his innovative concept, a startling number of "me-toos" copied his idea.

Not only does the Internet make it easier to start a business, but it allows small companies to compete on a level playing field with larger ones. Small businesses can use the Internet to communicate with customers and suppliers all over the world—any time of the day—and to access the types of resources and information that were previously available only to larger firms.

Besides the Internet, technological advances such as computer-aided manufacturing equipment and affordable data processing systems enable small companies to customize their products and deliver them as efficiently as their larger rivals. One small company that is successful because of technology is Isis, a pharmaceutical company. Being first to introduce a new drug in the market is critical in the pharmaceutical industry. But it takes years of research and data analysis to get the required agency approvals. In the past, small companies could not afford to spend millions of dollars on data-crunching systems to process the information efficiently. But today, less expensive versions of these sophisticated systems are available. As a result, a small firm like Isis can file its 40,000-page reports with the U.S. Food and Drug Administration in one-third the time by compressing the information onto one CD-ROM.[17]

Technology also makes it easier to start a small home-based business. With the Internet and online resources accountants, writers, lawyers, and consultants can set up shop at home. According to one study, about 24 million home-based businesses exist in the United States, and an additional 11 million people telecommute.[18] Some predict that as much as half the workforce soon may be involved in full- or part-time home-based businesses.[19]

### Rise in Number of Women and Minority Small-Business Owners

The number of women-owned small businesses has increased sharply over the past three decades—from 5 percent to 38 percent of all small businesses. These businesses now employ more than 18.5 million people and ring up more than $3.1 trillion in annual sales.[20]

As Exhibit 4.3 shows, women are starting small businesses for a number of reasons. Some choose to run their own companies so they can enjoy a more flexible work arrangement; others leave the corporate world because of advancement barriers—known as the glass ceiling. Take Josie Natori, for a perfect example. By her late twenties, Natori was earning six figures as the first female vice president of investment banking at Merrill Lynch. Where could she go from there? Today Natori is the owner of a $33 million fashion empire that sells elegant lingerie and evening wear.[21] Nevertheless, going solo does not guarantee success. Many women business owners still struggle to be taken seriously.

What women with companies less than a decade old say is the main reason they started a business:

| | |
|---|---|
| Entrepreneurial idea | 35% |
| Glass ceiling | 22% |
| Bored in job | 14% |
| Downsized | 10% |
| Fell into it | 10% |
| Family event | 5% |
| Born entrepreneur | 3% |
| Reenter workforce | 1% |

**EXHIBIT 4.3**

Women Starting Businesses

More than half of all women business owners started their own businesses because they had an entrepreneurial idea or wished to further advance their careers.

Similar advances are also showing up in minority segments of the population. Data from the U.S. Small Business Administration show that between 1987 and 1997, the number of minority-owned firms grew 168 percent—more than triple the 47 percent rate of U.S. businesses overall. Minority-owned firms now employ an estimated 3.9 million people.[22]

### Downsizing and Outsourcing

Beginning in the late 1980s and continuing through the 1990s, many big corporations dramatically reduced their number of employees to improve their profits. Such downsizing ushered in an age in which "small became beautiful." Some companies, such as Procter & Gamble, were able to function with fewer people once they redesigned their business systems to operate more efficiently.[23] Others made up for the layoffs of permanent staff by **outsourcing** or subcontracting special projects and secondary business functions to experts outside the organization. Still others turned to outsourcing as a way to permanently eliminate entire company departments.

Regardless of the reason, the increased use of outsourcing provides opportunities for smaller businesses to service the needs of larger enterprises. Many employees who leave big corporations find it more fulfilling to work as independent contractors or to join smaller firms. Some, like Harold Jackson, are even wooing their former employers as customers. After working several years as Coca-Cola's manager of media relations in Atlanta, Jackson left to found JacksonHeath Public Relations International, taking Coke with him as his most valuable client.[24]

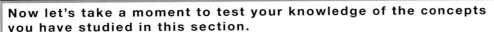

**> active concept check**

**Now let's take a moment to test your knowledge of the concepts you have studied in this section.**

**> Starting and Expanding a Small Business**

People in the United States are starting new businesses at dizzying rates. Could you or should you join the thousands of entrepreneurs like Josie Natori, Bill Gross, and Harold Jackson who start new businesses every year? What qualities would you need?

## CHARACTERISTICS OF ENTREPRENEURS

Contrary to what you might expect, most entrepreneurs are not glamorous adventurers; instead, they are often ordinary people like Bill Gross who have a good idea. But even Gross knows it takes more than a good idea to launch a successful business. Most entrepreneurs have these qualities in common: They prefer excitement, are highly disciplined, like to control their destiny, listen to their intuitive sense, relate well to others, are eager to learn whatever skills are necessary to reach their goal, learn from their mistakes, stay abreast of market changes, are willing to exploit new opportunities, seldom follow trends (rather, they spot and interpret trends), are driven by ambition, think positively, and prefer the excitement and potential rewards of risk taking over security.[25] Moreover, while many are anxious to become their own boss, surprisingly they cite making money as the secondary reason for starting their own business.[26] Exhibit 4.4 lists some successful entrepreneurs and the key factor contributing to their success.

Many entrepreneurs start with relatively small sums of money and operate informally from their homes, at least for a while.[27] Most have diverse backgrounds in terms of education and business expe-

| Key Success Factor | Company |
| --- | --- |
| Persistence | *Breed Technologies:* It took Allen Breed over 10 years to convince carmakers that air bags could save several thousand lives a year. Today Breed Technologies is one of the most profitable suppliers in the automotive industry—his company makes the sensors that trigger the air-bag system. With more than 5,000 employees and branches in eight countries, this company's sales went from zero to nearly half a billion dollars in less than a decade. |
| Skill | *La Tempesta:* Using Aunt Isa's recipe for biscotti (twice-baked Italian cookies), Bonnie Tempesta baked them and sold them at a fancy San Francisco chocolate shop. While attending a fancy-foods trade show one day, she noticed that she was the only one there with biscotti. Today she sells over $9 million worth through 65 separate regional distributors to 5,000 stores, including Starbucks, Nordstrom, and Neiman Marcus. |
| Passion | *Transmissions by Lucille:* Lucille Treganowan didn't grow up yearning to repair cars. In fact, she didn't know a transmission from a turnip. So she began asking mechanics questions, reading, and working on cars. In 1973 she started her business. Today, transmissions are more than a business; they are a passion. |
| Hobby | *Rusty Cos:* Russell Preisendorfer is an avid surfer. To support his habit he began shaping surfboards. Last year his privately owned Rusty Cos grossed $57 million from sales of surfboards and royalties from a line of surfing apparel he helps design. |
| Common Sense | *Auntie Anne's:* To bring in some extra cash, Anne Beiler managed a food stand at a farmer's market in Maryland. She noticed that the fastest-selling items at the stand were hand-rolled pretzels that sold for 55 cents each. Not bad for 7 cents worth of ingredients. So Beiler decided to try the pretzel business herself. Today Beiler's mini-empire consists of over 300 franchised pretzel shops in about 35 states. |
| Talent | *S.C.R.U.B.S.:* Sue Callaway's colorful, carefree, handmade scrubs were admired by more than the children in the neonatal intensive-care unit where she worked. Callaway's creations are graced with playful dogs, happy dolphins, smiling teddy bears, and other whimsical designs. When Callaway began getting orders from other hospital care professionals, this creative seamstress quit her nursing job and went into business for herself. Within two years, her business was bursting at the seams with orders. To attract new customers, Callaway's company mails over 18 million catalogs each year and has opened a small number of retail stores in shopping malls across the country. |

**EXHIBIT 4.4**

Entrepreneurial Success

If you like a product, chances are an entrepreneur is behind it.

rience. Some come from companies unlike the ones they start; others use their prior knowledge and skills—such as editing, telemarketing, public relations, or selling—to start their own businesses. Still others have less experience but an innovative idea or a better way of doing something. Like Bill Gross, they find an overlooked corner of the market, exploit a demographic trend unnoticed by others, or meet an unsatisfied consumer need through better service or a higher-quality product. Moreover, they often plan and develop their product quickly, while the rest of the business world ponders whether a market for the product exists.

## IMPORTANCE OF PREPARING A BUSINESS PLAN

Although many successful entrepreneurs claim to have done little formal planning, even the most intuitive of them have *some* idea of what they're trying to accomplish and how they hope to do it. No amount of hard work can turn a bad idea into a profitable one: The health-food store in a meat-and-potatoes neighborhood and the child-care center in a retirement community are probably doomed from the beginning. Before you rush in to supply a product, you need to be sure that a market exists.

You must also try to foresee some of the problems that might arise and figure out how you will cope with them. For instance, what will you do if one of your suppliers suddenly goes out of business? Can you locate another supplier quickly? What if the neighborhood starts to change—even for the better? An influx of wealthier neighbors may cause such a steep increase in rent that your business must move. Also, tough competition may move into the neighborhood along with the fatter pocketbooks. Do you have an alternative location staked out? What if styles suddenly change? Can you switch quickly from, say, hand-painted crafts to some other kind of artwork?

One of the first steps you should take toward starting a new business is to develop a **business plan,** a written document that summarizes an entrepreneur's proposed business venture, communicates the company's goals, highlights how management intends to achieve those goals, and shows how consumers will benefit from the company's products or services. Preparing a business plan serves two important functions: First, it guides the company operations and outlines a strategy for turning an idea into reality; Second, it helps persuade lenders and investors to finance your business. In fact, without a business plan, many investors won't even grant you an interview. Keep in mind that sometimes the greatest service a business plan can provide an entrepreneur is the realization that "the concept just won't work." Discovering this on paper can save you considerable time and money. (See the Appendix, "Getting Started with Business PlanPro Software.")

> ## active exercise

**Take a moment to apply what you've learned.**

## SMALL-BUSINESS OWNERSHIP OPTIONS

Once you've done your research and planning, if you decide to take the risk, you can get into business for yourself in three ways: Start from scratch, buy an existing business, or obtain a franchise. Roughly two-thirds of business founders begin **start-up companies;** that is, they start from scratch rather than buying an existing operation or inheriting the family business. Starting a business from scratch has many advantages and disadvantages, as Exhibit 4.5 points out. Of the three options for going into business for yourself, starting a new business is the most common route, and in many cases, the most difficult. Exhibit 4.6 provides a checklist of some of the many tasks involved in starting a new business.

Another way to go into business for yourself is to buy an existing business. This approach tends to reduce the risks—provided, of course, that you check out the company carefully. When you buy a business, you generally purchase an established customer base, functioning business systems, a proven product or service, and a known location. You don't have to go through the painful period of building a reputation, establishing a clientele, finding suppliers, and hiring and training employees. In addition, financing an existing business is often much easier than financing a new one; lenders are reassured by the company's history and existing assets and customer base. With these major details already settled, you can concentrate on making improvements.

| Advantages | Disadvantages |
|---|---|
| + Control over your own destiny | − Uncertainty of income |
| + Ability to reach your full potential | − Risk of losing your entire investment |
| + Unlimited profits | − Long hours and hard work |
| + Recognition for your efforts | − Complete responsibility |
| + Doing what you enjoy | − High levels of stress |

**EXHIBIT 4.5**

Weighing the Advantages and Disadvantages of Starting a New Business

Owning a business has many advantages, but you must also consider the potential drawbacks.

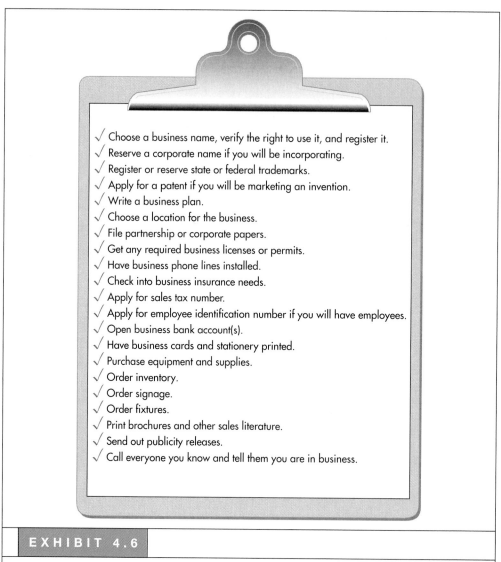

√ Choose a business name, verify the right to use it, and register it.
√ Reserve a corporate name if you will be incorporating.
√ Register or reserve state or federal trademarks.
√ Apply for a patent if you will be marketing an invention.
√ Write a business plan.
√ Choose a location for the business.
√ File partnership or corporate papers.
√ Get any required business licenses or permits.
√ Have business phone lines installed.
√ Check into business insurance needs.
√ Apply for sales tax number.
√ Apply for employee identification number if you will have employees.
√ Open business bank account(s).
√ Have business cards and stationery printed.
√ Purchase equipment and supplies.
√ Order inventory.
√ Order signage.
√ Order fixtures.
√ Print brochures and other sales literature.
√ Send out publicity releases.
√ Call everyone you know and tell them you are in business.

**EXHIBIT 4.6**

Business Start-Up Checklist

You have many tasks to perform before you start your business. Here are just a few.

Still, buying an existing business is not without disadvantages. For one thing, the business may be overpriced. For another, inventories and equipment may be obsolete. Furthermore, the location may no longer be satisfactory, the previous owner may have created ill will, your personality may clash with those of existing managers and employees, and outstanding bills owed by customers may be difficult to collect. Keep in mind that no matter how fast you learn and how much investigating you do, you're likely to find that the challenges of running an existing business are far greater than you anticipated.[28]

> active exercise

Take a moment to apply what you've learned.

## THE FRANCHISE ALTERNATIVE

An alternative to buying an existing business is to buy a **franchise** in somebody else's business. This approach enables the buyer to use a larger company's trade name and sell its products or services in a specific territory. In exchange for this right, the **franchisee** (the small-business owner who contracts to sell the goods or services) pays the **franchisor** (the supplier) an initial fee (and often monthly royalties as well). Franchises are a factor of rising importance in the U.S. economy. Franchising now accounts for roughly $1 trillion, or about 50 percent of all U.S. retail sales.[29]

### Types of Franchises

Franchises are of three basic types. A *product franchise* gives you the right to sell trademarked goods, which are purchased from the franchisor and resold. Car dealers and gasoline stations fall into this category. A *manufacturing franchise,* such as a soft-drink bottling plant, gives you the right to produce and distribute the manufacturer's products, using supplies purchased from the franchisor. A *business-format franchise* gives you the right to open a business using a franchisor's name and format for doing business. Fast-food chains such as KFC, Taco Bell, and Pizza Hut typify this form of franchising.

### How to Evaluate a Franchise

How do you protect yourself from a poor franchise investment? The best way is to study the opportunity carefully before you commit. Since 1978 the Federal Trade Commission has required franchisors to disclose information about their operations to prospective franchisees. By studying this information, you can determine the financial condition of the franchisor and ascertain whether the company has been involved in lawsuits with franchisees. Before signing a franchise agreement, it's also wise to consult an attorney. Exhibit 4.7 suggests some points to consider as you study the package of information on the franchise.

Nevertheless, some people find out too late that franchising isn't the best choice for them. They make a mistake common among prospective franchisees—buying without really understanding the day-to-day business. Often, prospects simply don't get beyond the allure of the successful name or concept—or the mistaken notion that a franchise brings instant success. "People go into a sub shop at the noon hour and see the cash register opening and closing," says the president of Franchise Solutions. "What they don't see is having to get there at 4 A.M. to bake the bread." Buying a franchise is much like buying any other business: It requires analyzing the market, finding capital, choosing a site, hiring employees, and buying equipment. The process also includes an element not found in other businesses—evaluating the franchisor.[30]

One of the best ways to evaluate a prospective franchisor is by talking to other franchisees. At a minimum, you should find out what other franchisees think of the opportunity. If they had it to do over again, would they still invest? You might even want to spend a few months working for someone who already owns a franchise you're interested in. Fabiola Garcia did. She worked at a 7-Eleven evenings and swing shifts, learning all aspects of the business as part of the screening and training process for prospective 7-Eleven franchise owners. This was in addition to a two-week special session at headquarters, where Garcia learned the franchisor's paperwork procedures.[31]

Nevertheless, as Jim and Laura White discovered, evaluating a franchise means more than assessing the current operation. What the market will be like tomorrow is just as important an issue to address. For example, when the Whites opened their Body Shop franchise in 1994, they expected to earn a comfortable living on their $300,000 investment. Instead, the outlet lost money every year.

1. What does the initial franchise fee cover? Does it include a starting inventory of supplies and products?

2. How are the periodic royalties calculated and when are they paid?

3. Are all trademarks and names legally protected?

4. Who provides and pays for advertising and promotional items?

5. Who selects the location of the business?

6. Is the franchise assigned an exclusive territory?

7. If the territory is not exclusive, does the franchisee have the right of first refusal on additional franchises established in nearby locations?

8. Is the franchisee required to purchase equipment and supplies from the franchisor or other suppliers?

9. Under what conditions can the franchisor and/or the franchisee terminate the franchise agreement?

10. Can the franchise be assigned to heirs?

### EXHIBIT 4.7

**Ten Questions to Ask before Signing a Franchise Agreement**

A franchise agreement is a legally binding contract that defines the relationship between the franchisee and the franchisor. Because the agreement is drawn up by the franchisor, the terms and conditions generally favor the franchisor. Before signing the franchise agreement, be sure to consult an attorney.

What they hadn't taken into account was that less than a year after the Whites' Body Shop opened, Bath & Body would come into the same mall. So did Crabtree & Evelyn, followed a year later by Garden Botanika (these chains sell products that compete directly with Body Shop's, and each of the stores was bigger than the Whites').[32]

### Advantages of Franchising

Why is franchising so popular? For one thing, when you invest in a franchise, you know you are getting a viable business, one that has "worked" many times before. If the franchise is well established, you get the added benefit of instant name recognition, national advertising programs, standardized quality of goods and services, and a proven formula for success. Buying a franchise also gives you instant access to a support network, and in many cases a ready-made blueprint for building a business. For an initial investment (from a few thousand dollars to upward of a million, depending on the franchise), you get services such as site-location studies, market research, training, and technical assistance, as well as assistance with building or leasing your structure, decorating the building, purchasing supplies, and operating the business for 6 to 12 months. Because few franchisees are able to write a check for the amount of the total investment, some franchisors also provide financial assistance.

### Disadvantages of Franchising

Although franchising offers many advantages, it is not the ideal vehicle for everyone. First, owning a franchise is no guarantee of wealth. Even though it may be a relatively easy way to get into business, not all franchises are hugely profitable. Some franchisees barely survive, in fact. One of the biggest disadvantages of franchising is the monthly payment, or royalty, that must be turned over to the franchisor. This fee varies from nothing at all to 20 percent of sales. High royalties are not necessarily bad as long as the franchisee gets ongoing assistance in return.

Another drawback of franchises is that many allow individual operators little independence. Franchisors can prescribe virtually every aspect of the business, down to the details of employee uniforms and the color of the walls. Furthermore, when a chain loses its cutting edge in the marketplace, being stuck with a franchise can be painful. By contrast, if independent retailers run into trouble with their product lines, they can change suppliers or perhaps switch rapidly to a whole new line of business. Franchisees can't. They're usually bound by contracts to sell only authorized goods, often supplied by the franchisor itself at whatever price the franchisor wants to charge.

For 23 years, the Body Shop, a high-quality skin and hair care manufacturer and retailer with nearly $1 billion in sales and more than 1,700 outlets in 48 countries, has served consumers for whom natural, no-frills cosmetics products have been both beneficial and culturally relevant. But competition from savvy, better-looking, and in some cases, lower-priced competitors has seriously eroded the Body Shop's market share. To shake things up, the Body Shop has reduced the number of franchisees in favor of company-owned stores and has begun an extensive store renovation campaign.

Although franchisors can make important decisions without consulting franchisees, the days of franchisors' exercising such control are ending. In many cases the relationship between franchisor and franchisee is becoming more of a joint venture. Some franchisors are rewriting contracts to become less dictatorial, says the CEO of U.S. Franchise Systems. Newer contracts offer stock options, automatic contract renewals, and empowerment through franchise advisory boards. Great Harvest Bread, for instance, promotes innovation among its franchisees. Owners are free to run their bakeries as they see fit—on just one condition: they must share what they learn along the way with other franchise owners.[33] Some franchisors are giving franchisees a voice in how advertising funds are used. Moreover, legislative proposals are being considered that would require franchisors to meet certain criteria (something like an accreditation) before they can sell a franchise in the United States.[34]

> ## active exercise

**Take a moment to apply what you've learned.**

### WHY NEW BUSINESSES FAIL

Even if you carefully evaluate a prospective franchisor or write a winning business plan, you have no guarantee for success. In fact, you may have heard some depressing statistics about the number of new businesses that fail. Some reports say your chances of succeeding are only one in three; others claim that the odds are even worse, stating that 85 percent of all new business ventures fail within 10 years. Actual statistics, however, show otherwise. Of the 857,000 small businesses that closed their doors in 1997, only 16 percent closed because they failed or went bankrupt.[35] Moreover, the true failure rate is much lower if you remove those operations that Dun & Bradstreet (D&B) business analysts say aren't "genuine businesses." For instance, a freelancer who writes one article for a magazine and then stops writing would be counted as a failed business under the traditional measurement (which is based on tax returns).[36]

Most new businesses fail for a number of reasons, as Exhibit 4.8 suggests. Moreover, once the signs of failure begin to surface, some entrepreneurs don't pull the plug fast enough. Jeff Schwarz worked three years without drawing a salary and used up $100,000 of his personal savings before closing his photography business, Remarkable Moments.[37]

Another thing to keep in mind is that failure isn't always the end of the world. Many presidents of big, successful companies, including Fred Smith of FedEx, can spin long tales about how failure got them where they are today or how failure was a valuable learning experience.[38] Still, not everybody bounces back. Experts advise that you can increase your chances for success by thinking about these important points before embarking on your entrepreneurial journey:[39]

1. Management incompetence
2. Lack of industry experience
3. Inadequate financing
4. Poor business planning
5. Unclear or unrealistic goals
6. Failure to attract and keep target customers
7. Uncontrolled growth
8. Inappropriate location
9. Poor inventory and financial controls
10. Inability to make the entrepreneurial transition

**EXHIBIT 4.8**

Why New Businesses Fail

Experts have identified these 10 reasons as the most likely causes of new business failure.

- *Know yourself and what you want to accomplish.* Ask yourself whether you have what it takes to start and operate a business. Consider whether you like dealing with people, enjoy the intricacies of making or selling the product or service, and get satisfaction from meeting the needs of your customers. Find out whether you have the technical knowledge and business management skills to do a better job than your competitors.

- *Know how to find the money you need.* Financing is one of the biggest challenges small businesses face. Many banks shy away from lending money to new businesses because they consider new businesses risky investments. (Financing the enterprise will be discussed later in this chapter.)

- *Know how to register and insure your business.* Having all the proper registrations, certifications, licenses, and insurance protects you from violations that could eventually shut down your business. In Component Chapter D we will discuss insurance and risk management.

- *Know who your customers are and how to reach them.* One of the most important parts of preparing a business plan is to learn who your customers are and to develop strategies for reaching those customers. Nonetheless, most businesspeople make the mistake of assuming that all you need is a good idea and that as soon as you open your doors, customers will come rushing in.

- *Know where to go for help.* Experts advise that you always seek professional assistance before beginning your entrepreneurial journey. For instance, you should pull together a team of professionals and consultants to whom you can turn for advice on a regular basis. These professionals include a good lawyer, accountant, bookkeeper, banker, insurance agent, and marketing expert. Besides using these professionals, a number of business resources exist that can help you with your undertaking, as the next section shows.

## active exercise &lt;

### Take a moment to apply what you've learned.

### SOURCES OF SMALL-BUSINESS ASSISTANCE

Many local business professionals are willing to serve as mentors and can help you avoid the pitfalls of business. As a small-business owner, you may turn to small-business resources such as the Service Corps of Retired Executives (SCORE—a resource partner of the SBA), incubators, and the Internet. These resources can help you evaluate your business idea, develop a business plan, locate start-up funding sources, and show you how to package your business image professionally.

### SCORE

Some of the best advice available to small businesses costs little or nothing. It's delivered by SCORE's 12,000 volunteers. These men and women are working and retired executives and active small-business owners who offer advice and one-to-one counseling sessions on topics such as developing a business plan, securing financing, and managing business growth. To date, more than 3.5 million clients, such as New York Bagel, have been helped by SCORE counselors.[40]

Whether you use a SCORE counselor or find a private mentor, having someone to bounce your ideas off of or help you create a five-year financial forecast can increase the chances of your business's survival, as Lynelle and John Lawrence discovered. Owners of the Mudhouse Café in Charlottesville, Virginia, the Lawrences used a SCORE representative to help them prepare a detailed business plan and obtain financing. "There's no way we would be here without SCORE," confesses the couple.[41]

### Incubators

As this chapter's opening vignette highlights, **incubators** are centers that provide "newborn" businesses with just about everything a company needs to get started—office space, expert advice, legal and accounting services, clerical services, marketing support, contacts, and more.[42]

Some incubators are open to businesses of all types; others specialize, such as Bill Gross's idealab! Regardless, the goal is to convert "tenant" firms into "graduates," so most incubators set limits—from 18 months to five years—on how long a company can stay in the nest. Most Internet fledglings, however, are up and running within 90 days.[43]

Incubators, of course, are not a new idea. Thousands of them hatch successful businesses each year. Create-A-Saurus, producer of a line of playground equipment assembled from recycled and reconditioned tires, was hatched from the Oakland (California) Small Business Growth Center. Similarly, a Milwaukee, Wisconsin, business incubator gave Yolanda Cross the chance to move her catering-related business from her home into a more professional setting, where it has flourished.[44] Studies show that firms that start out in incubators typically increase sales by more than 400 percent from the time they enter until the time they leave.[45] Furthermore, 8 out of 10 businesses nurtured in incubators succeed. "Our companies are like children—we will do anything to make them succeed," says Gross.[46]

### The Internet

The Internet is another source of small-business assistance. Sonja Edmond, owner of Heavenly Bounty Giftbaskets, a hand-crafted gift-basket business, had to look no farther than her computer screen when she needed help. Although she enjoyed making gift baskets as a hobby, she wasn't sure whether a viable market existed to support a home-based business. So she posted a price-setting question on CompuServe's Working from Home and Handcrafts forum. Within 24 hours, her e-mail box was flooded with answers from forum members, who "convinced me I could do this," she says. Edmond struck a resource gold mine: Not only did she find the encouragement she needed to plunge into entrepreneurship; she also got valuable business leads and advice on licensing her product.[47]

> ## active exercise

**Take a moment to apply what you've learned.**

## IMPORTANCE OF MANAGING GROWTH

Growing from start-up enterprise into a professionally managed organization creates a number of challenges for most small businesses. While the benefits of growth are many—it creates jobs, provides a stimulating and exciting environment to work in, and offers a potential for new wealth—growth has its drawbacks too. Growth forces change throughout the organization, affecting every aspect of the business operation. When growth is too rapid, it can force so much change that things spin out of control. And nothing can kill a successful business faster than chaos.[48]

Doug and Jill Smith learned this the hard way. With a 50 percent increase in sales—in one year alone—their company, Buckeye Beans & Herbs, was spinning out of control. They needed more people to take the orders, fill them, package the product, and so on. It took them a while to realize they weren't running a little mom-and-pop operation anymore. "We just couldn't do it all, and we didn't have the people in place yet," note the Smiths, who eventually got things back on the right track.[49]

Like the Smiths, many small-business owners find they know little about managing a larger company. "There are times I have moments of sheer panic," notes the president of Creedon Controls, an electrical contractor. "Where am I going to get the money? How am I going to cover the payroll? How am I going to get the job done?"[50] These are just a few of the challenges owners of a growing business must face. In general, growing companies need to install more sophisticated systems and processes.

They must staff positions that never existed and learn how to delegate responsibilities and control. And they must hire experienced managers. For some owners, managing a larger company means losing what they like most about being small—the ability to work closely with employees in a hands-on environment.

As you move from one level to the next in a growing company, experts advise that you take these steps:[51]

- *Get help.* Although some entrepreneurs are good at launching companies, they sometimes lack the skills needed to manage companies over the long term. The person who excels during the start-up phase might know the industry and the product or service very well but may have problems figuring out how to run the expanded business. Therefore, as a company grows, you need to hire advisers with good business expertise.

- *Prepare to change your role.* As a company grows, the owner's role must change. The leader of a growing concern needs to become the strategic thinker and the planner—and must learn to delegate day-to-day responsibilities. The CEO needs to be in charge of tomorrow while other people are in charge of today.

- *Modify your systems.* A growing company usually needs new technology, more inventory, new product-ordering systems, and new communication systems. Growth means there will be many more vendors, more bills, and more checks to write. "If you double the size of the company, the number of bills you have to pay goes up by a factor of six," notes one entrepreneur.[52]

- *Stay focused.* One of the biggest mistakes entrepreneurs make is straying too far from the original product or market. Take Lifeline Systems, a provider of personal-response systems for the elderly. Fewer than 10 years after it was founded, the company went public and was distributing its monitoring devices in more than 700 hospitals across the United States. Fearing that its focus was too small, the company diversified by introducing a new version of its monitoring device that could be used by children and college students in emergencies. It sold these devices to drug, electronics, and department stores at roughly half the price of the original model. But the mass-market strategy found few buyers. Worse, it alienated the company's hospital customers, whose demand for the original product was already falling as a result of slashed hospital budgets. Lifeline began reporting losses. When a new CEO was hired to turn things around, one of the first things he did was undo the company's diversification efforts and restore the company's original focus.[53]

## active concept check <

**Now let's take a moment to test your knowledge of the concepts you have studied in this section.**

## > Financing a New Business

Once you've decided to go into business for yourself, you will probably need some money to get started. Choosing the right sources of capital can be just as important as choosing the right location. Your decision will affect your company forever. Moreover, undercapitalization is a leading factor of small-business failure, as shown in this chapter's Focusing on E-Business Today feature.

### PRIVATE FINANCING SOURCES

Most new companies must borrow money from private sources. Obtaining money from family and friends is, of course, one possibility for financing a new enterprise. Bank loans are another. Keep in mind that obtaining a bank loan can be a challenge because many banks shy away from lending money to new businesses. For one thing, banks consider start-ups risky. For another, the risk inherent in some start-ups justifies higher interest rates than banks are allowed to charge by law. Thus, most banks will finance a start-up only if they can obtain payment guarantees from other financially sound parties or to the extent that the business has marketable collateral, such as buildings and equipment, to back the loan.[54] (In Chapter 17, we'll discuss the advantages, the disadvantages, and the risk of financing with borrowed money or debt versus financing with equity by selling shares of stock in your firm to the public.) In addition to friends and bank loans, other sources of private financing assistance include venture capitalists, angel investors, credit cards, and the SBA.

### Venture Capitalists

**Venture capitalists** are investment specialists who raise pools of capital from large private and institutional sources (such as pension funds) to fund ventures that have a high, rapid growth potential and a need for large amounts of capital. Venture capitalists, or VCs as they're called in entrepreneurial circles, do not simply lend money to a small business as a bank would. Instead they provide money and management expertise in return for a sizable ownership interest in the business. Once the business becomes profitable, venture capitalists reap the reward by selling their interest to other long-term investors for a sizable profit.

Overwhelmed by the number of potential start-ups and a flood of investment funds, most venture capitalist firms will only finance firms that need $10 million or more.[55] Moreover, because it takes the same commitment to watch a small company as a large one, most VCs limit their investments to companies that have the capability of generating $100 million in revenues within a three-year time frame.[56] Thus, if you're looking for only $1 or $2 million of financing, you might want to find an angel instead.

### Angel Investors

Comfortable with risks that scare off many banks, *angel investors* put their own money into start-ups with the goal of eventually selling their interest for a large profit. These wealthy individuals are willing to loan smaller amounts of money than are VCs and to stay involved with the company for a longer period of time.

In 1999, some 400,000 angels invested about $30 billion in 40,000 U.S. companies.[57] Start-ups that seek out angels typically have spent their first $50,000 to $100,000 and are now looking for the next $250,000 to grow their business.[58] In addition to providing financing, angels can be a great source of business expertise and credibility. High-profile angels include such experts as Bill Gates (chairman of Microsoft), Marc Andresseen (founder of Netscape), and others.[59]

### Credit Cards

According to a recent study by Arthur Andersen Company, one-third of businesses with 19 or fewer employees use credit cards to finance their new business ventures.[60] Many people turn to credit cards because credit card companies don't care how borrowers spend the money just as long as they pay the bill. Others use credit cards because they are the only source of funding available to them. But with high interest rates, credit cards are a risky way to finance a business, as Jorge de la Riva discovered. He used personal credit cards to start up his industrial wholesale business—an experience he calls "playing with the tiger." As de la Riva put it, "You can make it work only if you have a definite plan to pay back the debt."[61] Unfortunately, many do not. (Credit cards are discussed in greater detail in Chapter 17.)

## SMALL BUSINESS ADMINISTRATION ASSISTANCE

If your business doesn't fit the profile of high-powered venture-capital start-ups, or you can't find an angel, you might be able to qualify for a bank loan backed by the SBA. To get an SBA-backed loan, you apply to a regular bank, which actually provides the money; the SBA guarantees to repay up to 80 percent of the loan if you fail to do so. The average SBA-backed loan is about $100,000; the upper limit is $1 million with a 75 percent guarantee.[62] Guaranteed loans provided by the SBA launched FedEx, Intel, and Apple Computer. These three now pay more annual taxes to the federal government than the entire yearly cost of running the SBA.[63] In addition to operating its loan guarantee program, the SBA provides a limited number of direct loans to minorities, women, and veterans.[64]

From the businessperson's standpoint, SBA-backed loans are especially attractive because most have longer repayment terms than conventional bank loans—nine years as opposed to two or three. A longer repayment term translates into lower monthly payments. Unfortunately, demand for SBA loans vastly outstrips the agency's budget.[65] Nevertheless, Karla Brown is one of the lucky ones. With plenty of perseverance and a $19,000 microloan from the SBA, Brown was able to start her business, Ashmont Flowers Plus. The SBA microloan program began in 1992 to help people realize the American dream—to own a business and be self-sufficient. Microloans range from $100 to $25,000, with the average loan of $10,000 paid back over four years.[66]

Another option for raising money is one of the investment firms created by the Small Business Administration. Small Business Investment Companies (SBICs) and Minority Enterprise Small Business Investment Companies (MESBICs), which finance minority-owned businesses, are similar in operation to venture-capital firms, but they tend to make smaller investments and are willing to consider businesses that VCs may not want to finance.[67]

The partners in a start-up called WebTaggers.com, a computer application provider, recently spent an anxious day and a half preparing to present their business plan to venture capitalists. "In that 10-minute pitch I've got to give the whole story and ask for $10 million," says CEO David Chevalier.

## GOING PUBLIC

Whenever a corporation offers its shares of ownership, or **stock,** to the public for the first time, the company is said to be *going public*. The initial shares offered for sale are the company's **initial public offering (IPO).** Going public is an effective method of raising needed capital, but it can be an expensive and time-consuming process filled with regulatory nightmares. Before deciding to finance your company by selling stock, you should weigh the advantages and disadvantages of financing with stock, bonds, and bank loans, as Chapter 17 discusses in detail. Keep in mind that going public is one of the most difficult transactions a business can undertake. For one thing, it requires years of advance planning—sometimes as long as five years before the target date. For another, IPO candidates must have audited financial reports and a solid management team in place.[68]

Because of the high costs and complexity of an IPO, some companies choose to sell their stock directly to the public—a practice known as a **direct public offering (DPO).**[69] The number of DPOs is steadily growing, thanks to the Internet, and DPOs are expected to become an increasingly popular financing option.

The biggest advantage of a DPO is cost savings. DPOs provide businesses with fresh capital at less than half the cost of an IPO. Electronic printing and distribution of a firm's **prospectus,** a preliminary printed statement that is distributed to prospective investors, and the use of virtual sales presentations instead of live ones can save a company hundreds of thousands of dollars in travel, printing, and distribution costs.[70] In spite of these savings, most companies still go the traditional IPO route. For one thing, DPO shares are not traded on public security exchanges, making it difficult for shareholders to find subsequent buyers for their shares. (Security exchanges are discussed in Chapter 18.) For another, lack of security coverage and support before, after, and during the offering make it difficult to find investors.[71] Even Spring Street Brewing, one of the most highly publicized DPOs, admits that reaching out directly to investors on the Internet will not be as easy for others as it was for Spring Street Brewing, as the company benefited from unusually high levels of publicity because it was the first Internet DPO.[72]

If a company chooses to go the DPO route, it must still follow rules and regulations for selling securities privately. For example, Rule 504 of Regulation D of the Securities and Exchange Commission (also known as "504 offerings" or "Regulation D" offerings) allows companies to raise up to $1 million every 12 months by selling stock, provided they register the securities with the state. Regulation A extends the size of the offering to $5 million but requires a registration with the Small Business Office of the SEC.[73]

> ## video exercise

**Take a moment to apply what you've learned.**

> ## active concept check

**Now let's take a moment to test your knowledge of the concepts you have studied in this section.**

> ### Chapter Wrap-Up

Now that you've reached the end of the chapter, you may wish to explore the concepts you've been reading about in greater detail, or test yourself to see how well you've comprehended the material. In the box below you'll find a number of links. Click on any one of these links to find additional chapter resources.

> ## end-of-chapter resources

- **Summary of Learning Objectives**
- **Practice Quiz**
- **Focusing on E-Business Today**
- **Key Terms**
- **Test Your Knowledge**
- **Practice Your Knowledge**
- **Expand Your Knowledge**
- **A Case for Critical Thinking**

# Forms of Business Ownership and Business Combinations

## > What's Ahead

### INSIDE BUSINESS TODAY
### RESTRUCTURING KINKO'S PARTNERSHIPS TO DUPLICATE SUCCESS

Paul Orfalea knew he would run a big company someday. He just never envisioned Kinko's as that dream. At 22 Orfalea borrowed enough money to open a copying service near the University of California, Santa Barbara. The store was so small that he had to wheel the single copier onto the sidewalk to make room for customers. Nevertheless, it serviced the needs of local college students.

By 1995 (some 25 years later), Kinko's—named after Orfalea's reddish, curly hair—had grown into a chain of 815 stores operating in five countries. But Kinko's wasn't managed as a single entity. Instead, the business consisted of 130 separate partnerships, each operating groups of stores. Even though Orfalea retained a majority interest in each partnership, the partners were free to operate their stores as they saw fit. Therefore, not all Kinko's were the same, and that was a problem. Some partners reinvested their earnings in high-tech equipment; others cashed in their profits. This meant that traveling customers would find varing equipment and services from store to store: from color copiers and high-speed Internet access at spruced-up outlets in one city to dilapidated storefronts with little more than black-and-white copy machines in another.

Orfalea knew that to succeed in a high-tech marketplace, all Kinko's stores would have to look alike and offer comparable services. Moreover, with more and more people working from home and other remote locations, the stores would have to invest in expensive equipment such as digital printers, high-speed copiers, fast Internet connections, and even videoconferencing equipment to service growing customer needs. Orfalea also knew that such changes would require additional financing and the help of experts. So in 1997 Orfalea selected private investors Clayton, Dublier & Rice (CD&R) to help turn things around.

Kinko's, once known simply as the leading chain of printing and copy shops, has recast itself for the work-obsessed digital age.

Paying out $220 million in exchange for a 33 percent share of Kinko's, CD&R rolled the 130 individual partnerships into a single privately held corporation, giving each partner shares of stock in the newly formed organization. It took the original partners some time to adjust to the new corporate structure, but eventually they came around. Besides, the partners knew that having a private equity stake in Kinko's could be worth a sizable fortune if the company went public.

As a corporate entity, everyone was now working in the same direction. The store managers lobbied aggressively for new equipment and expanded their services to include on-site computer rentals, document binding and finishing, custom printing, passport photos, mailing services, videoconference facilities, and more. In addition, the company launched KinkonetSM, a proprietary document distribution and print network that allows customers to submit projects at one Kinko's site and pick up finished projects at another.

With annual sales now topping $1 billion, Kinko's is indeed the leader in the $7 billion copy-services market. Today customers can go into any of the 1,000 Kinko's in such far-flung places as Australia, Japan, South Korea, and the United Kingdom and find the same equipment, supplies, and services, making it possible for small-business owners and travelers to rely on Kinko's as their office away from home.[1]

## objectives                                                                              <

Take a moment to familiarize yourself with the key objectives of this chapter.

> **gearing up**

Before you begin reading this chapter, try a short warm-up activity.

As Paul Orfalea knows, one of the most fundamental decisions you must make when starting a business is selecting a form of business ownership. This decision can be complex and have far-reaching consequences for your business. Furthermore, as your business grows, chances are you may change the original form you selected, as Orfalea did.

The three most common forms of business ownership are sole proprietorship, partnership, and corporation. Each form has its own characteristic internal structure, legal status, size, and fields to which it is best suited. Each has key advantages and disadvantages for the owners. Exhibit 5.1 contrasts the characteristics of the three forms of business ownership.

## SOLE PROPRIETORSHIPS

A **sole proprietorship** is a business owned by one person (although it may have many employees), and it is the easiest and least expensive form of business to start. Many farms, retail establishments, and small service businesses are sole proprietorships, as are many home-based businesses (such as caterers, consultants, and computer programmers).

### Advantages of Sole Proprietorships

A sole proprietorship has many advantages. One is ease of establishment. All you have to do to launch a sole proprietorship is obtain necessary licenses, start a checking account for the business, and open your doors. Another advantage is the satisfaction of working for yourself. As a sole proprietor, you can make your own decisions, such as which hours to work, whom to hire, what prices to charge, whether to expand, and whether to shut down. Best of all, you can keep all the after-tax profits, and profits are taxed at individual income tax rates not at the higher corporate rates.

As a sole proprietor, you also have the advantage of privacy; you do not have to reveal your performance or plans to anyone. Although you may need to provide financial information to a banker if you need a loan, and you must provide certain financial information when you file tax returns, you do not have to prepare any reports for outsiders as you would if the company were a public corporation.

### Disadvantages of Sole Proprietorships

One major drawback of a sole proprietorship is the proprietor's **unlimited liability.** From a legal standpoint, the owner and the business are one and the same. Any legal damages or debts incurred by the business are the owner's responsibility. As a sole proprietor, you might have to sell personal assets, such as your home, to satisfy a business debt. And if someone sues you over a business matter, you might lose everything you own if you do not have the proper types and amount of business insurance (see Component Chapter C).

In some cases, the sole proprietor's independence can also be a drawback because it means that the business depends on the talents and managerial skills of one person. If problems crop up, the sole proprietor may not recognize them or may be too proud to seek help, especially given the high cost of hiring experienced managers and professional consultants. Other disadvantages include the difficulty of a single-person operation obtaining large sums of capital and the limited life of a sole proprietorship. Although some sole proprietors pass their business on to their heirs as part of their

| Corporate Structure | Ownership Rules and Control | Tax Considerations | Liability Exposure | Ease of Establishment and Termination |
|---|---|---|---|---|
| Sole proprietorship | One owner has complete control. | Profits and losses flow directly to the owners and are taxed at individual rates. | Owner has unlimited personal liability for business debts. | Easy to set up but leaves owner's personal finances at risk. Owner must generally sell the business to get his or her investment out. |
| General partnership | Two or more owners; each partner is entitled to equal control unless agreement specifies otherwise. | Profits and losses flow directly to the partners and are taxed at individual rates. Partners share income and losses equally unless the partnership agreement specifies otherwise. | Personal assets of any operating partner are at risk from business creditors. | Easy to set up. Partnership agreement recommended but not required. Partners must generally sell their share in the business to recoup their investment. |
| Limited partnership | Two or more owners; the general partner controls the business; limited partners do not participate in the management. | Same as for general partnership. | Limited partners are liable only for the amount of their investment. | Same as for general partnership. |
| Corporation | Unlimited number of shareholders; no limits on stock classes or voting arrangements. Ownership and management of the business are separate. Shareholders in public corporations are not involving in daily management decisions; in private or closely held corporations, owners are more likely to participate in managing the business. | Profits and losses are taxed at corporate rates. Profits are taxed again at individual rates when they are distributed to the investors as dividends. | Investor's liability is limited to the amount of their investment. | Expense and complexity of incorporation vary from state to state; can be costly from a tax perspective. In a public corporation, shareholders may trade their shares on the open market; in a private corporation, shareholders must find a buyer for their shares to recoup their investment. |

**EXHIBIT 5.1**

Characteristics of the Forms of Business Ownership

The "best" form of ownership depends on the objectives of the people involved in the business.

estate, the owner's death may mean the demise of the business. And even if the business does transfer to an heir, the founder's unique skills may have been crucial to the successful operation of the business.

## PARTNERSHIPS

If starting a business on your own seems a little intimidating, you might decide to share the risks and rewards of going into business with a partner. In that case, you would form a **partnership**—a legal association of two or more people as co-owners of a business for profit. You and your partners would share the profits and losses of the business and perhaps the management responsibilities. Your partnership might remain a small, two-person operation or it might have multiple partners, like Kinko's did.

Partnerships are of two basic types. In a **general partnership,** all partners are considered equal by law, and all are liable for the business's debts. In a **limited partnership,** one or more people act as *general partners* who run the business, while the remaining partners are passive investors (that is, they are not involved in managing the business). These partners are called *limited partners* because their liability (the amount of money they can lose) is limited to the amount of their capital contribution. Many states now recognize *limited liability partnerships* (LLPs) in which all partners in the business are limited partners and have only limited liability for the debts and obligations of the partnership. Most states restrict LLPs to certain types of professionals such as attorneys, physicians, dentists, and accountants.[2] Of the three forms of business ownership, partnerships are the least-common form (see Exhibit 5.2).

### Advantages of Partnerships

Proprietorships and partnerships have some of the same advantages. Like proprietorships, partnerships are easy to form. Partnerships also provide the same tax advantages as proprietorships, because profits are taxed at individual income-tax rates rather than at corporate rates.

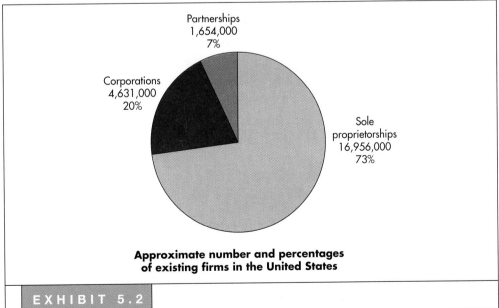

Partnerships
1,654,000
7%

Corporations
4,631,000
20%

Sole
proprietorships
16,956,000
73%

**Approximate number and percentages
of existing firms in the United States**

**EXHIBIT 5.2**

Popular Forms of Business Ownership

The most popular form of business ownership is a sole proprietorship, followed by a corporation and then a partnership.

However, in a couple of respects, partnerships are superior to sole proprietorships, largely because there's strength in numbers. When you have several people putting up their money, you can start a more ambitious enterprise. In addition, the diversity of skills that good partners bring to an organization leads to innovation in products, services, and processes, which improves your chances of success.[3] The partnership form of ownership also broadens the pool of capital available to the business. Not only do the partners' personal assets support a larger borrowing capacity, but the ability to obtain financing increases because general partners are legally responsible for paying off the debts of the group. Finally, by forming a partnership you increase the chances that the organization will endure, because new partners can be drawn into the business to replace those who die or retire. For example, even though the original partners of the accounting firm KPMG Peat Marwick (founded in 1897) died many years ago, the company continues.

### Disadvantages of Partnerships

Except in limited liability partnerships, at least one member of every partnership must be a general partner. All general partners have unlimited liability. Thus, if one of the firm's partners makes a serious business or professional mistake and is sued by a disgruntled client, all general partners are financially accountable. At the same time, general partners are responsible for any debts incurred by the partnership. Of course, malpractice insurance or business-risk insurance offers some financial protection (see Component Chapter C), but these types of insurance are costly.

Another disadvantage of partnerships is the potential for interpersonal problems. Difficulties often arise because each partner wants to be responsible for managing the organization. Electing a managing partner to lead the organization may diminish the conflicts, but disagreements are still likely to arise. Moreover, the partnership may have to face the question of what to do with unproductive partners. And if a partner wants to leave the firm, conflicts can arise over claims on the firm's profits and on capital the partner invested. Provisions for handling the departure and addition of partners are usually covered in the partnership agreement.

### Partnership Agreement

A *partnership agreement* is a written document that states all the terms of operating the partnership by spelling out the partners' rights and responsibilities. Although the law does not require a written partnership agreement, it is wise to work with a lawyer to develop one. One of the most important features of the agreement is that it addresses in advance sources of conflict that could result in battles between partners. To avoid disagreements later on, begin by spelling out such details as the division of profits, decision-making authority, expected contributions, and dispute resolution. Moreover, a key element of this document is the buy/sell agreement, which defines the steps a partner must take to sell his or her partnership interest or what will happen if one of the partners dies.

## active exercise

**Take a moment to apply what you've learned.**

## CORPORATIONS

A **corporation** is a legal entity with the power to own property and conduct business. The modern corporation evolved in the nineteenth century when large sums of capital were needed to build railroads, coal mines, and steel mills. Such endeavors required so much money that no single individual or group of partners could hope to raise it all. The solution was to sell shares in the business to numerous investors, who would get a cut of the profits in exchange for their money. These investors got a chance to vote on certain issues that might affect the value of their investment, but they were not involved in managing day-to-day operations. The investors were protected from the risks associated with such large undertakings by having their liability limited to the amount of their investment.

It was a good solution, and the corporation quickly became a vital force in the nation's economy. As rules and regulations developed to define what corporations could and could not do, corporations acquired the legal attributes of people. Like you, a corporation can receive, own, and transfer property; make contracts; sue; and be sued. Unlike the case with sole proprietorships and partnerships, a corporation's legal status and obligations exist independently of its owners.

The corporation is owned by its **shareholders,** who are issued shares of stock in return for their investments. These shares are evidenced by a **stock certificate,** and they may be bequeathed or sold to someone else. As a result, the company's ownership may change drastically over time while the company and its management remain intact (as long as the company is economically sound). The corporation's unlimited life span, combined with its ability to raise capital, gives it the potential for significant growth.

**COMMON STOCK** Most stock issued by corporations is **common stock.** Owners of common stock have voting rights and get one vote for each share of stock they own. They can elect the company's board of directors in addition to voting on major policies that will affect ownership—such as mergers, acquisitions, and takeovers. Besides conferring voting privileges, common stock frequently pays **dividends,** payments to shareholders from the company's profits. Dividends can be paid in cash or stock (called *stock dividends*). They are declared by the board of directors but their payment is not mandatory. For example, some companies, especially young or rapidly growing ones, pay no dividends. Instead, they reinvest their profits in new product research and development, equipment, buildings, and other assets so they can grow and earn future profits.

In addition to dividends, common shareholders can earn a return on their investment. If shareholders sell their stock in good times for more than they paid for it, they stand to pocket a handsome gain. But because the value or price of a company's common stock is subject to many economic variables besides the company's own performance, common-stock investments are risky and shareholders may not get any profit at all. In fact, if investors sell shares of common stock for less than they paid for it, they could incur a sizable financial loss. Common stock, risk, and financial investments are discussed in detail in Chapter 18.

**PREFERRED STOCK** In contrast to common stock, **preferred stock** does not usually carry voting rights. It does, however, give preferred shareholders the right of first claim on the corporation's assets (in the form of dividends) after all the company's debts have been paid. This right is especially important if the company ever goes out of business. Moreover, preferred shareholders get their dividends before common shareholders do. The amount of preferred dividend is usually set (or fixed) at the time the preferred stock is issued and can provide investors with a source of steady income. Like common stock, however, dividends on preferred stock may be omitted in times of financial hardship. Still, most preferred stock is *cumulative preferred stock,* which means that any unpaid dividends must be paid before dividends are paid to common shareholders.

**PUBLIC VERSUS PRIVATE OWNERSHIP** The stock of a **private corporation** such as Kinko's is held by only a few individuals or companies and is *not publicly traded.* By withholding their stock from public sale, the owners retain complete control over their operations and ownership. Such famous companies as Hallmark and Hyatt Hotels have opted to remain private corporations (also

Avis has never paid cash dividends to shareholders. The company believes that shareholders are best served by reinvesting profits back into the company to foster long-term growth.

referred to as *closed corporations* or *closely held companies*). These companies finance their operating costs and growth from either company earnings or other sources, such as bank loans. By contrast, the stock of a **public corporation** is held by and available for sale to the general public; thus the company is said to be *publicly traded.*

In Chapter 4 we discussed the concept of going public in the context of financing the enterprise. Bear in mind that in addition to providing a ready supply of capital, public ownership has other advantages and disadvantages. Among the advantages are increased liquidity, enhanced visibility, and the establishment of an independent market value for the company. Moreover, having a publicly traded stock gives companies flexibility to use such stock to acquire other firms. This was one of the primary reasons UPS decided to sell 10 percent of its stock to the public in 1999, after nearly a century of remaining a privately held organization.[4] Nevertheless, selling your stock to the public has distinct disadvantages: (1) the cost of going public is high (ranging from $50,000 to $500,000), (2) the filing requirements with the SEC (Securities and Exchange Commission) are burdensome, (3) you lose ownership control, (4) management must be ready to handle the administrative and legal demands of heightened public exposure, and (5) it subjects the value of the company's stock to external forces that are beyond the company's control.

### Advantages of Corporations

No other form of business ownership can match the success of the corporation in bringing together money, resources, and talent; in accumulating assets; and in creating wealth. As it grows, a corporation gains from a diverse labor pool, greater financing options, and expanded research-and-development capabilities. The corporation has certain inherent qualities that make it the best vehicle for reaching those objectives. One such quality is limited liability. Although a corporate entity can assume tremendous liabilities, it is the corporation that is liable and not the private shareholders. Take Johannes Schwartlander, who ran his San Francisco marble and granite business as a sole proprietorship for seven years. When the company began to grow, Schwartlander decided to incorporate to protect himself. "When we had so many employees and started installing marble panels ten stories up, I realized that if five years later something fell down, I would be responsible," he says.[5] Incorporation also protects him from personal liability should his business go bankrupt.

In addition to limited liability, corporations that sell stock to the general public have the advantage of **liquidity,** which means that investors can easily convert their stock into cash by selling it on the open market. This option makes buying stock in a corporation attractive to many investors. In contrast, liquidating the assets of a sole proprietorship or a partnership can be difficult. Moreover, shareholders of public corporations can easily transfer their ownership by selling their shares to someone else. Thus, corporations tend to be in a better position than proprietorships and partnerships to make long-term plans as a result of their unlimited life span and the funding available through the sale of stock. As they grow, corporations can benefit from the diverse talents and experience of a large pool of employees and managers. Moreover, large corporations are often able to finance projects internally.

Keep in mind that a company need not be large to incorporate. Most corporations, like most businesses, are relatively small, and most small corporations are privately held. The big ones, however, are *really* big. The 500 largest corporations in the United States, as listed by *Fortune* magazine, have combined sales of over $6.3 trillion. Wal-Mart stores alone employ 1,400,000 people, which is greater than the population of Detroit, Michigan.[6]

### Disadvantages of Corporations

Corporations are not without some disadvantages. As mentioned earlier, publicly owned companies are required by the government to publish information about their finances and operations. These reporting requirements increase the pressure on corporate managers to achieve short-term growth and earnings targets in order to satisfy shareholders and to attract potential investors. In addition, having to disclose financial information increases the company's vulnerability to competitors and to those who might want to take over control of the company against the wishes of the existing management.

The paperwork and costs associated with incorporation can also be burdensome, particularly if you plan to sell stock. The complexity varies from state to state, but regardless of where you live, it is wise to consult an attorney and an accountant before incorporating. In addition, corporations are taxed twice. They must pay federal and state corporate income tax on the company's profits, and individual shareholders must pay income taxes on their share of the company's profits received as dividends.

### Special Types of Corporations

Certain types of corporations enjoy special privileges provided they adhere to strict guidelines and rules. One special type of corporation is known as the **S corporation** (or subchapter S corporation). An S corporation is a distinction that is made only for federal income tax purposes and is, in terms of legal characteristics, no different from any other corporation. Basically, the owners receive the tax advantages of a partnership while they raise money through the sale of stock. In addition, income and tax deductions from the business flow directly to the owners, who are taxed at individual income-tax rates, just as they are in a partnership. Corporations seeking "S" status must meet certain criteria: (1) they must have no more than 75 investors, none of whom may be nonresident aliens; (2) they must be a domestic (U.S.) corporation; and (3) they can only issue one class of common stock, which means that all stock must share the same dividend and liquidation rights (but may have different voting rights).[7]

**Limited liability companies (LLCs)** are another special type of corporation. These flexible business entities combine the tax advantages of a partnership with the personal liability protection of a corporation. Furthermore, LLCs are not restricted in the number of shareholders they can have, and members' participation in management is not restricted as it is in limited partnerships. Members of an LLC normally adopt an operating agreement (similar to a partnership agreement) to govern the entity's operation and management. These agreements generally are flexible and permit owners to structure the allocation of income and losses any way they desire, so long as certain tax rules are followed. In addition, the agreements can be designed to meet the special needs of owners, such as special voting rights, management controls, and buyout options. The only limit to what can be done is the owners' imagination.[8]

Some corporations are not independent entities; that is, they are owned by a single entity. **Subsidiary corporations,** for instance, are partially or wholly owned by another corporation known as a **parent company,** which supervises the operations of the subsidiary. A **holding company** is a special type of parent company that owns other companies for investment reasons and usually exercises little operating control over those subsidiaries.

Corporations can also be classified according to where they do business. An *alien corporation* operates in the United States but is incorporated in another country. A *foreign corporation,* sometimes called an *out-of-state corporation,* is incorporated in one state (frequently the state of Delaware, where incorporation laws are lenient) but does business in several other states where it is registered. And a *domestic corporation* does business only in the state where it is chartered (incorporated).

### Corporate Governance

Although a corporation's common shareholders own the business, they are rarely involved in managing it, particularly if the corporation is publicly traded. Instead, the common shareholders elect a board of directors to represent them, and the directors, in turn, select the corporation's top officers, who actually run the company (see Exhibit 5.3).

The center of power in a corporation often lies with the **chief executive officer,** or **CEO.** Together with the chief financial officer (CFO) and the chief operating officer (COO), the CEO is responsible for establishing company policies, managing corporate direction, and making the big decisions that will affect the company's growth and competitive position. In Chapter 6, we'll discuss in detail the functions and roles of management. Keep in mind that the chief executive officer may also be the chairman of the board, the president of the corporation, or both. Moreover, because corporate ownership and management are separate, the owners may get rid of the managers (in theory, at least) if the owners vote to do so.

**SHAREHOLDERS** Shareholders of a corporation can be individuals, other companies, not-for-profit organizations, pension funds, and mutual funds. All shareholders who own voting shares are invited to an annual meeting to choose directors, select an independent accountant to audit the company's financial statements, and attend to other business. Those who cannot attend the annual meeting in person vote by **proxy,** signing and returning a slip of paper that authorizes management to vote on their behalf. Because shareholders elect the directors, in theory they are the ultimate governing body of the corporation. In practice, however, most individual shareholders in large corporations—where the shareholders may number in the millions—accept the recommendations of management.

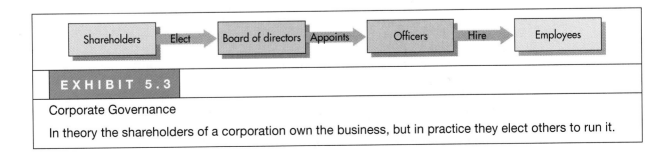

**EXHIBIT 5.3**

Corporate Governance

In theory the shareholders of a corporation own the business, but in practice they elect others to run it.

Typically, the more shareholders a company has, the less tangible the influence each shareholder has on the corporation. However, some shareholders have more influence than others. In recent years, *institutional investors,* such as pension funds, insurance companies, mutual funds, and college endowment funds, have accumulated an increasing number of shares of stock in U.S. corporations. As a result, these large institutional investors are playing a more powerful role in governing the corporations in which they own substantial shares, especially with regard to the election of a company's board of directors.[9] Furthermore, at companies such as Avis and United Airlines, employees are major shareholders and so have a significant voice in how the company is run. For example, when United Airlines employees did not endorse management's decision to promote company president John Edwardson to the CEO position, Edwardson resigned.[10]

**BOARD OF DIRECTORS** Representing the shareholders, the **board of directors** is responsible for declaring dividends, guiding corporate affairs, reviewing long-term strategic plans, selecting corporate officers, and overseeing financial performance. The board has the power to vote on major management decisions, such as building a new factory, hiring a new president, or buying a new subsidiary. Depending on the size of the company, the board might have anywhere from 3 to 35 directors, although 15 to 25 is the typical range for traditional corporations, with a smaller number for e-businesses. At most large corporations, boards are composed exclusively of directors from outside the company, with only the CEO and a senior executive or two from inside the organization. This helps ensure that the board provides diligent and independent oversight. Still, outside directors may be large company shareholders, and many serve on the boards of several companies.[11]

The board's actual involvement in running a corporation varies from one company to another. Some boards are strong and independent and serve as a check on the company's management. Others act as a "rubber stamp," simply approving management's recommendations. Hands-on boards are becoming far more common these days. Every Home Depot director, for instance, must make formal visits to at least 20 stores each year to gain a hands-on perspective of the company's operation.[12]

To compensate directors for their time and contributions, most large companies pay their directors a sizable fee and issue them stock options, the right to purchase a set number of shares of stock at a specific price (see Chapter 11). Some think compensation in the form of company stock aligns the directors' interests with those of other stockholders. But, critics of this practice claim it could compromise the directors' independence, nevertheless evidence shows that companies in which directors own large amounts of stock and take an active role in guiding the company usually outperform those with more passive boards.

## video exercise <

**Take a moment to apply what you've learned.**

## active concept check <

**Now let's take a moment to test your knowledge of the concepts you have studied in this section.**

 **Understanding Business Combinations**

Companies have been combining in various configurations since the early days of business. Joining two companies is a complex process because it involves every aspect of both companies. For instance, executives have to agree on how the combination will be financed and how the power will be transferred and shared. Marketing departments often need to figure out how to blend advertising campaigns and sales forces. Data processing and information systems, which seldom mesh, must be joined together seamlessly. And companies must deal with layoffs, transfers, and changes in job titles and work assignments.

## MERGERS, CONSOLIDATIONS, AND ACQUISITIONS

Two of the most popular forms of business combinations are mergers and consolidations. The difference between a merger and a consolidation is fairly technical, having to do with how the financial and legal transaction is structured. Basically, in a **merger,** one company buys another company, or parts of another company, and emerges as the controlling corporation. The controlling company assumes all the debts and contractual obligations of the company it acquires, which then ceases to exist. A **consolidation** is similar to a merger except that an entirely new firm is created by two or more companies that pool their interests. In a consolidation, both firms terminate their previous legal existence and become part of the new firm.

A third way that a company may acquire another firm is by purchasing that firm's voting stock. This transaction is generally referred to as an **acquisition** and is completed when the shareholders of the acquired firm tender their stock for either cash or shares of stock in the acquiring company. Keep in mind that the purpose and outcome of these three business combinations are basically the same, which is why you will often hear these terms used interchangeably.

> ## active exercise

**Take a moment to apply what you've learned.**

### Advantages of Mergers, Consolidations, and Acquisitions

Business combinations provide several financial and operational advantages. Combined entities hope to eliminate expenditures for redundant resources; increase their buying power as a result of their larger size; increase revenue by cross-selling products to each other's customers; increase market share by combining product lines to provide more comprehensive offerings; eliminate manufacturing overcapacity; and gain access to new expertise, systems, and teams of employees who already know how to work together.

Often these advantages are grouped under umbrella terms such as *economies of scale, efficiencies,* or *synergies,* which generally mean that the benefits of working together will be greater than if each company continued to operate independently. For instance, when Daimler-Benz and Chrysler merged, they expected to gain competitive advantages that were unavailable to either before the merger, as this chapter's case study explains.

### Disadvantages of Mergers, Consolidations, and Acquisitions

Despite the promise of economies of scale, studies of merged companies show that 65 to 85 percent of these deals fail to actually achieve promised efficiencies.[13] One such study even found that the profitability of acquired companies on average declined.[14] Keep in mind that "bigger" does not always equate to "better." Honda is only a fraction of GM's size, yet it has consistently outperformed GM for the past 20 years. Moreover, a recent study by Accenture found that, since 1995, small banks have consistently operated more efficiently per customer than their much larger competitors.[15] As one expert put it, if you combine two lumbering companies, you get one that runs worse, not better.[16]

Part of the problem with mergers is that companies often borrow immense amounts of money to acquire a firm, and the loan payments on this corporate debt use cash that is needed to run the business. Moreover, managers must help combine the operations of the two entities and this pulls them away from their normal day-to-day responsibilities. Another obstacle that companies face when combining forces is *culture clash.*

In Chapter 6 we discuss organizational culture in detail. A company's culture is the way people in the organization do things. Culture clash occurs when two joining companies have different beliefs about what is really important, how to make decisions, how to supervise people, how to communicate, and so on. Experts note that in too many deals the acquiring company imposes its values and management systems on the acquired company without any regard to what worked well there. When Quaker Oats acquired Snapple, for example, it immediately dismantled Snapple's distribution system, a key factor in Snapple's success. Ultimately, Quaker Oats paid the price by discovering that if you destroy another company's systems, you often end up buying nothing.[17]

Keep in mind that culture includes not only management style and practices but also the way people dress, how they communicate, or whether they punch a time clock. Recent studies have shown that underestimating the difficulties of merging two cultures was the major factor in failed mergers, and experts contend that the increasing number of worldwide mergers, consolidations, and acquisitions will make culture clash an even bigger challenge.[18] When Ford acquired Volvo, for example, Swedish autoworkers were nervous that they might lose their health club benefits and other perks that Swedish companies give to workers to compensate them for the high income taxes they pay the government.[19] Similarly, culture clash has been an issue at DaimlerChrysler as this chapter's case study will show.

### Types of Mergers

Mergers tend to happen in waves, in response to changes in the economy. One of the biggest waves of merger activity occurred between 1881 and 1911, when capitalists created giant monopolistic trusts, buying enough stock of competing companies in basic industries such as oil and steel to control the market. These trusts were **horizontal mergers,** or combinations of competing companies performing the same function. The purposes of a horizontal merger are to achieve the benefits of economies of scale and to fend off competition. The rise of a government antitrust movement and the dissolution of Standard Oil in 1911 marked the end of this wave.

A second great wave occurred in the boom decade of the 1920s. This era was marked by the emergence of **vertical mergers,** in which a company involved in one phase of an industry absorbs or joins a company involved in another phase of the same industry. The aim of a vertical merger is often to guarantee access to supplies or to markets. For example, until fairly recently, both Ford and General Motors owned the companies that supplied most of the parts for their cars.

A third wave of mergers occurred in the late 1960s and early 1970s, when corporations acquired strings of unrelated businesses, often in an attempt to moderate the risks of a volatile economy. These **conglomerate mergers** were designed to augment a company's growth and to diversify its risks. Theoretically, when one business was down, another would be up, thus creating a balanced performance picture for the company as a whole. At their peaks, some of these conglomerates had hundreds of companies. TLC Beatrice (formerly Beatrice Foods Company), for example, at one time owned companies as diverse as Tropicana (juice), Samsonite (luggage), Stiffle (lamps), and Eckrich (meats). Since the late 1960s, many of the superconglomerates have been dismantled or slimmed down to streamline operations, to build up capital for other endeavors, or to get rid of unprofitable subsidiaries.

In the 1980s, a wave of **leveraged buyouts (LBOs)** also occurred. In an LBO, one or more individuals purchase a company's publicly traded stock by using borrowed funds. The debt is expected to be repaid with funds generated by the company's operations and, often, by the sale of some of its assets. For an LBO to be successful, a company must have a reasonably priced stock and easy access to borrowed funds. Unfortunately, in many cases, the acquiring company must make huge interest and principle payments on the debt; this depletes the amount of cash that the company has for operations and growth.

Also during the 1980s, some investors purchased large companies because they were actually worth more by the piece than by the whole. These purchasers, often referred to as "corporate raiders," would buy undervalued companies and quickly sell off divisions to realize a quick and handsome gain.[20] Consider Beatrice. In 1986 investors Kohlberg Kravis Roberts bought the giant conglomerate and shortly thereafter broke it into pieces by selling off the subsidiaries.[21]

In the 1990s, a new wave of mergers, consolidations, and acquisitions began that were motivated by long-term strategies. Instead of using debt to take over and dismantle a company for a quick profit, corporate buyers used cash and stock to selectively acquire businesses to enhance their position in the marketplace. From 1992 through 2000, 71,811 corporate mergers, consolidations, and acquisitions at a combined value of $6.66 trillion were completed.[22]

## active exercise

**Take a moment to apply what you've learned.**

### Current Trends in Mergers, Consolidations, and Acquisitions

Today "corporate mergers have grown so frequent and so large," says Robert Pitofsky, chairman of the Federal Trade Commission (FTC), that "there's not a week that goes by that we're not called upon to review a big merger that has significant implications in the marketplace."[23] Some even predict that mergers that looked like earthquakes in the past may look like mere tremors years from now.[24]

Consider, for instance, the $160 billion merger of America Online (the world's biggest Internet provider) and Time Warner (the world's biggest media company). This megadeal, announced only 10 days into the new millennium, linked AOL's twenty-some million subscribers and unmatched e-commerce capabilities with Time Warner's sprawling cache of world-class media, entertainment, news brands, and broadband delivery systems to produce the world's first fully integrated media and communications company.[25]

One key factor contributing to this merger frenzy is fierce global competition. In today's global environment, large domestic companies must compete with foreign competitors even in their home markets. Tough competitive conditions have prompted the U.S. government to relax its regulatory standards. Rather than opposing any merger that might allow a company to develop a dominant position in the market, the FTC and the Anti-Trust Division of the Justice Department are stepping back to ensure that industries remain competitive in the global marketplace.

As Chapter 1 and Component Chapter B discuss, the relaxation of existing industry regulations is designed to make industries more competitive and to provide consumers with improved products and lower prices. But some think industry deregulation has backfired by spurring mass consolidation instead. Take the telecommunications industry, for example. Some see the 1999 consolidation of SBC and Ameritech as nothing more than a reassembly of the Ma Bell monopoly splintered by the Justice Department in 1984. As one naysayer put it: "First there were seven Baby Bells, then six, then five, and now four."[26] Moreover, Bell Atlantic's recent merger with GTE (to form Verizon) has reduced the number of Baby Bells to three, and they aren't babies.

The airline industry is also flirting with consolidation. Merger talks between UAL (United's parent) and US Airways in 2000 set off a raft of merger proposals between major airline carriers that could end with United, American, and Delta controlling 85 percent of U.S. air traffic. U.S. airlines now say that the only viable way to get significantly larger is to acquire competitors. "There's no other industry where consolidation and mergers probably makes more sense," says one U.S. airline board member. "But there's also no other industry where it's more difficult." Critics of such megamergers say that there's a limit on how far mergers and consolidations should go. They point out that the promise of deregulation—some 20 years ago—was lots of new competitors, not mergers and consolidations.[27]

Like the telecommunications and airline industries, the banking industry is also undergoing mass consolidation as a result of relaxed industry regulation. Since 1990 over 3,300 banks have been gobbled up by larger ones. Furthermore, the 1998 acquisition of Travelers by Citicorp (valued at $83 billion) spliced together a global bank, an insurance company, a brokerage firm, a credit-card operation, and some 100 million customers in 100 countries.[28] As Chapter 17 points out, the repeal of the Glass-Steagall Act now paves the way for banking, securities, and insurance industries to expand into one another's businesses and sets the stage for another wave of consolidations.[29]

This megamerger trend is also occurring in the oil and automobile industries. The $81 billion marriage of Exxon and Mobil in 1999 created the world's largest oil company, whereas the $36 billion combination of Daimler-Benz and Chrysler in 1998 was the biggest acquisition of any U.S. company by a foreign buyer—and one that is destined to transform the way the auto industry operates worldwide. Some believe that by combining product and sales networks, DaimlerChrysler has set the pace for the global car wars to come. As one economist put it, "If you don't play the game as a global company, you're going to wind up a niche player."[30]

> active poll

**What do you think? Voice your opinion and find out what others have to say.**

### Merger, Consolidation, and Acquisition Defenses

About 95 percent of all business combinations are friendly deals, as opposed to **hostile takeovers,** where one party fights to gain control of a company against the wishes of the existing management.[31] But not all hostile takeovers are bad. In November 1999 pharmaceutical giants Warner-Lambert and American Home Products (AHP) announced a $54.5 billion merger. The two were caught off guard when that same day rival Pfizer launched an unfriendly takeover bid for Warner-Lambert and eventually sweetened its bid as an inducement to wrap things up quickly. In February 2000, Pfizer succeeded in its hostile bid to buy Warner-Lambert for $90 billion. Warner-Lambert conceded that Pfizer's hostile bid was better for shareholders than its planned merger with AHP.[32]

As mentioned earlier, every corporation that sells stock to the general public is potentially vulnerable to takeover by any individual or company that buys enough shares to gain a controlling interest. Basically, a hostile takeover can be launched in one of two ways: by tender offer or by proxy fight. In a *tender offer,* the raider offers to buy a certain number of shares of stock in the corporation at a specific price. The price offered is generally more than the current stock price so that shareholders are motivated to sell. The raider hopes to get enough shares to take control of the corporation and to replace the existing board of directors and management. In a *proxy fight,* the raider launches a public relations battle for shareholder votes, hoping to enlist enough votes to oust the board and management. Proxy fights sound easy enough, but they are tough to win. The insiders have certain advantages: They can get in touch with shareholders, and they can use money from the corporate treasury in their campaign.

During the 1980s, when many takeovers were uninvited and even openly hostile, corporate boards and executives devised a number of schemes to defend themselves against unwanted takeovers:

- *The poison pill.* This plan, triggered by a takeover attempt, makes the company less valuable in some way to the potential raider; the idea is to discourage the takeover from actually happening. A good example is a special sale of newly issued stock to current stockholders at prices below the market value of the company's existing stock. Such action increases the number of shares the raider has to buy, making the takeover more expensive. Many shareholders believe that poison pills are bad for a company because they can entrench weak management and discourage takeover attempts that would improve company value.[33]

- *The golden parachute.* This method is designed to benefit a company's top executives by guaranteeing them generous compensation packages if they ever leave or are forced out after a takeover. These packages often total millions of dollars for each executive and therefore make the takeover much more expensive for the acquiring company. In this way, a golden parachute has an effect similar to that of a poison pill.

- *The shark repellent.* This tactic is more direct; it is simply a requirement that stockholders representing a large majority of shares approve of any takeover attempt. Of course, such a plan is viable only if the management team has the support of the majority of shareholders.

- *The white knight.* This tactic uses a friendly buyer to take over the company before a raider can. White knights usually agree to leave the current management team in place and to let the company continue to operate in an independent fashion. Starwood Lodging Trust, a large hotel investment firm, used this tactic to block the hostile takeover attempt of ITT by Hilton Hotels.[34]

Sometimes a group of investors is able to take a publicly traded company off the open market by purchasing all of the company's stock. This tactic is known as "taking the company private." Descendants of Levi Strauss, for example, borrowed $3 billion to buy back all the shares of Levi's stock so that the family could maintain control of the company.[35]

Companies sometimes go private to thwart unwanted takeovers. But this is a radical action. First of all, stockholders must be willing to sell, and second, buyers must have enough cash on hand to repurchase all the company's stock. Moreover, going private eliminates the firm's ability to raise future capital by selling authorized shares to the public, so it's not a move that many corporations make.

## STRATEGIC ALLIANCES AND JOINT VENTURES

In Chapter 3 we discussed strategic alliances and joint ventures from the perspective of international expansion. We defined a strategic alliance as a long-term partnership between companies to jointly develop, produce, or sell products, and we defined a joint venture as a special type of strategic alliance in which two or more firms jointly create a new business entity that is legally separate and distinct from its parents. In this chapter we will look at these forms of business combinations as an alternative to a merger, consolidation, or acquisition.

Strategic alliances can accomplish many of the same goals as a merger, consolidation, or acquisition without requiring a painstaking process of integration.[36] One of the biggest benefits of a strategic alliance is that the companies involved need not become fast friends for life. Pharmaceutical companies, for example, typically form strategic alliances to jointly develop products, but they go their separate ways once the patents on the drugs expire.

Many strategic alliances are driven by the realization that no single company can offer customers everything they need. Consider the alliance between Pacific Bell (a San Francisco–based local telecommunications provider) and Orconet (an Orange County, California, Internet service provider). Pacific Bell refers its telephone customers to Orconet for Internet connections, and Orconet promotes Pacific Bell's speedy DSL data-dedicated lines. Each company brings its pool of traditional customers to the other, expanding the potential markets for both.[37]

Companies can also form joint ventures to accomplish the same growth objectives. Joint ventures are similar to partnerships except that they are formed for a specific, limited purpose. America Online, Philips Electronics, and Direct TV recently formed a joint venture to develop and offer an interactive service that lets customers access the Internet via their TV sets. Joint ventures have many advantages. They allow companies to use each other's complementary strengths that might otherwise take too long to develop on their own, and they allow companies to share what may be the substantial cost and risk of starting a new operation.[38]

## > active concept check

**Now let's take a moment to test your knowledge of the concepts you have studied in this section.**

## > Chapter Wrap-Up

Now that you've reached the end of the chapter, you may wish to explore the concepts you've been reading about in greater detail, or test yourself to see how well you've comprehended the material. In the box below you'll find a number of links. Click on any one of these links to find additional chapter resources.

## > end-of-chapter resources

- Summary of Learning Objectives
- Practice Quiz
- Key Terms
- Test Your Knowledge
- Practice Your Knowledge
- Expand Your Knowledge
- A Case for Critical Thinking
- Business Plan Pro: Starting a Small Business

# C H A P T E R  6

# Functions and Skills of Management

## Chapter Outline

## > What's Ahead

### INSIDE BUSINESS TODAY
### TRANSFORMING THE WORLD: STEVE CASE'S VISION FOR AOL TIME WARNER

Industry experts laughed in his face. The Silicon Valley crowd sneered at his audacity. Back in 1995, Steve Case's predictions about the future of his fledgling company, America Online, seemed outrageous to everyone—except Steve Case. "We could be bigger than AT&T," Case predicted. "The future is online."

It was a vision that Case refused to abandon, in spite of the odds against him. Long before others dreamed of connecting the world through digital networks, Case saw infinite possibilities in cyberspace. A brief experiment with some online services during the early 1980s was the spark that ignited his imagination. "There was something magical about being able to sit at home . . . and talk to people over the world," he recalled. "It wasn't a great leap of faith to think that if you made it affordable and easy to use, people would want it."

Determined to turn his vision into reality, Case took the reins of an unsuccessful online business in 1985. Although the techies scoffed at his strategy of building a simple service for ordinary people, Case doggedly pursued his dream. He continuously assessed the needs of his customers, and he responded to their desires for an easier way to access information over the Internet by replacing arcane codes with simple graphics.

By 1992 Case had given his company a catchy name—America Online (AOL)—and had taken the company public. All the while, he continued analyzing other online services to understand the competitive and constantly changing world of cyberspace. He reacted to the intense

When the Federal Communications Commission approved the merger of AOL and Time Warner, Steve Case became the chairman of the world's biggest media business.

competition by developing and executing a strategy for dominating the online market. To attract more customers, Case introduced a flat monthly rate for unlimited Internet access and blanketed the country with millions of free AOL disks. Millions of customers signed up for AOL's services—far more than the company's communication networks could handle. But Case moved quickly and decisively to resolve the immediate crisis, regaining customer confidence by expanding the network's capacity.

Still, crisis after crisis threatened to topple Case's online kingdom. By 1995 AOL was losing money, agitating customers, and fighting intense competition. Although critics predicted the company's demise, Case remained focused on his original vision, to establish a global communications medium that would change people's lives. He knew where he was headed and why. Ignoring his detractors, Case concentrated on long-range goals. He examined AOL's existing resources and determined which outside resources he needed to help push AOL to the top. Then he expanded his customer base by acquiring such existing businesses as Netscape Communications and rival CompuServe.

By millennium's end, AOL was a profitable Internet powerhouse, serving more than 22 million customers around the globe. Case continued to look toward the future. He examined the changing technological environment and decided that AOL needed high-speed cable lines to build the Web's infrastructure for the new century. Determined to strengthen AOL as a global communications company, Case orchestrated the largest merger in history by joining forces with Time Warner, the world's largest media company.

Case's stunning move silenced the mockery of his critics. Driven by a vision that never wavered, he defied odds that seemed insurmountable to create the world's first fully integrated media and communications company. AOL Time Warner can change the way people live, work, learn, and communicate throughout the twenty-first century.[1]

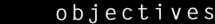

> **objectives**

Take a moment to familiarize yourself with the key objectives of this chapter.

> **gearing up**

Before you begin reading this chapter, try a short warm-up activity.

## > What Is Management?

Much of Steve Case's success comes from his ability to envision the future and find the best managers to help him turn his vision into reality and run his organization. But as Case knows, not everyone is equipped to be an effective manager. **Management** entails four basic functions: planning, organizing, leading, and controlling resources (land, labor, capital, and information) to efficiently reach a company's goals.[2] Managers are the employees responsible for performing these four functions in addition to a number of other duties to coordinate the organization's work. These duties, or **roles,** fall into three main categories:

- *Interpersonal roles.* Managers perform ceremonial obligations; provide leadership to employees; build a network of relationships with bosses, peers, and employees; and act as liaison to groups and individuals both inside and outside the company (such as suppliers, competitors, government agencies, consumers, special-interest groups, and interrelated work groups).

- *Informational roles.* Managers spend a fair amount of time gathering information by questioning people both inside and outside the organization. They also distribute information to employees, other managers, and outsiders.

- *Decisional roles.* Managers use the information they gather to encourage innovation, to resolve unexpected problems that threaten organizational goals (such as reacting to an economic crisis), and to decide how organizational resources will be used to meet planned objectives. They also negotiate with many individuals and groups, including suppliers, employees, and unions.[3]

Being able to move among these roles while performing the four basic management functions is just one of the many skills that managers must possess.

## > The Four Basic Functions of Management

Steve Case demonstrates that when managers possess the right combination of vision, skill, experience, and determination, they can lead an organization to success. To do this, however, they must perform the four basic functions of management: (1) planning, (2) organizing, (3) leading, and (4) controlling (see Exhibit 6.1). These functions are not discrete; they overlap and influence one another. Let's examine these four functions in detail.

### THE PLANNING FUNCTION

Planning is the primary management function, the one on which all others depend. Managers engaged in **planning** develop strategies for success, establish goals and objectives for the organization, and translate their strategies and goals into action plans. To develop long-term strategies and goals, managers must be well informed on a number of key issues and topics that could influence their decisions. A closer look at the strategic planning process will give you a clearer idea of the types of information managers need to help them plan for the company's future.

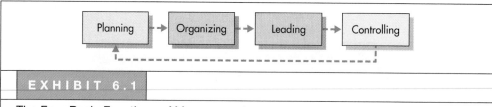

EXHIBIT 6.1

The Four Basic Functions of Management

Some managers, especially those in smaller organizations, perform all four managerial functions. Although these functions tend to occur in a somewhat progressive order, sometimes they occur simultaneously, and often the process is ongoing.

### Understanding the Strategic Planning Process

**Strategic plans** outline the firm's long-range (two to five years) organizational goals and set a course of action the firm will pursue to reach its goals. These long-term goals encompass eight major areas of concern: market standing, innovation, human resources, financial resources, physical resources, productivity, social responsibility, and financial performance.[4] A good strategic plan answers: Where are we going? What is the environment? How do we get there?

To answer these questions and establish effective long-term goals, managers require extensive amounts of information. For instance, managers must study budgets, production schedules, industry and economic data, customer preferences, internal and external data, competition, and so on. Managers use this information to set a firm's long-term course of direction during a process called strategic planning. Consisting of seven interrelated critical tasks, the strategic planning process is an ongoing event as Exhibit 6.2 suggests.[5]

**DEVELOP A CLEAR VISION** Most organizations are formed in order to realize a **vision**, a realistic, credible, and attainable view of the future that grows out of and improves on the present.[6] Henry Ford envisioned making affordable transportation available to every person. Fred Smith (founder of FedEx) envisioned making FedEx an information company (besides being a transportation company). Bill Gates (chairman of Microsoft) envisioned empowering people through great software, anytime, anyplace, and on any device. And Steve Case was able to see, before others, a global medium that would

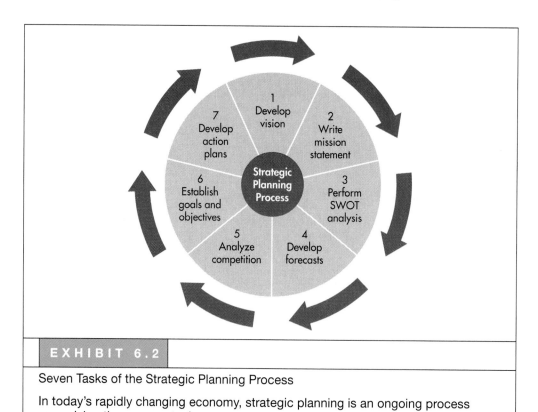

EXHIBIT 6.2

Seven Tasks of the Strategic Planning Process

In today's rapidly changing economy, strategic planning is an ongoing process comprising these seven tasks.

change the way people live, learn, and work. Case envisioned a world where everyone was connected by computers.[7] Without such visionaries, who knows how the world would be different. Thus, developing a clear vision is a critical task in the strategic planning process. But having a vision alone is no guarantee of success; it must also be communicated to others, executed, and modified as conditions change.

**TRANSLATE THE VISION INTO A MEANINGFUL MISSION STATEMENT** To transform vision into reality, managers must define specific organizational goals, objectives, and philosophies. A starting point is to write a company **mission statement,** a brief document that defines why the organization exists, what it seeks to accomplish, and the principles that the company will adhere to as it tries to reach its goals (see Exhibit 6.3). Put differently, a mission statement communicates who we are, what we do, and where we're headed. Typical components of a mission statement include the company's product or service; primary market; fundamental concern for survival, growth, and profitability; managerial philosophy; and commitment to quality and social responsibility.

Another important function of a mission statement is to bring clarity of focus to members of the organization. A mission statement helps employees understand how their role is tied to the organization's greater purpose. Thus, it should inspire and guide employees and managers in a way that they can understand the firm's vision and identify with it. Furthermore, the statement must be congruent with the organization's core values. Managers should refer to it to assess whether new project proposals are within the scope of the company's mission.[8]

Consider Edge Learning Institute, an employee-training firm based in Tempe, Arizona. Edge executives were considering mass-marketing their training videos through television "infomercials." However, they realized that this was contrary to the company's mission of using "the human touch when providing individuals and organizations with information." So they decided instead to expand Edge's reach by developing a network of franchises that follow the company's training methods.[9]

**ASSESS THE COMPANY'S STRENGTHS, WEAKNESSES, OPPORTUNITIES, AND THREATS** Before establishing long-term goals, a firm must have a clear assessment of its strengths and weaknesses compared with the opportunities and threats it faces. Such analysis is commonly referred to as SWOT, which stands for strengths, weaknesses, opportunities, and threats.

*Strengths* are positive internal factors that contribute to a company's success such as having a steady supply of knowledgeable employees or having a dynamic leader such as Steve Case at the helm.

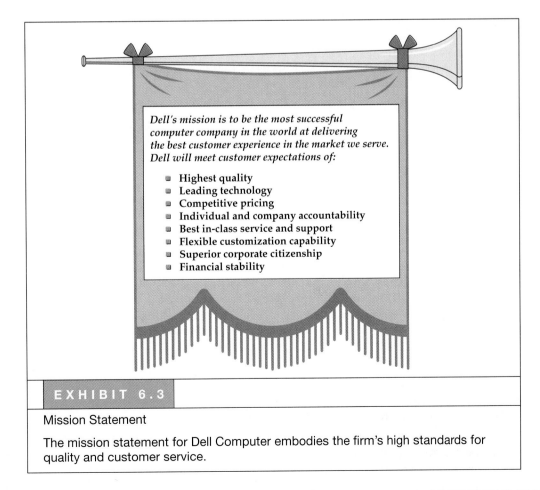

*Dell's mission is to be the most successful computer company in the world at delivering the best customer experience in the market we serve. Dell will meet customer expectations of:*

- **Highest quality**
- **Leading technology**
- **Competitive pricing**
- **Individual and company accountability**
- **Best in-class service and support**
- **Flexible customization capability**
- **Superior corporate citizenship**
- **Financial stability**

**EXHIBIT 6.3**

Mission Statement

The mission statement for Dell Computer embodies the firm's high standards for quality and customer service.

*Weaknesses* are negative internal factors that inhibit the company's success such as obsolete facilities, inadequate financial resources to fund the company's growth, or lack of managerial depth and talent. Identifying a firm's internal strengths and weaknesses helps management understand its abilities and current operating position. Management uses this internal analysis as a guide when establishing future goals.

One particular strength worth noting is a firm's *core competence.* A **core competence** is a bundle of skills and technologies that enable a company to provide a particular benefit to customers. A firm's core competence sets the company apart from its competitors and is difficult for competitors to duplicate. Sony's core competence, for example, is miniaturization. Federal Express's core competence is its efficient delivery process. America Online's core competence is the simplicity of its software. In most cases a core competence represents the sum of knowledge across the organization. Thus, it lasts even though individual employees may leave the firm.

Once managers have taken inventory of a company's internal strengths and weaknesses, they must next identify the external opportunities and threats that might significantly affect their ability to attain certain goals. *Opportunities* are positive external factors, such as new potential markets or customers. *Threats* are negative external forces that could inhibit the firm's ability to achieve its objectives. Threats include new competitors or entrants into the market, new government regulations, economic recession, increase in interest rates, technological advances that could make a company's product obsolete, and so on. Harvard Business School Professor Clayton Christensen notes that graveyards are full of big firms that ignored the competitive threats from start-ups.[10] (Threats and external analysis will be discussed in detail in Chapter 12 in the context of developing a strategic marketing plan.)

**DEVELOP FORECASTS** To plan for the future, managers must make a number of educated assumptions about future trends and events and modify those assumptions once new information becomes available. But as Steve Case knows, forecasting is not an exact science. In fact, Case once told a reporter, "What I've figured out is that I can predict the future. I just can't predict when."[11] To predict the future managers rely on expert forecasts that can be found in publications such as *Industry Week*'s "Trends and Forecasts," *Business Week*'s "Survey of Corporate Performance," and Standard & Poor's *Earnings Forecast.* However, these sources may not always include key variables specific to an individual company or industry. Therefore, managers must also develop their own forecasts.

Managerial forecasts fall under two broad categories: *quantitative forecasts,* which are typically based on historical data or tests and which involve complex statistical computations; and *qualitative forecasts,* which are based on intuitive judgments or consumer research. Statistically analyzing the cycles of economic growth and recession over several decades to predict when the economy will take a downward turn is an example of quantitative forecasting. Making predictions about sales of a new product on the basis of experience and consumer responses to a survey is an example of qualitative forecasting. Neither method is foolproof, but both are valuable tools, enabling managers to fill in the unknown variables that inevitably crop up in the planning process.

**ANALYZE THE COMPETITION** "Business is like any battlefield. If you want to win the war, you have to know who you're up against," says one management consultant.[12] Thus, sizing up the competition is another important task in planning for a company's future. It gives management a realistic view of the market, the company's position in it, and its ability to attain certain goals.

Managers begin the competitive analysis process by identifying existing and potential competitors. Next they determine the competencies, strengths, and weaknesses of their major competitors—just as they did for their own organization. Armed with competitive information, they look for ways to capitalize on a competitor's weaknesses or match or surpass their strengths to gain a competitive edge.

A company can gain a competitive edge through at least one of three competitive strategies:

- *Differentiation.* A company using differentiation develops a level of service, a product image, unique product features (including quality), or new technologies that distinguish its product from competitors' products. Volvo, for instance, stresses the safety of its cars. Caterpillar Tractor emphasizes product durability.

- *Cost leadership.* Businesses that pursue this strategy aim to become the low-cost leader in an industry by producing or selling products more efficiently and economically than competitors. Cost leaders have a competitive advantage by reaching buyers whose primary purchase criterion is price. Wal-Mart is a typical industry cost leader.

- *Focus.* When using a focus strategy, companies concentrate on a specific regional market or consumer group, such as the Southwest United States or economy car drivers. This type of strategy enables organizations to develop a better understanding of their customers and to tailor their products specifically to customer needs.[13] Examples of focused strategies include Abercrombie and Fitch (high-end apparel for young adults) and Williams Sonoma (quality cookware and appliances for serious cooks).

**ESTABLISH COMPANY GOALS AND OBJECTIVES** As mentioned earlier, establishing goals and objectives is the key task in the planning process. Although these terms are often used interchangeably, a **goal** is a broad, long-range accomplishment that the organization wishes to attain in typically five or more years, whereas an **objective** is a specific, short-range target designed to help reach that goal. For AOL, a goal might be to become the number-one Internet service provider in the Brazilian marketplace, and an objective might be to add 100,000 new Brazilian subscribers by year-end.

To be effective, organizational goals and objectives should be specific, measurable, relevant, challenging, attainable, and time-limited. For example it is better to state "increase our customer base by 10 percent over the next three years" than "substantially increase our customer base."

Setting appropriate goals has many benefits: it increases employee motivation, establishes standards for measuring individual and group performance, guides employee activity, and clarifies management's expectations. By establishing organizational goals, managers set the stage for the actions needed to achieve those goals. If actions aren't planned, the chances of reaching company goals are slim.

**DEVELOP ACTION PLANS** Once managers have established a firm's long-term strategic goals and objectives, they must then develop a plan of execution. **Tactical plans** lay out the actions and the allocation of resources necessary to achieve specific, short-term objectives that support the company's broader strategic plan. Tactical plans typically focus on departmental goals and cover a period of one to three years. Their limited scope permits them to be changed more easily than strategic plans. **Operational plans** designate the actions and resources required to achieve the objectives of tactical plans. Operational plans usually define actions for less than one year and focus on accomplishing a firm's specific objectives such as increasing the number of new subscribers by 5 percent over the next six months.

Keep in mind that many highly admired CEOs have stumbled, not because they didn't have strategies for success, but because they didn't execute their strategies or deliver on their commitments. That's because developing a strategy or vision is less than half the battle. It's executing it that counts. In today's information age, strategies quickly become public property. Everyone knows Dell's direct business model, for example, yet few companies, if any, have successfully copied its execution.

## Planning for a Crisis

No matter how well a company plans for its future, any number of problems can arise to threaten its existence. An ugly fight for control of a company, a product failure, a breakdown in routine operations (as a result of fire, for example), or an environmental accident could develop into a serious and crippling crisis. Managers can help a company survive these setbacks through **crisis management,** a plan for handling such unusual and serious problems.

The goal of crisis management is to keep the company functioning smoothly both during and after a crisis. Successful crisis management requires comprehensive contingency plans in addition to speedy, open communication with all who are affected by the crisis. Experts suggest selecting in advance a communications team and a knowledgeable spokesperson to handle the many requests for information that arise during a crisis. The individuals selected should be able to remain honest and calm when a crisis hits. Moreover, top managers should be visible in the hours immediately following the crisis to demonstrate that the company will do whatever is necessary to control the situation as best it can, find the cause, and prevent a future occurrence.[14]

Ford and Bridgestone/Firestone were criticized for not taking these actions when reports started surfacing about the faulty tires manufactured by Bridgestone/Firestone and fitted on Ford Explorer sports utility vehicles. When the vehicles were driven at high speed, the treads separated from the tires, causing the car to roll over and injuring—even killing—passengers. Although both Ford and Firestone eventually recalled 6.5 million tires, both companies are paying the price for making serious mistakes in handling the crisis. Some say that Firestone's reputation may even be damaged beyond repair.[15]

Responding to a crisis, of course, is much easier when management has prepared for problems by actively looking for signs of a disaster in the making. When Belgian and French consumers became ill after drinking cans of Coke produced with substandard carbon dioxide, Coca-Cola officials were caught off guard. "No one would have thought that this would happen to Coke. But they should have planned for it," notes one beverage industry expert. Instead, Coca-Cola's officials made the situation worse by denying that Coke could have been the problem. Company officials eventually issued an apology, but even today Coca-Cola suffers the consequences of its delayed response. The company has had far higher marketing costs in Europe because of the incident.[16]

Keep in mind that crisis planning is not only for large corporations, as Rocket USA will attest. Ready for takeoff in 1997, this five-person manufacturer of collectible windup toys had planned for

Cans of banned Coke were dumped at Coca-Cola depot in Evere, Belgium, as part of the largest recall in the company's history.

everything—except a UPS strike. The company found itself with orders streaming in and inventory stacked high in the warehouse, yet no way to fill orders. "We were totally in the dark about how we were going to ship," confesses the company president. The company had no backup plan.[17]

## active exercise

**Take a moment to apply what you've learned.**

### THE ORGANIZING FUNCTION

**Organizing,** the process of arranging resources to carry out the organization's plans, is the second major function of managers. During the organizing stage, managers think through all the activities that employees carry out (from programming the organization's computers to mailing its letters), as well as all the facilities and equipment employees need in order to complete those activities. They also give people the ability to work toward organizational goals by determining who will have the authority to make decisions, to perform or supervise activities, and to distribute resources.

The organizing function is particularly challenging because most organizations undergo constant change. Long-time employees leave, and new employees arrive. Equipment breaks down or becomes obsolete, and replacements are needed. The public's tastes and interests change, and the organization has to reevaluate its plans and activities. Shifting political and economic trends can lead to employee cutbacks—or perhaps expansion. Long-time competitors take unexpected actions, and new competitors enter the market. Every week the organization faces new situations, so management's organizing tasks are never finished. Consider Microsoft. The company continually challenges itself by asking: "Are we making what customers want and working on products and technologies they'll want in the future? Are we staying ahead of all our competitors? What don't our customers like about what we do, and what are we doing about it? Are we organized most effectively to achieve our goals?"[18]

The organizing function will be discussed in detail in Chapter 7. In this chapter, however, we will discuss the three levels of a corporate hierarchy—top, middle, bottom—commonly known as the **management pyramid.** In general, **top managers** are the upper-level managers who have the most power and who take overall responsibility for the organization. An example is the chief executive officer (CEO). Top managers establish the structure for the organization as a whole, and they select the people who fill the upper-level positions. Top managers also make long-range plans, establish major policies, and represent the company to the outside world at official functions and fund-raisers.

**Middle managers** have similar responsibilities, but usually for just one division or unit. They develop plans for implementing the broad goals set by top managers, and they coordinate the work of first-line managers. In traditional organizations, managers at the middle level are plant managers, division managers, branch managers, and other similar positions—reporting to top-level managers. But in more innovative management structures, middle managers often function as team leaders who are expected to supervise and lead small groups of employees in a variety of job functions. Similar to consultants, they must understand every department's function, not just their own area of expertise. Furthermore, they are granted decision-making authority previously reserved for only high-ranking executives.[19]

At the bottom of the management pyramid are **first-line managers** (or *supervisory managers*). They oversee the work of operating employees, and they put into action the plans developed at higher levels. Positions at this level include supervisor, department head, and office manager.[20] Even though more managers are at the bottom level than at the top, as illustrated in Exhibit 6.4, today's leaner companies tend to have fewer levels, flattening the organizational structure, as Chapter 7 points out.

> active poll

**What do you think? Voice your opinion and find out what others have to say.**

## THE LEADING FUNCTION

**Leading**—the process of influencing and motivating people to work effectively and willingly toward company goals—is the third basic function of management. Leading becomes even more challenging

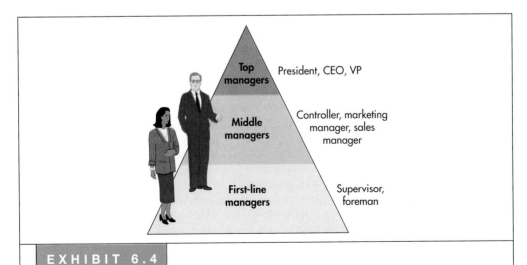

**EXHIBIT 6.4**

The Management Pyramid

Separate job titles are used to designate the three basic levels in the management pyramid.

in today's business environment, where individuals who have different backgrounds and unique interests, ambitions, and personal goals are melded into a productive work team. Managers with good leadership skills have greater success in influencing the attitudes and actions of others, both through the demonstration of specific tasks and through the manager's own behavior and spirit. Furthermore, effective leaders are good at *motivating,* or giving employees a reason to do the job and to put forth their best performance (see Chapter 10).

What makes a good leader? When early researchers studied leadership, they looked for specific characteristics, or *traits,* common to all good leaders. At the time, they were unable to prove any link between particular traits and leadership ability. However, researchers found that leaders who have specific traits, such as decisiveness and self-confidence, are likely to be more effective.[21] Additional studies have shown that managers with strong interpersonal skills and high emotional quotients (EQs) tend to be more effective leaders. The characteristics of a high EQ include:[22]

- *Self-awareness.* Self-aware managers have the ability to recognize their own feelings and how they, their job performance, and other people are affected by those feelings. Moreover, managers who are highly self-aware know where they are headed and why.

- *Self-regulation.* Self-regulated managers have the ability to control or reduce disruptive impulses and moods. They can suspend judgment and think before acting. Moreover, they know how to utilize the appropriate emotion at the right time and in the right amount.

- *Motivation.* Motivated managers are driven to achieve beyond expectations—their own and everyone else's.

- *Empathy.* Empathetic managers thoughtfully consider employees' feelings, along with other factors, in the process of making intelligent decisions.

- *Social skill.* Socially skilled managers tend to have a wide circle of acquaintances, and they have a knack for finding common ground with people of all kinds. They assume that nothing important gets done by one person alone and have a network in place when the time for action comes.

Keep in mind that these traits alone do not define a leader. Different leadership traits are appropriate under different leadership situations.[23]

### Adopting an Effective Leadership Style

*Leadership style* is the way a manager uses authority to lead others. Every manager, from the baseball coach to the university chancellor, has a definite style. The three broad categories of leadership style are *autocratic, democratic,* and *laissez-faire.*

**Autocratic leaders** make decisions without consulting others. "My way or the highway" summarizes this style, which tends to go with traditional, hierarchical organizational structures. Although autocratic leadership can be highly effective when quick decisions are necessary, it does little to empower employees or encourage innovation. Al Dunlop, past CEO of Sunbeam, used an autocratic leadership style to try to turn the failing household appliance maker around, as this chapter's Case for Critical Thinking shows.

In contrast, **democratic leaders** delegate authority and involve employees in decision making. Even though their approach can lead to slower decisions, soliciting input from people familiar with particular situations or issues may result in better decisions. As more companies adopt the principles of teamwork, democratic leadership continues to gain in popularity. For example, managers at Rhone-Poulenc, the U.S. subsidiary of France's leading chemical and pharmaceutical manufacturer, gradually made the transition from autocratic to democratic leadership as the organization moved from a hierarchical structure to a team-based environment. CEO Peter Neff says, "I don't look over people's shoulders anymore. . . . My role now is to enable people to do the best they know how to do." For Neff, this means acting as an opportunity seeker, coach, facilitator, motivator, and mentor rather than as a controller or problem solver.[24]

The third leadership style, laissez-faire, is sometimes referred to as free-rein leadership. The French term *laissez faire* can be translated as "leave it alone," or more roughly as "hands off." **Laissez-faire leaders** take the role of consultant, encouraging employees' ideas and offering insights or opinions when asked. The laissez-faire style may fail if workers pursue goals that do not match the organization's. However, the style has proven effective in some situations. Managers at Hewlett-Packard's North American distribution organization adopted a laissez-faire style when they were given nine months to reorganize their order-fulfillment process. The managers eliminated all titles, supervision, job descriptions, and plans, and they made employees entirely responsible for the project. At first there was chaos. However, employees soon began to try new things, make mistakes, and learn as they went. In the end, the team finished the reorganization ahead of schedule, reduced product delivery times from 26 days to 8 days, and cut inventory by 20 percent. Moreover, the employees experienced a renewed sense of challenge, commitment, and enjoyment in their work.[25]

| Boss-centered leadership ← | | | | | | → Employee-centered leadership |
|---|---|---|---|---|---|---|
| **Use of authority by the manager** | | | | | | **Area of freedom for workers** |
| Manager makes decision, announces it. | Manager "sells" decision. | Manager presents ideas, invites questions. | Manager presents tentative decision subject to change. | Manager presents problems, gets suggestions, makes decisions. | Manager defines limits, asks group to make decision. | Manager permits workers to function within defined limits. |

**EXHIBIT 6.5**

Continuum of Leadership Behavior

Leadership style occurs along a continuum, ranging from boss-centered to employee-centered. Situations that require managers to exercise greater authority fall toward the boss-centered end of the continuum. Other situations call for a manager to give workers leeway to function more independently.

More and more businesses are adopting democratic and laissez-faire leadership as they reduce the number of management layers in their corporate hierarchies and increase the use of teamwork. However, experienced managers know that no one leadership style works every time. In fact, new research shows that leaders with the best results do not rely on only one leadership style; instead they adapt their approach to match the requirements of the particular situation.[26] Adapting leadership style to current business circumstances is called **contingency leadership.** You can think of leadership styles as existing along a continuum of possible leadership behaviors, as suggested by Exhibit 6.5.

> ## active exercise

**Take a moment to apply what you've learned.**

### Coaching and Mentoring

Managers can provide effective leadership by coaching and mentoring their employees. On a winning sports team, the coach focuses on helping all team members perform at their highest potential. In a similar way, *coaching* managers strive to bring out the best in their employees.

   **Coaching** involves taking the time to meet with employees, discussing any problems that may hinder their ability to work effectively, and offering suggestions and encouragement to help them find their own solutions to work-related challenges. This process requires keen powers of observation, sensible judgment, and both a willingness and an ability to take appropriate action. However, just as a sports coach cannot play the game for team members, a coaching manager must step back and let employees perform when it's "game time." Coaching managers develop a solid game plan and empower their team to carry it out. If the team gets behind, the manager offers encouragement to boost morale. And when team members are victorious, the manager recognizes and praises their outstanding achievement.[27] Tom Gegax, co-founder of Tires Plus stores, has been using internal coaches in his organization for years. "People are more willing to take feedback from a coach than from a boss because so many of us have been coached before," says Gegax.[28]

   Acting as a mentor is similar to coaching, but mentoring also emphasizes helping employees understand how the organization works. A **mentor** is usually an experienced manager or employee who can help guide other employees through the corporate maze. Mentors have a deep knowledge of the business and a useful network of industry colleagues. In addition, they can explain office politics, serve as a role model for appropriate business behavior, and provide valuable advice about how to succeed within the organization.

Your mentor won't necessarily be your boss. Relationships with mentors often develop informally between the individuals involved. However, some companies have established formal mentoring programs. In the program at Xerox, women employees can spend a few hours every month discussing work or career issues with any of the participating women executives.[29] Mentoring offers benefits for both parties: The less-experienced employee gains from the mentor's advice and ideas; the mentor gains new networking contacts, in addition to personal satisfaction.

## video exercise  <

**Take a moment to apply what you've learned.**

### Managing Change

Another important function of leaders is to manage the process of change. As competitive pressures get worse, the pace of change accelerates while companies search for even higher levels of quality, service, and overall speed. Sometimes managers initiate change; other times change imposes itself from outside the company. Nonetheless, effective leaders refrain from launching new initiatives until current ones are embedded in the company's DNA. Take GE's Jack Welch, for example. He has introduced just five major initiatives in his 18 years as CEO.[30] Leaders such as Welch provide a powerful vision to pull people in a desired direction.[31] Then they work with employees to ensure that the change process goes smoothly.

According to one recent study, about 70 percent of all change initiatives fail.[32] Resistance to change often arises because people don't understand how it will affect them. Mention change and most people automatically feel victimized. Some worry that they may have to master new skills—ones that might be difficult. Others fear that their jobs will be in jeopardy. Experts advise that if managers want less resistance to change, they should build trust with employees long before the change arrives and, when it does, explain to them how it will affect their jobs. Moreover, cultivating constant change on a small scale can prepare employees for even larger changes; it's the difference between asking someone to run a race who has never even practiced before versus asking someone to run a race who jogs every day.[33]

### Building a Strong Organizational Culture

Strong leadership is a key element in establishing a productive **organizational culture**—the set of underlying values, norms, and practices shared by members of an organization. When you visit an organization, observe how the employees work, dress, communicate, address each other, and conduct business. Each organization has a special way of doing things. In corporations, this force is often referred to as *corporate culture.*

A company's culture influences the way people treat and react to each other. It shapes the way employees feel about the company and the work they do; the way they interpret and perceive the actions taken by others; the expectations they have regarding changes in their work or in the business; and how they view those changes.[34] Look at Southwest Airlines. As one manager puts it, "Our whole culture drives everything. So many companies, while they don't put it in writing, create a culture that says, 'Leave your personality at home; all we want you to do is work.' At Southwest, we say, 'Bring your personality and your sense of humor to work.' Our ads, our recruitment techniques, and our interview process—all of it attracts a certain type of individual who values hard work, family, and, yes, fun."[35]

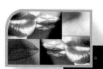

## active poll  <

**What do you think? Voice your opinion and find out what others have to say.**

## THE CONTROLLING FUNCTION

Controlling is the fourth basic managerial function. In management, **controlling** means monitoring a firm's progress toward meeting its organizational goals and objectives, resetting the course if goals or objectives change in response to shifting conditions, and correcting deviations if goals or objectives are not being attained.

### The Control Cycle

Managers strive to maintain a high level of **quality**—a measure of how closely goods or services conform to predetermined standards and customer expectations. Many firms control for quality through a four-step cycle that involves all levels of management and all employees. In the first step, top managers set **standards,** or criteria for measuring the performance of the organization as a whole. At the same time, middle and first-line managers set departmental quality standards so they can meet or exceed company standards. Establishing control standards is closely tied to the planning function and depends on information supplied by employees, customers, and other external sources. Examples of specific standards might be "Produce 1,500 circuit boards monthly with less than 1 percent failures."

In the second step of the control cycle, managers assess performance, using both quantitative (specific, numerical) and qualitative (subjective) performance measures. In the third step, managers compare performance with the established standards and search for the cause of any discrepancies. If the performance falls short of standards, the fourth step is to take corrective action, which may be done by either adjusting performance or reevaluating the standards. If performance meets or exceeds standards, no corrective action is taken. As Exhibit 6.6 shows, if everything is operating smoothly, controls permit managers to repeat acceptable performance. If results are below expectations, controls help managers take any necessary action.

Take America Online. Suppose the company does not reach its objectives of adding 100,000 new Brazilian customers by year-end. With proper control systems in place, managers will evaluate why these objectives were not reached. Perhaps they will find that a shortage of phone lines prevented expansion. Or perhaps the market where expansion was targeted became saturated with new Internet service providers. Regardless, management will search for the cause of the discrepancies before modifying the company's objectives or trying a different approach to achieve the company's long-term goals. Control methods are examined in greater detail in Chapter 9.

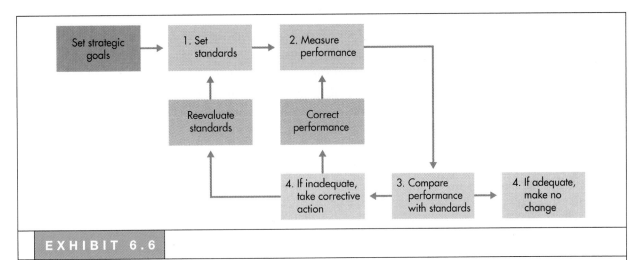

**EXHIBIT 6.6**

The Control Cycle

The control cycle has four basic steps: (1) On the basis of strategic goals, top managers set the standards by which the organization's overall performance will be measured. (2) Managers at all levels measure performance. (3) Actual performance is compared with the standards. (4) Appropriate corrective action is taken (if performance meets standards, nothing other than encouragement is needed; if performance falls below standards, corrective action may include improving performance, establishing new standards, changing plans, reorganizing, or redirecting efforts).

## Total Quality Management

The controlling function is an important part of total quality management, which is sometimes referred to as *total quality control*. In the past, *control* often meant those little sticky tags attached to new items that say, "inspected by #47." Companies would inspect finished products and rework or discard items that didn't meet quality standards. Today, this inspection step is only one small part of the total control process.

**Total quality management (TQM)** is both a management philosophy and a strategic management process that focuses on delivering the optimum level of quality to customers by building quality into every organizational activity (see Exhibit 6.7). Total quality management draws its ideas, principles, and tools from psychology, sociology, statistics, management, and marketing. The goal of TQM is to create an environment that encourages people to grow as individuals and to learn to bring about continuous and breakthrough improvements. Companies that adopt TQM create a value for all stakeholders—customers, employees, owners, suppliers, and the community.[36] The four key elements of TQM are employee involvement, customer focus, benchmarking, and continuous improvement.

1. **Create constancy of purpose for the improvement of goods and services.** The organization should constantly strive to improve quality, productivity, and consumer satisfaction to improve performance today and tomorrow.
2. **Adopt a new philosophy to reject mistakes and negativism.** Customers, managers, and employees all need to change their attitudes toward unacceptable work quality and sullen service.
3. **Cease dependence on mass inspection.** Instead of inspecting products after production to weed out bad quality, improve the process to build in good quality.
4. **End the practice of awarding business on price alone.** Create long-term relationships with suppliers who can deliver the best quality.
5. **Improve constantly and forever the system of production and service.** Improvement is not a one-time effort; managers must lead the way to continuous improvement of quality, productivity, and customer satisfaction.
6. **Institute training.** Train all organization members to do their jobs consistently well.
7. **Institute leadership.** Managers must provide the leadership to help employees do a better job.
8. **Drive out fear.** Create an atmosphere in which employees are not afraid to ask questions or to point out problems.
9. **Break down barriers between units.** Ensure that people in organizational departments or units do not have conflicting goals and are able to work as a team to achieve overall goals.
10. **Eliminate slogans, exhortations, and targets for the workforce.** These alone cannot help anyone do a better job, and they imply that employees could do better if they tried harder; instead, management should provide methods for improvement.
11. **Eliminate numerical quotas.** Quotas count only finished units, not quality or methods, and they generally lead to defective goods, wasted resources, and demoralized employees.
12. **Remove barriers to pride in work.** Most people want to do a good job but are prevented from doing so by misguided management, poor communication, faulty equipment, defective materials, and other barriers that managers must remove to improve quality.
13. **Institute a vigorous program of education and retraining.** Both managers and employees have to be educated in the new quality methods.
14. **Take action to accomplish the transformation.** With top-management commitment, have the courage to make the changes throughout the organization that will improve quality.

**EXHIBIT 6.7**

Total Quality Management

These 14 points, based on the work of W. Edwards Deming, can help managers improve their goods and services through total quality management.

- *Employee involvement.* Total quality management involves every employee in quality assurance. Workers are trained in quality methods and are empowered to stop a work process if they feel that products or services are not meeting quality standards. Managers also encourage employees to speak up when they think of better ways of doing things. This approach exemplifies a **participative management** style, the sharing of information at all levels of the organization (also known as *open-book management*). By directly involving employees in decision making, companies increase employees' power in an organization and improve the flow of information between employees and managers. At Borg-Warner Automotive (BWA), manufacturer of highly engineered components and systems for vehicle engines and transmissions, participatory management is ingrained in the company's culture. The product emphasis there is high-tech and the workforce emphasis is high-involvement. Management understands that people are the true drivers of improvement.[37]

- *Customer focus.* Focusing on the customer simply means finding out what customers really want and then providing it. This approach requires casting aside assumptions about customers and relying instead on accurate research. It also requires developing long-term relationships with customers, as Chapter 12 discusses in detail.

- *Benchmarking.* This element of TQM involves comparing your company's processes and products against the standards of the world's best companies and then working to match or exceed those standards. This process entails rating the manufacturing process, product development, distribution, and other key functions against those of acknowledged leaders; analyzing how those role models achieve their outstanding results; and then applying that knowledge to make quality improvements. Among the world-class organizations frequently cited as benchmarks for production are Toyota, IBM, and Hewlett-Packard; for distribution, L.L. Bean and FedEx; and for customer service, American Express and Nordstrom.[38]

- *Continuous improvement.* This key feature of TQM requires an ongoing effort to reduce defects, cut costs, slash production and delivery times, and offer customers innovative products.

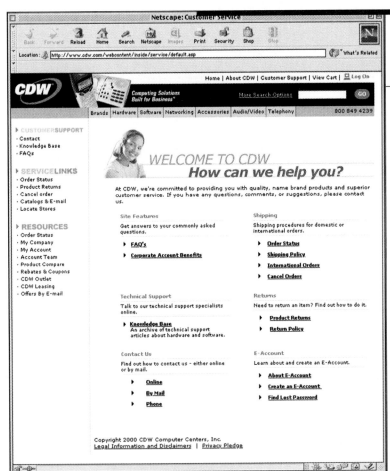

Computer Discount Warehouse's (CDW) Customer Service Web page is dedicated to finding out what customers want so the company can provide it.

Improvements are often small, incremental changes that add up to greater competitiveness over the long run. Because responsibility for such improvement often falls on employees, it becomes management's job to provide employee incentives that will motivate them to want to improve. Geon, a manufacturer of polyvinyl chloride (PVC) resins, motivates its employees through two programs. The first links employee bonuses to improvements in productivity, quality, and manufacturing. In recent years, employees have received an average bonus of 11 percent of their annual salaries through the program. The second program is a success-sharing plan tied to sales gains and stock price. This plan pays out millions of dollars in stock each year. Both initiatives have helped Geon produce 20 percent more PVC resin with 25 percent less manufacturing capacity, putting the company in a much better financial position.[39]

Although many U.S. companies are enjoying greater success as a result of total quality initiatives, a recent study of the largest U.S. companies indicates that such initiatives have fallen short of expectations in a large number of companies. However, the fact that total quality principles played a significant role in propelling Japanese businesses from postwar ruins to pillars of innovation and productivity suggests that much can be gained from the process. What may be lacking in the United States is a firm commitment to TQM. Many companies have jumped on the TQM bandwagon hoping for a quick boost in performance without really thinking about how to make total quality a part of their long-term strategy. Such companies often fail to provide the necessary managerial and financial support for the programs. In about half of the firms studied, less than 40 percent of workers and less than 80 percent of management teams were sufficiently knowledgeable about TQM philosophy, concepts, and tools.[40] Experts agree that the entire organization—from the bottom all the way up to the CEO—must be actively and visibly involved for TQM to work. Companies that make a halfhearted commitment should not expect dramatic improvements.[41]

At the same time, pursuing TQM is not necessarily a prerequisite for success. Many successful companies do not have TQM programs.[42] However, no business that operates in a competitive environment can expect long-term success unless managers strive to meet customers' needs, improve processes, lower costs, and empower employees in one way or another.

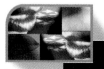

## active poll    <

**What do you think? Voice your opinion and find out what others have to say.**

## active concept check    <

**Now let's take a moment to test your knowledge of the concepts you have studied in this section.**

## > Management Skills

Managers rely on a number of skills to perform their functions and maintain a high level of quality in their organizations. These skills can be classified into three basic categories: *interpersonal, technical,* and *conceptual.* As managers rise through the organization's hierarchy, they may need to strengthen their abilities in one or more of these skills; fortunately, managerial skills can usually be learned.[43]

### INTERPERSONAL SKILLS

The various skills required to communicate with other people, work effectively with them, motivate them, and lead them are **interpersonal skills.** Because they mainly get things done through people, managers at all levels of the organization use interpersonal skills in countless situations. Encouraging employees to work together toward common goals, interacting with employees and other managers, negotiating with partners and suppliers, developing employee trust and loyalty, and fostering innovation—all these activities require interpersonal skills.

Communication, or exchanging information, is the most important and pervasive interpersonal skill that managers use. Effective communication not only increases the manager's and the organization's productivity but also shapes the impressions made on colleagues, employees, supervisors, investors, and customers. Communication allows you to perceive the needs of these stakeholders (your first step toward satisfying them), and it helps you respond to those needs.[44] Moreover, as the workforce becomes more and more diverse, managers will need to adjust their interactions with others, communicating in a way that considers the different needs, backgrounds, and experiences of people.

## TECHNICAL SKILLS

A person who knows how to operate a machine, prepare a financial statement, program a computer, or pass a football has **technical skills;** that is, the individual has the knowledge and ability to perform the mechanics of a particular job. Technical skills are most important at lower organizational levels because managers at these levels work directly with employees who are using the tools and techniques of a particular specialty, such as automotive assembly or computer programming. Still, twenty-first-century managers must have a strong technology background. They must find new computer applications that can complete daily work routines faster or provide more accurate information sooner.

Managers at all levels use **administrative skills,** which are the technical skills necessary to manage an organization. Administrative skills include the abilities to make schedules, gather information, analyze data, plan, and organize. Managers often develop such skills through education and then improve them by working in one or more functional areas of an organization, such as accounting or marketing.[45] Project management skills are becoming an increasingly important administrative skill. Managers must know how to start a project or work assignment from scratch, map out each step in the process to its successful completion, develop project costs and timelines, and establish checkpoints at key project intervals.

## CONCEPTUAL SKILLS

Managers need **conceptual skills** to see the organization as a whole, in the context of its environment, and to understand how the various parts interrelate. Conceptual skills are especially important to top managers. These managers are the strategists who develop the plans that guide the organization toward its goals. Entrepreneurs such as Steve Case use their conceptual skills to acquire and analyze information, identify both problems and opportunities, understand the competitive environment in which their companies operate, develop strategies, and make decisions.

A key managerial activity requiring conceptual skills is **decision making,** a process that has five distinct steps: (1) recognizing the need for a decision, (2) identifying, analyzing, and defining the problem or opportunity, (3) generating alternatives, (4) selecting an alternative and implementing it, and (5) evaluating the results. Managers monitor the results of decisions over time to see whether the chosen alternative works, whether any new problem or opportunity arises because of the decision, and whether a new decision must be made (see Exhibit 6.8).[46]

Keep in mind that a company's managerial structure defines the way decisions are made. Today's flatter organizations, for example, allow information to flow more freely among all levels of the organization, and they push decision making down to lower organizational levels. As Chapter 7 discusses in detail, more and more organizations are empowering their employees and teams by giving them increasing discretion over work-related issues.[47] This is especially true for e-businesses whose organizational and management structures must facilitate independent decision-making flexibility, risk taking, and open communication.

> **active poll**

**What do you think? Voice your opinion and find out what others have to say.**

> **active concept check**

**Now let's take a moment to test your knowledge of the concepts you have studied in this section.**

**Coca-Cola**

During WWII, Robert Woodruff, president of Coca-Cola, committed to selling bottles of Coke to members of the armed services for a nickel a bottle. Customer loyalty never came cheaper.

**Diners Club**

In 1950, when Frank McNamara found himself in a restaurant with no money, he came up with the idea of the Diners Club Card. The first credit card changed the nature of buying and selling throughout the world.

**Holiday Inn**

When the Wilson family of Memphis went on a motoring vacation, they discovered it was not much fun staying in motels that were either too expensive or too slovenly. So Kemmons Wilson built his own. The first Holiday Inn opened in Memphis in 1952.

**Honda**

When Honda arrived in America in 1959 to launch its big motor bikes, customers weren't keen on their problematic performance. However, they did admire the little Supercub bikes Honda's managers used. So Honda bravely changed direction and transformed the motorbike business overnight.

**Weight Watchers**

When Jean Nidetch was put on a diet by the Obesity Clinic at New York Department of Health, she invited six dieting friends to meet in her apartment every week. In 1961 she created Weight Watchers and launched the slimming industry.

**CNN**

Ignoring market research, Ted Turner launched the Cable News Network in 1980. No one thought a 24-hour news network would work.

**Sony**

Sony chief Akito Morita noticed that young people liked listening to music wherever they went. So in 1980 he and the company developed what became the Walkman. There was no need for market research, because according to Morita, "The public does not know what is possible. We do."

**Tylenol**

When Johnson & Johnson pulled Tylenol from store shelves in 1982 after capsules were found to be poisoned, the company put customer safety before corporate profit. And it provided a lesson in media openness.

**Dell**

In 1984 Michael Dell decided to sell PCs direct and built to order. Now everybody in the industry is trying to imitate Dell Computer's strategy.

**EXHIBIT 6.8**

Greatest Management Decisions Ever Made

Great decisions change things. Here are some of the greatest management decisions made in the twentieth century.

## > Chapter Wrap-Up

Now that you've reached the end of the chapter, you may wish to explore the concepts you've been reading about in greater detail, or test yourself to see how well you've comprehended the material. In the box below you'll find a number of links. Click on any one of these links to find additional chapter resources.

# > end-of-chapter resources

- Summary of Learning Objectives
- Practice Quiz
- Focusing on E-Business Today
- Key Terms
- Test Your Knowledge
- Practice Your Knowledge
- Expand Your Knowledge
- A Case for Critical Thinking

# Organization, Teamwork, and Communication

## > What's Ahead

### INSIDE BUSINESS TODAY
### DON'T LEAVE HOME TO GO TO WORK: AMERICAN EXPRESS COMPANY'S VIRTUAL ENVIRONMENT

Don't leave home without it!" sends a powerful message about the dangers of traveling without an American Express card tucked into your pocket. Millions of customers heed that advice each day, making American Express Company the world's largest travel agency and a leading provider of financial services. But providing a seamless network of services for customers around the globe requires effective teamwork from all employee's, whether they're working from the New York headquarters or telecommuting from home in Los Angeles. David House makes sure that his employees have everything they need to work together and contribute to the company's success—even if they don't leave home to go to work.

As president of American Express Global Establishment Services, the division that recruits new American Express merchants, House encourages his staff members to work together to achieve their goals. But uniting employees in sales offices across the country demands more than a few rousing pep talks. To build a successful team, House uses technology to promote communication within his division. He provides every employee with access to the company's highly efficient computer network. He offers employees the opportunity to work from home, eliminating the time, expense, and stress of daily commutes to the office.

American Express has continuously transformed itself to become a leading global travel, financial, and network services provider.

Furthermore, he contracts with outside sources to set up the home offices, arranging for everything from installation of phone lines to home safety checks for such things as carbon monoxide levels and availability of fire extinguishers. He even provides employees with computer training, software and hardware setup, and selection and delivery of office furniture to complete their virtual office environment.

Nevertheless, House knows that effective teams need more than equipment to produce quality work. They need to communicate. House's telecommuters conduct virtual meetings with colleagues around the world, taking advantage of e-mail and videoconferencing to brainstorm and collaborate on projects. Several units in House's division use a buddy system that requires remote workers to chat with on-site colleagues by phone every morning, covering topics from new customers to office politics. Other telecommuters report to a local or regional office several times each week, meeting with co-workers for specific purposes. Office meetings have predetermined agendas and follow regular schedules to reduce wasted meeting time and to allow team members to communicate face-to-face.

To encourage team members to work together, House commends outstanding team efforts. Each year, he awards lavish prizes to the top 75 sales reps for their contributions, and he makes a special point to recognize team members who share information with their peers. For example, House acknowledged one outstanding rep who focused on her team's regional sales objectives instead of her own quotas. She not only accompanied other reps on sales calls in her region, but made an effort to share her sales strategies by distributing copies of her winning presentations to every rep in the country.

House's knack for developing and using virtual teams at American Express has indeed paid off. Not only do virtual teams save the company time and travel costs, but they have increased employee productivity and improved customer satisfaction rates. Moreover, by using virtual teams, House has reduced the number of field offices from 85 to 7, resulting in additional cost savings for the company.[1]

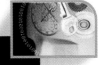

> **objectives**

Take a moment to familiarize yourself with the key objectives of this chapter.

> **gearing up**

Before you begin reading this chapter, try a short warm-up activity.

> **Designing an Effective Organization Structure**

Whether you're working from home as a member of David House's virtual team or in a traditional office setting, the decision-making authority of employees and managers is supported by the company's **organization structure.** This structure helps the company achieve its goals by providing a framework for managers to divide responsibilities, effectively distribute the authority to make decisions, coordinate and control the organization's work, and hold employees accountable for their work. In some organizations, this structure is a relatively rigid, vertical hierarchy like the management pyramid described in Chapter 6. In other organizations, such as American Express, teams of employees and managers from across levels and functions work together to make decisions and achieve the organization's goals.[2]

When managers design the organization's structure, they use an **organization chart** to provide a visual representation of how employees and tasks are grouped and how the lines of communication and authority flow. Exhibit 7.1 shows the organization chart for a grocery store chain. An organization chart depicts the official design for accomplishing tasks that lead to achieving the organization's goals, a framework known as the *formal organization.* Every company also has an **informal organization**—the network of interactions that develop on a personal level among workers. Sometimes the interactions among people in the informal organization parallel their relationships in the formal organization, but often interactions transcend formal boundaries. Crossing formal boundaries can help establish a more pleasant work environment, but it can also undermine formal work processes and hinder a company's ability to get things done.[3]

How do companies design an organization structure, and which organization structure is the most effective? As management guru Peter Drucker sees it, "There is no such thing as one right organization. Each has distinct strengths, distinct limitations, and specific applications." Drucker further notes that managers of the future will require a toolbox full of organization structures and will have to select the right tool for each specific task: on some tasks employees will be working in teams; on others, under a traditional command-and-control hierarchy.[4] Nevertheless, four factors must be taken into consideration when designing an effective organization structure: work specialization, chain of command, vertical organization, and horizontal organization and coordination.

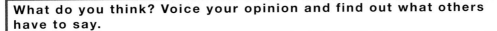

> **active poll**

What do you think? Voice your opinion and find out what others have to say.

## WORK SPECIALIZATION

Before designing an organizational structure, management must first decide on the optimal level of **work specialization**—the degree to which organizational tasks are broken down into separate jobs.[5] Few employees have the skills to perform every task a company needs. Therefore, work specialization

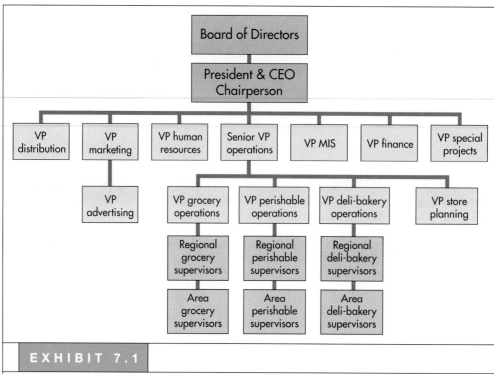

**EXHIBIT 7.1**

Organization Chart for Food Lion Grocery Store Chain

At first look, organization charts may appear very similar. In fact, the traditional model of an organization is a pyramid in which numerous boxes form the base and lead up to fewer and fewer boxes on higher levels, ultimately arriving at one box at the top. A glance at Food Lion's organization chart reveals who has authority over whom, who is responsible for whose work, and who is accountable to whom.

can improve organizational efficiency by enabling each worker to perform tasks that are well defined and that require specific skills. For example, in 1776 Scottish economist Adam Smith found that if each of 10 workers went through every step needed to make a pin, the entire group could make 200 pins a day. However, if each worker performed only a few steps and no one made a pin from start to finish, the same 10 workers could make 48,000 pins a day. When employees concentrate on the same specialized tasks, they can perfect their skills and perform their tasks more quickly. A classic example of work specialization is the automobile assembly line.

However, organizations can overdo specialization. If a task is defined too narrowly, employees may become bored with performing the same tiny, repetitive job over and over. They may also feel unchallenged and alienated. Managers must think carefully about how specialized or how broad each task should be. In fact, a growing number of companies are balancing specialization and employee motivation through teamwork. This approach enables group members to decide how to break down a complex task, and it allows employees to rotate among the jobs that the team is collectively responsible for. The team then shares credit for the results, and workers feel that they have created something of value. The team approach to organization is discussed in more depth later in this chapter.

## CHAIN OF COMMAND

Besides incorporating work specialization into an organizational structure, companies must also establish a **chain of command,** the unbroken line of authority that connects each level of management with the next level. The chain of command helps organizations function smoothly by making two things clear: who is responsible for each task, and who has the authority to make official decisions.

All employees have a certain amount of **responsibility**—the obligation to perform the duties and achieve the goals and objectives associated with their jobs. As they work toward the organization's goals, employees must also maintain their **accountability,** their obligation to report the results of their work to supervisors or team members and to justify any outcomes that fall below expectations. Managers ensure that tasks are accomplished by exercising **authority,** the power to make decisions, issue orders, carry out actions, and allocate resources to achieve the organization's goals. Authority is vested in the positions that managers hold, and it flows down through the management pyramid. **Delegation** is the assignment of work and the transfer of authority and responsibility to complete that work.[6]

Look again at Exhibit 7.1. The senior vice president of operations delegates responsibilities to the vice presidents of grocery operations, perishable operations, deli-bakery operations, and store planning. These department heads have the authority to make certain decisions necessary to fulfill their roles, and they are accountable to the senior VP for the performance of their respective divisions. In turn, the senior VP is accountable to the company CEO.

The simplest and most common chain-of-command system is known as **line organization** because it establishes a clear line of authority flowing from the top down, as Exhibit 7.1 depicts. Everyone knows who is accountable to whom, as well as which tasks and decisions each is responsible for. However, line organization sometimes falls short because the technical complexity of a firm's activities may require specialized knowledge that individual managers don't have and can't easily acquire. A more elaborate system called **line-and-staff organization** was developed out of the need to combine specialization with management control. In such an organization, managers in the chain of command are supplemented by functional groupings of people known as *staff,* who provide advice and specialized services but who are not in the line organization's chain of command (see Exhibit 7.2).

### Span of Management

The number of people a manager directly supervises is called the **span of management** or *span of control.* When a large number of people report directly to one person, that person has a wide span of management. This situation is common in **flat organizations** with relatively few levels in the management hierarchy. Sun Microsystems, Visa, and Oticon (a hearing-aid manufacturer in Denmark) are all companies that have flat organizations. British Petroleum (BP) is also amazingly flat and lean for an organization with $70 billion in revenues, 53,000 employees, and 90 business units that span the globe. At BP there is no level between the general managers of the business units and the group of nine operating executives who oversee the businesses.[7]

In contrast, **tall organizations** have many hierarchical levels, usually with only a few people reporting to each manager. In such cases, the span of management is narrow (see Exhibit 7.3). General Motors has traditionally had a tall organization structure with as many as 22 layers of management. However, as are many companies, GM is flattening its organization structure by delegating some middle management responsibilities to work teams.[8]

No formula exists for determining the ideal span of management. How well people work together is more important than the number of people reporting to one person. Still, several factors affect the

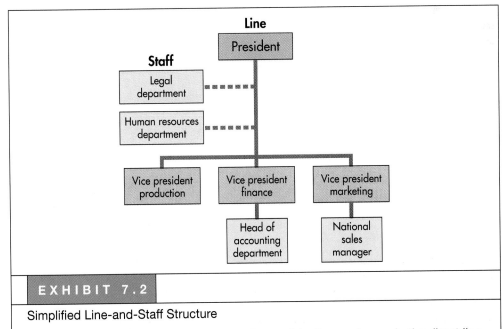

**EXHIBIT 7.2**

Simplified Line-and-Staff Structure

A line-and-staff organization divides employees into those who are in the direct line of command (from the top level of the hierarchy to the bottom) and those who provide staff (or support) services to line managers at various levels. Staff reports directly to top management.

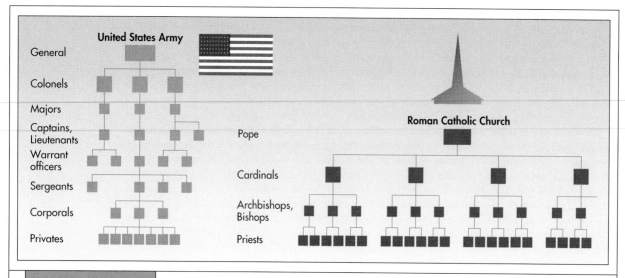

EXHIBIT 7.3

Tall Versus Flat Organizations

A tall organization has many levels with a narrow span of management at each level so that relatively few people report to each manager on the level above them. In contrast, a flat organization has relatively few levels with a wide span of management so that more people report to each manager.

number of people a manager can effectively supervise, including the manager's personal skill and leadership ability, the skill of the workers, the motivation of the workers, and the nature of the job. In general, employees who are highly skilled or who are trained in many work tasks don't require as much supervision as employees who are less skilled.

### Centralization Versus Decentralization

Organizations that focus decision-making authority near the top of the chain of command are said to be centralized. **Centralization** benefits a company by utilizing top management's rich experience and broad view of organizational goals. Both line organizations and line-and-staff organizations tend to be centralized.

However, the trend in business today is to decentralize. **Decentralization** pushes decision-making authority down to lower organizational levels—such as department heads—while control over essential companywide matters remains with top management. Implemented properly, decentralization can stimulate responsiveness because decisions don't have to be referred up the hierarchy.[9] Consider General Electric. Managers at each of GE's 13 independent businesses have $25 million they can spend as they see fit without having to get the approval of the board of directors or the CEO. Giving each core business more decision-making authority has helped GE achieve tremendous growth in sales and profits.[10]

However, decentralization does not work in every situation or in every company. At times, strong authority from the top of the chain of command may be needed to keep the organization focused on immediate goals. Managers should select the level of decision making that will most effectively serve the organization's needs given the individual circumstances.[11]

## active exercise &lt;

**Take a moment to apply what you've learned.**

### VERTICAL ORGANIZATION

Choosing between a vertical and a horizontal model is one of the most critical decisions a company can make. Many organizations use a traditional vertical structure to define formal relationships and the division of tasks among employees and managers. **Vertical organization** links the activities at the top of the organization with those at the middle and lower levels.[12] This structure also helps managers delegate authority to positions throughout the organization's hierarchy. Besides authority, the structure defines specific jobs and activities across vertical levels. In a vertical organization, companies define jobs and activities by using **departmentalization**—the arrangement of activities into logical groups that are then clustered into larger departments and units that form the total organization.[13] Four common ways of departmentalizing are by function, division, matrix, and network. An organization may use more than one method of departmentalization, depending on its particular needs.

### Departmentalization by Function

**Departmentalization by function** groups employees according to their skills, resource use, and expertise. Common functional departments include marketing, human resources, operations, finance, research and development, and accounting, with each department working independently of the others.[14] As depicted in Exhibit 7.1, functional departmentalization is highly centralized. In this structure, work doesn't flow through the company, it bounces around from department to department.

Splitting the organization into separate functional departments offers several advantages: (1) Grouping employees by specialization allows for the efficient use of resources and encourages the development of in-depth skills; (2) centralized decision making enables unified direction by top management; and (3) centralized operations enhance communication and the coordination of activities within departments. Despite these advantages, functional departmentalization can create communication barriers between departments, thereby slowing response to environmental change, hindering effective planning for products and markets, and overemphasizing work specialization (which alienates employees).[15] For these reasons, most large companies have abandoned the functional structure in the past decade or so.

### Departmentalization by Division

**Departmentalization by division** establishes self-contained departments that encompass all the major functional resources required to achieve their goals—such as research and design, manufacturing, finance, and marketing. These departments are typically formed according to similarities in product, process, customer, or geography.

- *Product divisions.* Many organizations use a structure based on **product divisions**—grouping around each of the company's products or family of products. The logic behind this organizational structure is that each department can manage all the activities needed to develop, manufacture, and sell a particular product or product line.

- *Process divisions.* **Process divisions,** also called *process-complete* departments, are based on the major steps of a production process. For example, a table-manufacturing company might have three divisions, one for each phase of manufacturing a table. Astra/Merck, a company that markets antiulcer and antihypertension drugs, is organized around six process divisions, including drug development and distribution.[16]

- *Customer divisions.* The third approach, **customer divisions,** concentrates activities on satisfying specific groups of customers. For example, Acer America, manufacturer of computer equipment, restructured into six customer-centric divisions to facilitate the fulfillment of the company's mission—to provide customers with the highest level of quality, reliability, and support (see Exhibit 7.4).[17]

- *Geographic divisions.* **Geographic divisions** enable companies spread over a national or an international area to respond more easily to local customs, styles, and product preferences. For example, Quaker Oats has two main geographic divisions: (1) U.S. and Canadian Grocery Products and (2) International Grocery Products. Each division is further subdivided to allow the company to focus on the needs of customers in specific regions.

Divisional departmentalization offers both advantages and disadvantages. First, because divisions are self-contained, they can react quickly to change, thus making the organization more flexible. In addition, because each division focuses on a limited number of products, processes, customers, or locations, divisions can offer better service to customers. Moreover, top managers can focus on problem areas more easily, and managers can gain valuable experience by dealing with the various functions in their divisions. However, divisional departmentalization can also increase costs by duplicating the use of resources such as facilities and personnel. Furthermore, poor coordination between divisions may cause them to focus too narrowly on divisional goals and neglect the organization's overall goals. Finally, divisions may compete with one another for employees, money, and other resources, causing rivalries that hurt the organization as a whole.[18]

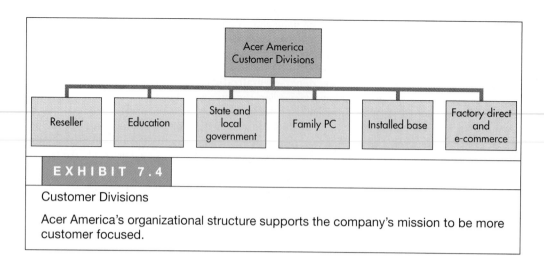

EXHIBIT 7.4

Customer Divisions

Acer America's organizational structure supports the company's mission to be more customer focused.

### Departmentalization by Matrix

**Departmentalization by matrix** is a structural design in which employees from functional departments form teams to combine their specialized skills (see Exhibit 7.5). This structure allows the company to pool and share resources across divisions and functional groups. The matrix may be a permanent feature of the organization's design, or it may be established to complete a specific project. Consider Black & Decker, which formed a matrix organization in the early 1990s. Departments such as mechanical design, electrical engineering, and model shop assigned employees with specific technical skills to work on product-development projects in such categories as saws, cordless appliances, and woodworking.[19]

Matrix departmentalization can help big companies function like smaller ones by allowing teams to devote their attention to specific projects or customers without permanently reorganizing the company's structure. But matrix structures are not without drawbacks. One problem of a matrix structure is that team members usually continue to report to their functional department heads as well as to a project team leader. Another drawback is that authority tends to be more ambiguous and up for grabs, creating power struggles and other interpersonal conflicts. Black & Decker realized this soon after it implemented the matrix organization. The manager with the most authority was always the functional department head, and the project team did not really hold any control. The company has since redesigned its organization structure, which is now based on product divisions that employ teams of people from many functional areas.[20]

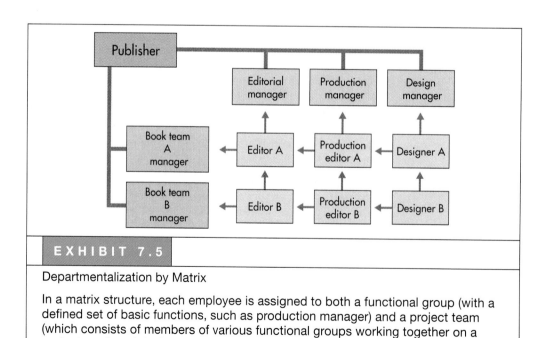

EXHIBIT 7.5

Departmentalization by Matrix

In a matrix structure, each employee is assigned to both a functional group (with a defined set of basic functions, such as production manager) and a project team (which consists of members of various functional groups working together on a project, such as bringing out a new consumer product).

In a matrix organization, excellent communication and coordination are necessary to avoid conflicts. In addition, companies may find it difficult to coordinate the tasks of diverse functional specialists so that projects are completed efficiently.[21] However, because it facilitates the pooling of resources across departments, a matrix organization can also enable a company to respond better to changes in the business environment.

### Departmentalization by Network

**Departmentalization by network** is a method of electronically connecting separate companies that perform selected tasks for a headquarters organization. Also called a *virtual organization,* the network organization *outsources* engineering, marketing, research, accounting, production, distribution, or other functions. This means that the organization hires other organizations under contracts to handle one or more of those functions. In fact, companies such as Nike, Liz Claiborne, and Dell Computer sell hundreds of millions of dollars' worth of products even though they outsource most of their manufacturing. As these companies have learned, the network approach is especially appropriate for international operations, allowing every part of the business to draw on resources no matter where in the world they may be.[22]

A network structure can also enable small companies to compete on a large scale. For example, Barbara Schrager operates Attainment Marketing Partners with only one employee. By using a virtual staff of designers and copywriters who work under contract on specific projects, she is able to create marketing, advertising, and public relations campaigns for major clients in New York.[23]

As Barbara Schrager knows, a network structure is extremely flexible because it gives companies the ability to hire whatever services are needed and then change them after a short time. The limited hierarchy required to manage a network organization also permits the company to make decisions and react to change quickly. Additional advantages are that the organization can continually redefine itself, and a lean structure usually means employees have greater job variety and satisfaction. However, the network approach lacks hands-on control, because the functions are not in one location or company. Also, if one company in the network fails to deliver, the headquarters organization could suffer or even go out of business. Finally, strong employee loyalty and team spirit are less likely to develop, because the emotional connection between the employee and the organization is weak.[24]

## HORIZONTAL ORGANIZATION

More and more businesses are transforming their traditional bureaucratic and hierarchical vertical structure into a horizontal organization.[25] The horizontal organization rejects the separation of people and work into functional departments by using the team concept to flatten hierarchies and integrate the many tasks of a business into a few smooth-flowing operations. The biggest benefit of horizontal organization is that everyone works together. Employees from various departments or functions are grouped around a few organization-wide, cross-functional core processes, and they are responsible for an entire core process from beginning to end. Employees who create new product designs, for instance, work with engineers and marketing personnel to make sure the designs can be manufactured and marketed.

A typical core process group might include staff from finance, research and development, manufacturing, and customer service. All core processes lead to one objective: creating and delivering something of value to the customer. The Occupational Safety and Health Administration (OSHA), the U.S. agency charged with protecting the safety of workers, recently organized its 1,400 field employees around two basic core processes to benefit customers: (1) preventing workplace accidents and (2) responding to accidents and complaints.[26]

While some companies completely dismantle their vertical structure to create horizontal organizations, others prefer a hybrid organization—one that combines vertical and horizontal functions. In these firms, core processes are supported by organization-wide functional departments such as human resources and finance. The Xerox corporation, for example, organized its business operations around five core processes based on five types of products. The core processes are supported by two company-wide vertical operations: technology management and customer service. This way researchers are not constrained by specific markets, and customers face only one customer service representative even if they buy different product types.[27]

By now you can see that whether it uses a traditional vertical or an innovative horizontal organization structure, every organization must coordinate activities and communication among its employees. **Horizontal coordination** facilitates communication across departments without the need to go up and down the vertical chain of command. Horizontal coordination also gives employees the opportunity to share their views, which strengthens their willingness to understand, support, and implement innovative ideas. Without horizontal coordination, functional departments would be isolated from one another, and they would be unable to align their objectives.[28] Of course, one way to inject horizontal coordination into a vertical structure is by working in teams.

## active concept check  <

Now let's take a moment to test your knowledge of the concepts you have studied in this section.

### > Working in Teams

While the vertical chain of command is a tried-and-true method of organizing for business, it is limited by the fact that decision-making authority is often located high up the management hierarchy. Companies that organize vertically may become slow to react to change, and high-level managers may overlook many great ideas for improvement that originate in the lower levels of the organization. As this section will show, the value of involving employees from all levels and functions of the organization in the decision-making process can not be overstated. As a result, most companies today use a variety of team formats in day-to-day operations.

According to a recent survey of Fortune 1,000 executives, 83 percent said their firms are working in teams or moving in that direction.[29] Even though this approach has many advantages, shifting to a team structure often requires a fundamental shift in the organization's culture. For one thing, management must show strong support for team concepts by empowering teams to make important decisions about the work they do. For another, teams must have clear goals that are tied to the company's strategic goals, and their outcomes need to be measured and compared with benchmarks. Moreover, employees must be motivated to work together in teams. Such motivation requires extensive training and a compensation system that is based, at least in part, on team performance.

## active exercise  <

Take a moment to apply what you've learned.

### WHAT IS A TEAM?

A **team** is a unit of two or more people who work together to achieve a goal. Teams differ from work groups in that work groups interact primarily to share information and to make decisions to help one another perform within each member's area of responsibility. In other words, the performance of a work group is merely the summation of all group members' individual contributions.[30] By contrast team members have a shared mission and are collectively responsible for their work. By coordinating their efforts, team members generate a positive synergy and achieve a level of performance that exceeds what would have been accomplished if members had worked individually.[31]

At Microsoft, almost all work is completed in teams. Two factors that have made Microsoft teams so successful are clear goals and strong leadership.[32] Although the team's goals may be set either by the team or by upper management, it is the job of the team leader to make sure the team stays on track to achieve those goals. Team leaders are often appointed by senior managers, but sometimes they emerge naturally as the team develops. Westinghouse Hanford, an electric power company, also uses teams. As one employee notes, by using teams, "we come up with better ideas, work more cohesively and find better ways to solve problems." All of these factors help companies become more flexible and respond more quickly to the challenges of the competitive global workplace.[33]

## TYPES OF TEAMS

The type, structure, and composition of individual teams within an organization all depend on the organization's strategic goals and the objective for forming the team. The five most common forms of teams are *problem-solving teams, self-managed teams, functional teams, cross-functional teams,* and *virtual teams.* Such classifications are not unique. For example, a problem-solving team may also be self-managed and cross-functional. Similarly, some teams are established on an informal basis. That is, they are designed to encourage employee participation but do not become part of the formal organization structure.

### Problem-Solving Teams

The most common type of informal team is the **problem-solving team.** Also referred to as *quality circles,* problem-solving teams usually consist of 5 to 12 employees from the same department who meet voluntarily to find ways of improving quality, efficiency, and the work environment. Any recommendations they come up with are then submitted to management for approval.[34] Land Rover, a manufacturer of luxury sport-utility vehicles, was able to save millions of dollars, improve productivity, and sell more vehicles by using problem-solving teams.[35] If such teams are able to successfully contribute to the organization, as Land Rover's were, they may evolve into formal teams, a change that represents a fundamental shift in the way the organization is structured.

### Self-Managed Teams

Self-managed teams take problem-solving teams to the next level. As the name implies, **self-managed teams** manage their own activities and require minimum supervision. Typically they control the pace of work and determination of work assignments. Fully self-managed teams select their own members. As you might imagine, many managers are reluctant to embrace self-managed teams because it requires them to give up significant control.

At SEI Investments, administrator for $121 billion in investor assets, the defining unit of operation is the self-managed team. Finding itself indistinguishable from other competitors, SEI took a wrecking ball to the traditional corporate pyramid and formed 140 self-managed teams to speed up reaction time, innovate more quickly, and get closer to the customer. Some SEI teams are permanent, designed to serve big customers or important markets; others are temporary—they come together to solve a problem and disband when their work is done. This flexible team structure is supported by having all office furniture on wheels so that teams can easily create their own work areas. In fact, employees move their desks so often that SEI has created software to map every employee's location.[36]

### Functional Teams

**Functional teams,** or *command teams,* are organized along the lines of the organization's vertical structure and thus may be referred to as vertical teams. They are composed of managers and employees within a single functional department. For example, look again at Exhibit 7.1. Functional teams could be formed in Food Lion's marketing, human resources, and finance departments. The structure of a vertical team typically follows the formal chain of command. In some cases, the team may include several levels of the organizational hierarchy within the same functional department.[37]

### Cross-Functional Teams

In contrast to functional teams, **cross-functional teams,** or horizontal teams, draw together employees from various functional areas and expertise. In many cross-functional teams, employees are cross-trained to perform a variety of tasks. At Pillsbury the most experienced workers can handle 23 different jobs.[38] Cross-functional teams inject horizontal coordination into a typical vertical organization structure in several ways: (1) they facilitate the exchange of information between employees, (2) they generate ideas for how to best coordinate the organizational units that are represented, (3) they encourage new solutions for organizational problems, and (4) they aid the development of new organizational policies and procedures.[39]

Boeing, for instance, used hundreds of "design-build" teams that integrated design engineers and production workers to develop its 777 airplane.[40] Cross-functional teams have also become a way of life at Chrysler (now DaimlerChrysler). Under the old setup, the company relied on functional departmentalization in which each function (such as design, engineering, manufacturing, and so on) handed the results of its work to the next function in essentially a sequential process that was time-consuming, costly, and prone to errors. Now team members from various functions work simultaneously and communicate frequently to ensure that the shape of a particular body part will accommodate adjacent components. As a result, the company has reduced the time it takes to bring a new vehicle to market from five years to less than three years.[41] Cross-functional teams such as the ones used at Boeing and DaimlerChrysler can take on a number of formats:

- *Task forces.* A **task force** is a type of cross-functional team formed to work on a specific activity with a completion point. Several departments are usually involved so that all parties who have a stake in the outcome of the task are able to provide input. However, once the goal has been accomplished, the task force is disbanded.[42] Saint Francis Hospital in Tulsa, Oklahoma, established a task force to find ways to reduce the cost of supplies. The team members came from many departments, including surgery, laboratory, nursing, financial planning, administration, and food service. The team not only helped the hospital save money by curbing supply waste but also generated excitement among hospital employees about working together for common goals.[43]

- *Special-purpose teams.* Like task forces, **special-purpose teams** are created as temporary entities to achieve specific goals. However, special-purpose teams are different because they exist outside the formal organization hierarchy. Such teams remain a part of the organization but they have their own reporting structures, and members view themselves as separate from the normal functions of the organization. A special-purpose team might be used to develop a new product when complete creative freedom is needed. By operating outside the formal organization, the team would be able to test new ideas and new ways of accomplishing tasks.[44]

- *Committees.* In contrast to a task force, a **committee** usually has a long life span and may become a permanent part of the organization structure. Committees typically deal with regularly recurring tasks. For example, a grievance committee may be formed as a permanent resource for handling employee complaints and concerns. Because many committees require official representation in order to achieve their goals, committee members are usually selected on the basis of their titles or positions rather than their personal expertise.

### Virtual Teams

**Virtual teams,** such as those used by David House's division, are groups of physically dispersed members who work together to achieve a common goal. Virtual team members communicate using a variety of technological formats and devices such as company intranets, e-mail, electronic meeting software, and telephones. Occasionally, they may meet face-to-face. The biggest advantage of virtual teams is that members are able to work together even if they are thousands of miles and time zones apart. At Texas Instruments, for instance, microchip engineers in India, Texas, and Japan are able to pool ideas, design new chips, and collaboratively debug them—even though they're 8,000 miles and 12 time zones apart.[45]

The three primary factors that differentiate virtual teams from face-to-face teams are the absence of nonverbal cues, limited social context, and the ability to overcome time and space constraints. Because virtual teams must function with less direct interaction among members, team members require certain competencies. Among these are project-management skills, time management skills, ability to use electronic communication and collaboration technologies, ability to work across cultures, and heightened interpersonal awareness.[46]

In many cases, virtual teams are as effective as teams that function under a single roof. At British Petroleum, for example, virtual teams link workers in the Gulf of Mexico with teams working in the eastern Atlantic and around the globe. By using a virtual team network, the company has decreased the number of helicopter trips to offshore oil platforms, has avoided refinery shutdowns because technical experts at other locations were able to handle problems remotely, and has experienced a significant reduction in construction rework, among other benefits.[47]

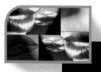

## active poll

**What do you think? Voice your opinion and find out what others have to say.**

### > Advantages and Disadvantages of Working in Teams

Even though teams can play a vital role in helping an organization reach its goals, they are not appropriate for every situation. Managers must weigh both the advantages and the disadvantages of teams when deciding whether to use them.[48]

One of the biggest advantages of teams is that the interaction of the participants leads to higher-quality decisions based on the combined intelligence of the group. Moreover, teams lead to increased acceptance of a solution. Team members who participate in making a decision are more likely to enthusiastically support the decision and encourage others to accept it.[49] Another big advantage is that teams have the potential to unleash vast amounts of creativity and energy in workers. Motivation and performance are often increased as workers share a sense of purpose and mutual accountability. Teams can also fill the individual worker's need to belong to a group. Furthermore, they can reduce boredom, increase feelings of dignity and self-worth, and reduce stress and tension between workers. Finally, teams empower employees to bring more knowledge and skill to the tasks they perform and thereby often lead to greater efficiency and cost reduction. Organizational flexibility is another key benefit of using teams in the workplace. Such flexibility means employees are able to exchange jobs, workers can be reallocated as needed, managers can delegate more authority and responsibility to lower-level employees, and the company can meet changing customer needs more effectively.

In short, using teams can add up to more satisfied employees performing higher-quality work that helps the organization achieve its goals. Studies of individual industries show that companies using teamwork to organize, plan, and control activities enjoy greater productivity, increased profits, fewer defects, lower employee turnover, less waste, and even increased market value.[50] Consider the results these companies achieved by using employee teams: Kodak has halved the amount of time it takes to move a new product from the drawing board to store shelves; Tennessee Eastman, a division of Eastman Chemical, increased labor productivity by 70 percent; Texas Instruments increased revenues per employee by over 50 percent; and Ritz-Carlton Hotels jumped to the top of the J. D. Power and Associates consumer survey of luxury hotels.[51]

Although teamwork has many advantages, it also has a number of potential disadvantages. For one thing, power within the organization sometimes becomes realigned with teams. Successful teams mean that fewer supervisors are needed, and usually fewer middle and front-line managers. Adjusting to their changing job roles, or even to the loss of their jobs, is understandably difficult for many people. Another potential disadvantage is **free riders**—team members who don't contribute their fair share to the group's activities because they aren't being held individually accountable for their work. The free-ride attitude can lead to the nonfulfillment of certain tasks. Still another drawback to teamwork is the high cost of coordinating group activities. Aligning schedules, arranging meetings, and coordinating individual parts of a project can eat up a lot of time and money. Moreover, a team may develop *groupthink,* a situation in which pressures to conform to the norms of the group cause members to withhold contrary or unpopular opinions. Groupthink can hinder effective decision making because some possibilities will be overlooked.[52]

## > active concept check

**Now let's take a moment to test your knowledge of the concepts you have studied in this section.**

## > Characteristics of Effective Teams

Team size is one factor that contributes to a team's overall effectiveness. The optimal size for teams is generally thought to be between 5 and 12 members. Teams smaller than 5 may be lacking in skill diversity and may, therefore, be less effective at solving problems. Teams of more than 12 may be too large for group members to bond properly and may discourage some members from sharing their ideas. Larger groups are also prone to disagreements and factionalism because so many opinions must be considered, thus making the team leader's job more difficult. Moreover, studies have shown that turnover and absenteeism are higher in larger teams because members tend to feel that their presence makes less of a difference.

For a team to be successful over time, it must also be structured to accomplish its task and to satisfy its members' needs for social well-being. Effective teams usually fulfill both requirements with a combination of members who assume one of four roles: task specialist, socioemotional role, dual role, or nonparticipator. People who assume the *task-specialist role* focus on helping the team reach its goals. In contrast, members who take on the *socioemotional role* focus on supporting the team's emotional needs and strengthening the team's social unity. Some team members are able to assume *dual roles,* contributing to the task and still meeting members' emotional needs. These members often make effective team leaders. At the other end of the spectrum are members who are *nonparticipators,*

| High | Task specialist role | Dual role |
|---|---|---|
| | Focuses on task accomplishment over human needs | Focuses on task and people |
| | | May be a team leader |
| | Important role, but if adopted by everyone, team's social needs won't be met | Important role, but not essential if members adopt task specialist and socioemotional roles |
| Member task behavior | Nonparticipator role | Socioemotional role |
| | Contributes little to either task or people needs of team | Focuses on people needs of team over task |
| | Not an important role—if adopted by too many members, team will disband | Important role, but if adopted by everyone, team's tasks won't be accomplished |
| Low | | |
| | Low    Member social behavior    High | |

**EXHIBIT 7.6**

Team Member Roles

Team members assume one of these four roles. Members who assume a dual role often make effective team leaders.

contributing little to reaching the team's goals or to meeting members' emotional needs. Exhibit 7.6 outlines the behavior patterns associated with each of these roles.

Other characteristics of effective teams include the following:[53]

- *Clear sense of purpose.* Team members clearly understand the task at hand, what is expected of them, and their role on the team.

- *Open and honest communication.* The team culture encourages discussion and debate. Team members speak openly and honestly, without the threat of anger, resentment, or retribution. They listen to and value feedback from others. As a result, all team members participate.

- *Creative thinking.* Effective teams encourage original thinking, considering options beyond the usual.

- *Focused.* Team members get to the core issues of the problem and stay focused on key issues.

- *Decision by consensus.* All decisions are arrived at by consensus. No easy, quick votes are taken.

Of course, learning effective team skills takes time and practice, so many companies now offer employees training in building their team skills. At Saturn, for example, every team member goes through a minimum of 92 hours of training in problem solving and people skills. Saturn teaches team members how to reach a consensus point they call "70 percent comfortable but 100 percent supportive." At that level of consensus, everybody supports the solution.[54] For a brief review of characteristics of effective teams, see Exhibit 7.7.

### FIVE STAGES OF TEAM DEVELOPMENT

Developing an effective team is an ongoing process. Like the members who form them, teams grow and change as time goes by. You may think that each team evolves in its own way. However, research shows that teams typically go through five definitive stages of development: forming, storming, norming, performing, and adjourning.[55]

- *Forming.* The forming stage is a period of orientation and breaking the ice. Members get to know each other, determine what types of behaviors are appropriate within the group, identify what is expected of them, and become acquainted with each other's task orientation.

- *Storming.* In the storming stage, members show more of their personalities and become more assertive in establishing their roles. Conflict and disagreement often arise during the storming stage as members jockey for position or form coalitions to promote their own perceptions of the group's mission.

**Build a sense of fairness in decision making**
✓ Encourage debate and disagreement without fear of reprisal
✓ Allow members to communicate openly and honestly
✓ Consider all proposals
✓ Build consensus by allowing team members to examine, compare, and reconcile differences
✓ Avoid quick votes
✓ Keep everyone informed
✓ Present all the facts

**Select team members wisely**
✓ Involve stakeholders
✓ Limit size to no more than 12 to 15 members
✓ Select members with a diversity of views
✓ Select creative thinkers

**Make working in teams a top management priority**
✓ Recognize and reward individual and group performance
✓ Provide ample training opportunities for employees to develop interpersonal, decision-making, and problem-solving skills
✓ Allow enough time for the team to develop and learn how to work together

**Manage conflict constructively**
✓ Share leadership
✓ Encourage equal participation
✓ Discuss disagreements
✓ Focus on the issues, not the people
✓ Keep things under control

**Stay on track**
✓ Make sure everyone understands the team's purpose
✓ Communicate what is expected of team members
✓ Stay focused on the core assignment
✓ Develop and adhere to a schedule
✓ Develop rules and obey norms

**EXHIBIT 7.7**

Characteristics of Effective Teams

Effective teams practice these good habits.

- *Norming.* During the norming stage, these conflicts are resolved, and team harmony develops. Members come to understand and accept one another, reach a consensus on who the leader is, and reach agreement on what each member's roles are.

- *Performing.* In the performing stage, members are really committed to the team's goals. Problems are solved, and disagreements are handled with maturity in the interest of task accomplishment.

- *Adjourning.* Finally, if the team has a limited task to perform, it goes through the adjourning stage after the task has been completed. In this stage, issues are wrapped up and the team is dissolved.

**> video exercise**

**Take a moment to apply what you've learned.**

As the team moves through the various stages of development, two things happen. First, the team develops a certain level of **cohesiveness,** a measure of how committed the members are to the team's goals. The team's cohesiveness is reflected in meeting attendance, team interaction, work quality, and goal achievement. Cohesiveness is influenced by many factors. Two primary factors are competition and evaluation. If a team is in competition with other teams, cohesiveness increases as the team strives to win. In addition, if a team's efforts and accomplishments are recognized by the organization, members tend to be more committed to the team's goals. Strong team cohesiveness generally results in high morale. Moreover, when cohesiveness is coupled with strong management support for team objectives, teams tend to be more productive.

The second thing that happens as teams develop is the emergence of **norms**—informal standards of conduct that members share and that guide their behavior. Norms define what is acceptable behavior. They also set limits, identify values, clarify what is expected of members, and facilitate team survival. Norms can be established in various ways: from early behaviors that set precedents for future actions, from significant events in the team's history, from behaviors that come to the team through outside influences, and from a leader's or member's explicit statements that have an impact on other members.[56]

## TEAM CONFLICT

By now you can see that being an effective team member requires many skills. However, none is more important than the ability to handle *conflict*—the antagonistic interactions resulting from differences in ideas, opinions, goals, or ways of doing things. Conflict can be both constructive and destructive to a team's effectiveness. Conflict is constructive if it increases the involvement of team members and results in the solution to a problem. Conflict is destructive if it diverts energy from more important issues, destroys the morale of teams or individual team members, or polarizes or divides the team.[57]

## active exercise <

**Take a moment to apply what you've learned.**

### Causes of Team Conflict

Team conflicts can arise for a number of reasons. First, teams and individuals may feel they are in competition for scarce or declining resources, such as money, information, and supplies. Second, team members may disagree about who is responsible for a specific task; this type of disagreement is usually the result of poorly defined responsibilities and job boundaries. Third, poor communication can lead to misunderstandings and misperceptions about other team members or other teams. In addition, intentionally withholding information can undermine trust among members. Fourth, basic differences in values, attitudes, and personalities may lead to clashes. Fifth, power struggles may result when one party questions the authority of another or when people or teams with limited authority attempt to increase their power or exert more influence. Sixth, conflicts can arise because individuals or teams are pursuing different goals.[58] For example, a British cardboard-manufacturing company switched from a hierarchical, functionally oriented organization to a team-based structure with the hope of empowering employees and reducing scrap. However, once they got started, the teams realized that the company had many problems to solve. Conflicts resulted when team members couldn't agree on which problems to tackle first.[59]

### How to Resolve Team Conflict

Each team member has a unique style of dealing with conflict, but the members' styles are primarily based on how competitive or cooperative team members are when a conflict arises. Depending on the particular situation, the same individual may use one of several styles, which include avoidance, defusion, and confrontation.[60] *Avoidance* may involve ignoring the conflict in the hope that it will subside on its own, or it may even involve physically separating the conflicting parties. *Defusion* may involve several actions, including downplaying differences and focusing on similarities between team members or teams, compromising on the disputed issue, taking a vote, appealing to a neutral party or higher authority, or redesigning the team. *Confrontation* is an attempt to work through the conflict by getting it out in the open, which may be accomplished by organizing a meeting between the conflicting parties.

These three styles of conflict resolution come into play after a conflict has developed, but team members and team leaders can take several steps to prevent conflicts. First, by establishing clear goals that require the efforts of every member, the team reduces the chance that members will battle over their objectives or roles. Second, by developing well-defined tasks for each member, the team leader ensures that all parties are aware of their responsibilities and the limits of their authority. And finally, by facilitating open communication, the team leader can ensure that all members understand their own tasks and objectives as well as those of their teammates. Keep in mind that communication builds respect and tolerance, and it provides a forum for bringing misunderstandings into the open before they turn into full-blown conflicts.

> active poll

What do you think? Voice your opinion and find out what others have to say.

> active concept check

Now let's take a moment to test your knowledge of the concepts you have studied in this section.

## > Managing the Flow of Information in the Organization

Whether an organization has a vertical or horizontal structure or is made up of functional or cross-functional teams, communication provides the crucial link between individuals, teams, departments, and divisions. The sharing of information among the parts of an organization, as well as between the organization and the outside world, is the glue that binds the organization together. In a large organization, transmitting the right information to the right people at the right time is a real challenge. To meet this challenge, organizations depend on both formal and informal communication channels.

### FORMAL AND INFORMAL COMMUNICATION CHANNELS

The **formal communication network** is aligned with the official structure of the organization. As we have seen, this structure is illustrated by an organization chart such as the one in Exhibit 7.1. Each box in the chart represents a link in the chain of command, and each line represents a formal channel for the transmission of official messages. Information may travel down, up, and across channels in the organization's formal hierarchy.

When managers depend too heavily on formal channels for communicating, they risk encountering **distortion**, or misunderstanding. Every link in the communication chain opens up a chance for error. So by the time a message makes its way all the way up or down the chain, it may bear little resemblance to the original idea. As a consequence, people at lower levels may have only a vague idea of what top management expects of them, and executives may get an imperfect picture of what's happening lower down the chain. This is less of a problem in flat organizations than it is in tall organizations, as fewer levels means fewer links in the communication chain.

Formal organization charts illustrate how information is supposed to flow; in actual practice lines and boxes on a piece of paper cannot prevent people from developing other communication channels. The **informal communication network,** or grapevine, is the invisible side of the organization: It consists of who talks to whom, who listens to whom, and who is really making the decisions and moving the work forward. This informal network isn't reflected in the formal chart. The formal and informal organizations coexist in the same space and time, but they are often independent entities, operating sometimes in concert and sometimes at cross-purposes.[61] Exhibit 7.8 illustrates a typical informal communication network, which is often a very powerful structure within the company.

### BARRIERS TO COMMUNICATION

Many individual and organizational barriers to effective communication exist within firms. Perhaps the most common barrier to communication is simply a lack of attention on the receiver's part. We all let our minds wander now and then, regardless of how hard we try to concentrate, especially if we are tired or if we feel that the information is too difficult or is unimportant. Communication can also break down if either the sender or the receiver has strong emotions about a subject.

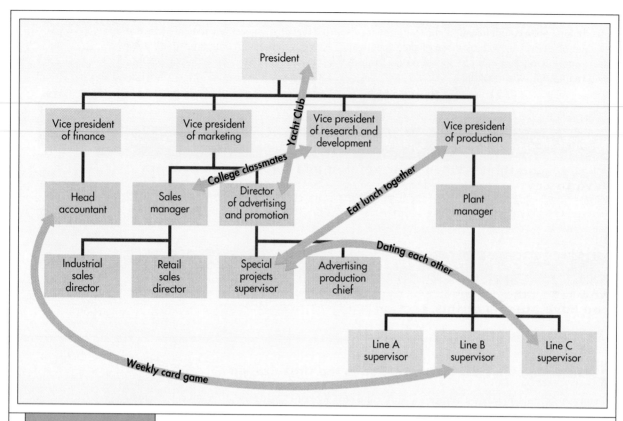

**EXHIBIT 7.8**

Informal Communication Network

In addition to its formal channels of communication, every company has an informal communication network. This network is often formed without regard for hierarchy or departmentalization.

Other persuasive barriers to communication include:

- *Perceptual differences.* How people perceive meanings of words, gestures, tone of voice, and other symbols is affected by their background, including age, culture, education, gender, economic position, religion, or political views.

- *Incorrect filtering.* People often screen out or abbreviate information before passing a message on to someone else. In business, secretaries, assistants, associates, and voice mail are just a few of the filters that exist between you and your receiver.

- *Language.* Even among people of the same culture, language can become a barrier to communication. If you have ever tried to read a legal contract, you know the problem. Lawyers, doctors, accountants, and computer programmers all use specialized vocabularies that affect their ability to communicate ideas.

Of course, many other factors can distort both the messages you send and those you receive in an organization. In fact, executives say that 14 percent of each 40-hour workweek is wasted because of poor communication between staff and management. [62] Nonetheless, as this chapter shows, such barriers can be reduced by designing an effective organization structure, by providing opportunities for employees to communicate, and by encouraging employees to work together in teams.

## active exercise    ◄

**Take a moment to apply what you've learned.**

## > active concept check

**Now let's take a moment to test your knowledge of the concepts you have studied in this section.**

### > Chapter Wrap-Up

Now that you've reached the end of the chapter, you may wish to explore the concepts you've been reading about in greater detail, or test yourself to see how well you've comprehended the material. In the box below you'll find a number of links. Click on any one of these links to find additional chapter resources.

### > end-of-chapter resources

- Summary of Learning Objectives
- Practice Quiz
- Focusing on E-Business Today
- Key Terms
- Test Your Knowledge
- Practice Your Knowledge
- Expand Your Knowledge
- A Case for Critical Thinking

# CHAPTER 8

# Technology and Information Management

## > What's Ahead

### INSIDE BUSINESS TODAY
### MEET MR. INTERNET: JOHN CHAMBERS—CISCO'S LIVE WIRE

Nobody is more responsible for fueling the Internet revolution than John Chambers, CEO of Cisco Systems. His company makes routers—souped-up computers that act as traffic cops—converting, sorting, and directing data throughout the Internet. Pretty basic stuff, but considering that about 70 percent of all Internet traffic passes through a Cisco router before it reaches its final destination, it's a very big business. So with Internet usage projected to grow exponentially, why is Chambers looking for new territory to conquer?

Chambers believes that the Internet is about to undergo a dramatic change, merging with the telephone and cable TV businesses and creating one mammoth voice-video-data network worldwide. As he sees it, tomorrow's homes will become much like today's offices—networks of linked devices and appliances connected to a server. And Chambers wants Cisco to play a key role in that transformation, putting the company squarely into competition with telecom equipment suppliers Lucent Technologies and Northern Telecom, both of whom are many times Cisco's size. Chambers is also stepping up efforts in two booming markets—wireless and optical—and going after leaders Nokia, Motorola, and Ericsson. "I want Cisco to be a dynasty," he says. "I think it can be the company that changes the world."

Chambers's confidence seems particularly astounding considering that Cisco is probably the most faceless dynasty-in-training ever. Popular as Cisco is with technology gurus its products are boring and invisible to most. "The joke around here," says one Cisco staffer, "is that

John Chambers, CEO of Cisco, has turned the company into the world's most comprehensive end-to-end supplier of networking equipment.

we're the most important company no one's ever heard of." But Chambers is working hard to put an end to that joke. He wants people to think of Cisco as a communications company, not a mere router company.

Part of Chambers's drive comes from his past experience. Before joining Cisco Systems in January 1991, he spent six years at IBM and eight years at minicomputer maker Wang Laboratories watching both companies get hammered by the PC revolution. He learned the hard way that selling all technology products to all people doesn't work. He got a chance to put his experience to work when he was appointed Cisco's CEO in 1994. It was an unconventional appointment because Chambers was a salesman—not a technology visionary like Microsoft's Bill Gates or Apple's Steve Jobs. But it turned out to be a wise move for Cisco.

As CEO, Chambers has orchestrated a series of acquisitions and developed critical partnerships to turn Cisco into the world's most comprehensive end-to-end supplier of networking equipment. Moreover, he reorganized Cisco's entire operation so that all business functions—from finance to employee communications—are Internet based. Some 90 percent of the company's sales and 80 percent of customer inquiries are transacted over the Web. "We provide the majority of company information and communications via the Web, which empowers employees to make decisions at all levels of the organization and to move at an Internet pace," says Chambers.

Since going public in 1990, Cisco has increased revenues by 30 to 40 percent each year. But in 2001, that pattern changed. Growing disarray among telecom customers, a sharp economic slowdown, and stepped up heat from Juniper, its major competitor, stalled Cisco's hypergrowth, and the company was forced to trim its workforce by 17 percent. Even though Cisco's annual sales top $13 billion, some believe that its glory days are history. Chambers, of course, disagrees. Cisco has the leading product in the marketplace, and with Internet traffic doubling every 100 days or so, Chambers insists that Cisco can keep up the pace. Based on his track record, few would bet against him.[1]

> # objectives

Take a moment to familiarize yourself with the key objectives of this chapter.

> # gearing up

Before you begin reading this chapter, try a short warm-up activity.

> ## What Is Effective Information Management?

As John Chambers knows, all businesses rely on the fast distribution of information for just about everything they do. Businesspeople need information to increase organizational efficiencies, stay ahead of competitors, find new customers, keep existing customers, develop new products, and so on. Fortunately, we live in the Information Age, where information is easily accessible and readily available. But having too much information can be overwhelming and at times counter-productive.

It has been estimated that humans have produced more information in the past 30 years than in the previous 5,000 and that most of it has been added in the past few years thanks to the Internet and other electronic media.[2] As the amount of information continues to increase, employees must learn how to discriminate between useful and useless information and between what is truly important and what is routine. Technology, of course, plays a key role in managing a company's information. Computers, computer networks, and telecommunication devices enable organizations to track, store, retrieve, process, and share information that can be leveraged to achieve competitive advantages. But in addition to using technology to gather and manage information, companies must develop strategies and systems for analyzing and presenting information so managers and employees can use it in their daily decision making.

According to Bill Gates, "The most meaningful way to differentiate your company from your competition is to do an outstanding job with information."[3] But what exactly does this involve? For one thing, information is most useful to those people who can act on it. A computer technician, for example, doesn't need to know the costs of office supplies, and the advertising manager doesn't need to know the repair schedules for the company's fleet of delivery equipment. Therefore, a key element of an effective information management system is the ability to *filter* information: making sure that the *right information* reaches the *right people* at the *right time,* and in the *right form.*[4] Moreover, for information to be useful, it must be accurate, timely, complete, relevant, and concise.[5] The closer information comes to meeting these five criteria, the more it will facilitate the company's decision-making process.

Of course, information in the real world is rarely perfect, and managers must often make do with whatever data they can get. So another key element of effective information management is understanding the difference between data and information and learning how to turn data into information.

### TURNING DATA INTO INFORMATION

Each day companies collect, generate, and store vast quantities of *data* (recorded facts and statistics) that are relevant to a particular decision or problem. For example, the accounting department may have price and sales data for hundreds of different products, the marketing department may have customer data, the purchasing department may have inventory data, and so on (see Exhibit 8.1). These data are stored in *databases,* centralized collections of data that can be used by people throughout an organization. However, these data do not become information until they are used to solve a problem, answer a question, or make a decision.

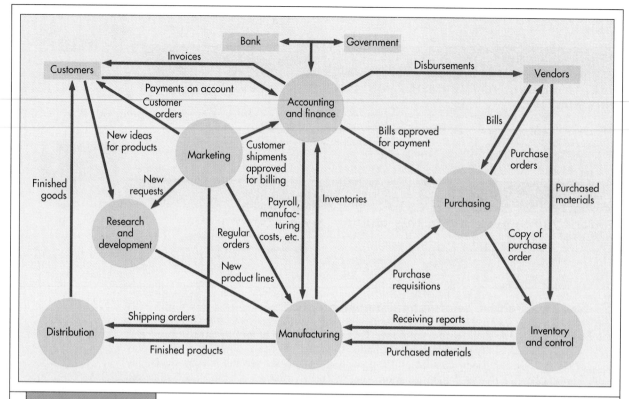

EXHIBIT 8.1

Information Flow in a Typical Manufacturing Company

Many kinds of manipulations and transfers of information support daily operations and decision making in a manufacturing company.

## active exercise

**Take a moment to apply what you've learned.**

When managers want to know the average monthly sales of products X, Y, and Z, they must cross-reference the data. Through a process known as **data warehousing,** data are moved from separate databases into a well-organized central database where they are sorted, summarized, and stored. Managers from the different functional areas can then make complex *queries,* or ask questions of the central database to review the data, analyze it, solve problems, answer questions, or make decisions (see Exhibit 8.2). Such multidepartmental queries are not possible when data are stored in separate databases throughout the organization.[6]

When a query is made, the computer software sifts through huge amounts of data, identifying what is valuable to the specific query and what is not. This process, known as **data mining,** allows computers to look for patterns and turn mountains of data into useful information.[7] For example, MCI WorldCom has marketing records on 140 million households, each of which may have as many as 10,000 separate attributes. By mining these data, the company can detect patterns that indicate which customers are most likely to switch to a different long-distance provider. Marketing personnel can use this information to decide which customers to target for special promotions and which incentives to offer current customers.[8]

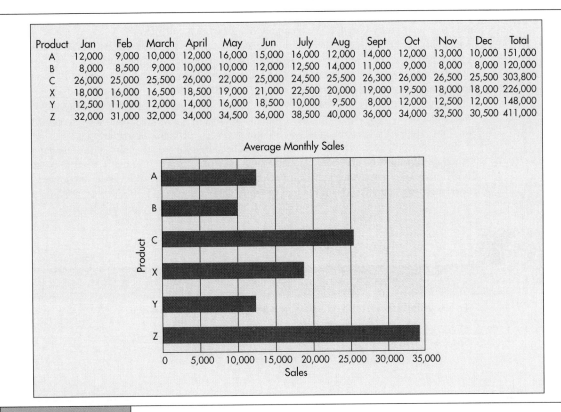

| Product | Jan | Feb | March | April | May | Jun | July | Aug | Sept | Oct | Nov | Dec | Total |
|---------|-----|-----|-------|-------|-----|-----|------|-----|------|-----|-----|-----|-------|
| A | 12,000 | 9,000 | 10,000 | 12,000 | 16,000 | 15,000 | 16,000 | 12,000 | 14,000 | 12,000 | 13,000 | 10,000 | 151,000 |
| B | 8,000 | 8,500 | 9,000 | 10,000 | 10,000 | 12,000 | 12,500 | 14,000 | 11,000 | 9,000 | 8,000 | 8,000 | 120,000 |
| C | 26,000 | 25,000 | 25,500 | 26,000 | 22,000 | 25,000 | 24,500 | 25,500 | 26,300 | 26,000 | 26,500 | 25,500 | 303,800 |
| X | 18,000 | 16,000 | 16,500 | 18,500 | 19,000 | 21,000 | 22,500 | 20,000 | 19,000 | 19,500 | 18,000 | 18,000 | 226,000 |
| Y | 12,500 | 11,000 | 12,000 | 14,000 | 16,000 | 18,500 | 10,000 | 9,500 | 8,000 | 12,000 | 12,500 | 12,000 | 148,000 |
| Z | 32,000 | 31,000 | 32,000 | 34,000 | 34,500 | 36,000 | 38,500 | 40,000 | 36,000 | 34,000 | 32,500 | 30,500 | 411,000 |

## EXHIBIT 8.2

### Data Versus Information

The table at the top represents sales data for a small company's six products. In this form, the data are just statistics that answer no particular question and solve no particular problem. Therefore, they are not considered information. But when a manager queries the database to identify the average monthly sales for each product, specific information is required. The sales data are used to generate the graph that illustrates the requested information.

### Gathering Data

Before you can turn data into meaningful information, however, you must first know where and how to obtain data. Data are frequently classified in two main ways: (1) according to where they are located, and (2) according to the purpose for which they were gathered.

Data grouped according to location are either internal data or external data. **Internal data** are those available in the company's own records—invoices, purchase orders, personnel files, and the like. **External data** are those obtained from outside sources. These include government agencies, such as the Census Bureau, and nongovernment sources, such as trade associations and trade periodicals. Internal data are sometimes easier to obtain and more specific to the company, but outside sources often have better resources for gathering data on broad economic and social trends.

Data grouped by purpose are either primary or secondary. **Primary data** are facts, statistics, and information not previously published that you gather on your own for the study of a specific problem. **Secondary data** consist of facts, statistics, and information previously published or collected by others. Sometimes the collection of secondary data is characterized as "library research." In business research, government and trade organizations are the major sources of secondary data.

Businesspeople usually examine secondary data first because these data often have three advantages over primary data:

- *Speed.* Secondary data sources provide information at a moment's notice.
- *Cost.* Collecting primary data may be an expensive process.
- *Availability.* The owner of a business can hardly expect the owner of a competing firm to make information available. Trade associations and the government, on the other hand, collect information from all firms and make it available to everyone.

Secondary data do have some drawbacks, however. The information may be out of date, or it may not be as relevant as it first seems. The company or agency that collected the data may not be as impartial as it should be. Furthermore, the source may lack expertise. The best way to overcome the disadvantages of secondary data may be to collect primary data through original research.

Some data obtained through primary and secondary research pertain to people's likes and dislikes, their opinions and feelings; other data are of a more factual nature. Factual data presented in numerical form are referred to as **statistics.** Examples of statistics include the batting averages of ballplayers, the number of highway deaths in a year, and the number of ice cream cones eaten in August. Statistics are often expressed as percentages—an inflation rate of 7 percent, for instance.

Businesspeople rely on statistical information because of its relative precision and analytical value. Although they must be able to understand such statistics, they do not really need to be statisticians. Today many microcomputer software packages are available that allow even those who have little experience with statistics to analyze and interpret data.

# active exercise <

## Take a moment to apply what you've learned.

### Analyzing Data

Once you have gathered enough data, you must analyze it so that you can turn the data into meaningful information. In other words, raw data—lists and tables of numbers—are of little practical value by themselves. Instead, they must be manipulated to bring forward certain key numbers, such as averages, index numbers, and trends.

**AVERAGES** One way to present data in an easily understood way is to find an *average,* a number typical of a group of numbers or quantities. A marketing manager, for example, may want to know the

Electric Library is one of the many Internet resources for secondary data. This Web site contains the latest newspaper and magazine articles on a variety of topics.

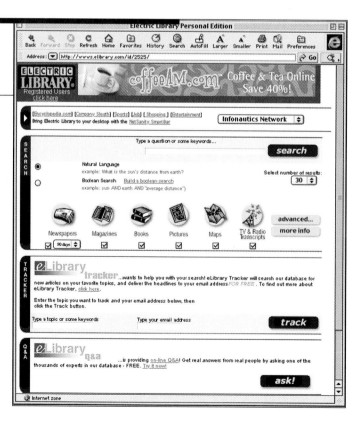

average age of potential consumers of a new product in order to slant advertising toward that age group. The most widely used averages are the *mean,* the *median,* and the *mode.*

- *The Mean.* The statistic most often thought of as an average is the **mean,** the sum of all the items in a group divided by the number of items in the group. The mean is invaluable when comparing one item or individual with a group.

- *The Median.* When items or numbers are arranged from lowest to highest, as in Exhibit 8.3, it is possible to find the **median**—the midpoint, or the point at which half the numbers are above and half are below.

- *The Mode.* The **mode** is the number that occurs most often in any series of data or observations. The mode answers the question, How frequently? or What is the usual size or amount? One important use of the mode is to supply marketing information about common sizes of shoes and clothing. If you were the owner of a shoe store, you would not want to stock 4 pairs of every shoe size in each style. You might find that for every 40 pairs of size 8 sold, only 2 of size 12 were sold.

As Exhibit 8.3 demonstrates, a single set of data may be used to produce all three averages.

**INDEX NUMBERS** In business, it is often important to know how results in one period compare with those of another. To express this comparison conveniently, an index number is used. An **index number** is a percentage that represents the amount of fluctuation between a base figure, such as a price or cost at one period, and the current figure.

Say an oil company wants to keep an index on the number of workers it employs. It chooses as a base year 1999, when it employed 5,000 workers. In 2000 employment slipped to 4,900 workers. In 2001 it surged to 5,300. The index numbers for the years 2000 and 2001 are obtained by dividing the base-year figure into the current-year figure and then multiplying by 100 to change the resulting decimal to a percentage:

$$\frac{Current\text{-}year\ employment\ (2000)}{Base\text{-}year\ employment} = \frac{4,900}{5,000}$$

$$= 0.98,\ or\ 98\%$$

$$\frac{Current\text{-}year\ employment\ (2001)}{Base\text{-}year\ employment} = \frac{5,300}{5,000}$$

$$= 1.06,\ or\ 106\%$$

These figures tell us that employment was off 2 percent in 2000 but up 6 percent in 2001.

**TRENDS** Managers must often determine whether the variations in business activity indicated by statistics have any regular pattern. Suppose that a department store's monthly index of sales shows an increase of 6 percent for June. Before deciding whether to increase the number of salesclerks and the

| Salesperson | Sales | |
|---|---|---|
| Wilson | $3,000 | |
| Green | 5,000 | |
| Carrick | 6,000 | |
| Wimper | 7,000 | — Mean |
| Keeble | 7,500 | — Median |
| Kemble | 8,500 | |
| O'Toole | 8,500 | — Mode |
| Mannix | 8,500 | |
| Caruso | 9,000 | |
| Total | $63,000 | |

**EXHIBIT 8.3**

Mean, Median, and Mode

The same set of data can be used to produce three kinds of averages, each of which has important business applications.

amount of inventory, the manager must know whether the increase in sales will continue into July and August and beyond. **Trend analysis** is the examination of data over a sufficiently long time so that regularities and relationships can be detected, interpreted, and used as the basis for forecasts of business activity.

## PRESENTING INFORMATION

Even the most carefully planned and painstakingly prepared data analysis may be a waste of time if your analysis is poorly presented. Presentations of information must be clear and easy to follow. Tables and graphs help, and such visual aids may even be crucial to giving readers a clear picture of the situation.

With all the graphics software available for computers, there is little reason not to present information in a form that has visual impact. Several types of diagrams are used to display relationships among data so that they are turned into meaningful information (see Exhibit 8.4):

- A *line graph* is a line connecting points. Line graphs show trends, such as an increase in profits or a decrease in sales.

- A *bar chart* uses either vertical or horizontal bars to compare information. Because of its simplicity, the bar chart is frequently used in business reports.

- A *pictograph* is a variation of the bar chart, with symbols or pictures instead of bars used to represent data. Pictographs are good attention-getters, but using them can often mean sacrificing some accuracy.

- A *pie chart* is a circle divided into slices. The slices are labeled as percentages of the whole circle, or 100 percent. A pie chart provides a vivid picture of relationships, but it is not good for showing precise data.

- A *statistical map* shows both locations and quantities by variations in color, texture, or shading or by a concentration of dots. Like the pie chart, it shows general relationships better than it shows specifics.

A **table,** a grid of words and numbers, is commonly used to present data when there is a large amount of precise numerical information to convey. Exhibit 8.5 shows the standard parts of a table.

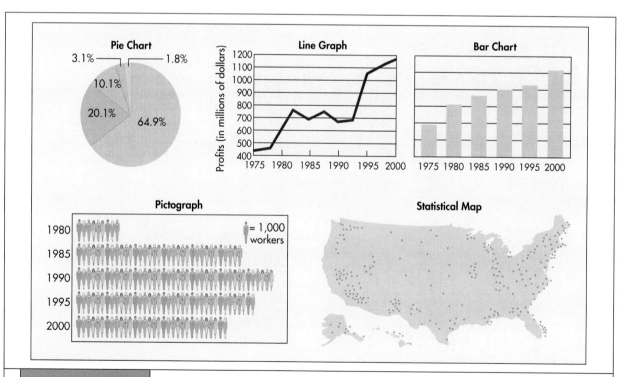

### EXHIBIT 8.4

Diagrams Used in Business Reports

These types of diagrams—pie chart, line graph, bar chart, pictograph, and statistical map—are most often used to present business data.

| GROSS REVENUES BY SOURCE (in thousands of dollars) | | | | |
|---|---|---|---|---|
| **Source of Revenue** | **1998*** | **1999** | **2000** | **2001** |
| Entertainment and recreation | 445,165 | 508,444 | 571,079 | 643,380 |
| Motion pictures | 118,058 | 152,135 | 134,785 | 161,400 |
| Consumer products and other | 66,602 | 80,564 | 90,909 | 109,725 |
| TOTAL REVENUES | 629,825 | 741,143 | 796,773 | 914,505 |

*Reclassified for comparative purposes and to comply with reporting requirements adopted in 1996.
*Source:* Company Annual Reports, 1998, 1999, 2000, 2001.

**EXHIBIT 8.5**

The Parts of a Table

All tables, whether long or short, simple or complicated, contain a title, column heads (across the top), line heads (down the left side), and entries to complete the matrix. They may also include footnotes and a source note.

> **active exercise**

**Take a moment to apply what you've learned.**

## DESIGNING EFFECTIVE INFORMATION SYSTEMS

As you can see, turning data into useful information requires a lot of work and analysis. Organizations depend on quality information to make good decisions and to help them accomplish their goals. Imagine how much harder it would be for Cisco Systems to offer new products without knowing sales trends and other vital statistics. Think of how much longer it would take Chambers to respond to customer requests if employees were not able to share their information with management. In fact, the design and development of effective information systems is of such vital importance to a company that some companies hire a top-level manager, called a **chief information officer (CIO),** to oversee the management of a company's information systems.

The CIO's responsibilities include finding out who in the organization needs what types of information, how these individuals will use this information, how often they will need it, and how they will share it with others. Once the company's information needs have been assessed, the CIO plans what types of data to track and develops systems to collect, track, store, process, retrieve, and distribute the data. Additionally, the CIO oversees the purchase and installation of computer hardware and software and other technologies to facilitate the collection and distribution of information. The types of information systems the CIO designs generally fall into two major categories: operations information systems and management support systems.[9] As Exhibit 8.6 illustrates, each category typically corresponds to business operations at specific levels of the organization.

### Operations Information Systems

Operations information systems include transaction processing systems, process and production control systems, and office automation systems. These systems typically support daily operations and decision making for lower-level managers and supervisors.

Much of the daily flow of data into and out of the typical business organization is handled by a **transaction processing system (TPS),** which captures and organizes raw data and converts these data into information. Common transaction processing systems take care of customer orders, billing, employee payroll, inventory changes, and other essential transactions. For example, credit

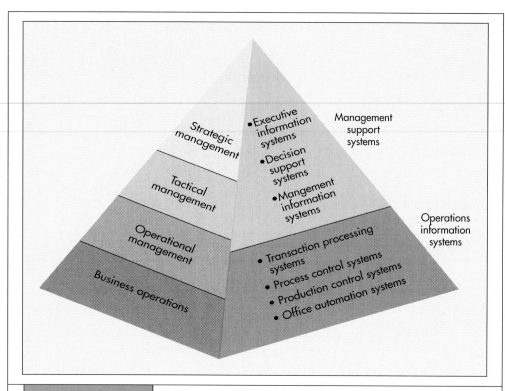

**EXHIBIT 8.6**

Information Systems and Organizational Levels

Managers and employees at the various levels of an organization rely on different types of information systems to help them accomplish their goals.

card companies use TPSs to accept charges and to bill cardholders. Another example is the computer that an airline representative uses to assign you a seat on your flight. These TPSs interact with human beings. However, sometimes a TPS interacts directly with another computer system, as when a drugstore's computer senses the need for more products and transmits orders to a drug wholesaler's computers via **electronic data interchange (EDI).** EDI systems transmit specially formatted documents (such as invoices and purchase orders) from one company's computers to another's. This can greatly reduce the time, paperwork, and cost associated with placing and processing orders, thereby making it easier and more profitable for a customer to do business with the company. Nevertheless, EDI systems are costly and complex. As a result, many companies are now moving EDI transactions to the Internet, as Chapter 9 points out.

Operations information systems are also used to make routine decisions that control operational processes. **Process control systems** monitor conditions such as temperature or pressure change in physical processes. These systems use special sensing devices that take measurements, enabling a computer to make any necessary adjustments to the process.[10]

**Production control systems** are used to manage the production of goods and services by controlling production lines, robots, and other machinery and equipment. In Chapter 9 we will discuss how computer-aided manufacturing can increase efficiency and improve quality by automating production processes. In some cases, manufacturing software is linked with design software to automate the entire design-and-production cycle. For instance, an engineer designing a new component for a car engine can electronically transfer the design to the production department, which will then control a milling machine that automatically carves the part from a block of steel.

**Office automation systems (OAS)** include any type of operations information system that helps you execute typical office tasks. Whether the job is producing a report or calculating next year's budget, an OAS allows you to complete the task more efficiently by converting the process into an electronic format. Office automation systems range from a single personal computer with word-processing software to networks of computers that allow people to send electronic mail and share work among computers.

> ## active exercise

**Take a moment to apply what you've learned.**

### Management Support Systems

Management support systems are designed to help managers make decisions. A variety of such systems exist, which allow users to analyze data, identify business trends, and make forecasts. A **management information system (MIS)** provides managers with information and support for making effective routine decisions. An MIS takes data from a database and summarizes or restates the data into useful information such as monthly sales figures, daily inventory levels, product manufacturing schedules, employee earnings, and so on. This information is generally organized in a report or graphical format, making it easier for managers to read and interpret.

Whereas a management information system provides structured, routine information for managerial decision making, a **decision support system (DSS)** assists managers in solving highly unstructured and nonroutine problems with the use of decision models and specialized databases. Compared with an MIS, a DSS is more interactive (allowing the user to interact with the system instead of simply receiving information), and it usually relies on both internal and external information.[11] Similar in concept to a DSS is an **executive information system (EIS),** which helps executives make the necessary decisions to keep the organization moving forward. An EIS usually has a more strategic focus than a DSS, and it is used by higher management to plan for the future.

Perhaps the greatest potential for computers to aid decision making and problem solving lies in the development of **artificial intelligence**—the ability of computers to solve problems through reasoning and learning and to simulate human sensory perceptions.[12] One type of computer system that can simulate human reasoning by responding to questions, asking for more information, and making recommendations is the **expert system.**[13] As its name implies, an expert system essentially takes the place of a human expert by helping less knowledgeable individuals make critical decisions. For instance, the troubleshooting methods used by an experienced auto mechanic could be programmed into an expert system. A beginning mechanic could describe a sick engine's symptoms to the system, which would then apply the expert mechanic's facts and rules to suggest which troubleshooting methods might reveal the cause of the problem.

Several software companies have taken expert systems a step further by giving them the ability to suggest innovative solutions for problem solving. Drawing on their preprogrammed knowledge of inventive principles, physics, chemistry, and geometry, such systems often come up with solutions to problems that lead to new-product inventions. One example is a flash for pocket cameras that eliminates "red eye."[14]

A second advance in artificial intelligence to make its way into business is the **speech-recognition system.** Using computer software, a generic vocabulary database, and a microphone, speech-recognition systems enable the user to interact with the computer verbally. Today the average microcomputer can accept spoken words at speeds of up to 125 words per minute. Artificial intelligence techniques enable the computer to learn the user's speech patterns and update its vocabulary database continually. In this way, the system evolves, becoming more intelligent, versatile, and easy to use. Although most systems are still limited to a single user, some systems are able to recognize words spoken by anyone. Business uses for this technology include both navigation, which uses voice commands in place of a mouse to open files, launch programs, and move around in document, and dictation, which enables the user to enter data verbally rather than through the keyboard.[15]

> ## active concept check

**Now let's take a moment to test your knowledge of the concepts you have studied in this section.**

Now that you have an idea of what is involved in effective information management, it's time to take a closer look at the role computers play in the information management process. To understand what makes computers tick, we must first distinguish hardware from software and discuss the types of computers that are used in today's workplace. **Hardware** represents the tangible equipment used in a computer system, such as disk drives, keyboards, modems, and *integrated circuits* (small pieces of silicon containing thousands of transistors and electronic circuits). **Software,** on the other hand, encompasses the programmed instructions, or applications, that direct the activity of the hardware.

## TYPES OF COMPUTERS

Computers can be found in a variety of shapes and sizes. However, the most distinguishing characteristic of any computer is its computing capacity, or the amount of processing that it can accomplish in a unit of time. Four popular classifications of computers by capacity are mainframes, microcomputers, workstations, and supercomputers.

- *Mainframe computers.* A **mainframe computer** is a large and powerful system capable of handling vast amounts of data. Smaller mainframes are commonly referred to as *midsize computers.*[16] Mainframes are especially useful when large-scale number crunching is involved, as with finance and accounting activities. Other common uses include controlling a manufacturing process in a factory, managing a company's payroll, and maintaining very large databases. As you'll read later in the chapter, many mainframes are being replaced by *client/server systems* composed of groups of smaller computers. However, an estimated 70 to 80 percent of the world's corporate data are still stored on mainframes. Moreover, organizations are discovering that their mainframe computers make excellent "Web servers." This means that the companies are able to use their existing mainframes to support the Internet applications that are becoming an increasingly important part of their business. These applications include sharing documents, sending and receiving e-mail, taking customer orders, and processing transactions.[17]

- *Microcomputers.* A **microcomputer,** often referred to generically as a *personal computer* or *PC,* represents the smallest and least-expensive class of computers. Unlike large mainframes, a microcomputer is built around a single microprocessor. Computers in this category are now available in several sizes, designated by *desktop, laptop, notebook,* and even *palmtop* (for computers that fit in your hand). Because of their versatility, made possible by a huge variety of software applications, microcomputers are now common in homes as well as in both large and small businesses.

- *Workstations.* A **workstation** marries the speed of a midsize computer with the desktop convenience of microcomputers. Workstations are used primarily by designers, engineers, scientists, and other power users who need fast computing and powerful graphics capabilities to solve mathematically challenging problems. Workstations look like microcomputers and are just as "personal" because they are typically used by one person. But they are distinguished from microcomputers by their speed and input/output devices. A typical workstation will have a high-resolution (high-clarity) monitor and other devices that enable the user to create precision drawings and perform other specialized functions.

- *Supercomputers.* While mainframes are capable of processing huge amounts of data quickly, they are limited in the complexity of calculations they can perform. A scientific calculation, for example, might tie up a university's mainframe for days at a time.[18] **Supercomputers** represent the leading edge in computer performance. They are capable of handling the most complex processing tasks with speeds in excess of 12 trillion calculations per second (a measure of computer speed known as teraflops).[19] Seismic analysis, weather forecasting, complex engineering modeling, and genetic research are among the common uses of supercomputers. Virtual reality design simulators are another application. For instance, Caterpillar designs new tractors and earth movers using virtual reality that lets engineers see how the machines will look and operate before they build physical prototypes.[20]

## HARDWARE COMPONENTS

Whether it's a palmtop computer keeping track of your appointment schedule or a supercomputer modeling the structure of a DNA molecule, every computer is made up of a basic set of hardware components. Of course, the hardware in a supercomputer differs greatly from the hardware in a hand-held unit, but the concepts are similar. Hardware can be divided into four basic groups: input devices, the central processing unit, output devices, and storage (see Exhibit 8.7).

Delta Airlines relies on supercomputers to handle massive amounts of data at its Operations Control Center in Atlanta.

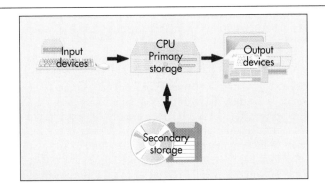

Hardware Elements in a Computer System

The primary elements of computer hardware are input devices, the central processing unit, output devices, and storage.

### Input Devices

Before it can perform any calculations, a computer needs data. Such data can be entered through a keyboard, mouse, computerized pen, microphone (for speech-recognition systems), or optical scanner. With the growth of the Internet and *multimedia* computer applications, video cameras and digital cameras have also become increasingly important input devices.

### Central Processing Unit

A computer's calculations are made in the **central processing unit (CPU),** which interprets and executes program instructions. The CPU performs the three basic functions of arithmetic, logic, and control/communication.[21] In microcomputers the CPU consists of a single integrated circuit, known as a **microprocessor,** and some associated support circuitry. In workstations, mainframes, and supercomputers, the CPU can be either a single processing unit made of multiple integrated circuits or multiple processing units operating in parallel, a scheme known as **parallel processing.** In such a setup, each processor takes one part of the problem—rather like 10 students working on 10 parts of an assignment at the same time.

### Output Devices

Once the data have been successfully entered and the CPU has processed them, they won't be of any use unless they are sent back to the outside world. The first place a computer's output usually goes is the *display,* or monitor. The display acts in the same basic manner as a television, providing the user with text, graphics, or a combination of both. However, when you need a permanent record or when you need to share hard copy with someone, you will probably use a printer. Engineers and scientists also use *plotters,* output devices that use pens to reproduce a displayed image by drawing it on paper.

In addition, as with input devices, specialized equipment can provide output for particular applications. For example, a *projection panel* is a special display device that connects to your computer and sits on top of a regular overhead projector. These panels can display everything from regular computer screens to videotape from a VCR. When combined with presentation and multimedia software that use graphics, projection panels enable computer users to develop unique and impressive business presentations.

### Storage

Input, processing, and output complete the basic computing cycle, but this cycle can't happen without some form of storage for the data being processed and for the software that is in charge of the operation. A **primary storage device** stores data and programs while they are being used in the computer. This device usually involves a set of semiconductor components known as **random-access memory (RAM),** so called because the computer can access any piece of data in such memory at random. Computers use RAM for temporary storage of programs and data during input, processing, and output operations. Unless it is provided with special backup circuitry, RAM is erased when electrical power is removed from the computer. RAM's counterpart is called **read-only memory (ROM),** which uses special circuits for permanent storage. ROM keeps its contents even when power is cut off, and it cannot be accessed by the user for everyday data storage. ROM typically stores programs such as the start-up routines that computers go through when they are first turned on, which involves checking for problems and getting ready to go to work.

**Secondary storage** takes care of data and programs that aren't needed at the moment and provides a permanent record of those data and programs. For instance, if you've finished working on a report that you might need to modify in a month, you put it in secondary storage. The most common mechanism for secondary storage is the **disk drive,** which can be of three types: a hard disk drive, a floppy disk drive, or a CD-ROM drive. *Hard disk drives* are usually enclosed inside the computer and can store data internally on rigid magnetic disks. *Floppy disk drives,* on the other hand, store data on removable magnetic disks. Although they are easily portable, floppy disks, (also called *diskettes*) can store far less information than hard disks. **CD-ROMs** are based on the same technology as music compact discs (CDs) and can store the equivalent of about 477 floppy diskettes. Run on *CD-ROM drives,* they are a key component in multimedia computing, which combines regular computer data with audio, computer animation, photography, and full-motion video.[22] The rapid and universal acceptance of the CD-ROM has given rise to another technology: CD-Re-Writable (CD-RW), which allows you to write and rewrite to a CD just as you do to a diskette.[23]

## COMPUTER SOFTWARE

Computer applications in today's business world are almost limitless. Companies use them to set goals, hire employees, order supplies, manage inventory, sell products, store data, communicate with employees, and perform countless other tasks. The term *application* refers both to an actual task, such as preparing reports and memos, and to the *software* that is used to complete the task.

### Systems Software

Systems software is perhaps the most important software category because it includes **operating systems,** which control such fundamental actions as storing data on disk drives and displaying text or graphics on monitors. Commonly used operating systems include MS-DOS, Windows (which increases the usability of MS-DOS by incorporating a graphical user interface), UNIX, IBM's OS/2, and Apple's Macintosh system. When you first turn on a computer, the operating system begins to direct the actions that enable the various computer hardware devices and software applications to interact in ways that are useful to you. A word-processing program, for instance, can't read the disk or write text to the display by itself; it relies on the operating system to direct the computer's hardware and to manage the flow of data into, around, and out of the system.

### Application Software

**Application software** encompasses programs that perform specific user functions, such as word processing, database management, desktop publishing, and so on. Application software can be either *custom* (developed specifically for a single user or set of users and not sold to others) or *general purpose* (developed with the goal of selling it to multiple users). Commercially available general-purpose software products are commonly referred to as *packages,* as in a *word-processing package.* In today's business-software market, the array of software packages is vast, including products that can prepare books and newspapers, monitor the stock market, locate potential customers on a map, track employee records, and produce sales reports, to name just a few. Exhibit 8.8 highlights the features of fundamental business software applications. Keep in mind that many of these individual programs are sold bundled together as integrated software programs such as Microsoft Office or Claris Works, making it easier to incorporate the work from one program into another.

### Communications Software

Today computers play a central role in business communications. A computer can exchange information with other computers through communications software, which opens up an entirely new spectrum of business capabilities: *electronic mail,* or *e-mail,* enables users to transmit written messages in electronic format between computers; *bulletin board systems (BBS)* and *newsgroups* are electronic

---

#### Software Application Programs

**Word processing:** Word processing programs enable users to type, store, edit, format, and print documents for almost any purpose. Text and graphics can be added, deleted, and moved without retyping the entire document. Special word-processing features include spelling checkers, grammar checkers, automatic text entry, mail merge (a feature that allows you to insert names into a generic form letter, giving the appearance that the letter is personalized), and automatic page numbering. Repetitive keystrokes or tasks can be recorded in a *macro,* a customized program you create to handle the typing or task automatically.

**Desktop publishing (DTP):** Desktop publishing software goes a step beyond typical word processors by allowing designers to lay out printer-ready pages that incorporate artwork, photos, and a large variety of typographic elements. Together with scanners and other specialized input devices, publishing programs let businesspeople create sophisticated documents on their computers in a fraction of the time it once took. Flyers, brochures, user manuals, annual reports, and newsletters are just a few of the documents that can be produced in camera-ready formats that go directly to the print shop.

**Spreadsheets:** A spreadsheet is a program designed to let users organize and manipulate data in a row-column matrix. The intersection of each row-and-column pair is called a *cell,* and every cell can contain a number, a mathematical formula, or text used as a label. Among the spreadsheet's biggest strengths is the ability to quickly update masses of calculations when conditions change. This is possible because a spreadsheet will automatically update a record if one of the records to which it is linked is changed. Businesspeople use spreadsheets to solve a wide variety of problems, ranging from statistical analysis to simulation models used in decision support systems.

**Databases:** Database management software allows users to create, store, maintain, rearrange, and retrieve contents of databases. Almost anywhere you find a sizable amount of data in electronic format, you'll find a database management program at work. Such programs help users produce useful information by allowing users to look at data from various perspectives.

**Graphics:** Graphic programs allow users to create and modify charts, graphs, tables, and diagrams. Together with specialized output devices such as plotters and color printers, business graphics software can produce overhead transparencies, 35 mm slides, posters, and signs. The graphic images created with these software packages can be imported in publishing and word-processing programs for incorporation into documents and presentations.

---

**EXHIBIT 8.8**

Business Software Applications

Software applications have been developed to satisfy almost every business need. Here's a quick review of their features.

versions of traditional bulletin boards that allow users to exchange ideas, news, and other information; file transfer software enables the transfer of digital files—including data, programs, text, images, sounds, and videos—from one computer to another; and EDI systems permit computers to communicate with each other to handle transactions that used to require human intervention.[24] Computers can also send and receive faxes as easily as a fax machine if they have the right software and hardware. Furthermore, computers enable people in different locations to communicate face-to-face through videoconferencing and other telecommunication devices. In fact, new developments in communications software and computer languages promise even more exciting possibilities.

For years, programmers all over the world have been quietly developing XML, short for Extensible Markup Language. Simply put, XML provides a standard way for computer applications and Web sites to understand each other and pass data—such as text, spreadsheet numbers, pricing lists, employee records, and so on—back and forth.[25] Today, to check your finances on the Internet, you use your PC to access the Web site of each financial institution you do business with. But with XML and any kind of digital device, in the future you will soon be able to ask a single "Web service" to give you a composite picture by combining the information from multiple Web sites. With a few keystrokes, you might even be able to transfer money from your Schwab account to your Chase checking account. Moreover, users will be able to excerpt text or numerical tables directly from a Web page, paste them into a word-processing or spreadsheet application on a PC, and then edit or annotate the text or manipulate the numbers. (In the past, when using the cut-and-paste feature on a Web site, text lost its formatting and spreadsheets become impossible to manipulate.)[26]

## TELECOMMUNICATIONS AND COMPUTER NETWORKS

It used to be that each piece of equipment in an office was self-contained. Even in the early years of business computing, the computer was used for word and data processing, the fax machine was used for transmitting data, the telephone was a device for communicating verbally, and the pager was for contacting people when they weren't near a telephone. Similarly, at home the computer, the television, the radio, and the telephone were all separate appliances that served individual purposes. However, all of these distinctions are now becoming blurred, thanks to advances in telecommunications and computer technology.

This linking of computers and communication devices is creating new opportunities for companies to accomplish their goals more efficiently and more effectively. For one thing, businesspeople can now easily stay in touch with their offices, their computers, their associates, and their families while they travel the world. It is also much easier for workers in remote locations to share work, ideas, and resources. What makes all of this possible are complex networks of linked computers and communication devices such as those manufactured by Cisco.

### Types of Networks

The brief discussion of communications earlier in this chapter hinted at one of the most important issues in business computing: connecting multiple computers in one way or another and allowing them to exchange data, a process known as **data communications.** Data communications systems connect users to all sorts of information both inside and outside the organization, as well as to expensive resources such as supercomputers and high-speed laser printers. However, computers are not limited to data communications only; audio and video communications between computers are also becoming increasingly common. How do they do it? Through networks.

As defined in Component Chapter A, a *network* is a collection of hardware, software, and communications media that are linked so they can share data and expensive hardware. Networks are classified by the size of their geographic area. In a **wide area network (WAN),** computers at different geographic locations are linked through one of several transmission media. In contrast, a **local area network (LAN),** as its name implies, meets data communications needs within a small area, such as an office or a university campus. As we discussed in Component Chapter A, intranets are wide area private corporate networks that allow employees to communicate with each other quickly, regardless of their location.

In the past, computer networks were highly centralized, usually consisting of a number of terminals connected to a mainframe host. However, the affordability and power of today's microcomputers has led to the emergence of client/server networks as the new standard. In a **client/server system,** a server computer—which can be anything from a microcomputer to a supercomputer—performs certain functions for its clients, such as data and applications software storage. The client computer, which is typically a microcomputer or workstation, relies on the server for processing support, but it also runs certain applications and performs certain functions on its own. By sharing processing duties, the client and server optimize application efficiency. For example, the server might store and maintain a centralized corporate database. Using *front-end software,* the client user downloads part of the database from the server to the client. The user can then process the data on the client computer without burdening the server. When finished, the user uploads the processed data to the server's *back-end software* for processing and storage.

### Network Hardware

Any computer can be part of a network, provided it has the right hardware, software, and transmission media. To communicate over standard telephone lines, a computer must be equipped with a **modem** (modulator-demodulator), which can be either a stand-alone unit or a circuit board that is plugged into the computer. The transmitting computer's modem converts digital computer signals to analog signals so that they can be transmitted over telephone lines. The receiving computer's modem converts the signals from analog back to digital. Modems are always required for data transmission via telephone lines, but are not necessarily required for other transmission media. For instance, some Internet-ready digital phones, pagers, computers, and other wireless communication devices transmit digital information over networks through antennas, satellites, cables, and special phone lines.[27]

In addition to modems, networks may depend on several other components to keep the network running smoothly. Front-end processors, multiplexers, and routers all work behind the scenes to help the network operate efficiently, and to enable different networks to communicate with each other. Exhibit 8.9 explains the role that each of these components plays in a network.

### Network Transmission Media

When people speak of a computer as being "online," they mean that it is part of a network. The "lines" that link the computers in the network may actually be one of several different transmission media. Currently the most common medium is telephone lines. These lines consist of two insulated copper wires bundled in pairs. Because virtually all homes and businesses in the United States are wired for telephones, these lines have been the natural choice for wide area networks and the Internet.

**CABLE** The speed at which standard telephone lines can transmit data is limited. Therefore, many LANs use *coaxial cable* to achieve high-speed data transmission. Coaxial cable is the same type of wire used to bring cable channels to your television. Many cable television companies now offer Internet access over their coaxial lines, which requires using a specially designed *cable modem.*[28]

Standard telephone lines and coaxial cable transmit data as electrical signals. In contrast, **fiber optic cable** transmits data as laser-generated pulses of light at incredibly fast speeds. Transmitted data is measured in bits; a standard phone line can transmit up to 56,000 bits per second. However, researchers at Lucent Bell Labs recently transmitted 3.28 terabits per second of data over a 180-mile stretch of fiber optic cable—that's roughly 20 million times faster than the speed of today's phone lines. Put differently, a 3.28 terabit capacity would be capable of moving three times today's global Internet traffic every second.[29]

Fiber optic cable now links the major countries and cities of the world for both voice and data transmission. However, because of the high cost involved, it will probably be quite a while before homes and businesses are linked by a universal fiber optic network. Instead, telephone companies are developing technologies to increase the data transmission capacity, or **bandwidth**, of common telephone lines.

**WIRELESS COMMUNICATION** Wireless communication offers an alternative to standard telephone, coaxial, and fiber optic lines. Just as humans can now communicate without wires via cellular telephones and pagers, so can computers send and receive data without being "hardwired" to a network. This feat is accomplished by transmitting data as microwave signals or radio signals to the receiving computer via stations located on mountains, towers, or tall buildings or by satellites orbiting the earth. **Wireless transceivers** are small devices attached to the computer that transmit and receive data. The mobility offered by this configuration is ideal for many applications.

At Wal-Mart Stores, for example, customers no longer pace the aisles while an employee checks whether an item missing from the shelf is available. With a few keystrokes on a wireless handheld computer, employees can find out on the spot whether merchandise is in the stockroom or at a nearby store. Similarly, handheld wireless computers do double duty as order pads and cash registers at some restaurants. Orders can be transmitted and credit cards electronically billed, right at tables.[30]

Wireless technology is also changing the traditional office setup. At Postnet, the Swedish postal service's Internet subsidiary, for example, wireless technology is a part of the company's culture. There are no desks at Postnet, just tables with electrical and data-connection cables. Few people work at the same table from one day to the next. Most simply pick any free table, plug in a laptop, and get down to business. "When people go home, the only thing left on the table is cables," says Lisbeth Gustafsson, Postnet's CEO. Gustafsson spends most of her day walking around the office

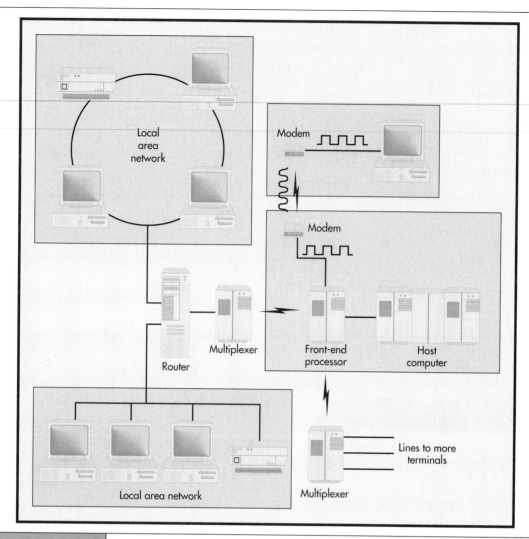

## EXHIBIT 8.9

Hardware Components in Computer Networks

Computer networks often rely on several hardware components to help them transmit data more efficiently. The *front-end processor* establishes a link between the source of the transmission and the destination, thereby freeing up the host to take care of other processing duties. The *multiplexer's* job is to gather data from several low-speed devices, such as terminals and printers, and concentrate it for transmission over a single communications channel, saving both time and expense. *Routers* link networks that use different operating systems and communications protocols. When a message is sent from a computer in one network to a computer in an incompatible network, the router converts the message to the necessary protocol and routes it to its final destination.

carrying her mobile phone, which is connected to the company's main switchboard. "If I had a fixed phone, I would have to be in a fixed place, and that's not part of our concept. The concept here is mobility." And it's a concept that promises to change the way people shop, work, and go about their daily lives.[31]

## active exercise

**Take a moment to apply what you've learned.**

An employee at the Electronic Boutique in Schaumburg, Illinois, scans a shopper's selections, charges his card, and prints a receipt using a portable check-out station.

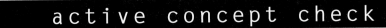

## > active concept check

Now let's take a moment to test your knowledge of the concepts you have studied in this section.

### > Technology Issues Affecting Today's Workplace

Computers are machines, and most machines can be used either well or poorly. Just as automobiles are both convenient and dangerous, computers can be both a help and a hindrance. A computer can greatly improve an employee's productivity, but it can also create new ways for employees to shirk responsibility, such as playing computer games and surfing the Internet. Computers can be a terrific source of customer information, but if put in the hands of a wrongdoer, serious damage can be inflicted on a person's privacy or on a company's ability to operate. As you can imagine, the use of technology in the workplace is continually challenged with a variety of issues.

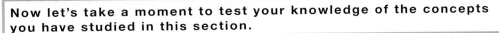

## > active exercise

Take a moment to apply what you've learned.

### DATA SECURITY

Before computers, a typical company conducted the vast majority of its business on paper. Important files and documents were kept under lock and key, and when something was sent to someone across the office or in another part of the country, security precautions were almost always used. Furthermore, only a limited number of people had access to vital company data. But today's move from paper-based systems to electronic data management poses a real threat to corporate security.[32]

Global networks increase the possibility that crucial information sent over an intranet or the Internet can fall into the wrong hands. Of course, cyberterrorism—orchestrated attacks on a company's information systems for political or economic purposes—is a very real threat. But an even greater security threat is a network without proper safeguards. Vulnerable networks can become a high-tech sieve that lets crooks steal or destroy sensitive data. That's because digital data are far easier to duplicate and disseminate. Furthermore, a PC without the proper password protections can easily become a fountain of insider information.

For these reasons, experts advise companies to install proper security systems and take these security measures: (1) Provide ongoing security education; (2) conduct background checks on all new employees; and (3) maintain clearly defined security policies that at a minimum encourage employees to use passwords, turn computer systems off when not in use, and rely on encryption when sending sensitive e-mail. Taking these measures, will of course, deter potential offenders, but it will not guarantee the security of your information. Systems protected by some of the world's foremost computer engineers can be vulnerable to attack, a lesson Microsoft learned after hackers broke into the company's computer network and viewed confidential data.[33]

### INFORMATION PRIVACY

Information privacy in today's workplace is another hot issue. Employers must find the right balance between protecting valuable company information and respecting employees' privacy rights. For instance, many employees erroneously believe that their e-mail and voice mail messages are private, and they're surprised when e-mail ends up in places they did not intend it to go. But employers have the legal right to monitor everything from an employee's Web access to the content of their company e-mail or voice mail messages. According to a survey by the American Management Association, about 35 percent of major U.S. companies keep tabs on workers by recording phone calls or voice mail and by checking employees' computer files and e-mail.[34] Moreover, both e-mail and voice mail can be used as evidence in court cases.[35] Therefore, a good rule of thumb is not to say anything in e-mail or voice mail that you would not want to see published in a newspaper.

### EMPLOYEE PRODUCTIVITY

Maintaining a high level of employee productivity is another challenge companies are facing. E-mail, voice mail, conference calls, and faxes interrupt employees while they work. Chat or real-time conversation windows can pop up on computer screens and demand immediate conversation. And the percentage of employees who use company resources for personal business is astounding (see Exhibit 8.10). Sending personal e-mail and faxes and surfing the Net are the three most common employee abuses.[36] Still, it's hard to be productive if you can't use the Internet when you need it, so restricting employees' access may be counterproductive.

### SABOTAGE AND THEFT

Today, criminals are doing everything from stealing intellectual property and committing fraud to committing pranks or, worse yet, acts of cyberterrorism in which political groups or unfriendly governments nab crucial information. For all the sophisticated work on firewalls, intrusion-detection systems, encryption, and computer security, it takes a relatively simple technique (like dialing a telephone number repeatedly) to tie up some of the biggest e-commerce sites. EBay, Yahoo!, Amazon.com, CNN, and others discovered this fact the hard way when traffic to their sites was virtually choked off in February 2000 by a prankster. It was a huge wake-up call for businesses as they realized that they need to spend as much time protecting their Web sites and networks as they do linking them with customers, suppliers, and contractors.[37]

Computer viruses, hidden programs that can work their way into computer systems and erase or corrupt data and programs, are the most common form of computer sabotage. Computer viruses behave much like human viruses by invisibly attaching themselves to computer data and programs that come into contact with them. They can be spread by diskettes, electronic bulletin boards, or computer networks, including the Internet. The "love bug" virus, which shut down the e-mail systems of the Pentagon, Congress, Ford Motor, British Parliament, the Danish government, and thousands of others in May 2000, was spread via e-mail. The virus originated in Asia and swept across Europe and throughout North and South America as quickly as the morning sun moved around the globe.[38]

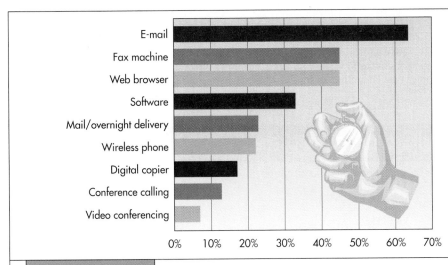

Percentage of Employees Who Use Office Resources for Personal Business

Everyone's doing it: Photocopying tax returns on the office copier, faxing a loan application, slipping personal mail into an overnight delivery envelope. According to a recent Ziff Davis survey, the Net is still the top company resource most workers use for personal business.

There is no way to entirely stop the spread of computer viruses, as new ones are created all the time. However, a number of excellent "vaccine" software programs exist that search for and destroy viruses and prevent new ones from infecting your computer system. You can reduce the chances of your system becoming infected by using such software to periodically scan your hardware and software for viruses and by being very cautious about what programs and files you load onto your hard drive.

Regardless of the type of sabotage, the FBI now estimates that reported computer losses add up to $10 billion a year, and the biggest threat comes from within. Up to 60 percent of computer break-ins are from employees. Still, most attacks go unreported because corporate victims want to avoid bad publicity.[39] And the situation could get worse. The United States will soon be awash in Web-browsing televisions, networked game consoles, smart refrigerators, and all kinds of wireless telecommunication devices—all of which have powerful processors, all of which are connected to the Net, and all of which are vulnerable to attacks.

> active poll

What do you think? Voice your opinion and find out what others have to say.

> active concept check

Now let's take a moment to test your knowledge of the concepts you have studied in this section.

Now that you've reached the end of the chapter, you may wish to explore the concepts you've been reading about in greater detail, or test yourself to see how well you've comprehended the material. In the box below you'll find a number of links. Click on any one of these links to find additional chapter resources.

## > end-of-chapter resources

- **Summary of Learning Objectives**
- **Practice Quiz**
- **Key Terms**
- **Test Your Knowledge**
- **Practice Your Knowledge**
- **Expand Your Knowledge**
- **A Case for Critical Thinking**

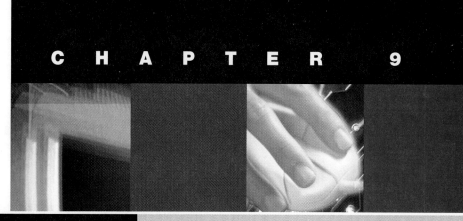

# Production of Quality Goods and Services

## C H A P T E R  9

 **What's Ahead**

### INSIDE BUSINESS TODAY
### SWEET SUCCESS: PRODUCING PERFECT KRISPY KREME DOUGHNUTS

Take one bite of a Krispy Kreme doughnut, and you'll understand why people have been buying them by the dozen for more than 60 years. They're doughnuts to die for—sinfully sweet with a delicate sugar glaze and a light, airy melt-in-your-mouth taste that keeps customers coming back for more. In fact, people in the United States treat themselves to more than 3 million Krispy Kreme doughnuts each day, buying more than 11,000 *dozen* of those tasty confections every hour. And the Krispy Kreme Company makes sure that every doughnut meets the high standards of taste and quality that its customers have come to expect.

More than 150 Krispy Kreme stores across the country produce and sell about 20 different types of doughnuts, ranging from dunking sticks to the popular glazed variety. Stores feature glass walls that allow customers to view the automated doughnut-making process in action. Between mixing the dough with water and sugar-glazing the finished product, the procedure for making Krispy Kreme doughnuts takes about an hour. But the manufacturing process begins long before stores in Arizona or Nebraska crank up their doughnut production lines. Every

With such a strong customer following, it's not uncommon to hear tales of driving several hours just to have a Krispy Kreme doughnut.

Krispy Kreme doughnut starts from a special mix created at the company's headquarters in Winston-Salem, North Carolina.

Whether you're indulging in a doughnut in New York or California, Krispy Kreme wants you to enjoy the same delicious taste with every bite. So the company maintains consistent product quality by carefully controlling each step of the production process. First, Krispy Kreme tests all raw ingredients—such as shortening, sugars, and flours—against established quality standards. For instance, every delivery of wheat flour is sampled and measured for such characteristics as moisture content and protein levels. If a sample from a 25-ton delivery fails to meet Krispy Kreme's quality standards, the entire delivery is rejected.

After blending the approved ingredients, the company seasons the mix in its warehouse for at least a week. Then Krispy Kreme tests the doughnut mix for quality. Technicians in the company's test kitchen make doughnuts from every 2,500-pound batch of mix to make sure that all ingredients have been blended correctly. Since the characteristics of the flour produced from different crops of wheat may require adjustments in the mixing time or the amount of water added to the dough mix, the technicians note such differences and pass the information along to the stores.

But it takes more than a quality mix to produce perfect Krispy Kreme doughnuts all the time. To ensure consistent quality, Krispy Kreme supplies its stores with everything they need to produce premium doughnuts. The company produces all of its own icings and fillings, shipping the goods by truck from its North Carolina warehouse to stores across the country. Krispy Kreme even makes the production machinery and equipment for its retail sites, following the tradition established by founder Vernon Rudolph, who invented and built the world's first doughnut-making equipment. Today, the company continues to craft everything from conveyors to fryers in its own metal shop. These high standards of product quality have created sweet success for Krispy Kreme. With a loyal customer base that extends far beyond the company's Southern roots, Krispy Kreme sells more than $238 million of doughnuts every year.[1]

**>** objectives

Take a moment to familiarize yourself with the key objectives of this chapter.

**>** gearing up

Before you begin reading this chapter, try a short warm-up activity.

## > Understanding Production and Operations Management

As managers of Krispy Kreme know, the extremely competitive nature of the global business environment requires companies to produce high-quality goods and services in the most efficient way possible. Few defects, fast production, low costs, excellent customer service, broad market reach, innovative products and processes, less waste, and high flexibility are all objectives that improve quality by adding value to the good or service being produced. Companies pursue these objectives to maintain a competitive advantage.[2] Moreover, managers understand that the level of quality that a company aspires to in the production of goods and services affects its long-term ability to address the needs of its customers.

### WHAT IS PRODUCTION?

What exactly is production and what does it involve? To many people, the term *production* suggests images of factories, machines, and assembly lines staffed with employees making automobiles, computers, furniture, Krispy Kreme doughnuts, or other tangible goods. That's because in the past people used the terms *production* and *manufacturing* interchangeably. With the growth in the number of service-based businesses and their increasing importance to the economy, however, the term **production** is now used to describe the transformation of resources into goods and services that people need or want. The broader term **production and operations management (POM),** or simply *operations management,* refers to all the activities involved in producing a firm's goods and services.

Like other types of management, POM involves the basic functions of planning, organizing, leading, and controlling. It also requires careful consideration of a company's goals, the strategies for attaining those goals, and the standards against which results will be measured. In both manufacturing and service organizations, the production and operations manager is the person responsible for performing these functions. One of the principal responsibilities of the production and operations manager is to design and oversee an efficient conversion process—one which lowers costs by optimizing output from each resource used in the process. These resources include money, materials, inventories, people, buildings, and time.

### WHAT IS THE CONVERSION PROCESS?

At the core of production is the *conversion process,* the sequence of events that convert resources (or inputs) into products and services. This process applies to both intangible services and tangible goods. For an airline to serve its customers, for example, it transforms tangible and intangible inputs such as the plane, pilot's skill, fuel, time, and passengers through processes such as booking flights, flying airplanes, maintaining equipment, and training crews. The output of this process is the arrival of customers at their destinations. For a clothing manufacturer to produce a jacket, inputs such as cloth, thread, and buttons are transformed by the seamstress into the finished product (see Exhibit 9.1).

Conversion is of two basic types. An **analytic system** breaks raw materials into one or more distinct products, which may or may not resemble the original material in form and function. In meatpacking, for example, a steer is divided into hide, bone, steaks, and so on. A **synthetic system** combines two or more materials to form a single product. For example, in steel manufacturing, iron is combined with small quantities of other minerals at high temperatures to make steel.

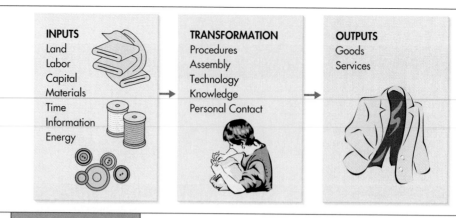

The Conversion Process

Production of goods or services is basically a process of conversion. Inputs (the basic ingredients) are transformed (by the application of labor, equipment, and capital) into outputs (the desired product or service).

| System | Inputs | Transformation Components | Transformation Function | Typical Desired Output |
|---|---|---|---|---|
| Hospital | Patients, medical supplies | Physicians, nurses, equipment | Health care | Healthy individuals |
| Restaurant | Hungry customers, food | Chef, waitress, environment | Well-prepared and well-served food | Satisfied customers |
| Automobile factory | Sheet steel, engine parts | Tools, equipment, workers | Fabrication and assembly of cars | High-quality cars |
| College or university | High school graduates, books | Teachers, classrooms | Impart knowledge and skills | Educated individuals |
| Department store | Shoppers, stock of goods | Displays, salesclerks | Attract shoppers, promote products, fill orders | Sales to satisfied customers |

EXHIBIT 9.2

Input-Transformation-Output Relationships for Typical Systems

Both goods and services undergo a conversion process, but the components of the process vary to accommodate the differences between tangible and intangible outputs.

Another thing to keep in mind is that the conversion process for a service operation and goods-production operation is similar in terms of *what* is done—that is, inputs are transformed into outputs. But the two differ in how the processes are performed (see Exhibit 9.2). That's because the production of goods results in a tangible output—something you can see or touch, such as a jacket, doughnut, desk, or bicycle—and the production of a service results in an intangible act. As such, the production of services involves a much higher degree of customer contact, is subject to greater variability, is more labor intensive, and results in a lower uniformity of output than the production of goods.

active exercise   <

Take a moment to apply what you've learned.

## MASS PRODUCTION VERSUS MASS CUSTOMIZATION

**Mass production**—manufacturing goods in large quantities—means little or no customization. Because of the high volume of similar goods produced, this process reduces production costs per unit and makes products available to more people. Even though mass production has economic advantages, the competitive pressures of the global economy often require production techniques that are flexible, customer-focused, and quality-oriented.

Consider Andersen Windows. Throughout most of its long history, Andersen mass-produced a range of standard windows in large batches. However, in the early 1990s customer demands and an increasing error rate caused Andersen to rethink the way it built windows. To better meet customer needs, the company developed an interactive computer catalog that allows customers to add, change, and remove features of Andersen's standard windows until they've designed the exact windows they want. Once the customers select their design, the computer automatically generates a price quote and sends the order to the factory, where standardized parts are tailored to customer specifications. Today the company offers close to 200,000 different products that are virtually error-free. Andersen's current production system is known as **mass customization**—using mass production techniques to produce customized goods. The company also uses *batch-of-one manufacturing,* in which every product is made to order from scratch.[3] The basic idea behind mass customization is that consumers have individual needs and are best served by products that can be easily customized for them.

Like Andersen Windows, many companies are adopting manufacturing techniques that let them tailor goods to individuals on a large scale. The key to customizing on a mass scale is digital technology—a combination of hardware, software, and new machines that fine-tune the production process. Levi Strauss & Company and Brooks Brothers are among those offering machine-customized clothing, thanks to new technologies that handle single items on the assembly line, or take body measurements that are then zapped to a manufacturing plant through the Web. Nike has Nike ID, which allows customers to alter the color, design, and even the construction of their shoes. Meanwhile, Mattel is hawking "My Design" dolls, customized "friends" of Barbie with clothing, skin color, hair styles, and even personalities picked by each owner.[4]

> **active concept check**

**Now let's take a moment to test your knowledge of the concepts you have studied in this section.**

> ## Designing the Production Process

Designing an effective production process is one of the key responsibilities of production and operations managers. It involves five important tasks: forecasting demand, planning for capacity, choosing a facility location, designing a facility layout, and scheduling work.

### FORECASTING DEMAND

The first step in designing an effective production process for a manufacturing operation is to determine how much product the company will need to produce in a certain time span. Using customer feedback, market research, past sales figures, industry analyses, and educated guesses about the future behavior of the economy and competitors, operations managers prepare **production forecasts,** estimates of future demand for the company's products. These estimates are then used to plan, budget, and schedule the use of resources. Of course, many factors in the business environment cannot be predicted or controlled with certainty. For this reason, managers must regularly review and adjust their forecasts to account for these uncertainties.

Service companies must also forecast demand. For example, dentists must be able to project approximately how many patients they will treat in a given time period so they can staff their offices properly and have enough dental supplies on hand. Without such forecasts, dentists can't run their production process (treating patients) efficiently. Similarly, cruise ship operators must forecast exactly how much food and supplies to stock for one week's journey, because once the ship sets sail, there are no last-minute deliveries. On the basis of years of experience, operation managers for Carnival's Elation Cruise Line can now forecast that a one-week Caribbean cruise will require some 10,000 pounds of meat, 10,080 bananas, and 41,600 eggs.[5]

## PLANNING FOR CAPACITY

Once product demand has been estimated, management must determine the company's capacity to produce the goods or services. The term *capacity* refers to the volume of manufacturing or service capability that an organization can handle. For example, a doctor's office with only one examining room limits the number of patients the doctor can see each day. And a cruise ship with 750 staterooms limits the number of passengers that the ship can accommodate in any given week. Similarly, a beverage bottling plant with only one conveyor belt and one local warehouse limits the company's ability to manufacture beverage products.

**Capacity planning** is a long-term strategic decision that establishes the overall level of resources needed to meet customer demand. The neighborhood convenience store needs to consider traffic volume throughout the day and night in order to plan staffing levels appropriately. At the other extreme of complexity, when managers at Boeing plan for the production of an airliner, they have to consider not only the staffing of thousands of people but also factory floor space, material flows from hundreds of suppliers, internal deliveries, cash flow, tools and equipment, and dozens of other factors. Because of the potential impact on finances, customers, and employees, capacity planning involves some of the most difficult decisions that managers have to make.

Top management uses long-term capacity planning to make significant decisions about an organization's ability to produce goods and services, such as expanding existing facilities, constructing new facilities, or phasing out unneeded ones. Such decisions entail a great deal of risk, for two reasons: (1) large shifts in demand are difficult to predict accurately, and (2) long-term capacity decisions can be difficult to undo. For example, if a new facility is built to produce a new product that then fails, or if demand for a popular product suddenly declines, the company will find itself with expensive excess capacity. Managers must decide what they should do with this excess capacity. If they keep it, they might try to find an alternate use for this space. If they eliminate it and demand picks up again, the company will have to forgo profits because it is unable to meet customer demand.[6]

## video exercise  &lt;

### Take a moment to apply what you've learned.

## CHOOSING A FACILITY LOCATION

One long-term issue that management must resolve early when designing the production process for goods and services is the location of production facilities. The goal is to choose a location that minimizes costs while increasing operational efficiencies and product quality. To accomplish this goal, management must consider such regional costs as land, construction, labor, local taxes, energy, and local living standards. In addition, management must consider whether the local labor pool has the skills that the firm needs. For example, firms that need highly trained accountants, engineers, or computer scientists often locate in areas near university communities, such as Boston. On the other hand, if most of the jobs can be filled by unskilled or semiskilled employees, firms can choose locations where such labor is available at a relatively low cost. The search for low-cost labor has led many U.S. companies to locate their manufacturing operations in countries such as Mexico, Taiwan, and Indonesia, where wages are relatively lower. However, companies that fail to compensate foreign workers fairly are risking strong consumer backlash in the United States.

Also affecting location decisions are transportation costs, which cover the shipping of supplies and finished goods. Almost every company needs easy, low-cost access to ground transportation such as highways and rail lines. Moreover, companies that sell a lot of products overseas must be able to arrange for efficient air or water transportation. Finally, companies must consider raw materials costs. For example, the location of a coal-based power plant must be chosen to minimize the cost of distributing electrical power to customers and to minimize the cost and *lead time* of shipping coal to the plant.

Location considerations may be different for some service organizations. Although they may also take regional costs into consideration, the main objective for many service firms is to locate where profit potential is greatest. Unlike manufacturing operations, in which low production costs are an important consideration, services tend to focus on more customer-driven factors.[7] Because they often require one-on-one contact with customers, service organizations such as gas stations, restaurants, department stores, and charities must locate where their target market is large and sustainable. Therefore, market research often plays a central role in site selection. However, for service companies that reach customers primarily by telephone, mail, or the Internet, proximity to customers is less of a consideration.

## DESIGNING A FACILITY LAYOUT

Once a site has been selected, managers must turn their attention to *facility layout,* the arrangement of production work centers and other elements (such as materials, equipment, and support departments) needed to process goods and services. Layout includes the efforts involved in selecting specific locations for each department, process, machine, support function, and other activity required for the operation or service. The need for a new layout design can occur for a number of reasons besides new construction; for instance, a new process or method might become available, the volume of business might change, a new product or service may be offered, an outdated facility may be remodeled, the mix of goods or services offered may change, or an existing product or service may be redesigned.[8]

Facility layout affects the amount of on-hand inventory, the efficiency of materials handling, the utilization of equipment, and the productivity and morale of employees. In goods manufacturing, the primary concern is the efficient movement of resources and inventory. In the production of services, facility layout controls the flow of customers through the system and influences the customer's satisfaction with the service.[9] In both services and goods operations, the major goals of a good layout design are to minimize materials-handling costs, reduce bottlenecks in moving material or people, provide flexibility, provide ease of supervision, use available space effectively and efficiently, reduce hazards, and facilitate coordination and communications wherever appropriate.[10] Four typical facility layouts are the *process layout, product layout, cellular layout,* and *fixed-position layout* (see Exhibit 9.3).[11]

A **process layout** is also called a *functional layout* because it concentrates everything needed to complete one phase of the production process in one place. Specific functions, such as drilling or welding, are performed in one location for different products or customers (see Exhibit 9.3A). The process layout is often used in machine shops as well as in service industries. For example, a medical clinic might dedicate one room to X-rays, another room to routine examinations, and still another to outpatient surgery.

An alternative to the process layout is the **product layout,** also called the assembly-line layout, in which the main production process occurs along a line, and products in progress move from one workstation to the next. Materials and subassemblies of component parts may feed into the main line at several points, but the flow of production is continuous. Electronics and personal-computer manufacturers are just two of many industries that typically use this layout (see Exhibit 9.3B).

Some production of services is also organized by product. For example, when you go to your local department of motor vehicles to get a driver's license, you usually go through a series of steps administered by several people: registering, taking a written or computerized test, having an eye exam, paying a cashier, and getting your picture taken. You emerge from this system a licensed driver (unless, of course, you fail one of the tests).

A **cellular layout** groups dissimilar machines into work centers (or cells) to process parts that have similar shapes and processing requirements (see Exhibit 9.3C). Arranging work flow by cells can improve the efficiency of a process layout while maintaining its flexibility. At the same time, grouping smaller numbers of workers in cells facilitates teamwork and joint problem solving. Employees are also able to work on a product from start to finish, and they can move between machines within their cells, thus increasing the flexibility of the team. Cellular layouts are commonly used in computer chip manufacture and metal fabricating.[12]

Finally, the **fixed-position layout** is a facility layout in which labor, materials, and equipment are brought to the location where the good is being produced or the customer is being served. Buildings, roads, bridges, airplanes, and ships are examples of the types of large products that are typically constructed using a fixed-position layout (see Exhibit 9.3D). Service companies also use fixed-position layouts; for example, a plumber goes to a job site bringing the tools, material, and expertise needed to repair a broken pipe.

**Routing** is the task of specifying the sequence of operations and the path through the facility that the work will take. The way production is routed depends on the type of product and the layout of the plant. A table-manufacturing company, for instance, uses a process layout because it has three departments, each handling a different phase of the table's manufacture and each equipped with specialized tools, machines, and employees. Department 1 cuts wood into tabletops and legs. These pieces are then sent to department 2, where holes are drilled and rough finishing is done. Finally, the individual pieces are routed to department 3, where the tables are assembled and painted.

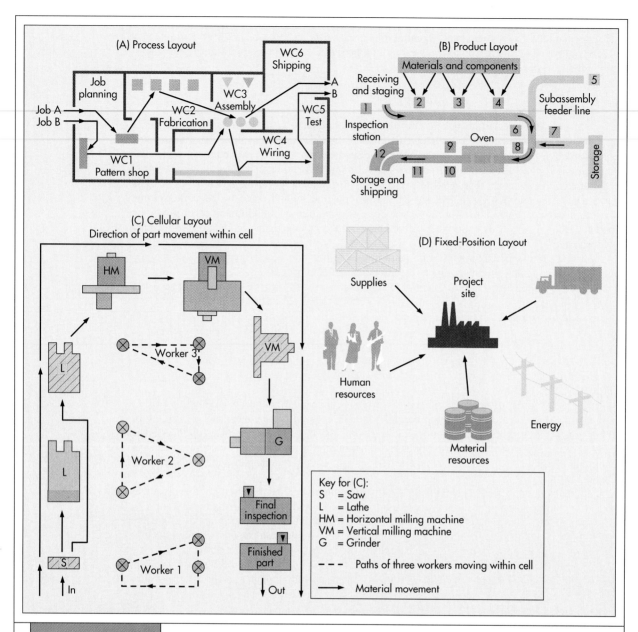

EXHIBIT 9.3

Types of Facility Layouts

Facility layout is often determined by the type of product an organization is producing.

(A) Process layout: Typically, a process layout is used for an organization producing made-to-order products. A process layout is arranged according to the specialized employees and materials involved in various phases of the production process.

(B) Product layout: A product layout is used when an organization is producing large quantities of just a few products. In a product or assembly-line layout, the developing product moves in a continuous sequence from one workstation to the next.

(C) Cellular layout: A cellular layout works well in organizations that practice mass customization. In a cellular layout, parts with similar shapes or processing requirements are processed together in work centers, an arrangement that facilitates teamwork and flexibility.

(D) Fixed-position layout: A fixed-position layout requires employees and materials to be brought to the product and is used when the product is too large to move.

## SCHEDULING WORK

In any production process, managers must use **scheduling**—determining how long each operation takes and setting a starting and ending time for each. A master schedule, often called a *master production schedule (MPS)*, is a schedule of planned completion of items. In services such as a doctor's office, the appointment book serves as the master schedule.

When a job has relatively few activities and relationships, many production managers keep the process on schedule with a **Gantt chart.** Developed by Henry L. Gantt in the early 1900s, the Gantt chart is a bar chart showing the amount of time required to accomplish each part of a process. It allows managers to see at a glance whether the process is in line with the schedule they had planned (see Exhibit 9.4).

For more complex jobs, the **program evaluation and review technique (PERT)** is helpful. It is a planning tool that helps managers identify the optimal sequencing of activities, the expected time for project completion, and the best use of resources within a complex project. To use PERT, the manager must (1) identify the activities to be performed, (2) determine the sequence of activities, (3) establish the time needed to complete each activity, (4) diagram the network of activities, (5) calculate the longest path through the network that leads to project completion, and (6) refine the network's timing or use of resources as activities are completed. The longest path through the network is known as the **critical path** because it represents the minimum amount of time needed to complete the project.

In place of a single time projection for each task, PERT uses four figures: an *optimistic* estimate (if things go well), a *pessimistic* estimate (if they don't go well), a *most likely* estimate (how long the task usually takes), and an *expected* time estimate, an average of the other three estimates.[13] The expected time is used to diagram the network of activities and determine the length of the critical path.

Consider the manufacture of shoes in Exhibit 9.5. At the beginning of the process, three paths deal with heels, soles, and tops. All three processes must be finished before the next phase (sewing tops to soles and heels) can be started. However, one of the three paths—the tops—takes 33 days, whereas the other two take only 18 and 12 days. The shoe tops, then, are on the critical path because they will delay the entire operation if they fall behind schedule. In contrast, soles can be started up to 21 days after starting the tops without slowing down production. This free time in the soles schedule is called *slack time* because managers can choose to produce the soles anytime during the 33-day period required by the tops.

Included in the scheduling process is the **dispatching** function, or the issuing of work orders to department supervisors. These orders specify the work to be done and the schedule for its completion. Work orders also inform department supervisors of their operational priorities and the schedule they must maintain.

| ID | Task Name | Start Date | End Date | Duration | 2001 |
|----|-----------|-----------|----------|----------|------|
| 1 | Make legs | 8/1/01 | 8/28/01 | 20d | |
| 2 | Cut tops | 8/22/01 | 8/28/01 | 5d | |
| 3 | Drill | 8/29/01 | 9/4/01 | 5d | |
| 4 | Sand | 9/5/01 | 9/11/01 | 5d | |
| 5 | Assemble | 9/12/01 | 9/25/01 | 10d | |
| 6 | Paint | 9/19/01 | 9/25/01 | 5d | |

**EXHIBIT 9.4**

A Gantt Chart

A chart like this one enables a production manager to see immediately the dates on which production steps must be started and completed if goods are to be delivered on schedule. Some steps may overlap to save time. For instance, after three weeks of cutting table legs, cutting tabletops begins. This overlap ensures that the necessary legs and tops are completed at the same time and can move on together to the next stage in the manufacturing process.

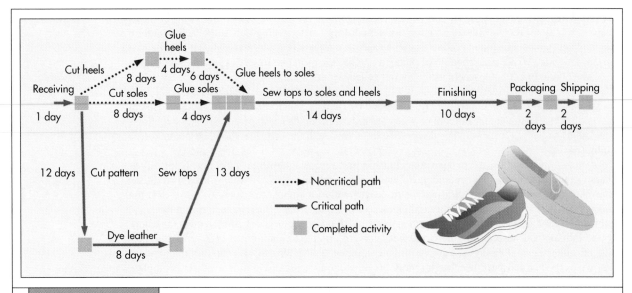

**EXHIBIT 9.5**

PERT Diagram for Manufacturing Shoes

In the manufacture of shoes, the critical path involves receiving, cutting the pattern, dyeing the leather, sewing the tops, sewing the tops to soles and heels, finishing, packaging, and shipping—a total of 61 days.

Of course, once the schedule has been set and the orders dispatched, a production manager cannot just sit back and assume that the work will get done correctly and on time. Even the best scheduler may misjudge the time needed to complete an operation, and production may be delayed by accidents, mechanical breakdowns, or supplier problems. Therefore, the production manager needs a system for handling delays and preventing a minor disruption from growing into chaos. A successful system is based on good communication between the employees and the production manager.

Suppose a machine breakdown causes department 2 of a manufacturing company to lose half a day of drilling time. If the schedule is not altered to direct other work to department 3 (the next department), the employees and equipment in department 3 will sit idle for some time. However, if department 2 informs the production manager of its machine problem right away, the production manager can immediately reschedule some fill-in work for department 3.

**active exercise** **<**

Take a moment to apply what you've learned.

**active concept check** **<**

Now let's take a moment to test your knowledge of the concepts you have studied in this section.

Today more and more companies are taking advantage of new production technologies to improve their efficiency and productivity. Alliant Food Services, for example, ships about 1 million cases of food and supplies daily. Historically, the shipping process was fraught with errors. But by using the Internet and wireless technology, the company has reduced shipping errors by more than 60 percent.[14]

Two of the most visible advances in production technology are computers and **robots**—programmable machines that work with tools and materials to perform various tasks. Although industrial robots may seem exotic, like some science fiction creation, they are quite common and are really nothing more than smart tools. Industrial robots can easily perform precision functions as well as repetitive, strenuous, or hazardous tasks.[15] When equipped with machine vision, or electronic eyes, robots can place doors on cars in precise locations, cull blemished vegetables from frozen-food processing lines, check the wings of aircraft for dangerous ice buildup, make sure that drug capsules of the right color go into the correct packages before they are shipped to pharmacies, and even assist with surgery.[16]

In addition to robots, other major developments in manufacturing automation include computer-aided design and engineering, computer-aided manufacturing, computer-integrated manufacturing, flexible manufacturing systems, and electronic information systems. Let's look a little closer at each of these.

### COMPUTER-AIDED DESIGN AND COMPUTER-AIDED ENGINEERING

Widely used today is **computer-aided design (CAD),** the application of computer graphics and mathematical modeling to the design of products. A related process is **computer-aided engineering (CAE),** in which engineers use computer-generated three-dimensional images and computerized calculations to test products. With CAE, engineers can subject proposed products to changing temperatures, various stresses, and even simulated accidents without ever building preliminary models. Moreover, the *virtual reality* capability of today's computers allows designers to see how finished products will look and operate before physical prototypes are built.

Using computers to aid design and engineering saves time and money because revising computer designs is much faster than revising hand-drafted designs and building physical models. In fact, computer technology allows companies to perfect a product or abandon a bad idea before production even begins. The result is better overall product quality. For example, when Boeing engineers designed the 777 airplane, they corrected problems and tried out new ideas entirely on their computer screens. Digitally preassembling the 3 million parts of the 777 allowed Boeing to exceed its goals for reducing errors, changes, and rework.[17]

### COMPUTER-AIDED MANUFACTURING AND COMPUTER-INTEGRATED MANUFACTURING

The use of computers to control production equipment is called **computer-aided manufacturing (CAM).** In a CAD/CAM system, computer-aided design data are converted automatically into processing instructions for production equipment to manufacture the part or product. This integration of design and production can increase the output, speed, and precision of assembly lines, as well as make customized production much easier.[18] In addition, the latest CAD/CAM software allows company departments to share designs and data over intranets and the Internet, enabling geographically dispersed departments to work together on complex projects.[19] For example, Ford uses a CAD/CAM/CAE system it calls C3P to develop new vehicle prototypes. Whereas it once took two to three months to build, assemble, and test a car chassis prototype, with C3P the entire process can now be completed in less than two weeks. Although the program is still quite new, Ford expects it to improve engineering efficiency by 35 percent and reduce prototype costs by up to 40 percent.[20]

The highest level of computerization in operations management is **computer-integrated manufacturing (CIM),** in which all the elements of production—design, engineering, testing, production, inspection, and materials handling—are integrated into one automated system. Computer-integrated manufacturing is not a specific technology but rather a strategy that uses technology for organizing and controlling a factory. Its role is to link the people, machines, databases, and decisions involved in each step of producing a good.[21]

> **active exercise**

**Take a moment to apply what you've learned.**

## FLEXIBLE MANUFACTURING SYSTEMS

Advances in design technology have been accompanied by changes in the way the production process is organized. Traditional automated manufacturing equipment is *fixed* or *hard-wired,* meaning it is capable of handling only one specific task. Although fixed automation is efficient when one type or model of good is mass produced, a change in product design requires extensive equipment changes. Such adjustments may involve high **setup costs,** the expenses incurred each time a manufacturer begins a production run of a different type of item. In addition, the initial investment for fixed automation equipment is high because specialized equipment is required for each of the operations involved in making a single item. Only after much production on a massive scale can a company recoup the cost of that specialized equipment.

An alternative to a fixed manufacturing system is a **flexible manufacturing system (FMS).** Such systems link numerous programmable machine tools by an automated materials-handling system of conveyors known as automatic guided vehicles (AGVs). These driverless computer-controlled vehicles move materials from any location on the factory floor to any other location. Changing from one product design to another requires only a few signals from a central computer. Each machine changes tools automatically, making appropriate selections from built-in storage carousels that can hold more than 100 tools. In addition, the sequence of events involved in building an item can be completely rearranged.[22] This flexibility saves both time and setup costs. Moreover, producers can outmaneuver less agile competitors by moving swiftly into profitable new fields. Flexible manufacturing also allows producers to adapt their products quickly to changing customer needs.[23] Such systems are particularly suited for *job shops,* such as small machine shops, which make dissimilar items or produce at so irregular a rate that repetitive operations won't help.

As a $10 million manufacturer of precision metal parts, Cook Specialty is one small company able to compete with larger manufacturers through flexible manufacturing. Cook used to make only certain products, such as basketball hoops and display racks. However, the company has transformed its production facilities so that it is now capable of manufacturing custom-engineered medical instruments and precision parts for high-tech equipment. Technical innovations for these devices advance rapidly, but Cook is able to adapt its production facilities to keep up with the changes. In fact, almost one-third of the products Cook manufactures each year are new.[24]

## WISE USE OF TECHNOLOGY

Of course, none of the production technologies mentioned so far will increase profits unless the company designs products to fit customer needs. As Chapter 8 discussed, today, many companies recognized for their quality link themselves with their customers through information systems. These systems enable companies to respond immediately to customer issues, support rapid changes in customer needs, and offer "made-to-order" products. Moreover, information technology allows customers to track their products and obtain status reports throughout the production cycle. It can also promote better communication within the company, thereby improving the way a company designs, manufacturers, and delivers goods and services.

While the benefits of using technology in the manufacturing process are many, one of the worst mistakes a company can make is to automate a series of tasks without first examining the underlying process. If the basic process creates the wrong products or involves needless steps, nothing is gained by automating it without first cleaning it up. Otherwise a business runs the risk of simply doing the wrong things faster. Problems can also result from installing production technology without properly preparing the workforce to implement and use the technology.

TRW is a global manufacturing and service company that targets the automotive, space, and defense industries. TRW regularly and carefully checks its automated production systems to make sure it is improving the production process without wasting capital. One employee focuses full-time on auditing machines for output mistakes, developing strategies for error reduction, and training other employees. Rather than automating for speed, the company focuses its efforts on designing "mistake-proofing" technology into its equipment, ensuring that it uses technology to work smarter as well as faster.[25]

### active concept check

**Now let's take a moment to test your knowledge of the concepts you have studied in this section.**

During the production design phase, operations managers forecast demand, plan for capacity, choose facility locations, design facility layouts and configurations, and develop production schedules and sequences. Once the design of the production process has been completed, operations managers are responsible for managing and controlling these processes and systems. In this section, we will discuss two important management and control concepts: inventory management and quality assurance.

## INVENTORY MANAGEMENT

Forward-thinking companies have realized that maintaining a competitive advantage requires continuously seeking ways to reduce costs, increase manufacturing efficiency, and improve customer value. They know how wasteful it is to tie up large sums of money in **inventory**—the goods and materials kept in stock for production or sale. On the other hand, not having an adequate supply of inventory can delay production and result in unhappy customers. That's why more and more companies are changing the way they purchase and handle the materials they use to produce goods and services.

**Purchasing** is the acquisition of the raw materials, parts, components, supplies, and finished products required to produce goods and services. The goal of purchasing is to make sure that the company has all of the materials it needs, when it needs them, at the lowest possible cost. To accomplish this goal, a company must always have enough supplies on hand to cover a product's **lead time**—the period that elapses between placing the supply order and receiving materials.

In the past, companies would buy large enough supply inventories to make sure they would not run out of parts during peak production times. As soon as inventory levels dropped to a predetermined level, the purchasing department would order new parts. Many companies continue to operate this way, which does offer certain benefits. For example, companies typically get a better price when they buy inventory in bulk, and having a large supply on hand enables them to meet customer demand quickly. Unfortunately, carrying a large inventory also ties up the company's money and increases the risk that products will become obsolete.

To minimize this risk and cost, and to increase manufacturing efficiency, many companies establish a system of **inventory control**—some way of (1) determining the right quantities of supplies and products to have on hand and (2) tracking where those items are. Three methods that companies use to control inventory and manage the production process are *just-in-time systems, material requirements planning,* and *manufacturing resource planning.*

### Just-in-Time Systems

An increasingly popular method of managing operations, including inventory control and production planning, is the **just-in-time (JIT) system.** The goal of just-in-time systems is to have only the right amounts of materials arrive at precisely the times they are needed. Because supplies arrive just as they are needed, and no sooner, inventories are eliminated and waste is reduced.

The maintenance of a "zero inventory" under JIT does have some indirect benefits. For instance, reducing stocks of parts to practically nothing encourages factories to keep production flowing smoothly, from beginning to end, without any holdups. And a constant production flow requires good teamwork. On the other hand, JIT exposes a company to greater risks, as a disruption in the flow of raw materials from suppliers can slow or stop the production process. A JIT system also places a heavy burden on suppliers because they must be able to meet the production schedules of their customers. For instance, an increasingly strong demand for electronic and computer components at the beginning of the twenty-first century left many electronic equipment manufacturers battling one another for computer chips and other components. "Just-in-time has become just-in-trouble," says the chief financial officer of one electronics company.[26]

Thus, to be effective, JIT systems must be designed to include multifunctional teamwork, flexible manufacturing, small-batch production, strict production control, quick setups, consistent production levels, preventive maintenance, and reliable supplier networks. Furthermore, poor quality simply cannot be tolerated in a stockless manufacturing environment because one defective part can bring production to a grinding halt. In other words, JIT cannot be implemented without a commitment to total quality control.[27] When all of these factors work together in sync, the manufacturer achieves *lean production;* that is, it can do more with less.[28]

In those cases where it is difficult for manufacturers and suppliers to coordinate their schedules, JIT may not work. For example, shoemaker Allen-Edmonds cannot get its principal raw material whenever it wants because calfskin hides come on the market only at certain times each year.[29] Additional factors can also affect JIT: whether a product is seasonal or promotional or perishable; whether it has unusual handling characteristics; its size; its weight; and the volatility of the sales cycle.[30]

Keep in mind that JIT concepts can also be used to reduce inventory and cycle time for service organizations. Consider Koley's Medical Supply, which manages inventory for hospitals using what it calls "stockless distribution." Rather than making large, general deliveries to the stockroom, the company delivers specific items in just the right quantities to the various floors and rooms in the hospital. Doing so isn't always easy: At one hospital, Koley's has to make deliveries to 168 individual receiving points. But the system creates value for Koley's customers. For example, in Omaha, Nebraska, Bishop Clarkson Memorial Hospital reduced its annual inventory costs from $500,000 to just $7,000.

## active poll

**What do you think? Voice your opinion and find out what others have to say.**

### Material Requirements Planning (MRP)

**Material requirements planning (MRP)** is another inventory-control technique that helps a manufacturer get the correct materials where they are needed, when they are needed, and without unnecessary stockpiling. Managers use computer programs to calculate when certain materials will be required, when they should be ordered, and when they should be delivered so that storage costs will be minimal. These systems are so effective at reducing inventory levels that they are used almost universally in both large and small manufacturing firms.

A more automated form of material requirements planning is the **perpetual inventory** system, in which computers monitor inventory levels and automatically generate purchase orders when supplies fall below a certain level. The price scanners found at the checkout counters of many stores are part of perpetual inventory systems. Every time a product is purchased, the scanner deletes that particular item from the computer system's inventory data. When inventory of the product reaches a predetermined level, the system generates an order for more. Often the store's system is linked to the supplier's own computer system, which enables the order to be placed with virtually no human involvement.

### Manufacturing Resource Planning (MRP II)

The MRP systems on the market today are made up of various modules, including inventory control, purchasing, customer order entry, production planning, shop-floor control, and accounting. With the addition of more and more modules that focus on capacity planning, marketing, and finance, an MRP system evolves into a **manufacturing resource planning (MRP II)** system.

Because it draws together all departments, an MRP II system produces a companywide game plan that allows everyone to work with the same numbers (see Exhibit 9.6). Employees can now draw on data, such as inventory levels, back orders, and unpaid bills, once reserved for only top executives. Moreover, the system can track each step of production, allowing managers throughout the company to consult other managers' inventories, schedules, and plans. In addition, MRP II systems are capable of running simulations (models of possible operations systems) that enable managers to plan and test alternative strategies.[31] An extension of MRP II is **enterprise resource planning (ERP),** which expands the scope of the production planning process to include customer and supplier information. ERP is based on software developed by SAP AG, a German software company. Using this software and ERP, manufacturers can tap into huge databases of company information to improve production processes.

### QUALITY ASSURANCE

Besides maintaining optimal inventory levels, companies today must produce high-quality goods as efficiently as possible. In almost every industry you can name, this global challenge has caused companies to reexamine their definition of quality and reengineer their production processes. Still, adopting high quality standards is not an easy task, because the manufacture of complex goods is not simply a matter of adding part A to part B to part C and so forth until a product emerges ready to ship. For example, the Mercedes M-Class sport-utility vehicle is assembled from subunits built by 65 major suppliers and many other smaller ones.[32] Making sure that all the pieces are put together in the proper sequence and at the proper time requires large-scale planning and scheduling. The same is true for the production of complex services.

The traditional means of maintaining quality is called **quality control**—measuring quality against established standards after the good or service has been produced and weeding out any defects. A more comprehensive approach is **quality assurance,** a system of companywide policies, practices, and proce-

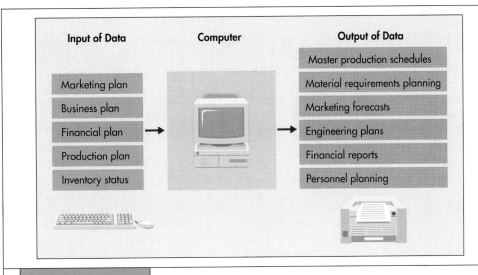

| Input of Data | Computer | Output of Data |
|---|---|---|
| Marketing plan | | Master production schedules |
| Business plan | | Material requirements planning |
| Financial plan | | Marketing forecasts |
| Production plan | | Engineering plans |
| Inventory status | | Financial reports |
| | | Personnel planning |

**EXHIBIT 9.6**

MRP II

An MRP II computer system gives managers and workers in every department easy access to data from all other departments, which in turn makes it easier to generate—and adhere to—the organization's overall plans, forecasts, and schedules.

dures to ensure that every product meets preset quality standards. Quality assurance includes quality control as well as doing the job right the first time by designing tools and machinery properly, demanding quality parts from suppliers, encouraging customer feedback, training employees, empowering them, and encouraging them to take pride in their work. As discussed in Chapter 6, total quality management takes things to even a higher level by building quality into every activity within an organization.

Companies approach quality assurance in various ways. As a builder of sheet-metal components and electromechanical assemblies, Trident Precision Manufacturing empowers workers to make decisions on the shop floor, and it spends 4.7 percent of payroll on employee training.[33] High-end computer maker Sequent Computer Systems has a "customer process engineering manager" whose primary responsibility is to continually communicate with customers and identify any recurring problems. These companies know that eliminating only one inefficiency, such as a defect or an excessively complex process, can reduce total product costs because less money is spent on inspection, complaints, and product service.[34]

> ## active exercise

**Take a moment to apply what you've learned.**

### Statistical Quality Control and Continuous Improvement

Quality assurance also includes the now widely used concept of **statistical quality control (SQC),** in which all aspects of the production process are monitored so that managers can see whether the process is operating as it should. The primary tool of SQC is **statistical process control (SPC),** which involves taking samples from the process periodically and plotting observations of the samples on a *control chart.* A large enough sample provides a reasonable estimate of the entire process. By observing the random fluctuations graphed on the chart, managers and workers can identify whether such changes are normal or whether they indicate that some corrective action is required in the process. In this way SPC can prevent poor quality.[35]

Statistical quality control is not limited to goods-producing industries. For example, financial services provider GE Capital uses statistical control methods to make sure the bills it sends to customers are correct. The company's use of SQC lowers the cost of making adjustments while improving customer satisfaction.[36]

In addition to using SQC, companies can empower each employee to continuously improve the quality of goods production or service delivery. The Japanese word for continuous improvement is *kaizen*. Japanese manufacturers learned long before many U.S. manufacturers that continuous improvement is not something that can be delegated to one or a few people. Instead it requires the full participation of every employee. This means encouraging all workers to spot quality problems, halt production when necessary, generate ideas for improvement, and adjust work routines as needed.[37]

### Global Quality Standards

Companies that do business in Europe have to leap an extra quality hurdle. Many manufacturers and service providers in Europe require that suppliers comply with **ISO 9000,** a set of international quality standards that establishes a minimum level of acceptable quality. Set by the International Organization for Standardization, a nongovernment entity based in Geneva, Switzerland, ISO 9000 focuses on internal production and process issues that affect quality, but it doesn't measure quality in terms of customer satisfaction or business results. Usually the standards are applied to products that have health- and safety-related features. However, even companies that manufacture products not covered by ISO 9000 standards are being forced to gain accreditation by customers seeking quality assurance. The standards are now recognized in over 100 countries, and one-fourth of all of the world's corporations insist that all their suppliers be ISO 9000 certified. Even the U.S. Navy requires its suppliers to meet ISO 9000 standards.[38]

ISO 9000 helps companies develop *world-class manufacturing,* a term used to describe the level of quality and operational effectiveness that puts a company among the top performers in the world. Companies seeking world-class quality can use as benchmarks those companies that are globally recognized quality leaders. They can also follow the guidelines of various national quality awards. In Japan, the Deming Prize is a highly regarded industrial quality award, and in the United States, the Malcolm Baldrige National Quality Award honors the quality achievements of U.S. companies. Of course, even if an organization doesn't want to actually apply for an award, it can improve quality by measuring its performance against the award's standards and working to overcome any problems uncovered by this process (see Exhibit 9.7).

---

- LEADERSHIP. Have senior leaders clearly defined the company's values, goals and ways to achieve the goals? Is the company a model "corporate citizen"?

- INFORMATION AND ANALYSIS. Does the company effectively use data and information to support customer-driven performance excellence and marketplace success?

- STRATEGIC PLANNING. How does the company develop strategies and business plans to stengthen its performance and competitive position?

- HUMAN RESOURCES DEVELOPMENT AND MANAGEMENT. How does the company develop the full potential of its work force? How are its human resource capabilities and work systems aligned with its strategic and business plans?

- PROCESS MANAGEMENT. How does the company design, manage, and improve key processes, such as customer-focused design and product and service delivery?

- BUSINESS RESULTS. How does the company address performance and improvement in key business areas—product and service quality, productivity and operational effectiveness, supply quality, and financial performance indicators linked to these areas?

- CUSTOMER FOCUS AND SATISFACTION. How does the company determine requirements, expectations, and preferences of customers? What are its customer satisfaction results?

**EXHIBIT 9.7**

Criteria for the Malcolm Baldrige National Quality Award

The Malcolm Baldrige National Quality Award is given annually to companies that demonstrate an outstanding commitment to quality. Named after former Secretary of Commerce Malcolm Baldrige, the awards are given to companies in each of four categories: manufacturing, services, small businesses, and universities and hospitals. This chart lists the criteria on which companies are judged for the award.

> **active exercise**

Take a moment to apply what you've learned.

> **active concept check**

Now let's take a moment to test your knowledge of the concepts you have studied in this section.

 **Managing the Supply Chain**

A company's ability to deliver quality products and services is often tied to the dynamics of its suppliers. One faulty part, one late shipment, can send rippling effects through the production system and can even bring operations to a grinding halt. When a surge of orders for new Boeing 747s stepped up demand for parts, for instance, Boeing's suppliers were caught flat-footed. "We had $25,000 engine mounts that couldn't be finished because we were waiting for $40 nuts and bolts," noted one Boeing supplier. As a result, promised aircraft delivery dates were delayed and Boeing suffered huge losses. To avoid such problems in the future, Boeing now works hand in hand with its suppliers to refine products and delivery schedules.[39]

The group of firms that provide all the various processes required to make a finished product is called the *supply chain.* The chain begins with the provider of raw materials and ends with the company that produces the finished product that is delivered to the final customer. The members of the

Computer failures at Hong Kong's huge new airport, Chek Lap Kok, left cargo, including perishables, sitting on the tarmac for days.

supply chain vary according to the nature of the operation and type of product but typically include suppliers, manufacturers, distributors, and retailers. For example, if the finished product is a wood table, the supply chain going backward would include the retail store where it was sold, the shipping company that delivered it to the retail store, the furniture manufacturer, the hardware manufacturer, and the lumber company that acquired the wood from the forest.[40]

Through a process known as **supply-chain management,** many companies now integrate all of the facilities, functions, and activities involved in the production of goods and services going from suppliers to customers.[41] The process is based on the belief that because one company's output is another company's (or consumer's) input, all companies involved will benefit from working together more closely.[42] Building high-trust relationships was once thought possible only with internal suppliers. But today more and more companies are reducing the number of outside suppliers they use, working collaboratively with them, sharing information with them, and even involving them in the production and design processes.

Honda, for example, has developed a process called Design In, which focuses directly on early supplier involvement. Honda will invite suppliers to work side by side with Honda's engineers, designers, and technologists in the very early stages of a new project. In addition, Honda believes in maintaining a frank, open, and collaborative relationship with its suppliers and even extends this philosophy to sharing cost data. "We show our suppliers our logic in coming up with the cost, and they show us theirs," notes Honda's senior purchasing manager.[43] This sharing of information with members of the supply chain has many benefits. Among them are increased sales, cost savings, inventory reductions, improved quality, accelerated delivery time, and improved customer service.[44]

Some companies are taking things one step further and actually involving suppliers in the manufacturing of their product. For example, at Volkswagen's factory in Resende, Brazil, seven main suppliers build components and assemble them onto vehicles inside the Volkswagen factory, using the suppliers' own equipment and workers. Volkswagen figures that integrating the suppliers so deeply into the production process is a strong incentive for the suppliers to deliver high-quality components in unprecedented time.[45]

## active poll  <

**What do you think? Voice your opinion and find out what others have to say.**

## > Outsourcing the Manufacturing Function

As companies strive to find better ways to produce goods, some are learning that outsourcing the manufacturing function can provide tremendous cost efficiencies. For one thing, outsourcing allows companies to redirect the capital and resources spent on manufacturing to new product research, marketing, and customer service. As a result, some manufacturers today don't really "manufacture" products at all. Instead, they design them, market them, and support them. This is especially true with high-tech products. Cisco Systems, for instance, owns only two of the 34 plants that produce its products. Cisco outsources its production to contract electronic manufacturers (CEMs).[46]

Solectron is a California CEM. The company has 24 production lines, which simultaneously assemble everything from pagers to printers to television decoding boxes for some of the biggest brand names in electronics. With sales topping $13 billion, Solectron is the only company that has twice won the Malcolm Baldrige Award for manufacturing excellence.[47] Similarly, Ingram Micro, the world's largest wholesale distributor of computers, does assembly work for archrivals that together control more than one-third of the U.S. computer market. In some cases these supercontractors even manage their customers' entire product lines by offering an array of services from design to inventory management and by providing delivery and after-sales service.[48]

Companies that outsource their manufacturing operations, of course, claim that their products are differentiated from those of their competitors (even if they are all assembled by the same contractor) because unique features and levels of quality are designed into a company's products. As one Hewlett-Packard vice president commented, "We own all the intellectual property; we farm out the direct labor; we don't need to screw the motherboard into the metal box and attach the ribbon cable." Still, others fear that outsourcing the manufacturing function could jeopardize a company's control over the product's intellectual property or quality. Intel, National Semiconductor, and Merck are among the corporate giants that have chosen to keep manufacturing in-house to protect their competitive edge.[49]

Besides outsourcing, another trend sweeping manufacturing organizations is relegating more work to suppliers. In some companies, in-house manufacturing operations consist of nothing more than bolting together fabricated chunks that have been manufactured by suppliers. Consider Airbus's jetliner factory in Toulouse, France, for example. Large sections of Airbus jets manufactured at factories throughout Europe are flown to Toulouse in giant modified cargo jets called Belugas. There, small teams "snap together" the largely complete components, attach the landing gear, and drill holes to fasten wings to fuselages. The result is a much more modern and efficient production system than the one used by the industry leader, Boeing. In fact, Airbus now produces more revenue per employee than Boeing's commercial airplane division and is narrowing the gap between the number one and two spots of this industry duopoly. As competition heats up, Airbus recognizes that the company's competitor is not the Boeing of today, but rather "the Boeing that will be."[50]

## > active exercise

**Take a moment to apply what you've learned.**

## > active concept check

**Now let's take a moment to test your knowledge of the concepts you have studied in this section.**

 **Chapter Wrap-Up**

Now that you've reached the end of the chapter, you may wish to explore the concepts you've been reading about in greater detail, or test yourself to see how well you've comprehended the material. In the box below you'll find a number of links. Click on any one of these links to find additional chapter resources.

## > end-of-chapter resources

- Summary of Learning Objectives
- Practice Quiz
- Focusing on E-Business Today
- Key Terms
- Test Your Knowledge
- Practice Your Knowledge
- Expand Your Knowledge
- A Case for Critical Thinking
- Business Plan Pro: Managing a Business

# CHAPTER 10

# Motivation, Today's Workforce, and Employee-Management Relations

 **What's Ahead**

### INSIDE BUSINESS TODAY
### CREATING COMPANY LOYALTY: TRUE BLUE EMPLOYEES AT SAS INSTITUTE

Job loyalty often takes a backseat to the lure of generous salaries and enticing stock options in today's fast-paced software industry. But as owner and CEO of SAS Institute (which stands for "statistical analysis software"), Jim Goodnight bucks the trend of offering stock options to employees. Plus, SAS salaries are merely competitive. Nevertheless, the 6,000 employees of the world's largest private software company have no desire to work anywhere else.

What's Goodnight's secret? Basically he does everything he can to create a corporate culture that respects employees and their needs for balancing work with their personal lives. Goodnight manages and motivates his workforce by relying on the philosophy that some things are more important to employees than money or stock offerings. The result? SAS employees are loyal. The company boasts a turnover rate of less than 5 percent—five times lower than the industry average.

It all began in 1981 when Goodnight realized that his small software company couldn't afford to lose talented workers. So he persuaded female employees to return to work after their maternity leaves by offering a powerful motivator: on-site day care. Today, the Cary, North Carolina, company operates the state's largest in-house day care operation, with a capacity of 700 children.

SAS Institute CEO Jim Goodnight takes a snack break with children at the company's on-site day care center.

But child care is only part of Goodnight's approach to keeping his staff happy and productive. Goodnight believes employees are more creative when they aren't preoccupied with worries about their families or outside responsibilities. So he gives workers everything they need to do a good job—a rare bonanza of benefits, including peace of mind about their personal lives and an enjoyable work environment.

SAS encourages employees to take care of their personal health and the health of their loved ones. The company provides everything from free health insurance and unlimited sick days to the services of a full-time elder-care consultant and an on-site health clinic staffed by doctors and nurse practitioners. Employees also have free access to a country-club-style haven of sports and exercise facilities at corporate headquarters. An on-site gym, for example, includes basketball courts, workout areas, space for aerobics classes, a dance studio, and meditation rooms. SAS even provides employees with such luxuries as a putting green, massage services, free juice and soda, three subsidized cafeterias, and overnight laundering of sweaty gym clothes at no cost.

To encourage employees to spend more time with their families, the company closes its doors promptly at six o'clock each evening. And SAS supplies baby seats and highchairs in company cafeterias so that children can eat lunch with their parents. Moreover, flexible work hours and a standard 35-hour workweek are the norm, along with three weeks of annual vacation and an additional week off with pay during Christmas.

In return for the lavish benefits, Goodnight expects performance from his employees. And they deliver in a big way. Not only are employees motivated to do their best, but such motivation gives SAS a competitive edge against giants like Oracle, Microsoft, and IBM. Furthermore, it shows up in the company's bottom line. With customers in more than 115 countries around the world, SAS maintains a 30 percent profit margin on $1 billion in annual sales. As Jim Goodnight puts it "Doing the right thing—treating people right—is also the right thing to do for the company."[1]

> # objectives

**Take a moment to familiarize yourself with the key objectives of this chapter.**

> # gearing up

**Before you begin reading this chapter, try a short warm-up activity.**

## > Understanding Human Relations

As Jim Goodnight knows, organizations need human resources to run their businesses. In fact, employees are a company's most valuable asset. "Ninety-five percent of our assets drive out the gate every afternoon at five," says Goodnight. "I want them to come back in the morning. I need them to come back in the morning."[2] But like most companies today, SAS faces an increasing need for qualified, skilled employees in an environment plagued by labor shortages and annual employee turnover rates that average about 20 percent. So Goodnight must offer employees benefits and reasons to return to SAS each morning.

Employee turnover, unscheduled absenteeism, and waning morale cost companies an estimated $200 billion or more annually, says one report—and that does not include the impact on a company's productivity.[3] For instance, if you have employees managing territories that generate from $1 to $2 million in company sales and one of them leaves, it might take you three to four months to find a replacement—and another three to four months before that individual becomes productive.[4] Which is why companies today can't afford to ignore the needs of their workforce. "If you do, it will have a significantly negative impact on the bottom line, and also be reflected in more lost workdays, more tardiness, poor morale, and low productivity," says one DaimlerChrysler director.[5]

In organizations, the goal of **human relations**—interactions among people within the organization—is to balance the diverse needs of employees with those of management. For instance, employers must motivate employees and keep them satisfied. But they must also remain competitive in the marketplace to ensure the organization's long-term success. Of course, achieving this balance becomes increasingly difficult because companies today face many staffing and demographic challenges. In this chapter we'll explore these challenges, and we'll discuss the role that labor unions play in the human relations function. Then in Chapter 11 we'll take a close look at what human resources managers do, as we explain the details of the hiring process, employee compensation, and specific employee benefits.

## > Motivating Employees

Every employee, by human nature, needs to feel valued, challenged, and respected. But when it comes to attracting and keeping talented people, even Jim Goodnight knows that money alone won't do it. Although compensation and employee benefits are indeed important, research shows that employees who maintain a high **morale** or a positive attitude toward both their job and organization perform better.[6]

Employees, regardless of their status, want and expect their employers to treat them fairly. They want more than a good paycheck and satisfying work. They want to balance their careers and their family lives. "There's an increasing interest in people finding meaning in their lives and in their work," notes Don Kuhn, the executive director of the International University Consortium for Executive Education. "People are no longer content with income and acquisition alone, but are looking for personal satisfaction."[7] They want to be part of something they can believe in, something that confers meaning on their work and on their lives. They want to be motivated.[8]

## WHAT IS MOTIVATION?

**Motivation** is an inner force that moves individuals to take action. In some cases, fear of management or of losing a job may move an employee to take action, but such negative motivation is much less effective than encouraging an individual's own sense of direction, creativity, and pride in doing a good job. Some managers rely on various kinds of rewards to motivate and reinforce the behavior of hardworking employees. These rewards include gifts, certificates, medals, dinners, trips, and so forth. Others, such as Jim Goodnight, motivate their employees by providing a culture that makes it enjoyable to come to work. Still others use positive and negative reinforcement to motivate their employees.

### Positive and Negative Reinforcement

Some companies try to control or change employee actions by using **behavior modification.** They systematically encourage those actions that are desirable and discourage those that are not. A manager can encourage or discourage employee behavior through the use of *reinforcement.* If an action results in pleasant consequences, the employee is likely to repeat the action; if the consequences are unpleasant, the employee is unlikely to repeat the action.

*Positive reinforcement* offers pleasant consequences (such as a gift or praise) for completing or repeating a desired action. Experts recommend the use of positive reinforcement because it emphasizes the desired behavior rather than the unwanted behavior. In contrast, *negative reinforcement* allows people to avoid unpleasant consequences by behaving in the desired way. Imagine, for example, that employees know they will have to work late if they don't finish a project on time. In this case, employees can avoid working late (unpleasant consequences) by finishing on time (desired behavior).

### Management by Objectives

Another proven motivation technique used by many organizations is **management by objectives (MBO),** a companywide process that empowers employees and involves them in goal setting and decision making. The process consists of four steps: setting goals, planning actions, implementing plans, and reviewing performance (see Exhibit 10.1). Because employees at all levels are involved in all four steps, they learn more about company objectives and feel that they are an important part of the companywide team. Furthermore, they understand how even their small job function contributes to the organization's long-term success.

One of the key elements of MBO is a collaborative goal-setting process. Together, a manager and employee define the employee's goals, the responsibilities for achieving those goals, and the means of evaluating individual and group performance so that the employee's activities are directly linked to achieving the organization's long-term goals. Jointly setting clear and challenging—but achievable—goals can encourage employees to reach higher levels of performance. At Aptar Group, a manufacturer of aerosol valves, finger pumps, and other caps for bottles, employee work teams set their own goals and report on their progress to senior management. Rob Revak, director of human resources at one of Aptar's divisions, finds that employees who set their own goals strive hard to reach them.[9]

MBO, of course, is just one of the ways companies motivate employees to perform. As you can imagine, humans are motivated by many factors. Thus, the challenge for managers is to select motivators that will inspire employees to achieve organizational goals. But which ones are the most effective? Several theories of motivation have attempted to answer that question.

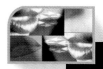

## active poll                                              <

**What do you think? Voice your opinion and find out what others have to say.**

## THEORIES OF MOTIVATION

Motivation has been a topic of interest to managers for more than a hundred years. Frederick W. Taylor was a machinist and engineer from Philadelphia who became interested in employee efficiency and motivation late in the nineteenth century. Taylor developed **scientific management,** an approach that seeks to improve employee efficiency through the scientific study of work. In Taylor's view, people were motivated almost exclusively by money, so he set up pay systems that rewarded employees when they were productive.

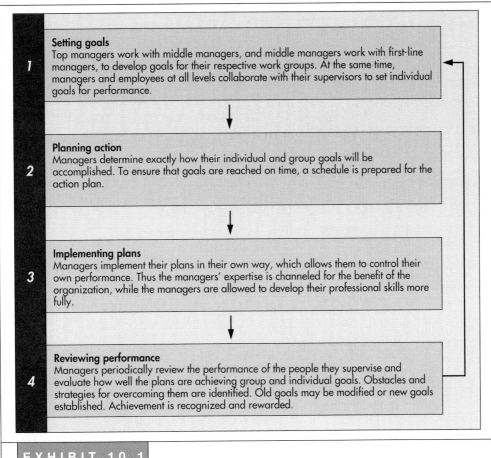

| 1 | **Setting goals**<br>Top managers work with middle managers, and middle managers work with first-line managers, to develop goals for their respective work groups. At the same time, managers and employees at all levels collaborate with their supervisors to set individual goals for performance. |

| 2 | **Planning action**<br>Managers determine exactly how their individual and group goals will be accomplished. To ensure that goals are reached on time, a schedule is prepared for the action plan. |

| 3 | **Implementing plans**<br>Managers implement their plans in their own way, which allows them to control their own performance. Thus the managers' expertise is channeled for the benefit of the organization, while the managers are allowed to develop their professional skills more fully. |

| 4 | **Reviewing performance**<br>Managers periodically review the performance of the people they supervise and evaluate how well the plans are achieving group and individual goals. Obstacles and strategies for overcoming them are identified. Old goals may be modified or new goals established. Achievement is recognized and rewarded. |

**EXHIBIT 10.1**

Management by Objectives

The MBO process has four steps. This cycle is refined and repeated as managers and employees at all levels work toward establishing goals and objectives, thereby accomplishing the organization's strategic goals.

Under Taylor's piecework system, for example, employees who just met or fell short of the quota were paid a certain amount for each unit produced. Those who produced more were paid a higher rate for *all* units produced, not just for those that exceeded the quota; this pay system gave employees a strong incentive to boost productivity.

Although money has always been a powerful motivator, scientific management fails to take into account other motivational elements, such as opportunities for personal satisfaction or individual initiative. Thus, scientific management can't explain why a person still wants to work even though that person's spouse already makes a good living or why a Wall Street lawyer will take a hefty pay cut to serve in government. Therefore, other researchers have looked beyond money to discover what else motivates people.

### Maslow's Hierarchy of Needs

In 1943 psychologist Abraham Maslow proposed the theory that behavior is determined by a variety of needs. He organized these needs into five categories and then arranged the categories in a hierarchy. As Exhibit 10.2 shows, the most basic needs are at the bottom of this hierarchy, and the more advanced needs are toward the top. In Maslow's hierarchy, all of the requirements for basic survival—food, clothing, shelter, and the like—fall into the category of *physiological needs.* These basic needs must be satisfied before the person can consider higher-level needs such as *safety needs, social needs* (the need to give and receive love and to feel a sense of belonging), and *esteem needs* (the need for a sense of self-worth and integrity).

At the top of Maslow's hierarchy is *self-actualization*—the need to become everything one can become. This need is also the most difficult to fulfill. Employees who reach this point work not only to make money or to impress others but also because they feel their work is worthwhile and satisfying

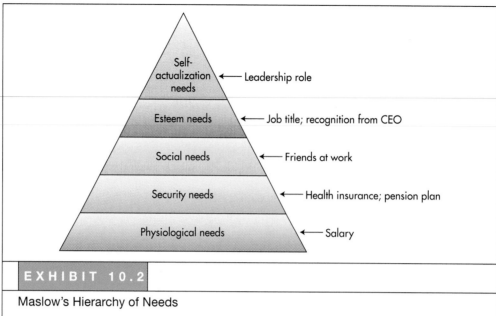

**EXHIBIT 10.2**

Maslow's Hierarchy of Needs

According to Maslow, needs on the lower levels of the hierarchy must be satisfied before higher-level needs can be addressed.

in itself. Self-actualization needs partially explain why some people make radical career changes or strike out on their own as entrepreneurs.

Although Maslow's hierarchy is a convenient way to classify human needs, it would be a mistake to view it as a rigid sequence. A person need not completely satisfy each level of needs before being motivated by a higher need. Indeed, at any one time, most people are motivated by a combination of needs.

### Two-Factor Theory

In the 1960s, Frederick Herzberg and his associates undertook their own study of human needs. They asked accountants and engineers to describe specific aspects of their jobs that made them feel satisfied or dissatisfied. Upon analyzing the results, they found that two entirely different sets of factors were associated with satisfying and dissatisfying work experiences: *hygiene factors* and *motivators* (see Exhibit 10.3).

What Herzberg called **hygiene factors** are associated with dissatisfying experiences. The potential sources of dissatisfaction include working conditions, company policies, and job security. Management can lessen worker dissatisfaction by improving hygiene factors that concern employees, but such improvements seldom influence satisfaction. On the other hand, managers can help employees feel more motivated and, ultimately, more satisfied, by paying attention to **motivators** such as achievement, recognition, responsibility, and other personally rewarding factors. Herzberg's theory is related to Maslow's hierarchy of needs: The motivators closely resemble the higher-level needs, and the hygiene factors resemble the lower-level needs.

Should managers concentrate on motivators or on hygiene factors? It depends. A skilled, well-paid, middle-class, middle-aged employee may be motivated to perform better if motivators are supplied. However, a young, unskilled worker who earns low wages, or an employee who is insecure, will probably still need the support of strong hygiene factors to reduce dissatisfaction before the motivators can be effective.[10]

### Theory X and Theory Y

In the 1960s, psychologist Douglas McGregor identified two radically different sets of assumptions that underlie most management thinking. He classified these sets of assumptions into two categories: *Theory X* and *Theory Y* (see Exhibit 10.4).

According to McGregor, **Theory X**–oriented managers believe that employees dislike work and can be motivated only by the fear of losing their jobs or by *extrinsic rewards* such as money, promotions, and tenure. This management style emphasizes physiological and safety needs and tends to ignore the higher-level needs in Maslow's hierarchy. In contrast, **Theory Y**–oriented managers

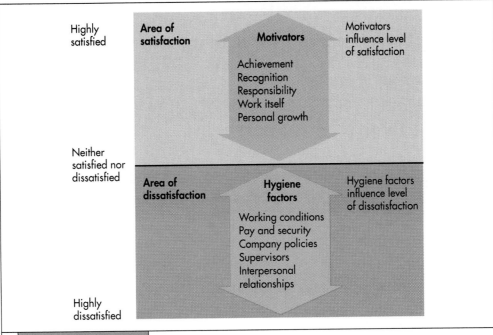

**EXHIBIT 10.3**

Two-Factor Theory

Hygiene factors such as working conditions and company policies can influence employee dissatisfaction. On the other hand, motivators such as opportunities for achievement and recognition can influence employee satisfaction.

| Theory X | Theory Y |
|---|---|
| 1. Employees inherently dislike work and will avoid it whenever possible. | 1. Employees like work and consider it as natural as play and rest. |
| 2. Because employees dislike work, they must be threatened with punishment to achieve goals. | 2. People naturally work toward goals they are committed to. |
| 3. Employees will avoid responsibilities whenever possible. | 3. The average person can learn to accept and even seek responsibility. |
| 4. Employees value security above all other job factors. | 4. The average person's intellectual potential is only partially realized. |

**EXHIBIT 10.4**

Theory X and Theory Y

McGregor proposed two distinct views of human beings: The assumptions of Theory X are basically negative, whereas those of Theory Y are basically positive.

believe that employees like work and can be motivated by working for goals that promote creativity or for causes they believe in. Thus, Theory Y-oriented managers seek to motivate employees through *intrinsic rewards.*

The assumptions behind Theory X emphasize authority; the assumptions behind Theory Y emphasize growth and self-direction. It was McGregor's belief that, although some employees need the strong direction demanded by Theory X, those who are ready to realize their social, esteem, and self-actualization needs will not work well under Theory X assumptions.[11]

## video exercise  <

**Take a moment to apply what you've learned.**

## active concept check  <

**Now let's take a moment to test your knowledge of the concepts you have studied in this section.**

## > Keeping Pace with Today's Workforce

Although motivational theories shed some light on what managers can do to motivate employees to work efficiently and effectively toward achieving the organization's goals, managers must also address the needs of today's workforce. They must manage a diverse group of individuals and recognize that all employees have interests and obligations outside of work, such as family, volunteer activities, and hobbies. Addressing employees' many needs becomes even more critical in a work environment plagued with a number of staffing challenges.

### STAFFING CHALLENGES

If you ask business leaders what their biggest challenges are today, you will most likely get these answers: finding, attracting, and keeping talented people; rightsizing their workforces; and satisfying employees' desire for a work–life balance.[12] Finding and keeping good workers is especially hard for small-company owners, who often trail bigger companies in salary, benefits, job security, and other criteria that lead workers to choose one company over another. Larger companies can woo top job applicants with hiring bonuses, flexible work schedules, job training, and other incentives. But because such enticements are costly, they are not feasible for smaller concerns.

#### Shortage of Skilled Labor

A close look at Component Chapter B confirms that many of today's growing occupations require specialized skills or training, whereas the shrinking occupations involve activities that require fewer skills or ones that are increasingly being automated. In fact, nearly all jobs today require computer literacy. Machinists, for example, need computer skills to operate chip-controlled equipment. Telemarketers must know how to keyboard. Even package delivery involves data entry. But finding technology-literate employees is a dilemma for most companies today.

By one estimate there are already 190,000 unfilled high-tech jobs, and the demand for people with engineering, computer, and other technical skills is mushrooming. An additional 1 million such jobs are expected to be created in this decade, with virtually no increase in supply.[13] Furthermore, the gap is widening between what employers will require of new employees in the years ahead and the actual skills of these employees.

One factor contributing to the skilled-labor shortage is the robust U.S. economy. An increasing demand for U.S. goods and services has put pressure on U.S. companies to operate at breakneck speeds. But with unemployment hovering at around 4 to 5 percent, the economy is considered to be at full employment.[14] So companies are exploring different options to attract and keep employees in their organizations.

Some companies are revamping rigid pay systems to make it easier for employees to move laterally and enhance their skills. Others are installing new career-development programs to help employees plan their career moves. Managers at International Paper, for example, sit down with every employee once a year to discuss their career desires, separate from their annual performance reviews.[15] Still others are instituting educational programs to attract and keep skilled employees. Cisco Systems, a manufacturer of computer network routers, runs its own Networking Academy. This in-house vocational program teaches students how to build and manage the computer-server networks the company sells. Cisco hopes that eventually the students will return to the company for permanent jobs.[16]

UPS took a particularly creative approach with its staffing dilemma when Louisville, Kentucky, could not supply the 6,000 additional employees the company needed to staff its growing $6 billion air-freight business. Rather than moving its main U.S. air hub from Louisville to another location, UPS partnered with the city of Louisville to attract new employees to the area. Together they built "UPS University," and special dormitories so student-workers could sleep during the day, attend classes taught by professors from the University of Louisville at night, and then work the UPS grave-yard shift (from 11:30 P.M. to 3:30 A.M.) and still have time to study. With over 15,000 employees in Louisville alone, UPS is now Kentucky's largest employer.[17]

### Rightsizing

The increasing demand for educated workers and the continuing conversion from a manufacturing-based economy to a service-based economy (as discussed in Chapter 1) are also forcing companies to pull apart their workforce and then piece it back together differently. More than 4.6 million job cuts were announced in the 1990s. Factors contributing to *downsizing* decisions included company reor-ganizations, business downturns, elimination of unprofitable product lines, outsourcing, mergers and acquisitions, and a general mismatch between employee job skills and job demands. Even though cor-porate downsizing continues today, what is puzzling is a concurrent trend toward "upsizing," or mas-sive hiring—and often within the same firm.[18]

This phenomenon can best be explained by the needs of companies to *rightsize,* or realign their workforces into business growth areas. For example, employees from Department A are let go while new hires are sought to keep up with the growth demands of Department B. Such was the case with defense electronics giant Raytheon. Even though the company slashed 8,700 defense jobs, or 10 per-cent of its workforce, it redeployed 5,000 engineers to its booming commercial units.[19]

**DECLINING EMPLOYEE LOYALTY** As you can imagine, rightsizing is a contributing factor to declining employee loyalty. Devastated by the lack of job security, employees quickly learn to "do what's best for me." In fact, today's employees are cautious. They recognize that the old idea of a paternal company taking care of employees has, for the most part, died. Employee expectations are now more realistic. Hardworking, loyal employees no longer expect to move up the organizational hierarchy. They realize that companies are going to do whatever they have to do to succeed and to survive. And this may mean manufacturing in South America, eliminating three layers of management, or closing down plants.[20] Even the Japanese tradition of lifetime employment is under attack. After years of severe economic recession and intense global competition, the Japanese are realizing that unconditional loyalty is becoming too expensive to justify. To remain competitive, Japanese companies are chipping away at their seniority-based management system and are forcing executives to perform or go—bringing Japan a little closer to the U.S. model.[21]

**INCREASING EMPLOYEE BURNOUT** Rightsizing is also putting pressure on remaining employees to work longer hours. When 3M spun off its data-storage and medical-imaging divisions, for example, some employees began putting in 80-hour weeks. One 3M customer service consultant summed up the feelings of many employees when he said, "I always perceived work to be a means to an end, but not *the* end."[22] Others are working longer hours just to keep up. "It seems like you work, work, work," says one Michigan chemist.[23]

On average, workers are putting in 260 more hours a year than a decade ago—many without over-time pay.[24] Moreover, the Bureau of Labor Statistics says the proportion of professionals and man-agers working extremely long hours—49 or more a week—has risen by as much as 37 percent since 1985.[25] Such long hours can lead to employee *burnout,* which is characterized by emotional exhaus-tion, depersonalization, and lower levels of achievement. Severe burnout or stress may even lead to clinical depression.[26] Other causes of employee burnout are job insecurity, technological advance-ments, and information overload:

- *Job insecurity.* Workers anxious about job security feel they have to give 150 percent (or more) or risk being seen as expendable. What once were considered crises-mode workloads have now become business as usual. These extra hours, which don't always bring extra pay, can leave employees feeling burned out and resentful.[27]

- *Technological advancements.* New technology allows employees to work from home, but being wired to the office 24 hours a day can add extra pressure. Employees feel compelled to answer that voice mail or e-mail whatever the hour. "We have all these great tools to save our time," notes one career expert. "Instead, it just extends our week. We're never out of touch anymore."[28]

- *Information overload.* Managers claim they're unable to handle the vast amounts of informa-tion they now receive. In fact, more information has been produced in the last 30 years than the previous 5,000, and the total quantity of printed material is doubling every 5 years, and accelerating.[29]

How does burnout affect the ability of workers to do their jobs? "When you feel under stress, you find your mental wheels spinning and you work mechanically rather than creatively," says one human resources expert. "The tasks that normally would take a few minutes sit unfinished for days because you lose the capacity to prioritize and you put off larger, important projects that take more energy and concentration."[30]

## active poll

**What do you think? Voice your opinion and find out what others have to say.**

### Quality of Work Life

A recent survey by jobtrack.com found that 42 percent of all job seekers identified work–life issues as the most important consideration in their choice of a new job. For some employees the primary work–life issue is caring for an elder parent; for others it's child care, rising college tuition costs, or a desire to return to school part-time.[31] Regardless, achieving a work–life balance is especially difficult when both parents work or in situations where downsizing and restructuring have left remaining employees with heavier workloads than in the past.

To help employees balance the demands of work and family, businesses are offering child care assistance, family leave, flexible work schedules, telecommuting, and other solutions that are explored later in this chapter and in Chapter 11. Many, such as SAS, are also focusing on improving the **quality of work life (QWL),** the environment created by work and job conditions.[32] An improved QWL benefits both the individual and the organization. Employees gain the chance to use their specialized abilities, improve their skills, and balance their lives. The organization gains a more motivated and loyal employee.

Two common ways of improving QWL are through **job enrichment,** which reduces specialization and makes work more meaningful by expanding each job's responsibilities, and through **job redesign,** which restructures work to provide a better fit between employees' skills and their jobs. As this chapter's opening vignette shows, quality of work life can be improved in other ways, too. Like SAS, many organizations are providing their employees with a number of benefits designed to help them balance their work with personal responsibilities. Accenture (formerly Andersen Consulting), for instance, will send someone to pick up an employee's car from the repair shop; Pepsi has an on-site dry cleaning drop-off at its New York headquarters; and American Banker's Insurance Group and Hewlett-Packard have sponsored schools at company sites that allow employees to visit their children during lunchtime and after school. All of these measures can improve employees' lives by freeing up their time and by making work a more enjoyable place to be.[33]

## active exercise

**Take a moment to apply what you've learned.**

## DEMOGRAPHIC CHALLENGES

The U.S. workforce is undergoing significant changes that require major alterations in how managers keep employees happy and productive. One of the most significant demographic trends facing companies today is increasing workforce diversity.

### Workforce Diversity

The U.S. workforce is diverse in race, gender, age, culture, family structures, religion, and educational backgrounds—and will become even more so in the years ahead. Although nearly three-fourths of the U.S. population is still classified as white, that's changing fast. By 2050 whites will represent only

53 percent of the U.S. population. Hispanics will make up about 24 percent, African Americans 14 percent, Asian Americans 8 percent, and Native Americans 1 percent.[34]

Managing this changing mixture of ages, faces, values, and views is, of course, increasingly difficult. Not only does a diverse workforce bring with it a wide range of skills, traditions, backgrounds, experiences, outlooks, and attitudes toward work that can affect individuals' behavior on the job, but managers must be able to communicate with and motivate this diverse workforce while fostering cooperation and harmony among employees. Two trends contributing to the diversity of the U.S. workforce are the influx of immigrants and the aging population.

**INFLUX OF IMMIGRANTS** Today foreign-born engineers jam the corridors of the U.S. Silicon Valley, hoping to reap the benefits of the nation's information technology boom. Meanwhile tens of thousands of Mexicans slip across the border each year. At the same time employers are clamoring for more foreign-born workers to fill their critical labor shortages, and they are pressuring Congress to enact legislation that would admit hundreds of thousands of additional immigrants each year. As a result, the percentage of immigrant workers in the U.S. labor force has climbed to its highest level in seven decades.[35] This trend is having profound effects on the economy—helping to hold down wages in unskilled jobs and giving many companies the employees they need to expand.

**AGING POPULATION** The population in the United States is aging, a situation that creates new challenges and concerns for employers and employees alike. The general aging of the population and the declining number of young people entering the workforce is largely due to the decisions of baby boomers (born 1946–1960) to marry later, to postpone or forgo starting a family, and to have fewer children. About 84 percent of baby boomers participate in today's labor market.[36] Experts predict that because of inadequate pensions, high medical costs, and a general desire to stay active, baby boomers will put off retirement until they are in their seventies.

Widespread delayed retirement will indeed present challenges for all parties involved. For one thing, even though the 1967 Age Discrimination in Employment Act (ADEA) makes workers over 40 a protected class, many suspect that age discrimination is widespread.[37] For another, older, more experienced employees command higher salaries. "For my salary, the company could hire two twenty

Putting more people of various ethnicities on the floor—and in executive positions—is a no-brainer for Wal-Mart, which was recently ranked by *Fortune* magazine as one of America's 50 best companies for Asian, black, and Hispanic Americans. This group, for instance, includes two senior vice presidents, four vice presidents, and two corporate counsels.

somethings," says a 41-year-old. "I'm good at what I do. But am I better than two people? Even I know that's not true." Not only do older employees earn more, but the costs of employee benefits such as medical insurance and pensions rise with age as well.[38] Furthermore, as the speed of change gets faster, it can be difficult for older employees to keep up unless they have the stamina of a 25-year-old.

Age has its advantages, of course. According to one recent study, older employees have more experience, better judgment, and a greater commitment to quality. They are also more likely to show up on time and less likely to quit. But these traits pale by comparison with the highly desired traits characteristic of younger workers, who appear more flexible, more adaptable, more accepting of new technology, and better at learning new skills. Studies also show that the difference in job performance between someone with 20 years experience and someone with just 5 years does not always justify the higher costs of maintaining a senior workforce.[39]

**DIVERSITY INITIATIVES** To cope with increasing workforce diversity, many companies offer employees sensitivity or awareness training to help them understand the different attitudes and beliefs that women, minorities, and immigrants bring to their jobs.[40] At Allstate Insurance, for example, all nonagent employees with service of more than one year are expected to complete diversity training—a company investment in excess of 540,000 hours of classroom time.[41] And at the Marriott Marquis Hotel in New York, mandatory diversity-training classes teach managers how to avoid defining problems in terms of gender, culture, or race. These classes also help managers become more sensitive to the behavior and communication patterns of employees with diverse backgrounds.

Although encouraging sensitivity to employee differences is important, a company stands to benefit most when it incorporates its employees' diverse perspectives into the organization's work. This assimilation enables the company to uncover new opportunities by rethinking primary tasks and redefining markets, products, strategies, missions, business practices, and even cultures. Consider the small public-interest law firm of Dewey & Levin. In the mid-1980s the firm had an all-white legal staff. Concerned about its ability to serve ethnically diverse populations, the firm hired a Hispanic female attorney. She introduced Dewey & Levin to new ideas about what kinds of cases to take on, and many of her ideas were pursued with great success. Hiring more women of color brought even more fresh perspectives. The firm now pursues cases that the original staff members would never have considered because they would not have understood the link between the issues involved in the cases and the firm's mission.[42] In short, diversity is an asset, and one of the challenges of corporate human relations is to make the most of this asset.

## Gender-Related Issues

Another demographic challenge companies have been grappling with for years is the gender gap in compensation. Women today earn about 76 percent of men's median pay.[43] Moreover, even though women now hold 46 percent of executive, administrative, and managerial positions (up from 34 percent in 1983), only 10 percent of the top managerial positions at the nation's 500 largest companies are held by women. At levels of vice president or higher, the figure is only 2.4 percent.[44] Some attribute this inequality to the *glass ceiling.*

**THE GLASS CEILING** The **glass ceiling** is an invisible barrier that keeps women and minorities from reaching the highest-level positions. One theory about the glass ceiling suggests that top management has long been dominated by white males who tend to hire and promote employees who look, act, and think as they do. Another theory states that stereotyping by male middle managers leads them to believe that family life will interfere with a woman's work. As a result, women are relegated to less visible assignments in the company, so their work goes unnoticed by top executives and their careers stagnate.[45]

In recent years, women have made significant strides toward overcoming job discrimination on the basis of gender, or **sexism,** thanks to a combination of changing societal attitudes and company commitments to workplace diversity. Such initiatives include long-term commitments to hiring more women, company-sponsored networking and career planning for women, diversity training and workshops, and mentoring programs designed to help female employees move more quickly through the ranks.

Pitney Bowes's long-term commitment to diversity, for instance, has resulted in women holding 5 of the top 11 jobs at the company. Patagonia boasts that women now hold more than half of the company's top-paying jobs and almost 60 percent of managerial jobs. And the appointment of Carly Fiorina to CEO of Hewlett-Packard (HP) was hailed by many as a milestone for women. With more than a quarter of HP's managers being women, it seems that the glass ceiling at this company has been shattered.[46]

**SEXUAL HARASSMENT** Another sensitive issue that women often face in the workplace is sexual harassment. As defined by the EEOC, **sexual harassment** takes two forms: the obvious request for sexual favors with an implicit reward or punishment related to work and the more subtle creation of a sexist environment in which employees are made to feel uncomfortable by off-color jokes, lewd remarks, and posturing. Even though male employees may also be targets of sexual harassment, and both male and female employees may experience same-sex harassment, sexual harassment of female employees by male colleagues continues to make up the majority of reported cases.

To put an end to sexual harassment, many companies are now enforcing strict harassment policies. Recent Supreme Court rulings explain (for the first time) how all employers—both large and small—can insulate themselves from potential sexual harassment lawsuits. In short, a company can defend itself successfully if it can prove that it had an effective policy against sexual harassment in place and that the employee alleging harassment failed to take advantage of this policy. To be effective, the policy must be in writing, communicated to all employees, and enforced.[47] This means that the company must train all employees on the policy, and the company must have clear procedures for reporting such behavior—including allowing employees access to management other than their supervisors. Without such policies, companies can be held indirectly responsible for a harasser's actions even when top managers had no idea that such practices were going on.[48]

> **active exercise**

**Take a moment to apply what you've learned.**

## ALTERNATIVE WORK ARRANGEMENTS

To meet today's staffing and demographic challenges, many companies are adopting alternative work arrangements. Three of the most popular arrangements are flextime, telecommuting, and job sharing. Many organizations find that a mix of these arrangements and other employee benefits works better than a one-size-fits-all approach.[49]

### Flextime

An increasingly important alternative work arrangement, **flextime** is a scheduling system that allows employees to choose their own hours within certain limits. Approximately 66 percent of all companies now offer some form of flextime.[50] For instance, a company may require everyone to be at work between 10:00 A.M. and 2:00 P.M., but employees may arrive or depart whenever they want as long as they work a total of 8 hours every day. Another popular flextime schedule is to work four 10-hour days each week, taking one prearranged day off (see Exhibit 10.5).

Full-time, permanent employees and independent contractors who say these are "extremely important" in job satisfaction

|  | Full-time | Independent |
|---|---|---|
| Ability to work from home | 15% | 44% |
| Flexible work schedule | 40% | 62% |
| Freedom from office politics | 44% | 60% |
| Believing in what they do | 72% | 83% |
| Making right amount of money | 50% | 46% |
| Work they find challenging | 55% | 59% |

**EXHIBIT 10.5**

9-to-5 Not for Everyone

For many full-time employees and independent contractors, their degree of job satisfaction is closely linked to the availability of these job conditions or attributes.

At SAS Institute, for instance, every white-collar employee has the opportunity to create a flexible schedule.[51] Other companies nationally recognized for having superior flextime policies are Pillsbury, Deloitte & Touche, and Aetna Life & Casualty.[52] Of course, flextime is more feasible in white-collar businesses that do not have to maintain standard customer-service hours. For this reason, it is not usually an option for employees on production teams, in retail stores, or in many offices where employees have to be on hand to wait on customers or answer calls.

The sense of control employees get from arranging their own work schedules is motivating for many. Companies have found that flextime reduces turnover, enables the company to adapt to business cycles, allows operation of a round-the-clock business, and helps maintain morale and performance after reengineering or downsizing. Still, flextime is not without drawbacks. They include supervisors who feel uncomfortable and less in control when employees are coming and going, and co-workers who resent flextimers because they assume that people who work flexible hours don't take their jobs seriously enough.[53]

### Telecommuting

Related to flexible schedules is **telecommuting**—working from home or another location using computers and telecommunications equipment to stay in touch with the employer's offices. Depending on which study you read, between 20 and 58 percent of employers now offer telecommuting arrangements for their employees. In fact, current estimates now put the number of U.S. telecommuters at about 16 million.[54]

Of course, some company operations clearly are not designed for telecommuting. For example, a printer who runs giant color presses can't run the presses from home. But for the kinds of jobs that can be performed from remote sites, telecommuting helps meet employees' needs for flexibility while boosting their productivity as much as 20 percent. Half of AT&T's 50,000 managers worldwide now telecommute.[55] Companies such as AT&T, IBM, and Lucent Technologies provide employees with laptops, dedicated phone lines, software support, fax-printer units, help lines, and full technical backup at the nearest corporate facility. Some even provide employees who work at home with a generous allowance for furnishings and equipment to be used at their discretion.[56]

Telecommuting offers many advantages. For one thing, it can save the company money by eliminating offices people don't need, consolidating others, and reducing related overhead costs.[57] Telecommuting also enables a company to hire talented people in distant areas without requiring them to relocate. This option expands the company's pool of potential job candidates while benefiting employees who have an employed spouse, children in school, or elderly parents to care for.[58] Employees also like telecommuting because they can set their own hours, reduce job-related expenses such as commuting costs, and spend more time with their families.

Telecommuting does have its limitations. The challenges of managing the cultural changes required by telecommuting are substantial. In telecommuting situations, midlevel managers relinquish direct, visual employee supervision. Some find it scary to be in the position of managing people they can't see. Others are concerned that people working at home will slack off or that telecommuting could cause resentment among office-bound colleagues or weaken company loyalty.[59] Regardless, companies are learning that you can't just give people computers, send them home, and call them telecommuters. You have to teach an employee how to think like a telecommuter.

Merrill Lynch recognizes this fact. Prospective telecommuters at Merrill Lynch must submit a detailed proposal that covers when and how they're going to work at home, and even what their home office will look like. Next they participate in a series of meetings. Finally, they spend two weeks in a simulation lab that lets employees and their managers experience the change. Once at home, telecommuters are required to document their at-home working hours and submit weekly progress reports.[60] But even for those companies that provide support, some telecommuters are finding that this "ideal setup" is not for everyone.

## active exercise <

### Take a moment to apply what you've learned.

### Job Sharing

**Job sharing,** which lets two employees share a single full-time job and split the salary and benefits, has been slowly gaining acceptance as a way to work part-time in a full-time position. According to a recent survey by Hewitt Associates (a firm specializing in employee benefits), 37 percent of employers offer job-sharing arrangements to their employees.[61] But such arrangements are usually offered to people who already work for the company and who need to cut back their hours. Rather than lose a good employee or have to find and train someone new, the company finds a way to split responsibilities.

Consider UnumProvident, a leading provider of insurance products. When two of its employees approached the company about sharing a job, the company decided to let them do it. Now one employee works all day Monday and Tuesday, the other works all day Thursday and Friday, and the two overlap on Wednesday. The personal benefits are exactly what the employees hoped for—more time at home. The company benefits because the position is rarely left uncovered during times of vacation or illness and because two people, instead of just one person, bring their ideas and creativity to the job.[62]

## > active concept check

**Now let's take a moment to test your knowledge of the concepts you have studied in this section.**

## > Working with Labor Unions

Not only do today's employees want alternative work arrangements, but they want safe and comfortable working conditions and pay that rewards their contributions to the organization. At the same time, however, business owners must focus on using company resources to increase productivity and profits. In the best of times and in the most enlightened companies, these two sets of needs can often be met simultaneously. However, when the economy slows down and competition speeds up, balancing the needs of employees with those of management can be a challenge.

Because of this potential for conflict, many employees join **labor unions,** organizations that seek to protect employee interests by negotiating with employers for better wages and benefits, improved working conditions, and increased job security. (See Exhibit 10.6 for a summary of the most significant laws relating to labor unions.) Employees are most likely to turn to unions if they are deeply dissatisfied with their current job and employment conditions, if they believe that unionization can be helpful in improving those job conditions, and if they are willing to overlook negative stereotypes that have surrounded unions in recent years.[63]

One advantage of joining labor unions is that it gives employees stronger bargaining power. By combined forces, union employees can put more pressure on management than they could as individuals. For instance, in August 1997, the International Brotherhood of Teamsters called a national strike against United Parcel Service (UPS) to fight for better pay for part-time workers, more full-time jobs, and better pension benefits. UPS finally agreed to most of the union's demands but only after the U.S. public supported the strike and began taking their business elsewhere. The 15-day labor dispute cost UPS about $1 billion in lost revenues.[64]

Not all employees support labor unions, of course. Many believe that unions stifle individual initiative and are not necessary to ensure fair treatment from employers. Moreover, companies that have most successfully resisted unionization seem to have adopted participative management styles and an enhanced sense of responsibility toward employees. Consider Marriott International. Marriott has recognized that the primary reasons employees consider unionizing is because they feel they are not treated well by management. In order to demonstrate to workers that they are valued, Marriott offers its employees stock options, social-service referral networks, day care, training classes, and opportunities for advancement. As a result, Marriott's employee turnover is well below that of most companies, and its employees' enthusiasm is high.[65]

Still, even the best working conditions are no guarantee that employees won't seek union representation. For instance, although Starbucks is renowned for its generous employee benefit programs and supportive work environment, employees of stores in Vancouver, British Columbia, organized and successfully bargained for higher wages.[66]

## HOW UNIONS ARE STRUCTURED

Many unions are organized at local, national, and international levels. **Locals,** or local unions, represent employees in a specific geographic area or facility; an example is Local 1853, which represents

| Legislation | Provision |
|---|---|
| Norris–La Guardia Act of 1932 | Limits companies' ability to obtain injunctions against union strikes, picketing, membership drives, and other activities. |
| National Labor Relations Act of 1935 (Wagner Act) | Gives employees the right to form, join, or assist labor organizations; the right to bargain collectively with employers through elected union representatives; and the right to engage in strikes, pickets, and boycotts. Prohibits certain unfair labor practices by the employer and union. Establishes the National Labor Relations Board to supervise union elections and to investigate charges of unfair labor practices by management. |
| Labor-Management Relations Act of 1947 (Taft-Hartley Act) | Amends Wagner Act to reaffirm employees' rights to organize and bargain collectively over working conditions. Establishes specific unfair labor practices both for management and for unions, and prohibits strikes in the public sector. |
| Landrum-Griffin Act of 1959 | Amends Taft-Hartley Act and Wagner Act to control union corruption and to add the secondary boycott as an unfair labor practice. A secondary boycott occurs when a union appeals to firms or other unions to stop doing business with an employer who sells or handles goods of a company whose employees are on strike. The act requires all unions to file annual financial reports with the U.S. Department of Labor, making union officials more personally responsible for the union's financial affairs. The act guarantees individual member rights such as the right to vote in union elections, the right to sue unions, and the right to attend and participate in union meetings. |
| Plant-Closing Notification Act of 1988 | Requires employers to give employees and local elected officials 60 days advance notice of plant shutdowns or massive layoffs. |

**EXHIBIT 10.6**

Key Legislation Relating to Unions

Most major labor legislation was enacted in the 1930s and 1940s. However, some more recent legislation has also been passed to protect organized labor.

GM's Saturn employees. Each local union is a hierarchy with a broad base of *rank-and-file* members, the employees the union represents. These members pay an initiation fee, pay regular dues, and vote to elect union officials. Each department or facility also has or elects a **shop steward,** who works in the facility as a regular employee and serves as a go-between with supervisors when a problem arises. In large locals and in locals that represent employees at several locations, an elected full-time **business agent** visits the various work sites to negotiate with management and enforce the union's agreements with those companies.

By comparison, a **national union** is a nationwide organization composed of many local unions that represent employees in specific locations; examples are the United Auto Workers (UAW) of America and the United Steelworkers of America. *International unions* have members in more than one country, such as the Union of Needletrades, Industrial, and Textile Employees (UNITE). A national union is responsible for such activities as organizing new areas or industries, negotiating industrywide contracts, assisting locals with negotiations, administering benefits, lobbying Congress, and lending assistance in the event of a strike. Local unions send representatives to the national delegate convention, submit negotiated contracts to the national union for approval, and provide financial support in the form of dues. They have the power to negotiate with individual companies or plants and to undertake their own membership activities.

The AFL-CIO is a **labor federation** consisting of a variety of national unions and of local unions that are not associated with any other national union. The AFL-CIO's two primary roles are to promote the political objectives of the labor movement and to provide assistance to member unions in their collective bargaining efforts.[67] In recent years, the AFL-CIO has also become much more active in recruiting new members, organizing new locals, and publicizing unions in general.

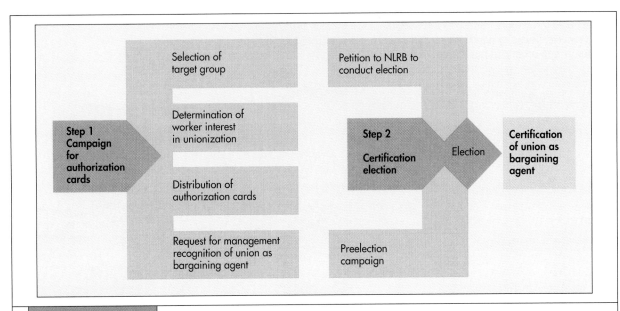

EXHIBIT 10.7

The Union-Organizing Process

This diagram summarizes the steps a labor union takes when organizing a group of employees and becoming certified to represent them in negotiations with management. The certification election is necessary only if management is unwilling to recognize the union.

## HOW UNIONS ORGANIZE

Union organizers, whether professional or rank-and-file, generally start by visiting with employees, although dissatisfied employees may also approach the union (see Exhibit 10.7). The organizers survey employees by asking questions such as "Have you ever been treated unfairly by your supervisor?" Employees who express interest are sent information about the union along with **authorization cards**—sign-up cards used to designate the union as their bargaining agent. If 30 percent or more of the employees in the group sign the union's authorization cards, the union may ask management to recognize it. Usually, however, unions do not seek to become the group's bargaining agent unless a majority of the employees sign.

Often the company's management is unwilling to recognize the union at this stage. The union can then ask the National Labor Relations Board (NLRB), an independent federal agency created in 1935 to administer and enforce the National Labor Relations Act, to supervise a **certification** election, the process by which a union becomes the official bargaining agent for a company's employees. If a majority of the affected employees choose to make the union their bargaining agent, the union becomes certified. If not, that union and all other unions have to wait a year before trying again.

Once a company becomes aware that a union is seeking a certification election, management may mount an active campaign to point out the disadvantages of unionization. A company is not allowed, however, to make specific threats or promises about how it will respond to the outcome of the election, and it is not allowed to change general wages or working conditions until the election has been concluded.

Even when a union wins a certification election, there's no guarantee that it will represent a particular group of employees forever. Sometimes employees become dissatisfied with their union and no longer wish to be represented by it. When this happens, the union members can take a **decertification** vote to take away the union's right to represent them. If the majority votes for decertification, the union is removed as bargaining agent.

> active poll

**What do you think? Voice your opinion and find out what others have to say.**

Maurice Miller, a meat cutter at Wal-Mart in Jacksonville, Texas, got the unionizing ball rolling when he was promised management training that didn't materialize, as this chapter's Case for Critical Thinking explains.

## THE COLLECTIVE BARGAINING PROCESS

As long as a union has been recognized as the exclusive bargaining agent for a group of employees, its main job is to negotiate employment contracts with management. In a process known as **collective bargaining,** union and management negotiators work together to forge the human resources policies that will apply to the unionized employees—and other employees covered by the contract—for a certain period, usually three years.

Most labor contracts are a compromise between the desires of union members and those of management. The union pushes for the best possible deal for its members, and management tries to negotiate agreements that are best for the company (and the shareholders, if a corporation is publicly held). Exhibit 10.8 illustrates the collective bargaining process.

### Meeting and Reaching an Agreement

When the negotiating teams made up of representatives of the union and management actually sit down together, they state their opening positions and each side discusses its position point by point. Labor usually wants additions to the current contract. In a cooperative atmosphere, the real issues behind the demands gradually come to light. For example, management may begin by demanding the right to determine the sizes of work crews when all it really wants is smaller work crews; the union, however, wants to protect the jobs of its members and keep crew sizes as large as possible but may agree to certain reductions in exchange for, say, higher pay. After many stages of bargaining, each party presents its package of terms, and any gaps between labor and management demands are then dealt with.

If negotiations reach an impasse, outside help may be needed. The most common alternative is **mediation**—bringing in an impartial third party to study the situation and make recommendations for resolution of the differences. Mediators are generally well-respected community leaders whom both sides will listen to. However, mediators can only offer suggestions, and their solutions are not binding. When a legally binding settlement is needed, the negotiators may submit to **arbitration**—a process in which an impartial referee listens to both sides and then makes a judgment by accepting one side's view. In *compulsory arbitration,* the parties are required by a government agency to submit to arbitration; in *voluntary arbitration,* the parties agree on their own to use arbitration to settle their differences.

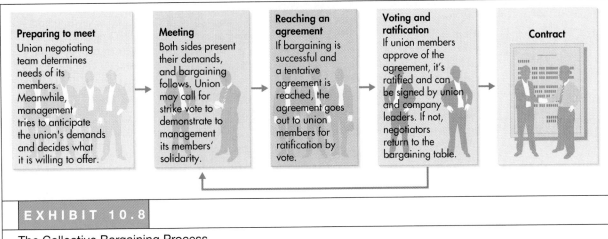

| Preparing to meet | Meeting | Reaching an agreement | Voting and ratification | Contract |
|---|---|---|---|---|
| Union negotiating team determines needs of its members. Meanwhile, management tries to anticipate the union's demands and decides what it is willing to offer. | Both sides present their demands, and bargaining follows. Union may call for strike vote to demonstrate to management its members' solidarity. | If bargaining is successful and a tentative agreement is reached, the agreement goes out to union members for ratification by vote. | If union members approve of the agreement, it's ratified and can be signed by union and company leaders. If not, negotiators return to the bargaining table. | |

**EXHIBIT 10.8**

The Collective Bargaining Process

Contract negotiations go through the four basic steps shown here.

### Exercising Options When Negotiations Break Down

The vast majority of management–union negotiations are settled quickly, easily, and in a businesslike manner. Nevertheless, sometimes negotiations reach an impasse, and neither side is willing to compromise. Both labor and management are able to draw on many powerful options when negotiations or mediation procedures break down.

**LABOR'S OPTIONS** Strikes and picket lines are perhaps labor's best-known tactics, but other options are also used.

- *Strike.* The most powerful weapon that organized labor can use is the **strike,** a temporary work stoppage aimed at forcing management to accept union demands. The basic idea behind the strike is that, in the long run, it costs management more in lost earnings to resist union demands than to give in. A 54-day strike at General Motors (GM) in 1998, for instance, cost the automaker over $2 billion in lost production revenues. Even though the union eventually won temporary reprieves on the closing of unprofitable plants, the settlement agreement failed to directly address important national issues, such as GM's push to open new factories overseas and trim its U.S. workforce. As a result, some observers pegged this costliest strike in decades as a lose-lose situation for both the company and the union.[68] An essential part of any strike is **picketing,** in which union members positioned at entrances to company premises march back and forth with signs and leaflets, trying to persuade nonstriking employees to join them and to persuade customers and others to stop doing business with the company.

- *Boycott.* A less direct union weapon is the **boycott,** in which union members and sympathizers refuse to buy or handle the product of a target company. Millions of union members form an enormous bloc of purchasing power, which may be able to pressure management into making concessions. One of the best-known boycotts was the grape boycott organized by Cesar Chavez in the early 1970s. To pressure California growers into accepting the United Farm Workers (UFW) as the bargaining agent for previously unorganized farm laborers, he and his colleagues persuaded an estimated 17 million people in the United States to stop buying grapes. Eventually, the California legislature passed the country's first law guaranteeing farmworkers the right to hold union elections.[69]

- *Publicity.* Increasingly, labor is pressing its case by launching publicity campaigns, often called *corporate campaigns,* against the target company and companies affiliated with it. These campaigns might include sending investors alerts that question the firm's solvency, staging rallies during peak business hours, sending letters to charitable groups questioning executives' motives, handing out leaflets that allege safety and health-code violations, and stimulating negative stories in the press.

Labor's other options include *slowdowns,* in which employers continue to do their jobs but at a snail's pace, and *sickouts,* in which employees feign illness and stay home. Both can cripple a company. For instance, in 2000 United Airlines was forced to cancel more than 20,000 flights during the peak summer travel months because company pilots refused to fly overtime hours and called in sick to protest the slow pace of contract negotiations.[70] Similarly, American Airlines was forced to cancel more than 6,600 flights when its pilots staged a sickout in 1999 to protest a lower wage scale for pilots of newly acquired Reno Air. A federal judge later ordered the pilots' union at American Airlines to pay the carrier $45.5 million to compensate the company for the costs it incurred and the business it lost as a result of the sickout.[71]

**MANAGEMENT'S OPTIONS**  As powerful as the union's tactics are, companies are not helpless when it comes to fighting back. Management can use a number of legal methods to pressure unions when negotiations stall:

- *Strikebreakers.* When union members walk off their jobs, management can legally replace them with **strikebreakers,** nonunion workers hired to do the jobs of striking workers. (Union members brand them as "scabs.") For example, when over 2,000 union workers struck at the *Detroit News* and *Detroit Free Press* newspapers, management kept the presses rolling by hiring 1,400 replacement workers. Although the strike caused both papers to lose customers, advertisers, and profits, the papers persevered for 19 months until the union gave in. By that time, many temporary replacements had been hired permanently, an action that management is legally permitted to take if it's necessary to keep a business going.[72]

- *Lockouts.* The U.S. Supreme Court has upheld the use of **lockouts,** in which management prevents union employees from entering the workplace in order to pressure the union to accept a contract proposal. A lockout is management's counterpart to a strike. It is a preemptive measure designed to force a union to accede to management's demands. Lockouts are legal only if the union and management have come to an impasse in negotiations and the employer is defending a legitimate bargaining position. During a lockout, the company may hire temporary replacements as long as it has no antiunion motivation and negotiations have been amicable.[73]

- *Injunctions.* An **injunction** is a court order prohibiting union workers from taking certain actions. Management used this weapon without restriction in the early days of unionism, when companies typically sought injunctions to order striking employees back to work on the grounds that the strikers were interfering with business. Today injunctions are legal only in certain cases. For example, the president of the United States has the right, under the Taft-Hartley Act, to obtain a temporary injunction to halt a strike deemed harmful to the national interest. In 1997 Bill Clinton used that power to intervene in American Airlines' labor dispute with its pilots' union. The president designated a 60-day period during which a specially appointed arbitration panel was to help the two sides reach an agreement. Although the workers were free to strike after 60 days, an agreement was reached and the strike was avoided.[74]

## active exercise

**Take a moment to apply what you've learned.**

### THE LABOR MOVEMENT TODAY

Unions remain a significant force in employee-management relations in the United States. But their membership continues to decline. Unions now represent only 14 percent (16.4 million) of workers in the United States (down from 20 percent in 1983).[75] One key reason for the decrease in union membership is the shift from a manufacturing-based economy to one dominated by service industries, which tend to appeal less to unions. Another factor contributing to the decline is the changing nature of the labor force. Women, young workers, and highly skilled workers have been harder to organize with traditional methods, as have workers in less hierarchical organizations.[76]

Dynamic labor leaders have recognized that their own inertia is partly to blame for the unions' decline, and they are taking corrective measures. Even though unions are sticking to their traditional causes—good wages, safe conditions, and benefits—progressive labor leaders are pursuing new workplace issues such as job security, increasing health care costs, labor involvement in decisions, child care, and more job training.[77] In the United States, AFL-CIO president John Sweeney has beefed up recruiting efforts, especially among low-wage service workers, minorities, and women. In addition, new industries are being targeted, including high technology and health care. Sweeney has also launched a highly visible public relations campaign and has begun to target people in smaller businesses and self-employed workers to bring them into the union fold. Some unions have already begun to show increases in membership as a result.[78]

What does the future hold for employee-management relations? It is difficult to make predictions. Although John Sweeney's leadership is boosting enthusiasm and political action among union members, as well as generating a new wave of recruiting and organizing, many experts agree that today's global economic conditions severely limit the ability of unions to regain the strength they once had. This is the case both in the United States and in other countries.

## > active concept check

**Now let's take a moment to test your knowledge of the concepts you have studied in this section.**

## > Chapter Wrap-Up

Now that you've reached the end of the chapter, you may wish to explore the concepts you've been reading about in greater detail, or test yourself to see how well you've comprehended the material. In the box below you'll find a number of links. Click on any one of these links to find additional chapter resources.

## > end-of-chapter resources

- Summary of Learning Objectives
- Practice Quiz
- Key Terms
- Test Your Knowledge
- Practice Your Knowledge
- Expand Your Knowledge
- A Case for Critical Thinking

# C H A P T E R 1 1

# Human Resources Management

 **What's Ahead**

### INSIDE BUSINESS TODAY
### BLENDING A SUCCESSFUL WORKFORCE: JAMBA JUICE WHIPS UP CREATIVE RECRUITING STRATEGIES

Finding and keeping employees in a tight labor market is no easy feat—especially for a high-growth company in the fast-food industry. But as a leading retailer of smoothies, freshly squeezed juices, healthy soups, and breads, Jamba Juice meets the challenge of building a successful workforce with an appealing blend of savvy recruiting strategies and creative incentive tools.

Since founder Kirk Perron opened his first smoothie store in 1990, Jamba Juice has grown to 300 locations in 15 states. The majority of Jamba's 4,000 employees are part-time workers, primarily high school and college students who whip up healthy concoctions between classes and during school breaks. To attract part-time "team members," Perron promotes the key ingredients of the company's success: nutrition, fitness, and fun. And he quickly points out that the company's name reflects the enjoyable working environment. *Jamba* is a West African word meaning "to celebrate."

As Jamba Juice expands its operations, Perron and his human resources staff work closely with the company's real estate committee to forecast demand for the number of workers needed in specific locations. Human resources begins the search at least four months before an official store opening, allowing time for finding, interviewing, and training new employees.

Searches are conducted using a variety of resources, and they are customized for each market. For instance, to attract young, cyber-savvy candidates who fit the profile of a typical

The Jamba Juice HR team conducts a thorough hiring process. Their goal is to get employees to stick around for the long term.

Jamba employee, human resources uses the Internet. Jamba Juice lists job openings on recruiting Web sites such as restaurantrecruit.com, a popular site with managers in the food industry. These sites, in turn, provide a direct link to Jamba Juice's Web site so that job seekers can find out more about the company or send an e-mail requesting additional information.

Of course, Internet ads can generate responses from applicants who live as far away as Australia and France. So Perron and his staff must sift through the piles of applications and identify the strongest candidates to interview. Initial interviews are conducted by telephone. During 30-minute phone screenings, human resources looks for personable candidates with a strong work ethic—the type of candidate who wants to stick with the company.

But recruiting new staff is only one of the challenges that Jamba Juice faces. Perron must also retain current store managers. To do that, Perron offers incentives to reward store performance. Managers receive a percentage of their store's sales every eight weeks. Furthermore, managers accrue retention bonuses for building the store's business. After accumulating three years of retention bonuses, managers receive a cash payment for their efforts. And managers who sign up for three more years of employment are rewarded with a three-week paid sabbatical.

Indeed Jamba's aggressive recruiting strategies and management incentives have paid off. The company's turnover rate dipped by 8 percent in one year. That's pretty impressive considering that annual employee turnover for the restaurant industry can reach 100 percent.[1]

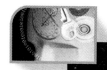

## objectives

**Take a moment to familiarize yourself with the key objectives of this chapter.**

## > Understanding What Human Resources Managers Do

As Kirk Perron knows, hiring the right people to help a company reach its goals and then overseeing their training and development, motivation, evaluation, and compensation is critical to a company's success. These activities are known as **human resources management (HRM),** which encompasses all the activities involved in acquiring, maintaining, and developing an organization's human resources. Because of the accelerating rate at which today's workforce, economy, and corporate cultures are being transformed, the role of HRM is increasingly viewed as a strategic one.

Human resources (HR) managers must figure out how to attract qualified employees from a shrinking pool of entry-level candidates; how to train less-educated, poorly skilled employees; how to keep experienced employees when they have few opportunities for advancement; and how to lay off employees equitably when downsizing is necessary. They must also retrain employees to enable them to cope with increasing automation and computerization, manage increasingly complex (and expensive) employee benefits programs, shape workplace policies to address changing workforce demographics and employee needs (as discussed in Chapter 10), and cope with the challenge of meeting government regulations in hiring practices and equal opportunity employment.

In short, human resources managers and staff members keep the organization running smoothly at every level by planning for a company's staffing needs, recruiting and hiring employees, training and developing employees and managers, and appraising employee performance. The HR staff also administers compensation and employee benefits and oversees changes in employment status (promotion, reassignment, termination or resignation, and retirement). This chapter explores each of these human resources responsibilities, beginning with planning (see Exhibit 11.1).

1. Planning for staffing needs
2. Recruiting and hiring
3. Training and development
4. Appraising performance
5. Administering compensation and benefits
6. Overseeing changes in employment status

**EXHIBIT 11.1**

The Functions of the Human Resources Department

Human resources departments are responsible for these six important functions.

One of the six functions of the human resources staff members is to plan for a company's staffing needs. Proper planning is critical because a miscalculation could leave a company without enough employees to keep up with demand, resulting in customer dissatisfaction and lost business. Yet if a company expands its staff too rapidly, profits may be eaten up by payroll, or the firm may have to lay off people who were just recruited and trained at considerable expense. The planning function consists of two steps: (1) forecasting supply and demand and (2) evaluating job requirements (see Exhibit 11.2).

## FORECASTING SUPPLY AND DEMAND

Planning begins with forecasting *demand*, the numbers and kinds of employees that will be needed at various times. For example, suppose Jamba Juice is planning to open another store in San Francisco within six months. The HR department would forecast that the store will need a store manager and an assistant manager as well as part-time salespeople. Although Jamba Juice might start looking immediately for someone as highly placed as the manager, hiring salespeople might be postponed until just before the store opens.

The next task is to estimate the *supply* of available employees. In many cases, that supply is within the company already—perhaps just needing training to fill future requirements. Jamba Juice may well find that the assistant manager at an existing store can be promoted to manage the new store, and one of the current salespeople can be named assistant manager. If existing employees cannot be tapped for new positions, the human resources manager must determine how to find people outside the company who have the necessary skills. In some cases, managers will want to consider strategic staffing alternatives such as hiring part-time and temporary employees to avoid drastic overstaffing or understaffing.

### Part-Time and Temporary Employees

More and more businesses try to save money and increase flexibility by building their workforces around part-time and temporary employees, or "temps," whose schedules can be rearranged to suit the company's needs. As a result, this segment of the labor force has increased by leaps and bounds in recent years. The Bureau of Labor Statistics projects that the temp-agency workforce will reach 4 million by 2006 (an increase of over 200 percent since 1997).[2] The temporary ranks include computer systems analysts, human resources directors, accountants, doctors, and even CEOs, with technical fields making up the fastest-growing segment of temporary employment.[3] Of the 19,000 Microsoft employees in the Puget Sound area, for example, 5,000 to 6,000 are temporary workers.[4]

The use of temps is an excellent recruiting technique because it allows companies to try out employees before hiring them permanently. Thus, what often begins as a temp assignment can turn into multiyear employment. Some 29 percent of workers employed by temp agencies remain on the job assignment for one year or more, says the Bureau of Labor Statistics. Many of these "permatemps" hold high-prestige, high-skilled technology jobs at firms such as Microsoft. In fact, they often do the same work as the company's permanent employees, but because they are temps, they do not qualify for the benefits enjoyed by regular workers.

Of course, for many, using permatemps is a win-win situation. Companies get a steady, knowledgeable labor supply, and workers have the flexibility to work for six months and then take some time off. But a recent spate of lawsuits could undo this mutually beneficial work arrangement. Some permatemps are suing companies, saying that they are, in fact, full-time employees and as such deserve employee benefits.[5]

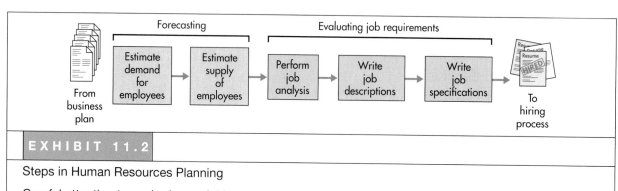

**EXHIBIT 11.2**

Steps in Human Resources Planning

Careful attention to each phase of this sequence helps ensure that a company will have the right human resources when it needs them.

## Outsourcing

Outsourcing is another way that companies fulfill their human resources needs without hiring permanent employees. Companies may outsource for a variety of reasons. Chief among them are that the outside source can provide materials, parts, or services better, at a lower price, and more efficiently. Expertise and flexibility are other reasons for outsourcing. Of course, outsourcing has many advantages: It gives companies access to new resources and world-class capabilities; it shares the risk of getting the work done; and it frees company resources for other purposes. Still, outsourcing has its share of risks. Among them are loss of control, greater dependency on suppliers, and loss of in-house skills. Some companies have also experienced work delays, unhappy customers, and labor union battles as a result of outsourcing.[6]

> ### active exercise

**Take a moment to apply what you've learned.**

## EVALUATING JOB REQUIREMENTS

The second step of the planning function is to evaluate job requirements. If you were the owner of a small business, you might have a good grasp of the requirements of all the jobs in your company. However, in large organizations where hundreds or thousands of employees are performing a wide variety of jobs, management needs a more formal and objective method of evaluating job requirements. That method is called **job analysis.**

To obtain the information needed for a job analysis, the human resources staff asks employees or supervisors several questions: What is the purpose of the job? What tasks are involved in the job? What qualifications and skills are needed to do it effectively? In what kind of setting does the job take place? Is there much public contact involved? Does the job entail much time pressure? Sometimes they obtain job information by observing employees directly. Other times they ask employees to keep daily diaries describing exactly what they do during the workday.

Once job analysis has been completed, the human resources staff develops a **job description,** a formal statement summarizing the tasks involved in the job and the conditions under which the employee will work. In most cases, the staff will also develop a **job specification,** a statement describing the skills, education, and previous experience that the job requires.

> ### active exercise

**Take a moment to apply what you've learned.**

> ### active concept check

**Now let's take a moment to test your knowledge of the concepts you have studied in this section.**

> ## Recruiting, Hiring, and Training New Employees

Having forecast a company's supply and demand for employees and evaluated job requirements, the next step is to match the job specification with an actual person or selection of people. This task is accomplished through **recruiting,** the process of attracting suitable candidates for an organization's jobs. Recruiters are specialists on the human resources staff who are responsible for locating job candidates. They use a variety of methods and resources, including internal searches, newspaper and Internet advertising, public and private employment agencies, union hiring halls, college campuses and career offices, trade shows, corporate "headhunters" (people who try to attract people at other companies), and referrals from employees or colleagues in the industry (see Exhibit 11.3). One of the fastest-growing recruitment resources for both large and small businesses is the Internet. Today many companies recruit online through their Web sites in addition to using popular online recruiting services.

## THE HIRING PROCESS

After exploring at least one—but usually more—of the available recruitment channels to assemble a pool of applicants, the human resources department may spend weeks and sometimes months on the hiring process. Most companies go through the same basic stages in the hiring process as they sift through applications to come up with the person (or persons) they want.

The first stage is to select a small number of qualified candidates from all of the applications received. Finalists may be chosen on the basis of a standard application form that all candidates fill out or on the basis of a résumé—a summary of education, experience, and personal data compiled by each applicant (see "Preparing Your Résumé" in Component Chapter D for further details). Sometimes both sources of information are used. Many organizations now use computer scanners to help them quickly sort through résumés and weed out those that don't match the requirements of the job.

The second stage in the hiring process is to interview each candidate to clarify qualifications and to fill in any missing information (see "Interviewing with Potential Employers" in Component Chapter D for further details). Another goal of the interview is to get an idea of the applicant's personality and ability to work well with others. Depending on the type of job at stake, candidates may also be asked to take a test or a series of tests.

After the initial prescreening interviews comes the third stage, when the best candidates may be asked to meet with someone in the human resources department who will conduct a more probing interview. For higher-level positions, candidates may go through a series of interviews with managers, potential co-workers, and the employees who will make up the successful candidate's staff. Sometimes this process can take weeks. Consider Southwest Airlines. To fill 4,200 job openings in one year, the company interviewed nearly 80,000 people. For many positions, candidates undergo a rigorous interview process that can take as long as six weeks before they are hired. Southwest wants to make sure that new employees will fit in with the company's culture. The payback: low turnover and high customer satisfaction.[7]

After all the interviews have been completed, the process moves to the final stages. In the fourth stage, the position's supervisor evaluates the candidates, sometimes in consultation with a higher-level manager, the human resources department, and staff. During the fifth stage, the employer checks the references of the top few candidates. The employer may also research the candidates' education, previous employment, and motor vehicle records. A growing number of employers are also checking candidates' credit histories, a practice that is drawing criticism as a violation of privacy.[8] In the sixth stage, the supervisor selects the most suitable person for the job. Now the search is over—provided the candidate accepts the offer.

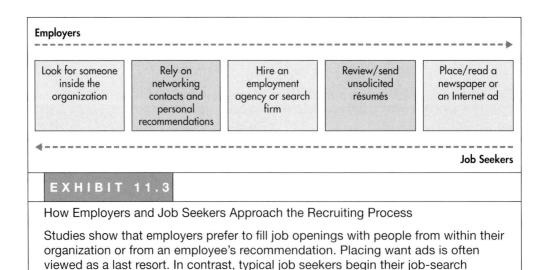

**Employers**

| Look for someone inside the organization | Rely on networking contacts and personal recommendations | Hire an employment agency or search firm | Review/send unsolicited résumés | Place/read a newspaper or an Internet ad |

**Job Seekers**

### EXHIBIT 11.3

How Employers and Job Seekers Approach the Recruiting Process

Studies show that employers prefer to fill job openings with people from within their organization or from an employee's recommendation. Placing want ads is often viewed as a last resort. In contrast, typical job seekers begin their job-search process from the opposite direction (starting with reading a newspaper or Internet ads).

### Background Checks

Violence in the workplace is an increasing threat that can harm employees and customers, hurt productivity, and lead to expensive lawsuits and higher health care costs. More than 1 million physical assaults and thousands of homicides occur at work each year. If an employer fails to prevent "preventable violences," that employer will likely be found liable. This means that companies need to be especially careful about negligent hiring.[9] In one case, Saks Fifth Avenue hired an undercover security officer at its flagship store in New York without adequately checking his background. After he raped a young woman executive twice in her office, it was discovered that the security officer had been convicted of sexually abusing an 11-year-old girl in Kentucky.[10]

This and similar cases emphasize the need for employers to conduct thorough background checks on job applicants, including verifying all educational credentials and previous jobs, accounting for any large time gaps between jobs, and checking references (see Exhibit 11.4). Background checks are particularly important for jobs in which employees are in a position to possibly harm others. For example, a trucking company must check applicants' driving records to avoid hiring a new trucker with poor driving skills.

### Hiring and the Law

Federal and state laws and regulations govern many aspects of the hiring process. In particular, employers must be careful to avoid discrimination in the wording of their application forms, in interviewing, and in testing. Employers must also respect the privacy of applicants. Consider the dilemma this presents for employers.

On the one hand, asking questions about unrelated factors such as citizenship, marital status, age, and religion violates the Equal Employment Opportunity Commission's regulations because they may lead to discrimination. In addition, employers are not allowed to ask questions about whether a person has children, whether a person owns or rents a home, what caused a physical disability, whether a person belongs to a union, whether a person has ever been arrested, or when a person attended school. The exception is when such information is related to a bona fide occupational qualification for the specific job.

On the other hand, employers must also obtain sufficient information about employees to avoid becoming the target of a negligent-hiring lawsuit. Moreover, the Immigration Reform and Control Act (passed in 1986) forbids almost all U.S. companies from hiring illegal aliens. The act also prohibits discrimination in hiring on the basis of national origin or citizenship status. This results in a sticky situation for many employers who must try to determine their applicants' citizenship so they can verify that the newly hired are legally eligible to work without asking questions that violate the law. As you can imagine, striking the balance can be quite a challenge.

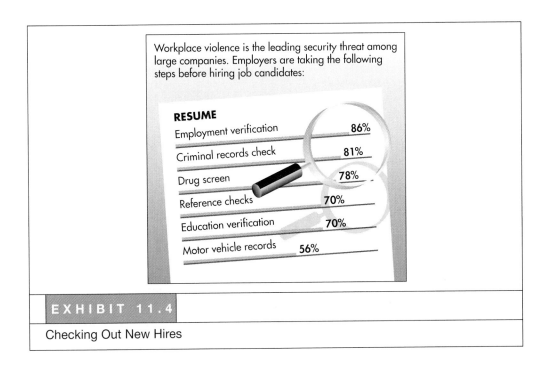

Workplace violence is the leading security threat among large companies. Employers are taking the following steps before hiring job candidates:

**RESUME**

| | |
|---|---|
| Employment verification | 86% |
| Criminal records check | 81% |
| Drug screen | 78% |
| Reference checks | 70% |
| Education verification | 70% |
| Motor vehicle records | 56% |

**EXHIBIT 11.4**

Checking Out New Hires

### Testing

One much-debated aspect of the hiring process is testing—using not only the tests that prospective employers give job applicants but any devices that can evaluate employees when making job decisions. Tests are used to gauge abilities, intelligence, interests, and sometimes even physical condition and personality.

Many companies rely on preemployment testing to determine whether applicants are suited to the job and whether they'll be worth the expense of hiring and training. Companies use three main procedures: job-skills testing, psychological testing, and drug testing. Job-skills tests are the most common type, designed to assess competency or specific abilities needed to perform a job. Psychological tests usually take the form of questionnaires. These tests can be used to assess overall intellectual ability, attitudes toward work, interests, managerial potential, or personality characteristics—including dependability, commitment, and motivation. People who favor psychological testing say that it can predict how well employees will actually perform on the job. However, critics say that such tests are ineffective and potentially discriminatory.

To avoid the increased costs and reduced productivity associated with drug abuse in the workplace (estimated to cost industry some $100 billion a year), many employers require applicants to be tested for drug use. Studies show that substance abusers have two to four times as many workplace accidents as people who do not use drugs. Moreover, drug use can be linked to over 40 percent of industry fatalities. Nevertheless, some employers prefer not to incur the extra expense to administer drug tests; others consider such tests an invasion of privacy.[11]

## active poll  <

**What do you think? Voice your opinion and find out what others have to say.**

## TRAINING AND DEVELOPMENT

To make sure that all new employees understand the company's goals, policies, and procedures, most large organizations and many small ones have well-defined **orientation** programs. Although they vary, such programs usually include information about company background and structure, equal opportunity practices, safety regulations, standards of employee conduct, company culture, employee compensation and benefit plans, work times, and other topics that newly hired employees might have questions about.[12] Orientation programs help new employees understand their role in the organization and feel more comfortable.

At Intel, for instance, all new hires participate in a six-month "integration" curriculum. Day One begins when new hires receive a packet at their home. The packet contains material about the company's culture and values, along with some forms to fill out. During the first month, all new hires attend a class called "Working at Intel," a formal eight-hour introduction to the company's corporate culture. At the end of the six-month period, each new hire participates in a two-hour structured question-and-answer session, in which an executive reviews the employee's transition into Intel and then asks a final long-term question: "What do you think it will take to succeed at Intel?"[13]

In addition to orientation programs, most companies offer training (and retraining), because employee competence has a direct effect on productivity and profits. Wal-Mart's senior vice president of human resources Coleman Peterson believes that training is the most important part of human resources management. As Peterson puts it, "Wal-Mart is in the business of keeping and growing talent."[14] Although some employers worry that employees who develop new or improved skills might leave them for higher-paying jobs, studies show that the contrary is true. The more training given to employees, the more likely they will want to stay, because training gives them a sense that they are going somewhere in their careers, even if they're not getting a promotion.[15]

In most companies, training takes place at the work site, where an experienced employee oversees the trainee's on-the-job efforts, or in a classroom, where an expert lectures groups of employees. Tires Plus is one of a growing number of companies that invests heavily in employee training to become more competitive. Some 1,700 employees spend a total of 60,000 hours annually attending formal training programs at Tires Plus University. Additionally, Tires Plus offers special training programs to develop inexperienced but promising workers into mechanics and managers. While training programs cost Tires Plus more than $3 million a year, they help the company retain talented workers and fill

Hoping to create a better workforce, appliance maker Whirlpool sends a group of new hires to live together in a large house, where during the course of their eight-week stay, they prepare over 900 meals, wash over 120 bags of laundry, and perform countless hours of reloading Whirlpool dishwashers and dryers. This group of recruits will then use their knowledge to train sales staffs at retailers such as Sears that sell the company's appliances.

leadership positions—a small price to pay in today's tight labor market.[16] Southwest Airlines is another company that offers its employees training through its "University for People." Employees can choose courses that will help them to do their jobs more effectively and be more flexible in the tasks they can perform.[17]

Employee training may also involve a self-study component using training manuals, computers, tests, and interactive modules. For example, employees at Days Inn of America participate in interactive self-paced Web-based training to learn reservation operations, housekeeping duties, supervision, and even how to deal with surly guests.[18]

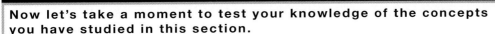

**> active concept check**

**Now let's take a moment to test your knowledge of the concepts you have studied in this section.**

 **Appraising Employee Performance**

How do employees know whether they are doing a good job? How can they improve their performance? What new skills should they learn? Most human resources managers attempt to answer these questions by developing **performance appraisal** systems to objectively evaluate employees according to set criteria. Such systems promote fairness because their standards are usually job-related.

The ultimate goal of performance appraisals is not to judge employees but rather to improve their performance. Thus, experts recommend that performance reviews be an ongoing discipline—not just a once-a-year event linked to employee raises. Periodic performance evaluations are especially important in today's project-driven, results-oriented workplace. Employees need fast feedback so they can correct their deficiencies in a timely manner.[19]

Most companies require regular, written evaluations of each employee's work. To ensure objectivity and consistency, firms generally use a standard company performance appraisal form to evaluate employees (see Exhibit 11.5). The evaluation criteria are in writing so that both employee and supervisor understand what is expected and are therefore able to determine whether the work is being done adequately. Written evaluations also provide a record of the employee's performance, which may protect the company in cases of disputed terminations.

| Name | Title | Service Date | Date |
|---|---|---|---|
| Location | Division | Department | |
| Length of Time in Present Position | Period of Review | Appraised by | |
| | From: _____ To: _____ | Title of Appraisor | |

| Area of Performance | Comment | Rating |
|---|---|---|
| **Job Knowledge and Skill**<br>Understands responsibilities and uses background for job. Adapts to new methods/techniques. Plans and organizes work. Recognizes errors and problems. | | 5  4  3  2  1 |
| **Volume of Work**<br>Amount of work output. Adherence to standards and schedules. Effective use of time. | | 5  4  3  2  1 |
| **Quality of Work**<br>Degree of accuracy–lack of errors. Thoroughness of work. Ability to exercise good judgment. | | 5  4  3  2  1 |
| **Initiative and Creativity**<br>Self-motivation in seeking responsibility and work that needs to be done. Ability to apply original ideas and concepts. | | 5  4  3  2  1 |
| **Communication**<br>Ability to exchange thoughts or information in a clear, concise manner. Dealing with different organizational levels of clientele. | | 5  4  3  2  1 |
| **Dependability**<br>Ability to follow instructions and directions correctly. Performs under pressure. Reliable work habits. | | 5  4  3  2  1 |
| **Leadership Ability/Potential**<br>Ability to guide others to the successful accomplishment of a given task. Potential for developing subordinate employees. | | 5  4  3  2  1 |

**5. Outstanding** — Employee who consistently exceeds established standards and expectations of the job.

**4. Above Average** — Employee who consistently meets established standards and expectations of the job. Often exceeds and rarely falls short of desired results.

**3. Satisfactory** — Generally qualified employee who meets job standards and expectations. Sometimes exceeds and may occasionally fall short of desired expectations. Performs duties in a normally expected manner.

**2. Improvement Needed** — Not quite meeting standards and expectations. An employee at this level of performance is not quite meeting all the standard job requirements.

**1. Unsatisfactory** — Employee who fails to meet the minimum standards and expectations of the job.

| I have had the opportunity to read this performance appraisal. | How long has this employee been under your supervision? |
|---|---|
| Signature        Date | Signature of Supervisor        Date |

**EXHIBIT 11.5**

Sample Performance Appraisal Form

Many companies use forms like this one to ensure performance appraisals are as objective as possible.

Many performance appraisal systems require the employee to be rated by several people (including more than one supervisor and perhaps several co-workers). This practice further promotes fairness by correcting for possible biases. One appraisal format that moves the review process from a one-dimensional perspective to a multidimensional format is the 360-degree review. Designed to provide employees with a broader range of perspectives, the 360-degree review solicits feedback from colleagues above, below, and around the employee to provide observations of the person's performance in several skill and behavioral categories. This means that employees rate the performance of their superiors as well as that of their peers.[20]

One of the biggest problems with any employee appraisal system is finding a way to measure productivity. In a production job, the person who types the most pages of acceptable copy or who assembles the most defect-free microprocessors in a given amount of time is clearly the most productive. But how does an employer evaluate the productivity of the registration clerk at a hotel or the middle manager at a large television station? Although the organization's overall productivity can be measured (number of rooms booked per night, number of viewers per hour), often the employer can't directly relate the results to any one employee's efforts.

Evaluating productivity becomes an even greater challenge in organizations where employees work in teams. Some companies, such as Con-Way Transportation Services, meet this challenge by having teams evaluate themselves. About every three months a neutral facilitator leads a discussion in which team members rate team performance on a 1 to 5 scale for 31 criteria, which can include customer satisfaction, the ability to meet goals, employee behavior toward co-workers and customers, job knowledge, motivation, and skills. During the meetings, members discuss the team's performance. Individual performance is also discussed but only in the context of the team. Each person creates two columns on a sheet of paper, one labeled "strengths" and the other, "something to work on." Team members self-assess and then pass the list around the room so other team members can add their comments.[21]

> ## video exercise

**Take a moment to apply what you've learned.**

> ## Administering Compensation and Employee Benefits

On what basis should employees be paid? How much should they be paid? When should they be paid? What benefits should they receive? Every day, company leaders confront these types of decisions. Administering **compensation,** a combination of payments in the form of wages or salaries, incentive payments, employee benefits, and employer services, is another major responsibility of a company's human resources department.

## WAGES AND SALARIES

Many blue-collar (production) and some white-collar (management and clerical) employees receive compensation in the form of **wages,** which are based on calculating the number of hours worked, the number of units produced, or a combination of both time and productivity. Wages provide a direct incentive to an employee: The more hours worked or the more pieces completed, the higher the employee's paycheck. Moreover, employers in the United States must comply with the Fair Labor Standards Act of 1938, which sets a minimum hourly wage for most employees and mandates overtime pay for employees who work longer than 40 hours a week. Most states also have minimum wage laws intended to protect employees not covered by federal laws or to set higher wage floors.[22]

Employees whose output is not always directly related to the number of hours worked or the number of pieces produced are paid **salaries.** As with wages, salaries base compensation on time, but the unit of time is a week, two weeks, a month, or a year. Salaried employees such as managers normally receive no pay for the extra hours they sometimes put in; overtime is simply part of their obligation. However, they do get a certain amount of leeway in their schedules.

Both wages and salaries are, in principle, based on the contribution of a particular job to the company. Thus, a sales manager, who is responsible for bringing in sales revenue, is paid more than a secretary, who handles administrative tasks but doesn't sell or supervise. However, as the tables in Component Chapter D show, pay varies widely by position, industry, and location. Among the best-paid employees in the world are chief executive officers of large U.S. corporations.

## INCENTIVE PROGRAMS

To encourage employees to be more productive, innovative, and committed to their work, many companies such as Jamba Juice provide managers and employees with **incentives,** cash payments that are linked to specific individual, group, and companywide goals; overall productivity; and company success. In other words, achievements, not just activities, are made the basis for payment. The success of these programs often depends on how closely incentives are linked to actions within the employee's control:

- *Bonuses.* For both salaried and wage-earning employees, one type of incentive compensation is the **bonus,** a payment in addition to the regular wage or salary. As an incentive to reduce turnover during the year, some firms pay an annual year-end bonus, amounting to a certain percentage of each employee's wages. Other cash bonuses are tied to company performance.

- *Commissions.* In contrast to bonuses, **commissions** are a form of compensation that pays employees a percentage of sales made. Used mainly for sales staff, they may be either the sole compensation or an incentive payment in addition to a regular salary.

- *Profit sharing.* Employees may be rewarded for staying with a company and encouraged to work harder through **profit sharing,** a system in which employees receive a portion of the company's profits. Depending on the company, profits may be distributed quarterly, semiannually, or annually.

- *Gain sharing.* Similar to profit sharing, **gain sharing** ties rewards to profits (or cost savings) achieved by meeting specific goals such as quality and productivity improvement. For example, gain sharing is one tool that the city of College Station, Texas, uses to encourage savings and innovative ideas. In 1997, 520 full-time city employees each received $460 as a reward for helping to save the city $884,000.[23]

- *Pay for performance.* A variation of gain sharing, **pay for performance,** requires employees to accept a lower base pay but rewards them if they reach production targets or other goals. Experts estimate that 30 percent of U.S. companies have already adopted at least some pay-for-performance measures. Many have realized productivity gains as well as greater flexibility in keeping employees during hard times.[24] However, some critics point out that such incentives can actually lead to lower quality because employees become focused on working fast rather than working well.

- *Knowledge-based pay.* Another approach to compensation being explored by companies is **knowledge-based pay,** or skill-based pay, which is tied to employees' knowledge and abilities rather than to their job per se. Typically, the pay level at which a person is hired matches that person's current level of skills; as the employee acquires new skills, the pay level goes up. Because employees do not compete with each other to increase their pay through promotions, knowledge-based pay enhances teamwork, flexibility, and motivation.[25]

- *Broadbanding.* Like knowledge-based pay, **broadbanding** gives pay raises without promoting employees. Instead of having many narrow pay grades, the company has fewer, broader pay grades. For example, instead of a range of $30,000 to $40,000 for a particular job, a broadband range may be $20,000 to $50,000. This approach allows today's flatter organizations to reward employees without having to move them up a hierarchy. It also allows companies to move employees to different positions without being restricted by the pay grades normally associated with specific jobs.

Although these incentive programs are popular in today's workplace, some companies find it difficult to change the way workers think about pay. For a long time, businesses have trained their employees to associate higher job grades with status, titles, and eligibility for additional benefits. Furthermore, some critics say that broadbanding and other incentives don't really benefit employees, but are just another way for companies to keep labor costs down. One study by compensation consulting firm William M. Mercer reported that under broadbanding, employees' long-term career earnings actually decrease between 10 and 50 percent.[26]

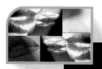

**active poll**  <

**What do you think? Voice your opinion and find out what others have to say.**

## EMPLOYEE BENEFITS AND SERVICES

Companies also regularly provide **employee benefits**—financial benefits other than wages, salaries, and incentives. For example, Starbucks offers medical and dental insurance, vacation and holiday pay, stock options, discounts on Starbucks products, and a free pound of coffee every week. The benefits package is available to part-time as well as full-time employees, so Starbucks attracts and retains good people at every level.[27]

Some companies offer employee benefits as a preset package; that is, the employee gets whatever insurance, paid holidays, pension plan, and other benefits the company sets up. But a growing number of companies recognize that people have different priorities and needs at different stages of their lives. So they offer employees flexible benefits. Such plans allows employees to pick their benefits—up to a certain dollar amount—to create a benefits package that is tailored to their individual needs. Moreover, they smooth out imbalances in benefits received by single employees and workers with families.[28] An employee with a young family might want extra life or health insurance, for example, and might feel no need for a pension plan, whereas a single employee might choose to "buy" an extra week or two of vacation time by giving up some other benefit.

The benefits most commonly provided by employers are insurance, retirement benefits, employee stock-ownership plans, stock options, and family benefits. In the next sections, we will explore how these benefits and services are undergoing considerable change to meet the needs of today's workforce.

### Insurance

Although it is entirely optional, insurance is the most popular employee benefit. Many businesses offer substantial compensation in the form of life and health insurance, but dental and vision plans, disability insurance, and long-term-care insurance are also gaining in popularity (see Component Chapter C for a discussion of types of employee insurance coverage). Today only about 62 percent of employees are covered by a company health plan.[29]

Often a company will negotiate a group insurance plan for employees and pay most of the premium costs. However, faced with exploding health costs, many companies now require employees to pay part of their insurance premiums or more of the actual doctor bills.[30] In addition, more companies are hiring part-time and temporary workers, who typically receive very few company benefits. Nonetheless, some companies, such as Schlotzky's company-owned restaurants provide employees with fully paid health coverage because doing so discourages employee turnover. "The benefits plan is a positive incentive for people to come on board; it helps hire people who might have gone to Wendy's or Burger King," says Schlotzky's human resources director, Alice Klepac.[31]

### Retirement Benefits

In the past, few people were able to save enough money in the course of their working years for their retirement. The main purpose of the Social Security Act was to provide basic support to those who could not accumulate the retirement money they would need later in life. Today, nearly everyone who works regularly has become eligible for Social Security payments during retirement. This income is paid for by the Social Security tax, part of which is withheld by the employer from employees' wages and part of which is paid by the employer.

In addition to Social Security, many employees receive company-sponsored retirement benefits. Studies show that 72 percent of workers at large firms (more than 500 employees) have some form of company-sponsored retirement coverage.[32] The most popular type of retirement coverage is the **pension plan,** which is funded by company contributions. Each year, enough money is set aside in a separate pension account to cover employees' future retirement benefits. These plans are regulated by the Employees' Retirement Income Security Act of 1974 (ERISA), which established a federal agency to insure the assets of pension plans.

Three of the most popular types of company-sponsored pension plans are *defined contribution plans, defined benefit plans,* and *401(k) plans.* About 51 percent of company pension plans are defined contribution plans, which are similar to savings plans that provide a future benefit based on annual employer contributions, voluntary employee matching contributions, and accumulated investment earnings. Less popular are defined benefit plans, which are offered by only 27.4 percent of those companies offering pension plans.[33] Defined benefit plans are formula-based plans in which employers typically promise to pay their employees a benefit upon retirement based on the employee's retirement age, final average salary, and years of service.[34] Another popular type of retirement plan is the employer-sponsored 401(k) plan, which allows eligible participants to contribute pre-tax dollars to a tax-qualified retirement plan. One special feature of a 401(k) plan is the deferral of federal and state income taxes and Social Security taxes on contributions up to a maximum of $10,500 until the time of withdrawal.[35]

In addition to these three plans, a number of employers are now offering employees "hybrid" plans that combine the features of both defined benefit and defined contribution plans. One example is a cash-balance plan, which is a defined benefit plan that provides a defined-contribution–type lump sum distribution consisting of contributions and interest earnings for employees who leave before retirement age.[36]

### Employee Stock-Ownership Plans

Another employee benefit being offered by a number of companies is the **employee stock-ownership plan (ESOP),** under which a company places a certain amount of its stock in trust for some or all of its employees, with each employee entitled to a certain share. These plans allow employees to later purchase the shares at a fixed price. If the company does well, the ESOP may provide a substantial employee benefit.

Of course, linking the financial success of employees to the success of the company is indeed a worthy goal, but some say that in the long run ESOPs are not effective performance motivators. Consider United Airlines. In 1994, United Airlines' pilots made major wage concessions in exchange for receiving a 55 percent equity stake in the company via an ESOP. As a result of those concessions, United's pilots trailed the industry in pay. Nevertheless, the pilots hoped to recover the equivalence of their lost wages and more through increased market value of their ESOP shares, and the company hoped to gain enhanced employee morale and improved customer service by making the employees stockholders. Neither occurred. "I was one of the people who believed it [employee stock ownership] would make a difference and that life would be better than it has been," says one United pilot spokesperson. "But it doesn't seem to have made a great deal of difference in the way the company was run." Moreover, because ESOP rules bar employees from selling their shares until they retire or quit, the shares were useless for financing a mortgage or a college education. In short, the pilots felt they had been taken for a ride.[37] So after a summer of tense union negotiations and thousands of cancelled United flights, in September 2000 management finally agreed to give the pilots substantial wage hikes and to terminate the ESOP.[38]

### Stock Options

A related method for tying employee compensation to company performance is the stock option plan. The National Center for Employee Ownership estimates that between 7 to 10 million employees received stock options in 1999 (an increase of 20 percent from 1998). **Stock options** grant employees the right to purchase a set number of shares of the employer's stock at a specific price, called the *grant price,* during a certain time period. Options typically "vest" over five years, at a rate of 20 percent annually. This means that at the end of one year employees can purchase up to 20 percent of the shares in the original grant, at the end of two years 40 percent, and so on.

For example, in 1997 paper products maker Kimberly-Clark gave its 57,000 employees a grant of 25 to 125 options each at $52.125 a share (the grant price). The options could be exercised from January 2, 2000, to October 21, 2004. If the market price of Kimberly-Clark's stock climbs above the grant price during this exercise period, employees can purchase their set number of shares at the grant price, sell them at the market price, and pocket the profit. If the market price does not exceed $52.125, employees will let their options expire.[39]

Stock options can be a win-win situation for employers and employees. From the employer's perspective, stock options cost very little and provide long-term incentives for good people to stay with the company. From the employee's perspective, stock options can generate a handsome profit if the stock's market price exceeds the grant price. But stock options lose their appeal when the stock does not perform as expected. Employees could lose considerable profits if the stock's price falls below the option grant price.[40]

### Family Benefits

The Family Medical and Leave Act (FMLA), signed into law in 1993, requires employers with 50 or more workers to provide them with up to 12 weeks of unpaid leave per year for childbirth, adoption, or the care of oneself, a child, a spouse, or a parent with serious illness.[41] Although the intent of the law is noble, the fact is that the average person can't afford to take extended periods of time off without pay.

Day care is another important family benefit, especially for two-career couples. Although only 10 percent of companies provide day care facilities on the premises, 86 percent of companies surveyed by Hewitt & Associates offer child-care assistance. Types of assistance include dependent-care spending accounts and resource and referral (R&R) services, which help employees find suitable child care. Firms estimate that they save anywhere from $2.00 to $6.75 in lost productivity and employee absenteeism for every $1.00 they spend on R&R programs.[42]

A related family issue is care for aging parents. An estimated 50 percent of employers offer some form of elder-care assistance, ranging from referral services that help find care providers to dependent-care allowances. Some companies will even agree to move elderly relatives when they transfer an employee to another location.[43]

### Other Employee Benefits

Although sometimes overlooked, paid holidays, sick pay, premium pay for working overtime or unusual hours, and paid vacations are important benefits.[44] Companies handle holiday pay in various ways. To provide incentives for employee loyalty, most companies grant employees longer paid vacations after they've been with the organization for a prescribed number of years. Some companies let employees buy additional vacation time or sell unused days back to the employer. Sick-day allowances also vary from company to company and from industry to industry. Some U.S. companies, including Texas Instruments, have begun offering paid-time-off banks that combine vacation, personal use, and sick days into one package. Employees can then take a certain number of days off each year for whatever reason necessary, with no questions asked.[45]

Among the many other benefits that companies sometimes offer are sabbaticals, tuition loans and reimbursements, professional development opportunities, personal computers, financial counseling and legal services, assistance with buying a home, paid expenses for spouses who travel with employees, employee assistance programs, nap time, and wellness programs. Typical wellness programs include health screenings, health and wellness education programs, and fitness programs. Children's clothier Osh Kosh B'Gosh, for example, provides wellness education classes in nutrition, heart disease, cancer, diabetes, prescription medication, and others.[46] Wellness programs have been reported to reduce absenteeism, health care costs, sickness, and work-related accidents.[47]

According to the U.S. Labor Department, 48 percent of all employers with more than 100 workers now offer **employee assistance programs (EAPs).** EAPs offer private and confidential counseling to employees who need help with issues related to drugs, alcohol, finances, stress, family, and other personal problems. Studies by the National Council on Alcoholism and Drug Dependence (NCADD) show that the average annual cost for EAP services run from $12 to $20 per employee. But, on average, these services save between $5 and $16 for each dollar spent as a result of improved safety and productivity, as well as reduced employee turnover.[48]

Benefits such as company cars, paid country club memberships, free parking, and expanded casual dress days are often referred to as perks. With today's tight job market, perks are being offered more frequently to attract the best managers (see Exhibit 11.6).[49] "But recruitment perks only go so far," says one compensation expert. "Organizations must offer the total work experience to attract talent." And to keep talent from leaving, they must offer workers challenging jobs and training, more family-related benefits, and better management supervision.[50]

## > active exercise

**Take a moment to apply what you've learned.**

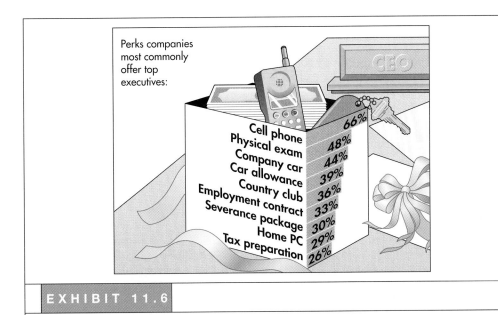

Perks companies most commonly offer top executives:

| | |
|---|---|
| Cell phone | 66% |
| Physical exam | 48% |
| Company car | 44% |
| Car allowance | 39% |
| Country club | 36% |
| Employment contract | 33% |
| Severance package | 30% |
| Home PC | 29% |
| Tax preparation | 26% |

**EXHIBIT 11.6**

Life Is Not Shabby at the Top

## > Overseeing Changes in Employment Status

Of course, providing competitive compensation and good employee benefits is no guarantee that employees will stay with the company. A recent survey shows that all things being equal, 25 percent would leave their current jobs for a pay increase of 10 percent or less, and more than 55 percent would leave for an increase of at least 20 percent.[51] Employees may also leave for reasons other than compensation. Some may decide to retire or may resign voluntarily to pursue a better opportunity. On the other hand, the company may take the initiative in making the change—by promoting, reassigning, or terminating employees. Whatever the reason, losing an employee usually means going to the trouble and expense of finding a replacement, whether from inside or outside the company. Overseeing changes in the employment status is another responsibility of the human resources department.

### PROMOTING AND REASSIGNING EMPLOYEES

When a person leaves or is promoted to a position of more responsibility, the company has to find someone else for the open job. As Exhibit 11.3 shows, many companies prefer to look within the organization for such candidates. In part, this "promote from within" policy allows a company to benefit from the training and experience of its own workforce. This policy also rewards employees who have worked hard and demonstrated the ability to handle more challenging tasks. In addition, morale is usually better when a company promotes from within because employees see that they can advance.

However, a potential pitfall of internal promotion is that a person may be given a job beyond that person's competence. A common practice is for someone who is good at one kind of job to be made a manager. Yet managing often requires a completely different set of skills. Someone who consistently racks up the most sales in the company, for example, is not necessarily a good candidate for sales manager. If the promotion is a mistake, the company not only loses its sales leader but also risks losing the employee altogether. People who can't perform well in a new job generally become demoralized and lose confidence in the abilities they do have. At the very least, support and training are needed to help promoted employees perform well.

One big issue these days is *relocation* of promoted and reassigned employees. In the past, companies transferred some employees fairly often, especially those being groomed for higher management positions. Now, however, fewer and fewer employees are willing to accept transfers. The reasons are many: disruption of a spouse's career; strong ties to family, friends, and community; disinterest in the proposed new location; the expense of relocating (buying and selling homes, planning around the reduction of a spouse's income, facing a higher cost of living in the new location); availability of good schools and child care; and the possibility that relocating won't be good for the employee's career.[52]

To encourage employee relocation, many employers today are covering the costs of house-hunting trips, moving, storage, transportation, and temporary living expenses. In addition, many employers are now helping spouses find good jobs in new locations, assisting transferees with home sales, providing school and day care referral services, and sometimes reimbursing employees for spouses' lost wages or for financial losses resulting from selling and buying houses. Many companies are also reconsidering their transfer policies and asking employees to transfer only when it is absolutely necessary.[53]

### TERMINATING EMPLOYEES

A company invests time, effort, and money in each new employee it recruits and trains. This investment is lost when an employee is removed by **termination**—permanently laying the employee off because of cutbacks or firing the employee for poor performance. Many companies facing a downturn in business have avoided large-scale layoffs by cutting administrative costs (curtailing travel, seminars, and so on), freezing wages, postponing new hiring, implementing job-sharing programs, or encouraging early retirement. However, sometimes a company has no alternative but to reduce the size of its workforce, leaving the human resources department to handle layoffs and their resulting effects on both the terminated and the remaining employees.

### Layoffs

**Layoffs** are the termination of employees for economic or business reasons unrelated to employee performance. To help ease the pain of layoffs, many companies provide laid-off employees with job-hunting assistance. *Outplacement* aids such as résumé-writing courses, career counseling, office space, and secretarial help are offered to laid-off executives and blue-collar employees alike. Moreover, outplacement centers offer courses and tests to help employees decide what types of jobs are best suited for them.[54]

Some companies adopt no-layoff, or guaranteed-employment, policies. This means that in an economic downturn, employees may be shifted to other types of jobs, perhaps at reduced pay, or given the chance to participate in work-sharing programs. Such no-layoff policies help promote employee loyalty and motivation, which benefit the company over the long run. Rhino Foods realized the benefit of this policy when the company hit a downturn in the mid-1990s. Employees voluntarily took temporary jobs with other companies, which Rhino helped them find. If the new companies paid lower wages than the employees normally received, Rhino made up the difference. Employees also kept their Rhino seniority, benefits, and accrued vacation time. When business picked up again, the employees returned. As a result of the exchange program, Rhino enjoys much higher employee morale, loyalty, and trust than it would had it laid off workers.[55]

### Firings and Employment at Will

It has long been illegal for any U.S. company to fire employees because they are would-be union organizers, have filed a job-safety complaint, or are of a particular race, religion, gender, or age. Beyond those restrictions, the courts have traditionally held that any employee not covered by a contract may be fired "at will." **Employment at will** is the right of the employer to keep or terminate employees as it sees fit. Recently, however, a number of legal decisions have begun to alter this doctrine. The most far-reaching decisions have held that there may be an implied contract between employer and employee requiring that any firing be done "fairly." **Wrongful discharge** suits—lawsuits that contend the employee was fired without adequate advance notice or explanation—have been plentiful in light of the massive layoffs in recent years. Some fired employees have even argued that their being called "permanent" employees by the company should protect them from firing—or at least from unfair firing. To combat this problem, many companies require employees to sign an "employment at will" statement acknowledging that they may be fired at any time at the company's discretion.

> **active poll**

**What do you think? Voice your opinion and find out what others have to say.**

### RETIRING EMPLOYEES

As Chapter 10 discussed, the U.S. population is aging rapidly. For the business community, an aging population presents two challenges. The first is to give job opportunities to people who are willing and able to work but who happen to be past the traditional retirement age. Many older citizens are concerned about their ability to live comfortably on fixed retirement incomes. Others simply prefer to work. For several decades, many companies and industries had **mandatory retirement** policies that made it necessary for people to quit working as soon as they turned a certain age. Then in 1967 the federal Age Discrimination in Employment Act outlawed discrimination against anyone between the ages of 40 and 65. In 1986 Congress amended the act to prohibit mandatory retirement for most employees. As a corollary, employers are also forbidden to stop benefit contributions or accruals because of age.

The second challenge posed by an aging workforce is to find ways to encourage older employees to retire early. One method a company may use is to offer older employees financial incentives to resign, such as enhanced retirement benefits or one-time cash payments. Inducing employees to depart by offering them financial incentives is known as a **worker buyout.** This method can be a lot more expensive than firing or laying off employees. However, the method has several advantages: The morale of the remaining employees is preserved because they feel less threatened about their own security, younger employees see a rise in their chances for promotion, and the risk of age-discrimination lawsuits is minimized.

## > Chapter Wrap-Up

Now that you've reached the end of the chapter, you may wish to explore the concepts you've been reading about in greater detail, or test yourself to see how well you've comprehended the material. In the box below you'll find a number of links. Click on any one of these links to find additional chapter resources.

## > end-of-chapter resources

- Summary of Learning Objectives
- Practice Quiz
- Key Terms
- Test Your Knowledge
- Practice Your Knowledge
- Expand Your Knowledge
- A Case for Critical Thinking
- Business Plan Pro: Managing Human Resources and Labor Relations

# CHAPTER 12

# Fundamentals of Marketing and Customer Service

## > What's Ahead

**INSIDE BUSINESS TODAY**
**DRIVEN BY DATA: BANKING ON INFORMATION AT CAPITAL ONE**

If you think credit cards are merely banking products, think again. According to the co-founder, chairman, and CEO of Capital One Financial Corp, "Credit cards aren't banking—they're information." In fact, information is the driving force behind Richard Fairbank's successful strategy for building Capital One into one of America's leading credit card companies.

Fairbank collects extensive records on millions of consumers, maintaining massive databases on everything from customer demographics to individual card transactions. Then he uses that information not only to identify customers who would make good credit risks but also to develop customized marketing strategies for different customer segments.

First, Fairbank applies data mining techniques to his records of potential customers to find individuals who match the profile of the ideal credit card holder: the person who maintains a credit card balance but always makes a minimum monthly payment on time. And to build his customer base, he creates customized mailing lists by studying such demographics as educational levels and club memberships. For instance, Fairbank used data mining to develop his own profile of college students after he discovered that the credit card industry's mailing lists covered only one-third of the college population. Students overlooked by other credit card companies responded eagerly to Capital One's offers, returning 70 percent more applications than the industry's standard lists.

Capital One is winning big the cutthroat world of credit cards by analyzing customer information.

Next, Fairbank analyzes information about current Capital One customers to figure out how customers use their cards and to find meaningful patterns in consumer buying behavior. Finally, he conducts 40,000 tests each year, experimenting with everything from annual credit card fees to the color of the envelopes used for mailings. One of Fairbank's early experiments, featured the "teaser rate," offering low interest rates for an introductory period. When the experiment attracted millions of new customers, competitors launched similar programs.

With test results in hand, Fairbank produces and sells 7,000 types of customized credit cards—each with slightly different terms and conditions—aimed at different customer segments. Some customers pay $20 per year for a card with $200 worth of credit. Others carry no-fee cards with credit lines of $10,000 or $20,000. And many of the cards cater to customer preferences or interests, featuring images that range from Mt. Fuji to a Mercedes-Benz or a Canadian moose.

Fairbank even uses data mining to predict what customers might buy and how Capital One can sell those products and services to them. For example, after tests revealed that customers preferred to buy things when they call Capital One—rather than when Capital One calls them—Fairbank decided to offer additional products and services to incoming callers. He partnered with other businesses to sell callers such products as MCI long distance, Hartford insurance, and Damark International catalog club memberships. And he used an analysis of each customer's buying habits and demographics to develop a computer software system that recommends which products to sell specific customer types when they call Capital One.

Such aggressive marketing tactics have indeed paid off. Capital One sells more than 1 million non–credit card products annually. Furthermore, half of all new Capital One customers buy another product from the company within 12 months of signing up for their credit card. Meanwhile, Fairbank continues to bank on Capital One's extensive databases to identify new marketing opportunities—using the databases to test, produce, and sell a constant stream of new products to Capital One's 21 million customers.[1]

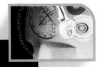

> # objectives

**Take a moment to familiarize yourself with the key objectives of this chapter.**

> # gearing up

**Before you begin reading this chapter, try a short warm-up activity.**

> ## What Is Marketing?

Even though you are just beginning a formal classroom study of business, you probably already know quite a bit about marketing. Companies like Capital One have been trying to sell you things for years, and you've learned something about their techniques—contests, advertisements, tantalizing displays of merchandise, price markdowns, and product giveaways, to name but a few. However, marketing involves much more than a fancy display of merchandise, a clever commercial, or a special contest. In fact, a lot of planning and execution are needed to develop a new product, set its price, get it into stores, and convince people to buy it.

Think about all the decisions you would have to make if you worked for Richard Fairbank, for example. How many credit card customers would you need in order to be profitable? Which types of customers would you serve? How would you attract new customers? What fees would you charge for your service? What would you do if another credit card operation offered more attractive services or lower fees? These are just a few of the many marketing decisions that all companies make in order to be successful.

The American Marketing Association (AMA) defines **marketing** as planning and executing the conception, pricing, promotion, and distribution of ideas, goods, and services to create exchanges that satisfy individual and organizational objectives.[2] With respect to products, marketing involves all decisions related to determining a product's characteristics, price, production specifications, market-entry date, distribution, promotion, and sales. With respect to customers, marketing involves understanding customers' needs and their buying behavior, creating consumer awareness, providing **customer service**—which is everything a company does to satisfy its customers—and maintaining relationships with customers long after the sales transaction is complete (see Exhibit 12.1).

Most people, of course, think of marketing in connection with selling tangible goods for a profit (the term *product* refers to any "bundle of value" that can be exchanged in a marketing transaction). But marketing applies to services, not-for-profit organizations, people, places, and causes too. Politicians always market themselves. So do places (such as Paris or Poland) that want to attract residents, tourists, and business investment. **Place marketing** describes efforts to market geographical areas ranging from neighborhoods to entire countries. **Cause-related marketing** promotes a cause or a social issue—such as physical fitness, recycling, or highway safety. *Permission marketing* asks customers for permission before sending them marketing messages. American Airlines, for example, requests your permission before sending you weekly e-mail notices listing discounted air fares.

### THE ROLE OF MARKETING IN SOCIETY

Take another look at the AMA definition of marketing. Notice that marketing involves an exchange between two parties—the buyer and the selling organization—both of whom must obtain satisfaction from the transaction. This definition suggests that marketing plays an important role in society by helping people satisfy their needs and wants and by helping organizations determine what to produce.

### Needs and Wants

To survive, people need food, water, air, shelter, and clothing. A **need** represents a difference between your actual state and your ideal state. You're hungry and you don't want to be hungry; you

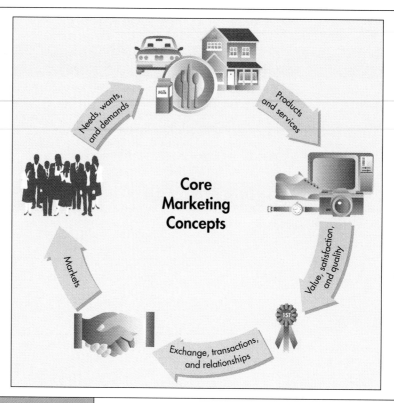

**EXHIBIT 12.1**

What Is Marketing?

Each of the core marketing concepts—needs, wants, demands, products, services, values, satisfaction, quality, exchanges, transactions, relationships, and markets—building on the ones before it.

need to eat. Needs create the motivation to buy products and are therefore at the core of any discussion of marketing.

Your **wants** are based on your needs but are more specific. Producers do not create needs, but they do shape your wants by exposing you to alternatives. For instance, when you need some food, you may want a Snickers bar or an orange. A fundamental goal of marketing is to direct the customer's basic need for various products into the desire to purchase specific brands. Al Ries and Jack Trout, co-authors of *The 22 Immutable Laws of Marketing,* note that customers' wants are directed by changing people's perception of products.[3] After all, what's the real difference between Viva and Bounty paper towels? Is one actually more absorbent than the other, or do you only perceive it that way?

### Exchanges and Transactions

When you participate in the **exchange process,** you trade something of value (usually money) for something else of value, whether you're buying an airline ticket, a car, or a college education. When you make a purchase, you cast your vote for that item and encourage the producer of that item to make more of it. In this way, supply and demand are balanced, and society obtains the goods and services that are most satisfying.

When the exchange actually occurs, it takes the form of a **transaction.** Party A gives Party B $1.29 and gets a medium Coke in return. A trade of values takes place. Most transactions in today's society involve money, but money is not necessarily required. For example, when you were a child, you may have traded your peanut butter sandwich for a friend's bologna and cheese in a barter transaction that involved no money.

### The Four Utilities

To encourage the exchange process, marketers enhance the appeal of their products and services by adding **utility,** something of value to customers (see Exhibit 12.2). When organizations change raw materials into finished goods, they are creating **form utility** desired by consumers. For example, when

| Utility | Example |
| --- | --- |
| Form utility | Sunkist Funs Fruits are nutritious, bite-sized snacks that appeal to youngsters because of their shapes—numbers, letters, dinosaurs, spooks, and animals. |
| Time utility | LensCrafters has captured a big chunk of the market for eyeglasses by providing on-the-spot, one-hour service. |
| Place utility | By offering convenient home delivery of the latest fashion apparel and accessories, the Delia*s catalog and Web site have become favorites of teenaged girls. |
| Possession utility | RealNetworks, producer of software for listening to music from the Internet, allows customers to download and install its programs directly from the company's Web site. |

**EXHIBIT 12.2**

Examples of the Four Utilities

The utility of a good or service has four aspects, each of which enhances the product's value to the consumer.

Nokia combines plastic, computer chips, and other materials to make digital phones, the company is providing form utility. In other cases, marketers try to make their products available when and where customers want to buy them, creating **time utility** and **place utility.** Overnight couriers such as Airborne Express create time utility, whereas coffee carts in offices and ATM machines in shopping malls create place utility. The final form of utility is **possession utility**—the satisfaction that buyers get when they actually possess a product, both legally and physically. First Union Mortgage, for example, creates possession utility by offering loans that allow people to buy homes they could otherwise not afford.

> active poll

**What do you think? Voice your opinion and find out what others have to say.**

## TECHNOLOGY AND THE EVOLUTION OF MARKETING

Technology has always played a significant role in the evolution of the marketing function. Today, the Internet opens new channels for distributing tangible goods and intangible services worldwide, and it is changing the way marketers sell and advertise products, and communicate with customers. Moreover, the Internet provides customers with options they never had before—countless brands to choose from, searchable databases, personal attention, shipping and delivery options, built-to-order merchandise, instant access to information, and more.

Advances in other technologies are also changing today's marketing function. Mobil Speedpass, for example, is a tiny radio transmitter that attaches to a car window or a key chain and sends the user's credit card number to the gas station's computerized pump during a fuel stop.[4] Small free-standing electronic structures, called *kiosks,* vend products and services in convenient locations and introduce new products in dynamic ways. Located in showrooms or shopping areas, kiosks can inform customers about inventory, products, and store promotions; take and process orders; help people fill out applications; and sell small items such as entertainment and transportation tickets. Wild Oats, a chain of natural-foods grocery stores headquartered in Boulder, Colorado, for instance, uses kiosks to deliver health and nutritional information to customers.[5]

Not only do these new technologies improve the speed and convenience of customer transactions, but at the same time they provide marketers with information about customers' lifestyles, product preferences, and buying habits. Of course, without such technological advances, the world of marketing might resemble earlier eras.

### Production Era and Sales Era

During the *production era* (which lasted until the 1930s), many business executives viewed marketing simply as an offshoot of production. Product design was based more on the demands of mass-production techniques than on customers' wants and needs. This type of **sellers' market** existed in many industries where demand for products exceeded supply. Thus, manufacturers were generally able to sell all that they produced. They relied on a good, solid product to sell itself, and they comfortably limited their marketing efforts to taking orders and shipping goods.

Once technological advancements increased production capacity, however, the market for manufactured goods became more competitive. Business leaders, realizing that they would have to persuade people to buy all the goods they could make, expanded their marketing activities. To stimulate demand for their products, firms spent more on advertising, but they still focused on selling whatever the company produced. Consequently, this period (1930s to 1950s) was labeled the *sales era*. It lasted until companies began facing a new challenge: an overabundance of products, or **buyers' market**—that is, supply exceeded demand. Faced with excess product, companies shifted from pushing whatever they produced on all consumers to finding out what buyers wanted and then filling that specific need. They became more customer-centered. This shift in focus began the *marketing era* that continues to develop and evolve today (see Exhibit 12.3).

### Marketing Era and Relationship Era

Although some companies still operate with sales- or production-era values, today most have adopted the **marketing concept,** stressing customer needs and wants, concentrating on specific target markets, seeking long-term profitability, and coordinating their own marketing efforts. Some organizations take the marketing concept to a higher level by maintaining long-term relationships with customers. Thus, the relationship between customer and company does not end with the sales transaction; instead it is viewed as an ongoing process.[6]

**Relationship marketing** is the process of building long-term satisfying relationships with key parties—customers, suppliers, distributors—to retain their long-term business. Frequently referred to as customer relationship management (CRM), relationship marketing focuses on establishing a learning relationship with each customer. The relationship gets smarter with each interaction—you learn something about your customer and you change your product or service to meet the customer's needs.

As Exhibit 12.4 shows, the Internet is a terrific vehicle for learning about and building relationships with customers. It brings the outside world closer and allows businesses to reach out and establish relationships with customers beyond their borders and market to the world. In addition, many companies are using the Internet to obtain information about customers, answer customers' questions, test their reaction to new products, sell products, obtain customer feedback, and better understand who their customers are and what they want.

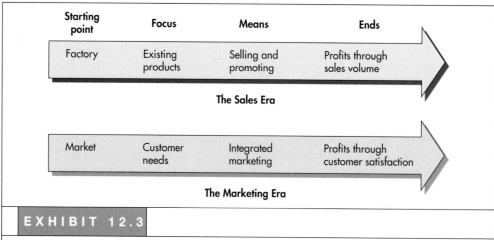

**EXHIBIT 12.3**

The Selling and Marketing ERAs Contrasted

During the sales era, firms sold what they made rather than focusing on what buyers wanted. But in today's marketing era, firms determine the needs and wants of a market and strive to deliver desired products or services more effectively and efficiently than their competitors do.

| Internet capability → | Marketing and product research | Sales and distribution | Support and customer feedback |
|---|---|---|---|
| Benefits to company → | • Provides data for market research<br><br>• Establishes consumer response to new products | • Reaches new customers<br><br>• Provides a low-cost distribution method<br><br>• Allows for electronic catalogs | • Improves customer access<br><br>• Puts more staff in contact with customers<br><br>• Allows immediate response to customer problems |
| Opportunities → | Increased market share | Lower costs | Enhanced customer satisfaction |

**EXHIBIT 12.4**

How the Internet Enhances Customer Relations

The Internet is a powerful tool for marketing research, establishing new markets, testing customer interest in emerging products, and conducting a dialogue with customers.

## > active concept check

**Now let's take a moment to test your knowledge of the concepts you have studied in this section.**

## > The Importance of Understanding Customers

According to management consultant Peter Drucker, "The aim of marketing is to know and to understand the customer so well that the product or service fits him and sells itself."[7] This is a challenge because customers today are not very easy to understand. Consider SkyMall's experience. SkyMall, which sells gifts and other items through in-flight catalogs and the Web, got into trouble because it didn't really understand its customers. CEO Robert Worsley wanted to please customers by hand-delivering their in-flight purchases as soon as the airplane landed. This was a costly service, requiring large warehouses filled with inventory. As it turned out, however, customers, already burdened with luggage, were not eager to carry more packages. They enjoyed ordering from SkyMall while in the air, but they didn't want to pick up their packages once they arrived at the airport.[8] Worsley's mistake was to offer costly extra services his customers didn't want. Fortunately, the company discovered and corrected its mistake early. But it shows just how easy it is to lose touch with the needs of today's customers.

### FOCUSING ON TODAY'S CUSTOMERS

Today's customers are sophisticated, price sensitive, and demanding. They live time-compressed lifestyles and have little patience for retailers who do not understand them or will not adapt their business practices to meet their needs. They expect products and services to be delivered faster and more conveniently. And they have no qualms about switching to competitors if their demands are not met.

Armed with facts, prices, data, product reviews, advice, how-to guides, and databases, today's customers are informed, and this places them in an unprecedented position of control.[9] They walk into car dealerships reading spec sheets downloaded from such Web sites as CarSmart, Auto-by-Tel, or

CarSmart has helped over 2 million consumers get a low competitive price without any hassles or haggling. Not only does the Web site provide consumers with free automobile price quotes and links to dealers, but it locates vehicles and arms consumers with just about everything they need to know before purchasing a car.

Edmunds.com that disclose the dealer's invoice cost, dealer rebates, and other purchasing incentives.[10] Prior to the Internet, of course, consumers had no way of knowing such detail—and many car dealers liked it this way. After all, ill-informed prospects are easily manipulated whereas educated buyers are not. But the Internet has changed all that. What does this mean for traditional car companies and dealers? As Robert Eaton, past co-chairman of DaimlerChrysler put it, "The customer is going to grab control of the process and we are all going to salute smartly and do exactly what the customer tells us if we want to stay in business."[11]

Of course, auto dealers aren't the only ones experiencing this power shift. "The realtor of yesterday was totally in control of basic information," notes George Stephens, chairman of the Houston Association of Realtors. Now home buyers use real estate Web sites to gain more control of the house-hunting process. Home descriptions, photographs, room dimensions, property tax information, and school and town information are all provided on Web sites—making it possible for customers to do their research online before setting foot in the real estate office.[12]

From travel agents to supermarkets to auto dealers to furniture stores to realtors—today's customers are indeed calling the shots. Which is why more and more businesses are striving to understand customers and satisfy their changing needs.

### SATISFYING CUSTOMERS

How do you know whether your customers are satisfied? Better still, why do companies care if their customers return? Companies strive to satisfy their customers and keep them coming back for these reasons:[13]

- Acquiring a new customer can cost up to five times as much as keeping an existing one.
- Long-term customers buy more, take less of a company's time, bring in new customers, and are less price-sensitive.
- Satisfied customers are the best advertisement for a product.
- Firms perceived to offer superior customer service find that they can charge as much as 10 percent more than their competitors.
- Research shows that dissatisfied customers may tell as many as 20 other people about their bad experiences.

One of the best ways to measure customer satisfaction, of course, is to analyze your customer base: Are you getting new customers? Are good ones leaving? What is your customer retention rate? What are you doing to keep your customers loyal?

Look at Capital One. When a current customer calls the company to close his or her account, the customer is immediately transferred to a customer retention specialist, whose job is to offer the customer a better deal (interest rate, line of credit, and so on) to keep the customer's business. Some companies, of course, promote loyalty by offering extra-long product guarantees: Hewlett-Packard, for example, guarantees 99.999 percent product reliability and availability so that customers are loyal and are willing to buy additional goods and services;[14] A.T. Cross pens carry a lifetime guarantee; and Le Creuset cookware is guaranteed for 101 years.[15] Software maker Intuit is so focused on retaining customers that every employee—including the president—spends a few hours each month working the customer-service phone lines. This intense focus helps Intuit make its Quicken program so user-friendly that customers are fiercely loyal. As one marketing consultant put it: "People would rather change their bank than switch from Quicken."[16]

But such customer loyalty is the exception, not the norm. On average, U.S. companies lose half their customers every five years. Why are customers less loyal today? First, they have more choices; more styles, options, services, and products are available than ever before. Second, customers have more information from brochures, consumer publications, the Internet, and more, which empowers buyers and raises expectations. Third, when more and more products start to look the same, nothing stands out for customers to be loyal to. And fourth, time is scarce. If it's easier to buy gas at a different service station each week, customers will.[17] Furthermore, customer loyalty must be earned every day, because customer needs and buying habits change constantly (see Exhibit 12.5).

Keep in mind that not every customer is worth keeping. Some customers cost a great deal to service; others spend little but demand a lot. "We've gotten a lot smarter about separating the customers we do want from the customers we don't want," says C. Michael Armstrong, CEO of AT&T. Facing $500 million in yearly losses on the millions of customers who make few long-distance calls, AT&T routes customer service calls from low spenders to automated systems and lavishes human attention on higher-spending customers.[18]

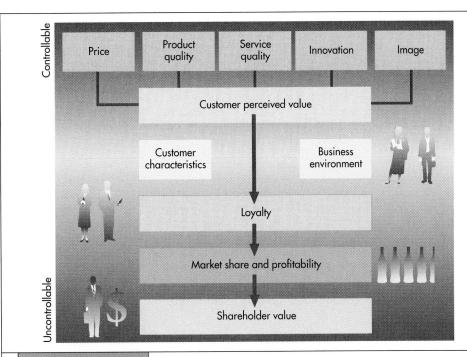

**EXHIBIT 12.5**

Beyond Customer Satisfaction

Satisfying the customer is no longer the ultimate business virtue. Companies today are looking for more and better ways of cementing customer loyalty to boost market share, profitability, and shareholder value.

## LEARNING ABOUT CUSTOMERS

According to management expert Peter Drucker, the most important sources of information for strategic decision making come from customers.[19] Amazon.com, for example, uses the information it obtains from customers to make buying recommendations for them. But it also uses that information to, as CEO Jeff Bezos puts it, "invent things we suspect people will want."[20]

In the past, most companies obtained information about changing customer preferences, changing market trends, and new competitor products by utilizing a variety of marketing research techniques. But today, companies are tapping into this valuable source of information by using technology to engage in two-way, ongoing dialogues with customers through e-mail, Web pages, fax machines, and toll-free telephone numbers. Like Capital One, they are constructing and using customer databases to capture insights about customers in great detail, to remember customer preferences and priorities, and to make the customer experience more personal and compelling. Some are even using this data to serve up personalized marketing messages, create Web pages that display products and services that suit the customer's specific requirements, and present specific segments of a company's online catalog instead of requiring customers to click through multiple Web pages.

### Consumer Buying Behavior

To learn what induces individuals to buy one product instead of another, companies study **consumer buying behavior.** For instance, when Israeli-based Sky Is the Ltd. needed to know where and how U.S. consumers buy crackers, its executives researched the behavior of U.S. shoppers. After conducting marketing research studies, they found that the firm's little-known brand would get lost among the sea of crackers on supermarket shelves but could attract some attention in gourmet food stores.[21]

Three things that companies must take into consideration when analyzing consumer buying behavior are the differences between organizational and consumer markets, the buyer's decision process, and factors that influence the buyer's decision process.

**ORGANIZATIONAL VERSUS CONSUMER BUYERS** The **organizational market** is made up of three main subgroups: the industrial/commercial market (companies that buy goods and services to produce their own goods and services, such as Toyota), the reseller market (wholesalers such as Ingram Micro, which wholesales computers, and retailers such as Ann Taylor, which sells women's clothing), and the government market (federal, state, and local agencies such as the state of Texas and the city of Dallas).

Organizations buy raw materials (grain, steel, fabric) and highly technical and complex products (printing presses, management consultation, buildings). They also buy many of the same products that consumers do—such as food, paper products, cleaning supplies, and landscaping services—but they generally purchase larger quantities and use a more complex buying process. By contrast, the **consumer market** consists of individuals or households that purchase goods and services for personal use. In most cases, consumers purchase smaller quantities of items and use a process similar to the one outlined in Exhibit 12.6.

**THE BUYER'S DECISION PROCESS** Suppose you want to buy a car. Do you rush to the dealer, plunk down money, and buy the first car you see? Of course not. Like most buyers, you go through a decision process, outlined in Exhibit 12.6, that begins with identifying a problem, which in this case is the need for a car. Your next step is to look for a solution to your problem. Possibilities occur to you on the basis of your experience (perhaps you recently drove a certain car) and on your exposure to marketing messages. If none of the obvious solutions seems satisfying, you gather additional information. The more complex the problem, the more information you are likely to seek from friends or relatives, magazines, salespeople, store displays, and sales literature.

Once you have all the information in hand, you are ready to make a choice. You may select one of the alternatives, such as a new Chevy Blazer or a used Ford Explorer. You might even postpone the decision or decide against making any purchase at all, depending on the magnitude of your desire, the outside pressure to buy, and your financial resources. If you decide to buy, you will evaluate the wisdom of your choice. If the item you bought is satisfying, you might buy the same product again under similar circumstances, thus developing a loyalty to the brand. If it is not satisfying, you will probably not repeat the purchase.

If the purchase was a major one, you will sometimes suffer from **cognitive dissonance,** commonly known as buyer's remorse. You will think about all the alternatives you rejected and wonder whether one of them might have been a better choice. At this stage, you're likely to seek reassurance that you have done the right thing. Realizing this tendency, many marketers try to reinforce their sales with guarantees, phone calls to check on the customer's satisfaction, user hot lines, follow-up letters, and so on. Such efforts help pave the way for repeat business.

**EXHIBIT 12.6**

The Consumer Decision Process

Consumers go through a decision-making process that can include up to five steps.

**FACTORS THAT INFLUENCE THE BUYER'S DECISION PROCESS** Throughout the buying process, various factors may influence a buyer's purchase decision. An awareness of the following factors and consumer preferences enables companies to appeal to the group most likely to respond to its products and services:

- *Culture.* The cultures and subcultures people belong to shape their values, attitudes, and beliefs and influence the way people respond to the world around them. Understanding culture is therefore an increasingly important step in international business and in marketing to diverse populations within a country such as the United States.

- *Social class.* In addition to being members of a particular culture, people also belong to a certain social class—be it upper, middle, lower, or somewhere in between. In general, members of various classes pursue different activities, buy different goods, shop in different places, and react to different media.

- *Reference groups.* A reference group consists of people who have a good deal in common: family members, friends, co-workers, sports enthusiasts, music lovers, computer buffs. Individuals are members of many such reference groups, and they use the opinions of the appropriate group as a benchmark when they buy certain types of goods or services.

- *Self-image.* The tendency to believe that "you are what you buy" is especially prevalent among young people. Marketers capitalize on people's need to express their identity through their purchases by emphasizing the image value of goods and services. That's why professional athletes and musicians frequently appear as product endorsers—so that consumers will incorporate part of these celebrities' public image into their own self-image.

- *Situational factors.* These factors include events or circumstances in people's lives that are more circumstantial but that can influence buying patterns. Such factors might include having a coupon, being in a hurry, celebrating a holiday, being in a bad mood, and so on.

### Marketing Research

Conducting marketing research is another way companies learn about the needs and wants of their customers. **Marketing research** is the process of gathering and analyzing information about customers, markets, and related marketing issues. It is one of the tools used by managers to help understand the market. Companies rely on research when they set product goals, develop new products, and plan future marketing programs. They also use research to monitor a program's effectiveness by analyzing the number of consumers using a product or purchasing it more than once. In addition, they use marketing research to keep an eye on the competition, track industry trends, and measure customer satisfaction. Popular marketing research tools include personal observations, customer surveys and questionnaires, experiments, telephone or personal interviews, studies of small samples of the consumer population, and focused interviews of 6 to 10 people (called focus groups).

**> video exercise**

**Take a moment to apply what you've learned.**

**LIMITATIONS OF MARKETING RESEARCH** Focus groups, consumer surveys, and other marketing research tools for probing customers wants and needs can indeed be useful, but they have limitations. In 1985 when Bell Labs first invented the cell phone, AT&T asked a big consulting firm to do a customer survey. The results convinced management that there was no market for the cell phone, and AT&T shelved the new product. Eight years later, AT&T ended up acquiring McCaw Cellular to catch up with the irreversible trend of cell phone usage.[22]

Part of the problem with surveys is that they are administered in artificial settings that do not accurately represent the marketplace. Moreover, surveys generally measure the level of service that the company currently provides instead of identifying ways to propel a company beyond its current state of service. Furthermore, if not carefully worded and administered, surveys can be misleading, as well as poor predictors of future buying behavior. For example, more than 90 percent of car buyers are either "satisfied" or "very satisfied" when they drive away from the dealer's showroom, but less than half wind up buying the same car the next time around.[23]

Keep in mind that marketing research can suggest, in a narrow way, what people might prefer or dislike today, but it is seldom a good predictor of what will excite consumers in the future.[24] Successful business people such as Barry Diller understand this. Diller forged ahead with Fox Broadcasting even though surveys said there was no need for another network. Sony is another classic example. The Walkman is one of the most successful consumer products ever introduced, yet it was greeted by skepticism during the prototype test.[25] FedEx and CNN were also met with public naysaying. So was the Chrysler minivan.[26]

Finally, marketing research is not a substitute for good judgment. When used inappropriately, research can be the source of expensive mistakes. Coca-Cola's experience with new Coke is a classic example of how marketing research can lead a company astray when data are not used correctly. In an effort to stem the growth of archcompetitor Pepsi, Coca-Cola conducted extensive taste tests to find a cola taste that consumers liked better than either Coke or Pepsi. On the basis of this research, the company launched New Coke, replacing the 100-year-old Coca-Cola formula. But New Coke simply did not sell, and Coca-Cola had to mount an expensive marketing effort to salvage the brand. At the same time, public outcry drove the company to bring back the original formula, renamed Coke Classic.

What went wrong? First researchers focused only on taste and failed to look at the emotional attachment consumers had to traditional Coke soft drink. Second, many of the people who participated in the test did not realize that old Coke would be taken off the shelf. If the company had asked the right questions, the rocky course of New Coke's introduction might have been smoother.[27]

**VIRTUAL REALITY** One especially effective marketing research tool is three-dimensional modeling (also known as virtual reality). Modeling allows the marketer to quickly and inexpensively re-create the atmosphere of an actual retail store on a computer screen. Consumers can view model shelves stocked with any kind of product, pick up the package from the shelf by touching its image on the monitor, turn the package to examine it from all sides, and move the product to the virtual shopping cart—as though it were an actual store. Meanwhile the computer records the amount of time the consumer spends shopping in each product category and examining the package, the quantity of products purchased, and the order in which they are purchased.

The advantages of virtual reality research over traditional marketing research methods include realistic settings; quick setup; easy reconfiguration of brands, pricing, and shelf space; fast and error-free data collection; low costs and flexibility; and the ability to test new concepts before incurring manufacturing or advertising costs. For instance, when Goodyear Tire wanted to expand its distribution to general merchandise outlets (previously the tires were only available in company-owned retails stores), Goodyear used a series of virtual reality simulations to assess consumer brand-name loyalty and pricing strategies. The simulations even identified which of Goodyear's competitors posed the greatest threat to its business.[28]

### Database Marketing

Another way to learn about customer preferences—and more specifically about a customer's lifetime value—is to gather and analyze all kinds of customer-related data. As CEO Richard Fairbank knows, every credit card transaction, Internet sale, and frequent buyer purchase leaves behind a trail of information that retailers can use to their advantage. Frequent-shopper card programs, good for a wealth of discounts at checkout, have convinced customers to share some of the most intimate details about their lives. For instance, customer grocery purchases reveal preferences for everything from hygiene products to junk food to magazines.

**Database marketing** is the process of recording and analyzing customer interactions, preferences, and buying behavior for the purpose of contacting and transacting with customers. Although the terms *database marketing* and *relationship marketing* are sometimes used interchangeably, they are not the same. Database marketing is the act of gathering and analyzing customer information, whereas relationship marketing focuses on conducting two-way communication between the company and the customer in order to build long-term relationships. The underlying principle of database marketing is simple: All customers share some common needs and characteristics but each customer has his or her own twist. By analyzing data collected on each customer's key attributes, companies can determine which customers to target, which to avoid, and how to customize marketing offers for the best response (see Exhibit 12.7).[29]

Allstate, for example, uses database marketing to amass huge amounts of data about applicants (credit reports, driving records, claims histories) in order to swiftly price a customer's insurance policy.[30] Ritz Carlton records all customer requests, comments, and complaints in a worldwide database that now contains individual profiles of more than 500,000 guests. By accessing these profiles, employees at any Ritz Carlton hotel can accommodate the individual tastes of its customers from anywhere in the world.[31] And Capital One has enough customer information in its databases to fill the hard drives of more than 200,000 personal computers.[32]

As Chapter 8 explains, some companies take database marketing a step further by gathering details about customer transactions, requests, and preferences from every department. Using customer relationship management software, companies interact with customers, remember customer preferences and priorities, capture insights about customers in great detail, calculate customers' profitability and future potential, build sophisticated but easily accessible customer profiles, and share these data throughout the organization. As a result, salespeople, marketers, and service representatives all have access to a single, unified view of the customer.[33]

Companies store this information in computerized data warehouses. Through data mining, they analyze the data electronically and find meaningful patterns that lead the way to more effective, more targeted and individualized marketing. But as Chapter 2 points out, many companies are struggling to find a balance between satisfying their needs for customer information and respecting the customer's right to privacy (see this chapter's Focusing on E-Business Today Feature).

> # active exercise

**Take a moment to apply what you've learned.**

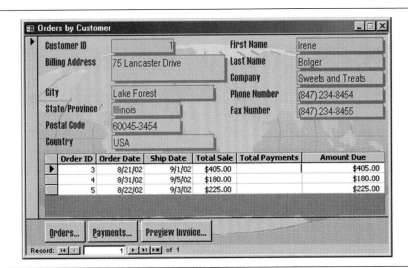

## EXHIBIT 12.7

Typical Database for Customers' Orders

Designing a user-friendly database to record customer information is the key to building an effective database marketing program. The information from this simple order-entry screen will eventually be transferred to a customer history file so that the company can rank its customers by total dollars spent and other criteria.

## TREATING CUSTOMERS INDIVIDUALLY

Companies used to rely primarily on differentiating their products and services to compete in the marketplace. But today many companies are gaining a competitive edge by differentiating the customer experience, making it more personal and compelling. Capital One, for instance, attracts millions of customers by presenting itself a little differently to each customer. The company offers more than 7000 variations of its credit card and up to 20,000 variations of other products, from phone cards to insurance.[34]

*One-to-one marketing* involves individualizing a firm's marketing efforts for a single customer to accommodate the specific customer's needs. The four key steps to putting an effective one-to-one marketing program in place are: (1) identifying your customers, (2) differentiating among them, (3) interacting with them, and (4) customizing your product or service to fit each individual customer's needs.[35] Technology is, of course, a critical component of each of these steps. Here are some examples of successful one-to-one marketing programs:

- Dell computer, which builds every computer according to customer specifications, designs a special ordering Web site, called Premier Pages, for customers with over 400 employees. Dell offers millions of computing configurations, but employees accessing Premier Pages may only be allowed to choose from 1,000, 100, or only 1 or 2 options (selected by the employee's organization). By placing customized limits on ordering options, Dell keeps its corporate customers' accounting departments happy. Of course, customers aren't the only ones benefiting from Premier Pages. They're also good for Dell. The program cuts Dell's costs by minimizing ordering errors and freeing up valuable sales staff.[36]

- Nike's personalized shoe initiative, dubbed NikeID, allows customers to use the company's Web site to pick custom colors they want on their running shoes or cross trainers. Nike will even stitch a name (up to eight letters) next to the swoosh instead of having a celebrity name such as Michael Jordan.[37]

- Levi's Original Spin is designed for customers who are not entirely satisfied with the roughly 130 styles of jeans sold off the shelf by Levis. Customers can order a custom-fitted pair, choosing from three basic models, 10 fabrics, five leg styles, and two types of fly.[38]

- American Airlines displays a Web site that looks different to each of about one million registered AAdvantage flyers. Customers who log in are greeted by a name and sometimes by a direct marketing offer. The site is programmed to present a discount to any customer who has paid three visits without making a purchase.[39]

One-to-one marketing programs such as these require a thorough understanding of each customer's preferences and a detailed history of each customer's interactions with the company. But for compa-

At the Lands' End Web site, customers can get more than answers to their questions. Personal shoppers can recommend additional products that match customers' preferences and even split the computer screen to display apparel combinations.

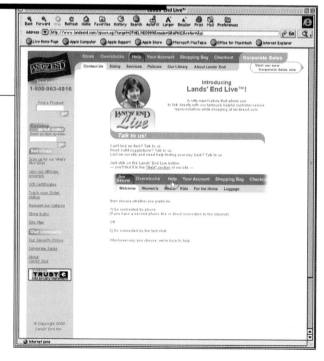

nies the payoff can result in increased customer loyalty: The more time and energy a customer spends teaching a firm about that customer's own preferences, the more difficult it becomes for the customer to obtain the same level of individualized service from a competitor.[40]

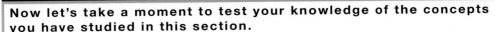

> active concept check

Now let's take a moment to test your knowledge of the concepts you have studied in this section.

## > How to Plan Your Marketing Strategies

By now you can see why successful marketing rarely happens without carefully analyzing and understanding your customers. Once you have learned about your customers, you're ready to begin planning your marketing strategies. *Strategic marketing planning* is a process that involves three steps: (1) examining your current marketing situation, (2) assessing your opportunities and setting your objectives, and (3) developing a marketing strategy to reach those objectives (see Exhibit 12.8). The purpose of strategic marketing planning is to help you identify and create a competitive advantage, something that sets you apart from your rivals and makes your product more appealing to customers.[41] Most companies record the results of their planning efforts in a document called the *marketing plan.* Here's a closer look at the three steps in the process.

### STEP 1: EXAMINING YOUR CURRENT MARKETING SITUATION

Examining your current marketing situation is the first step in the strategic marketing planning process; it includes reviewing your past performance (how well each product is doing in each market where you sell it), evaluating your competition, examining your internal strengths and weaknesses, and analyzing the external environment. The complexity of this step depends on the complexity of your business. Whereas giant multinational firms such as Xerox and Nestlé have to examine the current marketing situation for dozens of product lines and geographical divisions, smaller firms, such as individual Jiffy-Lube franchises, have far fewer products to think about.

#### Reviewing Performance

Unless you're starting a new business, your company has a history of marketing performance. Maybe sales have slowed in the past year; maybe you've had to cut prices so much that you're barely earning

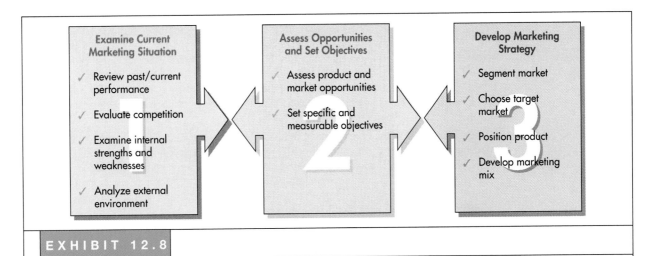

**EXHIBIT 12.8**

The Strategic Marketing Planning Process

Strategic marketing planning covers three steps: (1) examining your current marketing situation, (2) assessing your opportunities and setting objectives, and (3) developing your marketing strategy.

a profit; or maybe sales are going quite well and you have money to invest in new marketing activities. Reviewing where you are and how you got there is critical, because you will want to repeat your successes and learn from your past mistakes.

### Evaluating Competition

In addition to reviewing past performance, you must also evaluate your competition. If you own a Burger King franchise, for example, you need to watch what McDonald's and Wendy's are doing. You also have to keep an eye on Taco Bell, KFC, Pizza Hut, and other restaurants in addition to paying attention to any number of ways your customers might satisfy their hunger—including fixing a sandwich at home. Furthermore, you need to watch the horizon for competitors that do not yet exist, such as the next big food craze.

### Examining Internal Strengths and Weaknesses

Besides reviewing past performance and evaluating competition, successful marketers identify and examine their internal strengths and weaknesses. In other words they look at such things as management, financial resources, production capabilities, distribution networks, managerial expertise, and promotional capabilities. Next, they try to identify sources of competitive advantage in addition to areas that need improvement. This step is important because you can't develop a successful marketing strategy if you don't know your strengths as well as your limitations. On the basis of your internal analysis, you will be able to decide whether your business should (1) limit itself to those opportunities for which it possesses the required strengths or (2) challenge itself to reach higher goals by acquiring and developing new strengths.

Understanding your strengths and weaknesses is especially important when evaluating the merits of global expansion. Selling products overseas requires not only managerial expertise and financial resources but also the ability to adjust your operation to different cultures, customs, legal requirements, and product specifications. Even selling on the Internet requires technological expertise and commitment as well as a thorough understanding of customer buying behavior.

### Analyzing the External Environment

Marketers must also analyze a number of external environment factors when planning their marketing strategies. These factors include:

- *Economic conditions.* Marketers are greatly affected by trends in interest rates, inflation, unemployment, personal income, and savings rates. In tough times, consumers put off buying expensive items such as major appliances, cars, and homes. They cut back on travel, entertainment, and luxury goods. When the economy is good, consumers open their wallets and satisfy their pent-up demand for higher-priced goods and services.

- *Natural environment.* Changes in the natural environment can affect marketers, both positively and negatively. Interruptions in the supply of raw materials can upset even the most carefully conceived marketing plans. Floods, droughts, and cold weather can affect the price and availability of many products as well as the behavior of target customers.

- *Social and cultural trends.* Planners also study the social and cultural environment to determine shifts in consumer values. If social trends are running against a product, the producer might need more advertising to educate consumers about the product's benefits. After Campbell Soup saw its sales of condensed soups slump, it began running commercials and posting Web pages about the benefits of soup as a cooking ingredient.[42] Alternatively, businesses may have to modify their products to respond to changing tastes. Shiseido, for example, changed its nail polish line after studying what Japanese teens were using.[43]

- *Laws and regulations.* As is every other function in business today, marketing is controlled by laws at the local, state, national, and international levels. From product design to pricing to advertising, virtually every task you'll encounter in marketing is affected in some way by laws and regulations. For example, the Nutritional Education and Labeling Act of 1990 forced marketers to put standardized nutritional labels on food products. Although this regulation cost manufacturers millions of dollars, it was a bonanza for food-testing laboratories.

- *Technology.* When technology changes, so must your marketing approaches. Look at Encyclopedia Britannica. It didn't take long for new computer technology to almost wreck this 230-year-old publishing company with annual sales of $650 million. After all, with books costing over $1,500, weighing 118 pounds, and taking 4.5 feet of shelf space, consumers opted for affordable CD-ROM and Internet versions offered by competitors. Today Encyclopedia Britannica delivers information via the Internet and CD-ROMs, as the "Case for Critical Thinking" in Chapter 15 will explain.[44]

Marketers must not only keep on top of today's external environment, they must also think about tomorrow's changes. Sprint, for example, is leading the race in wireless Web users even though the company trailed competitors in its market share for mobile phone subscribers. How? By continually pushing for the best technology—a key factor when it comes to accessing Web sites via mobile phones.[45]

## STEP 2: ASSESSING YOUR OPPORTUNITIES AND SETTING YOUR OBJECTIVES

Once you've examined your current marketing situation, you're ready to assess your marketing opportunities and set your objectives. Successful companies are always on the lookout for new marketing opportunities, which can be classified into four options: selling more of your existing products in current markets (market penetration), creating new products for your current markets (new product development), selling your existing products in new markets (geographic expansion), and creating new products for new markets (diversification).[46] These four options are listed in order of increasing risk; trying new products in unfamiliar markets is usually the riskiest choice of all.

With opportunities in mind, you are ready to set your marketing objectives. A common marketing objective is to achieve a certain level of **market share,** which is a firm's portion of the total sales within a market. Objectives must be specific and measurable. Establishing a goal to "increase sales in the future" is not a good objective; it doesn't say by how much or by what date. On the other hand, a goal to "increase sales 25 percent by the end of next year" provides a clear target and a reference against which progress can be measured. Objectives should also be challenging enough to be motivating. As CEO Mitchell Leibovitz of the Pep Boys auto parts chain says: "If you want to have ho-hum performance, have ho-hum goals."[47] Whatever objectives you set, be sure all employees know and understand what the organization wants to accomplish. Every Ritz Carlton employee, for example, attends a daily 15-minute meeting in which managers reiterate the hotel chain's business goals and commitment to customer service.[48]

> ## active exercise

**Take a moment to apply what you've learned.**

## STEP 3: DEVELOPING YOUR MARKETING STRATEGY

Using your current marketing situation and your objectives as your guide, you're ready to move to the third step. This is where you develop your **marketing strategy,** which consists of dividing your market into *segments* and *niches,* choosing your *target markets* and the *position* you'd like to establish in those markets, and then developing a *marketing mix* to help you get there.

### Dividing Markets into Segments

A **market** contains all the customers or businesses that might be interested in a product and can pay for it. Most companies subdivide the market in an economical and feasible manner by identifying *market segments,* homogeneous groups of customers within a market that are significantly different from each other. This process is called **market segmentation;** its objective is to group customers with similar characteristics, behavior, and needs. Each of these market segments can then be targeted by offering products that are priced, distributed, and promoted differently.

Here are five factors marketers frequently use to identify market segments:

- *Demographics.* When you segment a market using **demographics,** the statistical analysis of population, you subdivide your customers according to characteristics such as age, gender, income, race, occupation, and ethnic group. *People en Español,* for example, is targeted to the Hispanic American segment.[49] Be aware, however, that according to recent studies, demographic variables are poor predictors of behavior.[50]

- *Geographics.* When differences in buying behavior are influenced by where people live, it makes sense to use **geographic segmentation.** Segmenting the market into different geographical units such as regions, cities, counties, or neighborhoods allows companies to customize and sell products that meet the needs of specific markets. For instance, car rental agencies stock more four-wheel-drive vehicles in mountainous and snowy regions than they do in the South.

- *Psychographics.* Whereas demographic segmentation is the study of people from the outside, **psychographics** is the analysis of people from the inside, focusing on their psychological makeup, including activities, attitudes, interests, opinions, and lifestyle. Psychographic analysis focuses on why people behave the way they do by examining such issues as brand preferences, media preferences, reading habits, values, and self-concept.

- *Geodemographics.* Dividing markets into distinct neighborhoods by combining geographical and demographic data is the goal of **geodemographics.** The geodemographic system developed by Claritas Corporation divides the United States into 40 neighborhood types, with labels such as "Blue Blood Estates" and "Old Yankee Rows." This system, known as PRIZM, uses postal ZIP codes for the geographic segmentation part, making it easy to use specialized marketing programs to reach people in targeted neighborhoods.[51]

- *Behavior.* Markets can also be segmented according to customers' knowledge of, attitude toward, use of, or response to products or product characteristics. This approach is known as **behavioral segmentation.** Web-based BizTravel knows that business travelers have definite preferences and attitudes toward airlines, hotels, pricing, and schedules. So when a customer logs on to plan a trip, BizTravel's automated system is set up to recommend a customized itinerary based on that customer's previous choices and purchases.[52]

When you segment your market, you end up with several customer groups, each representing a potentially productive focal point for marketing efforts. However, keep in mind that a single segment includes customers with a variety of needs. For example, people from the same neighborhood may purchase Colgate toothpaste, but some will buy it for its flavor, others because it prevents decay, and others because it has whiteners. One way to recognize such differing needs is to segment your market into smaller microsegments or niches.[53] Producing and marketing an all-purpose athletic shoe is an example of servicing a market segment, whereas producing and marketing specialized athletic shoes—running, walking, tennis, cross-training, biking, and so on—is an example of servicing a niche market.

## active exercise

**Take a moment to apply what you've learned.**

### Choosing Your Target Markets

Once you have segmented your market, the next step is to find appropriate target segments or **target markets** to focus your efforts on. Deciding exactly which segment to target—and when—is not an easy task. Sometimes the answer will be obvious, such as when you lack the necessary technological skills or financial power to enter a particular market segment. At other times, you'll have the resources to compete in several segments but not enough resources to compete in all of them. In general, marketers use a variety of criteria to narrow their focus to a few suitable market segments. These criteria can include size of segment, competition in the segment, sales and profit potential, compatibility with company resources and strengths, costs, growth potential, and risks.[54]

Targeting is such a critical part of strategic marketing that missteps can be costly, as Motorola found out. The company stayed focused on the traditional cell phone market segment long after rivals Nokia and Ericsson had expanded into the digital phone segment. Furthermore, Motorola didn't respond when it was asked to develop digital phones for AT&T's digital network. By the time Motorola began to work on digital phones, its competitors had grabbed market share and brand loyalty in that fast-growing segment.[55]

Exhibit 12.9 diagrams three popular strategies for reaching target market. Companies that practice *undifferentiated marketing* (or mass marketing) ignore differences among buyers and offer only one product or product line to satisfy the entire market. This strategy, which concludes that all buyers have similar needs that can be served with the same standardized product, was more popular in the past then it is today. Henry Ford, for instance, sold only one car type (the Model T Ford) and in one color (black) to the entire market.

By contrast, companies that manufacture or sell a variety of products to several target customer groups practice *differentiated marketing.* General Motors, for instance, manufactures a car for every personality, and Nike produces a shoe for every athlete. Differentiated marketing is a popular approach but it requires substantial resources because you have to tailor products, prices, promotional efforts, and distribution arrangements for each customer group.

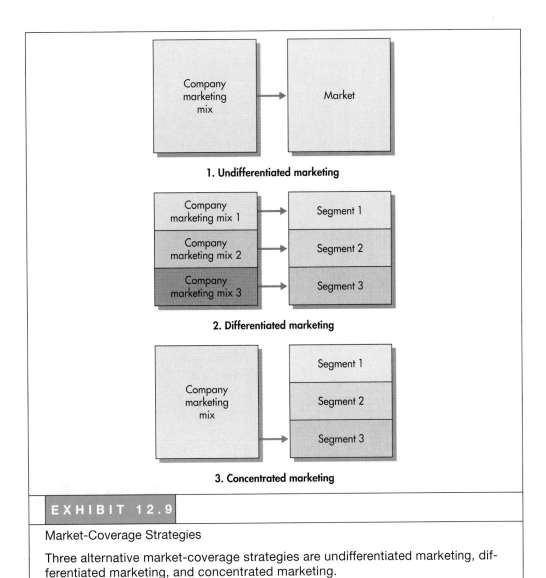

**EXHIBIT 12.9**

Market-Coverage Strategies

Three alternative market-coverage strategies are undifferentiated marketing, differentiated marketing, and concentrated marketing.

When company resources are limited, *concentrated marketing* may be the best marketing strategy. You acknowledge that different market segments exist and you choose to target just one. Southwest Airlines, for instance, began its operation by originally concentrating on servicing the submarket of intrastate, no-frills commuters.[56] The biggest advantage of concentrated marketing is that it allows you to focus all your time and resources on a single type of customer. The strategy can be risky, however, since you've staked your company's fortune on just one segment.

### Positioning Your Product

Once a company has decided which segments of the market it will enter, it must then decide what position it wants to occupy in those segments. **Positioning** your product is the act of designing your company's offering and image so that it occupies a meaningful and distinct competitive position in your target customers' minds.

Most companies position their products by choosing among several differentiating product factors, including features, performance, quality, durability, reliability, style, design, and customer service such as ordering ease, delivery and installation methods, and customer support. For example, Colgate Total is positioned as a toothpaste to prevent gum disease, cavities, and plaque, whereas Rembrandt's Dazzling White is positioned as a toothpaste to whiten teeth. By contrast, Aquafresh Whitening is positioned as a toothpaste that whitens, fights cavities, and tastes good.[57] Chapter 13 explores some positioning strategies based on product factors and pricing. Keep in mind, however, that companies also differentiate their products on the basis distribution, and promotion—the other elements in the firm's *marketing mix*.[58]

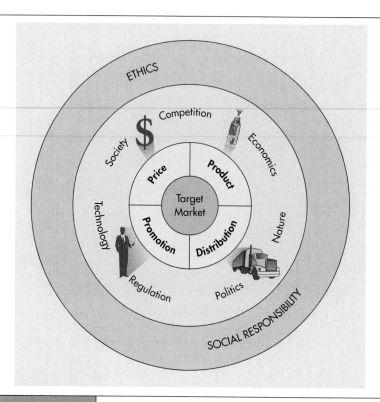

EXHIBIT 12.10

Positioning and the Marketing Environment

When positioning products for target markets, you need to consider the four marketing-mix elements plus the external environment.

### Developing the Marketing Mix

Once you've segmented your market, selected your target market, and positioned your product, your next task is to develop a marketing mix. A firm's **marketing mix** (often called the *four Ps*) consists of product, price, place (or distribution), and promotion (see Exhibit 12.10). The most basic marketing-mix element is *product,* which covers the product itself plus brand name, design, packaging, services, quality, and warranty. *Price,* the amount of money customers pay for the product (including any discounts) is the second marketing-mix element. *Place* (which is commonly referred to as *distribution*) is the third marketing-mix element. It covers the organized network of firms that move goods and services from the producer to the consumer. *Promotion,* the fourth marketing-mix element, includes all the activities the firm undertakes to communicate and promote its products to the target market. Among these activities are advertising, personal selling, public relations, and sales promotion.

We take a closer look at each of these four marketing-mix elements in the remaining chapters of this text part. Chapter 13 discusses product and pricing strategies, Chapter 14 focuses on distribution strategies, and Chapter 15 discusses promotional strategies.

## video exercise ◀

**Take a moment to apply what you've learned.**

## > active concept check

Now let's take a moment to test your knowledge of the concepts you have studied in this section.

### > Chapter Wrap-Up

Now that you've reached the end of the chapter, you may wish to explore the concepts you've been reading about in greater detail, or test yourself to see how well you've comprehended the material. In the box below you'll find a number of links. Click on any one of these links to find additional chapter resources.

### > end-of-chapter resources

- **Summary of Learning Objectives**
- **Practice Quiz**
- **Focusing on E-Business Today**
- **Key Terms**
- **Test Your Knowledge**
- **Practice Your Knowledge**
- **Expand Your Knowledge**
- **A Case for Critical Thinking**

# Product and Pricing Strategies

## > What's Ahead

### INSIDE BUSINESS TODAY
### A LIVING BRAND: MARTHA STEWART, AMERICA'S LIFESTYLE QUEEN

She wants to teach you how to create the good life—and sell you everything you need for it. Martha Stewart is the most famous U.S. homemaker, the living, human force behind a powerful personal brand that has become a household word.

Stewart established herself as a lifestyle expert during the 1980s by writing numerous books on such topics as entertaining, gardening, and cooking. By 1991 her popularity had snared the attention of Time, the publishing division of Time Warner. To capitalize on the public's recognition of Stewart's name, Time launched a magazine (*Martha Stewart Living*) featuring her image and advice, and it expanded her audience through a weekly syndicated television show, how-to books, and regular appearances on NBC's *Today* show.

As Stewart broadened her reach through a variety of media, she recognized the vast potential of supplying homemakers with affordable, quality products that they would need for tackling the projects featured in her magazine and on her TV show. So she made a lucrative deal with Kmart to provide consumers with a coordinated line of home products bearing her name. Her dominant image, already familiar to millions of fans, provided strong brand identity for the Kmart product line. Furthermore, the Kmart arrangement provided Stewart with the funds to purchase a controlling interest in *Martha Stewart Living* from Time in 1997.

Martha Stewart and Chuck Conaway, Chairman and CEO of Kmart, celebrate the debut of Martha Stewart Everyday, an extensive line of housewares available at Kmart stores.

The purchase gave Stewart complete control over the magazine's content—and the chance to refer readers to her brand-name products as she dispensed advice on everything from making beds to baking cakes. To introduce even more consumers to the Martha Stewart brand name, Stewart developed new approaches for promoting her products. First, she featured her products in a mail-order catalog, Martha by Mail, and on her Web site, www.marthastewart.com. Then she expanded her relationships with such big retailers as Kmart and Sears, broadening her product mix to include paints, baby items, and garden tools. Moreover, she formed Martha Stewart Living Omnimedia as the parent company for her expanding empire. She also increased her media presence with daily radio features, a syndicated newspaper column, and additional television appearances. In 1999 Stewart took the empire public.

Today Stewart coordinates and integrates all communications and promotions efforts to maximize the impact of her name among consumers and to increase brand identity for her product mix. For instance, if Stewart features an article about rose gardening in *Martha Stewart Living,* she uses the same information as the basis for a segment on her television show and for how-to articles about rose gardening on her Web site. Moreover, each message directs consumers to Stewart's product line of garden tools. For example, the television program guide on Stewart's Web site links the rose-gardening segment with Stewart's garden products for sale at her Web store.

Stewart's savvy product and promotional strategies have transformed the former caterer into one of the nation's leading brands, which features a product mix of nearly 3,000 items. Annual sales of Martha Stewart products currently exceed $225 million, and analysts expect sales to approach $400 million in the near future.[1]

# > objectives

**Take a moment to familiarize yourself with the key objectives of this chapter.**

# > gearing up

**Before you begin reading this chapter, try a short warm-up activity.**

## > Developing Product Strategies

Products such as ones bearing the Martha Stewart brand name are one of the four elements in a firm's marketing mix. From a marketing standpoint, a **product** is anything offered for the purpose of satisfying a want or a need in a marketing exchange. If you were asked to name three popular products off the top of your head, you might think of Doritos tortilla chips, the Volkswagen Beetle, and Gatorade drinks. You might not think of the Boston Celtics, Disney World, and the television show *60 Minutes*. That's because we tend to think of products as *tangible* objects, or things that we can actually touch and possess. Basketball teams, amusement parks, and television programs provide an *intangible* service for our use or enjoyment, not for our ownership; nevertheless, these and other services are products just the same.

### TYPES OF PRODUCTS

Think again about Doritos tortilla chips and Disney World. You wouldn't market these two products in the same way because buyer behavior, product characteristics, market expectations, competition, and other elements of the equation are entirely different. Acknowledging these differences, marketers most commonly categorize products on the basis of tangibility and use.

#### Tangible and Intangible Products

Although some products are predominantly tangible and others are mostly intangible, most products fall somewhere between those two extremes. When you buy software such as Norton Anti-Virus, for example, you get service features along with the product—such as virus updates, customer assistance, and so on. The *product continuum* indicates the relative amounts of tangible and intangible components in a product (see Exhibit 13.1). Education is a product at the intangible extreme, whereas salt and shoes are at the tangible extreme. TGI Friday's restaurants fall in the middle because they involve both tangible (food) and intangible (service) components.

Service products have some special characteristics that affect the way they are marketed. As we have seen, *intangibility* is one fundamental characteristic. You can't usually show a service in an ad, demonstrate it before customers buy, mass produce it, or give customers anything tangible to show for their purchase. Services marketers often compensate for intangibility by using tangible symbols or by adding tangible components to their products. Prudential Insurance, for example, uses the Rock of Gibraltar as a symbol of stability, and its ads invite you to get "your piece of the rock."

Another unique aspect of service products is *perishability*. Because services cannot usually be created in advance or held in storage until people are ready to buy, services are time sensitive. For instance, if airlines don't sell seats on a particular flight, once the flight takes off an unsold seat can never produce revenue. Hotel rooms and movie theatre seats are similar. For this reason, many services try to shift customer demand by offering discounts or promotions during slow periods. Movie theatres, for instance, offer discounted tickets before 6:00 P.M. and restaurants offer early-bird specials.

#### Consumer Products

As you saw in Chapter 12, organizational and consumer markets use many of the same products for different reasons and in different ways. Even though some products are sold to both markets, those

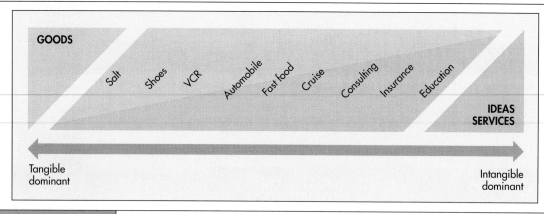

EXHIBIT 13.1

The Product Continuum

Products contain both tangible and intangible components; predominantly tangible products are categorized as goods, whereas predominantly intangible products are categorized as services.

known as *consumer products* are sold exclusively to consumers. Consumer products can be classified into four subgroups, depending on how people shop for them:

- *Convenience products* are the goods and services that people buy frequently, without much conscious thought, such as toothpaste, dry cleaning, film developing, and photocopying.

- *Shopping products* are fairly important goods and services that people buy less frequently: a stereo, a computer, a refrigerator, or a college education. Such purchases require more thought and comparison shopping to check on price, features, quality, and reputation.

- *Specialty products* include CK perfume, Armani suits, and Suzuki violin lessons—particular brands that the buyer especially wants and will seek out, regardless of location or price. Specialty products are not necessarily expensive, but they are products that customers go out of their way to buy and rarely accept substitutes for.

- *Unsought goods* are products that people do not normally think of buying, such as life insurance, cemetery plots, and new products they must be made aware of through promotion.[2]

### Organizational Products

*Organizational products,* or products sold to firms, are generally purchased in large quantities and are not for personal use. Two categories of organizational products are expense items and capital items. *Expense items* are relatively inexpensive goods and services that organizations generally use within a year of purchase. Examples are pencils and printer cartridges. *Capital items,* by contrast, are more expensive organizational products and have a longer useful life. Examples include desks, photocopiers, and computers.

Aside from dividing products into expense and capital items, organizational buyers and sellers often classify products according to their intended usage.

- *Raw materials* like iron ore, crude petroleum, lumber, and chemicals are used in the production of final products.

- *Components* like spark plugs and printer cartridges are similar to raw materials. They also become part of the manufacturers' final products.

- *Supplies* such as pencils, nails, and lightbulbs that are used in a firm's daily operations are considered expense items.

- *Installations* such as factories, power plants, airports, production lines, and semiconductor fabrication machinery are major capital projects.

- *Equipment* includes less expensive capital items such as desks, telephones, and fax machines that are shorter lived than installations.

- *Business services* range from simple and fairly risk-free services such as landscaping and cleaning to complex services such as management consulting and auditing.

## THE PRODUCT LIFE CYCLE

Few products last forever. Most products go through a **product life cycle,** passing through four distinct stages in sales and profits: introduction, growth, maturity, and decline (see Exhibit 13.2). As the product passes from stage to stage, various marketing approaches become appropriate.

The product life cycle can describe a product class (gasoline-powered automobiles), a product form (sports utility vehicles), or a brand (Ford Explorer). Product classes and forms tend to have the longest life cycles, whereas specific brands tend to have shorter life cycles. The amount of time that a product remains in any one stage depends on customer needs and preferences, economic conditions, the nature of the product, and the marketer's strategy. Still, the proliferation of new products, changing technology, globalization, and the ability to quickly imitate competitors is hurtling product forms and brands through their life cycles much faster today. The pace is so frenetic that in the words of GTE's president Kent Foster, "Companies are marketing products that are still evolving, delivered to a market that is still emerging, via technology that is changing on a daily basis."[3] Consider electronics, where product life is now a matter of months: Panasonic replaces its consumer electronic products with new models every 90 days.[4] Why? Smart companies know that if they don't keep innovating, competitors who do will capture the business.

### Introduction

The first stage in the product life cycle is the *introductory stage,* during which producers launch a new product and stimulate demand. In this stage, companies typically spend heavily on conducting research-and-development efforts to create the new product, on developing promotions to build awareness of the product, and on establishing the distribution system to get the product into the marketplace. Every product—from personal computers to digital cameras—gets its start in this stage. The producer makes little profit during the introduction; however, these start-up costs are a necessary investment if the new product is to succeed. Procter & Gamble, for example, has spent millions to develop entirely new products such as Dryel, a home dry-cleaning product.[5]

### Growth

After the introductory stage comes the *growth stage,* marked by a rapid jump in sales and, usually, an increase in the number of competitors and distribution outlets. As competition increases, so does the struggle for market share. This situation creates pressure to introduce new product features and to maintain large promotional budgets and competitive prices. In fact, marketing in this stage is so

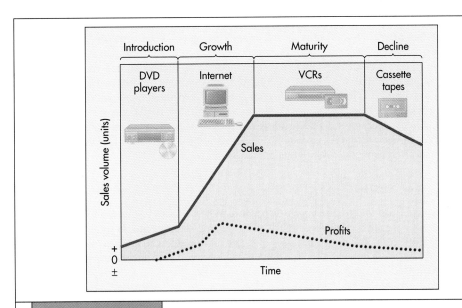

| EXHIBIT 13.2 |
| --- |

The Product Life Cycle

Most products and product categories move through a life cycle similar to the one represented by the curve in this diagram. However, the duration of each stage varies widely from product to product.

expensive that it can drive out smaller, weaker firms. With enough growth, however, a firm can often produce and deliver its products more economically than in the introduction phase. Thus, the growth stage can reap handsome profits for those who survive.

### Maturity

During the *maturity stage,* the longest in the product life cycle, sales begin to level off or show a slight decline. Most products are in the maturity stage of the life cycle where competition increases and market share is maximized—making further expansion difficult. Because the costs of introduction and growth have diminished in this stage, most companies try to keep mature products alive so they can use the resulting profits to fund development of new products. Some companies extend the life of a mature product by modifying the product's characteristics to improve the product's quality and performance.

Consider Nike. Far and away the market leader in sales of athletic shoes, Nike is attempting to renew interest in this mature product form by making such improvements as boosting cushioning in the midsole, reducing shoe weight, and improving the heel.[6] Similarly Whirlpool keeps adding new styles and features to its dishwashers and washing machines, and Hewlett-Packard adds new performance features to its printers and computers to extend the life of these mature products.

Apple Computer's colorful iMac personal computers are another example of the kinds of improvements companies make as products approach the maturity stage. Introduced in the early maturity phase of personal computers, iMac helped Apple grab badly needed market share from competitors in addition to generating a healthy dose of higher revenues and profits. Looking ahead, the company plans to maintain sales momentum through ongoing upgrades, such as adding faster chips without increasing the price of future iMac computers.[7]

### Decline

Although maturity can be extended for many years, most products eventually enter the *decline stage,* when sales and profits slip and then fade away. Declines occur for several reasons: changing demographics, shifts in popular taste, product competition, and advances in technology. When a product reaches this point in the life cycle, the company must decide whether to keep it or discontinue it and focus on developing newer products. For instance, as digital photography moves ahead, some predict that the film business will dwindle into a small niche market. The challenge for Kodak will be to replace lost film sales with sales of newer products.[8]

Sometimes all a declining product needs is some innovation. The Dean Food Company, for example, decided to keep its chocolate milk product despite a long-term decline in milk consumption. By introducing new single-serving plastic bottles called Chugs, the company increased sales for the product and brought new life to the entire chocolate milk category.[9] Mattel faced a similar decision about declining Barbie sales not long ago. For years, the company had been able to bring Barbie products back from periodic sales dips by introducing innovations such as limited-edition collectible Barbie dolls, customizable Barbie dolls, and even Barbie software. One of Mattel's biggest hits of the 1990s was Holiday Barbie, a limited-edition line of dolls that generated more than $100 million in sales during its peak year. After nearly a decade, however, Holiday Barbie sales began to decline. Long after the holidays were over, some retailers resorted to deep discounts to move any leftover dolls. Finally, Mattel decided to discontinue the line—but not the technique. Limited-edition dolls such as Millennium Barbie remain a major marketing tool for Mattel.[10]

## NEW-PRODUCT-DEVELOPMENT PROCESS

Suppose your company decides to develop a new product. Where do you begin? Many companies ask that question all the time. In fact, the possibility of developing a big winner is so alluring that U.S. companies spend billions of dollars a year trying to create new products or improve old ones.[11]

### active exercise

**Take a moment to apply what you've learned.**

In reality, however, most new products are not really new at all; only about 5 percent are true innovations.[12] The rest are variations of familiar products, created by changing the packaging, improving the formula, or modifying the form or flavor. For example, when Kraft took its decade-old Crystal Light powdered fruit drink, added water, and packaged it in fancy plastic bottles, sales of the reinvented brand swiftly surpassed those of Coke's lavishly launched Fruitopia.[13]

Nevertheless, coming up with a winning product is not an easy task. That's because many competitors are likely to get the same idea at the same time. So the victory often goes to the company with the best *product-development process*—the series of stages through which a product idea passes (see Exhibit 13.3). As noted by MIT researcher and journalist Michael Schrage: Effective *prototyping* (or turning an idea into a working model) may be the most valuable competitive advantage an innovative organization can have.[14]

Consider Sony. The company's competitors can take 6 to 10 months to turn an idea into a prototype, but on average Sony takes only 5 days.[15] This faster development time is possible because innovative companies like Sony, Hewlett-Packard, and 3M use cross-functional teams to push new products through development and onto the market.

How many of the new products created each year will endure? Nobody knows for sure, but the odds are that most new products will disappear within a few years. According to one authority, less than 1 percent of new product introductions will be around in five years; some will vanish within six months; others will never make it to market.[16] That's because not all ideas become new products. Some are killed midstream because they do not meet the exit criteria that specify what needs to be accomplished before a product moves from one stage into the next. Here are the six stages of the new-product-development process:

- *Idea generation.* The first step in the product-development process is to come up with ideas that will satisfy unmet needs. Customers, competitors, and employees are often the best source of new-product ideas. For instance, when Rubbermaid sent 15 two-person teams to willing consumers' homes to observe home-storage practices, the group returned with 300 new-product ideas in just three days.[17] Products such as Post-it notes and masking tape grew from 3M's 15 percent rule—which allows employees at 3M to spend up to 15 percent of their time working on a new-product idea without management's approval.[18]

- *Idea screening.* From the mass of ideas suggested, the company culls a few that appear to be worthy of further development, applying broad criteria such as whether the product can use existing production facilities and how much technical and marketing risk is involved. In the case of industrial or technical products, this phase is often referred to as a "feasibility study," in which the product's features are defined and its workability is tested. In the case of consumer products, marketing consultants and advertising agencies are often called in to help evaluate new ideas. In some cases, potential customers are asked what they think of a new product idea—a process known as concept testing.

- *Business analysis.* A product idea that survives the screening stage is subjected to a business analysis. During this stage the company reviews the sales, costs, and profit projections to see if they meet the company's objectives. For instance, one question the company must answer is whether the company can make enough money on the product to justify the investment. To answer this question, the company forecasts the probable sales of the product, assuming various pricing strategies. In addition, it estimates the costs associated with various levels of production. Given these

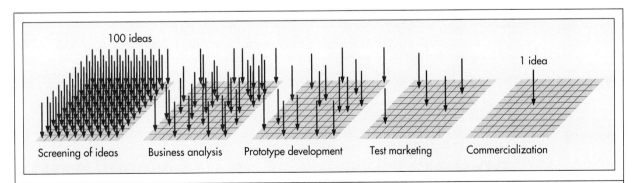

**EXHIBIT 13.3**

The Product-Development Process

For every hundred ideas generated, only one or two salable products may emerge from the lengthy and expensive process of product development.

After a long dry spell, Heinz is developing a number of new products. At this Heinz plant, workers sample prototypes of StarKist Tuna in a Pouch, the biggest innovation in tuna packaging since canned tuna was introduced 80 years ago. The company hopes the innovative package will make a big splash with consumers.

projections, the company calculates the potential profit that will be achieved if the product is introduced. If the product meets the company's objectives, it can then move to the prototype-development stage.

- *Prototype development.* At this stage the firm actually develops the product concept into a physical product. The firm creates and tests a few samples, or *prototypes,* of the product, including its packaging. During this stage, the various elements of the marketing mix are put together. In addition, the company evaluates the feasibility of large-scale production and specifies the resources required to bring the product to market.

- *Test marketing.* During **test marketing,** the firm introduces the product in selected areas of the country and monitors consumer reactions. Test marketing gives the marketer experience with marketing the product before going to the expense of a full introduction. It is most often used in cases where the cost of marketing a product far exceeds the cost of developing it. Still, test marketing is not without some risks. Testing a new product may give competitors a chance to find out about a company's newest ideas.[19]

- *Commercialization.* The final stage of development is **commercialization,** the large-scale production and distribution of those products that have survived the testing process. This phase (also referred to as a *product launch*) requires the coordination of many activities—manufacturing, packaging, distribution, pricing, and promotion. A classic mistake is letting marketing get out of phase with production by promoting the product before the company can supply it in adequate quantity. Many companies roll out their new products gradually, going from one geographic area to the next. This plan enables them to spread the costs of launching the product over a longer period and to refine their strategy as the rollout proceeds.

An estimated 50,000 new products are announced in the United States each year.[20] Sometimes companies launch new products because they have a terrific new concept, other times because they are following in the footsteps of their competitors. When a large organization develops a new product, it is often placed under the supervision of a product or brand manager. A **brand manager** is responsible for developing and implementing a strategic marketing plan for a specific brand and for creating a marketing mix for that brand's products as they move through the product life cycle.

## PRODUCT-LINE AND PRODUCT-MIX DECISIONS

To stay competitive, most companies continually add and drop products to ensure that declining items will be replaced by growth products. A **product line** is a group of products that are similar in terms of use or characteristics. The General Mills snack-food product line, for example, includes Bugles, Fruit Roll-Ups, Sweet Rewards Snack Bars, and Pop Secret Popcorn. Within each product line, a company confronts decisions about the number of goods and services to offer. Martha Stewart, for instance, must decide how many types of pie and cake tins the company should produce in its kitchenware line. Similarly, Home Depot must decide how many types of garden hoses it should sell in its retail stores.

An organization with several product lines has a **product mix,** a collection of goods or services offered for sale. For example, the General Mills product mix consists of cereals, baking products, desserts, snack foods, main meals, and so on (see Exhibit 13.4). Three important dimensions of a company's product mix are *width, length,* and *depth.* A company's product mix is *wide* if it has several different product lines. General Mills' product mix, for instance, is fairly wide with five or more product lines. A company's product mix is long if it carries several items in its product lines as General Mills does. A product mix is deep if it has a number of versions of *each* product in a product line. General Mills, for example, produces several different versions of Cheerios—frosted, multigrain, and honey nut. The same is true for many other products in the company's other product lines.

When deciding on the dimensions of a product mix, a company must weigh the risks and rewards associated with various approaches. Some companies limit the number of product offerings and focus on selling a few selected items to be economical: Doing so keeps the production costs per unit down and limits selling expenses to a single sales force. Other companies adopt a full-line strategy as a protection against shifts in technology, taste, and economic conditions.

As Exhibit 13.5 shows, you can expand your product line in a number of ways. You can introduce additional items in a given product category under the same brand name—such as new flavors, forms, colors, ingredients, or package sizes.[21] Frito Lay, for example, extended the Doritos line in 1997 when it introduced its new zesty flavors Salsa Verde and Flamin' Hot Sabrositos to target the U.S. Hispanic market.[22] You can extend the brand to include new products. Crest toothpaste, for example, extended

| Ready-to-Eat Cereals | Snack Foods and Beverages | Baking Products and Desserts | Main Meals and Side Dishes | Dairy Products |
| --- | --- | --- | --- | --- |
| Cheerios | Bugles Corn Snacks | Betty Crocker Cake Mixes | Bac*Os | Colombo Yogurt |
| Cinnamon Toast Crunch | Chex Snack Mix | Bisquick | Chicken Helper | Yoplait Yogurt |
| Cocoa Puffs | Fruit by the Foot | Creamy Deluxe Frosting | Hamburger Helper | |
| Kix | Fruit Roll-Ups | Gold Medal Flour | Potato Buds | |
| Nature Valley Granola | Nature Valley Granola Bars | Softasilk Cake Flour | Suddenly Salad | |
| Oatmeal Crisp | Pop Secret Popcorn | | Tuna Helper | |
| Raisin Nut Bran | Sweet Rewards Snack Bars | | | |
| Total | | | | |
| Wheaties | | | | |

### EXHIBIT 13.4

The Product Mix at General Mills

Selected products from General Mills show a product mix that is fairly wide but that varies in length and depth within each product line.

| Method of Expansion | How It Works | Example |
|---|---|---|
| Line filling | Developing items to fill gaps in the market that have been overlooked by competitors or have emerged as consumers' tastes and needs shift | Alka-Seltzer Plus cold medicine |
| Line extension | Creating a new variation of a basic product | Tartar Control Crest toothpaste |
| Brand extension | Putting the brand for an existing product category into a new category | Virgin Cola |
| Line stretching | Adding higher- or lower-priced items at either end of the product line to extend its appeal to new economic groups | Marriott Marquis hotel |

**EXHIBIT 13.5**

Expanding the Product Line

Knowing that no product or category has an unlimited life cycle, companies use one or more of these methods to keep sales strong by expanding their product lines.

its brand to include dental floss, mouthwash, and brightening solutions. Keep in mind, however, that line extensions involve some risk. An overextended brand name might lose its specific meaning, and sales of an extension may come at the expense of other items in the line. A line extension works best when it takes sales away from competing brands, not when it cannibalizes the company's other items.[23]

## PRODUCT POSITIONING STRATEGIES

In Chapter 12 we defined a product's position as the place it occupies in the consumer's mind relative to competing products. For example, BMW and Porsche are associated with performance, Mercedes Benz with luxury, and Volvo with safety. By organizing products and services into categories based on the perceived position, consumers simplify the buying process. Instead of test-driving all cars, for instance, they may focus on those they perceive to be high-performance vehicles.

Even though consumers position products with or without the help of marketers, marketers do not want to leave their product's position to chance. Companies define the position they want to occupy in the consumer's mind before developing their marketing strategies. Then they choose positions that will give their products the greatest advantage in selected target markets.[24] Marketers can follow several positioning strategies. They can position their products on specific product features or attributes (such as size, ease of use, style), on the services that accompany the product (such as convenient delivery or lifetime customer support), on the product's image (such as reliability or sophistication), on price (such as low cost or premium), on category leadership (such as the leading online bookseller), and so forth.

When choosing the number of distinguishing variables to promote, companies try to avoid three major positioning errors: underpositioning (failing to ever really position the product at all), overpositioning (promoting too many benefits so that no one actually stands out), and confused positioning (mixing benefits that confuse the buyer such as sophisticated image and low cost). Consider McDonald's, for instance. To convince U.S. consumers that McDonald's McCafe coffee shops stand for premium, McDonald's decided to locate the cafes in a separate area of its fast-food franchises. The cafes have their own counter, sign, and coffeehouse-like furniture. Employees wear upscale outfits, beans are gourmet quality, and drinks are served in ceramic mugs—but prices are lower than those of competitors such as Starbucks.[25]

## PRODUCT STRATEGIES FOR INTERNATIONAL MARKETS

In the course of developing strategies for marketing products internationally, companies must consider a variety of important factors. First, they must decide on which products and services to introduce in which countries. When selecting a country, they must take into consideration the type of government, market entry requirements, tariffs and other trade barriers, cultural and language differences, consumer preferences, foreign-exchange rates, and differing business customs. Then,

When Mars Incorporated designs and promotes its M&M candy products for the Russian market, it takes cultural context into account.

they must decide whether to *standardize* the product, selling the same product everywhere, or to *customize* the product to accommodate the lifestyles and habits of local target markets. Keep in mind that the degree of customization can vary. At times, a company may change only the product's name or packaging; if it decides to customize, however, the company will be offering a completely different product in different markets.

Of course, understanding the country's culture and regulations will help a company make these important choices, as Chapter 3 discussed. But even the most successful U.S. companies sometimes blunder. Look at Disney. After losing $1 billion in Euro-Disney's first year of operation, the company realized that Paris was not Anaheim or Orlando. For example, French employees were insulted by the Disney dress code, and European customers were not accustomed to standing in line for rides or eating fast food standing up. So rather than continue alienating the Europeans, Disney switched from a standardized to a customized strategy by adjusting its marketing mix for Europeans. The company ditched its controversial dress code, authorized wine with meals, lowered admission prices, hired a French investor relations firm, and changed the name of the complex from Euro-Disney to Disneyland Paris to lure the French tourists.[26]

Like Disney, many U.S. manufacturers have customized their products after learning that international customers are not all alike. For instance, Heinz now varies its ketchup recipe in different countries—after having discovered that consumers in Belgium and Holland use ketchup as a pasta sauce. In China, Cheetos are cheeseless because the Chinese people don't really like cheese.[27] On the other hand, Kellogg sells the same Corn Flakes in Europe that it sells in the United States. Only recently, however, has Kellogg made significant inroads in European markets, thanks to television advertising and lifestyle changes that favor bigger breakfasts.[28] The latest twist is for companies to adapt non–U.S. products for U.S. markets. For example, Hååagen-Dazs has successfully introduced a caramel ice cream from Argentina into U.S. markets.[29]

> ## video exercise

**Take a moment to apply what you've learned.**

## > Developing Brand and Packaging Strategies

Regardless of what type of product a company sells, it usually wants to create a **brand** identity by using a unique name or design that sets the product apart from those offered by competitors. Jeep, Levi's 501, Apple, and Martha Stewart are **brand names,** the portion of a brand that can be spoken, including letters, words, or numbers. McDonald's golden arches symbol is an example of a **brand mark,** the portion of a brand that cannot be expressed verbally.

The choice of a brand name and any associated brand marks can be a critical success factor. A well-known brand name, for instance, can generate more sales than an unknown name. As a result, manufacturers zealously protect their names. Brand names and brand symbols may be registered with the Patent and Trademark Office as trademarks. As Component Chapter B explains, a **trademark** is a brand that has been given legal protection so that its owner has exclusive rights to its use. Keep in mind, however, that when a name becomes too widely used it no longer qualifies for production under trademark laws. Cellophane, kerosene, linoleum, escalator, zipper, shredded wheat, and raisin bran are just a few of the many brand names that have passed into public domain, much to their creators' dismay.

Sometimes companies, such as Warner Brothers, *license* or sell the rights to specific well-known names and symbols—such as Looney Tunes cartoon characters—and then manufacturers use these licensed labels to help sell products. In fact, 65 percent of Fortune 500 companies have licensing agreements. Licensing can be a terrific source of revenue. General Mills alone has more than 1,200 licensing agreements that cover everything from clothes to cologne and generate annual revenues of $1.1 billion.[30]

## active exercise    <

**Take a moment to apply what you've learned.**

### BRAND CATEGORIES

Brand names may be owned by manufacturers, retailers, wholesalers, and a variety of business types. Brands offered and promoted by a national manufacturer, such as Procter & Gamble's Tide detergent and Pampers disposable diapers, are called **national brands. Private brands** are not linked to a manufacturer but instead carry a wholesaler's or a retailer's brand. DieHard batteries and Kenmore appliances are private brands sold by Sears. As an alternative to branded products, some retailers also offer **generic products,** which are packaged in plain containers that bear only the name of the product. Generic products can cost up to 40 percent less than brand-name products because of uneven quality, plain packaging, and lack of promotion. Yet generic goods have found a definite market niche, as a look at your local supermarket shelves will confirm.

### BRAND EQUITY AND LOYALTY

A brand name is often an organization's most valuable asset because it provides customers with a way of recognizing and specifying a particular product so that they can choose it again or recommend it to others. This notion of the value of a brand is also called *brand equity.* Strong brands often command a premium price in the marketplace, as Nike shoes, the North Face ski wear, Bobbie Brown cosmetics, and Evian water do.

Customers who buy the same brand again and again are evidence of the strength of **brand loyalty,** or commitment to a particular brand. Brand loyalty can be measured in degrees. The first level is **brand**

**awareness,** which means that people are likely to buy a product because they are familiar with it. The next level is **brand preference,** which means people will purchase the product if it is available, although they may still be willing to experiment with alternatives if they cannot find the preferred brand. The third and ultimate level of brand loyalty is **brand insistence,** the stage at which buyers will accept no substitute.

Companies can take various approaches to building brands. One approach is to create separate brands for products targeted to different customer segments. For example, Second Cup Limited, a Canadian company, uses three distinct coffeehouse brands—Coffee Plantation, Gloria Jean's, and Coffee People—to target three geographical segments. The opposite approach is illustrated by Starbucks, which operates under one brand everywhere in the world.[31] Yet another approach is illustrated by the Gap. The $8 billion company has put its main brand on BabyGap and GapBody stores as well as its GapScents fragrances. Yet it has maintained separate brand identities for Banana Republic and Old Navy, two chains aimed at distinctly different customer segments.[32]

### Family Branding

An increasing number of companies have been using **family branding** (using one brand on a variety of related products) to add to their product lines. Kraft, for example, has extended its Jell-O product line to include gelatin in a cup, pudding in a cup, and cheesecake snacks in a cup. These products build on the convenience-with-quality image of the Jell-O family brand.[33]

Building on the name recognition of an existing brand cuts the costs and risks of introducing new products. However, there are limits to how far a brand name can be stretched to accommodate new products and still fit the buyer's perception of what the brand stands for. Snickers ice cream bars and Dr. Scholl's socks and shoes worked as brand extensions, but Bic perfume and Rubbermaid computer accessories did not.

After years of being one of the coolest brands on the block, some think Tommy Hilfiger has overextended his brand. By plastering his name on everything from linens to infant clothes and pushing the brand into over 10,000 U.S. department stores and even discount outlets, Hilfiger alienated his loyal customers. As one customer put it, "Even cheap stores sell Tommy Hilfiger."[34] Richard Branson, founder of Virgin, has also been criticized of overextending the Virgin brand. Branson has slapped the Virgin name and logo on a chaotic jumble of hundreds of products—from airplanes to cola to financial services—putting it in danger of losing its identity. "Virgin makes no sense; it's completely unfocused," says the head of one New York communications firm.[35]

### Co-Branding

Co-branding is another way you can strengthen your brands and products. **Co-branding** occurs when two or more companies team up to closely link their names in a single product. Two examples of successful co-branding include Kellogg's Pop Tarts made with Smucker's jam and Nabisco Cranberry Newtons filled with Ocean Spray cranberries. Co-branding can help companies reach new audiences and tap the equity of particularly strong brands.[36] Moreover, it can help change a product's image. In an attempt to associate the Kodak brand with the output side of digital photography, the company has been co-branding its name with all things digital. The Kodak name sits above Lexmark's logo on an inkjet printer (one of the first to print photographic inkjet paper), and it's all over the Web sites of companies that trumpet their use of Kodak processing and papers.[37]

## PACKAGING AND LABELING YOUR PRODUCTS

Most products need some form of packaging to protect the product from damage or tampering and to make it convenient for customers to purchase. Packaging also makes products easier to display and facilitates the sale of smaller products. In addition, packaging can provide convenience, as with food products that are ready to eat right out of the wrapper. Quaker Oats, for example, has gained considerable market share by switching from bulky boxes to easy-open, lower-priced bags for its cereal products.[38] In some cases, packaging is an essential part of the product itself, such as microwave popcorn or toothpaste in pump dispensers.

Besides function, however, packaging plays an important role in a product's marketing strategy because most consumer buying decisions are made in the store. As a result, companies spend big bucks on packaging to attract consumer attention and to promote a product's benefits through the package's shape, composition, and design. Innovative packaging—such as Mentadent toothpaste's two-chamber package with pump—can give your product a powerful marketing boost, whereas a poorly designed package may drive consumers away.

Labeling is an integral part of packaging. Whether the label is a separate element attached to the package or a printed part of the container, it serves to identify a brand. Sometimes the label also gives grading information about the product or information about ingredients, operating procedures, shelf life, or risks. The labeling of foods, drugs, cosmetics, and many health products is regulated under various federal laws, which often require disclosures about potential dangers, benefits, and other issues consumers need to consider when making a buying decision.

Labels do more than communicate with consumers. They are also used by manufacturers and retailers as a tool for monitoring product performance and inventory. **Universal Product Codes (UPCs),** those black stripes on packages, give companies a cost-effective method of tracking the movement of goods. Store checkout scanners read UPC codes and relay the identity, sales, and prices of all products to the retailer's computer system. Such data can help retailers and manufacturers measure the effectiveness of promotions such as coupons and in-store displays.

## active poll  <

**What do you think? Voice your opinion and find out what others have to say.**

## active concept check  <

**Now let's take a moment to test your knowledge of the concepts you have studied in this section.**

## > Developing Pricing Strategies

Pricing, the second major component of a firm's marketing mix, is often one of the most critical decisions a company must make. Price is the only element in a company's marketing mix that produces revenue—all other elements represent cost. Thus, setting a product's price not only determines the amount of income your company will generate from sales of that product but it can differentiate the product from competition. As you can imagine, determining the right price is not an easy task. If a company charges too much, it will generate fewer sales; if it charges too little, it will sacrifice potential profits.

### BREAK-EVEN ANALYSIS

How does a company determine the amount of profit it will earn by selling a certain product? **Break-even analysis** is a tool companies use to determine the number of units of a product they must sell at a given price to cover all manufacturing and selling costs, or to break even. In break-even analysis, you consider two types of costs. **Variable costs** change with the level of production. These include raw materials, shipping costs, and supplies consumed during production. **Fixed costs,** by contrast, remain stable regardless of the number of products produced. These costs include rent payments, insurance premiums, and real estate taxes. The total cost of operating the business is the sum of a firm's variable and fixed costs.

The **break-even point** is the minimum sales volume the company must achieve to avoid losing money. Sales volume above the break-even point will generate profits, whereas sales volume below the break-even amount will result in losses. You can determine the break-even point in number of units with this simple calculation:

$$Break\text{-}even\ point = \frac{Fixed\ costs}{Selling\ price\ per\ unit - Variable\ costs\ per\ unit}$$

For example, if you wanted to price haircuts at $20 and you had fixed costs of $60,000 and variable costs per haircut of $5, you would need to sell 4,000 haircuts to break even:

$$Break\text{-}even\ point\ (in\ units) = \frac{\$60,000}{\$20 - \$5} = 4,000\ units$$

Of course, $20 isn't your only pricing option. Why not charge $30 instead? When you charge the higher price, you need to give only 2,400 haircuts to break even (see Exhibit 13.6). However, before

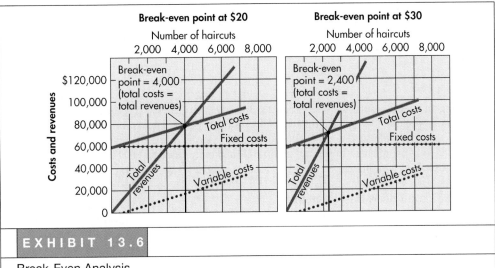

**Break-even point at $20**

Number of haircuts
2,000  4,000  6,000  8,000

**Break-even point at $30**

Number of haircuts
2,000  4,000  6,000  8,000

Break-even point = 4,000 (total costs = total revenues)

Break-even point = 2,400 (total costs = total revenues)

Costs and revenues

$120,000
100,000
80,000
60,000
40,000
20,000
0

Total costs
Fixed costs
Total revenues
Variable costs

**EXHIBIT 13.6**

Break-Even Analysis

The break-even point is the point at which revenues just cover costs. After fixed costs and variable costs have been met, any additional income represents profit. The graph shows that at $20 per haircut, the break-even point is 4,000 haircuts; charging $30 yields a break-even point at only 2,400 haircuts.

you raise your haircut prices to $30, bear in mind that a lower price may attract more customers and enable you to make more money in the long run.

Break-even analysis doesn't dictate what price you should charge; rather, it provides some insight into the number of units you have to sell at a given price to make a profit. This analysis is especially useful when you are trying to calculate the effect of running a special pricing promotion, and using spreadsheet software allows you to try different prices and see the results.

## FACTORS AFFECTING PRICING DECISIONS

A company's pricing decisions are determined by manufacturing and selling costs, competition, and the needs of wholesalers and retailers who distribute the product to the final customer. In addition, pricing is influenced by a firm's marketing objectives, government regulations, consumers' perceptions, and consumer demand.

- *Marketing objectives.* The first step in setting a price is to match it to the objectives you set in your strategic marketing plan. Is your goal to increase market share, increase sales, improve profits, project a particular image, or combat competition? Consider Intel. This Silicon Valley chipmaker slashed prices on its Pentium brand microprocessors to boost sales and fend off lower-priced rival brands.[39] Rolex takes a different approach, using premium pricing along with other marketing-mix elements to give its watches a luxury position.

- *Government regulations.* Government plays a big role in pricing in many countries. To protect consumers and encourage fair competition, the U.S. government has enacted various price-related laws over the years. Three important classes of pricing are regulated: (1) *price fixing*—an agreement among two or more companies supplying the same type of products as to the prices they will charge, (2) *price discrimination*—the practice of unfairly offering attractive discounts to some customers but not to others, and (3) *deceptive pricing*—pricing schemes that are considered misleading.

- *Consumer perceptions.* Another consideration is the perception of quality that your price will elicit from your customers. When people shop, they usually have a rough price range in mind. An unexpectedly low price triggers fear that the item is of low quality. South Korean carmaker Hyundai, for example, decided not to cut prices when the dollar gained strength against the Korean won, because the company did not want to reinforce an image of shoddy goods.[40] On the other hand, an unexpectedly high price makes buyers question whether the product is worth the money.

- *Consumer demand.* Whereas a company's costs establish a floor for prices, demand for a product establishes a ceiling. Theoretically, if the price for an item is too high, demand falls and the producers reduce their prices to stimulate demand. Conversely, if the price for an item is too low, demand increases and the producers are motivated to raise prices. As prices climb and profits improve, producers boost their output until supply and demand are in balance and prices stabilize. Nonetheless, the relationship between price and demand isn't always this perfect. Some goods and services are relatively insensitive to changes in price; others are highly responsive. Marketers refer to sensitivity as **price elasticity**—how responsive demand will be to a change in price.

## PRICING METHODS

Developing an effective price for your product is like a game of chess: Those who make their moves one at a time—seeking to minimize immediate losses or to exploit immediate opportunities—will be beaten by those who plan a few moves ahead. In other words, every element in the marketing mix must be carefully coordinated to support an overall marketing strategy. Here are a few methods that marketers use to set their prices.

### Cost-Based and Priced-Based Pricing

Many companies simplify the pricing task by using *cost-based pricing* (also known as cost plus pricing). They price by starting with the cost of producing a good or a service and then add a markup to the cost of the product. This form of pricing, while simple, makes little sense. First, any pricing that ignores demand and competitor prices is not likely to lead to the best price. Second, although cost-based pricing may ensure a certain profit, companies using this strategy tend to sacrifice profit opportunity.

Recent thinking holds that cost should be the last item analyzed in the pricing formula, not the first. Companies that use *priced-based pricing* can maximize their profit by first establishing an optimal price for a product or service. The product's price is based on an analysis of a product's competitive advantages, the users' perception of the item, and the market being targeted. Once the desired price has been established, the firm focuses its energies on keeping costs at a level that will allow a healthy profit. Keep in mind that although few businesses fail from overpricing their products, many more will fail from underpricing them.[41]

### Price Skimming

A product's price seldom remains constant and will vary depending on the product's stage in its life cycle. During the introductory phase, for example, the objective might be to recover product development costs as quickly as possible. To achieve this goal, the manufacturer might charge a high initial price—a practice known as **skimming**—and then drop the price later, when the product is no longer a novelty and competition heats up. Products such as HDTV and flat-screen monitors are perfect examples of this practice. Price skimming makes sense under two conditions: if the product's quality and image support a higher price, and if competitors cannot easily enter the market with competing products and undercut the price.

### Penetration Pricing

Rather than setting a high initial price to skim off a small but profitable market segment, a company might try to build sales volume by charging a low initial price, a practice known as **penetration pricing.** This approach has the added advantage of discouraging competition, because the low price (which competitors would be pressured to match) limits the profit potential for everyone. America Online (AOL) used this strategy when it adopted the $19.95 monthly flat rate Internet access charge several years ago. AOL wanted every desktop it could get, even at a financial loss. The strategy worked. Today AOL is the world's largest Internet service provider.

Penetration pricing can also help you expand the entire product category by attracting customers who wouldn't have purchased at higher, skim-pricing levels. Furthermore, if your company is new to a category pioneered by another company, this strategy can help you take customers away from the pioneer.[42] Still, the strategy makes most sense when the market is highly price sensitive so that a low price generates additional sales and the company can maintain its low-price position long enough to keep out competition.

## PRICE ADJUSTMENT STRATEGIES

Once a company has set a product's price, it may choose to adjust that price from time to time to account for changing market situations or changing customer preferences. Three common price adjustment strategies are price discounts, bundling, and dynamic pricing.

### Price Discounts

When you use **discount pricing,** you offer various types of temporary price reductions, depending on the type of customer being targeted and the type of item being offered. You may decide to offer a trade discount to wholesalers or retailers as a way of encouraging orders, or you may offer cash discounts to reward customers who pay cash or pay promptly. You may offer a quantity discount to buyers who buy large volumes, or you may offer a seasonal discount to buyers who buy merchandise or services out of season.

Another way to discount products is by *value pricing* them, charging a fairly affordable price for a high-quality offering. Many restaurants, including Friendly's, offer value menus for certain times of the day or certain customer segments, such as seniors. This strategy builds loyalty among price-conscious customers without damaging a product's quality image.

Although discounts are a popular way to boost sales of a product, the downside is that they can touch off price wars between competitors. Price wars encourage customers to focus only on a product's pricing, and not on its value or benefits. Thus, they can hurt a business—even an entire industry—for years. Consider the price war that Web-based Amazon.com started when it began selling *New York Times* best-selling books at a 50 percent discount in an effort to bring more customers to its site. Online rivals Barnesandnoble.com and Borders.com quickly matched Amazon.com's prices, and smaller bookstores were forced to lower their prices on best-sellers. To offset the loss of revenue, some small bookstores stocked their shelves with more profitable book categories, such as specialty books. Others could not compete and eventually closed up shop.[43]

### Bundling

Sometimes sellers combine several of their products and sell them at one reduced price. This practice, called **bundling,** can promote sales of products consumers might not otherwise buy—especially when the combined price is low enough to entice them to purchase the bundle. Examples of bundled products are season tickets, vacation packages, sales of computer software with hardware, and wrapped packages of shampoo and conditioner. Bundling products and services can make it harder for consumers to make price comparisons.

### Dynamic Pricing

**Dynamic pricing** is the opposite of fixed pricing. Using Internet technology, companies continually reprice their products and services to meet supply and demand. Dynamic pricing not only enables companies to move slow-selling merchandise instantly, but it also allows companies to experiment with different pricing levels. Because price changes are immediately posted to electronic catalogs or Web sites, customers always have the most current price information. Airlines and hotels are notorious for this type of continually adjusted pricing. In addition to posting current prices on their homepages and many travel Web sites, many major airlines and hotels send customers weekly e-mail notifications listing special discount fares.[44]

Three popular dynamic pricing tactics are:

- *Auction pricing,* where buyers bid against each other and the highest bid buys the product
- *Group buying,* where buyers obtain volume discount prices by joining buying groups
- *Name-your-price,* where buyers specify how much they are willing to pay for a product and sellers can choose whether to sell at that price

All three are changing the way buyers and sellers conduct electronic business, as this chapter's Focusing on E-Business feature discusses.

> **video exercise**

**Take a moment to apply what you've learned.**

> **active concept check**

**Now let's take a moment to test your knowledge of the concepts you have studied in this section.**

Thanks to the Internet, new pricing models such as name-your-own-price used by Priceline.com are becoming more and more popular. Priceline.com allows consumers to say what they're willing to pay for goods such as airline tickets, then tries to find sellers who will meet buyers' terms

## > Chapter Wrap-Up

Now that you've reached the end of the chapter, you may wish to explore the concepts you've been reading about in greater detail, or test yourself to see how well you've comprehended the material. In the box below you'll find a number of links. Click on any one of these links to find additional chapter resources.

## > end-of-chapter resources

- **Summary of Learning Objectives**
- **Practice Quiz**
- **Focusing on E-Business Today**
- **Key Terms**
- **Test Your Knowledge**
- **Practice Your Knowledge**
- **Expand Your Knowledge**
- **A Case for Critical Thinking**

# Distribution Strategies

## C H A P T E R  1 4

 **What's Ahead**

### INSIDE BUSINESS TODAY
### BUILDING A DISTRIBUTION STRATEGY: HOME DEPOT, THE ULTIMATE CATEGORY KILLER

It's the ultimate category killer, offering 125,000 square feet of everything you need for home repair and improvement projects. Home Depot is the world's largest home improvement retailer, stocking 40,000 to 50,000 products in every store. And the company keeps prices low and profits high by eliminating the middleman. Bypassing traditional retail distribution channels, Home Depot orders merchandise directly from manufacturers instead of purchasing from wholesale distributors. Furthermore, management negotiates deep discounts with producers for high-volume orders and passes the savings along to customers.

Today, with more than 1,000 stores, $40 billion in annual sales, and a huge traffic volume, Home Depot is an alluring distribution channel for producers. But first they must win Home Depot's business. And that's not easy. Home Depot's extensive store network and customer base give the retailer the upper hand in negotiating the best prices from suppliers. Keeping an eye on the bottom line, Home Depot conducts biannual reviews with every vendor. Hundreds of suppliers hawk their wares at the company's review sessions, vying to win, keep, or expand their shelf space at Home Depot. But management maintains a hard line with producers. Home Depot rarely agrees to price increases and constantly strives for additional discounts to improve the company's profit margins. "We've taken a lot of cost out of products through regular reviews with these vendors," says co-founder Arthur Blank.

Home Depot, the category killer that drove hundreds of mom-and-pop hardware stores out of business, is expanding its reach to the Internet.

Those who survive the ordeal get to sell their products to the legions of do-it-yourselfers who stuff their oversized shopping carts with every kind of home improvement product imaginable. Some producers are even willing to modify their traditional distribution channels for the chance to distribute their products through the retailing giant. Deere & Company, for example, has long distributed its riding mowers and heavy agricultural and construction equipment through established dealers. But those same dealers now face stiff competition from Home Depot's exclusive line of riding mowers produced by Deere under the brand name of Scotts. And that creates tension between Deere and its dealers.

Of course, the relationships between producers, dealers, and retailers have always been a bit tense. But now the Internet threatens to strain these connections more—even for giants such as Home Depot. Although the costs of shipping heavy or bulky goods prohibit many Home Depot suppliers from selling their wares directly to consumers, producers of smaller home improvement items are likely candidates for profitable e-commerce ventures. But not if Home Depot has anything to say about it. In fact, the company has no intention of competing against its suppliers for customers. And Blank indirectly told suppliers so in a letter which stated, "We realize that a vendor has a right to sell through whatever distribution channels it desires. However, we, too, have the right to be selective, . . . and we trust that you can understand that a company may be hesitant to do business with its competitors."

Will Home Depot have enough clout to prevent its suppliers from selling directly to customers on the Internet? Management thinks so. Home Depot plans to make its products available online in the future in addition to opening a new physical store every 53 hours. After all, as Arthur Blank sees it, "the Internet is really just another way that our customers are going to choose to shop with us."[1]

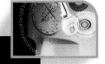

> ## Selecting the Most Effective Distribution Channels

Home Depot is just one example of how producers use intermediaries to get their products to market. Getting products to consumers is the role of distribution, the fourth element of a firm's marketing mix—also known as *place*. **Distribution channels,** or *marketing channels,* are an organized network of firms that work together to get goods and services from producer to consumer. Distribution channels come in all shapes and sizes. Some channels are short and simple such as the direct model Home Depot uses; others are complex and involve many people and organizations. Nonetheless, as Arthur Blank knows, a company's decisions about which combination of channels to use—the **distribution mix**—and its overall plan for moving products to buyers—the **distribution strategy**—play a major role in the firm's success.

## THE ROLE OF MARKETING INTERMEDIARIES

Think of all the products you buy: food, toiletries, clothing, sports equipment, train tickets, haircuts, gasoline, stationery, appliances, CDs, videotapes, books, and all the rest. How many of these products do you buy directly from the producer? For most people, the answer is not many.

Most companies do not sell their goods directly to the final users, even though the Internet is making it easier to do so these days. Instead, producers in many industries work with **marketing intermediaries** (also called *middlemen*) to bring their products to market. In some cases, these "go-betweens" represent the producers but do not actually buy the products they sell; in others, the intermediaries buy and own what they sell.

Without marketing intermediaries, the buying and selling process would be expensive and time-consuming (see Exhibit 14.1). Intermediaries are instrumental in creating three of the four forms of utility mentioned in Chapter 12: place utility, time utility, and possession utility. By providing an efficient process for transferring products from the producer to the customer, intermediaries reduce the number of transactions and ensure that goods and services are available at a convenient time and place.

Overall, intermediaries perform a number of specific distribution functions that make life easier for both producers and customers. They

- *Match buyers and sellers.* By making sellers' products available to multiple buyers, intermediaries reduce the number of transactions between producers and customers.
- *Provide market information.* Intermediaries such as Home Depot collect valuable data about customer purchases: who buys, how often, and how much. Collecting these data allows them to spot buying patterns and to share marketplace information with producers.
- *Provide promotional and sales support.* Many intermediaries create advertising, produce eye-catching displays, and use other promotional devices for some or all of the products they sell. Some employ a sales force, which can provide a number of selling functions, as illustrated in Chapter 15.
- *Gather an assortment of goods.* Home Depot, Macy's, and other intermediaries receive bulk shipments from producers and break them into more convenient units by sorting, standardizing, and dividing bulk quantities into smaller packages.

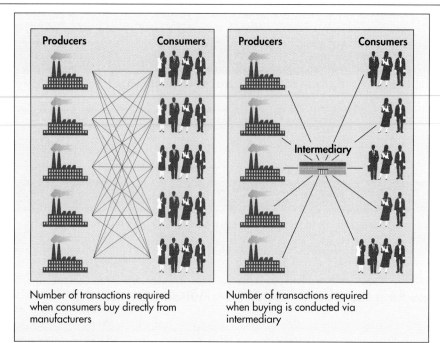

EXHIBIT 14.1

How Intermediaries Simplify Commerce

Intermediaries actually reduce the price customers pay for many goods and services because they reduce the number of contacts between producers and consumers that would otherwise be necessary. They also create place, time, and possession utility.

- *Transport and store the product.* Intermediaries such as retail stores maintain an inventory of merchandise that they acquire from producers so they can quickly fill customers' orders. In many cases retailers purchase this merchandise from wholesalers who, in addition to breaking bulk, may also transport the goods from the producer to the retail outlets.

- *Assume risks.* When intermediaries accept goods from manufacturers, they take on the risks associated with damage, theft, product perishability, and obsolescence.

- *Provide financing.* Large intermediaries sometimes provide loans to smaller producers.

Of course, the lines separating producers and their intermediaries are becoming fuzzier as some producers assume typical distribution functions. Producer S.C. Johnson Wax, for example, warehouses goods, stocks store shelves with Johnson Wax products, and even handles some retail functions for rival products as part of its contractual arrangement with Wal-Mart.[2] Similarly, Northern Telecom doesn't just send one gigantic shipment of telephones to Wal-Mart and other large intermediaries. Instead, the company has to inventory shipments, label boxes so they look like they come directly from the intermediaries, and perform other functions that minimize the intermediaries' inventory and handling costs.[3]

More and more intermediaries are performing functions once reserved exclusively for manufacturers. Computer wholesaler Ingram Micro, for instance, has been taking on such tasks as assembling PCs and handling inquiries from customers. Among the big-name producers that Ingram serves are Hewlett-Packard, Apple, and Compaq. Ingram also builds computers that dealers resell to consumers (and that bear the dealer's own name). Ingram is content to operate in the background and does not plan to enter the retail market with its own brand, says Ingram's CEO.[4]

Intermediaries such as Ingram Micro are expanding their functions to add value and to solidify their role within the distribution system. Ingram is responding to a dynamic environment filled with risks and opportunities. But some intermediaries feel threatened by the Internet. They worry that the Internet will allow manufacturers to bypass distributors and conduct business directly with end users. Others disagree. While they recognize that technology and the Internet are significantly changing the way intermediaries do business, they see the role intermediaries play as becoming more diverse and important now and in the future.

## TYPES OF DISTRIBUTION CHANNELS

The number and type of intermediaries in a distribution mix depend on the kind of product being sold and the marketing practices of the industry. An arrangement that works well for a power-tool and appliance manufacturer like Black & Decker or a book publisher like Prentice Hall would not necessarily work for an insurance company, a restaurant, a steel manufacturer, or a movie studio. In general, consumer products and business products tend to move through different channels (see Exhibit 14.2).

### Channel Levels

Most businesses purchase goods they use in their operations directly from producers, so the distribution channel is short. In contrast, the channels for consumer goods are usually longer and more complex than the channels for business goods. The four primary channels for consumer goods are:

- *Producer to consumer.* Producers who sell directly to consumers through catalogs, telemarketing, infomercials, and the Internet are using the shortest, simplest distribution channel. Dell Computer and other companies that sell directly to consumers are seeking closer relationships with customers and more control over pricing, promotion, service, and delivery.[5] Although this approach eliminates payments to channel members, it also forces producers to handle distribution functions such as storing inventory and delivering products.

- *Producer to retailer to consumer.* Some producers create longer channels by selling their products to retailers such as Home Depot, who then resell them to consumers. Ford vehicles, Benjamin Moore paint, and New Balance athletic shoes are typical of the many products distributed in this way.

- *Producer to wholesaler to retailer to consumer.* Most manufacturers of supermarket and drugstore items rely on even longer channels. They sell their products to wholesalers, who in turn sell to the retailers. This approach works particularly well for small producers who lack the resources to sell or deliver merchandise to individual retail sites.

- *Producer to agent/broker to wholesaler to retailer to consumer.* Additional channel levels are common in certain industries, such as agriculture, where specialists are required to negotiate transactions or to perform interim functions such as sorting, grading, or subdividing the goods.

### Channels for Services

So far we have examined how producers of tangible goods use various channels to reach consumers and businesses, but how do producers of intangible services reach their customers? Because delivery

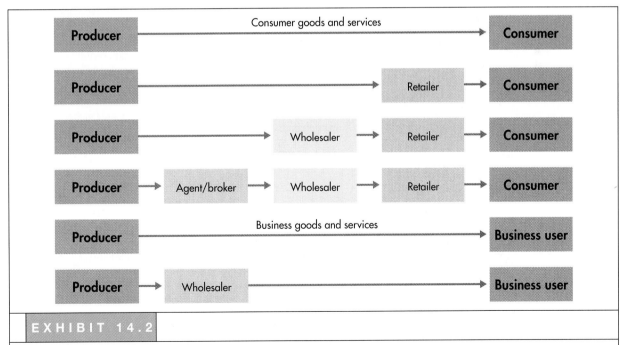

**EXHIBIT 14.2**

Alternative Channels of Distribution

Producers of consumer and business goods and services must analyze the alternative channels of distribution available for their products so they can select the channels that best meet their marketing objectives and their customers' needs.

of a service requires direct contact between providers and users, most service marketers use a direct channel to reach their customers. Hairstylists and lawyers, for example, deal directly with their clients, as do accounting firms such as H&R Block.

Some service businesses, however, do use other distribution channels. For example, Air France and other airlines typically sell tickets and vacation packages through travel agents. Similarly, State Farm and many other insurance companies market their policies through insurance agents and brokers. Technology is also increasing the number of options for distributing services. Banks, for instance, distribute financial services to customers all over the globe using automated teller machines in shopping centers, airports, and many other locations.

### Reverse Channels

Although most marketing channels move products from producers to customers, *reverse channels* move them in the opposite direction. The two most common reverse channels are those used for recycling and for product recalls and repairs. Recycling channels continue to grow in importance as consumers and businesses become more sensitive to solid-waste-disposal problems. The channels for some recycled goods, like returnable soft drink bottles, use traditional intermediaries—which in this case are retailers and bottlers. In other cases, recycling collection centers have been established to funnel material from consumers back to producers.

## video exercise <

### Take a moment to apply what you've learned.

## FACTORS TO CONSIDER WHEN SELECTING CHANNELS

Should you sell directly to end users or rely on intermediaries? Which intermediaries should you choose? Should you try to sell your product in every available outlet or limit its distribution to a few exclusive shops? Should you use more than one channel? These are some of the critical decisions that managers face when designing and selecting marketing channels for any product.

Keep in mind that building an effective channel system takes years and, like all marketing relationships, requires commitment. Once you commit to your intermediaries, changing your distribution arrangements may prove difficult. As Chris DeNove, a channel expert puts it, "It's much more difficult to modify an existing system than to start with a clean slate." Citing the automobile industry, for example, DeNove points out that "if an auto maker could start over now, none of them would create a franchise distribution system that looks like the existing one."[6]

Effective channel selection depends on a number of factors; some are related to the type of product and the target market, and others are related to the company—its strengths, weaknesses, and objectives. In general, however, choosing one channel over another is a matter of making trade-offs among four factors: the number of outlets that sell your product, the cost of distribution, the control of your product as it moves through the channel to the final customer, and the possibility of channel conflict.

### Market Coverage

The appropriate *market coverage*—the number of wholesalers or retailers that will carry your product—varies by type of product. Inexpensive convenience goods or organizational supplies such as Pilot pens sell best if they are available in as many outlets as possible. Such **intensive distribution** will require wholesalers and retailers of many types. In contrast, shopping goods (goods that require some thought before being purchased) such as General Electric appliances require different market coverage, because customers shop for such products by comparing features and prices. For these items, the best strategy is usually **selective distribution,** selling through a limited number of outlets that can give the product adequate sales and service support.

If producers of expensive specialty or technical products do not sell directly to customers, they may choose **exclusive distribution,** offering products in only one outlet in each market area. Vehicle manufacturers have traditionally relied on exclusive distribution agreements to sell through one dealership in each local area. By contrast, other firms use multiple channels to increase their market coverage and reach several target markets. Apparel manufacturers such as Champion frequently sell through a combination of channels, including department stores, specialty stores, the Internet, and cat-

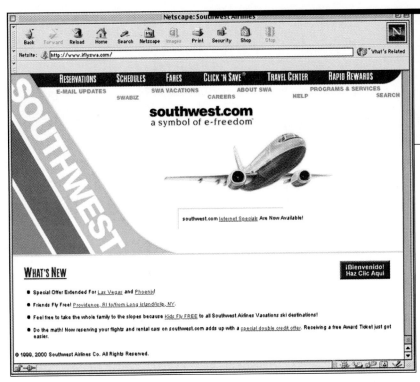

Southwest Airlines uses a multi-channel sales approach. Customers can purchase travel tickets from intermediaries such as travel agents, or they may purchase tickets directly from the company's customer service reps or over the Internet.

alogs. Using multiple channels is becoming increasingly popular as explained in this chapters' special feature, Focusing on E-Business Today.

### Cost

Costs play a major role in determining a firm's channel selection. It takes money to perform all the functions that are handled by intermediaries. Small or new companies often cannot afford to hire a sales force large enough to sell directly to end users or to call on a host of retail outlets. Neither can they afford to build large warehouses and distribution centers or to buy trucks to transport their goods. These firms need the help of intermediaries who can spread the cost of such activities across a number of noncompeting products. With time and a larger sales base, a producer may build enough strength to take over some of these functions and reduce the length of the distribution channel.

### Control

A third issue to consider when selecting distribution channels is control of how, where, and when your product is sold. Remember, you can't force any intermediary to promote, service, sell, or deliver your product. Longer distribution channels mean less control for producers, who become increasingly distant from sellers and buyers as the number of intermediaries multiplies.

On the other hand, companies may not want to concentrate too many distribution functions in the hands of too few intermediaries. Control becomes critical when a firm's reputation is at stake. For instance, a designer of high-priced clothing might want to limit distribution to exclusive boutiques, because the brand could lose some of its appeal if the clothing were sold in discount stores. In addition, producers of complex technical products such as X-ray machines don't want their products handled by unqualified intermediaries who can't provide adequate customer service.

In a conventional marketing channel, wholesalers and retailers are independent of one another. Each firm essentially pursues its own objectives, although maximizing sales is usually a shared goal. In contrast, a **vertical marketing system (VMS)** is one in which the producer, wholesaler, and retailer act as a unified system to conduct distribution activities. One channel member owns the others, has contracts with them, or wields so much power that they must all cooperate. Thus, the main advantage of a VMS is channel control (see Exhibit 14.3).

Vertical marketing systems vary in their level of formality:

- *Corporate vertical marketing system.* This is the most controlled vertical marketing system, in which a single firm handles production, wholesaling, and retailing functions. An example of this

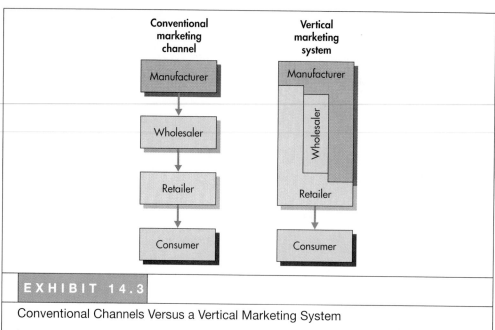

**Conventional marketing channel**

Manufacturer → Wholesaler → Retailer → Consumer

**Vertical marketing system**

Manufacturer / Wholesaler / Retailer → Consumer

**EXHIBIT 14.3**

Conventional Channels Versus a Vertical Marketing System

In a conventional channel structure no channel member has control over the other members, but in a vertical marketing system, one channel member has significant control over the other members.

arrangement would be a firm like Walt Disney that sells its merchandise through company-owned retail stores. In some cases, the entire distribution chain is controlled by a single firm, but often the channel contains a mix of corporate-controlled and independently owned operations.

- *Administered vertical marketing system.* This is a less formal arrangement in which one member of the distribution chain has enough power to influence the behavior of the others, but there are no ownership ties. The dominant company, known as the **channel captain,** performs functions that work to the mutual benefit of the entire chain. The channel captain can be a large manufacturer such as Procter & Gamble, Kraft Foods, or Gillette who, by virtue of the volume of product sold through the channel, can command unusual cooperation from resellers regarding displays, shelf space, promotions, and price policies. Or they can be a retailer such as Home Depot or Wal-Mart who can use its power to exert a strong influence on suppliers. Wal-Mart, for example, pushes its 65,000 suppliers to become lean operations so they can meet Wal-Mart's strict pricing requirements. "I went there [to Wal-Mart] knowing we were going to get squeezed and wrung and twisted—all in positive ways," says the CEO of Liz Claiborne, which designs the Ross clothing brand exclusively for Wal-Mart.[7]

- *Contractual vertical marketing system.* This system is a compromise between a corporate system and an administered system. With this approach, the members of the channel are legally bound by a contractual agreement that spells out their respective responsibilities. Franchising is the most common form of the contractual vertical marketing system. Many of the world's best-known retail outlets, from McDonald's to Radio Shack, rely on franchising to cover attractive markets.

### Channel Conflict

Because the success of individual channel members depends on the overall channel success, ideally all channel members should work together smoothly. However, individual channel members must also run their own businesses profitably. Which means that they often disagree on the roles each member should play. Such disagreements create *channel conflict.*[8]

Channel conflict may arise when suppliers provide inadequate support, when markets are oversaturated with intermediaries, or when companies sell products via multiple channels, each of which is competing for the same customers. For instance, Hallmark's decision to sell cards to mass-market outlets such as discount stores, supermarkets, and drugstores angered its 8,200 independent dealers who must now compete with large chains. To keep the peace, Hallmark launched a $175 million ad campaign and created new products exclusively for independents, but only time will tell whether these steps will be enough to save the card shops.[9]

Keep in mind that some channel conflict can be productive, especially when it leads to a more efficient channel system. Therefore, the challenge is not to eliminate channel conflict but rather to effectively manage it to avoid distribution system dysfunction and improve service to consumers. New channels, such as the Internet, are creating serious conflicts. Many producers are struggling for balance as they modify their channel arrangements to add Internet services while trying to maintain relationships with older, valued channel members.[10] Levi Strauss faced this challenge. In 1998 the jeans manufacturer announced that it was restricting online sales of Levis jeans to the manufacturer's Web site. Worried that they might lose jean sales, retail partners protested. Some even fought back by giving Levi's jeans less prominent display space in their stores. Eventually Levi Strauss caved in to retailer pressure and ceased selling merchandise directly to consumers via its company Web site.[11]

### Other Factors

In addition to market coverage, cost, control, and possible channel conflict, managers should consider several other factors when selecting distribution channels. These factors include the nature and price of the product, the market's growth rate, the geographical concentration of the customer base, customers' need for service, the importance of rapid delivery, the strengths and weaknesses of the various types of intermediaries within the channel, and international laws and customs when selling in other countries (see Exhibit 14.4).

| Factor | Explanation |
|---|---|
| Number of transactions | When many transactions are likely, the channel should provide for many outlets, and several levels of intermediaries. If only a few transactions are likely, the number of outlets can be limited, and the channel can be relatively short. |
| Value of transactions | If the value of each transaction is high, the channel can be relatively short and direct, because the producer can better absorb the cost of making firsthand contact with each customer. If each transaction has a low value, a long channel is used to spread the cost of distribution over many products and outlets. |
| Market growth rate | In a rapidly growing market, many outlets and a long channel of distribution may be required to meet demand. In a shrinking market, fewer outlets are required. |
| Geographic concentration of market | If customers are clustered in a limited geographic area, the channel can be short, because the cost of reaching each account is relatively low. If customers are widely scattered, a multilevel channel with many outlets is preferable. |
| Need for service and sales support | Complex, innovative, or specialized products require sophisticated outlets where customers can receive information and service support; short, relatively direct channels are generally used. If the product is familiar and uncomplicated, the consumer requires little assistance; long channels with many self-serve outlets can be used. |

**EXHIBIT 14.4**

Factors Involved in Selecting Distribution Channels

The choice of distribution channel depends on the product, the customer, and the company's capabilities.

## active exercise  <

**Take a moment to apply what you've learned.**

## active concept check  <

**Now let's take a moment to test your knowledge of the concepts you have studied in this section.**

### > Selling Products Through Intermediaries

Depending on the customer base and industry distribution patterns, products are normally distributed through two main types of intermediaries: wholesalers and retailers. **Wholesalers** sell primarily to retailers, to other wholesalers, and to organizational users such as government agencies, institutions, and commercial operations. In turn, the customers of wholesalers either resell the products or use them to make products of their own. Wholesalers that sell to organizational customers are often called **industrial distributors** to distinguish them from wholesalers that supply retail outlets.

Unlike wholesalers, **retailers** sell products to the final consumer for personal use. Retailers can operate out of a physical facility (supermarket or gas station), through vending equipment (soft drink machine, newspaper box, or automated teller), or from a virtual store (via telephone, catalog, or Web site). The form of contact affects the way intermediaries work with producers and customers, as explained in the following sections.

#### SELLING THROUGH WHOLESALERS

Because wholesalers seldom deal directly with consumers, you may not be familiar with this vital link in the distribution chain. Yet 453,000 U.S. wholesalers sell a whopping $4 trillion worth of goods every year.[12] Most U.S. wholesalers are independent, and they can be classified as *merchant wholesalers, agents,* or *brokers.*

The majority of wholesalers are **merchant wholesalers,** independently owned businesses that buy from producers, take legal title to the goods, then resell them to retailers or to organizational buyers. **Full-service merchant wholesalers** provide a wide variety of services, such as storage, selling, order processing, delivery, and promotional support. **Rack jobbers,** for example, are full-service merchant wholesalers that set up displays in retail outlets, stock inventory, and mark prices on merchandise displayed in a particular section of a store. **Limited-service merchant wholesalers,** on the other hand, provide fewer services. Natural resources such as lumber, grain, and coal are usually marketed through a class of limited-service wholesalers called **drop shippers,** which take ownership but not physical possession of the goods they handle.

In contrast to merchant wholesalers, **agents and brokers** never take title to the products they handle, and they perform fewer services. Their primary role is to bring buyers and sellers together, for which they are generally paid a commission (a percentage of the money received). Real estate agents, insurance brokers, and securities brokers, for example, match up buyers and sellers for a fee or a commission, but they don't own what they sell. Producers of commercial parts often sell to business customers through brokers. Georgia-based broker, Jerry Whitlock, has built a $1 million business by using the Internet to wholesale industrial seals made by nearly 100 producers to factories around the country.[13] Manufacturers' representatives, another type of agent, sell various noncompeting products to customers in a specific region and arrange for product delivery. By representing several manufacturers' products, these reps achieve enough volume to justify the cost of a direct sales call.

#### SELLING THROUGH STORE RETAILERS

In contrast to wholesalers, retailers are a highly visible element in the distribution chain. More than 1.1 million retail intermediaries ring up merchandise worth $2.5 trillion every year.[14] Store retailers include department stores, discount stores, off-price stores, warehouse clubs, factory outlets, specialty stores,

| Type of Retailer | Description | Examples |
|---|---|---|
| Category killer | Type of specialty store focusing on specific products on giant scale and dominating retail sales in respective products categories | Office Depot Toys "R" Us |
| Convenience store | Offers staple convenience goods, long service hours, quick checkouts | 7-Eleven |
| Department store | Offers a wide variety of merchandise under one roof in departmentalized sections and many customer services | Sears J.C. Penney Nordstrom |
| Discount store | Offers a wide variety of merchandise at low prices and few services | Kmart Wal-Mart |
| Factory/retail outlet | Large outlet store selling discontinued items, overruns, and factory seconds | Nordstrom Rack Nike outlet store |
| Hypermarket | Giant store offering food and general merchandise at discount prices | Super Kmart |
| Off-price store | Offers designer and brand-name merchandise at low prices and few services | T. J. Maxx Marshall's |
| Specialty store | Offers a complete selection in a narrow range of merchandise | Payless Shoes |
| Supermarket | Large, self-service store offering a wide selection of food and nonfood merchandise | Kroger |
| Warehouse club | Large, warehouse style store that sells food and general merchandise at discount prices; some require club membership | Sam's Club |

**EXHIBIT 14.5**

Types of Retail Stores

The definition of retailer covers many types of outlets. This table shows some of the most common types.

category killers, supermarkets, hypermarkets, convenience stores, and catalog stores (see Exhibit 14.5). They sell everything from rolling pins to Rolls-Royces and from hot dogs to haute cuisine.

Retail stores provide benefits to consumers in many ways. Retail stores like Home Depot save people time and money by providing an assortment of merchandise under one roof. Stores like Pier One Imports give shoppers access to goods and delicacies that they would have difficulty finding on their own. Still other retailers build traffic and add convenience by diversifying their product lines, a practice known as **scrambled merchandising.** For example, you can rent videos, eat pizza, and buy T-shirts at Grand Union supermarkets, and you can buy cosmetics, stationery, and toys at Walgreen's drugstores. Such mixed product assortments cut across retail classifications and blur store identities in the consumers' minds.

Many stores begin as discount operations and then upgrade their product offerings to become more like department stores in appearance, merchandise, and price. This process of store evolution, known as the **wheel of retailing,** follows a predictable pattern: An innovative retailer with low operating costs attracts a following by offering low prices and limited service. As this store adds more services over time to broaden its appeal, its prices creep upward, opening the door for lower-priced competitors. Eventually, these low-price competitors also upgrade their operations and are replaced by still other lower-priced stores that later follow the same upward pattern.

### Specialty Stores, Category Killers, and Discount Stores

Although department stores account for about 10 percent of overall U.S. retail sales, a much higher percentage of store sales are racked up by other types of retailers.[15] When you shop in a pet store, a shoe store, or a stationery store, you are in a **specialty store**—a store that carries only particular types of goods. The basic merchandising strategy of a specialty shop is to offer a limited number of product lines but an extensive selection of brands, styles, sizes, models, colors, materials, and prices within each line stocked. Specialty shops are particularly strong in certain product categories: books, children's clothing, or sporting goods, for example.

At the other end of the retail spectrum are the **category killers**—superstores that dominate a particular product category by stocking every conceivable variety of merchandise in that category. Home Depot, Toys "R" Us, Office Depot, and Barnes & Noble are examples. Category killers ring up as much as one-third of all U.S. retail sales, a dominant position.[16] Still, experts predict that with increasing competition, category killers will eventually become a diminishing force. To increase their market share, some category killers such as Comp USA, Staples, and even Home Depot (using the Villager's Hardware name) are opening stores that are one-half to one-third the size of their other stores. Smaller stores help boost profits because they are less costly to run and stock only top-selling items.[17]

In contrast to category killers, **discount stores** offer a wider variety of merchandise, lower prices, and fewer services. Some experts predict that "the discount department segment is going to be the fastest-growing."[18] In fact, discount stores such as Wal-Mart and Target are stopping category killers like Toys "R" Us in their tracks. That's because a specific product category such as toys accounts for only a fraction of general discounters' sales, so the discounters can afford to cut prices on that category as a way to lure shoppers. But toys are the only category at Toys "R" Us, so lowering prices can hurt this category killer far more than it can hurt the multiproduct discount store.[19]

One of the newest categories of discounters are supercenters, large discount stores that offer large selections of groceries, toys, household items, and more. Since the early 1990s, Wal-Mart has opened over 800 U.S. supercenters with an average size of 182,000 square feet. The company continues to open 160 or more new supercenters each year, in addition to new supermarket-style Wal-Mart Neighborhood Markets. By combining a broad selection of products and services and everyday low prices, supercenters have made Wal-Mart one of the nation's largest food retailers. Lower prices are a major advantage: Wal-Mart admits that it can sell groceries below cost because it compensates by selling other profitable merchandise. But the world's largest retailer is also counting on its high-efficiency distribution system to put fresher produce on the shelves and keep popular items in stock at all times.[20]

### Retail Industry Challenges

One of the biggest challenges facing the retail industry today is an oversupply of physical retail stores. An estimated 21.5 square feet of retail space exists for every man, woman, and child in the United States today, a 46 percent increase from the 14.7 square feet per person in 1986. As one retail expert puts it, "We are absolutely overmalled."[21]

Some of this excess retail space is being transformed into office space. But the oversupply and changing consumer shopping habits have thrown the industry into a state of turmoil. Competition among retailers is more intense than ever, forcing continued mergers among store chains. Shoppers are tired of tramping from one store to another or are attracted by the convenience of shopping online. In fact, the average time consumers spend shopping has dropped 25 percent since 1982, and the average number of stores visited during a mall trip has dropped by 32 percent.[22] Furthermore, many retail locations are looking their age; nearly half of the more than 2,800 enclosed malls in the United States were built in the 1970s or earlier.[23]

To entice shoppers, some malls are being re-invented through extensive remodeling and the addition of newer stores, restaurants, and short-term shows and exhibits. New stores are also popping up everywhere—from airport terminals to tiny towns—offering anytime, anyplace shopping convenience to draw consumers back again and again.[24] Some retailers are trying to make their stores exciting, memorable, and fun. This trend toward "retail-tainment" is adding a touch of friendly theatrics to local outlets of giant chains. Customers who can attend a cooking class at Williams Sonoma or get tips from golf pros at the Sports Authority are likely to come back for the latest in-store event—and buy something when they do.[25]

## video exercise ⟨

**Take a moment to apply what you've learned.**

## SELLING THROUGH NONSTORE RETAILERS

Nonstore retailing has its roots in the mail-order catalogs sent out by Sears and Montgomery Ward during the late 1800s, selling everything from household goods to ready-to-assemble housing materials. Today you can order clothing, electronics, flowers, and almost every other type of tangible and intan-

Toys "R" Us sells over $11 billion in merchandise annually but is facing increasing competition from discounter Wal-Mart and online toy retailers. In 2000, the company formed a strategic alliance with Amazon. By sharing each other's strengths in toy retailing, the partners hope to become the world's leading seller of toys on the Internet.

gible product from anywhere in the world at any time of day without actually visiting a store. Nonstore retailing includes mail-order firms such as L. L. Bean, vending machines such as those selling candy bars and soft drinks, telemarketers such as those selling British Telecom services, door-to-door direct sellers, and a variety of electronic venues such as the Internet, television home shopping networks, and interactive kiosks (free-standing information and ordering machines).

Even though nonstore retailing has many venues, about 93 percent of goods and services are still sold through physical stores.[26] However, nonstore retailing is growing at a much faster rate than traditional store retailing, and it is estimated that one-third to one-half of all general merchandise could soon be sold through nonstore channels.[27] In many cases, producers are reaching shoppers through a carefully balanced blend of store and nonstore retail outlets, as this chapter's Focusing on E-Business Today feature highlights. Nike, for example, sells its products on its Web site, in addition to selling Nike products through store retailers. To encourage customers to purchase through store retailers, Nike lists the locations of its retailers on its Web site—and offers the products it sells on the Web at full price (no discounts).[28]

Despite the convenience of nonstore retailing, most people will continue to shop in stores because they like to see, feel, smell, and try out goods before they buy.[29] This was the line of thinking behind Gateway's decision to open Gateway Country stores. The company hopes that giving customers the opportunity to test-drive the computers and achieve a comfort level with the technology will eventually pay off.[30]

### Mail-Order Firms

Among the most popular types of nonstore retailers are **mail-order firms.** These firms provide customers and businesses with a wide variety of goods ordered from catalogs and shipped by mail or private carrier. Catalog shopping is big business. In 1999, U.S. consumers spent more than $265 billion on mail-order goods and services, and businesses ordered another $190 billion worth through catalogs.[31] But this venue is facing stiff competition from the Internet and traditional stores. The annual growth rate for consumer catalog sales is expected to decline over the next few years from around 8 percent to 5 percent.[32]

To boost sales, catalog firms such as Harry and David, Delia*s, and L. L. Bean have developed Web sites to display their products and allow customers to place orders electronically. Some have even opened up small retail outlets in select cities. Why in this virtual age are catalogers opening physical stores? For one thing, retail stores soothe consumers' doubts about not seeing the product or gauging its quality. For another, some customers prefer to shop online versus paging through paper catalogs. As one retail expert put it, "the combination of bricks-and-mortar and the Internet is where we have to be."[33]

### Automatic Vending

For certain types of products, vending machines are an important nonstore retail outlet. In Japan, soda pop, coffee, candy, sandwiches, and cigarettes are all commonly sold this way. From the consumer's point of view, the chief attraction of vending machines is their convenience: They are open 24 hours a day and may be found in a variety of handy locations such as college dormitories. On the other hand, vending-machine prices are usually no bargain. The cost of servicing the machines is relatively high, and vandalism is a factor. So high prices are required in order to provide the vending-machine company and the product manufacturer with a reasonable profit.

### Telemarketing and Door-to-Door Sales

Telemarketing and door-to-door sales are also common forms of nonstore retailing. You have probably experienced telephone retailing, or *telemarketing,* in the form of calls from insurance agents, long-distance telephone companies, and assorted nonprofit organizations, all trying to interest you in their products and causes. Every year, U.S. consumers buy more than $186 billion worth of goods and services over the telephone, and business purchases by phone top $239 billion.[34]

Door-to-door sales, in which a large sales force calls directly on customers in their homes or offices to demonstrate merchandise, take orders, and make deliveries, is becoming less popular. Two famous names in door-to-door selling—and its variant, the party plan—are Avon and Tupperware. However, both companies are launching initiatives to sell directly to the customer over the Internet. After 115 years of selling exclusively door-to-door, Avon is pushing into traditional retail by establishing Avon centers in Sears and J.C. Penney stores. Avon had always avoided such a move for fear of competing against its 500,000 U.S. sales representatives. So to keep the peace, the company is creating a separate line of "Avon Gold" products to sell at its store-within-a-store concept, and it is establishing kiosks in shopping malls that will be run by Avon sales representatives.[35]

### Electronic Retailing

Whether you call it electronic retailing, digital commerce, e-shopping, e-tailing, cybershopping, or virtual retail, the amount of money spent by consumers online is projected to increase exponentially each year.[36] Electronic retailing has many advantages. From the retailer's viewpoint, electronic retailing costs less (no expensive store rent and store payroll); from the customer's viewpoint, electronic retailing means being able to shop around the clock for products and information tailored to individual needs.

Some electronic retailers—known as *pure-plays*—sell goods only via the Internet. They have no physical stores and make the Internet the cornerstone of their distribution strategies. Amazon.com, for instance, is a pure-play electronic retailer. The company offers an online-only assortment of CDs, videos, and scores of other products besides its extensive book listings. Other electronic retailers, such as Barnes & Noble, operate both physical stores and Web stores—this approach is becoming more and more common.[37]

Dell Computer originally sold computers only through mail-order catalogs and telemarketing. But now it is moving business to the Internet—where it already generates an eye-popping $40 million in sales each day. "We're trying to transform the way Dell does business," explains the director of Dell Online. "We want the Net to become a core part of your experience with Dell."[38]

Nonetheless, hanging out a shingle on the Internet does not guarantee visitors, let alone sales (see Exhibit 14.6). Those products and selling approaches that best fit the Internet will succeed; less-appropriate products and selling approaches will fail.[39] Look at iPrint, an Internet-only printer of business cards, letterhead, and other stationery items. Although print-to-order products are commonly sold in person at Mail Boxes Etc. and many independent print shops, iPrint is thriving on a user-friendly, self-service approach. "The success of our Web site depends on the fact that it's as easy to use as a bank ATM," says Royal P. Farras, iPrint's founder.[40] Among the ways you can sell your products online are through electronic catalogs and via cybermalls with virtual storefronts.

**active exercise**   **<**

**Take a moment to apply what you've learned.**

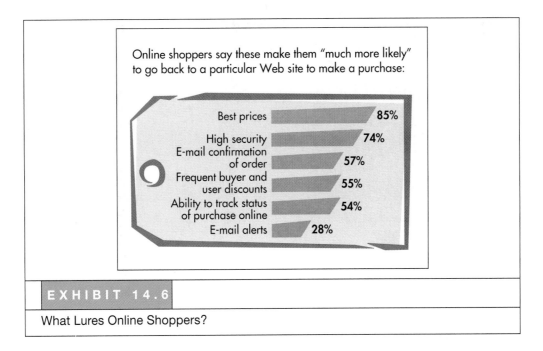

Online shoppers say these make them "much more likely" to go back to a particular Web site to make a purchase:

| | |
|---|---|
| Best prices | 85% |
| High security | 74% |
| E-mail confirmation of order | 57% |
| Frequent buyer and user discounts | 55% |
| Ability to track status of purchase online | 54% |
| E-mail alerts | 28% |

**EXHIBIT 14.6**

What Lures Online Shoppers?

**ELECTRONIC CATALOGS** Electronic catalogs (catalogs on computer disk or published over the Internet) have many advantages: they offer an easy way for customers to search for products, they allow businesses to reach an enormous number of potential customers at a relatively low cost, and they present timely information about a product's price and availability. Consider AMP, an electronics manufacturer in Harrisburg, Pennsylvania. The company was spending about $8 million to $10 million a year on its paper-based catalog, and some of the information was already out of date by the time the catalog was mailed. So, like many companies, AMP switched to electronic catalogs. W. W. Grainger, a 73-year-old industrial-parts supplier is another company that has moved its catalog, with over 80,000 items, to the Web. The company's annual Web sales now total about $400 million.[41]

**CYBERMALLS** A *cybermall* is a Web-based retail complex that houses dozens of *virtual storefronts,* or Internet-based stores. Consumers can buy everything from computer software to gourmet chocolates in cybermalls maintained by Yahoo!, America Online, and Microsoft. Like their physical counterparts, these Internet storefronts rely on a lot of "walk-in" traffic. For instance, cybermall shoppers interested in buying a CD might also click on the cyber shoe store. Besides exposure, another key advantage of a cybermall is that tenants do not have to create their own Web page or find a server to house it. Typically, the cybermall operator does all that for a sizable fee.[42]

Some cybermalls specialize. For example, MelaNet's African Marketplace specializes in goods and services provided by African Americans.[43] Other cybermalls feature a broader selection of retailers selling diverse goods and services. Yahoo!'s cybermall features well over 27,000 virtual storefronts, including big stores like J.C. Penney and smaller stores like the Amish Acres General Store. With cybermall sales increasing every day, Yahoo!'s chief operating officer predicts that online shopping will soon be bigger than catalog shopping.[44]

**> active concept check**

**Now let's take a moment to test your knowledge of the concepts you have studied in this section.**

**> Managing Physical Distribution**

Besides selecting the most effective channels for selling a product, companies must decide on the best way to move their products and services through the channels so that they are available to the customers at the right place, at the right time, and in the right amount. **Physical distribution** encompasses all the activities required to move finished products from the producer to the consumer,

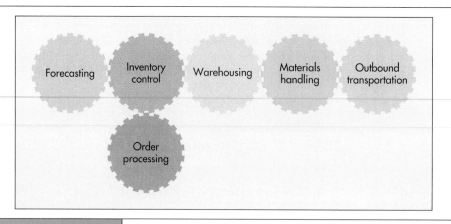

EXHIBIT 14.7

Steps in the Physical Distribution Process

The phases of a distribution system should mesh as smoothly as the cogs in a machine. Because the steps are interrelated, a change in one phase can affect the other phases. The objective of the process is to provide a target level of customer service at the lowest overall cost.

including inventory control, order processing, warehousing, materials handling, and outbound transportation (see Exhibit 14.7).

The distribution process may not appear very glamorous or exciting, but it is vital to a company's success. To illustrate the importance of physical distribution, consider this: A typical box of breakfast cereal can spend as long as 104 days getting from factory to supermarket, moving haltingly through a series of wholesalers, distributors, brokers, diverters, and consolidators, each of which has a warehouse. In fact, so many physical distribution systems are burdened with duplication and inefficiency that in industry after industry executives have been placing one item near the top of the corporate agenda: **logistics**—the planning and movement of goods and information throughout the supply chain.

Hard pressed to knock out competitors on quality or price, companies are trying to gain an edge through their ability to deliver the right stuff to the right place at the right time. For instance, PC Connection, a direct marketer selling computers and software, uses physical distribution to maintain an edge in customer service. Computer buyers who order as late as 2:45 A.M. can receive their purchases later that same day, nearly anywhere in the United States. PC Connection achieves this remarkable level of service by maintaining a warehouse at the Ohio airport used by its shipping partner, Airborne Express. When an order arrives by phone or fax, the merchandise can be loaded on the next Airborne flight. This dedication to customer service pays off for PC Connection in increased sales and a loyal customer base.[45] Plus, more skillful handling of logistics can put money back into a company's pocket by reducing inventory levels and holding time for finished goods.[46]

Keep in mind that streamlining processes that traverse companies and continents is not an easy task, but the payback can be enormous. Over a two-year period, National Semiconductor was able to cut its standard delivery time 47 percent, reduce distribution costs 2.5 percent, and increase sales 34 percent. How? By shutting down six warehouses around the globe and air-freighting its microchips to customers worldwide from a new distribution center in Singapore.[47]

## TECHNOLOGY AND PHYSICAL DISTRIBUTION

Some of today's most advanced physical distribution systems employ satellite navigation and communication, voice-input computers, machine vision, robots, onboard computer logbooks, and planning software that relies on artificial intelligence. Kansas-based trucking firm OTR Express operates almost as if it were a giant computer system that just happens to use trucks to get the job done. By using custom software to track everything from the location of trucks to the best places in the country to buy tires, OTR racks up profits while keeping the firm's prices competitive.[48]

FedEx also fully exploits the benefits of technology to automate its services and provide superior customer service. The company's $180 million small-package sorting system processes over 400,000 packages an hour. Each parcel is scanned four times, weighed, and measured, and its digital image is recorded on computer. In addition, the company's world shipping software streamlines customer billing, reduces shipping paperwork, and allows customers to track their shipments over the Internet.[49]

Regardless of the technology you use, the key to success in managing physical distribution is to coordinate the activities of everyone involved, from the sales staff that is trying to satisfy demanding customers to the production staff that is trying to manage factory workloads. The overriding objective should be to achieve a competitive level of *customer-service standards* (the quality of service that a firm provides for its customers) at the lowest total cost. In general, as the level of service improves, the cost of distribution increases. A producer must analyze whether it is worthwhile to deliver the product in, say, three days as opposed to five, if doing so increases the price of the item.

This type of trade-off can be difficult because the steps in the distribution process are all interrelated. A change in one affects the others. For example, if you use slower forms of transportation, you reduce your shipping costs, but you probably increase your storage costs. Similarly, if you reduce the level of inventory to cut your storage costs, you run the risk of being unable to fill orders in a timely fashion. The trick is to optimize the *total* cost of achieving the desired level of service. This optimization requires a careful analysis of each step in the distribution process in relation to every other step.

> active poll

**What do you think? Voice your opinion and find out what others have to say.**

## IN-HOUSE OPERATIONS

The steps in the distribution process can be divided into in-house operations and transportation. The in-house steps in the process include forecasting, order processing, inventory control, warehousing, and materials handling.

### Forecasting

To control the flow of products through the distribution system, a firm must have an accurate estimate of demand. To some degree, historical data can be used to project future sales; however, the firm must also consider the impact of unusual events (such as special promotions) that might temporarily boost demand. For example, if Home Depot decided to offer a special discount price on electric drills during September, management would need to purchase additional drills during the latter part of August to satisfy the extra demand.

### Order Processing

**Order processing** involves preparing orders for shipment and receiving orders when shipments arrive. It includes a number of activities, such as checking the customer's credit, recording the sale, making the appropriate accounting entries, arranging for the item to be shipped, adjusting the inventory records, and billing the customer. Because order processing involves direct interaction with the customer, it affects a company's reputation for customer service. Most companies establish standards for filling orders within a specific time period. PC Connection's guarantee of same-day shipping for orders received up to 2:45 A.M. is a good example.

### Inventory Control

As Chapter 9 discusses, in an ideal world, a company would always have just the right amount of goods on hand to fill the orders it receives. In reality, however, inventory and sales are seldom in perfect balance. Most firms like to build a supply of finished goods so that they can fill orders in a timely fashion. But how much inventory is enough? If your inventory is too large, you incur extra expenses for storage space, handling, insurance, and taxes; you also run the risk of product obsolescence. On the other hand, if your inventory is too low, you may lose sales when the product is not in stock. The objective of *inventory control* is to resolve these issues. Inventory managers decide how much product to keep on hand and when to replenish the supply of goods in inventory. They also decide how to allocate products to customers if orders exceed supply.

Today's distribution centers, such as this one for Amazon.com, are highly automated with advanced materials-handling systems controlled by a computer.

### Warehousing

Products held in inventory are physically stored in a **warehouse,** which may be owned by the manufacturer, by an intermediary, or by a private company that leases space to others. Some warehouses are almost purely holding facilities in which goods are stored for relatively long periods. Other warehouses, known as **distribution centers,** serve as command posts for moving products to customers. In a typical distribution center, goods produced at a company's various locations are collected, sorted, coded, and redistributed to fill customer orders.

### Materials Handling

An important part of warehousing activities is **materials handling,** the movement of goods within and between physical distribution facilities. One main area of concern is storage method—whether to keep supplies and finished goods in individual packages, in large boxes, or in sealed shipping containers. The choice of storage method depends on how the product is shipped, in what quantities, and to which locations. For example, a firm that typically sends small quantities of goods to widely scattered customers wouldn't want to use large containers. Materials handling also involves keeping track of inventory so that the company knows where in the distribution process its goods are located and when they need to be moved.

Using technology in the materials-handling process can make a big difference. When customers place orders at Amazon.com, for example, workers known as pickers race around large distribution centers, pulling the items off the shelves and loading them onto a giant conveyor belt. The products move from belt to belt until they drop into one of the 2,000 chutelike assembly bins assigned to customers when they clicked the Web site's "buy it now" button. As the conveyer moves, other items for the same customer fall into the bin. When the order is complete, a light flashes below the bin, and a worker puts all the binned items into a box, which then travels down another series of belts through machines that pack it, tape it, weigh it, affix a mailing label, and load it onto a truck at one of the loading docks.[50]

## TRANSPORTATION OPERATIONS

Firms that move freight are called *carriers,* and they fall into three basic categories: **Common carriers** offer their services to the general public, **contract carriers** haul freight for selected companies under written contract, and **private carriers** are company-owned systems that move their own company's products. Some firms use a combination of carriers, relying on common or contract carriers to help out when their private carriers are running at capacity.

For any business, the cost of transportation is normally the largest single item in the overall cost of physical distribution. When choosing transportation, however, managers must also evaluate other marketing issues: storage, financing, sales, inventory size, speed, product perishability, dependability, flexibility, and convenience—to name a few. The goal is to maximize the efficiency of the entire distribution process while minimizing overall cost. Each of the five major modes of transportation described here has distinct advantages and disadvantages. By utilizing intermodal transportation (a combination of multiple modes), shippers can compound the benefits of each mode.

- *Rail.* Railroads can carry heavier and more diverse cargo and a larger volume of goods than any other mode of transportation. However, trains are constrained to tracks, so they can rarely deliver goods directly to customers.

- *Truck.* Trucks are a preferred form of transportation for two reasons: (1) the convenience of door-to-door delivery and (2) the ease and efficiency of travel on public highways, which does not require the use of expensive terminals or the execution of the right-of-way agreements (customary for air and rail transportation). However, trucks cannot carry all types of cargo cost effectively; for example, commodities such as steel and coal are too large and heavy.

- *Water.* The lowest-cost method of transportation is water, the preferred method for such low-cost bulk items as oil, coal, ore, cotton, and lumber. However, ships are slow, and service to any given location is infrequent. Furthermore, another form of transportation is usually needed to complete delivery to the final destination, like it is for rail.

- *Air.* Air transportation offers the advantage of speed, but at a price. Airports are not always convenient to customers; airplanes have size, shape, and weight limitations; and planes are the least dependable and most expensive form of transportation. Weather may cause flight cancellations, and even minor repairs may lead to serious delays. But when speed is a priority, air is usually the only way to go.

- *Pipeline.* For products such as gasoline, natural gas, and coal or wood chips (suspended in liquid), pipelines are an effective mode of transportation. Although they are expensive to build, they are extremely economical to operate and maintain. The downside is that transportation via pipeline is slow (three to four miles per hour), and routes are inflexible.

## > Incorporating the Internet into Your Distribution Strategies

The Internet's efficient and effective global reach is revolutionizing the way goods and services are sold and distributed. Amazon.com's Jeff Bezos was a pioneer in recognizing the Internet's potential for making goods and services available to buyers. He reasoned that given a choice, many people would prefer the ease and convenience of online shopping to visiting a store every time they wanted to buy a book. He also believed that publishers would welcome Amazon.com as yet another way to get their books into the hands of readers.

Today, a growing number of businesses sell a huge selection of goods and services online. For some like Amazon, the Internet is their only marketing channel. For others like Recreational Equipment Inc. (REI), a sporting goods retailer, the Internet offers an additional way to sell to customers (see A Case For Critical Thinking, on p. 393). For an increasing number of businesses, the Internet represents an ideal way to communicate with customers, provide information, and promote their products or services. Funjet uses its Web site to advertise its charter vacations and provide potential customers with sufficient information to plan and price their trips. To book the trip, however, customers must still work through an authorized travel agent.[51]

Many intermediaries are using the Internet to improve the efficiency of their distribution systems and to expand their market reach. Herman Miller, an office furniture manufacturer, uses the Internet to target the home-office market, a segment that its traditional dealer network wasn't servicing. The company sees this as a terrific opportunity for the supplier and the distributor to reach new customers. An added benefit is that these home-office customers may eventually grow into corporate accounts (typically serviced by dealers).[52]

Some companies, of course, are using the Internet to eliminate the middleman entirely. After 110 years of offering medical insurance through 20,000 insurance agents, Provident American Life & Health Insurance Company dropped its agent network, changed its name to HealthAxis.com, and launched a Web site to sell a full line of insurance products directly to consumers. CEO Michael Ashker says that eliminating "costly middlemen in an industry where distribution is inefficient" allowed the company to cut its prices by 15 percent.[53]

The airline industry is another example of how some companies are using the Internet to eliminate intermediaries. For years, airlines have been encouraging fliers to bypass physical and online travel agencies and buy tickets direct from the carriers' own Web sites—a move that would save the airlines considerable commissions and fees. Orbitz.com, a joint venture owned by United Airlines, AMR (parent of American Airlines), Delta Airlines, Northwest Airlines, and Continental Airlines, now makes it easier for consumers to buy airline tickets direct from over 30 airlines. Critics of the joint venture claim that the purpose of Orbitz is to eliminate third-party travel agents and to transfer the ticketing business to the proprietary electronic channel. The airlines counter that Orbitz was established to create an additional channel for selling airline tickets and travel-related products such as hotel and car rental bookings, not clear the field of independent travel agents.[54]

As these examples show, the Internet is indeed a powerful force that is changing the role of traditional intermediaries. But jumping on the electronic-commerce bandwagon entails a variety of risks and costs that can complicate life for any company. Experts have, of course, recommended several strategies for incorporating the Internet into an existing channel structure. We explore these strategies in this chapter's special feature, Focusing on E-Business Today.

## video example    

**Take a closer look at the concepts and issues you've been reading about.**

## active concept check    

**Now let's take a moment to test your knowledge of the concepts you have studied in this section.**

> ### Chapter Wrap-Up

Now that you've reached the end of the chapter, you may wish to explore the concepts you've been reading about in greater detail, or test yourself to see how well you've comprehended the material. In the box below you'll find a number of links. Click on any one of these links to find additional chapter resources.

> ### end-of-chapter resources

- **Summary of Learning Objectives**
- **Practice Quiz**
- **Focusing on E-Business Today**
- **Key Terms**
- **Test Your Knowledge**
- **Practice Your Knowledge**
- **Expand Your Knowledge**
- **A Case for Critical Thinking**

# Promotional Strategies

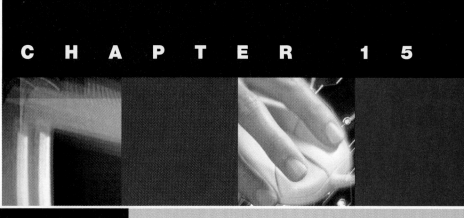

## C H A P T E R   1 5

## > What's Ahead

### INSIDE BUSINESS TODAY
### FLOORING IT: MINI-BILLBOARDS AT YOUR FEET FROM FLOORGRAPHICS

In-store advertisers try to influence your final purchasing decisions by planting messages on everything from shopping carts to end-of-aisle displays. But the CEO of Floorgraphics uses a different approach to catch the attention of store customers. Richard Rebh places colorful ads directly at the feet of shoppers, delivering messages that literally stop consumers in their tracks at the final point of sale.

Rebh's company produces, distributes, and installs mini-billboards on the floors of major retailers across the country, carefully positioning each advertiser's message directly below the shelf location of the featured product. Since studies show that 70 percent of brand decisions are made in the store, Rebh insists that floor ads make a powerful impact on final buying decisions. "We believe we have the most crucial piece of real estate in the media world—right where every manufacturer wants to be, right in front of their product, right at the moment of decision," Rebh contends.

Rebh paves the way for Floorgraphics ads by leasing advertising floor space from stores for periods of three to five years. Then he sells the space to advertisers for 4-, 8-, or 12-week cycles and oversees every detail necessary for properly producing and installing each ad. After transforming an advertiser's digital photographs into six square feet of colorful, laminated decals, Floorgraphics' technicians affix the mini-billboards to the floors of participating

Richard Rebh, founder of Floorgraphics, wants customers to walk all over his products.

merchants. Advertisers can promote their products with a single floor ad or divide their allotted space into smaller, separate components. Campbell Soup, for instance, uses a trail of small floor ads in the shape of Os to lead customers directly to the shelf location for SpaghettiOs.

Rebh of course avoids cluttering up every square inch of floor tile with splashy ads. To maintain the effectiveness of each message, he limits the number of floor ads to two per store aisle. Furthermore, he grants advertisers exclusive coverage in their brand categories. Floor ads for such competing brands as Pepsi and Coca-Cola, for example, do not appear in the same store.

To entice merchants to sign on with Floorgraphics, Rebh offers participating retailers a cut of ad revenue, usually about 25 percent of sales. And he provides advertisers a showcase for their advertising dollars that is economical, especially when compared to the costs of advertising on outdoor billboards, in TV commercials, and in other traditional media. For each mini-billboard, the cost-per-thousand impressions averages about $1 a day for advertisers, including production and installation charges.

Since the launch of Floorgraphics in 1998, Rebh has installed floor ads for more than 100 national advertisers in over 16,000 grocery, mass-merchandise, drug, and auto retail stores, including such retailing giants as Kmart and Food Lion. The unique promotional medium not only stimulates immediate sales but also reminds consumers of brand names and increases impulse purchases. Surveys commissioned by Floorgraphics reveal that floor ads increase brand sales by 25 to 27 percent, more than doubling the effect of advertising products such as shopping cart ads.

Rebh's future plans call for creating animated and electronic floor ads—complete with voice, sound, music, and full-motion images—that can be changed by remote control. And he envisions interactive floor displays that will allow customers to alter messages or register preferences by stepping on the ads. As far as Rebh is concerned, the floor's the limit for in-store consumer promotions.[1]

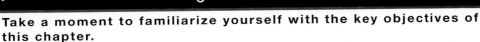

> ## objectives

**Take a moment to familiarize yourself with the key objectives of this chapter.**

> ## gearing up

**Before you begin reading this chapter, try a short warm-up activity.**

> ### The Promotional Mix

Richard Rebh knows that promotions such as floor ads can increase brand awareness and stimulate customers to buy. Although **promotion** is defined in many ways, it is basically persuasive communication that motivates people to buy whatever an organization is selling—goods, services, or ideas. Promotion may take the form of direct, face-to-face communication or indirect communication through such media as television, radio, magazines, newspapers, direct mail, billboards, the Internet, floor ads, and other channels.

Of the four ingredients in the marketing mix (product, price, distribution, and promotion), promotion is perhaps the one most often associated with marketing. Although it is no guarantee of success, promotion does have a profound impact on a product's performance in the marketplace. Moreover, your **promotional strategy** defines the direction and scope of the promotional activities you implement to meet your marketing objectives.

#### PROMOTIONAL GOALS

You can use promotion to achieve three basic goals: to inform, to persuade, and to remind. *Informing* is the first promotional priority, because people cannot buy something until they are aware of it and know what it can do for them. Potential customers need to know where the item can be purchased, how much it costs, and how to use it. *Persuading* is also an important priority, because most people need to be encouraged to purchase something new or switch brands. Advertising that meets this goal is classified as **persuasive advertising.** *Reminding* the customer of the product's availability and benefits is also important, because such reminders stimulate additional purchases. The term for such promotional efforts is **reminder advertising.**

Beyond these general objectives, your promotional strategy should accomplish specific objectives: They should attract new customers, increase usage among existing customers, aid distributors, stabilize sales, boost brand-name recognition, create sales leads, differentiate the product, and influence decision makers.

#### PROMOTIONAL ETHICS AND REGULATIONS

Although promotion serves many useful functions, critics argue that its goals are self-serving. Some contend that sellers use promotional tools to persuade people to buy unnecessary or potentially harmful goods like antiaging creams, baldness "cures," sweetened cereals, liquor, and cigarettes. Others argue that promotion encourages materialism at the expense of more worthwhile values, that it exploits stereotypes, and that it manipulates the consumer on a subconscious level. Still others argue that the money spent on promotion could be put to better use inventing new products or improving the quality of existing items.

Although abuses do occur, some of those charges are not justified. Take the charge about *subliminal advertising,* the notion that advertisers hide manipulative visual or audio cues in ads. Critics claim that flashing brief targeted messages across a movie screen (although too short to be recognized at the conscious level) can induce consumers to purchase the promoted products. However, there is no objective evidence of the existence of this sort of trickery and little psychological evidence to suggest that it would work even if anyone were doing it.[2]

Public concern about potential misuse of promotion has led the Federal Trade Commission (FTC) and other government agencies to pass strict rules and regulations that limit promotional abuses. One rule is that *all statements of fact must be supported by evidence.* For example, the Food and Drug Administration ordered Glaxo Wellcome PLC, makers of flu drug Relenza, to stop showing a widely aired commercial because it suggested that Relenza was "more effective than had been demonstrated."[3] Another rule is that *sellers must not create an overall impression that is incorrect.* So they cannot claim that doctors recommend a product if doctors do not; nor can they dress an actor in a doctor's white jacket to deliver the message; nor can they use whipped cream in a shaving-cream commercial to create an impression of a firm, heavy lather. Most states also regulate promotional practices by certain businesses, such as liquor stores, stock brokerages, employment agencies, and loan companies.

Many individual companies and industries also practice self-regulation to restrain false and misleading promotion. The National Advertising Review Board, whose members include advertisers, agencies and the general public, has a full-time professional staff that investigates complaints of deceptive advertising. If the complaint appears justified, the board tries to get the offending company to stop—even if it means referring the offender to proper government enforcement agencies.

## active poll   <

**What do you think? Voice your opinion and find out what others have to say.**

## FIVE ELEMENTS OF PROMOTION

Within the framework of these guidelines, marketers use a mix of five activities to achieve their promotional objectives: personal selling, advertising, direct marketing, sales promotion, and public relations. These elements can be combined in various ways to create a **promotional mix** for a particular product or idea (see Exhibit 15.1).

- *Personal selling.* **Personal selling** is the interpersonal arm of the promotional mix. It involves person-to-person presentation—either face-to-face, by phone, or by interactive media such as Web TV's video conferencing or customized Web sites—for the purpose of making sales and building customer relationships. Personal selling allows for immediate interaction between the buyer and seller. It also enables the seller to adjust the message to the specific needs, interests, and reactions of the individual customer. The chief disadvantage of face-to-face personal selling is its relatively high cost—about $170 per sales call according to one recent study.[4]

- *Advertising.* **Advertising** consists of messages paid for by an identified sponsor and transmitted through a mass-communication medium such as television, radio, or newspapers. The primary role of advertising is to create product awareness and stimulate demand by bringing a consistent message to a large targeted consumer group economically. As we shall see later in the chapter, advertising can take many forms—each with its own advantages and disadvantages.

- *Direct marketing.* **Direct marketing** is defined by the Direct Marketing Association as distributing one or more promotional materials directly to a consumer or business recipient for the purpose of generating (1) a response in the form of an order, (2) a request for further information, or (3) a visit to a store or other place of business for purchase of a specific product or service.[5] As this definition shows, direct marketing is both a distribution method and a form of promotion. This chapter covers the promotion side, and Chapter 14 discusses the distribution side.

- *Sales promotion.* **Sales promotion** includes a wide range of events and activities designed to stimulate immediate interest in and encourage the purchase of your product or service. The impact of sales promotion activities is often short-term; thus, sales promotions are not as effective as advertising or personal selling in building long-term brand preference.[6]

- *Public relations.* **Public relations** encompasses all the nonsales communications that businesses have with their many audiences—communities, investors, industry analysts, government agencies and officials, and the news media. Companies rely on public relations to build a favorable corporate image and foster positive relations with these groups.

In the next sections we'll explore the unique characteristics, tools, advantages, and disadvantages of each of these five elements of the promotional mix.

| Activity | Reach | Timing | Cost Flexibility | Exposure |
|---|---|---|---|---|
| Personal selling | Direct personal interaction with limited reach | Regular, recurrent contact | Message tailored to customer and adjusted to reflect feedback | Relatively high |
| Advertising | Indirect interaction with large reach | Regular, recurrent contact | Standard, unvarying message | Low to moderate |
| Direct marketing | Direct personal interaction with large reach | Intermittent, based on short-term sales objectives | Customized, varying message | Relatively high |
| Sales promotion | Indirect interaction with large reach | Intermittent, based on short-term sales objectives | Standard, unvarying message | Varies |
| Public relations | Indirect interaction with large reach | Intermittent, as newsworthy events occur | Standard, unvarying message | No direct cost |

**EXHIBIT 15.1**

The Five Elements of Promotion

The promotional mix typically includes a blend of various elements. The most effective mix depends on the nature of the market and the characteristics of the good or service being marketed. Over time the mix for a particular product may change.

## > Personal Selling

By almost any measure, personal selling is the dominant form of promotional activity. Most companies spend twice as much on personal selling as they do on all other marketing activities combined, even as technology is drastically changing the entire selling process.

Today's sales reps are plugged in—to headquarters and their customers. Many are walking electronic wonders, virtual offices with laptop computer, cell phone, and pager.[7] These new technologies provide online proposal-generation and order-management systems to relieve salespeople of nonproductive tasks, freeing them to spend more time attending to customers' specific needs. Consider the sales reps at Owens-Corning, for example. The company's newly developed Field Automation Sales Team system (FAST) has fundamentally changed the way salespeople do their jobs. Now they use laptops to learn about customers' backgrounds and sales histories, resolve customer service issues on the spot, modify pricing information as needed, print customized sales material, and more. By using the latest technology, Owens-Corning reps have become more empowered. "They become the real managers of their own business and their own territories," says Owens-Corning's regional general manager.[8]

### TYPES OF SALES PERSONNEL

The people who do personal selling go by many names: salespeople, account executives, marketing representatives, sales representatives, and sales consultants, to cite only a few. Regardless of their title, salespeople can be categorized according to three broad areas of responsibility: order getting, order

Owens-Corning's FAST sales force automation system makes working directly with customers easier than ever.

taking, and sales support services. Although some salespeople focus primarily on one area of responsibility, others may have broader responsibilities that span all three.

### Order Getters

**Order getters** are responsible for generating new sales and for increasing sales to existing customers. Order getters can range from telemarketers selling home security systems and stockbrokers selling securities to engineers selling computers and nuclear physicists selling consulting services. Order getting is sometimes referred to as **creative selling,** particularly if the salesperson must invest a significant amount of time in determining what the customer needs, devising a strategy to explain how the product can meet those needs, and persuading the customer to buy. This type of creative selling requires a high degree of empathy, and the salesperson focuses on building in a long-term relationship with the customer.

### Order Takers

**Order takers** do little creative selling; they primarily process orders. Unfortunately, the term *order taker* has assumed negative overtones in recent years because salespeople often use it to refer to someone too lazy to work for new customers or actively close orders, or they use it to refer to someone whose territory is so attractive that the individual can just sit by the phone and wait for orders to roll in. Regardless of how salespeople use the term, order takers in the true sense play an important role in the sales function.

With the aim of generating additional sales, many companies are beginning to train their order takers to think more like order getters. You've probably noticed that nearly every time you order a meal at McDonald's and don't ask for French fries, the person at the counter will ask, "Would you like an order of fries to go with that?" Such suggestions can prompt customers to buy something they may not otherwise order.

### Sales Support Personnel

**Sales support personnel** generally don't sell products, but they facilitate the overall selling effort by providing a variety of services. Their responsibilities can include looking for new customers, educating potential and current customers, building goodwill, and providing service to customers after the sale. The three most common types of sales support personnel are missionary, technical, and trade salespeople.

**Missionary salespeople** are employed by manufacturers to disseminate information about new products to existing customers (usually wholesalers and retailers) and to motivate them to sell the product to their customers. Manufacturers of pharmaceuticals and medical supplies use missionary salespeople to call on doctors and pharmacists. They leave samples and information, answer questions, and persuade doctors to prescribe their products.

**Technical salespeople** contribute technical expertise and assistance to the selling function. They are usually engineers and scientists or have received specialized technical training. In addition to providing support services to existing customers, they may also participate in sales calls to prospective customers. Companies that manufacture computers, industrial equipment, and sophisticated medical equipment use technical salespeople to sell their products as well as to provide support services to existing customers.

**Trade salespeople** sell to and support marketing intermediaries. Producers such as Hormel, Nabisco, and Sara Lee use trade salespeople to give in-store demonstrations, offer samples to customers, set up displays, restock shelves, and work with retailers to obtain more shelf space. Increasingly, producers work to establish lasting, mutually beneficial relationships with their channel partners, and trade salespeople are responsible for building those relationships.

## THE PERSONAL SELLING PROCESS

Although it may look easy, personal selling is not a simple task. Some sales, of course, are made in a matter of minutes. However, other sales, particularly for large organizational purchases, can take months to complete. Many salespeople follow a carefully planned process from start to finish as Exhibit 15.2 suggests. But personal selling involves much more than performing a series of steps. Successful salespeople help customers understand their problems and show them new and better solutions to those problems. Moreover, they're willing to invest the time and effort to build a long-term relationship with customers both before and after the sale.[9]

### Step 1: Prospecting

**Prospecting** is the process of finding and qualifying potential customers. This step involves three activities: (1) *generating sales leads*—names of individuals and organizations that *might* be likely prospects for the company's product; (2) *identifying prospects*—potential customers who indicate a need or a desire for the seller's product; and (3) *qualifying prospects*—the process of figuring out which prospects have both the authority and the available money to buy. Those who pass the test are called **qualified prospects.**

### Step 2: Preparing

With a list of hot prospects in hand, the salesperson's next step is to prepare for the sales call. Without this preparation, the chances of success are greatly reduced. Preparation starts with creating a prospect profile, which includes the names of key people, their role in the decision-making process, and other relevant information, such as the prospect's buying needs, motive for buying, current suppliers, income/revenue level, and so on.

Next, the salesperson decides how to approach the prospect. Possible options for a first contact include sending a letter or making a cold call in person or by telephone. For an existing customer, the salesperson can either drop by unannounced or call ahead for an appointment, which is generally preferred.

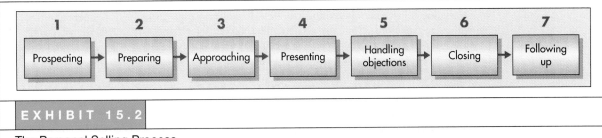

**EXHIBIT 15.2**

The Personal Selling Process

The personal selling process can involve up to seven steps, starting with prospecting for sales leads and ending with following up after the sale has been closed.

Before meeting with the prospect, the salesperson establishes specific objectives to achieve during the sales call. Depending on the situation, objectives can range anywhere from "getting the order today" to simply "persuading prospects to accept the company as a potential supplier." After establishing the objectives, the salesperson prepares the actual presentation, which can be as basic as a list of points to discuss or as elaborate as a product demonstration or multimedia presentation.

### Step 3: Approaching the Prospect

Whether the approach is by telephone, by letter, or in person, a positive first impression results from three elements. The first is an appropriate *appearance*—you wouldn't wear blue jeans to call on a banker, and you probably wouldn't wear a business suit to call on a farmer. Appearance also covers the things that represent you, including business cards, letters, and automobiles. Second, a salesperson's *attitude and behavior* can make or break a sale. A salesperson should come across as professional, courteous, and considerate. Third, a salesperson's *opening lines* should include a brief greeting and introduction, followed by a few carefully chosen words that get the prospect's attention and generate interest. The best way to get a prospect's attention is to focus on a benefit to the customer rather than on the product itself.

### Step 4: Making the Presentation

The most crucial step in the selling process is the presentation. It can take many forms, but its purpose never varies: to personally communicate a product message that will persuade a prospect to buy. Most sellers use one of two methods: The **canned approach** is a memorized presentation (easier for inexperienced sellers, but inefficient for complex products or for sellers who don't know the customer's needs). The **need-satisfaction approach** (now used by most professionals) identifies the customer's needs and creates a presentation to specifically address them.

### Step 5: Handling Objections

No matter how well a presentation is delivered, it doesn't always conclude with an immediate offer that might move the prospect to buy. Often the prospect will express various types of objections and concerns throughout the presentation. In fact, the absence of objections is often an indication that the prospect is not all that interested. Many successful salespeople look at objections as a sign of the prospect's interest and as an opportunity to develop new ideas that will strengthen future presentations. Smart salespeople know that objections to price are often a mask for some other issue. They also know *not* to argue with the customer. If you do, you may prove how smart you are by winning the argument, but you will probably lose the sale.

### Step 6: Closing

So far, you have invested considerable time and effort, but you haven't made a dime. You may have spent weeks or months to bring the customer to this point, but you don't make any money until the prospect decides to buy. This stage of the selling process, when you persuade the customer to place an order, is referred to as **closing.** How should you ask for the order? Closing techniques are numerous; among the more popular are the alternative proposal close, the assumptive close, the silent close, and the direct close. The *alternative proposal close* asks the prospect to choose between some minor details, such as method of shipment. Example: "Should we ship this standard freight or overnight?" With the *assumptive close,* you simply proceed with processing the order, assuming that the prospect has already decided to buy. Another alternative is the *silent close,* in which you finish your presentation and sit quietly, waiting for the customer to respond with a buying decision. Finally, many salespeople prefer the *direct close,* where you just come right out and ask for the order.

These closing techniques might strike you as tricks, and in the hands of unethical salespeople, some closing approaches certainly can be. However, the professional salesperson uses these techniques to make the selling process effective, and efficient, and as painless for the customer as possible—not to trick people into buying when they aren't ready.

### Step 7: Following Up

Most salespeople depend on repeat sales and referrals from satisfied customers, so it's important that they follow up on all sales and not ignore the customer once the first sale is made. During this follow-up stage of the selling process, you need to make sure that the product has been delivered properly and that the customer is satisfied. Inexperienced salespeople may avoid the follow-up stage because they fear facing an unhappy customer. However, an important part of a salesperson's job is to ensure customer satisfaction and to build goodwill.

> # active exercise

**Take a moment to apply what you've learned.**

> # active concept check

**Now let's take a moment to test your knowledge of the concepts you have studied in this section.**

> ## Advertising and Direct Marketing

Advertising and direct marketing are the two elements of a firm's promotional mix with which consumers are most familiar. The average U.S. resident is exposed to roughly 250 ads every day.[10] In addition to television, radio, and Internet ads, you receive phone calls from telemarketers, direct marketing letters, and a variety of communications—including floor ads—that try to sell you something.

All forms of advertising and direct marketing have three objectives: to create product awareness, to create and maintain the image of a product, and to stimulate consumer demand. Advertising and direct marketing are the promotional approaches that best reach mass audiences quickly at a relatively low per-person cost. Additionally, you have more control over these forms of promotion than over the others. For instance, you can say whatever you want, as long as you stay within the boundaries of the law and conform to the moral and ethical standards of the advertising medium and trade associations. Still, to be effective, your messages must be persuasive, stand out from competition, and motivate your target audience.

### ADVERTISING APPEALS

Well-designed ads make a carefully planned appeal to whatever motivates the audience. The specific motivator depends largely on the target audience. By segmenting along age, ethnic group, lifestyles, and other variables, advertisers try to identify which groups of people can be reached with various kinds of appeals. Nonetheless, all appeals fall into one of two general categories: logical or emotional.

Some ads use a logical appeal to persuade you with data; others target your emotions to get their point across. When selling technical products, some industrial and high-tech marketers assume that logic is the only reasonable approach. However, even with the most unemotional sort of product, emotions can be a significant factor in the decision process because all people have hopes, fears, desires, and dreams, regardless of the products they're buying.

Emotional appeals range from the most syrupy and sentimental to the downright terrifying. Fear appeals cover a broad range: personal and family safety, financial security, social acceptance, and business success or failure. Appeals to fear have to be managed carefully, however. Laying it on too thick can anger the audience or even cause them to block out the message entirely.[11] On the lighter side, some companies try to convince you of how good it will feel to use their products. Flowers, greeting cards, and gifts are among the products usually sold with a positive emotional appeal.

#### Price or Value Appeal

Promising to give buyers more for their money is one of the most effective appeals you can use, particularly in terms of audience recall.[12] A value appeal can be accomplished in several ways: lowering the price and making people aware of the new bargain price, keeping the price the same but adding value, or keeping the price and the product the same and trying to convince people that the product is worth whatever price you are charging.

#### Celebrity Appeal

A popular ad theme is celebrity attribution. The theory behind using celebrities in ads is that people will be more inclined to use products endorsed by celebrities and that some of the stars' image will rub

Sales of Salton's countertop grill soared when it signed on former heavyweight champ George Foreman as the product's spokesperson. The success of the grill can be attributed to both a good product and the credibility Foreman has with the public.

off on the products. After Tiger Woods won the 2000 PGA golf championship, his annual income increased by an estimated $50 to $200 million from celebrity product endorsements.[13] American Express chose Woods because he characterizes traits such as discipline, hard work, and preparation—the pillars of American Express. "It's hard to visualize anyone he wouldn't appeal to," says the company president.[14]

Similarly, Salton, a $500 million designer and seller of kitchen products, struck a deal with heavyweight champ George Foreman to promote a countertop grill. The promotion was such a success that the company eventually bought the rights to use George Foreman's name in perpetuity in association with its food preparation appliances.[15]

Nonetheless, celebrity ads are not always successful. Consumers don't always find them convincing (or at least don't claim to find them convincing). In one survey on the power of various advertising appeals, 70 percent of the respondents ranked celebrity endorsements as the least convincing. Another danger is that linking the celebrity to the product also links the celebrity's behavior (both good and bad) to the product. Madonna, Mike Tyson, O. J. Simpson, Michael Jackson, and Jennifer Capriati are among celebrities who have lost endorsement contracts when aspects of their private lives became public news.

### Sex Appeal

A tenant of advertising is, "sex sells." The classic technique is to have an attractive, scantily attired model share the page or TV screen with the product. The model may bring nothing to the ad beyond a visual focus point. The goal is to have the audience associate the product with pleasure. Guess Jeans and Calvin Klein's Obsession perfume are well-known examples of this approach. The sex appeal has to be used with some caution, however. At the extreme, using sex as the appeal can keep an ad from running, when print or electronic media refuse to accept it for publication or broadcast. In addition, attempts to present a sexy image may cross the line, offending some readers and viewers as simply sexist, not sexy.

### active poll

**What do you think? Voice your opinion and find out what others have to say.**

## ADVERTISING CATEGORIES

Despite the type of appeal used, advertising can be classified by type. **Product advertising** is the most common type, designed to sell specific goods or services, such as Kellogg's cereals, Sega video games, or Esteé Lauder cosmetics. Product advertising generally describes the product's features and may mention its price. Other advertising classifications include institutional, advocacy, competitive, and comparative advertising.

### Institutional Advertising

**Institutional advertising** is designed to create goodwill and build a desired image for a company rather than to sell specific products. As discussed in Chapter 2, many companies are now spending large sums for institutional advertising that focuses on *green marketing,* creating an image of companies as corporate conservationists. Institutional advertisers tout their actions, contributions, and philosophies not only as supporting the environmental movement but as leading the way. When utilized as *corporate advertising,* institutional advertising often promotes an entire line of a company's products. Institutional ads can also be used to remind investors that the company is doing well.

Institutional ads that address public issues are called **advocacy advertising.** Mobil and W. R. Grace are well known for running ads that deal with taxation, environmental regulation, and other issues. Advocacy advertising has recently expanded beyond issues in which the organization has a stake. Some companies now run advocacy ads that don't directly benefit their business, such as ads to project opinions and attitudes that support those of their target audiences.

### Competitive Versus Comparative Advertising

You can argue that all advertising is competitive in nature, but the term **competitive advertising** is applied to those ads that specifically highlight how a product is better than its competitors. When two or more products are directly contrasted in an ad, the technique being used is **comparative advertising.** In some countries, comparative ads are tightly regulated and sometimes banned; that is clearly not the case in the United States. Indeed, the Federal Trade Commission encourages advertisers to use direct product comparisons with the intent of better informing customers.

Comparative advertising is frequently used by competitors vying with the market leader, but it is useful whenever you believe you have some specific product strengths that are important to customers. Burger King used it on McDonald's, Pepsi used it on Coke, and car manufacturers from Ford to Toyota use it. This approach is bare-knuckle marketing, and, when done well, is effective. However, comparative advertising sometimes ends up getting neutralized by look-alike campaigns from the competition. Analgesics (painkillers) is one category cited as an example of comparative advertising taken too far. There are so many claims and counterclaims in this "ad war" that consumers can't keep it all straight anymore.[16]

### National Versus Local Advertising

Finally, advertising can be classified according to the sponsor. **National advertising** is sponsored by companies that sell products on a nationwide basis. The term *national* refers to the level of the advertiser, not the geographic coverage of the ad. If a national manufacturer places an ad in only one city, the ad is still classified as a national ad. As Exhibit 15.3 shows, national advertisers spend over $215 billion annually.[17]

By contrast, **local advertising** is sponsored by a local merchant. Grocery store ads in the local newspaper are a good example. **Cooperative advertising** is a financial arrangement whereby companies with products sold nationally share the costs of local advertising with local merchants and wholesalers. As a result, it is a cross between local and national advertising.

### Interactive Advertising

For years advertisers produced a standard commercial and distributed it to the masses via TV, magazines, or newspapers. But the Internet, interactive TV, video screens on shopping carts, and freestanding kiosks have expanded the advertiser's choices from one-way passive to two-way active marketing communication.

**Interactive advertising** is the two-way exchange between a merchant and a potential customer. With interactive advertising, the consumer uses a TV remote control, computer mouse, or other electronic device to communicate with the advertiser. For example, a consumer can click on a device to participate in a television poll, purchase an item, or obtain additional product information. Interactive ads generally include more information than can possibly be packed into a 30-second commercial, but they have a major drawback: the consumer can control the amount of information received and can even decide not to participate in the ad's interactive features. Those who choose to participate in the ad, however, tend to be interested in the message—making it more effective.

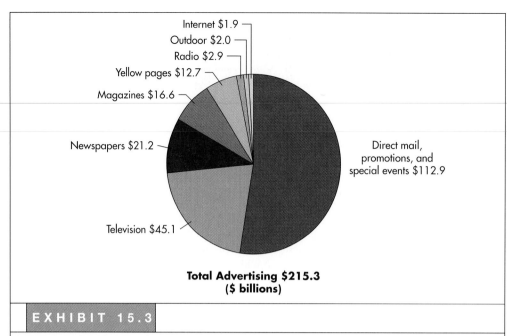

Internet $1.9
Outdoor $2.0
Radio $2.9
Yellow pages $12.7
Magazines $16.6
Newspapers $21.2
Television $45.1
Direct mail, promotions, and special events $112.9

**Total Advertising $215.3
($ billions)**

**EXHIBIT 15.3**

U.S. National Advertising Expenditures by Media Type

Despite downsizing, restructuring, and many changes in competitive marketing strategies, advertising is still being employed extensively by most marketers. U.S. national advertisers spent some $215.3 billion on a variety of media types for 1999.

### Media Categories

Advertising media fall into six major categories, each with its own strengths and weaknesses as highlighted in Exhibit 15.4. However, imaginative marketers are constrained only by their creativity. Free movie magazines are distributed in theater lobbies, commercial airlines carry in-flight advertising, and supermarkets run ads on their shopping bags, shopping carts, and now on their floors thanks to Floorgraphics. The most dramatic change in advertising is explored in the next section as we look at the opportunities afforded by marketing products through the Internet.

## DIRECT AND INTERNET MARKETING

Direct marketing has become the promotion tool of choice for many companies because it enables them to more precisely target and personalize messages to specific consumer and business segments and build long-term customer relationships.[18] The most popular direct marketing vehicles are direct mail, targeted e-mail, telemarketing, direct response television, and the Internet.

### Direct Mail and Targeted E-Mail

The principal vehicle for direct marketing is **direct mail,** which includes catalogs and other materials delivered through the U.S. Postal Service and private carriers. Mailing out letters, brochures, videotapes, disks, and other promotional items to customers and prospects can be an effective way to increase sales, although companies must take into account the cost of printing and postage.

Increasingly, companies are sending complex e-mails to highly targeted lists of prospects. This technique works much the same way as offline direct marketing campaigns. Companies build databases of e-mail addresses by enticing customers to register on a Web site in exchange for information or access to a special offer.[19] For example, when Jive Records wanted to push 'NSync's album *No Strings Attached,* it sent e-mails to thousands of the band's fans. The e-mail featured a click-and-play video message from band members, encouraging fans to spread the word about the album. As you can imagine, this form of direct marketing has many advantages. Besides impressive response rates, targeted e-mail campaigns allow marketers to gauge how many people open and forward the e-mail, as well as track how long the user views the message and whether or not they click through to the Web site.[20]

| Medium | Advantages | Disadvantages |
|--------|-----------|---------------|
| Newspapers | Extensive market coverage; low cost; short lead time for placing ads; good local market coverage; geographic selectivity | Poor graphic quality; short life span; cluttered pages; visual competition from other ads |
| Television | Great impact; broad reach; appealing to senses of sight, sound, and motion; creative opportunities for demonstration; high attention; entertainment carryover | High cost for production and air time; less audience selectivity; long preparation time; commercial clutter; short life for message; vulnerability to remote controls |
| Direct mail | Can deliver large amounts of information to narrowly selected audiences; excellent control over quality of message; personalization | High cost per contact; delivery delays; difficulty of obtaining desired mailing list; consumer resistance; generally poor image (junk mail) |
| Radio | Low cost; high frequency; immediacy; highly portable; high geographic and demographic selectivity | No visual possibilities; short life for message; commercial clutter; lower attention than television; easy to switch stations |
| Magazines | Good reproduction; long life; local and regional market selectivity; authority and credibility; multiple readers | Limited demonstration possibilities; long lead time between placing and publishing ads; high cost; less compelling than other major media |
| Internet | Fast-growing reach; low cost; ability to personalize; can appeal to senses of sight, sound, and motion | Difficulty in measuring audiences; consumer resistance; increasing clutter |

**EXHIBIT 15.4**

Advantages and Disadvantages of Major Advertising Media

When selecting the media mix, companies attempt to match the characteristics of the media audiences with the characteristics of the customer segments being targeted. A typical advertising campaign involves the use of several media.

### Telemarketing

Another popular form of direct marketing is **telemarketing,** or selling over the telephone, a low-cost way to efficiently reach many people. Time-pressed customers often appreciate the convenience of buying by phone.[21] With *outbound telemarketing,* companies place *cold calls* to potential customers who have not requested a sales call; *inbound telemarketing* establishes phone lines for customers to call in to place orders or request information. However, because outbound telemarketing has been criticized as being intrusive, several states have enacted legislation that (1) gives consumers the right to place their names on "do not call" lists, (2) restricts telemarketers from calling during certain hours, and (3) prohibits telemarketers from blocking caller ID technology.[22]

### Direct Response Television and Infomercials

Direct marketers use print, TV, and radio advertising much as mass advertisers do but with one critical difference. With direct response advertising, an offer is made and a response vehicle such as an 800 number is provided. Direct response television, for example, allows customers who view an ad to communicate directly with sellers using a computer keyboard, a television, and a modem. Customers can use their keyboards to ask questions or to place product orders. Experts predict that direct response or interactive TV will be available in 24 million households by 2004.[23]

Television *infomercials* are another widely used direct marketing technique. These longer forms of advertisement—approximately 30 minutes in length—have the appearance of regular TV programs but provide viewers with a toll-free number to place an order. Infomercials are useful selling tools for new products that need some form of demonstration or technical explanation. Tae-Bo infomercials, for example, sold more than $75 million worth of product videos in one year by demonstrating the grueling combination of punches and kicks that can help you lose weight, and free your spirit.[24] Still, only 10 percent of infomercials sell between $5 million and $120 million of products in one year.[25]

### Internet Advertising

Look back at Exhibit 15.3. Even though 95 percent of direct marketers use the Internet for sales or marketing applications, it still plays only a minor role in the overall media mix.[26] Nonetheless, the use of Internet advertising is expected to increase exponentially.[27]

The principal advantages of Internet advertising include:[28]

- *Timeliness.* Internet ads can be updated any time at a minimal cost.
- *Reach.* Internet ads can reach very large numbers of potential buyers globally.
- *Cost.* Internet ads can be less expensive than television, newspaper, or radio ads.[29]
- *Interactive options.* Chat, e-mail, and instant messaging can be incorporated in the ad at a reasonable cost.

Moreover, just like targeted e-mail, Internet ads can be sent to specific interest groups or individuals. Advertisers can tailor a unique pitch to the individual and use interactive options to gather information about each interaction. For example, companies can (1) track the exact information accessed by any particular visitor to their Web site, (2) develop a profile for each of their regular visitors, (3) present information that may be of special interest to a particular visitor, and (4) alert customers to special savings or remind them of past purchases.

**Banner ads** are one of the most popular forms of Internet advertising. Called banners because of their long, thin shape, the ads generally appear at the top and bottom of Web sites and contain a short text or graphical message that can be customized for target audiences. In addition to clicking on the ad to go to the advertiser's Web site, *rich media,* a combination of high-grade graphics with audio and interactive capabilities, allows users to interact with the banner ad by opening dropdown lists, selecting buttons, or performing other actions with a mouse inside the ad.

Another very important form of Internet advertising is a company's own Web site. This is the place where visitors can learn about your company, products, and services as demonstrated in this chapter's special feature, Focusing on E-Business Today. Sponsorships are another increasingly popular form of Internet advertising. Similar to co-branding, advertisers sponsor a Web site that provides content, while the advertiser gets to offer information about its own products. Hi-C, for example, sponsored a children's game area on the Web site MaMaMedia and cross-promoted the sponsorship on the back of Hi-C juice boxes.[30] For a list of Internet advertising terms, consult Exhibit 15.5.

## active exercise <

**Take a moment to apply what you've learned.**

## MEDIA PLANS

Regardless of which form of advertising you use, you must get your message to your target audience by choosing suitable **media,** or channels of communication. Your **media plan** is a document that shows your advertising budget, how you will divide your money among various media, and when your ads will appear. The goal of your media plan is to make the most effective use of your advertising dollar.

### The Media Mix

The critical task in media planning is to select a **media mix,** the combination of print, broadcast, and other media for the advertising campaign. In Exhibit 15.4, we pointed out the advantages and disadvantages of popular advertising media types. When selecting the media mix, the first step is to determine the characteristics of the target audience and the types of media that will reach the greatest audience at the lowest cost per exposure. The choice is also based on what the medium can do (show the product in use, list numerous sale items and prices, and so on). The second step in choosing the media mix is to pick specific vehicles in each of the chosen media categories, such as individual magazines *(Time, Rolling Stone, Sports Illustrated)* or individual radio stations (a rock station, a classical station).

| Term | Explanation |
|---|---|
| Banner | Small, usually rectangular graphic display that appears on a Web site like a roadside billboard. Clicking on the banner will transfer you to the advertiser's Web site. |
| Click through | How often a viewer will respond to an ad by clicking on it. |
| Cost per click (CPC) | The ad rate charged only if the Web surfer responds to a displayed ad. |
| CPM (cost per thousand impressions) | The cost of delivering an impression to 1,000 people. |
| Impressions | The total number of times users call up a page with a banner during a specific time. |
| Interactive advertisement | Any advertisement that requires or allows the viewer/consumer to take some action. |
| Interstitials | Brief ad message that appears as a new Web page downloads. Intrusive style can create an impact but can also be annoying. |
| Pointcasting | Mass delivery of Internet information using push technology. Also known as Webcasting. |
| Pop-up windows | Linked ad messages that appear within a new browser window. |
| Splash screen | An initial Web page used as a promotion or lead-in to the site homepage and designed to capture the user's attention for a short time by using multimedia effects. |

**EXHIBIT 15.5**

Popular Cybermarketing Terms

New Internet marketing terms keep cropping up as marketers find creative ways to use Internet technology to communicate their messages.

### Media Buying

Sorting through all the media is a challenging task. In fact, many companies rely on professional media planners or *advertising agencies*—firms of marketing specialists who assist companies in planning and preparing advertisements—to find the best combinations of media and to negotiate attractive terms. These professionals use four important types of data in selecting their media buys. The first is **cost per thousand (CPM),** a standardized ratio that converts the total cost of advertising space to the more meaningful cost of reaching 1,000 people with the ad. CPM is especially useful for comparing media that reach similar audiences.

Two other decision tools are reach and frequency, which represent the trade-off between breadth and depth of communication. **Reach** refers to the total number of audience members who will be exposed to a message at least once in a given time period; it is usually expressed as a percentage of the total number of audience members in a particular population. **Frequency** is the average number of times that each audience member is exposed to the message; it is calculated by dividing the total number of exposures by the total audience population.

The fourth decision tool is **continuity,** which refers to the period spanned by the media schedule and the timing of ad messages within the period evenly spread over the schedule or heavily concentrated in some periods. Obviously, within a fixed budget, a media plan cannot do everything: If it is important to reach a high percentage of a target group with significant frequency, the cost of doing so on a continuous basis may be prohibitive. Media planners often resort to airing messages in "waves" or "flights"—short periods of high reach and frequency that sacrifice continuity. This strategy is common in the travel industry, which crowds much of its annual media spending into the peak vacation seasons.

 **Sales Promotion**

The fourth element of promotion, sales promotion, consists of short-term incentives to encourage the purchase of a product or service. Over the past two decades, U.S. sales-promotion expenditures have grown so much they now exceed those for traditional forms of advertising.[31] Sales promotion can be broken down into two basic categories: consumer promotion and trade promotion.

## CONSUMER PROMOTION TOOLS

**Consumer promotion** is aimed directly at final users of the product. Companies use a variety of promotional tools and incentives to stimulate repeat purchases and to entice new users:

- *Coupons.* The biggest category of consumer promotion—and the most popular with consumers—is **coupons**, certificates that spur sales by giving buyers a discount when they purchase specified products. Customers redeem their coupons at the time of purchase.[32] Companies offer coupons on packages, in print ads, in direct mail, at the checkout, and on the Internet to encourage trial of new products, reach out to nonusers of mature products, encourage repeat buying, and temporarily lower a product's price.[33] Ford and General Motors, for example, have mailed coupons to owners of older-model vehicles to induce them to buy new cars.[34] Couponing is a fairly inefficient technique, however: A lot of money is wasted on advertising and delivering coupons that are never redeemed. Also, critics say couponing instills a bargain-hunting mentality, leading some people to avoid buying unless they have a coupon.[35]

- *Rebates.* Similar to coupons, rebates are another popular promotional tool. Instead of receiving the discount at the time of purchase, buyers generally get reimbursement checks from the manufacturer by submitting proofs of purchase along with a prepared manufacturer's rebate form. Here again, many buyers neglect to redeem the rebates, making the costs of running such programs relatively low. Moreover, rebates allow the manufacturer to promote the reduced price even though customers pay the full price at checkout.[36]

- *Point-of-purchase.* Another widely used consumer promotion technique is the **point-of-purchase (POP) display,** a device for showing a product in a way that stimulates immediate sales. It may be simple, such as the end-of-aisle stacks of soda pop in a supermarket or the racks of gum and mints at checkout counters. Simple or elaborate, point-of-purchase displays really work: Studies show that in almost every instance, such displays significantly increase sales.[37]

- *Samples.* Studies repeatedly show that the most effective way to get someone to try a product—and subsequently buy it—is to give that person a sample. Neutrogena many years ago began placing sample sizes of its glycerine soap in hotel bathrooms. Butler and Procter & Gamble give dentists toothbrushes to pass on to their patients. Hall's puts bins heaped with cough drops in theatre lobbies. And Kellogg hands out single-serving packs of Smart Start cereal on street corners. Samples are an effective way to introduce a new product, encourage nonusers to try an existing product, encourage current buyers to use the product in a new way, or expand distribution into new areas.[38]

- *Special-event sponsorship.* Sponsoring special events has become one of the most popular sales-promotion tactics. Thousands of companies spend billions of dollars to sponsor events ranging from golf to opera. The 2000 Summer Olympic Games in Sydney drew over $315 million alone in sponsorship revenue. Coke, Visa, Panasonic, McDonald's, and General Motors were the games' largest sponsors.[39]

- *Cross-promotion.* Another popular sales promotion vehicle is **cross-promotion,** which involves using one brand to advertise another noncompeting brand. One example is PepsiCo's arrangement with Yahoo! to cross-promote each others' products. Pepsi promoted the Yahoo! Web site on 1.5 billion soft drink bottles and in-store displays, while Yahoo! promoted Pepsi products on its Web site.[40] Another example is "Intel Inside," one of the most successful cross-promotion campaigns ever. In just two years following the campaign's inception, awareness of the Intel chip went from roughly 22 percent of PC buyers to more than 80 percent.[41]

Other popular consumer sales-promotion techniques include in-store demonstrations, loyalty and frequency programs such as frequent-flyer miles, and **premiums,** which are free or bargain-priced items offered to encourage the consumer to buy a product. Contests, sweepstakes, and games are also quite popular in some industries and can generate a great deal of public attention, particularly when valuable or unusual prizes are offered. **Specialty advertising** (on pens, calendars, T-shirts, and so on) helps keep a company's name in front of customers for a long period of time.

## TRADE PROMOTION TOOLS

Although shoppers are more aware of consumer promotion, trade promotion actually accounts for the largest share of promotional spending. **Trade promotions** are aimed at inducing distributors or retailers to sell a company's products by offering them a discount on the product's price, or a **trade allowance.** The distributor or retailer can pocket the savings and increase company profits or can pass the savings on to the consumer to generate additional sales. Besides discounts, other popular trade-allowance forms are display premiums, dealer contests or sweepstakes, and travel bonus programs. All are designed to motivate distributors or retailers to push particular merchandise.

Trade allowances can create the controversial practice of **forward buying,** in which the retailer takes advantage of a trade allowance by stocking up while the price is low. Say that the producer of Bumble Bee tuna offers retailers a 20 percent discount for a period of 6 weeks. A retailer might choose, however, to buy enough tuna to last 8 or 10 weeks. Purchasing this excessive amount at the lower price increases the retailer's profit, but at the expense of the producer's profit.

Many companies targeting business buyers participate in **trade shows,** gatherings where producers display their wares to potential customers. According to one estimate, the average industrial exhibitor can reach 60 percent of all its prospects at a trade show, and some exhibitors do 25 percent or more of annual sales at a single show. Apart from attracting likely buyers, trade shows have the advantage of enabling a producer to demonstrate and explain the product and to compile information about prospects.[42]

> ### video exercise

**Take a moment to apply what you've learned.**

> ## Public Relations

Public relations plays a vital role in the success of most companies, and that role applies to more than just the marketing of goods and services. Smart businesspeople know they need to maintain positive relations with their communities, investors, industry analysts, government agencies and officials, and the news media. All these activities fall under the umbrella of public relations. For many companies, public relations is the fastest growing element of the promotional mix.[43]

A good reputation is one of a business's most important assets. A recent study shows that companies with a good public image have a big edge over less-respected companies. Consumers are more than twice as likely to buy new products from companies they admire, which is why smart companies work hard to build and protect their reputations. Sometimes companies hire public relations firms to help them maintain or restore their public image. Tire maker Bridgestone/Firestone hired a public relations firm to help it restore its tattered image following the 2000 recall of 6.5 million Firestone tires that had been implicated to over 100 U.S. traffic deaths. A spokesperson for Bridgestone/Firestone acknowledged that the company had been slow to respond to public concerns. "We underestimated the intensity of the situation, and we have been too focused on internal details," he said. "We are determined to change all that."[44]

Another way that companies build and maintain good reputations is by maintaining good relations with both the general news media and specialized trade media. **Press relations** is the process of communicating with newspapers, magazines, and broadcast media. In the personal-computer industry, for example, manufacturers know that many people look to *ComputerWorld, PC, Byte,* and other computer publications as influential sources of information about new products. Editors and reporters often review new products and then make recommendations to their readers, pointing out both strengths and weaknesses. Companies roll out the proverbial red carpet for these media figures, treating them to hospitality suites at conventions, factory tours, and interviews with company leaders. When introducing products, manufacturers often send samples to reporters and editors for review, or they visit the media offices themselves.

Two standard public relations tools are the news release and the news conference. A **news release** is a short memo sent to the media covering topics that are of potential news interest; a *video news release* is a brief video clip sent to television stations. Companies use news releases to get favorable news coverage about themselves and their products. When a business has significant news to announce, it will often arrange a **news conference.** Both tools are used when the company's news is of widespread interest, when products need to be demonstrated, or when company officials want to be available to answer questions from the media.

## > Coordinating Your Marketing Efforts

With five major promotional methods available—personal selling, advertising, direct marketing, sales promotion, and public relations—how do you decide on the right mix for your product? There are no easy answers, because you must take many factors into account. In fact, when you consider all the ways that audiences can receive marketing messages today, the potential for confusion is not all that surprising. Besides the traditional media—radio, television, billboards, print ads, and direct-mail promotions—marketers are using Web sites, e-mail, faxes, kiosks, sponsorships, and many other channels to deliver messages to targeted audiences. Coordinating these diverse vehicles is becoming vital if you are to send a consistent message and boost its effectiveness.

### INTEGRATING YOUR MARKETING COMMUNICATIONS

**Integrated marketing communications (IMC)** is a strategy of coordinating and integrating all your communications and promotion efforts to provide customers with clarity, consistency, and maximum communications impact. "It's everything from running ads to developing new media, to creating custom media, licensing, promotion, sweepstakes—every aspect of communicating to consumers," says one media expert.[45] The basics of IMC are quite simple: communicating with one voice and one message to the marketplace, as Exhibit 15.6 suggests.

The need for communicating with one voice is even greater today. Consumers are exposed to a greater variety of marketing communications and don't necessarily distinguish between message sources the way marketers do. In the consumer's mind, messages from different sources blur into one single message about the company. Thus, conflicting messages from different sources can result in confused company images and brand positions.[46]

Properly implemented, IMC increases marketing and promotional effectiveness. Look at Southwest Airlines. The company coordinates all marketing to establish and maintain a consistent

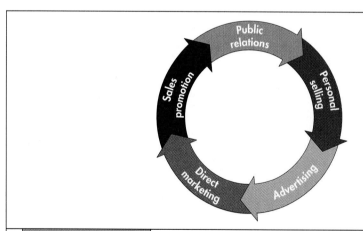

**EXHIBIT 15.6**

Integrated Marketing Communications

Coordinating the five elements of promotion delivers a consistent message to the marketplace.

image of low-fare, high-frequency service in new and existing markets. For example, when the Texas-based airline beefed up service on the East Coast, it used public relations, special events, and advertising to whip up excitement by promoting a special Thanksgiving Day cross-country flight from Baltimore, Maryland, to Oakland, California, at the bargain rate of $99. The resulting media coverage effectively communicated the airline's low-price, flyer-friendly position. "We always start out with the public relations side in announcing inaugural services. Then we integrate government relations, community affairs, service announcements, special events, advertising, and promotion," says the head of Southwest's ad agency. "We try to fire all guns at once so that by the time Southwest comes into the market, the airline already is part of the community."[47]

While integrating your communications and promotional efforts may seem logical and relatively simple, many organizations find IMC difficult to implement. They discover that over time their promotional mixes develop into collections of disconnected efforts. Organizational resistance is the primary cause for IMC failure. Many marketing departments are accustomed to autonomy and see IMC as a threat to their resources and decision-making power. Besides, moving to an IMC approach requires new ways of organizing, planning, and managing all marketing functions, and some marketing departments are not up to the task.[48]

> **video exercise**

**Take a moment to apply what you've learned.**

## FINE-TUNING YOUR PROMOTIONAL STRATEGIES

Besides integrating your marketing efforts, you must consider other factors when deciding on the right promotional mix. For one thing, most companies have limited resources, so establishing a promotional budget is often the first step in developing a promotional strategy. Next, you should consider the nature and appeal of the product, its position in the life cycle, the size and interests of its targeted segments, its competitive situation, any country and cultural differences, and its desired market position.

### Product Considerations

Various types of products lend themselves to differing forms of promotion. Simple, familiar items like laundry detergent can be explained adequately through advertising, but personal selling is generally required to communicate the features of unfamiliar and sophisticated goods and services such as office-automation equipment or municipal waste-treatment facilities. Direct, personal contact is particularly important in promoting customized services such as interior design, financial advice, or legal counsel. In general, consumer and organizational goods usually require differing promotional mixes.

The product's price is also a factor in the selection of the promotional mix. Inexpensive items sold to a mass market are well suited to advertising and sales promotion, which have a relatively low per-unit cost. At the other extreme, products with a high unit price lend themselves to personal selling because the high cost of a sales call is justified by the size of the order. Furthermore, the nature of the selling process often demands face-to-face interaction between the buyer and seller.

Another factor that influences both the level and mix of promotional activity is the product's position in its life cycle. Early on, when the seller is trying to inform the customer about the product and build the distribution network, promotional efforts are in high gear. Selective advertising, sales promotion, and public relations are used to build awareness and to encourage early adopters to try the product; personal selling is used to gain the cooperation of intermediaries. For example, Gillette spent $300 million to promote the launch of the Mach3 razor during its first year—on top of $750 million-plus in development costs to accelerate the Mach3's transition from the costly introduction stage to the profitable growth stage faster than any previous Gillette razors. So far this strategy has paid off. In just 18 months after the Mach3 was launched, sales for the product hit $1 billion, making it the company's most successful new product ever.[49]

As the market expands during the growth phase, the seller broadens the advertising and sales-promotion activities to reach a wider audience and continues to use personal selling to expand the distribution network. When the product reaches maturity and competition is at its peak, the seller's primary goal is to differentiate the product from rival brands. Advertising generally dominates the promotional mix during this phase, but sales promotion is an important supplemental tool, particularly for low-priced consumer products. As the product begins to decline, the level of promotion generally tapers off. Advertising and selling efforts are carefully targeted toward loyal, steady customers.

### Market Considerations

To some extent, the promotional mix depends on whether the seller plans to focus the marketing effort on intermediaries or final customers. If the focus is on intermediaries, the producer uses a **push strategy** to persuade wholesalers and retailers to carry the item. Personal selling and sales promotions aimed at intermediaries dominate the promotional mix. If the marketing focus is on end users, the producer uses a **pull strategy** to appeal directly to the ultimate customer, using advertising, direct mail, contests, discount coupons, and so on. With this approach, consumers learn of the product through promotion and request it from retailers, who respond by asking their wholesalers for it or by going directly to the producer (see Exhibit 15.7).

Most companies use both push and pull tactics to increase the impact of their promotional efforts. For example, when Schering-Plough introduced Claritin antihistamine, it used push tactics to educate physicians about the prescription drug's use and efficacy while using pull tactics such as television and print advertising to increase market awareness and encourage consumers to ask for the new medication. This diverse, high-powered promotional mix helped Claritin capture a whopping 54 percent of the antihistamine drug market within a short time.[50]

The promotional mix is also influenced by the size and concentration of the market. In markets with many widely dispersed buyers, advertising is generally the most economical way of communicating the product's features. In markets with relatively few customers, particularly when they are clustered in a limited area, personal selling is a practical promotional alternative. Many marketers use a combination of methods, often relying on advertising and public relations to build awareness and interest, following up with personal selling to complete the sale.

### Positioning Considerations

The strategic importance of positioning is discussed in Chapter 13. Although promotion is just one aspect of the positioning process, it is certainly one of the most important. Consequently, positioning strategies should play a key role in the design of every company's promotional mix. The nature of a company's advertising, the type of salespeople it hires, its policy regarding coupons, its support for cultural events—decisions like these have a dramatic effect on the position that a company and its products will occupy in the minds of potential customers.

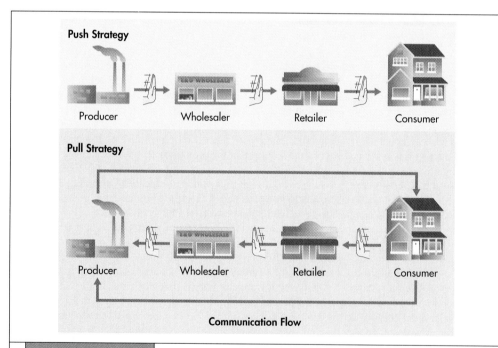

**EXHIBIT 15.7**

Push and Pull Strategies

Push strategies "push" products through distribution channels to final consumers by persuading wholesalers and retailers to carry the product. Pull strategies use consumer promotions and advertising to induce consumers to buy the product and "pull" the product through the distribution channels.

**International Considerations**

Businesses operating in international markets face another layer of strategic and tactical decisions when it comes to promotion. The *global* and *local* approaches to international advertising represent two extremes. With the global approach, the advertiser tries to keep the strategy and tactics identical in every country, with necessary exceptions made for local laws and media. With the local approach, the advertiser allows its divisions or representatives in each country to design and implement their own advertising. Most international campaigns fall somewhere between these two extremes. Advertisers who opt for the regional approach strike a compromise between the efficiency of the global approach and the cost and complexity of the local approach by grouping similar countries together under a single campaign. This grouping strategy is frequently adopted by e-businesses that created multiple Web sites to meet the language and cultural needs of international customers in the global marketplace.

> ## active concept check

**Now let's take a moment to test your knowledge of the concepts you have studied in this section.**

> ## Chapter Wrap-Up

Now that you've reached the end of the chapter, you may wish to explore the concepts you've been reading about in greater detail, or test yourself to see how well you've comprehended the material. In the box below you'll find a number of links. Click on any one of these links to find additional chapter resources.

> ## end-of-chapter resources

- Summary of Learning Objectives
- Practice Quiz
- Key Terms
- Test Your Knowledge
- Practice Your Knowledge
- Expand Your Knowledge
- A Case for Critical Thinking
- Business Plan Pro: Developing Marketing Strategies to Satisfy Customers

# Accounting

## Chapter Outline

## > What's Ahead

### INSIDE BUSINESS TODAY
### DRILLING FOR DOLLARS AT DENTAL LIMITED

Most people don't think of their dentist's office as a business, but "running a dental practice is no different from running any other service business," says Dr. Arthur Schatzman, co-owner of Dental Limited in Wheeling, Illinois. "We have customers (patients), accounts receivable, accounts payable, depreciable equipment, employee profit-sharing plans, building insurance—and we face the same challenges that most small-business owners face." But there's a twist.

Unlike many small-business owners and professionals, dentists aren't trained to run a business. "We had one lecture in dental school about the cost of dental supplies," says Schatzman, "but that's about all the business we were taught. Everything I learned about running the business side of a dental practice I learned on my own—by reading business magazines, networking with other business owners, and talking with accountants and other business professionals." In fact, one of the first things Schatzman and his partner Dr. Robert Crane did when they established Dental Limited was to hire an independent accountant. The accountant helped the dentists set up their bookkeeping systems and taught them some accounting fundamentals.

Today, all bookkeeping and record processing at Dental Limited is automated. Patient records, routing slips, billing, insurance claims, and accounts receivable are processed electronically using a proprietary software package called Soft Dent. In addition to using Soft Dent, Dental Limited uses Intuit's Quick Books to pay bills and process patients' payments

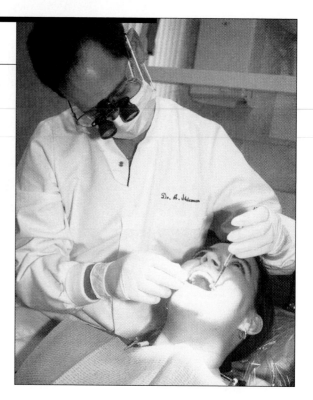

Dr. Arthur Schatzman, co-owner of Dental Limited, relies on his accountant for sound financial advice.

electronically. Quick Books generates cash receipts and disbursements journals along with a variety of financial reports and statements, which the dentists submit to their accountant. The accountant uses this information to prepare the company's quarterly payroll reports, compile the company's quarterly and annual financial statements, and prepare the company's tax return. But first the accountant reviews the daily computerized accounting transactions (to make sure they have been recorded properly) and prepares adjusted journal entries if errors are found.

Periodically the accountant meets with the dentists to advise them of changes in employment laws and tax laws or to assist them with important financial decisions. For example, several years ago Schatzman and Crane expanded Dental Limited by purchasing an existing dental practice from a retiring dentist. "Overnight we doubled the number of our patients and employees. We moved our existing practice into the larger space occupied by the retiring dentist, but we weren't thrilled about purchasing the entire office building—a requirement of the deal. We had to negotiate tenant leases and leasehold improvements, enter into building maintenance contracts, market vacant office space, and more" recalls Schatzman. "It was a big financial commitment."

To help them evaluate the merits of the acquisition, Schatzman and Crane relied on their accountant for financial advice. The accountant calculated a number of possible financial outcomes for the purchase of the practice and building using best-case and worst-case scenarios. For example, what if, say, 20 percent of the acquired patients decided not to stay with Dental Limited, or 30 percent of the current tenants decided not to renew their leases. "It's one thing to look at numbers on financial statements," says Schatzman, "but it takes a good accountant to teach you how to analyze the numbers and prepare for a possible range of financial outcomes."

Looking back, the dentists don't remember too many financial surprises—just some awfully big headaches. "We knew the upside and the downside of the deal," recalls Schatzman. "And thanks to our careful financial analysis, we were prepared."[1]

> objectives

Take a moment to familiarize yourself with the key objectives of this chapter.

> gearing up

Before you begin reading this chapter, try a short warm-up activity.

## > What Is Accounting?

As Schatzman and Crane know, it's difficult to manage a business today without accurate and up-to-date financial information. **Accounting** is the system a business uses to identify, measure, and communicate financial information to others, inside and outside the organization. Financial information is important to businesses such as Dental Limited for two reasons: First, it helps managers and owners plan and control a company's operation and make informed business decisions. Second, it helps outsiders evaluate a business. Suppliers, banks, and other lenders want to know whether a business is creditworthy; investors and shareholders are concerned with a company's profit potential; government agencies are interested in a business's tax accounting.

Because outsiders and insiders use accounting information for different purposes, accounting has two distinct facets. **Financial accounting** is concerned with preparing financial statements and other information for outsiders such as stockholders and *creditors* (people or organizations that have lent a company money or have extended them credit); **management accounting** is concerned with preparing cost analyses, profitability reports, budgets, and other information for insiders such as management and other company decision makers. To be useful, all accounting information must be accurate, objective, consistent over time, and comparable to information supplied by other companies.

### THE RULES OF ACCOUNTING

Much of accounting information is *proprietary,* which means it is not divulged to outsiders. Schatzman and Crane, for example, produce a variety of proprietary financial reports and analyses that help them run their dental practice more efficiently and profitably. But because they do not share these reports with outsiders, they are free to organize them in a format that suits their company's specific needs.

All U.S. public companies must prepare their published financial statements according to **generally accepted accounting principles (GAAP),** basic accounting standards and procedures that have been agreed on by the accounting profession. All U.S. public companies must publish their financial statements in accordance with GAAP. This requirement makes it possible for external users to compare the financial results of one company with those of another and to gain a general idea of a firm's relative effectiveness and its standing within a particular industry.

In the United States, the Financial Accounting Standards Board (FASB) is responsible for establishing GAAP. Other countries, of course, have similar governing boards, which means that foreign companies such as Nissan or Toyota may report accounting data using rules that are different from those used by U.S. companies such as Ford or General Motors. Nonetheless, foreign companies that list their securities on a U.S. stock exchange must publish a set of financial statements that conform to GAAP. Converting financial statements prepared under foreign accounting rules to GAAP puts all companies listed on U.S. stock exchanges on even ground. For example, when Toyota Motor Corporation listed its stock on the New York Stock Exchange the company's earnings dropped four percentage points because of a difference between Japanese accounting rules and U.S. accounting rules.[2]

To eliminate such confusion and simplify bookkeeping for multinational companies, the London-based International Accounting Standards Committee (IASC) is developing a uniform set of global rules for accounting. The committee hopes its proposed International Accounting Standards (IAS) will be adopted by all countries and accepted by all U.S and foreign stock exchanges. But such global rules are meeting strong resistance from the U.S. Securities and Exchange Commission (SEC) and FASB, which are concerned that many of the International Accounting Standards are not as strict as GAAP.[3]

Keep in mind that accounting rules set forth the principles and guidelines that companies and accountants must follow when preparing financial reports or recording accounting transactions (which we will discuss later in this chapter). But, as with any rules, they can be interpreted aggressively or conservatively. Furthermore, management and accountants often make estimates or financial projections in the course of their accounting work. Sometimes these numbers need to be adjusted because unexpected events happen or because the estimates were too optimistic or too conservative. In fact, pick up any newspaper business section and chances are you'll read about a company that is taking a "big charge against earnings" or is restating its financial reports because of revised projections. Interpreting accounting rules, establishing financial systems, preparing reports, and projecting the future are just some of the challenging tasks that accountants perform on the job.

## WHAT ACCOUNTANTS DO

Some people confuse the work accountants do with **bookkeeping,** which is the clerical function of recording the economic activities of a business. Although some accountants do perform some bookkeeping functions, their work generally goes well beyond the scope of this activity. Accountants design accounting systems, prepare financial statements, analyze and interpret financial information, prepare financial forecasts and budgets, prepare tax returns, interpret tax law, and do much more. In fact, the entire accounting profession is undergoing sweeping changes. As one spokesperson for the American Institute of Certified Public Accounts (AICPA) put it, "Users no longer want to look back— they want to look forward, and supplying forward-looking information is the kind of service businesses will be paying for in the future."[4]

Of course, one of the forces driving this change is the availability of new technology (see Exhibit 16.1). Today, financial data are produced, collected, analyzed, and distributed faster and in greater detail than ever before. New software programs, more powerful computers, and the ability to store vast amounts of data now make it possible to automate many accounting tasks. Thus, today's accountants have time to redirect their efforts to more important business functions, such as helping clients improve business processes, plan for the future, evaluate product performance, analyze profitability by customer and product groups, and design and install new computer systems. Not only are today's accountants involved in company decision making, but many assist clients such as Dental Limited in planning for the future.

Performing these functions, requires a strong business background and a variety of business skills beyond accounting (see Exhibit 16.2). For instance, many accountants work on cross-functional teams so they must be able to convey technical messages to a nontechnical audience. In other words, accountants must be able to communicate effectively and relate comfortably to others outside their field.[5] To prepare accountants for these additional responsibilities, most U.S. states have increased the educational eligibility requirement to sit for the CPA examination from 120 to 150 semester hours.[6] This exam is prepared by the AICPA and is a requirement for accountants to become **certified public accountants (CPAs).**

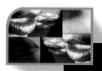

### active poll ◄

**What do you think? Voice your opinion and find out what others have to say.**

### Public Accountants

**Public accountants,** such as the one hired by Dental Limited, are independent of the businesses, organizations, and individuals they serve. These accountants perform a variety of accounting functions for their clients. Perhaps the most widely recognized functions are compiling financial statements and preparing tax returns. Although all accountants can handle these tasks, only public accountants who have passed the CPA exam may ensure the integrity and reliability of a company's financial statements. They do this by conducting an **audit**—a formal evaluation of the fairness and reliability of financial statements. Companies whose stock (ownership shares) is publicly traded in the United States are required to file audited financial statements with the SEC.

During an audit, CPAs who work for an independent accounting firm (also known as *external* auditors) review a client's financial records to determine whether the statements that summarize these

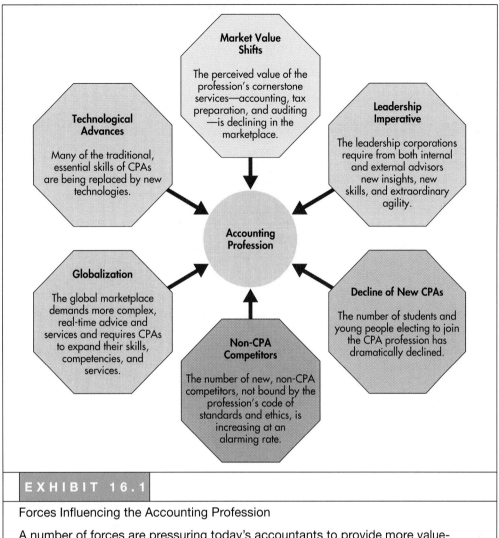

**Market Value Shifts**

The perceived value of the profession's cornerstone services—accounting, tax preparation, and auditing—is declining in the marketplace.

**Technological Advances**

Many of the traditional, essential skills of CPAs are being replaced by new technologies.

**Leadership Imperative**

The leadership corporations require from both internal and external advisors new insights, new skills, and extraordinary agility.

**Accounting Profession**

**Globalization**

The global marketplace demands more complex, real-time advice and services and requires CPAs to expand their skills, competencies, and services.

**Non-CPA Competitors**

The number of new, non-CPA competitors, not bound by the profession's code of standards and ethics, is increasing at an alarming rate.

**Decline of New CPAs**

The number of students and young people electing to join the CPA profession has dramatically declined.

| EXHIBIT 16.1 | |
| --- | --- |

Forces Influencing the Accounting Profession

A number of forces are pressuring today's accountants to provide more value-added services.

records have been prepared in accordance with GAAP and fairly present the financial position and operating results of the firm. Once the auditors have completed an audit, they attach a report summarizing their findings to the client's published financial statements. Sometimes these reports disclose information that might materially affect the client's financial position, such as the bankruptcy of a major supplier, a large obsolete inventory, costly environmental problems, or questionable accounting practices. For example, when auditors at Arthur Andersen discovered falsified shipping documents and purchase orders at Aviation Distributors, the auditors could no longer attest to the accuracy of the company's financial results.[7] Most companies, however, receive a clean audit report, which means that to the best of the auditors' knowledge the company's financial statements are accurate.

In addition to hiring external auditors, many large companies also have **internal auditors**— employees who investigate and evaluate a company's internal operations and data to determine whether they are accurate and whether they comply with GAAP, federal laws, and industry regulations. Although this self-checking process is vital to an organization's financial health, an internal audit is not a substitute for having an independent auditor look things over and render an unbiased opinion. Many people, such as creditors, shareholders, investors, and government agencies, rely on the integrity of a company's financial statements and place great trust and confidence in the independence of auditors whose detached position allows them to be objective and, when necessary, critical.

Today, 90 percent of all publicly held U.S. corporations are audited by the world's five largest accounting firms: PricewaterhouseCoopers, KPMG Peat Marwick, Arthur Andersen, Ernst & Young, and Deloitte & Touche.[8] In addition to auditing and accounting services, many accounting firms provide a variety of management consulting services for their clients. Some accounting firms have become multiline service organizations in which accounting and auditing are rapidly becoming

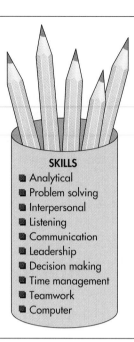

**SKILLS**
- Analytical
- Problem solving
- Interpersonal
- Listening
- Communication
- Leadership
- Decision making
- Time management
- Teamwork
- Computer

**EXHIBIT 16.2**

Ten Most Important Skills for Accountants

Besides having a thorough knowledge of accounting, today's accountants need the right mix of personal and business skills to increase their chances for a successful career.

secondary activities.[9] Others have established separate business consulting units—many of which now rank among the world's leading consulting firms. Nonetheless, regulators are concerned that the increasing amount of work performed by public accountants for their clients places their independence at risk.[10]

## active exercise &lt;

**Take a moment to apply what you've learned.**

### Private Accountants

Of the 1.9 million accountants worldwide, only 35 percent are in public practice. The remaining 65 percent are, for the most part, **private accountants** (sometimes called corporate accountants) working for a business, a government agency (such as the Internal Revenue Service, a school, or a local police department), or a nonprofit corporation (such as a church, charity, or hospital).[11] Although many private accountants are CPAs, a growing number are **certified management accountants (CMAs),** who earn certification by passing a two-day exam (given by the Institute of Management Accountants) that is comparable in difficulty to the CPA exam.[12]

Some accountants specialize in certain areas of accounting, such as **cost accounting** (computing and analyzing production costs), **tax accounting** (preparing tax returns and tax planning), or **financial analysis** (evaluating a company's performance and the financial implications of strategic decisions such as product pricing, employee benefits, and business acquisitions). Most company accountants work together as a team under the supervision of the company **controller,** who reports to the vice president of finance. Exhibit 16.3 shows the typical finance department of a large company. In smaller organizations, the controller may be in charge of the company's entire finance operation and report directly to the president.

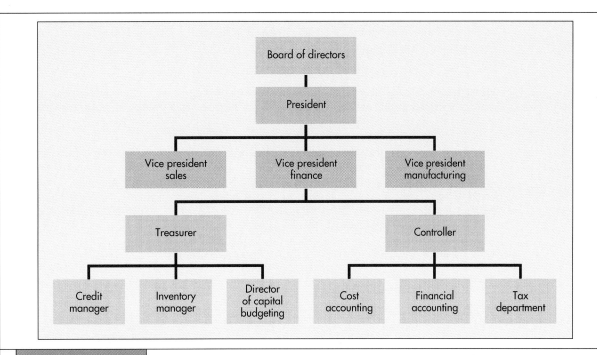

**EXHIBIT 16.3**

Typical Finance Department

Here is a typical finance department of a large company. In smaller companies, the controller may be the highest ranking accountant and report directly to the president.

Of course, maintaining an accounting staff with the expertise businesses require to operate in today's competitive environment can be a costly proposition—even for large organizations. For this reason, more and more companies are assigning many of their accounting tasks and financial projects to outside accountants and consultants who specialize in an area of accounting or in an industry. Experts predict that outsourcing a company's accounting and finance functions will become even more widespread in the future.[13]

> ## active concept check

**Now let's take a moment to test your knowledge of the concepts you have studied in this section.**

> ## What Are the Fundamental Accounting Concepts?

Regardless of who performs a company's accounting functions, all accountants must master the fundamental accounting concepts. Knowing the rules of accounting is critical to an organization's financial health. Without rules and standards, there would be no consistencies for comparisons. Moreover, assessing a company's performance or likelihood of continued success would be anyone's best guess.

In their work with financial data, accountants are guided by three basis concepts: the *fundamental accounting equation, double-entry bookkeeping,* and the *matching principle.*

### THE ACCOUNTING EQUATION

For thousands of years, businesses and governments have kept records of their **assets**—valuable items they own or lease, such as equipment, cash, land, buildings, inventory, and investments. Claims against those assets are **liabilities,** or what the business owes to its creditors—such as banks and suppliers. For example, when a company borrows money to purchase a building, the lender or creditor has a claim against the company's assets. What remains after liabilities have been deducted from assets is **owners' equity:**

$$Assets - Liabilities = Owners' equity$$

Using the principles of algebra, this equation can be restated in a variety of formats. The most common is the simple **accounting equation,** which serves as the framework for the entire accounting process:

$$Assets = Liabilities + Owners' equity$$

This equation suggests that either creditors or owners provide all the assets in a corporation. Think of it this way: If you were starting a new business, you could contribute cash to the company to buy the assets you needed to run your business or you could borrow money from a bank (the creditor) or you could do both. The company's liabilities are placed before owners' equity in the accounting equation because creditors get paid first. After liabilities have been paid, anything left over belongs to the owners or, in the case of a corporation, to the shareholders. As a business engages in economic activity, the dollar amounts and composition of its assets, liabilities, and owners' equity change. However, the equation must always be in balance; in other words, one side of the equation must always equal the other side.

## DOUBLE-ENTRY BOOKKEEPING

To keep the accounting equation in balance, companies use a **double-entry bookkeeping** system that records every transaction affecting assets, liabilities, or owners' equity. For example, if Dental Limited purchased a $6,000 dental chair on credit, assets would increase by $6,000 (the cost of the chair) and liabilities would also increase by $6,000 (the amount the company owes the vendor), keeping the accounting equation in balance. But if Dental Limited paid cash outright for the chair (instead of arranging for credit), then the company's total assets and total liabilities would not change because the $6,000 increase in equipment would be offset by an equal $6,000 reduction in cash. In fact, the company would just be switching assets—cash for equipment.

Even though software programs such as Quick Books do much of the tedious recording of accounting transactions such as the one just discussed, accountants must program the computer software so that all transactions are recorded properly. Furthermore, once these individual transactions are recorded and then summarized, accountants must review the resulting transaction summaries and adjust or correct all errors or discrepancies before they can **close the books,** or transfer net revenue and expense items to retained earnings.

## THE MATCHING PRINCIPLE

The **matching principle** requires that expenses incurred in producing revenues be deducted from the revenue they generated during the same accounting period. This matching of expenses and revenue is necessary for the company's financial statements to present an accurate picture of the profitability of a business. Accountants match revenue to expenses by adopting the **accrual basis** of accounting, which states that revenue is recognized when you make a sale or provide a service, not when you get paid. Similarly, your expenses are recorded when you receive the benefit of a service or when you use an asset to produce revenue—not when you pay for it. Accrual accounting focuses on the economic substance of the event instead of on the movement of cash. It's a way of recognizing that revenue can be earned either before or after cash is received and that expenses can be incurred when you receive a benefit (such as a shipment of supplies) whether before or after you pay for it.

If a business runs on a **cash basis,** the company records revenue only when money from the sale is actually received. Your checkbook is an easy-to-understand cash-based accounting system: You record checks at the time of purchase and deposits at the time of receipt. Revenue thus equals cash received, and expenses equal cash paid. The trouble with cash-based accounting, however, is that it can be misleading. You can misrepresent expenses and income by the way you time payments. It's easy to inflate income, for example, by delaying the payment of bills. For that reason, public companies are required to keep their books on an accrual basis.

**Depreciation,** or the allocation of the cost of a tangible long-term asset over a period of time, is another way that companies match expenses with revenue. During the normal course of business, a company enters into many transactions that benefit more than one accounting period—such as the purchase of buildings, inventory, and equipment. When you buy a piece of real estate or equipment, instead of deducting the entire cost of the item at the time of purchase, you depreciate it, or spread its cost over the asset's useful life (because the asset will likely generate income for years to come). If the company were to expense long-term assets at the time of purchase, the financial performance of the company would be distorted in the year of purchase as well as in all future years when these assets generate revenue.

> # active exercise

**Take a moment to apply what you've learned.**

> # active concept check

**Now let's take a moment to test your knowledge of the concepts you have studied in this section.**

> ## How Are Financial Statements Used?

An accounting system is made up of thousands of individual transactions—debits and credits to be exact. During the accounting process, sales, purchases, and other transactions are recorded and classified into individual accounts. Exhibit 16.4 presents the process for putting all of a company's financial data into standardized formats that can be used for decision making, analysis, and planning. To make sense of these individual transactions, accountants summarize them by preparing financial statements.

### UNDERSTANDING FINANCIAL STATEMENTS

Financial statements consist of three separate yet interrelated reports: the *balance sheet,* the *income statement,* and the *statement of cash flows.* Together these statements provide information about an organization's financial strength and ability to meet current obligations, the effectiveness of its sales and collection efforts, and its effectiveness in managing its assets. Organizations and individuals use

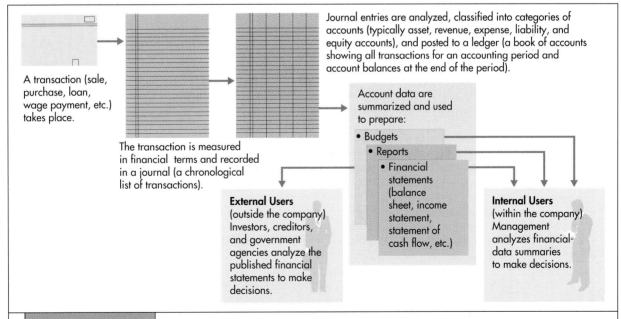

**EXHIBIT 16.4**

The Accounting Process

The traditional printed accounting forms are shown here. Today, nearly all companies use the computer equivalents of these forms.

financial statements to spot opportunities and problems, to make business decisions, and to evaluate a company's past performance, present condition, and future prospects. In sum, they're indispensable.

In the following sections we will examine the financial statements of Computer Central, a company engaged in direct sales and distribution of brand-name personal computers (such as Compaq, Toshiba, and Macintosh) and related computer products (such as software, printer cartridges, and scanners). The company conducts its primary business from a combined telemarketing, corporate office, warehouse, and showroom facility located in Denver, Colorado. There, Computer Central's 600-plus account executives service over 634,000 customers annually. In 2002 the company shipped over 2.3 million orders, amounting to more than $1.7 billion in sales—a 35 percent increase in sales from the prior year. The company's daily sales volume has grown exponentially over the last decade—from $232,000 to $6.8 million. Because of this tremendous growth and the increasing demand for new computer products, the company recently purchased a 276,000-square-foot building. Keep these points in mind as we discuss Computer Central's financial statements in the next sections.

### Balance Sheet

The **balance sheet,** also known as the statement of financial position, is a snapshot of a company's financial position on a particular date, such as December 31, 2002. In effect, it freezes all business actions and provides a baseline from which a company can measure change. This statement is called a balance sheet because it includes all elements in the accounting equation and shows the balance between assets on one side of the equation and liabilities and owners' equity on the other side. In other words, as in the accounting equation, a change on one side of the balance sheet means changes elsewhere. Exhibit 16.5 is the balance sheet for Computer Central as of December 31, 2002.

In reality, however, no business can stand still while its financial condition is being examined. A business may make hundreds of transactions of various kinds every working day. Even during a holiday, office fixtures grow older and decrease in value, and interest on savings accounts accumulates. Yet the accountant must set up a balance sheet so that managers and other interested parties can evaluate the business's financial position as if it were static, rather than ever-changing.

Every company prepares a balance sheet at least once a year, most often at the end of the **calendar year,** covering from January 1 to December 31. However, many business and government bodies use a **fiscal year,** which may be any 12 consecutive months. For example, a company may use a fiscal year of June 1 to May 31 because its peak selling season ends in May. Its fiscal year would then correspond to its full annual cycle of manufacturing and selling. Some companies prepare a balance sheet more often than once a year, perhaps at the end of each month or quarter. Thus, every balance sheet is dated to show the exact date when the financial snapshot was taken.

By reading a company's balance sheet you should be able to determine the size of the company, the major assets owned, any asset changes that occurred in recent periods, how the company's assets are financed, and any major changes that have occurred in the company's debt and equity in recent periods. Most companies classify assets, liabilities, and owners' equity into categories like those shown in the Computer Central balance sheet.

**ASSETS** As discussed earlier in this chapter, an asset is something owned by a company that will be used to generate income. Assets can consist of cash, things that can be converted into cash (such as investments), and equipment needed to make products or to provide services. For example, Computer Central needs a warehouse and a sizable inventory to sell computer products to its customers. Most often, the asset section of the balance sheet is divided into current assets and *fixed assets*. **Current assets** include cash and other items that will or can become cash within the following year. **Fixed assets** (sometimes referred to as property, plant, and equipment) are long-term investments in buildings, equipment, furniture and fixtures, transportation equipment, land, and other tangible property used in running the business. Fixed assets have a useful life of more than one year. Computer Central's principal fixed asset is the company's warehouse facility.

Assets are listed in descending order by *liquidity,* or the ease with which they can be converted into cash. Thus, current assets are listed before fixed assets. The balance sheet gives a subtotal for each type of asset and then a grand total for all assets. Computer Central's current assets consist primarily of cash, investments in short-term marketable securities such as money-market funds, accounts receivable (or amounts due from customers), and inventory (such as computers, software, and other items the company sells to customers).

**LIABILITIES** Liabilities come after assets because they represent claims against the company's assets, as shown in the basic accounting equation: *Assets = Liabilities + Owners' equity.* Liabilities may be current or long-term, and they are listed in the order in which they will come due. The balance sheet gives subtotals for **current liabilities** (obligations that will have to be met within one year of the date of the balance sheet) and **long-term liabilities** (obligations that are due one year or more after the date of the balance sheet), and then it gives a grand total for all liabilities.

## Computer Central
### Balance Sheet
### As of December 31, 2002
### (in thousands)

### ASSETS

| Current Assets | | |
|---|---:|---:|
| Cash | $4,230 | |
| Marketable Securities | 36,458 | |
| Accounts Receivable | 158,204 | |
| Inventory | 64,392 | |
| Miscellaneous Prepaid and Deferred Items | 6,504 | |
| **Total Current Assets** | | **$269,788** |
| | | |
| Fixed Assets | | |
| Property and Equipment | 53,188 | |
| Less: Accumulated Depreciation | −16,132 | |
| **Total Fixed Assets** | | 37,056 |
| | | |
| Other Assets | | 4,977 |
| **Total Assets** | | **$311,821** |

### LIABILITIES AND SHAREHOLDERS' EQUITY

| Current Liabilities | | |
|---|---:|---:|
| Accounts Payable | $41,358 | |
| Accrued Expenses | 29,700 | |
| **Total Current Liabilities** | | **$71,058** |
| | | |
| Long-Term Liabilities | | |
| Loans Payable | $15,000 | |
| **Total Long-Term Liabilities** | | 15,000 |
| **Total Liabilities** | | 86,058 |
| | | |
| Shareholders' Equity | | |
| Common Stock | | |
| (21,571 shares @ $.01 par value) | $216 | |
| Less: Treasury Stock (50,000 shares) | −2,089 | |
| Paid-in Capital | 81,352 | |
| Retained Earnings | 146,284 | |
| **Total Shareholders' Equity** | | 225,763 |
| **Total Liabilities and Shareholders' Equity** | | **$311,821** |

**Current Assets**
Cash and other items that will or can be converted to cash within one year.

**Fixed Assets**
Long-term investments in buildings, equipment, furniture, and any other tangible property expected to be used in running the business for a period longer than one year.

**Current Liabilities**
Amounts owed by the company that are to be repaid within one year.

**Long-Term Liabilities**
Debts that are due a year or more after the date of the balance sheet.

**Shareholders' Equity**
Money contributed to the company for ownership interests, as well as the accumulation of profits that have not been paid out as dividends (retained earnings).

**EXHIBIT 16.5**

Balance Sheet for Computer Central

The categories used on Computer Central's year-end balance sheet are typical.

Computer Central's current liabilities consist of accounts payable and accrued expenses. Accounts payable includes the money the company owes its suppliers (such as Compaq and Toshiba) as well as money it owes vendors for miscellaneous services (such as electricity and telephone charges). *Accrued expenses* are expenses that have been incurred but for which bills have not yet been received. According to the matching principle, Computer Central records its expenses when the company receives the benefit of the service, not when the company pays for it. For example, Computer Central's account executives earn commissions on computer sales to customers. The company has a liability to its account executives once the sale is made, regardless of when a check is issued to the employee. The company must record this liability because it represents a claim against company assets. If such expenses and their associated liabilities were not recorded, the company's financial statements would be misleading and would violate the matching principle (because the commission expenses that were earned at the time of sale would not be matched to the revenue generated from the sale).

Computer Central's long-term liabilities are relatively small for a company its size. In 2002, the company purchased a new $30 million warehouse facility with $15 million in cash it had saved over many years and a five-year, $15 million bank loan. The company invests its excess cash in short-term marketable securities so it can earn interest on these funds until they are needed for future projects.

**OWNERS' EQUITY** The owners' investment in a business is listed on the balance sheet under owners' equity (or shareholders' equity for a corporation such as Computer Central). Sole proprietorships list owner's equity under the owner's name with the amount (assets minus liabilities). Small partnerships list each partner's share of the business separately, and large partnerships list the total of all partners' shares. Shareholders' equity for a corporation is presented in terms of the amount of common stock that is outstanding, meaning the amount that is in the hands of the shareholders. The combined amount of the assigned or par value of the common stock plus the amount paid over the par value (paid-in capital) represents the shareholders' total investment. Roughly $81 million was paid into the corporation by Computer Central shareholders at the time the company's shares were issued. In 2002 the company repurchased 50,000 shares of the company's own stock in the open market for $948,000. The company will use this *treasury stock* for its employee stock option plan and other general corporate purposes.

Shareholders' equity also includes a corporation's **retained earnings**—the portion of shareholders' equity that is not distributed to its owners in the form of dividends. Computer Central's retained earnings amount to $146 million. The company did not pay dividends. Instead it is building its cash reserves for future asset purchases and to finance future growth.

### Income Statement

If the balance sheet is a snapshot, the income statement is a movie. The **income statement** shows how profitable the organization has been over a specific period of time, typically one year. It summarizes all **revenues** (or sales), the amounts that have been or are to be received from customers for goods or services delivered to them, and all **expenses,** the costs that have arisen in generating revenues. Expenses and income taxes are then subtracted from revenues to show the actual profit or loss of a company, a figure known as **net income**—profit, or the *bottom line.* By briefly reviewing a company's income statements you should have a general sense of the company's size, its trend in sales, its major expenses, and the resulting net income or loss. Owners, creditors, and investors can evaluate the company's past performance and future prospects by comparing net income for one year with net income for previous years. Exhibit 16.6 is the 2002 income statement for Computer Central, showing net income of almost $66 million. This is a 32 percent increase over the company's net income of $50 million for the previous year.

Expenses, the costs of doing business, include both the direct costs associated with creating or purchasing products for sale and the indirect costs associated with operating the business. Whether a company manufactures or purchases its inventory, the cost of storing the product for sale (such as heating the warehouse, paying the rent, and buying insurance on the storage facility) is added to the difference between the cost of the beginning inventory and the cost of the ending inventory in order to compute the actual cost of items that were sold during a period—or the **cost of goods sold.** The computation can be summarized as follows:

Cost of goods sold = Beginning inventory + Net purchases − Ending inventory

As shown in Exhibit 16.6, cost of goods sold is deducted from sales to obtain a company's **gross profit**—a key figure used in financial statement analysis. In addition to the costs directly associated with producing goods, companies deduct **operating expenses,** which include both *selling expenses* and *general expenses,* to compute a firm's *net operating income,* or the income that is generated from business operations. **Selling expenses** are operating expenses incurred through marketing and distributing the product (such as wages or salaries of salespeople, advertising, supplies, insurance for the sales operation, depreciation for the store and sales equipment, and other sales department expenses such as telephone charges). **General expenses** are operating expenses incurred in the overall administration of a business. They include professional services (accounting and legal fees), office salaries, depreciation of office equipment, insurance for office operations, supplies, and so on.

A firm's net operating income is then adjusted by the amount of any nonoperating income or expense items such as the gain or loss on the sale of a building. The result is the firm's net income or loss before income taxes (losses are shown in parentheses), a key figure used in budgeting, cash flow analysis, and a variety of other financial computations. Finally, income taxes are deducted to compute the company's net income or loss for the period.

## Computer Central

### Income Statement
### Year ended December 31, 2002
### (in thousands)

| | | |
|---|---:|---:|
| **Revenues** | | |
| Gross Sales | $1,991,489 | |
| Less Sales Returns and Allowances | −258,000 | |
| | | |
| Net Sales | | $1,733,489 |
| | | |
| **Cost of Goods Sold** | | |
| Beginning Inventory | $61,941 | |
| Add: Purchases During the Year | 1,515,765 | |
| Cost of Goods Available for Sale | −1,577,706 | |
| Less: Ending Inventory | 64,392 | |
| | | |
| Total Cost of Goods Sold | | −1,513,314 |
| | | |
| Gross Profit | | $220,175 |
| | | |
| **Operating Expenses** | | |
| Selling Expenses | $75,523 | |
| General Expenses | 40,014 | |
| | | |
| Total Operating Expenses | | 115,537 |
| | | |
| Net Operating Income (Gross Profit less Operating Expenses) | | 104,638 |
| Other Income | | 4,373 |
| | | |
| Net Income Before Income Taxes | | 109,011 |
| Less: Income Taxes | | −43,170 |
| | | |
| **Net Income After Taxes** | | $65,841 |

**Revenues**
Funds received from sales of goods and services to customers as well as other items such as rent, interest, and dividends. Net sales are gross sales less returns and allowances.

**Cost of Goods Sold**
Cost of merchandise or services that generate a company's income by adding purchases to beginning inventory and then subtracting ending inventory.

**Operating Expenses**
Generally classified as selling and general expenses. Selling expenses are those incurred through the marketing and distributing of the company's products. General expenses are operating expenses incurred in the overall administration of a business.

**Net Income After Taxes**
Profit or loss over a specific period determined by subtracting all expenses and taxes from revenues.

### EXHIBIT 16.6

Income Statement for Computer Central

An income statement summarized the company's financial operations over a particular accounting period, usually a year.

### Statement of Cash Flows

In addition to preparing a balance sheet and an income statement, all public companies and many privately owned companies prepare a **statement of cash flows** to show how much cash the company generated over time and where it went (see Exhibit 16.7). The statement of cash flows reveals not only the increase or decrease in the company's cash for the period but also the accounts (by category) that caused that change. From a brief review of this statement you should have a general sense of the amount of cash created or consumed by daily operations, the amount of cash invested in fixed or other assets, the amount of debt borrowed or repaid, and the proceeds from the sale of stock or payments for dividends. In addition, an analysis of cash flows provides a good idea of a company's ability to pay its short-term obligations when they become due. Computer Central's statement of cash flows shows that the company used $15 million of its cash reserves and the proceeds of a $15 million bank loan in 2002 to pay for its new facility.

### > active exercise

**Take a moment to apply what you've learned.**

## Computer Central
### Statement of Cash Flows
### Year ended December 31, 2002
### (in thousands)

**Cash flows from operating activities:***

| | | |
|---|---:|---:|
| Net Income | $65,841 | |
| Adjustments to reconcile net income to net cash provided by operating activities | −61,317 | |
| *Net cash provided by operations* | | $4,524 |

**Cash flows from investing activities:**

| | | |
|---|---:|---:|
| Purchase of property and equipment | −30,110 | |
| Purchase of securities | −114,932 | |
| Redemptions of securities | 112,463 | |
| *Net cash used in investment activities* | | −32,579 |

**Cash flows from financing activities**

| | | |
|---|---:|---:|
| Loan proceeds | 15,000 | |
| Purchase of treasury stock | −2,089 | |
| Proceeds from exercise of stock options | 1,141 | |
| *Net cash used in financing activities* | | 14,052 |

| | |
|---|---:|
| **Net (decrease) increase in cash** | −14,003 |
| **Cash and cash equivalents at beginning of year** | $18,233 |
| **Cash and cash equivalents at end of year** | $4,230 |

*Note: Numbers preceded by minus sign indicates cash outflows.

---

**EXHIBIT 16.7**

Statement of Cash Flows for Computer Central

A statement of cash flows shows a firm's cash receipts and cash payments as a result of three main activities—operating, investing, and financing—for a period.

## ANALYZING FINANCIAL STATEMENTS

Once financial statements have been prepared, managers and outsiders use these statements to evaluate the financial health of the organization, make business decisions, and spot opportunities for improvements by looking at the company's performance in relation to its past performance, the economy as a whole, and the performance of its competitors.

### Trend Analysis

The process of comparing financial data from year to year in order to see how they have changed is known as *trend analysis.* You can use trend analysis to uncover shifts in the nature of the business over time. Most large companies provide data for trend analysis in their annual reports. Their balance sheets and income statements typically show three to five years or more of data (making comparative statement analysis possible). Changes in other key items—such as revenues, income, earnings per share, and dividends per share—are usually presented in tables and graphs.

Of course, when you are comparing one period with another, it's important to take into account the effects of extraordinary or unusual items such as the sale of major assets, the purchase of a new line of products from another company, weather, or economic conditions that may have affected the company in one period but not the next. These extraordinary items are usually disclosed in the text portion of a company's annual report or in the notes to the financial statements.

## Ratio Analysis

Managers and others compute financial ratios to facilitate the comparison of one company's financial results with those of competing firms and with industry averages. **Ratio analysis** compares two elements from the same year's financial figures. They are called ratios because they are computed by dividing one element of a financial statement by another. The advantage of using ratios is that it puts companies on the same footing; that is, it makes it possible to compare different-size companies and changing dollar amounts. For example, by using ratios, you can easily compare a large supermarket's ability to generate profit out of sales with a similar statistic for a small grocery store.

The benefit of converting numbers into ratios can be explained by the following example: Suppose you wanted to know how well your favorite baseball player was performing this year. To find out, you would check the player's statistics—batting average, runs batted in (RBIs), hits, and home runs. In other words, you would look at data that have been arranged into meaningful statistics that allow you to compare present performance with past performance and with the performance of other players in the league. Financial ratios do the same thing. They convert the raw numbers from the current and prior years' financial statements into ratios that highlight important relationships or measures of performance.[14]

Just as baseball statistics focus on various aspects of performance (such as hitting or pitching), financial ratios help companies understand their current operations and answer key questions: Is inventory too large? Are credit customers paying too slowly? Can the company pay its bills? Ratios also set standards and benchmarks for gauging future business by comparing a company's scores with industry averages that show the performance of competition. Every industry tends to have its own "normal" ratios, which act as yardsticks for individual companies. Dun and Bradstreet, a credit rating firm, and Robert Morris Associates publish both average financial figures and ratios for a variety of industries and company sizes.

Before reviewing specific ratios, consider two rules of thumb: First, avoid drawing too strong a conclusion from any one ratio. For instance, even with a low batting average, a baseball player's RBIs may prove valuable in the team's lineup. Second, once ratios have presented a general indication, refer back to the specific data involved to see whether the numbers confirm what the ratios suggest. In other words do a little investigating, because statistics can be misleading. Remember, a baseball player who has been at bat only two times and has one hit has a batting average of .500.

## Types of Financial Ratios

Financial ratios can be organized into the following groups, as Exhibit 16.8 shows: profitability, liquidity, activity, and leverage (or debt).

**PROFITABILITY RATIOS** You can analyze how well a company is conducting its ongoing operations by computing **profitability ratios,** which show the state of the company's financial performance or how well it's generating profits. Three of the most common profitability ratios are **return on sales,** or profit margin (the net income a business makes per unit of sales); **return on investment (ROI),** or return on equity (the income earned on the owner's investment); and **earnings per share** (the profit earned for each share of stock outstanding). Exhibit 16.8 shows how to compute these profitability ratios by using the financial information from Computer Central.

**LIQUIDITY RATIOS** **Liquidity ratios** measure the ability of the firm to pay its short-term obligations. As you might expect, lenders and creditors are keenly interested in liquidity measures. Liquidity can be judged on the basis of *working capital,* the *current ratio,* and the *quick ratio.* A company's **working capital** (current assets minus current liabilities) is an indicator of liquidity because it represents current assets remaining after the payment of all current liabilities. The dollar amount of working capital can be misleading, however. For example, it may include the value of slow-moving inventory items that cannot be used to help pay a company's short-term debts.

A different picture of the company's liquidity is provided by the **current ratio**—current assets divided by current liabilities. This figure compares the current debt owed with the current assets available to pay that debt. The **quick ratio,** also called the *acid-test ratio,* is computed by subtracting inventory from current assets and then dividing the result by current liabilities. This ratio is often a better indicator of a firm's ability to pay creditors than the current ratio because the quick ratio leaves out inventories—which at times can be difficult to sell. Analysts generally consider a quick ratio of 1.0 to be reasonable whereas a current ratio of 2.0 is considered a safe risk for short-term credit. Exhibit 16.8 shows that both the current and quick ratios of Computer Central are well above these benchmarks and industry averages.

**ACTIVITY RATIOS** A number of **activity ratios** may be used to analyze how well a company is managing its assets. The most common is the **inventory turnover ratio,** which measures how fast a company's inventory is turned into sales; in general, the quicker the better, because holding excess inventory can be expensive. When inventory sits on the shelf, money is tied up without earning

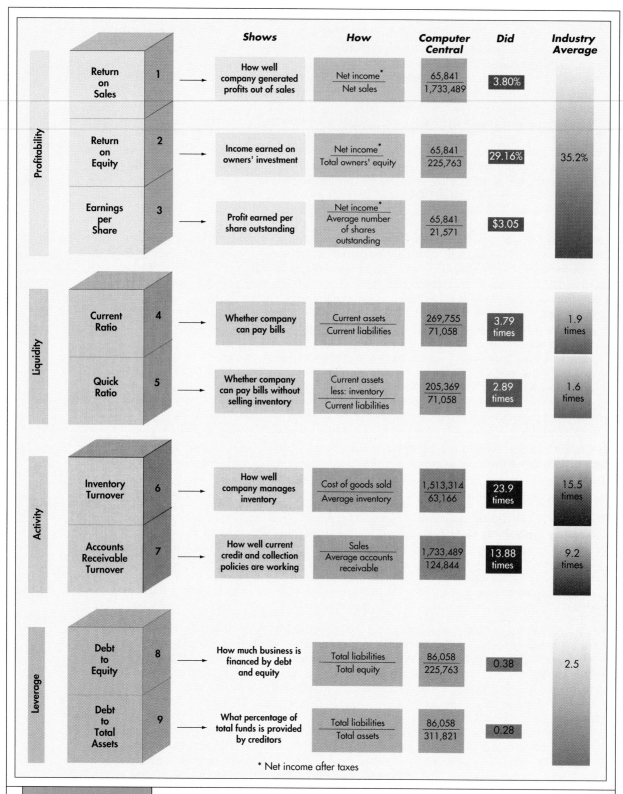

| | | Shows | How | Computer Central | Did | Industry Average |
|---|---|---|---|---|---|---|
| **Profitability** | Return on Sales | 1 | How well company generated profits out of sales | $\dfrac{\text{Net income}^*}{\text{Net sales}}$ | $\dfrac{65,841}{1,733,489}$ | 3.80% | |
| | Return on Equity | 2 | Income earned on owners' investment | $\dfrac{\text{Net income}^*}{\text{Total owners' equity}}$ | $\dfrac{65,841}{225,763}$ | 29.16% | 35.2% |
| | Earnings per Share | 3 | Profit earned per share outstanding | $\dfrac{\text{Net income}^*}{\text{Average number of shares outstanding}}$ | $\dfrac{65,841}{21,571}$ | $3.05 | |
| **Liquidity** | Current Ratio | 4 | Whether company can pay bills | $\dfrac{\text{Current assets}}{\text{Current liabilities}}$ | $\dfrac{269,755}{71,058}$ | 3.79 times | 1.9 times |
| | Quick Ratio | 5 | Whether company can pay bills without selling inventory | $\dfrac{\text{Current assets less: inventory}}{\text{Current liabilities}}$ | $\dfrac{205,369}{71,058}$ | 2.89 times | 1.6 times |
| **Activity** | Inventory Turnover | 6 | How well company manages inventory | $\dfrac{\text{Cost of goods sold}}{\text{Average inventory}}$ | $\dfrac{1,513,314}{63,166}$ | 23.9 times | 15.5 times |
| | Accounts Receivable Turnover | 7 | How well current credit and collection policies are working | $\dfrac{\text{Sales}}{\text{Average accounts receivable}}$ | $\dfrac{1,733,489}{124,844}$ | 13.88 times | 9.2 times |
| **Leverage** | Debt to Equity | 8 | How much business is financed by debt and equity | $\dfrac{\text{Total liabilities}}{\text{Total equity}}$ | $\dfrac{86,058}{225,763}$ | 0.38 | 2.5 |
| | Debt to Total Assets | 9 | What percentage of total funds is provided by creditors | $\dfrac{\text{Total liabilities}}{\text{Total assets}}$ | $\dfrac{86,058}{311,821}$ | 0.28 | |

\* Net income after taxes

**EXHIBIT 16.8**

How Well Does This Company Stack Up?

Nearly all companies use ratios to evaluate how well the company is performing in relation to prior performance, the economy as a whole, and the company's competitors.

interest; furthermore, the company incurs expenses for its storage, handling, insurance, and taxes. In addition, there is always a risk that the inventory will become obsolete before it can be converted into finished goods and sold. The firm's goal is to maintain enough inventory to fill orders in a timely fashion at the lowest cost.

Keep in mind that it's difficult to judge a company by its inventory level. For example, lower inventories might mean one of many things: You're running an efficient operation; the right inventory is not being stocked; or sales are booming and you need to increase your orders. Likewise, higher inventories could signal a decline in sales, careless ordering, or stocking up because of favorable pricing. The "ideal" turnover ratio varies with the type of operation. In 2002 Computer Central turned its inventory 23.9 times (see Exhibit 16.8). This rate is unusually high when compared with industry averages, and it suggests that the company stocks only enough inventory to fill current orders and cover a product's reorder time, as discussed in Chapter 9.

Another popular activity ratio is the **accounts receivable turnover ratio,** which measures how well a company's credit and collection policies are working by indicating how frequently accounts receivable are converted to cash. The volume of receivables outstanding depends on the financial manager's decisions regarding several issues, such as who qualifies for credit and who does not, how long customers are given to pay their bills, and how aggressive the firm is in collecting its debts. Be careful here as well. If the ratio is going up, you need to determine whether the company is doing a better job of collecting or sales are rising. If the ratio is going down, it may be because sales are decreasing or because collection efforts are sagging. In 2002 Computer Central turned its accounts receivable 13.88 times—considerably higher than the industry average (see Exhibit 16.8).

**LEVERAGE, OR DEBT, RATIOS**  You can measure a company's ability to pay its long-term debts by calculating its **debt ratios,** or leverage ratios. Lenders look at these ratios to determine whether the potential borrower has put enough money into the business to serve as a protective cushion for the loan. The **debt-to-equity ratio** (total liabilities divided by total equity) indicates the extent to which a business is financed by debt, as opposed to invested capital (equity). From the lender's standpoint, the lower this ratio, the safer the company, because the company has less existing debt and may be able to repay additional money it wants to borrow. However, a company that is conservative in its long-term borrowing is not necessarily well managed; often a low level of debt is associated with a low growth rate. Computer Central's low debt-to-equity ratio of 38 percent (as shown in Exhibit 16.8) reflects the company's practice of financing its growth by using excess cash flow from operations and by selling shares of common stock to the public.

The **debt-to-total-assets ratio** (total liabilities divided by total assets) also serves as a simple measure of a company's ability to carry long-term debt. As a rule of thumb, the amount of debt should not exceed 50 percent of the value of total assets. For Computer Central, this ratio is a very low 28 percent and again reflects the company's policy of using retained earnings to finance its growth (see Exhibit 16.8). However, this ratio, too, is not a magic formula. Like grades on a report card, ratios are clues to performance. Managers, creditors, lenders, and investors can use them to get a fairly accurate idea of how a company is doing. But remember, one ratio by itself doesn't tell the whole story.

> **video exercise**

**Take a moment to apply what you've learned.**

## USING ACCOUNTING INFORMATION TO MAKE FINANCIAL DECISIONS

Suppose your company is considering changing the way it pays your sales force. Instead of paying them a fixed salary, the company would like to pay salespeople a base salary plus a commission, hoping that the commissions will motivate them to sell more product. How would you determine the best commission rate? Would this new pay structure cost the company more money? How could you guarantee that your sales force would benefit from this change? What if sales increased by 10 percent instead of the 20 percent you had projected? These are the types of questions accountants deal with daily. Sometimes questions are even more complex because there are more variables. Asking "what-if" questions is certainly not new. What is new, however, is the application of computing technology to the process.

By using electronic spreadsheet programs such as Microsoft Excel or Lotus 1-2-3, companies can analyze the financial costs and benefits of just about any decision. For example, when Schatzman and Crane were deciding whether to purchase the retiring dentist's practice and building, their accountant analyzed the merits of the investment using a series of spreadsheet calculations.

Financial analysis begins with a firm's financial data. Typically, the accountant will enter these data into an electronic spreadsheet and manipulate the numbers by converting total costs to unit costs such as cost per passenger-mile (for airlines) or cost per package delivered (for companies such as FedEx). Next, the accountant will compute a range of outcomes using expected, best-case, and worst-case scenarios—such as unit costs will increase by 5 percent, 2 percent, or 10 percent. Armed with such information, management can make more educated decisions.

Building decision models with spreadsheet software is just one of the many tasks accountants perform, as this chapter demonstrates. In Chapter 17 we'll discuss other functions that accountants perform such as financial planning, budgeting, and managing a company's cash flow. But first we'll explore some accounting issues that are surfacing as more and more companies transact e-commerce.

## active exercise &lt;

**Take a moment to apply what you've learned.**

## active concept check &lt;

**Now let's take a moment to test your knowledge of the concepts you have studied in this section.**

### &gt; Chapter Wrap-Up

Now that you've reached the end of the chapter, you may wish to explore the concepts you've been reading about in greater detail, or test yourself to see how well you've comprehended the material. In the box below you'll find a number of links. Click on any one of these links to find additional chapter resources.

## &gt; end-of-chapter resources

- Summary of Learning Objectives
- Practice Quiz
- Focusing on E-Business Today
- Key Terms
- Test Your Knowledge
- Practice Your Knowledge
- Expand Your Knowledge
- A Case for Critical Thinking

# Financial Management and Banking

## > What's Ahead

### INSIDE BUSINESS TODAY
### VIRTUAL FINANCIAL MANAGEMENT: INTUIT'S ONE-STOP MONEY SHOP

Balancing the family checkbook was a regular battle for Scott Cook's wife—until Cook came up with Quicken, an easy-to-use software program for managing personal finances. Today 12 million consumers and 3 million small-business owners track their finances with software developed and marketed by Intuit, under the Quicken brand name. And as co-founder of the world's largest maker of personal finance software, Cook is providing consumers with everything they need for money management through Quicken.com, Intuit's one-stop financial supermarket on the Web.

Ever since Cook developed the first edition of Quicken in 1984, Intuit has dominated the market for personal finance software with its three best-selling products—Quicken for personal financial management, QuickBooks for small-business accounting, and TurboTax for tax preparation. But the Internet boom in the mid-1990s convinced Cook that Intuit could no longer rely solely on sales of traditional software products. After all, computer manufacturers were offering free financial software with new computers, and Internet-savvy consumers had little desire to pay $50 for personal finance software when they could find financial tools on the Web for free. So Cook decided to transform the traditional software company into an Internet financial services provider.

Banking on the strength of the Quicken brand, Cook launched Quicken.com in 1997. Although the site initially offered stock quotes, financial planning advice, and online banking, Cook quickly expanded the scope of Intuit's online services. First, he integrated the site into Intuit's software products, allowing users of Quicken software programs to download data from

Scott Cook, co-founder of Intuit, is betting the company's future on the Internet.

Quicken.com with the click of a mouse. Then he partnered with more than 50 banks and dozens of mortgage lenders and insurance carriers to turn the site into a full-service financial supermarket.

Today Quicken.com serves as a personal finance center, offering customers everything from bill payment to mortgages under one virtual roof. Using the "do-it-yourself" approach, consumers can download stock research, electronically file their tax returns, create a portfolio, or choose from an array of recommended mutual funds. Moreover, the site serves as a "virtual financial adviser" by directing consumers to the ideal financial instrument for their needs at the most reasonable price. Consumers in search of an auto loan, for example, can log on to Quicken.com to get quotes and compare rates from several different banks. But to complete the transactions, users will have to go to the bank's Web site. That's because Quicken.com doesn't actually sell financial products; rather, it acts as an intermediary—matching buyers and sellers and earning a commission for its services.

The site also attracts small-business owners by offering such services as CashFinder to entrepreneurs in search of capital and loans, and payroll services that work with QuickBooks. Furthermore, the site's online marketplace offers discounts on purchases of office supplies from such retailers as Office Depot and Gateway.

A firm believer that technology allows anyone to manage finances—even "people who think General Ledger is a World War II hero"—Cook continues to improve Intuit's range of online services. For example, Intuit became the first Internet provider to offer "pay anyone" capabilities by providing payment of electronic or traditional paper bills through Quicken's Web site. Another site feature consolidates bills, investments, credit card transactions, and bank balances on one screen, permitting consumers to keep track of all their financial information in one place.

And Cook's vision for a one-stop money shop is paying off. Intuit now derives more than one-third of its revenue from Internet services, generating income through customer payments for such services as electronic tax filings and payroll services, through advertising and sponsorships, and through commissions on such transactions as loans and mortgages.[1]

## > objectives

Take a moment to familiarize yourself with the key objectives of this chapter.

## > gearing up

Before you begin reading this chapter, try a short warm-up activity.

## > What Does Financial Management Involve?

As Intuit founder Scott Cook knows, all companies need to pay their bills and still have some money left over to improve the business. Furthermore, a key goal of any business is to increase the value to its owners (and other stakeholders) by making it grow. Maximizing the owner's wealth sounds simple enough: Just sell a good product for more than it costs to make. Before you can earn any revenue, however, you need money to get started. Once the business is off the ground, your need for money continues—whether it's to buy new road repair equipment or to build a new warehouse.

Planning for a firm's current and future money needs is the foundation of **financial management,** or finance. This area of concern involves making decisions about alternative sources and uses of funds with the goal of maximizing a company's value (see Exhibit 17.1). To achieve this goal, financial managers develop and implement a firm's financial plan; monitor a firm's cash flow and decide how to create or use excess funds; budget for current and future expenditures; recommend specific investments; develop a plan to finance the enterprise for future growth; and interact with banks and capital markets.

We begin this chapter by taking a close look at each of these activities. Next we discuss the banking environment in which financial managers operate. But first, keep in mind that in most smaller companies the owner is responsible for the firm's financial decisions, whereas in larger operations

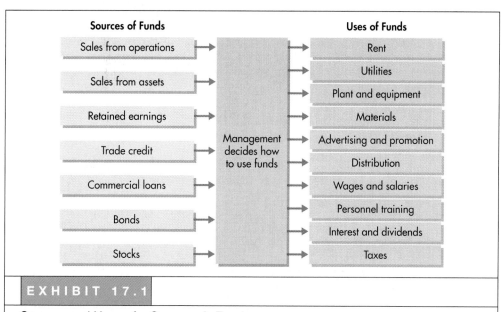

| Sources of Funds | Uses of Funds |
|---|---|
| Sales from operations | Rent |
| Sales from assets | Utilities |
| Retained earnings | Plant and equipment |
| Trade credit | Materials |
| Commercial loans | Advertising and promotion |
| Bonds | Distribution |
| Stocks | Wages and salaries |
| | Personnel training |
| | Interest and dividends |
| | Taxes |

Management decides how to use funds

**EXHIBIT 17.1**

Sources and Uses of a Company's Funds

Financial management involves finding suitable sources of funds and deciding on the most appropriate uses for those funds.

financial management is the responsibility of the finance department, which reports to a vice president of finance or a chief financial officer (CFO). This department includes the accounting function. In fact, most financial managers are accountants.

## DEVELOPING AND IMPLEMENTING A FINANCIAL PLAN

One way companies make sure they have enough money is by developing a *financial plan.* Normally in the form of a budget, a **financial plan** is a document that shows the funds a firm will need for a period of time, as well as the sources and uses of those funds. When you prepare a financial plan for a company, you have two objectives: achieving a positive cash flow and efficiently investing excess cash flow to make your company grow. Financial planning requires looking beyond the four walls of the company to answer questions such as: Is the company introducing a new product in the near future or expanding its market? Is the industry growing? Is the national economy declining? Is inflation heating up? Would an investment in new technology improve productivity?[2]

### Monitoring Cash Flow

An underlying concept of any financial plan is that all money should be used productively. This concept is important because without cash a company cannot purchase the assets and supplies it needs to operate or pay dividends to its shareholders. In accounting, we focused on the net income of a firm. Cash flows are generally related to net income; that is, companies with relatively high accounting profits generally have relatively high cash flows, but the relationship is not precise. That's because net income can be generated from a variety of accounting transactions that do not directly impact a firm's cash on hand.

One way financial mangers improve a company's cash flow is by monitoring its *working capital accounts:* cash, inventory, accounts receivable, and accounts payable. They use commonsense procedures such as shrinking accounts receivable collection periods, dispatching bills on a timely basis without paying bills earlier than necessary, controlling the level of inventory, and investing excess cash.

**MANAGING ACCOUNTS RECEIVABLE AND ACCOUNTS PAYABLE** Keeping an eye on accounts receivable—the money owed to the firm by its customers—is one way to manage cash flow effectively. The volume of receivables depends on the financial manager's decisions regarding several issues: who qualifies for credit and who does not; how long customers have to pay their bills; and how aggressive the firm is in collecting its debts. In addition to setting guidelines and policies to handle these issues, the financial manager analyzes the firm's outstanding receivables to identify patterns that might indicate problems and establishes procedures for collecting overdue accounts.

The flip side of managing receivables is managing payables—the bills that the company owes to its creditors. Here the objective is generally to postpone paying bills until the last moment, since accounts payable represent interest-free loans from suppliers. However, the financial manager also needs to weigh the advantages of paying promptly if doing so entitles the firm to cash discounts. In addition, paying on time is a good way to maintain the company's credit standing, which it turn influences a lender's decision to approve a loan. Of course, paying bills online with programs such as Intuit's Quicken and Microsoft Money is one way to manage cash aggressively and efficiently. As more and more companies deliver their bills electronically to customers via the Internet, and as such services become more reliable, online bill paying is expected to take off.[3]

**MANAGING INVENTORY**
Inventory is another area where financial managers can fine-tune the firm's cash flow. In Chapter 9 we discussed that inventory sitting on the shelf represents capital that is tied up without earning interest. Furthermore, the firm incurs expenses for storage and handling, insurance, and taxes. Additionally, there is always the risk that inventory will become obsolete before it can be converted into finished goods and sold. Thus, the firm's goal is to maintain enough inventory to fill orders in a timely fashion at the lowest cost. To achieve this goal, financial managers work with operations managers and marketing managers to determine the economic order quantity (EOQ), or quantity of materials that, when ordered regularly, results in the lowest ordering and storage costs. (Inventory control techniques and efficient ordering systems are discussed in Chapter 9.)

### Managing Cash Reserves

Sometimes companies find themselves with more cash on hand than they need. A seasonal business may experience a quiet period between the time when revenues are collected from the last busy season and the time when suppliers' bills are due. Department stores, for example, may have excess cash during a few weeks in February and March. A firm may also accumulate cash to meet a large financial commitment in the future or to finance future growth. Using a company's own money instead of borrowing from an outside source such as a bank has one chief attraction: No interest payments are required. Finally, every firm keeps some surplus cash on hand as a cushion in case its needs are greater than expected.

Part of the financial manager's job is to make sure that excess cash is invested so that it earns as much interest as possible. Aggressive financial managers use electronic cash management (the ability to access bank account information online) to move cash between accounts and pay bills on a daily basis; they also invest excess cash on hand in short-term investments called **marketable securities.** These interest-bearing or dividend-paying investments include money-market funds or publicly traded stocks such as IBM or Sears. They are said to be "marketable" because they can be easily converted back to cash. Because marketable securities are generally used as contingency funds, however, most financial managers invest these funds in securities of solid companies or the government—ones with the least amount of risk. (Securities are discussed in detail in Chapter 18.)

> ## active exercise
### Take a moment to apply what you've learned.

## BUDGETING

In addition to developing a financial plan and monitoring cash flow, financial managers are responsible for developing a **budget,** a financial blueprint for a given period (often one year). Master (or operating) budgets help financial managers estimate the flow of money into and out of the business by structuring financial plans in a framework of a firm's total estimated revenues, expenses, and cash flows. Accountants provide much of the data required for budgets and are important members of the budget development team because they have a complete understanding of the company's operating costs.

The master budget sets a standard for expenditures, provides guidelines for controlling costs, and offers an integrated and detailed plan for the future. For example, by reviewing the budget of any airline you can determine whether the company plans on increasing its fleet of aircraft, adding more routes, hiring more employees, increasing employees' pay, or continuing or abandoning any discounts for travelers. No wonder companies like to keep their budgets confidential. Once a budget has been developed, the finance manager compares actual results with projections to discover variances and then recommends corrective action—a process known as **financial control.**

### Capital Budgeting

In contrast to operating budgets, capital budgets forecast and plan for a firm's **capital investments,** such as major expenditures in buildings or equipment. Capital investments generally cover a period of several years and help the company grow. Before investments can be made, however, a firm must decide on which of the many possible capital investments to make, how to finance those that are undertaken, and even whether to make any capital investments at all. This process is called **capital budgeting.**

The process generally begins by having all divisions within a company submit their capital requests—essentially, "wish lists" of investments that would make the company more profitable and thus more valuable to its owners over time. Next the financial manager decides which investments need evaluating and which don't. For example, the routine replacement of old equipment probably wouldn't need evaluating; however, the construction of a new manufacturing facility would. Finally, a financial evaluation is performed to determine whether the amount of money required for a particular investment will be greater than, equal to, or less than the amount of revenue it will generate. On the basis of this analysis, the financial manager can determine which projects to recommend to senior management for purchase approval.

### Forecasting Capital Requirements

Keep in mind that as with any major investment decision, an erroneous forecast of capital requirements can have serious consequences. If the firm invests too much in assets, it will incur unnecessarily heavy expenses. If it does not replace or upgrade existing assets on a regular basis, the assets will likely become obsolete. For example, old manufacturing equipment may be incapable of handling increasing capacities. This could even result in a loss of market share to competitors. For these important reasons, firms try to match capital investments with the company's goals. In other words, if the firm is growing, then projects that would produce the greatest growth rates would receive highest

priority. However, if the company is trying to reduce costs, those projects that enhance the company's efficiency and productivity would be ranked toward the top. Because asset expansion frequently involves large sums of money and affects the company's productivity for an extended period of time, finance managers must carefully evaluate the best way to finance or pay for these investments, another major responsibility of financial managers.

## FINANCING THE ENTERPRISE

Most companies can't operate and grow without a periodic infusion of money. Firms need money to cover the day-to-day expenses of running a business, such as paying employees and purchasing inventory. They also need money to acquire new assets such as land, production facilities, and equipment. Furthermore, as Chapter 4 pointed out, start-up companies need money to fund the costs involved in launching a new business.

Where can existing firms obtain the money they need to operate and grow? The most obvious source would be revenues: cash received from sales, rentals of property, interest on short-term investments, and so on. Another likely source would be suppliers who may be willing to do business on credit, thus enabling the company to postpone payment. Most firms also obtain money in the form of loans from banks, finance companies, or other commercial lenders. In addition, public companies can raise funds by selling shares of stock, and large corporations can sell bonds.

As you can imagine, financing an enterprise is a complex undertaking. The process begins by assessing the firm's financing needs and determining whether funds are needed for the short or long term. Next, the firm must assess the cost of obtaining those funds. Finally, it must weigh the advantages and disadvantages of financing through debt or equity, taking into consideration the firm's special needs and circumstances in addition to the advantages and disadvantages of public versus private ownership (as discussed in Chapter 5). The financing process is further complicated by the fact that many sources of long-term and short-term financing exist—each with their own special attributes, risks, and costs.

### Length of Term

Financing can be either short-term or long-term. **Short-term financing** is any financing that will be repaid within one year, whereas **long-term financing** is any financing that will be repaid in a period longer than one year. The primary purpose of short-term financing is to ensure that a company maintains its liquidity, or its ability to meet financial obligations (such as inventory payments) as they become due. By contrast, long-term financing is used to acquire long-term assets such as buildings and equipment or to fund expansion via any number of growth options. Long-term financing can come from both internal and external sources, as Exhibit 17.2 highlights.

### Cost of Capital

In general, a company wants to obtain money at the lowest cost and least amount of risk. However, lenders and investors want to receive the highest possible return on their investment, also at the lowest

When Intel needs funds to purchase new equipment, management will weigh the advantages and disadvantages of using internal or external financing sources.

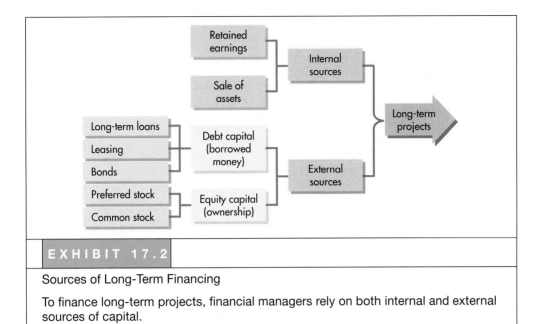

EXHIBIT 17.2

Sources of Long-Term Financing

To finance long-term projects, financial managers rely on both internal and external sources of capital.

risk. A company's **cost of capital,** the average rate of interest it must pay on its debt and equity financing, depends on three main factors: the risk associated with the company, the prevailing level of interest rates, and management's selection of funding vehicles.

**RISK** Lenders and investors who provide money to businesses expect their returns to be in proportion to the two types of risk they face: the quality and length of time of the venture. Obviously, the more financially solid a company is, the less risk investors face. However, time also plays a vital role. Because a dollar will be worth less tomorrow than it is today, lenders need to be compensated for waiting to be repaid. As a result, long-term financing generally costs a company more than short-term financing.

**INTEREST RATES** Regardless of how financially solid a company is, the cost of money will vary over time because interest rates fluctuate. The **prime interest rate (prime)** is the lowest interest rate offered on short-term bank loans to preferred borrowers. The prime changes irregularly and, at times, quite frequently—sometimes because of supply and demand and other times because the prime rate is closely tied to the **discount rate,** the interest rate Federal Reserve Banks charge on loans to commercial banks and other depository institutions. We will discuss the importance of the discount rate later in the chapter when we discuss the money supply.

Companies must take such interest rate fluctuations into account when making financing decisions. For instance, a company planning to finance a short-term project when the prime rate is 8.5 percent would want to reevaluate the project if the prime rose to 10 percent a few months later. Even though companies try to time their borrowing to take advantage of drops in interest rates, this option is not always possible. A firm's need for money doesn't always coincide with a period of favorable rates. At times, a company may be forced to borrow when rates are high and then renegotiate the loan when rates drop. Sometimes projects must be put on hold until interest rates become more affordable.

**OPPORTUNITY COST** Using a company's own cash to finance its growth has one chief attraction: No interest payments are required. Nevertheless, such internal financing is not free; this money has an *opportunity cost.* That is, a company might be better off investing its excess cash in external opportunities, such as another company's projects or stocks of growing companies, and borrowing money to finance its own growth. Doing so makes sense as long as the company can earn a greater *rate of return,* the percentage increase in the value of an investment, on external investments than the rate of interest paid on borrowed money. This concept is called **leverage** because the loan acts like a lever: It magnifies the power of the borrower to generate profits (see Exhibit 17.3). However, leverage works both ways: Borrowing may magnify your losses as well as your gains. Because most companies require some degree of external financing from time to time, the issue is not so much whether to use outside money; rather, it's a question of how much should be raised, by what means, and when. The answers to such questions determine the firm's **capital structure,** the mix of debt and equity.

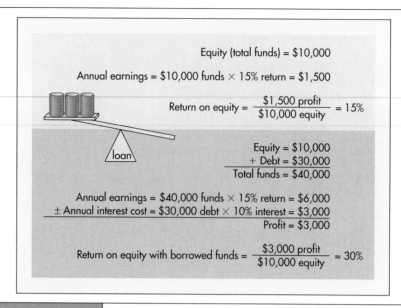

Equity (total funds) = $10,000

Annual earnings = $10,000 funds × 15% return = $1,500

$$\text{Return on equity} = \frac{\$1,500 \text{ profit}}{\$10,000 \text{ equity}} = 15\%$$

loan

Equity = $10,000
+ Debt = $30,000
Total funds = $40,000

Annual earnings = $40,000 funds × 15% return = $6,000
± Annual interest cost = $30,000 debt × 10% interest = $3,000
Profit = $3,000

$$\text{Return on equity with borrowed funds} = \frac{\$3,000 \text{ profit}}{\$10,000 \text{ equity}} = 30\%$$

### EXHIBIT 17.3

How Leverage Works

If you invest $10,000 of your own money in a business venture and it yields 15 percent (or $1,500), your return on equity is 15 percent. However, if you borrow an additional $30,000 at 10 percent interest and invest a total of $40,000 with the same 15 percent yield, the ultimate return on your $10,000 equity is 30 percent (or $3,000). The key to using leverage successfully is to try to make sure that your profit on the total funds is greater than the interest you must pay on the portion of it that is borrowed.

### Debt Versus Equity Financing

*Debt financing* refers to what we normally think of as a loan. A creditor agrees to lend money to a debtor in exchange for repayment, with accumulated interest, at some future date. *Equity financing* is achieved by selling shares of a company's stock. (The advantages and disadvantages of selling stock to the public are discussed in Chapter 5.) When choosing between debt and equity financing, companies consider a variety of issues, such as the cost of the financing, the claim on income, the claim on assets, and the desire for ownership control (see Exhibit 17.4)

### Common Types of Debt Financing

Two common types of short-term debt financing are **trade credit** (or open-account purchases) from suppliers—allowing purchasers to obtain products before paying for them; and **commercial paper**—short-term promissory notes of major corporations usually sold in denominations of $100,000 or more, with maturities of up to 270 days (the maximum allowed by the SEC without registration.

Loans, another common source of debt financing, can be long-term or short-term and secured or unsecured. **Secured loans** are those backed by something of value, known as **collateral,** which may be seized by the lender in the event that the borrower fails to repay the loan. The most common type of secured loan is a *mortgage,* in which a piece of property such as a building is used as collateral. Other types of loan collateral are accounts receivable, inventories, marketable securities, and other assets. **Unsecured loans** are ones that require no collateral. Instead, the lender relies on the general credit record and the earning power of the borrower. To increase the returns on such loans and to obtain some protection in case of default, most lenders insist that the borrower maintain some minimum amount of money on deposit at the bank—a **compensating balance**—while the loan is outstanding.

One example of an unsecured loan is a working capital **line of credit,** which is an agreed-on maximum amount of money a bank is willing to lend a business during a specific period of time, usually one year. Once a line of credit has been established, the business may obtain unsecured loans for any amount up to that limit, provided the bank has funds. The line of credit can be canceled at any time, so companies that want to be sure of obtaining credit when needed should arrange a revolving line of credit, which guarantees that the bank will honor the line of credit up to the stated amount.

| Characteristic | Debt | Equity |
|---|---|---|
| Maturity | **Specific:** Specifies a date by which it must be repaid. | **Nonspecific:** Specifies no maturity date. |
| Claim on income | **Fixed cost:** Company must pay interest on debt held by bondholders and lenders before paying any dividends to shareholders. Interest payments must be met regardless of operating results. | **Discretionary cost:** Shareholders may receive dividends after creditors have received interest payments; however, company is not required to pay dividends. |
| Claim on assets | **Priority:** Lenders have prior claims on assets. | **Residual:** Shareholders have claims only after the firm satisfies claims of lenders. |
| Influence over management | **Little:** Lenders are creditors, not owners. They can impose limits on management only if interest payments are not received. | **Varies:** As owners of the company, shareholders can vote on some aspects of corporate operations. Shareholder influence varies, depending on whether stock is widely distributed or closely held. |

**EXHIBIT 17.4**

Debt Versus Equity

When choosing between debt and equity financing, companies evaluate the characteristics of both types of funding.

Keep in mind that sometimes companies get into trouble by taking on too much debt. For example, when Quaker Oats unloaded Snapple for $300 million (after having plunked down a whopping $1.7 billion to purchase the brand from its creators less than three years earlier), the company recorded a $1.4 billion loss on the sale. Analysts estimate that Quaker lost $1.6 million for every day it owned Snapple because the net revenue generated from sales of the brand did not cover the costs of financing the acquisition.[4]

Rather than borrowing from a commercial lender to buy a piece of property or equipment, a firm may enter into a **lease,** under which the owner of an item allows another party to use it in exchange for regular payments. Leasing may be a good alternative for a company that has difficulty obtaining loans because of a poor credit rating. Creditors are more willing to provide a lease than a loan because, should the company fail, the lessor need not worry about a default on loan payments; it can simply repossess equipment it legally owns. Some firms use leases to finance up to 35 percent of their total assets, particularly in industries such as airlines, where assets are mostly large, expensive pieces of equipment.

When a company needs to borrow a large sum of money, it may not be able to get the entire amount from a single source. Under such circumstances, it may borrow from many individual investors by issuing *bonds*—certificates that obligate the company to repay a certain sum, plus interest, to the bondholder on a specific date. (Both bonds and stocks are traded on organized securities exchanges and are discussed in detail in Chapter 18.)

**>** video exercise

Take a moment to apply what you've learned.

## > The U.S. Financial System

Regardless of whether you finance your company's needs with debt, equity, or cash reserves, you will be interacting with financial institutions in a number of ways. The variety of financial institutions that operate within the U.S. banking environment can be classified into two broad categories: *deposit institutions* and *nondeposit institutions.* Deposit institutions accept deposits from customers or members and offer checking and savings accounts, loans, and other banking services. Among the many deposit institutions are the following:

- Commercial banks, which operate under state or national charters.

- Thrifts, including savings and loan associations (which use most of their deposits to make home mortgage loans) and mutual savings banks (which are owned by their depositors).

- Credit unions, which take deposits only from members, such as one company's employees or one union's members or another designated group.

Nondeposit institutions offer specific financial services but do not accept deposits. Among the many nondeposit institutions are the following:

- Insurance companies, which provide insurance coverage for life, property, and other potential losses; they invest the payments they receive in real estate, in construction projects, and in other ways.

- Pension funds, which are set up by companies to provide retirement benefits for employees; money contributed by the company and its employees is put into securities and other investments.

- Finance companies, which lend money to consumers and businesses for home improvements, expansion, purchases, and other purposes.

- Brokerage firms, which allow investors to buy and sell stocks, bonds, and other investments; many also offer checking accounts, high-paying savings accounts, and loans to buy securities. (Brokerage firms will be discussed more fully in Chapter 18.)

In the past, services such as checking, savings, and loans were not offered at all financial institutions; instead, each institution focused on offering a particular set of financial services for specific customer groups. However the competitive situation changed dramatically after the passage of the Depository Institutions Deregulation and Monetary Control Act of 1980. This law deregulated banking and made it possible for all financial institutions to offer a wider range of services—blurring the line between banks and other financial institutions and encouraging more competition between different types of institutions. Before we take a look at the changing U.S. banking environment, we must first discuss the types of traditional services offered by financial institutions.

### FINANCIAL SERVICES

No matter where in the world you live, work, or travel, today's businesses and individuals require a wide range of financial services. Banks of all sizes—from the largest multinational bank to the tiniest community bank—provide customers with a variety of financial services that include checking and savings accounts, loans, and credit, debit, and smart cards. Moreover, thanks to technological advances and Web sites such as Quicken.com, customers can now access their money and account information at any hour and from almost anywhere. Of course, the human touch is still a big part of banking. But in today's time-pressured world, more people want to handle banking transactions from different locations and at different times, not during traditional bankers' hours.

#### Checking and Savings Accounts

Money you put into your checking account is a *demand deposit,* available immediately (on demand) through the use of **checks,** written orders that direct your bank to pay the stated amount of money to you or to someone else. Banks traditionally paid no interest on money in checking accounts. Since the laws changed in 1980, however, financial institutions have been allowed to offer interest-bearing NOW checking accounts. Most NOW accounts limit the number of checks customers can write and impose a fee if the account balance falls below a minimum level.

You earn interest on the money you put away in savings accounts; credit unions typically pay slightly higher savings rates than commercial banks. Originally, these accounts were known as *passbook savings accounts* because customers received a small passbook in which the bank recorded all deposits, withdrawals, and interest. Today, banks send out statements instead of passbooks, so these accounts have become known as *statement savings accounts.* In general, money in savings accounts can be withdrawn at any time. Money in a *money-market deposit account* earns more interest, but you are allowed only a limited number of monthly withdrawals. Money held in a *certificate of deposit (CD)* earns an even higher interest rate, but you cannot withdraw the funds for a stated period, such as six months or more. If you want to make an early withdrawal from a CD, you will lose some or all of the interest you've earned.

### Loans

Banks are a major source of loans for customers who need money for a particular purpose. Individuals, for example, usually apply for mortgage loans when they want to buy a home. They also look to banks and financial services firms for auto loans, home-improvement loans, student loans, and many other types of loans. Businesses rely on banks to provide loans for expansion, purchases of new equipment, construction or renovation of plants and facilities, or other large-scale projects. Like consumers, businesses shop around to compare interest rates, fees, and repayment schedules before they take out a loan.

### Credit, Debit, and Smart Cards

For everyday access to short-term credit, banks issue **credit cards,** plastic cards that entitle customers to make purchases now and repay the loaned amount later. Many banks charge an annual fee for Visa and MasterCard credit cards, and all charge interest on any unpaid credit card balance. Nondeposit institutions such as American Express also issue credit cards.

Credit cards have become immensely popular with consumers because they are convenient and allow people to make purchases without cash. They also help people manage their finances by either choosing to repay the full amount when they are billed or making small payments month by month until the debt has been repaid. Credit card companies make money by charging customers interest on their unpaid account balances and by charging businesses a processing fee, which can range from 2 to 5 percent of the value of each sales transaction paid by credit card. Nearly every store accepts credit cards, and mail-order merchants and Internet retailers are especially dependent on credit cards to facilitate purchases.

In addition to credit cards, many banks offer **debit cards,** plastic cards that function like checks in that the amount of a purchase is electronically deducted from the user's checking account and is transferred to the retailer's account at the time of the sale. Debit cards are ideal for customers who must control their spending or stick to a budget. **Smart cards** are plastic cards with tiny computer chips that can store amounts of money (from the user's bank account) and selected data (such as shipping address, credit card information, frequent-flyer account numbers, health and insurance details, or other personal information). When a purchase is made, the store's equipment electronically deducts the amount from the value stored on the smart card and reads and verifies requisite customer information. Users reload money from their bank accounts to their smart cards as needed.

Although popular in Europe, smart cards have been slow to catch on in the United States for two reasons: Low U.S. telephone rates (compared to those of European countries) make it affordable to verify credit card transactions over the phone, and it is not cost-effective for most U.S. businesses to replace current credit card infrastructures with smart card readers and computer chip technology. Nevertheless, American Express has made inroads with its combination smart card and credit card, Blue. Designed to appeal to online shoppers, Blue comes with software and a small smart card reader that plugs into the user's serial port. Customers who purchase online simply insert Blue into the reader, type in a password, and the digital information stored on the smart card tells the vendor their credit card number, expiration date, and shipping address.[5]

> ## active exercise

**Take a moment to apply what you've learned.**

| | | Cost per transaction |
|---|---|---|
| | Bank with live teller | $1.07 |
| | Bank through debit card | .29 |
| | Bank through ATM | .27 |
| | Bank on the Internet | .04 |

**EXHIBIT 17.5**

Banking Transaction Costs

The average cost of having a teller handle a banking transaction is much higher than the cost for other ways of handling banking transactions. This is why banks want customers to bypass tellers whenever possible.

### Electronic Banking

Electronic banking includes various banking activities conducted from sites other than a physical bank location. For instance, all over the world, customers rely on **automated teller machines (ATMs)** to withdraw money from their demand-deposit accounts at any hour. In the United States, over 200,000 ATMs handle 11 billion electronic banking transactions every year. Look around: ATMs are everywhere, from banks, malls, and supermarkets to airports, resorts, and tourist attractions. By linking with regional, national, and international ATM networks, banks let customers withdraw cash far from home, make deposits, and handle other transactions. To compete, more banks are jazzing up their ATMs by allowing purchases of stamps, traveler's checks, movie tickets, ski lift tickets, and even foreign currency.[6]

**Electronic funds transfer systems (EFTS)** are another form of electronic banking. These computerized systems allow users to conduct financial transactions efficiently from remote locations. More than one-third of all U.S. workers take advantage of EFTS when their employers use *direct deposit* to transfer wages directly into employees' bank accounts. This procedure saves employers and employees the worry and headache of handling large amounts of cash.[7] Even the U.S. government uses EFTS for regular payments such as Social Security benefits.

In addition to automated teller machines and electronic funds transfer systems, most major banks and many thrifts and community banks now offer Internet or online banking to accommodate the growing number of individuals and businesses that want to transfer money between accounts, check account balances, pay bills, apply for loans, and handle other transactions at any hour. Online banking is not only fast and easy for customers but also extremely cost-efficient for banks (see Exhibit 17.5). But as discussed in this chapter's special feature, Focusing on E-Business Today, Internet banking has been slow to take off.[8]

## active exercise

**Take a moment to apply what you've learned.**

## THE EVOLVING U.S. BANKING ENVIRONMENT

Since the deregulation of the banking industry in 1980, financial institutions have changed radically in response to deregulation, competitive pressures, and financial problems. The most obvious evidence: industry consolidation and the repeal of the Glass-Steagall Act.

In 1934, there were 14,146 main bank offices in the United States; by 1999, the number had plummeted to only 8,581.[9] Seeking strength, efficiency, and access to more customers and markets, U.S. banks underwent a series of mergers, acquisitions, and takeovers during the 1980s and 1990s.

As banks and thrifts searched for higher profits in this competitive environment, some invested heavily in real estate and oil-drilling activities, loaned money to foreign governments, and financed company buyouts. Then the real estate market collapsed, oil prices plummeted, developers went bankrupt, and countries and companies hit hard by economic woes slowed or stopped payments on their loans. In many cases, failing institutions were taken over by stronger banks; in other cases, banks such as NationsBank and BankAmerica merged to cut costs and cover more territory with more services.

In 1999 Congress opened the floodgates for consolidation among banks, brokerage firms, and insurance companies by passing the 1999 Financial Services Modernization Act. This law repealed the Glass-Steagall Act (also known as the Banking Act of 1933) and portions of the 1956 Bank Holding Act, which for decades had kept banks out of the securities and insurance businesses. Originally enacted after the stock market crash of 1929 and the Great Depression, the Glass-Steagall Act was designed to restore confidence in U.S. financial houses by restricting investment banks and commercial banks from crossing into each others' businesses and potentially abusing their fiduciary duties at the expense of customers. Moreover, it ensured that a catastrophic failure in one part of the finance industry did not invade every other part, as it did in 1929. The 1956 Bank Holding Company Act restricted what banks could do in the insurance business.[10]

### Integration of Financial Services

The repeal of the Glass-Steagall Act and the lifting of other bank restrictions has fueled a raft of megamergers. Banks are combining with other banks and insurance companies to create financial supermarkets that offer customers a full range of services—from traditional loans to investment banking services to public stock offerings to insurance. The average U.S. resident now uses 15 banking and investment products (checking, credit cards, mortgage, mutual funds, life insurance, and so on) from five different companies. And financial supermarkets want to consolidate that scattered business into a single trusted brand name. For example, Merrill Lynch, a major brokerage firm, now offers federally insured interest-bearing savings and checking accounts among other bank products—in addition to securities trading. Similar offerings from other brokerage firms are expected.[11] Meanwhile, American Express has expanded beyond credit cards and now lends money to small businesses, Wal-Mart and E*Trade are purchasing banks, and tellers at Citibank are talking up mutual funds. Indeed, the line between brokers, bankers, and insurers is blurring beyond distinction.[12] And Scott Cook hopes that as competition heats up, customers will rely on Quicken.com for direction to the financial organization that will best match their particular needs at the most reasonable price.

### Community Banks and Interstate Banking

While consumer convenience, improved operating efficiencies, and integrated financial services are frequently cited as the chief benefits of industry consolidation, some worry that industry consolidation could concentrate too much power in large financial institutions. Others insist there will always be room for smaller, community banks.

*Community banks* are smaller banks that concentrate on serving the needs of local consumers and businesses. A number of factors are contributing to their increasing popularity. One is the void created by bank consolidations, which frequently lead to loan and other decisions being made by bank officials who are not local and don't know the applicants. Most community bankers, if they believe in a small business owner, will go out of their way to make a loan. They won't break the rules, but they might bend them a little. Moreover, community banks typically try to help their local customers by thinking creatively—offering customized services "that maybe a large branching operation just simply does not have the flexibility to do," explains Robert J. Wingert of the Community Bankers Association of Illinois. Another reason for their increasing popularity is that consolidations have made considerable talent available to start community banks. Finally, favorable economic conditions have also contributed to their resurgence.[13]

As community banks continue to operate in smaller, well-defined areas, midsize and larger banks have been expanding into new markets by opening branch operations or merging with banks across state lines. Such interstate operations were made possible by the Riegle-Neal Interstate Banking and Branching Efficiency Act of 1994, a landmark law that reversed legislation dating back to 1927.[14] As a result, customers can now make deposits, cash checks, or handle any banking transaction in any branch of their bank, regardless of location. Of course, banks benefit too. BankAmerica, for example, had to operate separate banking systems in 10 states until the Riegle-Neal Act was passed. Now the company can combine its banks under a single operating system to maximize efficiencies.[15] Looking beyond U.S. borders, BankAmerica and other banks have gone global with branches in many countries—just as foreign banks such as Japan's Dai-Ichi Kangyo Bank have long done business in the United States and around the world.

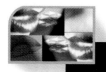

### BANK SAFETY AND REGULATION

Regardless of where or how you conduct your financial transactions, everyone (including Congress, regulators, and the financial community) worries about bank failure. As many as 9,000 U.S. banks failed during the Depression years from 1929 to 1934. In response to concerns about bank safety during that period, the government established the Federal Deposit Insurance Corporation (FDIC) to protect money in customer accounts. Today, money on deposit in U.S. banks is insured by the FDIC up to a maximum of $100,000 through the Savings Association Insurance Fund (for thrifts) and the Bank Insurance Fund (for commercial banks). Similarly, the National Credit Union Association protects deposits in credit unions.

In addition, a number of government agencies supervise and regulate banks. State-chartered banks come under the watchful eyes of each state's banking commission; nationally chartered banks are under the federal Office of the Comptroller of the Currency; and thrifts are under the federal Office of Thrift Supervision. The overall health of the country's banking system is, ultimately, the responsibility of the Federal Reserve System.

### > The Functions of the Federal Reserve System

The Federal Reserve System was created in 1913. Commonly known as the Fed, it is the most powerful financial institution in the United States, serving as the central bank. The Fed's primary role is to manage the money supply so that the country avoids both recession and inflation. It also supervises and regulates banks and serves as a clearinghouse for checks.

The Fed is a network of 12 district banks that controls the nation's banking system. The overall policy of the Fed is established by a seven-member board of governors who meet in Washington, D.C. To preserve the board's political independence, the members are appointed by the president to 14-year terms, staggered at two-year intervals. Although all national banks are required to be members of the Federal Reserve System, membership for state-chartered banks is optional. Still, the Fed exercises regulatory power over all deposit institutions, members and nonmembers alike. The Federal Reserve System has three major functions: influencing the U.S. money supply, supplying currency, and clearing checks.

### INFLUENCING THE U.S. MONEY SUPPLY

**Money** is anything generally accepted as a means of paying for goods and services. Before it was invented, people got what they needed by trading their services or possessions; in some societies, such as Russia, this system of trading, or bartering, still exists. However, barter is inconvenient and impractical in a global economy, where many of the things we want are intangible, come from places all over the world, and require the combined work of many people.

To be an effective medium of exchange, money must have these important characteristics: It must be divisible, portable (easy to carry), durable, and difficult to counterfeit; and it should have a stable value. In addition, money must perform three basic functions: First, it must serve as a medium of exchange—a tool for simplifying transactions between buyers and sellers. Second, it must serve as a measure of value so that you don't have to negotiate the relative worth of dissimilar items every time you buy something. Finally, money must serve as a temporary store of value—a way of accumulating your wealth until you need it.

The Fed's main job is to establish and implement *monetary policy*, guidelines for handling the nation's economy and the money supply. The U.S. money supply has three major components:

- **Currency:** Money in the form of coins, bills, traveler's checks, cashier's checks, and money orders
- **Demand deposit:** Money available immediately on demand, such as checking accounts
- **Time deposits:** Accounts that pay interest and restrict the owner's right to withdraw funds on short notice, such as savings accounts, certificates of deposit, and money-market deposit accounts

The Fed influences the money supply to make certain that enough money and credit are available to fuel a healthy economy. However, it must act carefully, because altering the money supply affects interest rates, inflation, and the economy. When the money supply is increased, more money is available for loans, so banks can charge lower interest rates to borrowers. On the other hand, an increased money supply can lead to more consumer spending and can result in the demand for goods exceeding supply. When demand exceeds supply, sellers may raise their prices, leading to inflation. In turn, inflation can slow economic growth—a situation the Fed wants to avoid. And, because so many companies now buy and sell across national borders, the Fed's changes may affect the interlinked economies of many countries, not just the United States.[16] That's why the Fed moves cautiously and keeps a close eye on the size of the money supply.

### How the Money Supply Is Measured

To get a rough idea of the size of the money supply, the Fed looks at various combinations of currency, demand deposits, and time deposits (see Exhibit 17.6). The narrowest measure, **M1,** consists of currency, demand deposits, and NOW accounts that are common forms of payment. **M2,** a broader measure of the money supply, includes M1 plus savings deposits, money-market funds, and time deposits under $100,000. **M3,** the broadest measure of the money supply, includes M2 plus time deposits of $100,000 and higher and other restricted deposits.

### Tools for Influencing the Money Supply

The Fed can use four basic tools to influence the money supply:

- *Changing the reserve requirement.* All financial institutions must set aside *reserves,* sums of money equal to a certain percentage of their deposits. The Fed can change the **reserve requirement,** the

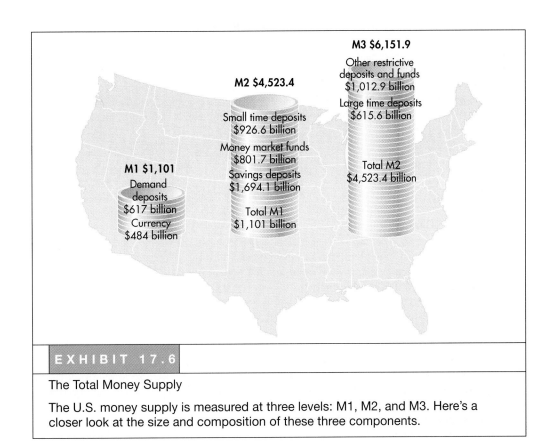

**EXHIBIT 17.6**

The Total Money Supply

The U.S. money supply is measured at three levels: M1, M2, and M3. Here's a closer look at the size and composition of these three components.

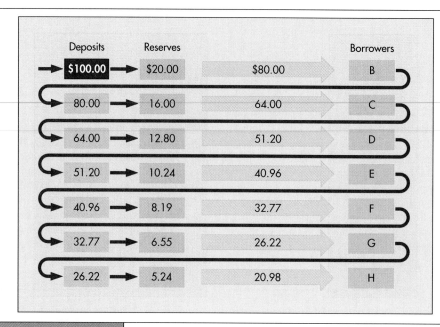

| Deposits | Reserves | | Borrowers |
|---|---|---|---|
| $100.00 | $20.00 | $80.00 | B |
| 80.00 | 16.00 | 64.00 | C |
| 64.00 | 12.80 | 51.20 | D |
| 51.20 | 10.24 | 40.96 | E |
| 40.96 | 8.19 | 32.77 | F |
| 32.77 | 6.55 | 26.22 | G |
| 26.22 | 5.24 | 20.98 | H |

## EXHIBIT 17.7

### How Banks Create Money

Banks stay in business by earning more on interest from loans than they pay out in the form of interest on deposits; they can increase their earnings by "creating" money. When customer A deposits $100, the bank must keep some in reserve but can lend, say, $80 to customer B (and earn interest on that loan). If customer B deposits the borrowed $80 in the same bank, the bank can lend 80 percent of *that* amount to borrower C. The initial $100 deposit therefore creates a much larger pool of funds from which customer loans may be made.

percentage of deposits that banks must set aside, to influence the money supply. However, the Fed rarely uses this technique because a small change can have a drastic effect. Increasing the reserve requirement slows down the economy: Banks have less money to lend, so businesses can't borrow to expand and consumers can't borrow to buy goods and services. Conversely, reducing this requirement boosts the economy, because banks have more money to lend to businesses and consumers (see Exhibit 17.7).

- *Changing the discount rate.* The Fed can also change the discount rate, the interest rate it charges on loans to commercial banks and other depository institutions. When the Fed raises the discount rate, member banks generally raise the prime interest rate. Thus, raising the discount rate discourages loans, and in so doing tightens the money supply, which can slow down economic growth. By contrast, lowering the discount rate results in lower lending rates, which can encourage more borrowing and stimulate economic growth.

- *Conducting open-market operations.* The tool the Fed uses most often to influence the money supply is the power to buy and sell U.S. government bonds. Because anyone can buy these bonds on the open market, this tool is known as **open-market operations.** If the Fed is concerned about inflation, it can reduce the money supply by selling U.S. government bonds, which takes cash out of circulation. And when the Fed wants to boost the economy, it can buy back government bonds, putting cash into circulation and increasing the money supply.

- *Establishing selective credit controls.* The Fed can also use **selective credit controls** to set the terms of credit for various kinds of loans. This tool includes the power to set *margin requirements,* the percentage of the purchase price that an investor must pay in cash when purchasing a stock or a bond on credit. By altering the margin requirements, the Fed is able to influence how much cash is tied up in stock market transactions.

Exhibit 17.8 summarizes the effects of using these four tools.

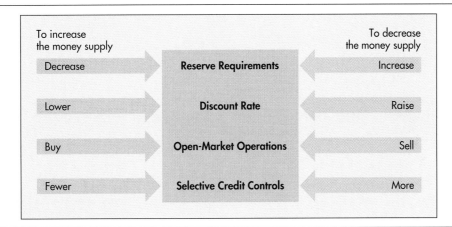

| To increase the money supply | | To decrease the money supply |
| --- | --- | --- |
| Decrease | **Reserve Requirements** | Increase |
| Lower | **Discount Rate** | Raise |
| Buy | **Open-Market Operations** | Sell |
| Fewer | **Selective Credit Controls** | More |

**EXHIBIT 17.8**

Influencing the Money Supply

The Federal Reserve uses four tools to influence the money supply as it attempts to stimulate economic growth while keeping inflation and interest rates at acceptable levels.

> active exercise

**Take a moment to apply what you've learned.**

## SUPPLYING CURRENCY AND CLEARING CHECKS

The second function of the Fed is to supply currency to keep the U.S. financial system running smoothly. Regional Federal Reserve Banks are responsible for providing member banks with adequate amounts of currency throughout the year. For example, in preparation for potential disruptions due to year-2000 computer problems, the Fed was ready to provide U.S. banks with another $50 billion in cash.[17]

Another function of the Federal Reserve is to act as a clearinghouse for checks. Today, money on deposit in banks or other financial institutions is recorded in computerized ledger entries. When a customer deposits or cashes a check drawn on a bank in another city or town, the customer's bank uses the Fed's check-processing system to clear the check and receive payment. In clearing this check, the Fed's computer system charges and credits the appropriate accounts. Exhibit 17.9 shows the operation of this automated clearinghouse function, which is invisible yet indispensable to consumers and businesses. Keep in mind that a number of factors are contributing to the decline in check usage. These include increased use of electronic payments, direct payroll deposits, direct drafts from consumer bank accounts, credit and debit cards, and online banking.

> active concept check

**Now let's take a moment to test your knowledge of the concepts you have studied in this section.**

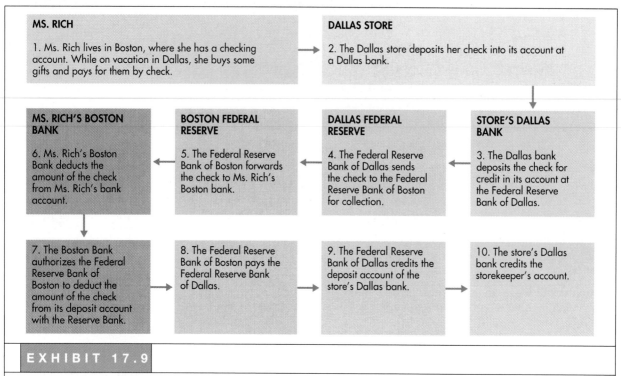

**MS. RICH**

1. Ms. Rich lives in Boston, where she has a checking account. While on vacation in Dallas, she buys some gifts and pays for them by check.

**DALLAS STORE**

2. The Dallas store deposits her check into its account at a Dallas bank.

**MS. RICH'S BOSTON BANK**

6. Ms. Rich's Boston Bank deducts the amount of the check from Ms. Rich's bank account.

**BOSTON FEDERAL RESERVE**

5. The Federal Reserve Bank of Boston forwards the check to Ms. Rich's Boston bank.

**DALLAS FEDERAL RESERVE**

4. The Federal Reserve Bank of Dallas sends the check to the Federal Reserve Bank of Boston for collection.

**STORE'S DALLAS BANK**

3. The Dallas bank deposits the check for credit in its account at the Federal Reserve Bank of Dallas.

7. The Boston Bank authorizes the Federal Reserve Bank of Boston to deduct the amount of the check from its deposit account with the Reserve Bank.

8. The Federal Reserve Bank of Boston pays the Federal Reserve Bank of Dallas.

9. The Federal Reserve Bank of Dallas credits the deposit account of the store's Dallas bank.

10. The store's Dallas bank credits the storekeeper's account.

**EXHIBIT 17.9**

How the Fed Clears Checks

The Federal Reserve acts as a clearinghouse for checks in the United States. This example shows how the Fed clears a check that has been drawn on a bank in one city but deposited by a store into a bank in another city.

## > Chapter Wrap-Up

Now that you've reached the end of the chapter, you may wish to explore the concepts you've been reading about in greater detail, or test yourself to see how well you've comprehended the material. In the box below you'll find a number of links. Click on any one of these links to find additional chapter resources.

### > end-of-chapter resources

- **Summary of Learning Objectives**
- **Practice Quiz**
- **Focusing on E-Business Today**
- **Key Terms**
- **Test Your Knowledge**
- **Practice Your Knowledge**
- **Expand Your Knowledge**
- **A Case for Critical Thinking**

# C H A P T E R  1 8

# Securities

 ## What's Ahead

### INSIDE BUSINESS TODAY
### TRICKS OF E*TRADE

In the early 1980s, Bill Porter was running a thriving business, providing Charles Schwab and other brokerage firms with electronic stock quotes and trading services. A physicist and inventor, Porter began to wonder why he and other individual investors had to pay brokers hundreds of dollars each time they bought or sold stocks, bonds, and mutual funds. Although personal computing was still in its infancy, he envisioned a more efficient, more direct method of placing trades directly from his PC keyboard. By 1992 Porter had translated his vision into E*Trade Securities, an all-electronic brokerage firm accessed through America Online and CompuServe. But E*Trade did not really take off until 1996, when the fledgling brokerage firm launched its multifaceted Web site, making online securities trading accessible and affordable for all Internet users.

E*Trade was at the forefront of a growing movement toward online investing, fueled in part by a healthy U.S. economy and by investors eager to participate in U.S. securities markets that were trending upward and setting record highs. Forecasts indicated that millions of investors would soon be trading online, and Porter wanted E*Trade to capture a large share of this fast-growing market.

Unlike traditional full-service brokers, E*Trade did not offer extensive research reports written by experts who investigated specific stocks and bonds in detail. And it did not offer the constant hand-holding of a personal broker. What it did offer was a quick, easy, and inexpensive way to buy and sell securities over the Internet. Investors who knew exactly what they wanted

To capture a large share of the fast-growing online trade market, E*Trade's CEO, Christos Cotsakos, has to juggle a variety of challenges.

could simply go to the E*Trade Web site, then point and click to make trades—paying a fraction of the commissions charged by full-service brokers.

In 1996, to build E*Trade into a world-class brokerage firm, Porter brought in Christos Cotsakos, a former executive with Federal Express and A.C. Nielsen. Under Cotsakos's leadership, the company launched an aggressive multimillion-dollar ad campaign, using the tagline "Someday we'll all invest this way," and enhanced E*Trade's services by offering customers personalized Web screens, online securities research, and more. In just a few years, E*Trade became an online investing powerhouse with 1.9 million accounts. But it wasn't long before Schwab, TD Waterhouse, Merrill Lynch, and Morgan Stanley Dean Witter copied E*Trade's e-broker strategy.

So to keep a competitive edge, Cotsakos changed E*Trade's course. While the big guys were busy adding the clicks, E*Trade got physical. In 2000 E*Trade purchased thousands of ATMs from Credit Capture Services, opened the first of 200 planned bricks-and-mortar outlets called E*Trade Zone in a SuperTarget discount store, and announced plans to open an old-fashioned 30,000-square-foot New York retail outlet—one with helpful salesclerks, kiosks, and reams of marketing material.

"Pushing our brand into the real world is the next evolution for E*Trade," explains one E*Trade officer. And Cotsakos plans on doing just that by turning E*Trade into a financial supermarket—a place where people can handle all their personal financial needs. Still, big questions linger. With more competitors and financial-services companies saying, "If you want cheaper trading you can get it from us," Cotsakos will have to decide whether E*Trade should go it alone or merge with the kind of old-line financial services that have been the target of E*Trade's humorous ads.[1]

> # objectives

> # gearing up

> ## Types of Securities Investments

As Christos Cotsakos knows, **securities**—stocks, bonds, options, futures, commodities, and other investments—are much in the news these days. Look at the business section of any newspaper or magazine, and you'll read about a corporation selling stocks or bonds to finance operations or expansion. In the same way, governments and municipalities issue bonds to raise money for building or public expenses—from national defense to road improvements. These securities are traded in organized markets where investors (individuals and institutions) can buy and sell them to meet their investment goals.

### STOCKS

As you saw in Chapter 5, a share of stock represents ownership in a corporation; it is evidenced by a stock certificate. If you are a shareholder—someone who owns stock—you may vote on important issues but you have no say in day-to-day business activities. You and other shareholders have the advantage of limited liability if the corporation gets into trouble. At the same time, as part owners, you share in the fortunes of the business and are eligible to receive dividends as long as you hold the stock.

Stock certificates issued to shareholders often include a **par value,** a dollar value assigned to the stock primarily for bookkeeping purposes and (for certain kinds of stock) for use in calculating dividends. Don't confuse par value with a stock's *market value,* the price at which a share currently sells, or its *book value,* the amount of net assets of a corporation represented by one share of common stock.

The number of stock shares a company sells depends on the amount of equity capital the company will require and on the price of each share it sells. A corporation's board of directors sets a maximum number of shares into which the business can be divided. In theory, all these shares—called **authorized stock**—may be sold at once. In practice, however, the company sells only a part of its authorized stock. The part sold and held by shareholders is called **issued stock;** the unsold portion is called **unissued stock.** Common stock is one of two classes of stock an investor can buy; the other is preferred stock.

### Common Stock

Most investors buy common stock, which represents an ownership interest in a publicly traded corporation. As discussed in Chapter 5, shareholders of this class of stock vote to elect the company's board of directors, vote on other important corporate issues, and receive dividends—payments from the company's profits. In addition, they stand to make a profit if the stock price goes up and they sell their shares for more than the purchase price. The reverse is also true: shareholders of common stock can lose money if the market price drops and they sell the stock for less than they paid for it.

From time to time a company may announce a **stock split,** in which it increases the number of shares that each stock certificate represents while proportionately lowering the value of each share. Companies generally use a stock split to make the share price more affordable. For instance, if a company with 1 million shares outstanding and a stock price of $50 per share announces a two-for-one split, it is doubling the number of shares. After the split, the company will have 2 million shares outstanding, and each original share will become two shares worth $25 each.

A special type of common stock is *tracking stock,* shares linked to the performance of a specific business unit of a public corporation. This type of stock allows a company to wring top market value from an attractive business unit as if it were an independent company. From the investor's perspective, tracking stock is a convenient way to own part of this business unit while taking advantage of the parent's financial stability. But tracking stocks are risky, as "Are Tracking Stocks on Track?" points out. Conservative investors often prefer **blue-chip stock,** stock in a corporation such as General Electric that is well established and has a long record of solid earnings and dividends.

### Preferred Stock

Investors who own preferred stock, the second major class of stock, enjoy higher dividends and a better claim (after creditors) on assets if the corporation fails. The amount of the dividend on preferred stock is printed on the stock certificate and set when the stock is first issued. If interest rates fluctuate, the market price of preferred stock will go up or down to adjust for the difference between the market interest rate and the stock's dividend.

Preferred stock often comes with special privileges. *Convertible preferred stock* can be exchanged, if the shareholder chooses, for a certain number of shares of common stock issued by the company. *Cumulative preferred stock* has an additional advantage: If the issuing company stops paying dividends for any reason, the dividends on these shares will be held (accumulate) until preferred shareholders have been paid in full—before common stockholders are paid.

# active exercise ◄

## Take a moment to apply what you've learned.

## BONDS

Unlike stock, which gives the investor an ownership stake in the corporation, bonds are debt financing. (See Chapter 17 for a detailed discussion of debt versus equity financing.) A **bond** is a method of raising money in which the issuing organization borrows from an investor and issues a written pledge to make regular interest payments and then repay the borrowed amount later. When you invest in this type of security, you are lending money to the company, municipality, or government agency that issued the bond. Bonds are usually issued in multiples of $1,000, such as $5,000, $10,000 and $50,000. Also like stocks, bonds are evidenced by a certificate, which shows the issuer's name, the amount borrowed (the **principal**), the date this principal amount will be repaid, and the annual interest rate investors receive.

The interest is stated in terms of an annual percentage rate but is usually paid at 6-month intervals. For example, the holder of a $1,000 bond that pays 8 percent interest due January 15 and July 15 could expect to receive $40 on each of those dates. A look at the financial section of any newspaper will show that some corporations sell new bonds at an interest rate two or three percentage points higher than that offered by other companies. Yet the terms of the bonds seem similar. Why? Because bonds are not guaranteed investments. The variations in interest rates reflect the degree of risk associated with the bond, which is closely tied to the financial stability of the issuing company. Agencies such as Standard & Poor's (S&P) and Moody's rate bonds on the basis of the issuers' financial strength. Exhibit 18.1 shows that the safest corporate bonds are rated AAA (S&P) and Aaa (Moody's). Low-rated bonds, known as *junk bonds,* pay higher interest rates to compensate investors for the higher risk.

### Corporate Bonds

*Corporate bonds*—those issued by companies—are big business. The New York Stock Exchange lists more corporate bonds than stocks, and the market value of all outstanding corporate bonds exceeds $2 trillion.[2]

Corporate bonds are issued in a variety of types. **Secured bonds** are backed by company-owned property (such as airplanes or plant equipment) that will pass to the bondholders if the issuer does not repay the amount borrowed. *Mortgage bonds,* one type of secured bond, are backed by real property owned by the issuing corporation. **Debentures** are unsecured bonds, backed only by the corporation's promise to pay. Because debentures are riskier than other types of bonds, investors who buy these bonds receive higher interest rates. **Convertible bonds** can be exchanged at the investor's option for a certain number of shares of the corporation's common stock. Because of this feature, convertible bonds generally pay lower interest rates.

| S&P | Interpretation | Moody's | Interpretation |
|---|---|---|---|
| AAA | Highest rating | Aaa | Prime quality |
| AA | Very strong capacity to pay | Aa | High grade |
| A | Strong capacity to pay; somewhat susceptible to changing business conditions | A | Upper-medium grade |
| BBB | More susceptible than A rated bonds | Baa | Medium grade |
| BB | Somewhat speculative | Ba | Somewhat speculative |
| B | Speculative | B | Speculative |
| CCC | Vulnerable to nonpayment | Caa | Poor standing; may be in default |
| CC | Highly vulnerable to nonpayment | Ca | Highly speculative; often in default |
| C | Bankruptcy petition filed or similar action taken | C | Lowest rated; extremely poor chance of ever attaining real investment standing |
| D | In default | | |

**EXHIBIT 18.1**

Corporate Bond Ratings

Standard & Poor's (S&P) and Moody's Investors Service are two companies that rate the safety of corporate bonds. When its bonds receive a low rating, a company must pay a higher interest rate to compensate investors for the higher risk.

### U.S. Government Securities and Municipal Bonds

Just as corporations raise money by issuing bonds, so too do federal, state, city, and local governments and agencies. As an investor, you can buy a variety of U.S. government securities, including three types of bonds issued by the U.S. Treasury, U.S. savings bonds, and bonds issued by various U.S. municipalities.

**Treasury bills** (also referred to as T-bills) are short-term U.S. government bonds that are repaid in less than one year. Treasury bills are sold at a discount and redeemed at face value. The difference between the purchase price and the redemption price is, in effect, the interest earned for the time periods. **Treasury notes** are intermediate-term U.S. government bonds that are repaid from 1 to 10 years after they were initially issued. **Treasury bonds** are long-term U.S. government bonds that are repaid more than 10 years after they were initially issued. In total, investors worldwide hold about $3.5 trillion in these three types of securities. Both treasury notes and treasury bonds pay a fixed amount of interest twice a year. But in general, U.S. government securities pay lower interest than corporate bonds because they are considered safer: There is very little risk that the government will fail to repay bondholders as promised. Another benefit is that investors pay no state or local income tax on interest earned on these bonds. Also, these bonds can easily be bought or sold through the Treasury or in organized securities markets.

A traditional choice for many individual investors, **U.S. savings bonds** are issued by the U.S. government in amounts ranging from $50 to $10,000. Investors who buy Series EE savings bonds pay just 50 percent of the stated value and receive the full face amount in as little as 17 years (the difference being earned interest). Once the bond's face value equals its redemption value, the bond continues to earn interest, but only until 30 years after the bonds were issued (the bond's final maturity date). Other savings bonds are Series HH, which can be bought only by exchanging Series EE bonds, and Series I, which pay interest indexed to the inflation rate.

**Municipal bonds** (often called *munis*) are issued by states, cities, and special government agencies to raise money for public services such as building schools, highways, and airports. Investors can buy two types of municipal bonds: general obligation bonds and revenue bonds. A **general obligation bond** is a municipal bond backed by the taxing power of the issuing government. When interest payments

Bell South Telecommunications Bond Certificate: (1) name of corporation issuing bond; (2) type of bond (debenture); (3) face value of the bond; (4) annual interest rate (8.25%); (5) maturity date (due 2032).

come due, the issuer makes payments out of its tax receipts. In contrast, a **revenue bond** is a municipal bond backed by the money to be generated by the project being financed. As an example, revenue bonds issued by a city airport are paid from revenues raised by the airport's operation. To encourage investment, the federal government doesn't tax the interest that investors receive from municipal bonds. Also exempt from state income tax is the interest earned on municipal bonds that are issued by the governments within the taxpayer's home state. However, **capital gains**—the return investors get from selling a security for more than its purchase price—are taxed at both the federal and state levels.

### Retirement of Debt

Issuers of bonds must eventually repay the borrowed amount to their bondholders. Normally, this is done when the bonds mature—say, 10, 15, or 20 years after the bond is issued. The cost of retiring the debt can be staggering because bonds are generally issued in large quantities—perhaps thousands of individual bonds in a single issue. To ease the cash flow burden of redeeming its bonds all at once, a company sometimes issues *serial bonds,* which mature at various times, as opposed to *term bonds,* which mature all at the same time.

Another way of relieving the financial strain of retiring many bonds all at once is to set up a **sinking fund.** When a corporation issues a bond payable by a sinking fund, it must set aside a certain sum of money each year to pay the debt. This money may be used to retire a few bonds each year, or it may be set aside to accumulate until the issue matures.

With most bond issues, a corporation retains the right to pay off the bonds before maturity. Bonds containing this provision are known as *callable bonds,* or *redeemable bonds.* If a company issues bonds when interest rates are high and interest rates fall later on, it may want to pay off its high-interest bonds and sell a new issue at a lower rate. However, this feature carries a price tag: Investors must be offered a higher interest rate to encourage them to buy callable bonds. The portion of the percentage rate that is above market rates is actually a "call premium."

## active exercise

### Take a moment to apply what you've learned.

## OTHER INVESTMENTS

Stocks and bonds are the most common marketable securities available for investors. However, other securities have been developed. For the most part, options, financial futures, commodities, and their variations are used by money managers and savvy traders. In recent years, some of these securities, particularly options, have been used more by individual investors.

### Options and Financial Futures

As Chapter 11 points out, a stock option is the purchased right—but not the obligation—to buy or sell a specified number of shares of a stock at a predetermined price during a specified period. Options can be used for wild speculation, or they can be used to **hedge** your positions—that is, partially protect against the risk of a sudden loss. By trading options, the investor doesn't have to own shares of stock in a company—only an option to buy or sell those shares. Investors who trade stock options are betting that the price of the stock will either rise or fall. The cost of buying an option on shares of stock is only the premium paid to the seller, or the price of the option.

All options fall into two broad categories: *puts* and *calls*. Exhibit 18.2 explains the rights acquired with each type of option. **Financial futures** are similar to options, but they are legally binding contracts to buy or sell a financial instrument (stocks, Treasury bonds, foreign currencies) for a set price at a future date.

### Commodities

For the investor who is comfortable with risky investments, nothing compares with speculating in **commodities**—raw materials and agricultural products, such as petroleum, gold, coffee beans, pork bellies, beef, and coconut oil. Commodities markets originally sprang up as a convenience for buyers and sellers interested in trading the actual commodities. A manufacturer of breakfast cereals, for example, must buy wheat, rye, oats, and sugar from hundreds of farmers. The easiest way to arrange these transactions is to meet in a forum where many buyers and sellers come to trade. Because the commodities are too bulky to bring to the marketplace, the traders buy and sell contracts for delivery of a given amount of these raw materials at a given time.

Trading contracts for immediate delivery of a commodity is called *spot trading,* or *cash trading.* Most commodity trading is for future delivery, usually months in advance, sometimes a year or more; this is called *trading commodities futures.* The original purpose of futures trading was to allow producers and consumers of commodities to hedge their position, or protect themselves against violent price swings. For example, say you're a cattle rancher in Montana and each month you purchase 20,000 bushels of feed corn. A big rise in corn prices resulting from a flood in the Midwest could ruin you. To hedge against such risk, you purchase futures contracts guaranteeing

| Right | Buyer's Belief | Seller's Belief |
|---|---|---|
| | **CALL OPTION** | |
| The right to buy the stock at a fixed price until the expiration date. | Buyer believes price of underlying stock will increase. Buyer can buy stock at a set price and sell it at higher price for a capital gain. | Seller believes price of underlying stock will decline and that the option will not be exercised. Seller earns a premium. |
| | **PUT OPTION** | |
| The right to sell the stock at a fixed price until the expiration date. | Buyer believes price of underlying stock will decline and wants to lock in a fixed profit. Buyer usually already owns shares of underlying stock. | Seller believes price of underlying stock will rise and that the option will not be exercised. Seller earns a premium. |

**EXHIBIT 18.2**

Options

All options fall into two broad categories: puts and calls.

you 20,000 bushels of corn at a given price when you need them at a later date. Now you know what you'll have to pay. But for every hedger, there must be a speculator—a person willing to take on the risk the hedger wants to shed. The person on the other end of your corn trade probably has no business interest in corn or cattle; the speculator simply wants to gamble on buying an offsetting corn contract at a lower price and thus make a profit on the deal.[3] But such speculation is risky—even seasoned veterans have been known to lose literally millions of dollars within a few days.

## active concept check <

**Now let's take a moment to test your knowledge of the concepts you have studied in this section.**

## > Investors and Investing

Whether you are a corporation or an individual, investing means putting your money to work to earn more money. Done wisely, it can help you meet your financial goals. But investing means you have to make decisions about how much you want to invest and where to invest it. To choose wisely, you need to know what options you have and what risks they entail.

### INSTITUTIONAL AND PRIVATE INVESTORS

Two types of investors buy and sell marketable securities (investments that can easily be converted to cash): institutions and individuals. **Institutional investors**—such as pension funds, insurance companies, investment companies, banks, and colleges and universities—dominate U.S. securities markets. Institutional investors buy and sell securities in large quantities, often in blocks of at least 10,000 shares per transaction. Because institutions have such large pools of money to work with, their investment decisions have a major impact on the marketability of a company's shares as well as the overall behavior of the securities markets.

### INVESTMENT OBJECTIVES

Many investors seek the highest **yield** or return to supplement their income. Yield on a stock is calculated by dividing the stock's dividends by its annualized market price. Some investors want to make a large profit in a short period of time. Others may be looking for a long-term steady return to fund retirement activities or provide money to send their children to college. In general, people make investment decisions on the basis of five criteria: *income, growth, safety, liquidity,* and *tax consequences.*

If an investor wants a steady, reasonably predictable flow of cash, he or she will seek an investment that provides fixed or dividend income. Fixed income investments include certificates of deposit, government securities, corporate bonds, and preferred stocks. A retired person wanting to supplement Social Security or pension benefits would be a customer for this type of investment.

Many investors are concerned with wealth accumulation, or growth. Their objective is to maximize capital gains. **Growth stocks** are issued by younger and smaller companies such as E*Trade that have strong growth potential. These companies normally pay no dividends because they reinvest earnings in the company to expand operations. High-growth stocks attract a breed of investors who buy stocks with rapidly accelerating earnings and sell them on the tiniest of disappointments over a company's prospects. For this reason, they are considered the most *volatile* in the market—that is, their stock prices tend to rise more quickly, but they can fall just as quickly.

Safety is another concern. Generally, the higher the potential for income or growth, the greater the risk of the investment. **Speculators** are investors who accept high risks in order to realize large capital gains. Of course, every investor must make some kind of trade-off. This is true for all investments. Government bonds are safer than corporate bonds, which are safer than common stocks, which are safer than futures contracts, which are safer than commodities.

Keep in mind that before you get too caught up in focusing on your own assessment of a specific security, you need to understand what other investors are thinking. You may see an abundance of value, or substantial growth potential, but if other investors don't share your view, your insights won't do you much good. The market is a voting machine, whereon countless individuals register choices—sometimes based on reason and sometimes based on emotion.[4]

Two additional investment objectives you should consider when selecting investments are liquidity and tax consequences. Liquidity is the measure of how quickly an investor can change an investment into cash. For example, common stock is more liquid than real estate; most financial assets can be changed into cash within a day. Some, like certificates of deposit, can be cashed in before maturity, but only after paying a penalty. All investors must consider the tax consequences of their decisions. Historically, dividend and interest income have been taxed heavily, and capital gains have been taxed relatively lightly. Also, as stated earlier in the discussion of municipal bonds, the income from most state and local municipal bonds is exempt from federal income tax.

## INVESTMENT PORTFOLIO

No single investment instrument will provide income, growth, and a high degree of safety. For this reason, all investors—whether institutions or individuals—build **investment portfolios,** or collections of various types of investments. Money managers and financial advisers are often asked to determine which investments should be in an investor's portfolio and to buy and sell securities and maintain the client's portfolio. Sometimes they must structure a portfolio to provide a desired **rate of return,** the percentage of gain or interest yield on investments.

### Asset Allocation and Diversification

Managing a portfolio to gain the highest rates of return while reducing risk as much as possible is known as **asset allocation.** A portion of the portfolio might be devoted to cash instruments such as money-market mutual funds, a portion to income instruments such as government and corporate bonds, and a portion to equities (mainly common stock). The money manager then determines how much each portion should be, on the basis of economic and market conditions—not an easy task. If the economy is booming and the stock market is performing well, the money manager might take advantage of the good environment by shifting 75 percent of the total portfolio into stocks, 20 percent into bonds, and 5 percent into cash. If the economy turns bad, the stock market heads downward, and inflation heats up, the money manager might readjust the portfolio and invest 30 percent in stocks, 40 percent in short-term government securities, and 30 percent in cash. This adjustment helps protect the value of the portfolio during poor investment conditions.[5]

Another major concern for these managers is **diversification**—reducing the risk of loss in a client's total portfolio by investing funds in several different securities so that a loss experienced by any one will not hurt the entire portfolio. One way to diversify is by investing in securities from unrelated industries and a variety of countries. Another way is by allocating your assets among different investment types. Both of these goals can be accomplished by investing in mutual funds.

### Mutual Funds

**Mutual funds** are financial organizations that pool money from many investors to buy a diversified mix of stocks, bonds, or other securities. These funds are particularly well suited for investors who wish to spread a fixed amount of money over a variety of investments and do not have the time or experience to search out and manage investment opportunities. *No-load* funds charge no fee to buy or sell shares, whereas *load funds* charge investors a commission to buy or sell shares. The most common types of loads are front end (assessed when you purchase the fund) and back end (assessed when you sell the fund).

Investment companies offer two types of mutual funds. An *open-end fund* issues additional shares as new investors ask to buy them. In essence, the fund's books never close. The number of shares outstanding changes daily as investors buy new shares or redeem old ones. These shares aren't traded in a separate market. *Closed-end funds,* on the other hand, raise all their money at once by distributing a fixed number of shares that trade much like stocks on major security exchanges. As soon as a certain number of shares are sold, the fund closes its books.

Various mutual funds have different investment priorities. Among the most popular mutual funds are **money-market funds,** which invest in short-term securities and other liquid investments. *Growth funds* invest in stocks of rapidly growing companies. *Income funds* invest in securities that pay high dividends and interest. *Balanced funds* invest in a carefully chosen mix of stocks and bonds. *Sector funds* (also known as specialty or industry funds) invest in companies within a particular industry. *Global funds* invest in foreign and U.S. securities, whereas *international funds* invest strictly in foreign securities. And *index funds* buy stocks in companies included in specific market averages, such as the Standard & Poor's 500. You can buy shares in mutual funds through your broker or directly from the mutual fund company.

## active poll

**What do you think? Voice your opinion and find out what others have to say.**

## active concept check

**Now let's take a moment to test your knowledge of the concepts you have studied in this section.**

---

> ### Securities Markets

Where can you purchase bonds, stocks, and other securities? Stocks and bonds are bought and sold in two kinds of marketplaces: primary markets and secondary markets. As discussed in Chapter 5, corporations sell their stock to the public to generate funds for expansion or other purposes. Newly issued shares or initial public offerings (IPOs) are sold in the **primary market.** Once these shares have been issued, subsequent investors can buy and sell them in the organized **secondary market** known as **stock exchanges** (or securities exchanges).

### SECURITIES EXCHANGES

The New York Stock Exchange (NYSE), also known as the "Big Board," is the world's largest securities exchange. The stocks and bonds of about 2,900 companies, with a combined market value topping $12 trillion, are traded on the exchange's floor.[6] Options, futures, and closed-end funds are also traded there. After the NYSE, some of the largest stock exchanges are located in Tokyo, London, Frankfurt, Paris, Toronto, and Montreal. Many companies list their securities on more than one securities exchange. Thus, NYSE-listed stocks can also be bought and sold at one or more of the U.S. regional exchanges, such as the Pacific or Philadelphia exchanges, or in the *over-the-counter market.*

The **over-the-counter (OTC) market** consists of a network of registered stock and bond representatives who are spread out across the United States—and in some cases around the world. Most use a nationwide computer network owned by the National Association of Securities Dealers (NASD). This network is called **NASDAQ (National Association of Securities Dealers Automated Quotations).** NASDAQ, which now represents a total market value of about $4.8 trillion, is home to many of the world's leading technology firms—Microsoft, Intel, Oracle, and a host of others. This chips-and-code crowd is largely responsible for NASDAQ's huge daily trading volume, which frequently surpasses the NYSE even though the total market value of the shares listed on the NYSE is about three times larger than the total market value of shares listed on the NASDAQ.[7] In 1998 NASD (owners of NASDAQ) acquired the American Stock Exchange (the world's third-largest auction exchange), making NASDAQ an even stronger competitor.[8]

### Listing Requirements

To have its stock traded on a securities exchange, a publicly held company must become a member of the exchange and meet certain listing requirements related to net income, the number of shares outstanding, and the total market value of all outstanding shares—its *market capitalization.* These listing requirements differ from exchange to exchange but generally increase as one moves from the NASDAQ to the regional exchanges to the larger New York Stock Exchange. For example, as of 2000, the minimum NASDAQ listing requirements were 1.1 million shares outstanding with a minimum bid price of $1.00 and net tangible assets valued at $6 million. By contrast the minimum listing requirements for the American Stock Exchange was 500,000 public shares with a total minimum capitalization value of $3 million, whereas a listing on the NYSE required 1.1 million shares with a total minimum capitalization value of $60 million.[9]

Over the years, NASDAQ has developed into a formidable challenger to the NYSE. In part, this growth came about because NASDAQ's listing requirements were less stringent than those of other exchanges, so younger companies with low market capitalizations could only be traded over the counter. But recently the NYSE loosened its standards a bit to attract fast-growth firms that once gravitated toward NASDAQ.[10]

### Trading Systems

The process for buying and selling securities varies according to the type of exchange. As Exhibit 18.3 depicts, in an **auction exchange,** such as the New York Stock exchange, all buy and sell orders (and all information concerning companies traded on that exchange) are funneled onto an auction floor. There, buyers and sellers are matched by a **stock specialist,** a broker who occupies a post on the trading floor and conducts all the trades in specific stocks via a central clearinghouse. If buying or selling imbalances occur in that stock, a specialist can halt trading to prevent the price from plunging without adequate cause. Specialists can also sell stock to customers out of their own inventory.[11] In contrast, a **dealer exchange,** such as NASDAQ, has no central marketplace exists for making transactions. Instead, all buy and sell orders are executed through computers by **market makers,** registered stock and bond representatives who sell securities out of their own inventories.

**Electronic communication networks (ECNs)** use the Internet to link buyers and sellers. Frequently referred to as a virtual stock market or cybermarket, ECNs have no exchange floors, specialists, or market makers. In fact, they are nothing more than computer networks with software programs that match buy and sell orders directly, cutting out the once dominant market makers and specialists. Like other securities marketplaces, ECNs aim to make money by providing a place where stocks can be traded and by collecting commissions on each trade. Most ECNs operate globally and economically—which is why they are becoming increasingly popular. All told, the two biggest ECNs, Instinet and Island, together with seven others, now control nearly a third of all security trades.[12]

Keep in mind that even though a company's stock is listed on an auction or dealer exchange, its shares may also be traded on a ECN. For instance, many brokerage firms use a combination of auction exchanges, dealer exchanges, and ECNs to execute their trades. In fact, over 38 percent of NASDAQ shares are traded on ECNs, and new rules are letting ECNs take closer aim at the NYSE.[13]

### The Changing Nature of Securities Exchanges

Until recently, big Wall Street firms have lived with costly stock exchange floors, specialists, and market makers because the system worked well enough. But now these systems are under attack. As the Chairman of the NASD puts it, "the old methods of exchanging stocks no longer meet the needs of the investing consumer."[14] Discount brokers, ECNs, large securities institutions such as Merrill Lynch and Goldman Sachs (which are investing in ECNs), and consumers are pushing traditional securities exchanges to offer electronic trading options within their exchanges.[15] As a result, the NYSE recently rolled out Direct Plus, which automatically executes trading orders for up to 2,099 shares—80 percent of all transactions—in five seconds.[16] Moreover, some of Wall Street's largest brokers are lobbying the SEC to adopt a sweeping new market system that includes a central display of all stock quotes.[17]

Like the NYSE and a handful or other "open-outcry" marketplaces—where traders do transactions in face-to-face—encounters, the 152-year-old Chicago Board of Trade (CBOT) is under assault by technologically superior new rivals. The CBOT recently surrendered its title as the world's busiest futures exchange to an all-electronic Swiss-German exchange called Eurex, which didn't exist three years ago.[18] Now some think that the CBOT's reluctance to adopt computer technology and its stubborn defense of face-to-face pit trading may be its undoing. Instead of investing heavily in technology, several years ago, the CBOT spent $182 million to build the giant trading floor it now occupies—a big mistake, according to some. Moreover, even if the exchange decides to adopt a fully electronic trading system—and it is inching in that direction—some fear it may be too late.[19]

The push toward round-the-clock trading is another challenge securities markets are facing. Extending traditional trading hours of 9:30 A.M. to 4 P.M. (Eastern U.S. time zone) by adding early-morning and late-night trading sessions is the next revolution sweeping Wall Street. *After-hours trading* or *extended-hours trading* refers to the purchase and sale of publicly traded stocks after the major stock markets, such as the NYSE and NASDAQ, close. Many securities exchanges now offer after-hours trading via ECNs that typically operate from 8:00 A.M. to 9:15 A.M. and 4:15 P.M. to 7 or 8 P.M., although some operate 24 hours a day. The biggest advantage to extended-hours trading is that it accommodates traders who live in regions outside the Eastern U.S. time zone. The biggest disadvantage, however, is lack of volume. Most institutional investors close up shop after the NYSE closing bell. Nonetheless, to remain competitive, many traditional securities exchanges have already extended their traditional trading hours.[20]

## Old Way

*Stocks are traded by "specialists" on the New York Stock Exchange and by "market makers" in the NASDAQ market.*

## New Way

*Computers replace specialists and market makers on electronic communications networks, or ECNs.*

**Broker receives order**

### Buying on the NYSE

**1** Broker sends a buy order to a specialist on the exchange floor.

**Specialist**

**2** Specialist looks for sellers on the trading floor or in his electronic order book.

**3** If he finds enough sellers to match his offer price, he completes the transaction.

If there aren't enough sellers at that price, he can buy at a higher price, with customer permission.

If he still can't find enough willing sellers, he may sell the stock to the customer out of his own inventory.

### Buying on the NASDAQ

**1** Broker consults a trading screen that lists how many shares various market makers are offering to sell and at what prices.

**Market maker**

**2** Broker picks the best price and sends an electronic message to the market maker, who must sell the shares he has listed.

**3** If that satisfies the buyer's demand, the transaction is complete. If not, the market maker can offer to complete the order at an equal or higher price. If his offer is higher, the broker can accept it or seek a better price from a different market maker.

### Buying on an ECN

**1** Broker sends a buy order to an ECN.

**ECN**

**2** The computer looks for matching sell orders on the ECN and then on NASDAQ.

**3** If it finds enough sellers to complete the trade, the transaction is executed. If it doesn't, it's not.

**Broker**

---

### EXHIBIT 18.3

Old and New Ways to Buy Stocks

Some think that floor trading will become a thing of the past as electronic communication networks become increasingly popular.

## video exercise    <

**Take a moment to apply what you've learned.**

# HOW TO BUY AND SELL SECURITIES

Regardless of when you trade securities, where you trade securities, or how you trade securities, you must execute all trades by using a securities broker. Currently individuals cannot interact with securities marketplaces or ECNs directly; purchases must be made through traditional stock brokers—although some hope this will change soon.[21]

A **broker** is an expert who has passed a series of formal examinations and is legally registered to buy and sell securities on behalf of individual and institutional investors. As an investor, you pay *transaction costs* for every buy or sell order, to cover the broker's commission, which varies with the type of broker and the size of your trade: A *full-service broker* provides financial management services such as investment counseling and planning; a *discount broker* such as E*Trade provides fewer or limited services and generally charges lower commissions than a full-service broker.

For years, industry experts have been predicting the demise of the full-service broker. However, the traditional broker is not being erased by the click of a mouse just yet. Many customers still want and need personal financial advice that only an experienced professional can provide.

## Trading Online

E*Trade is part of the online trading phenomenon that has revolutionized the way investors buy and sell securities. Already, online trading is responsible for an estimated one-third of all stock trades made by individual investors.[22] Convenience, control, and cost are the main advantages of trading online. Rather than talk with your broker each time you want to trade, you can now visit your brokerage firm's or mutual fund's Web site, enter your buy or sell instructions, and pay a much lower broker's commission. In fact, full-service brokerages initially resisted online trading because they were concerned about losing their lucrative percentage commissions. But now even traditional firms like Merrill Lynch have jumped on the cyber-bandwagon, offering online trading with lower, flat-fee commissions in line with transaction charges levied by Schwab and others for Internet trades.[23]

Online trading is mostly about do-it-yourself investing; when you trade online, you trade alone, with no one to hold your hand, check for mistakes, or offer advice. Nonetheless, many online brokers, such as Charles Schwab's Internet site, offer a range of services and resources, including free or low-cost research, customized tracking of securities, e-mails confirming trades, electronic newsletters packed with investment tips, and more.[24] But online trading is far from perfect. Some sites have had problems that have prevented investors from placing online trades for minutes or even hours, as this chapter's Focusing on E-Business Today's special feature illustrates.

## Trading Procedures

Before you start to trade, take time to think about your objectives, both long term and short term. Next, look at how various securities match your objectives and your attitude toward risk, since investing in stocks and bonds can involve potential losses. Finally, consider the many ways you can have your broker buy or sell securities: A **market order** tells the broker to buy or sell at the best price that can be negotiated at the moment. A **limit order** specifies the highest price you are willing to pay when buying or the lowest price at which you are willing to sell. A **stop order** tells the broker to sell if the price of your security drops to or below the price you set, protecting you from losing more money if prices are dropping. You can also place a time limit on your orders. An **open order** instructs the broker to leave the order open until you cancel it. A **day order** is valid only on the day you place it, and should not be confused with a *day trader,* a stock trader who holds positions for a very short time (minutes to hours) and closes out these positions within the same day.

If you have special confidence in your broker's ability, you may place a **discretionary order,** which gives the broker the right to buy or sell your securities at the broker's discretion. In some cases, discretionary orders can save you from taking a loss, because the broker may have a better sense of when to sell a stock. If the broker's judgment proves wrong, however, you cannot hold the broker legally responsible for the consequences; so investigate your broker's background and think carefully before you give anyone the right to trade your securities.

Investors sometimes borrow cash to buy stocks, a practice known as **margin trading.** Instead of paying for the stock in full, you borrow some of the money from your stockbroker, paying interest on the borrowed money and leaving the stock with the broker as collateral. As we mentioned in Chapter 17, the Federal Reserve Board establishes margin requirements. Be aware, however, that margin trading increases risk. If the price of a stock you bought on margin goes down, you will have to give your broker more money or the broker will sell your stock. Such forced sales can cause prices to fall even further, triggering a vicious cycle of sales and margin calls.[25]

If you believe that a stock's price is about to drop, you may choose a trading procedure known as **short selling.** With this procedure, you sell stock you borrow from a broker in the hope of buying it back later at a lower price. After you return the borrowed stock to the broker, you keep the price difference. For example, you might decide to borrow 25 shares that are selling for $30 per share and sell short because you think the share price is going to plummet. When the stock's price declines to $15, you buy 25 shares on the open market and make $15 profit on every share (minus transaction costs). Selling short is risky. If the stock had climbed to $32, you would have had to buy shares at that higher price, even though you would be losing money.

# active exercise <

**Take a moment to apply what you've learned.**

## HOW TO ANALYZE FINANCIAL NEWS

Whether you trade online or off, you need to monitor financial news sources to see how your investments are doing. Start with daily newspaper reports on securities markets. Other sources include newspapers aimed specifically at investors (such as *Investor's Business Daily* and *Barron's*) and general-interest business publications that follow the corporate world and give hints about investing (such as the *Wall Street Journal, Forbes, Fortune,* and *Business Week*). Standard & Poor's, Moody's Investor Service, and Value Line also publish newsletters and special reports on securities. Online sources include your brokerage firm's Web site plus a growing number of excellent financial Web sites listed in "Put Your Money Where Your Mouse Is!"

What types of financial information should you be looking for? First, you want to determine the general direction of stock prices. If stock prices have been rising over a long period, the industry and the media will often describe this situation as a **bull market.** The reverse is a **bear market,** one characterized by a long-term trend of falling prices. You can see these broad market movements in Exhibit 18.4. Once you have the general picture, look at the timing. Has a bull market lasted for too long, suggesting that stocks are overvalued and a *correction* (tumbling prices) might be imminent? Also watch the volume of shares traded each day. If the stock market is down on heavy volume (that is, if prices are moving downward and a lot of trading is going on), investors may be trying to sell before prices go down further—a bearish sign.

### Watching Market Indexes and Averages

One way to determine whether the market is bullish or bearish is to watch **market indexes** and averages, which use the performance of a representative sampling of stocks, bonds, or commodities as a gauge of broader market activity. The most famous U.S. stock average is the Dow Jones Industrial Average (DJIA), which tracks the prices of 30 blue-chip stocks, each representing a particular sector of the U.S. economy. Critics say the Dow is too narrow and too susceptible to short-term swings, lacks the right stocks, and gives too much weight to higher-priced shares. But advocates say the Dow's 30 stocks serve as a general barometer of market conditions. Regardless, a recent shuffling of the index by the *Wall Street Journal* editors (guardians of the Dow) should make it more representative of the "new economy." In 1999 Microsoft, Intel, Home Depot, and SBC Communications replaced time-honored blue chips Chevron, Goodyear, Sears Roebuck, and Union Carbide.[26]

Another widely watched index is the Standard & Poor's 500 Stock Average (S&P 500), which tracks the performances of 500 corporate stocks, many more than the DJIA. This index is weighted by market value, not by stock price, so large companies carry far more weight than small companies.[27] The Wilshire 5000 Index, which actually covers some 7,000 stocks, is the broadest index measuring U.S. market performance. To get a sense of how technology stocks are doing, check the NASDAQ Composite Index, covering more than 3,000 over-the-counter stocks, including many high-tech firms. You can also look at indexes to learn about the performance of foreign markets, such as Japan's Nikkei 225 Index and the United Kingdom's FT-SE 100 Index.

### Interpreting the Financial News

In addition to watching market trends, you will want to follow the securities you own and others that look like promising investments. For stocks, you can turn to the stock exchange report in major daily newspapers. Exhibit 18.5 shows how to read this report, which includes high and low prices for the past 52 weeks, the number of shares traded (volume), and the change from the previous day's closing price. U.S. securities markets began quoting security prices in decimals (dollars and cents) in 2000. Prior to that year, prices were quoted in fractions as small as 1/16. Using decimals in trading makes stock prices easier for many investors to understand. Moreover, quoting shares down to the penny permits stocks to be priced in smaller increments.[28]

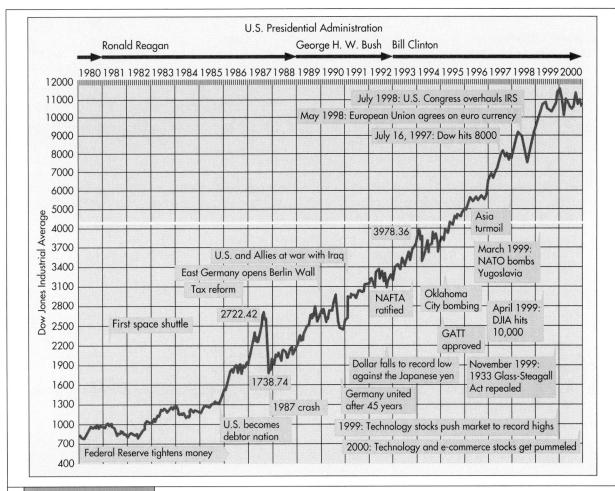

**EXHIBIT 18.4**

The Stock Market's Ups and Downs

The peaks and valleys on this chart represent swings in the Dow Jones Industrial Average, the most widely used indicator of U.S. stock prices.

Included in the stock exchange report is the **price-earnings ratio,** or *p/e ratio* (also known as the price-earnings multiple), which is computed by dividing a stock's market price by its *prior* year's earnings per share. Some investors also calculate a forward p/e ratio using *expected* year earnings in the ratio's denominator. Bear in mind that if a stock's p/e ratio is well below the industry norm, either the company is in trouble or it's an undiscovered gem with a relatively low stock price. For more detailed data on a stock, consult the company's annual reports or documents filed with the Securities and Exchange Commission (SEC).

To follow specific bonds, check the bond quotation tables in major newspapers (see Exhibit 18.6). When reading these tables, remember that the price is quoted as a percentage of the bond's value. For example, a $1,000 bond shown closing at 65 actually sold at $650. Newspapers and business publications also include tables of price quotations for investments such as mutual funds, commodities, options, and government securities (see Exhibit 18.7). These same publications also carry news about securities frauds and investor protection.

> **active exercise**

**Take a moment to apply what you've learned.**

| (1) | | (2) | (3) | (4) | (5) | (6) | (7) | (8) | | (9) | (10) |
| 50-Week High | 52-Week Low | Stock | Sym | Div | Yld % | PE | Vol 100S | Hi | Low | Close | Net Chg |
| --- | --- | --- | --- | --- | --- | --- | --- | --- | --- | --- | --- |
| 55.25 | 26.20 | NtlDataCp | NCD | .30 | .8 | 20 | 3580 | 40.75 | 38.20 | 39.95 | −.70 |
| 56.25 | 17.00 | Navistar | NAV | . . . | | 9 | 2570 | 45.95 | 44.40 | 45.75 | +1.30 |
| 33.75 | 15.00 | NeimanMarc | NMG | . . . | | 11 | 888 | 24.70 | 23.65 | 23.80 | −.80 |
| **22.90** | **10.75** | **NoblDrill** | **NE** | **. . .** | | **26** | **15762** | **24.00** | **22.75** | **24.00** | **+1.25** |

1. **520-week high/low:** Indicates the highest and lowest trading price of the stock in the past 52 weeks plus the most recent week but not the most recent trading day (adjusted for splits). Stocks are quoted in decimals. In most newspapers, boldfaced entries indicate stocks whose price changed by 5% or more if the previous closing price was $2 or higher.

2. **Stock:** The company's name abbreviated. A capital letter usually means a new word. In this example, NtlDataCp is National Data Corporation, NeimanMarc is Neiman-Marcus Group, and NoblDrill is Noble Drill.

3. **Symbol:** Symbol under which this stock is traded on stock exchanges.

4. **Dividend:** Dividends are usually annual payments based on the last quarterly or semiannual declaration, although not all stocks pay dividends. Special or extra dividends or payments are identified in footnotes.

5. **Yield:** The percentage yield shows dividends as a percentage of the share price.

6. **PE:** Price-to-earnings ratio, calculated by dividing the stock's closing price by the earnings per share for the latest four quarters.

7. **Volume:** Daily total of shares traded, in hundreds. A listing of 888 indicates 88,800 shares were traded during that day.

8. **High/Low:** The stock's highest and lowest price for that day.

9. **Close:** Closing price of the stock that day.

10. **Net change:** Change in share price from the close of the previous trading day.

Common Stock Footnotes: d—new 52 week low; n—new; pf—preferred; s—stock split or stock dividend of 25 percent or more in previous 52 weeks; u—new 52 week high; v—trading halted on primary market; vi—in bankruptcy; x—ex dividend (the buyer won't receive a recently declared dividend, but the seller will)

**EXHIBIT 18.5**

How to Read a Newspaper Stock Quotation

Even before you invest, you will want to follow the latest quotations for your stock. This table shows you how to read the newspaper stock quotation tables.

## REGULATION OF SECURITIES MARKETS

Whenever you buy and sell securities, your trades are governed by a network of state and federal laws. Combined with industry self-regulation, these laws are designed to ensure that you and all investors receive accurate information and that no one artificially manipulates the market price of a given security. Trading in stocks and bonds is monitored by the Securities and Exchange Commission. In addition, the SEC works closely with the stock exchanges and NASD to police securities transactions and maintain the system's integrity.

### SEC Filing Requirements

As mentioned earlier, companies must meet certain requirements (which include filing a blizzard of registration papers and reports) to be listed on any exchange (see Exhibit 18.8). Similarly, brokers must operate according to the rules of the exchanges, rules that are largely designed to protect investors. (See Component Chapter B for a list of major federal legislation governing the securities industry.) Overseeing all these details keeps the SEC very busy indeed. Every year the SEC screens over 15,200 annual reports, 40,000 investor complaints, 14,000 prospectuses (a legal statement that describes the objectives of a spe-

| (1)<br>Company | (2)<br>Cur Yld | (3)<br>Vol | (4)<br>Close | (5)<br>Net Chg |
|---|---|---|---|---|
| NYTel 6 1/8 10 | 6.6 | 11 | 93.40 | −.25 |
| PacBell 6 1/4 05 | 6.4 | 10 | 98.40 | +.25 |
| Safwy 9 7/8 07 | 8.4 | 20 | 117.50 | +3.60 |
| StoneC 11 1/4 | 11.1 | 24 | 103.50 | −1.10 |
| TimeWar 9 1/8 13 | 8.3 | 30 | 109.75 | −.50 |

1. **Company:** Name of company issuing the bond, such as New York Telephone, and bond description, such as 6 $\frac{1}{8}$ percent bond maturing in 2010.

2. **Current yield:** Annual interest on $1,000 bond divided by the closing price shown. The yield for New York Telephone is $61.25 ÷ $933.75 = 0.06559, or approximately 6.6 percent.

3. **Volume:** Number of bonds traded (in thousands) that day.

4. **Close:** Price of the bond at the close of the last day's business.

5. **Net change:** Change in bond price from the close of the previous trading day.

**EXHIBIT 18.6**

How to Read a Newspaper Bond Quotation

When newspapers carry bond quotations, they show prices as a percentage of the bond's value, which is typically $1,000.

cific investment), and 6,500 proxy statements (a shareholder's written authorization giving someone else the authority to cast his or her vote). The agency's Web site contains a mountain of public documents that investors can browse, download, or print to learn more about publicly traded companies.[29]

### Insider Trading

*Insider trading* occurs when people buy or sell a stock based on information that is not available to the general public. It comes in all flavors, from buying options in a company ahead of merger or earnings news to placing stock orders ahead of a big institution or group of retail investors (a practice called front-running). While insider trading can produce big profits for the unscrupulous, it also claims many victims. Acquisition companies, for example, are forced to pay higher-than-expected premiums to buy a target company when leaks trigger a run-up in the target's stock price. Most of the talk originates form loose-lipped company insiders.

One of the SEC's top priorities is to crack down on insider trading. But the SEC readily admits that success in the battle is about as likely as victory in the war against drugs. "As the volume of deals and the number of people involved in deals increases, it gets harder to enforce it," says SEC's associate enforcement director, William Baker. "People are getting access to information that they didn't have in the past." Moreover, the dizzying number of corporate mergers has given birth to a mountain of price-sensitive paperwork on Wall Street.

### Regulation Fair Disclosure

Regulation Fair Disclosure (FD) was adopted by the SEC in 2000 to create a level playing field for all investors. Specifically, the regulation mandates that any news with the potential to affect the price of a stock must be released to everyone simultaneously. In other words, the regulation prohibits companies from "selectively disclosing" important information (such as earnings estimates) to big institutional shareholders and Wall Street analysts ahead of regular investors. Otherwise, early news recipients would be able to "make a profit or avoid a loss at the expense of those kept in the dark."[30]

In spite of its good intentions, the regulation could have unintended consequences, say critics. Some worry that instead of giving small and large investors equal access to market-sensitive information, the regulation could cut down on the amount of information received by everyone. Part of the problem stems from the fact that the SEC has not clearly defined what it means by *market-sensitive* information, so companies are opting to err on the side of silence. Moreover, some companies claim

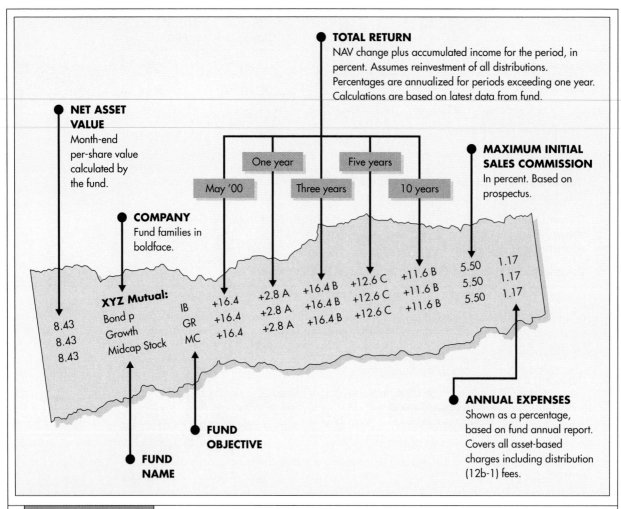

**TOTAL RETURN**
NAV change plus accumulated income for the period, in percent. Assumes reinvestment of all distributions. Percentages are annualized for periods exceeding one year. Calculations are based on latest data from fund.

**NET ASSET VALUE**
Month-end per-share value calculated by the fund.

**MAXIMUM INITIAL SALES COMMISSION**
In percent. Based on prospectus.

**COMPANY**
Fund families in boldface.

One year   Five years

May '00   Three years   10 years

XYZ Mutual:
Bond p        IB    +16.4   +2.8 A   +16.4 B   +12.6 C   +11.6 B   5.50   1.17
Growth        GR    +16.4   +2.8 A   +16.4 B   +12.6 C   +11.6 B   5.50   1.17
Midcap Stock  MC    +16.4   +2.8 A   +16.4 B   +12.6 C   +11.6 B   5.50   1.17

8.43
8.43
8.43

**FUND OBJECTIVE**

**FUND NAME**

**ANNUAL EXPENSES**
Shown as a percentage, based on fund annual report. Covers all asset-based charges including distribution (12b-1) fees.

### EXHIBIT 18.7

How to Read a Newspaper Mutual Fund Quotation

A mutual fund listing shows the new asset value of one share (the price at which one share is trading) and the change in trading price from one day to the next.

it's too difficult to give small investors the same level of information that they have selectively provided to investment analysts.[31]

### Online Securities Fraud

No longer do con artists need rooms full of cold-calling brokers. Today, with just an e-mail address list and a chat-board alias or two, penny-stock promoters can dupe tens of thousands (if not millions) of investors by making false claims about a company, watching investors eager to make a fast profit pump up the company's stock price, then selling or dump their penny shares at inflated prices and pocket a handsome profit.

The combination of a "get-rich" mindset and the huge number of people now investing online have made such cyberscamming schemes common. Online and off, investors are getting ripped off to the tune of an estimated $10 billion a year—that's more than $1 million an hour. And the SEC's Internet complaint hotline gets up to 200 messages a day.[32] In fact, so pervasive has the problem become that it has drawn the attention of the Department of Justice, the FTC, the U.S. Attorney's offices, and even the FBI. To help curb Internet stock scams, NASD has developed an Internet search engine to find phrases such as "too good to be true," and it monitors securities chat forums for fraudulent or misleading information.[33] As an investor, your best defense against fraud is to carefully research securities before you buy and to steer clear of any investment that seems too good to be true (see Exhibit 18.9).

| An Edgar Scorecard |
| --- |
| **10K ➡** The official version of a company's annual report, with a comprehensive overview of the business. |
| **10Q ➡** An abridged version of the 10K, filed quarterly for the first three quarters of a company's fiscal year. |
| **8K ➡** An interim report disclosing significant company events that occur before the company files its next 10Q or 10K. |
| **12B-25 ➡** Request for a deadline extension to file a required report, like a 10K or 10Q. When the late report is ultimately filed, NT is appended to the report's name. |
| **S1 ➡** Basic registration form for new securities, most often initial or secondary public offerings. |
| **Proxy Statement ➡** Information and ballot materials for shareholder votes, including election of directors and approval of mergers and acquisitions when required. |
| **Forms 3, 4, and 5 ➡** Directors, officers, and owners of more than 10 percent of a company's stock report their initial purchases on Form 3 and subsequent purchases or sales on Form 4; they file an annual statement of their holdings on Form 5. |

**EXHIBIT 18.8**

An Edgar Scorecard

To successfully navigate the Securities and Exchange Commission's Edgar database of corporate filings, it helps to know the most common filings required of publicly traded companies and their content.

> **active concept check**

**Now let's take a moment to test your knowledge of the concepts you have studied in this section.**

1. Is the investment registered with the SEC and your state's securities agency?
2. Have you read the company's audited financial statements?
3. Is the person recommending this investment a registered broker?
4. What does the person promoting the investment have to gain?
5. If the tip came from an online bulletin board or e-mail, is the author identifiable or using an alias? Is there any reason to trust that person?
6. Are you being pressured to act before you can evaluate the investment?
7. Does the investment promise you'll get rich quick, using words like "guaranteed," "high return," or "risk free"?
8. Does the investment match your objectives? Could you afford to lose all of the money you invest?
9. How easy would it be to sell the investment later? Remember, stocks with fewer shares are easy for promoters to manipulate and hard for investors to sell if the price starts falling.
10. Does the investment originate overseas? If yes, beware: It is tougher to track money sent abroad, and harder for burned investors to have recourse to justice.

**EXHIBIT 18.9**

Ten Questions to Ask Before You Invest

You can avoid getting taken in an online stock scam by asking yourself these 10 questions before you invest.

## > Chapter Wrap-Up

Now that you've reached the end of the chapter, you may wish to explore the concepts you've been reading about in greater detail, or test yourself to see how well you've comprehended the material. In the box below you'll find a number of links. Click on any one of these links to find additional chapter resources.

## > end-of-chapter resources

- Summary of Learning Objectives
- Practice Quiz
- Focusing on E-Business Today
- Key Terms
- Test Your Knowledge
- Practice Your Knowledge
- Expand Your Knowledge
- A Case for Critical Thinking
- Business Plan Pro: Managing Financial Information and Resources

## NOTES

### CHAPTER 1

1. Kara Swisher, "Behind the Portal," *Wall Street Journal,* 17 April 2000, R74–R76; Brent Schlender, "How a Virtuoso Plays the Web," *Fortune,* 6 March 2000, F79–F83; Brent Schlender, "The Customer Is the Decision-Maker," *Fortune,* 6 March 2000, F84–F86; Joseph Nocera, "Do You Believe? How Yahoo! Became a Blue Chip," *Fortune,* 7 June 1999, 76–92; Linda Himelstein, Heather Green, Richard Siklos, and Catherine Yang, "Yahoo! The Company, the Strategy, the Stock," *Business Week,* 7 September 1998, 661; Jonathan Littman, "Driven to Succeed: The Yahoo Story," *Upside,* September 1998, 70–75; Carol Pickering, "A Tale of Two Startups," *Forbes,* 5 October 1998, 85; Steven Levy, "Surfers, Step Right Up!," *Newsweek,* 25 May 1998, 74–82; Steve Rosenbush, "How Can Tim Koogle Stay So Cool in the Face of AOL's Assault," *Business Week E.Biz,* 15 May 2000, EB27; Ben Elgin and Linda Himelstein, "The Word at Yahoo! Yikes!" *Business Week,* 30 October 2000, 63; Quentin Hardy, "The Killer Ad Machines," *Forbes,* 11 December 2000, 168–178.

2. IBM 1997 Annual Report online, *Annual Report Gallery,* [accessed 21 April 1999] www.reportgallery.com.

3. Everette James, "Services—U.S. Firms Are Leaders in the Global Economy," *Business America,* April 1998, 5–7.

4. U.S. Department of Commerce, Bureau of Economic Analysis Web site, beadata.bea.doc.gov/bea/dn2/gpoc.htm [accessed 24 September 1999]; "Fortune 1000 Ranked Within Industry," *Fortune,* 26 April 1999, F51–F73.

5. *Survey of Current Business* (Washington, D.C.: GPO, November 1997), Table B8, 132; Infoplease Almanac, Infoplease.com, [accessed 22 September 1999], www.infoplease.com/ipa/A0302230.html.

6. *Statistical Abstract of the United States,* 1996 (Washington, D.C.: GPO, 1996), 56–59, 394, 396.

7. George Hager, "Fast-Growing Internet Industry Surges Startling 62%," *USA Today,* 6 June 2000, A1.

8. Thomas Stewart, "Brain Power," *Fortune,* 17 March 1997, 105–110; "Post-Capitalist Society," Soundview Executive Book Summaries 17, no. 3 (March 1995).

9. James Wilfong and Toni Seger, *Taking Your Business Global* (Franklin Lakes, N.J.: Career Press, 1997).

10. Robert L. Heilbroner and Lester C. Thurow, *Economics Explained* (New York: Simon & Schuster, 1994), 29–30.

11. Heilbroner and Thurow, *Economics Explained,* 250.

12. Heilbroner and Thurow, *Economics Explained,* 250.

13. Collin McMahon, "Russians at a Critical Crossroad," *Chicago Tribune,* 29 August 1998, 1; Patricia Kranz, "Russia; Is There a Solution?" *Business Week,* 7 September 1998, 27–29; Robert J. Samuelson, "Global Capitalism, R.I.P?" *Newsweek,* 14 September 1998, 40–42; Emily Thorton, "Russia—What Happens When Markets Fail," *Business Week,* 26 April 1999, 50–52; Bruce Nussbaum, "Time to Act," *Business Week,* 14 September 1998, 34–37.

14. Larry Derfner, "The Fight over Privatization: Netanyahu Has Pledged to End Israel's," *The Jewish Week,* 9 August 1996, 14+; "Israel to Privatize 49% of El Al Airlines," *New York Times,* 2 June 1998, C5; Pierre Tran, "Air France Head Hopes for Privatization," *Reuters Business Report,* 8 June 1997, 6; Nathan Gardels, "Socialism Fate Awaits the Welfare State," *New Perspectives Quarterly,* 22 March 1996, 2; "Air France Shares Jump on First Day of Trading," *New York Times,* 23 February 1999, C3; Greg Steinmetz, "Her Majesty May Sell Part of London's Tube, Angering Some in U.K.," *Wall Street Journal,* 14 October 1999, A1, A12.

15. Erik Eckholm, "Chinese Restate Goals to Reorganize State Companies," *New York Times,* 23 September 1999, A10; Mark L. Clifford, Dexter Roberts, Joyce Barnathan, and Pete Engardio, "Can China Reform Its Economy?" *Business Week,* 29 September 1997, 116–123; Nicholas D. Kristof and Sheryl WuDunn, "The World's Ills May Be Obvious, But Their Cure Is Not," *New York Times,* 15 February 1999, [accessed 16 February 1999], www.nytimes.com/library/world/ global/021699global-econ.html; Dexter Roberts, "China's New Revolution," *Business Week,* 27 September 1999, 72–78.

16. Gary Hamel and Jeff Sampler, "The E-Corporation," *Fortune,* 7 December 1998, 81–92.

17. Brian O'Reilly, "The Rent-a-Car Jocks Who Made Enterprise #1," *Fortune,* 28 October 1996, 125–128.

18. Jeff Wise, "How Skiboarding Became the New Snowboarding," *New York Times Magazine,* 21 March 1999, 58–61.

19. Joel Brinkley, "U.S. Judge Says Microsoft Violated Antitrust Laws with Predatory Behavior," *New York Times,* 4 April 2000, A1, C12; Merrill Goozner, "Microsoft Is Ruled an Illegal Monopoly," *Chicago Tribune,* 4 April 2000, sec. 1, 1, 16; Ted Bridis and John R. Wilke, "Judge Orders Microsoft Broken in Two, Imposes Tough Restriction on Practices," *Wall Street Journal,* 8 June 2000, A3, A12; "Judge Suspends Restrictions on Microsoft," *Wall Street Journal,* 21 June 2000, A3; John R. Wilke and Rebecca Buckman, "Justices Decline Early Look at Microsoft," *Wall Street Journal,* 27 September 2000, A3, A17.

20. Jon Van, "WorldCom, Sprint Fold Under Heft of Scrutiny," *Chicago Tribune,* 14 July 2000, sec.3, 1.

21. Patrick M. Reilly, "Barnes & Noble Closes Book on Attempt to Buy Ingram Amid FTC Objections," *Wall Street Journal,* 3 June 1999, B16.

22. Martin Kasindorf and Ken Fireman, "The Clinton Budget/2002 Solution," *Newsday,* 7 February 1997, A4; Gilbert C. Alston, "Balancing the Federal Budget," *Los Angeles Times,* 14 February 1997, B8; Jennifer Oldham, "The Budget Battle; Deficit and Debt: A Primer," *Los Angeles Times,* 6 January 1996, D1; Brian Naylor, Jacki Lynden, and Robert Siegel, "House Budget Debate," 1997 National Public Radio, 30 July 1997; U.S. Department of Treasury Web site, [accessed 19 April 1999], www.treas.gov.

23. Robert Kuttner, "What's Wrong With Paying Off the National Debt?" *Business Week,* 15 May 2000, 35; Budget of the United States Government Fiscal Year 2001, [accessed 21 April 2000], w3.access.gpo.gov/usbudget/index.html.

24. Kathleen Madigan, "Keep Your Nest Egg Safe—Watch Housing Data," *Business Week,* 17 April 2000, 208–210.

25. Elia Kacapyr, "The Well-Being Index," *American Demographics,* February 1996, 32–35; Beth Belton, "U.S. Brings Economy into Information Age," *USA Today,* 17 March 1999, B1.

26. Rona Gindin, "Dealing With a Multicultural Workforce," *Nation's Restaurant News,* September–October 1998, 31, 83; Howard Gleckman, "A Rich Stew in the Melting Pot," *Business Week,* 31 August 1998, 76+.

27. Nanette Byrnes and Paul C. Judge, "Internet Anxiety," *Business Week,* 28 June 1999, 79–88.

28. Robert D. Hof, Gary McWilliams, and Gabrielle Saveri, "The Click Here Economy," *Business Week,* 22 June 1998, 122–128.

29. Michael Moynihan, *The Coming American Renaissance* (New York: Simon & Schuster, 1987), 25.

30. William A. Sahlman, "The New Economy Is Stronger Than You Think," *Harvard Business Review,* November–December 1999, 99–106.

31. Sahlman, "The New Economy Is Stronger Than You Think," 99–106.

32. Michael van Biema and Bruce Greenwald, "Managing Our Way to Higher Service-Sector Productivity," *Harvard Business Review,* July/August 1997, 87–95.

33. Moynihan, *The Coming American Renaissance,* 42–43; "Through Seven Decades, Tracking Business and the World," *Business Week,* 4 October 1999, 118A–118P.

## CHAPTER 2

1. Roger Rosenblatt, "The Root of All Good: Reaching the Top by Doing the Right Thing," *Time,* 18 October 1999, 88–91; Stan Friedman, "Apparel with Conscience: The Givers," *Apparel Industry Magazine,* June 1999, 78–79; Andrea Adelson, "Wedded to Its Moral Imperatives," *New York Times,* 16 May 1999, 9; Michael Lear-Olimpi, "Management Mountaineer," *Warehousing Management,* January–February 1999, 23–30; Jennifer Bellantonio, "Fighting the Good Fight," Sporting Goods Business, 1999, S18–S22; Larry Armstrong, "Patagonia Sticks to Its Knitting," *Business Week,* 7 December 1998, 68; Nancy Rivera Brooks, "Companies Give Green Power the Green Light," *Los Angeles Times,* 27 September 1998, D8; Charlene Marmer Solomon, "A Day in the Life of Terri Wolfe: Maintaining Corporate Culture," *Workforce,* June 1998, 94–95; Jacqueline Ottman, "Proven Environmental Commitment Helps Create Committed Customers," *Marketing News,* 2 February 1998, 5–6; Dawn Hobbs, "Patagonia Ranked 24th by Magazine," *Los Angeles Times,* 23 December 1997, B1; Jim Collins, "The Foundation for Doing Good," *Inc.,* December 1997, 41–42; Paul C. Judge, "It's Not Easy Being Green," *Business Week,* 24 November 1997, 180; Melissa Downing, "A Lean, Green Fulfillment Machine," *Catalog Age,* June 1997, 63; Staci Bonner, "Patagonia, A Green Endeavor," *Apparel Industry Magazine,* February 1997, 46–48; Polly LaBarre, "Patagonia Comes of Age," *Industry Week,* 3 April 1995, 42–48; John Steinbreder, "Yvon Chouinard, founder and owner of the Patagonia Outdoor . . . " *Sports Illustrated,* 2 November 1991, 200.

2. Thomas Easton and Stephan Herrera, "J&J's Dirty Little Secret," *Forbes,* 12 January 1998, 42–44.

3. Easton and Herrera, "J&J's Dirty Little Secret," 42–44.

4. "For Heavy Drinkers, a Written Warning," *New York Times Abstracts,* 27 October 1998, sec. F, 8 [accessed 24 May 1999], nrstg2s. djnr.com/cgi-binDJ.

5. Dan Carney, "Fraud on the Net," *Business Week E.Biz,* 3 April 2000, EB58–EB64.

6. John Galvin, "The New Business Ethics: Cheating, Lying, Stealing, 15 May 2000, 86–99.

7. Jeffrey L. Seglin, "Dot.Con," *Forbes ASAP,* 21 February 2000, 135; Jerry Useem, "New Ethics . . . or No Ethics," *Fortune,* 20 March 2000, 83–86.

8. "FCC, Slam Door on This Idea," *Los Angeles Tribune,* 27 September 1999, 6; "Customer Complaints On Phone Slamming, Cramming Seen Rising," *Wall Street Journal,* 30 August 1999, B10.

9. Amy Zipkin, "Getting Religion On Corporate Ethics," *New York Times,* 18 October 2000, C1, C10.

10. John S. McClenahen, "Your Employees Know Better," *Industry Week,* 1 March 1999, 12–14.

11. Betsy Stevens, "Communicating Ethical Values: A Study of Employee Perceptions," *Journal of Business Ethics,* June 1999, 113–120.

12. Milton Bordwin, "The Three R's of Ethics," *Management Review,* June 1998, 59–61.

13. Mark Seivar, personal communication, 2 April 1998; "1-800-Jus-tice or 1-800-Rat-fink," *Reputation Management,* March–April 1995, 31–34; Margaret Kaeter, "The 5th Annual Business Ethics Awards for Excellence in Ethics," *Business Ethics,* December 1993, 26–29.

14. "Does It Pay to Be Ethical?" *Business Ethics,* March–April 1997, 14–16; Don L. Boroughs, "The Bottom Line on Ethics," *U.S. News & World Report,* 20 March 1995, 61–66.

15. Douglas S. Barasch, "God and Toothpaste," *New York Times Magazine,* 22 December 1996, 28.

16. Edward O. Welles, "Ben's Big Flop," *Inc.,* September 1998, 40+; Constance L. Hays, "Getting Serious at Ben & Jerry's," *New York Times,* 22 May 1998, C1, C3.

17. Welles, "Ben's Big Flop," 40+; Hays, "Getting Serious at Ben & Jerry's," C1, C3.

18. Constance L. Hays, "Ben & Jerry's To Unilever, With Attitude," *New York Times,* 13 April 2000, C1, C20; Fred Bayles, "Reviews In On Ben & Jerry's Sweet Deal," *USA Today,* 20 April 2000, 3A.

19. See letters in *New York Times,* 25 August 1918, and *New York Herald,* 1 October 1918.

20. Michael A. Verespej, "Why They're the Best," *Industry Week,* 16 August 1999, 102–109.

21. Thomas A. Fogarty, "Corporations Use Causes for Effect," *USA Today,* 10 November 1997, 7B; Peaceworks Web site [accessed 22 June 1999], www.peaceworks.net; Florence Fabricant, "A Young Entrepreneur Makes Food, Not War," *New York Times,* 30 November 1996, sec. International Business, 21.

22. Wal-Mart Web site [accessed 22 June 1999], www.walmart foundation.org/cmn.html; Microsoft Web site [accessed 22 June 1999], www.microsoft.com/giving/pages/O-givann.htm; American Express Web site [accessed 22 June 1999], www6.americanexpress.com/corp/philanthropy/community.asp.

23. Carrie Shook, "Dave's Way," *Forbes,* 9 March, 1998, 126–127.

24. Anna Muoio, ed., "Ways to Give Back," *Fast Company,* December–January 1998, 113+.

25. William H. Miller, "Cracks in the Green Wall," *Industry Week,* 19 January, 1998, 58–65.

26. "Why Ford Came Clean," *Newsweek,* 22 May 2000, 50.

27. Gil Adams, "Cleaning Up," *International Business,* February 1996, 32; Susan Moffat, "Asia Stinks," *Fortune,* 9 December 1996, 120–132; Pete Engardio, Jonathan Moore, and Christine Hill, "Time For a Reality Check in Asia," *Business Week,* 2 December 1996, 58–66.

28. Michael Castleman, "Tiny Particles, Big Problems: Our Air Is Cleaner, Yet the Body Count Climbs," *Sierra,* 21 November 1995, 26.

29. Chris Bury and Ted Koppel, "The Ad Campaign and the Kyoto Summit," *ABC Nightline,* 9 December 1997; Peter Passell, "Trading on the Pollution Exchange," *New York Times,* 24 October 1997, C1,

C4; Julia Flynn, Heidi Dawley, and Naomi Freundlich, "Green Warrior in Gray Flannel," *Business Week,* 6 May 1996, 96.

30. Kirk Spitzer, "Companies Divert Enough Waste to Fill Five Astrodomes," *Gannett News Service,* 2 November 1995; Michael Satchell, Betsy Carpenter, Kenan Pollack, "A New Day for Earth Lovers," *U.S. News & World Report,* 24 April 1994, 58–62.

31. David Brinkerhoff, "Honda Unveils Electric Car to Rival GM Version," *Reuters Business Report,* 3 January 1997; "Manhattan Beach Offers Free Charging for Electric Cars," *Los Angeles Times,* 27 March 1997, B5; Howard Rothman, "Interview: Amory Lovins," *Business Ethics,* March–April 1996, 34–36.

32. Joseph Weber, "3M's Big Cleanup," *Business Week,* 5 June 2000, 96–98.

33. Dan Charles, "Industrial Symbiosis," *Morning Edition (NPR),* 31 July 1997.

34. "Money to Burn?" *The Economist* 345, 6 December 1997; Donna Beckley, "Industrial Pollution Still Haunts Hudson, Group Says," *Gannet News Service,* 24 September 1996, S12; Jim Bradley, "Buying High, Selling Low," *E Magazine,* 17 July 1996, 14–15; Brian Doherty, "Selling Air Pollution," *Reason,* 1 May 1996, 32–37; Bill Nichols, "Four Years of Work, Debate Produce First Phase of EPA's Cluster Rules," *Pulp & Paper,* 1998, 71+.

35. Satchell, Carpenter, and Pollack, "A New Day for Earth Lovers," 58–62.

36. Spitzer, "Companies Divert Enough Waste to Fill Five Astrodomes," *Electric Library,* Online, [accessed 28 July 1997].

37. "The IW Survey: Encouraging Findings," *Industry Week,* 19 January 1998, 62.

38. Constance L. Hays, "Since 70's the World Has Become Safer for Consumerism," *New York Times,* 5 January 1998, C6.

39. Daniel Eisenberg and Adam Zagorin, "Firestone's Rough Road," *Time,* 18 September 2000, 38–40; Joann Muller and Nicole St. Pierre, "How Will Firestone and Ford Steer Through This Blowout?" *Business Week,* 28 August 2000, 54+.

40. Laura Shapiro, "The War of the Labels," *Newsweek,* 5 October 1992, 63, 66.

41. Karen Friefeld, "As Subtle As a Slap In the Face: New Ad Campaign Makes Certain Its Messages are Absolutely Clear," *Newsday,* 21 May 1995, A56.

42. Chris Burritt, "Fallout From the Tobacco Settlement," *Atlanta Journal and Constitution,* 22 June 1997, A14; Jolie Solomon, "Smoke Signals," *Newsweek,* 28 April 1997, 50–51; Marilyn Elias, "Mortality Rate Rose Through '80s," *USA Today,* 17 April 1997, B3; Mike France, Monica Larner, and Dave Lindorff, "The World War on Tobacco," *Business Week,* 11 November 1996; Richard Lacayo, "Put Out the Butt, Junior," *Time,* 2 September 1996, 51; Elizabeth Gleick, "Smoking Guns," *Time,* 1 April 1996, 50.

43. Anne Faircloth, "Denny's Changes Its Spots," *Fortune,* 13 May 1996, 133–142; Nicole Harris, "A New Denny's—Diner By Diner," *Business Week,* 25 March 1996, 166–168; Eric Smith, "Not Paid in Full," *Black Enterprise,* April 1996, 16; Mark Lowery, "Denny's New Deal Ends Blackout," *Black Enterprise,* 20 February 1995, 43; "Denny's Does Some of the Right Things," *Business Week,* 6 June 1994, 42; "Making Amends at Denny's," *Business Week,* 21 November 1994, 47.

44. "Does It Pay to Be Ethical?" *Business Ethics,* March–April 1997, 15.

45. John A. Byrne, Leslie Brown, and Joyce Barnathan, "Directors in the Hot Seat," *Business Week,* 8 December 1997, 100, 102, 104.

46. Suzanne Wooley, "The Hustlers Queue Up On the Net," *Business Week,* 20 November 1995, 146–148.

47. Robert Pear, "U.S. Proposes Rules to Bar Obstacles to the Disabled," *New York Times,* 22 January 1991, A1, 12.

48. "Vital Facts 1999," OSHA Web site, [accessed 29 September 1999], www.osha-slc.gov/OSHAFacts/OSHAFacts.html.

49. Yochi J. Dreazen, "New OSHA Proposal Enrages Businesses," *Wall Street Journal,* 8 November 2000, A2, A6; Robert Manor, "OSHA's Ergonomic Rules Rile Business," *Chicago Tribune,* 14 November 2000, sec. 1, 1.

50. Wendy Bounds and Hilary Stout, "Sweatshop Pact: Good Fit or Threadbare?" *Wall Street Journal,* 10 April 1997, A2; Ellen Neuborne, "Nike to Take a Hit In Labor Report," *USA Today,* 27 March 1997, B1; William J. Holstein et al., "Santa's Sweatshop," *U.S. News & World Report,* 16 December 1996, 50–60; Stephanie Strom, "From Sweetheart to Scapegoat," *New York Times,* 27 June 1996, C1, 16; Nancy Gibbs, "Cause Celeb: Two High-Profile Endorsers Are Props in a Worldwide Debate Over Sweatshops and the Use of Child Labor," *Time,* 17 June 1996; Ellen Neuborne, "Labor's Shopping List: No Sweatshops," *USA Today,* 5 December 1995, B1; Bob Herbert, "A Sweatshop Victory," *New York Times,* 22 December 1995, A15.

51. Skip Kaltenheuser, "Bribery Is Being Outlawed Virtually Worldwide," *Business Ethics,* May–June 1998, 11; Thomas Omestad, "Bye-bye to Bribes," *U.S.News & World Report,* 22 December 1997, 39, 42–44.

52. Kate Murphy, "Fighting Pollution—And Cleaning Up, Too," *Business Week,* 19 January, 1998, 90.

53. Martin Walker, "How Green Is Europe?" *Europe,* February 1998, 26, 28–29.

54. Del Jones, "FBI: Spies Cost U.S. Firms $2B a Month," *USA Today,* 10 February 1999, 2B.

55. Andrew Tanzer, "Tech-Savvy Pirates," *Forbes,* 7 September 1998 [accessed 28 June 1999], www.forbes.com/forbes/98/0907/6205162a. htm; Richard Rapaport, "Singapore Sting," *Forbes,* 7 April 1997 [accessed 28 June 1999], www.forbes.com/asap/97/0407/084.htm.

56. Barrie McKenna, "OECD Creates Corporate Conduct Code: Governance Principles Range from Shareholders' Rights to Responsibilities of Directors," *The Globe and Mail,* 29 April 1999, B13 [accessed 28 June 1999] nrstg2p.djnr.com.

## CHAPTER 3

1. Trek's Web site, www.trekbikes.com [accessed 26 May 2000]; Michele Wucker, "Keep on Trekking," *Working Woman,* December/January 1998, 32–36; Christopher Elliott, "Zero Defects through Design," *Chief Executive,* 1998, 36–38; Randy Weston, "Trek Design System Cranks Out Changes," *Computerworld,* 15 December 1997, 37.

2. John Alden, "What in the World Drives UPS?" *International Business,* March/April 1998, 6–7; UPS Web site, ups.com [accessed 16 May 2000].

3. "Getting It Right in Japan," *International Business,* May–June 1997, 19.

4. Gary M. Wederspahn, "Exporting Corporate Ethics," *Global Workforce,* January 1997, 29–30; Dana Milbank and Marcus W. Brauchli, "Greasing Wheels," *Wall Street Journal,* 29 September 1995, A1, A7.

5. James Wilfong and Toni Seger, *Taking Your Business Global* (Franklin Lakes, N.J.: Career Press, 1997), 289.

6. Jules Abend, "Jockey Colors Its World," *Bobbin,* February 1999, 50–54.

7. Ricky W. Griffin and Michael W. Pustay, *International Business* (Reading, Mass.: Addison-Wesley, 1999), 415.

8. "Padgett Surveys Franchise/Small Business Sectors," *Franchising World,* March–April 1995, 46; John Stansworth, "Penetrating the Myths Surrounding Franchise Failure Rates—Some Old Lessons for New Business," *International Small Business Journal,* January–March 1995, 59–63; Laura Koss-Feder, "Building Better Franchise

Relations," *Hotel & Motel Management,* 6 March 1995, 18; Carol Steinberg, "Franchise Fever," *World Trade,* July 1992, 86, 88, 90–91; John O'Dell, "Franchising America," *Los Angeles Times,* 25 June 1989, sec. IV, 1.

9. One World Web site, www.oneworldalliance.com/ [accessed 16 May 2000].

10. Lewis M. Simons, "High-Tech Jobs for Sale," *Time,* 22 July 1996, 59.

11. Alden, "What in the World Drives UPS?" 6–7.

12. Ernest Beck and Emily Nelson, "As Wal-Mart Invades Europe, Rivals Rush to Match Its Formula," *Wall Street Journal,* 6 October 1999, A1, A6.

13. "Foreign Investment in U.S. Reaches 54.4 Billion Dollars in 1995," *Xinhua News Agency,* 1996.

14. Thomas G. Condon and Kurt Badenhausen, "Spending Spree," *Forbes,* 26 July 1999, 208–18.

15. *Big Emerging Markets: 1996 Outlook* (Washington D.C.: GPO, 1996); Nicholas D. Kristof and Sheryl WuDunn, "The World's Ills May Be Obvious, But Their Cure Is Not," *New York Times,* 18 February 1999, www.nytimes.com/library/world/global/021699global-econ.html [accessed 19 February 1999].

16. Holley H. Ulbrich and Mellie L. Warner, *Managerial Economics* (New York: Barron's Educational Series, 1990), 190.

17. Patrick Lane, "World Trade Survey: Why Trade Is Good for You," *The Economist,* 3 October 1998, S4–S6.

18. Bureau of Economic Analysis Web site, www.bea.doc.gov/bea/di/ tradgs-d.htm [accessed 15 May 2000].

19. Maria Mallory, "Wheels of Fortune," *U.S. News & World Report,* 4 March 1996, 49–50.

20. "Overview of the Economy," Bureau of Economic Analysis Web site, www.bea.doc.gov/bea/glance.htm [accessed 15 May 2000]; Table 1—U.S. International Transactions, Bureau of Economic Analysis Web site, www.bea.doc.gov/bea/di/bopq/bop1./htm [accessed 27 October 1999].

21. Robert J. Samuelson, "Trading with the Enemy," *Newsweek,* 1 April 1996, 41; Amy Borrus, Pete Engardio, and Dexter Roberts, "The New Trade Superpower," *Business Week,* 16 October 1995, 56–57; David A. Andelman, "Marco Polo Revisited," *American Management Association,* August 1995, 10–12; John Greenwald, "Get Asia Now, Pay Later," *Time,* 10 October 1994, 61; Simons, "High-Tech Jobs for Sale," 59.

22. James Cox, "Tariffs Shield Some U.S. Products," *USA Today,* 6 May 1999, 1B.

23. Eric Schmitt, "U.S. Backs off Sanctions, Seeing Poor Effect Abroad," *New York Times,* 31 July 1998, A1, A6; Robert T. Gray, "Book Review," *Nation's Business,* January 1999, 47.

24. "Saudi Arabia Hopes to Join WTO by 2002," *Reuters Business Report,* 3 August 1997.

25. "Airbus to Resume Talks on Status," *New York Times,* 5 May 1999, C4; Daniel Michaels, "Airbus Industrie's Partners Are Close to Establishing a Single Corporation," *Wall Street Journal,* 8 June 2000, A20; Daniel Michaels, "Country by Country—Flying High," *Wall Street Journal,* 25 September 2000, R18.

26. "Japanese Steelmakers Face U.S. Penalties In Antidumping Case," *Wall Street Journal,* 3 August 2000, C19.

27. James Cox, "Tariffs Shield Some U.S. Products," *USA Today,* 6 May 1999, 1B, 2B.

28. "APEC Ministers Commit to Sustainable Development," *Xinhau News Agency,* 11 June 1997; Fred C. Bergsten, "An Asian Push for World-Wide Free Trade: The Case For APEC," *The Economist,* 6 January 1996, 62; "U.S. Must Press to Reduce Trade Barriers in Asia, Pacific, Congress Told," *Gannett News Service,* 1995.

29. Michael M. Phillips, "One by One," *Wall Street Journal,* 26 April 1999, R4, R7.

30. Christopher Koch. "It's a Wired, Wired World," *Webmaster,* March 1997, 50–55.

31. Masaaki Kotabe and Maria Cecilia Coutinho de Arruda, "South America's Free Trade Gambit," *Marketing Management,* Spring 1998, 39–46.

32. "Grand Illusions," *The Economist,* 4 March 1995, 87; Bob Davis, "Global Paradox: Growth of Trade Binds Nations, But It Also Can Spur Separatism," *Wall Street Journal,* 20 June 1994, A1, A6; Barbara Rudolph, "Megamarket," *Time,* 10 August 1992, 43–44; Peter Truell, "Free Trade May Suffer from Regional Blocs," *Wall Street Journal,* 1 July 1991, A1.

33. Patrice M. Jones, "Leaving Trade Pact's Woes Behind," *Chicago Tribune,* 10 May 2000, sec. 3, 42.

34. Rafael A. Lecuona, "Economic Integration: NAFTA and MER-COSUR, A Comparative Analysis," *International Journal on World Peace,* December 1999, 27–49.

35. Emeric Lepourte, "Europe's Challenge to the U.S. in South America's Biggest Market," *Christian Science Monitor,* 8 April 1997, 19; Mario Osava, "Mercosur: Free Trade with Europe More Advantageous Than FTAA," *Inter Press English News Wire,* 6 May 1997; Robert Maynard, "At a Crossroads in Latin America," *Nation's Business,* April 1996, 38–39; Gregory L. Miles and Loubna Freih, "Join the Caribbean Revolution," *International Business,* September 1994, 42–54; Matt Moffett, "Spreading the Gospel," *Wall Street Journal,* 28 October 1994, R12.

36. Lecuona, "Economic Integration: NAFTA and MERCOSUR, A Comparative Analysis."

37. Joel Russell, "NAFTA in the Real World," *Hispanic Business,* June 1996, 22–28; Scot J. Paltrow, "NAFTA's Job Impact Slight, Study Says," *Los Angeles Times,* 19 December 1996, D3.

38. "Sweden Says EU Enlargement Outweighs NATO Expansion," *Xinhau News Agency,* 16 July 1996; Helene Cooper, "The Euro: What You Need to Know," *Wall Street Journal,* 4 January 1999, A5, A6.

39. Thomas Kamm, "EU Certifies Participants for Euro," *Wall Street Journal,* 26 March 1998, A14.

40. Thane Peterson, "The Euro," *Business Week,* 27 April 1998, 90–94; Joan Warner, "The Great Money Bazaar," *Business Week,* 27 April 1998, 96–98; Gail Edmondson, "Industrial Evolution," *Business Week,* 27 April 1998, 100–101.

41. Bill Spindle, "A Flip of the Coins: Yen Dances, Euro Won't," *Wall Street Journal,* 10 May 2000, A21, A23.

42. Joshua Kurlantzick, "The Big Mango Bounces Back: Economic Recovery in Thailand and Southeast Asia," *World Policy Journal,* Spring 2000, 79–85.

43. Tom Petruno and Art Pine, "Indonesian Currency Fall Deepens Asia Crisis," *Los Angeles Times,* 9 January 1998, A1.

44. Pete Engardio, Christina Hoag, and Peter Coy, "Deja Vu?" *Business Week,* 21 December 1998, 34–35.

45. Mark Whitehouse, "Capital Flight Remains Draining Problem for Russia," *Wall Street Journal,* 19 April 1999, A19.

46. Jeffrey D. Sachs, "Rule of the Ruble," *New York Times,* 4 June 1998, A27; Richard Lacayo, "IMF to the Rescue," *Time,* 8 December 1997, 37–39; Paul Krugman, "Saving Asia: It's Time to Get Radical," *Fortune,* 7 September 1998, 75–80.

47. "IMF to East Asia: OOPS!" *Business Week,* 29 May 2000, 60; Sachs, "Rule of the Ruble"; Lacayo, "IMF to the Rescue."

48. Sachs, "Rule of the Ruble"; Lacayo, "IMF to the Rescue."

49. Nicholas D. Kristof and David E. Sanger, "How U.S. Wooed Asia to Let Cash Flow In," *New York Times* Web site www.nytimes.com/library/world/global/021699global-econ.html [accessed

15 February 1999]; Paul Krugman, "Saving Asia: It's Time to Get Radical," *Fortune,* 7 September 1998, 75–80; Phillips, "One by One."

50. Kristof and Sanger, "How U.S. Wooed Asia to Let Cash Flow In."

51. Kurlantzick, "The Big Mango Bounces Back: Economic Recovery in Thailand and Southeast Asia"; Diane Brady and Jonathan Moore, "Happy Days Are Here Again? Not Quite," *Business Week,* 27 September 1999, 44–45; Peter Montagnon, "Catching the Next Wave," *Financial Times,* 28 December 1999, 10+.

52. Kristof and WuDunn, "The World's Ills May Be Obvious, But Their Cure Is Not."

53. Jean-Michael Paul, "Asian Economies May Suffer a Relapse," *Wall Street Journal,* 5 May 1999, A22; Michael Schuman, "Korea's Fast Recovery Suggests That Reform Isn't the Only Answer," *Wall Street Journal,* 14 May 1999, A1, A6.

54. Neela Banerjee, "Good News and Bad News on the Economy of Russia," *New York Times on the Web,* www.nytimes.com/library/financial/122099outlook-russ.html [accessed 28 February 2000]; Patricia Kranz and Margaret Coker, "The Tidal Wave of Cash Gushing Out of Russia," *Business Week,* 13 September 1999, 158.

55. Laurence Zuckerman, "Boeing's Leaders Losing Altitude," *New York Times,* 13 December 1998, BU1, 11.

56. Rob Norton, "Not So Fast: The Little Crisis That Couldn't," *Fortune,* 17 April 2000, 100; Justin Fox, "Forecast for the U.S. Economy: Still Mostly Sunny," *Fortune,* 15 February 1999, 92–98; David E. Sanger, "U.S. Trade Deficit Soared in '98, Reaching Record $168.8 Billion," *New York Times,* 20 February 1999, A1, B2; Michael M. Phillips, "How Long Can the U.S. Stay Immune to What Ails the Economy?" *Wall Street Journal,* 5 February 1999, A1, A10.

57. Phillips, "How Long Can the U.S. Stay Immune to What Ails the Economy?"

## CHAPTER 4

1. Christopher Palmeri, "Is Idealab! Running Dry?" *Business Week,* 5 June 2000, EB50; Rhonda L. Rundle, "Idealab! Registers for Stocking Offering; Welch Joins Board," *Wall Street Journal,* 21 April 2000, B6; James Lardner, "Ideas on the Assembly Line," *U.S. News & World Report,* 20 March 2000, 48–50; Rhonda L. Rundle, "Idealab! Receives Funds from Firms Totaling $1 Billion," *Wall Street Journal,* 14 March 2000, B8; Karen Kaplan, "At Idealab, Rewards Outweigh the Risks," *Los Angeles Times,* 13 March 2000, C1; Arlene Weintraub and Jennifer Reingold, "That's One Hot Incubator," *Business Week,* 13 March 2000, 42–43; Warren S. Hersch, "The 1999 Top 25 Executives: Deepockets," *Computer Reseller News,* 15 November 1999, 167; Emily Barker, "Bright Lights, Big Opportunity," *Inc.,* 14 September 1999, 22; Larry Armstrong, "They Thought We Were Crazy," *Business Week,* 8 March 1999, 38; Ann Marsh, "Warring Wallets," *Forbes,* 28 December 1998, 103; Larry Armstrong and Ronald Grover, "Bill Gross, Online Idea Factory," *Business Week,* 29 June 1998, 100; Ann Marsh, "Promiscuous Breeding," *Forbes,* 7 April 1997, 74–77; "Ideas by the Gross," *Inc.,* February 1997, 50; Jerry Useem, "The Start-up Factory," *Inc.,* February 1997, 40–52; "Hatching Ideas," *Upside,* December 1996, 30; Joseph Nocera, "Bill Gross Blew Through $800 Million in 8 Months And He's Got Nothing to Show For It," *Fortune,* 5 March 2001, 71–82.

2. David Birch, "Thinking About Tomorrow," *Wall Street Journal,* 24 May 1999, R30–R31.

3. Claudia H. Deutsch, "When a Big Company Hatches a Lot of Little Ideas," *New York Times,* 23 September 1998, D4.

4. "Matters of Fact," *Inc.,* April 1985, 32.

5. David Leonhardt, "Big Airlines Should Follow Midwest's Recipe," *Business Week,* 28 June 1999, 40; Stephenie N. Mehta, "Small Talk," *Wall Street Journal,* 23 May 1996, R28–R30.

6. Michael Moeller, Steve Hamm, and Timothy J. Mullaney, "Remaking Microsoft," *Business Week,* 17 May 1999, 106–16.

7. Timothy D. Schelhardt, "David in Goliath," *Wall Street Journal,* 23 May 1996, R14; Deutsch, "When a Big Company Hatches a Lot of Little Ideas."

8. Donna Fenn, "The Buyers," *Inc.,* June 1996, 46–52.

9. Brian O'Reilly, "The New Face of Small Business," *Fortune,* 2 May 1994, 82–88.

10. "The Facts About Small Business 1999," U.S. Small Business Administration, Office of Advocacy, SBA Website [accessed 5 June 2000] www.sba.gov/ADVO/stats/facts99.pdf.

11. Janice Castro, "Big vs. Small," *Time,* 5 September 1988, 49; Steve Solomon, *Small Business USA* (New York: Crown, 1986), 124.

12. Lloyd Gite and Dawn M. Baskerville, "Black Women Entrepreneurs on the Rise," *Black Enterprise,* August 1996, 73–74.

13. Rachel Beck, *Wall Street Journal Interactive Edition—Small Business Suite,* 28 March 1998, [accessed 21 April 1998] interactive.wsj.com/public/currentarticles/SB891025783545694000.htm.

14. Bill Meyers, "It's a Small-Business World," *USA Today,* 30 July 1999, B1, B2.

15. James Lardner and Paul Sloan, "The Anatomy of Sickly IPOs," *U.S. News and World Report,* 29 May 2000, 42; Hoover's Online [accessed 2 June 2000] www.hoovers.com/hoov/ipo/features/mainstats.html.

16. "Small Businesses Skeptical of Internet Impact," *NUA Internet Surveys,* 1 June 2000, [accessed 1 June 2000] www.nua.ie/surveys/index.org; "U.S. Small Businesses Spending More Online," *NUA Internet Surveys,* 17 May 2000 [accessed 1 June 2000] www.nua.ie/surveys/index.org.

17. Joshua Macht, "The Two Hundred Million Dash," *Inc. Technology 1997,* 16 September 1997, 48–55.

18. Tim McCollum, "A High-Tech Edge for Home Offices," *Nation's Business,* December 1998, 52–54.

19. *Inc. Special Edition—The State of Small Business 1997,* 20 May 1997, 112; James Wilfong and Toni Seger, *Taking Your Business Global* (Franklin Lakes, N.J.: Career Press, 1997), 84.

20. "The Facts About Small Business 1999," U.S. Small Business Administration, Office of Advocacy, SBA Website [accessed 5 June 2000] www.sba.gov/ADVO/stats/facts99.pdf.

21. Stephanie Armour, "Many Turn to Start-Ups for Freedom," *USA Today,* 8 June 1998, 1B, 2B; "The Top 500 Women-Owned Businesses," *Working Woman,* May 1998, 50.

22. Jane Fritsch, "Big in Small Business, Straining to Grow," *New York Times,* 23 September 1998, D2; "Report on Statistical Information About Women-Owned Businesses," *U.S. Small Business Administration,* October 1998 [accessed 31 May 2000] www.sba.gov/library/reportsroom.html; "SBA FY1999 Annual Performance Report," *U.S. Small Business Administration* [accessed 31 May 2000] www.sba.gov/aboutsba/indexreports.html; "Report on Statistical Information About Minority-Owned Businesses," [accessed 31 May 2000] www.sba.gov/library/reportsroom.html; "The Facts About Small Business 1999," U.S. Small Business Administration, Office of Advocacy, SBA Website [accessed 5 June 2000] www.sba.gov/ADVO/ stats/facts99.pdf.

23. Gordon Fairclough, "P&G to Slash 13,000 Jobs, Shut 10 Plants," *Wall Street Journal,* 10 June 1999, A3, A10.

24. Carolyn Brown, "How to Make Your Ex-Boss Your Client," *Black Enterprise,* 30 April 1994, 951.

25. Wilfong and Seger, *Taking Your Business Global,* 78–80; Kelly J. Andrews, "Born or Bred?" *Entrepreneurial Edge* 3 (1998): 24–28.

26. Jane Applegate, *Succeeding in Small Business* (New York: Plume/ Penguin, 1992), 1.

27. Lisa J. Moore and Sharon F. Golden, "You Can Plan to Expand or Just Let It Happen," *U.S. News & World Report,* 23 October 1989, 78; John Case, "The Origins of Entrepreneurship," *Inc.,* June 1989, 56.

28. Norm Brodsky, "Caveat Emptor," *Inc.,* August 1998, 31–32; "Why Buy a Business?" CCH Toolkit Web site, [accessed 20 May 1999] aol. toolkit.cch.com/text/PO1_0820.asp.

29. Dale Buss, "New Dynamics for a New Era," *Nation's Business,* January 1999, 45–48.

30. Roberta Maynard, "Choosing a Franchise," *Nation's Business,* October 1996, 56–63.

31. Latonya West, "Success Is Convenient," *Minorities in Business,* [undated], 22–26.

32. Jeffrey A. Tannenbaum, "Taking a Bath," *Wall Street Journal,* 22 June 1998, 27.

33. Heath Row, "Great Harvest's Recipe for Growth," *Fast Company,* December 1998, 46–48.

34. Roberta Maynard, "The Changing Landscape," *Nation's Business,* January 1997, 54–55.

35. "Small Business Answer Card 1998," Small Business Administration, Office of Advocacy, SBA Website [accessed 5 June 2000] www.sba.gov/ ADVO/stats/answer.pdf.

36. Joseph W. Duncan, "The True Failure Rate of Start-Ups," *D&B Reports,* January–February 1994; Maggie Jones, "Smart Cookies," *Working Woman,* April 1995, 50–52; Janice Maloney, "Failure May Not Be So Bad After All," *New York Times,* 23 September 1998, 12.

37. Jerry Useem, "The Secret of My Success," *Inc.,* May 1998, 67–80.

38. Maloney, "Failure May Not Be So Bad After All."

39. Gerda D. Gallop and Roz Ayres-Williams, "Five Things You Should Know Before Starting a Business," *Black Enterprise,* September 1998, 66–72.

40. SCORE Web site [accessed September 18, 1997] www.score.org; J. Tol Broome Jr., "SCORE's Impact on Small Firms," *Nation's Business,* January 1999, 41–43.

41. Broome, "SCORE's Impact on Small Firms"; Robert McGarvey, "Peak Performance," *American Way,* July 1996, 56–60.

42. Loren Fox, "Hatching New Companies," *Upside,* February 2000, 144–52.

43. Dale Buss, "Bringing New Firms out of Their Shell," *Nations Business,* March 1997, 48–50; Fox, "Hatching New Companies."

44. Buss, "Bringing New Firms out of Their Shell."

45. Jonathan Katz, "Hatching Ideas," *Industry Week,* 18 September 2000, 63–65.

46. James Lardner, "Ideas on the Assembly Line Thanks to Internet Incubators, Starting a New Business May Never Be the Same," *U.S. News & World Report,* 20 March 2000, 48–50.

47. McGarvey, "Peak Performance."

48. Juan Hovey, "Risky Business," *Industry Week,* 15 May 2000, 75–76.

49. Sharon Nelton, "Coming to Grips with Growth," *Nation's Business,* February 1998, 26–32.

50. Nelton, "Coming to Grips with Growth."

51. Nelton, "Coming to Grips with Growth."

52. Nelton, "Coming to Grips with Growth."

53. Michael Selz, "Here's the Problem," *Wall Street Journal— Breakaway Special Report Winter 1999,* 22 February 1999, 12.

54. Bob Zider, "How Venture Capital Works," *Harvard Business Review,* November/December 1998, 131–39.

55. Barbara Darrow, "Touched By An Angel," *Computer Reseller News,* 17 April 2000, 152, 156.

56. Jill Andresky Fraser, "Where Has All the Money Gone?" *Inc.,* April 2000, 101–10.

57. Darrow, "Touched By An Angel," 152, 156.

58. Jane Easter Bahls, "Cyber Cash; "Startup Financing: Finding an Angel to Get Going," CCH Business Owners Toolkit Web site, [accessed 20 May 1999] aol.toolkit.cch.com/columns/Starting/225-99AngelR.asp.

59. Darrow, "Touched By An Angel," 152,156.

60. Rodney Ho, "Banking on Plastic," *Wall Street Journal,* 9 March 1998, A1, A8.

61. Joel Russell, "Credit Card Capitalism," *Hispanic Business,* March 1998, 40.

62. Henry Wichmann Jr., Charles Harter, and H. Charles Sparks, "Big Cash for Small Business," *Journal of Accountancy,* July 1999, 64–72.

63. Wilfong and Seger, *Taking Your Business Global,* 20.

64. Ronaleen R. Roha, "Big Loans for Small Businesses," *Changing Times,* April 1989, 105–09; "Small Loans, Big Problems," *Economist,* 28 January 1995, 73; Elizabeth Kadetsky, "Small Loans, Big Dreams," *Working Woman,* February 1995, 46–49; Reid Rutherford, "Securitizing Small Business Loans: A Banker's Action Plan," *Commercial Lending Review,* Winter 1994–1995, 62–74.

65. Roha, "Big Loans for Small Businesses," 105.

66. Susan Hodges, "Microloans Fuel Big Ideas," *Nation's Business,* February 1997, 34–35.

67. Karen Gutloff, "Five Alternative Ways to Finance Your Business," *Black Enterprise,* March 1998, 81–85.

68. Roberta Maynard, "Are You Ready to Go Public," *Nation's Business,* January 1995, 30–32.

69. Robert A. Mamis, "Face to Face—Andy Klein," *Inc.,* July 1996, 39–40; Sharon Nelton, "Using the Internet to Find Funds," *Nation's Business,* August 1998, 35–36.

70. "E-Business Case Studies," IBM Web site [accessed 10 March 2000] www.ibm.com/e-business/case_studies/dsm.phtml.

71. C. J. Prince, "This Little Company Went to Market," *Chief Executive,* April 1999, 22.

72. Nelton, "Using the Internet to Find Funds."

73. Stephanie Gruner, "When Mom & Pop Go Public," *Inc.,* December 1996, 66–73.

## CHAPTER 5

1. Adapted from Kinko's Web site, [accessed 13 December 1998] www.kinkos.com/info; Shawn Tully, "A Better Taskmaster Than the Market," *Fortune,* 26 October 1998, 277–86; Laurie J. Flynn, "For the Officeless, A Place to Call Home," *New York Times,* 6 July 1998, 1, 4; Michele Marchetti, "Getting the Kinks Out," *Sales and Marketing Management,* March 1997, 56–64; "Man of Few Words," *Sales and Marketing Management,* March 1997, 63; "Kinko's Improves Image of Businesses with Top-Notch Proposals and Presentations Capabilities; Presentations a Growing Percentage of Customer Work at Kinko's," *Business Wire,* 28 September 1997; "Kinko's Strengthens Office Product Assortment," *Discount Store News,* 17 November 1997, 6, 70; Ann Marsh, "Kinko's Grows Up— Almost," *Forbes,* 1 December 1997, 270–72; "Kinko's Strikes Deal for Mideast Growth," *Graphic Arts Monthly,* January 1998, 22; Lori Ioannou and Paul Orfalea, "Interview: The Brains Behind Kinko's," *Your Company,* 1 May 1999, 621.

2. Norman M. Scarborough and Thomas W. Zimmerer, *Effective Small Business Management* (Upper Saddle River, N.J.: Prentice Hall, 2000), 84.

3. James W. Cortada, "Do You Take This Partner," *Total Quality Review,* November–December 1995, 11.

4. Laurence Zuckerman, "UPS Hears Market's Song, and Plans to Sell Some Stock," *New York Times,* 22 July 1999, A1, C23.

5. Vivien Kellerman, "A Growing Business Takes the Corporate Plunge," *New York Times,* 23 July 1994, sec. Your Money, 31.

6. Noshua Watson, "The Lists," *Fortune,* 17 April 2000, 289–95.

7. Scarborough and Zimmerer, *Effective Small Business Management,* 90.

8. Robert G. Goldstein, Russell Shapiro, and Edward A. Hauder, "So Many Choices of Business Entities—Which One Is Best for Your Needs?" *Insight (CPA Society),* February/March 1999, 10–16.

9. Rana Dogar, "Crony Baloney," *Working Woman,* January 1997; Richard H. Koppes, "Institutional Investors, Now in Control of More Than Half the Shares of U.S. Corporations, Demand More Accountability," *National Law Journal,* 14 April 1997, B5; John A. Byrne, "The Best & Worst Boards," *Business Week,* 25 November 1996, 82–84; Anthony Bianco, John Byrne, Richard Melcher, and Mark Maremont, "The Rush to Quality on Corporate Boards," *Business Week,* 3 March 1997, 34–35.

10. Cliff Edwards, "President of United Airlines Resigns Under Union Pressure—Edwardson Steps Down to Sidestep Turmoil," *Denver Rocky Mountain News,* 19 September 1998, 2B.

11. Gary Strauss, "From Public Service to Private Payday," *USA Today,* 17 April 2000, 1B, 2B.

12. Geoffrey Colvin, "America's Worst Boards," *Fortune,* 17 April 2000, 241–48.

13. David A. Nadler, "10 Steps to a Happy Merger," *New York Times,* 15 March 1998, BU14.

14. Peter Passell, "Do Mergers Really Yield Big Benefits?" *New York Times,* 14 May 1998, C1, C2.

15. "Merger Mania, Sobering Statistics," *The Economist,* 20 June 1998, 89.

16. Alex Taylor III, "More Mergers. Dumb Idea," *Fortune,* 15 February 1999, 26–27.

17. Nadler, "10 Steps to a Happy Merger"; Glenn Rifkin, "How IBM and Lotus Work Together," *Strategy and Business,* Third Quarter 1998, 42–61.

18. J. Robert Carleton, "Cultural Due Diligence," *Training,* November 1997, 67–75; "How to Merge," *The Economist.*

19. Almar Latour, "Detroit Meets a Worker Paradise," *Wall Street Journal,* 3 March 1999, B1, B4.

20. Michael Oneal, Brian Bremner, Jonathan B. Levine, Todd Vogel, Zachary Schiller, and David Woodruff, "The Best and Worst Deals of the '80s," *Business Week,* 15 January 1990, 52.

21. Irving W. Bailey II and Alvin H. Schechter, "The Corporation as Brand: An Identity Dilemma," *Chief Executive,* October 1994, 421.

22. Stephen Labaton, "800-Pound Gorillas," *New York Times,* 11 June 2000, sec. 4, 1.

23. Labaton, "800-Pound Gorillas."

24. William Glasgall, John Rossant, and Thane Peterson, "The Citicorp-Travelers Deal May Point the Way to the Future of Financial Services," *Business Week,* 20 April 1998, 35–37.

25. Martin Peers, Nick Wingfield, and Laura Landro, "AOL, Time Warner Set Plan to Link in Mammoth Merger," *Wall Street Journal,* 11 January 2000, A1, A6; Thomas E. Weber, Martin Peers, and Nick Wingfield, "Two Titans in a Strategic Bind Bet on a Futuristic Megadeal," *Wall Street Journal,* 11 January 2000, B1, B12; "AOL and Time Warner Will Merge to Create World's First Internet-Age Media and Communications Company," America Online Web site, [accessed 11 January 2000] media.web.aol.com/media/press.cfm.

26. Jeffrey Taylor, "Alarm Bells," *Wall Street Journal,* 12 May 1998, A1, A8; Tim Jones and Frank James, "FCC Head: No Ring of Certainty for Deal," *Chicago Tribune,* 13 May 1998, sec. 1, 1, 22; Jeffrey A. Tannenbaum, "The Consolidators: Acquisitive Companies Set Out to 'Roll Up' Fragmented Industries," *Wall Street Journal,* 3 March 1997, A1; Jon Van, "Ameritech Deal Targets Stocks over Consumers," *Chicago Tribune,* 12 May 1998, sec. 1, 1, 10.

27. Scott McCartney and Bill Adair, "Merger Talk Fills Skies and Airline Regulators Have a Juggling Act," *Wall Street Journal,* 8 June 2000, A1, A16.

28. Eleena De Lisser, "Banking on Mergers," *Wall Street Journal,* 24 May 1999, R25.

29. Stephen Labaton, "U.S. Set to Clear a Merger between Exxon and Mobil," *New York Times,* 27 November 1999, A1, B2.

30. Merrill Goozner and John Schmeltzer, "Mass Exodus Hits Corporate Names," *Chicago Tribune,* 12 May 1998, sec. 3, 1, 3; Bill Vlasic, "The First Global Car Colossus," *Business Week,* 18 May 1998, 40–43; Abid Aslam, "Exxon-Mobil Merger Could Poison the Well," *Inter Press Service English News Wire,* 2 December 1998, Electric Library [accessed 2 June 1999]; Agis Salpukas, "Do Oil and Bigger Oil Mix?" *New York Times,* 2 December 1998, C1, C4.

31. Steve Lipen, "Concentration: Corporations' Dreams Converge in One Idea: It's Time to Do a Deal," *Wall Street Journal,* 26 February 1997, A1, A8.

32. "Business: Pfizer's Prize," *Economist,* 12 February 2000, 69; Nikheil Deogun and Robert Langreth, "P&G Walks Away From Merger Talks Stock Decline Prompts End to Warner-AHP Link; Bidder Pfizer Bolstered," *Wall Street Journal,* 25 January 2000, A3.

33. Joann S. Lublin, " 'Poison Pills' Are Giving Shareholders a Big Headache, Union Proposals Assert," *Wall Street Journal,* 23 May 1997, C1.

34. Thomas Mulligan, "ITT Takes Starwood Offer," *Los Angeles Times,* 13 November 1997, D2; Kathleen Morris, "Behind the New Deal Mania," *Business Week,* 3 November 1997, 36.

35. Martha Groves and Stuart Silverstein, "Levi Strauss Offers Year's Pay as Incentive Bonus," *Los Angeles Times,* 13 June 1996, A1.

36. Michael Hickins, "Searching for Allies," *Management Review,* January 2000, 54–58.

37. Hickins, "Searching for Allies," 54–58.

38. Gary Dessler, *Management,* 2d ed. (Upper Saddle River, N.J.: Prentice Hall, 2001), 45.

## CHAPTER 6

1. Jared Sandberg, "Case Study," *Newsweek,* 24 January 2000, 31–36; Fred Vogelstein, "The Talented Mr. Case," *U.S. News & World Report,* 24 January 2000, 41–42; David Lieberman, "Merger Fulfills Needs of Each," *USA Today,* 11 January 2000, 1B–2B; Kara Swisher, "How Steve Case Morphed into a Media Mogul," *Wall Street Journal,* 11 January 2000, B1, B12; Thomas E. Weber, Martin Peers, and Nick Wingfield, "Two Titans in a Strategic Bind Bet on a Futuristic Megadeal," *Wall Street Journal,* 11 January 2000, B1, B12; Joshua Cooper Ramo, "How AOL Lost the Battles But Won the War," *Time,* 22 September 1997, 46.

2. Richard L. Daft, *Management,* 4th ed. (Fort Worth, Tex.: Dryden Press, 1997), 8.

3. Courtland L. Bovée, John V. Thill, Marian Burk Wood, and George P. Dovel, *Management* (New York: McGraw-Hill, 1993), 220; David H. Holt, *Management: Principles and Practices,* 2d ed. (Upper Saddle River, N.J.: Prentice Hall, 1990), 10–12; James A. F. Stoner, *Management,* 4th ed. (Upper Saddle River, N.J.: Prentice Hall, 1989), 15–18.

4. Gillian Flynn, "A Flight Plan for Success," *Workforce,* July 1997, 72–78.

5. Norman M. Scarborough and Thomas W. Zimmerer, *Effective Small Business Management* (Upper Saddle River, N.J.: Prentice Hall, 2000), 41–56.

6. Stephen P. Robbins, *Managing Today* (Upper Saddle River, N.J.: Prentice Hall, 1997), 452.

7. David Bank and Don Clark, "Microsoft Broadens Vision Statement Beyond PCs," *Wall Street Journal,* 23 July 1999, A3, A4.

8. Leonard Goodstein, Timothy Nolan, and J. William Pfeiffer, *Applied Strategic Planning* (New York: McGraw-Hill, 1993), 169–92.

9. Aimee L. Stern, "Management: You Can Keep Your Staff on the Competitive Track If You . . . Inspire Your Team with a Mission Statement," *Your Company,* 1 August 1997, 36.

10. Toni Mack and Mary Summers, "Danger: Stealth Attack," *Forbes,* 25 January 1999, 88–92.

11. Joshua Cooper Ramo, "How AOL Lost the Battles But Won the War," *Time,* 22 September 1997, 46.

12. Scarborough and Zimmerer, *Effective Small Business Management,* 50.

13. Daft, *Management,* 221–23, 260–62.

14. Judy A. Smith, "Crisis Communications: The War on Two Fronts," *Industry Week,* 20 May 1996, 136; John F. Reukus, "Hazard Communication," *Occupational Hazards,* February 1998, 39; Kim M. Gibson and Steven H. Smith, "Do We Understand Each Other?" *Journal of Accountancy,* January 1998, 53.

15. Timothy Aeppel, Clare Ansberry, Milo Geyelin, and Robert L. Simison, "Road Signs: How Ford, Firestone Let the Warnings Slide By as Debacle Developed," *Wall Street Journal,* 6 September 2000, A1; Joann Muller, David Welch, Jeff Green, Lorraine Woellert, and Nicole St. Pierre, "A Crisis of Confidence," *Business Week,* 18 September 2000, 40–42.

16. William Echikson, Stephen Baker, and Dean Frost, "Things Aren't Going Better with Coke," *Business Week,* 28 June 1999, 49; Janine Reid, "Keeping a Crisis From Going Bad to Worse," *Air Conditioning, Heating & Refrigeration News,* 24 January 2000, 41+.

17. Edward A. Robinson, "America's Most Admired Companies," *Fortune,* 3 March 1997, 68; Susan Chandler, "Crisis Management: How TWA Faced the Nightmare," *Business Week,* 5 August 1996, 30; Kerri Selland, "Experts Say Corporations Ill-Prepared for Crises," *Reuters,* 23 July 1996; Thomas S. Mulligan, "TWA Garners Weak Marks for Crisis Management," *Los Angeles Times,* 20 July 1996, D1; Tom Incantalupo, "TWA's Image Polishing," *Newsday,* 23 July 1996, A49.

18. Michael Moeller, Steve Hamm, and Timothy J. Mullaney, "Remaking Microsoft," *Business Week,* 17 May 1999, 106–16.

19. Stephanie Armour, "Once Plagued by Pink Slips, Now They're in Driver's Seat," *USA Today,* 14 May 1998, 1B–2B.

20. Daft, *Management,* 219–21.

21. Gary A. Yukl, *Leadership in Organizations,* 2d ed. (Upper Saddle River, N.J.: Prentice Hall, 1989), 9, 175–76.

22. Daniel Goleman, "What Makes a Leader?" *Harvard Business Review,* November–December 1998, 92–102; Shari Caudron, "The Hard Case for Soft Skills," *Workforce,* July 1999, 60–66.

23. Daft, *Management,* 498–99.

24. Michael A. Verespej, "Lead, Don't Manage," *Industry Week,* 4 March 1996, 58.

25. Stratford Sherman, "Secrets of HP's 'Muddled' Team," *Fortune,* 18 March 1996, 116–20.

26. Daniel Goleman, "Leadership That Gets Results," *Harvard Business Review,* March–April 2000, 78–90.

27. Stephen P. Robbins and David A. De Cenzo, *Fundamentals of Management,* 2d ed. (Upper Saddle River, N.J.: Prentice Hall, 1998), 55–56; James Waldroop and Timothy Butler, "The Executive as Coach," *Harvard Business Review,* November–December 1996, 113.

28. Kathryn Tyler, "Scoring Big in the Workplace," *HR Magazine,* June 2000, 96–106.

29. "The Advantage of Female Mentoring," *Working Woman,* October 1991, 104.

30. Ram Charan and Geoffrey Colvin, "Why CEOs Fail," *Fortune,* 21 June 1999, 69–78.

31. James A. Belasco and Ralph C. Stayer, *Flight of the Buffalo* (New York: Warner Books, 1993), 138.

32. Michael Been and Nitin Nohria, "Cracking the Code of Change," *Harvard Business Review,* May–June 2000, 133–41.

33. Michael Barrier, "Managing Workers in Times of Change," *Nation's Business,* May 1998, 31–32.

34. J. Robert Carleton, "Cultural Due Diligence," *Training,* November 1997, 67–75.

35. Joanne Cole, "Flying High at Southwest," *HR Focus,* May 1998, 8+.

36. Kostas N. Dervitsiotis, "The Challenge of Managing Organizational Change," *Total Quality Management,* February 1998, 109–22.

37. George Taninecz, "Borg-Warner Automotive," *Industry Week,* 19 October 1998, 44–46.

38. Bovée et al., *Management,* 680.

39. Michael A. Verespej, "Stability Before Growth," *Industry Week,* 15 April 1996, 12–16.

40. James R. Lackritz, "TQM Within Fortune 500 Corporations," *Quality Progress,* February 1997, 69–72.

41. David Sirota, Brian Usilaner, and Michelle S. Weber, "Sustaining Quality Improvement," *Total Quality Review,* March–April 1994, 23; Joe Batten, "A Total Quality Culture," *Management Review,* May 1994, 61; Rahul Jacon, "More Than a Dying Fad?" *Fortune,* 18 October 1993, 66–72.

42. Lackritz, "TQM Within Fortune 500 Corporations."

43. Robert L. Katz, "Skills of an Effective Administrator," *Harvard Business Review,* September–October 1974. Reprinted in *Paths Toward Personal Progress: Leaders Are Made, Not Born* (Boston: Harvard Business Review, 1983), 23–35; Mike Dawson, "Leaders Versus Managers," *Systems Management,* March 1995, 32; R. S. Dreyer, "Do Good Bosses Make Lousy Leaders?" *Supervision,* March 1995, 19–20; Michael Maccoby, "Teams Need Open Leaders," *Research-Technology Management,* January–February 1995, 57–59.

44. Courtland L. Bovée and John V. Thill, *Business Communication Today,* 6th ed. (Upper Saddle River, N.J.: Prentice Hall, 2000), 4.

45. Daft, *Management,* 128; Kathryn M. Bartol and David C. Martin, *Management* (New York: McGraw-Hill, 1991), 268–72.

46. Bartol and Martin, *Management,* 268–72; Ricky W. Griffin, *Management,* 3d ed. (Boston: Houghton Mifflin, 1990), 131–37.

47. Robbins, *Managing Today,* 72.

## CHAPTER 7

1. American Express Company's Web site www.americanexpress.com; [accessed 29 July 2000] Sally Richards, "Make the Most of Your First Job," *Informationweek,* 21 June 1999, 183–86; Tim Greene, "American Express: Don't Leave Home to Go to Work," *Network World,* 8 March 1999, 25; Mahlon Apgar IV, "The Alternative Workplace: Changing Where and How People Work," *Harvard Business Review,* May/June 1998, 121–30; "How Senior Executives at American Express View the Alternative Workplace," *Harvard Business Review,* May/June 1998, 132–33; Michelle Marchetti, "Master Motivators," *Sales and Marketing Management,* April 1998, 38–44; Carrie Shook, "Leader, Not Boss," *Forbes,* 1 December 1997, 52–54.

2. Richard L. Daft, *Management,* 4th ed. (Fort Worth, Tex.: Dryden Press, 1997), 358.

3. Rob Goffee and Gareth Jones, "What Holds the Modern Company Together?" *Harvard Business Review,* November–December 1996, 134–45.

4. Peter F. Drucker, "Management's New Paradigms," *Forbes,* 5 October 1998, 152–76.

5. Stephen P. Robbins, *Managing Today!* (Upper Saddle River, N.J.: Prentice Hall, 1997), 193; Daft, *Management,* 320.

6. Stephen P. Robbins and David A. De Cenzo, *Fundamentals of Management,* 2d ed. (Upper Saddle River, N.J.: Prentice Hall, 1998), 201; Daft, *Management,* 321.

7. "Sharing Knowledge Through BP's Virtual Team Network," *Harvard Business Review*, September–October 1997, 152–53.

8. Alan Webber, "The Best Organization Is No Organization," *USA Today,* 13A; Eve Tahmincioglu, "How GM's Team Approach Works," *Gannett News Service,* 24 April 1996, S11.

9. Fred R. David, *Strategic Management*, 6th ed. (Upper Saddle River, N.J.: Prentice Hall, 1997), 225; Kathryn M. Bartol and David C. Martin, *Management* (New York: McGraw-Hill, 1991), 352.

10. Jeanne Dugan, Alison Rea, and Joseph Weber, "The BW 50: Business Week's Performance Rankings of the S&P 500 Best Performers," *Business Week,* 24 March 1997, 80.

11. Daft, *Management,* 325.

12. Bartol and Martin, *Management,* 345.

13. Courtland L. Bovée, John V. Thill, Marian Wood, George Dovel, *Management* (New York: McGraw-Hill, 1993), 285.

14. Bartol and Martin, *Management,* 370–71.

15. Gary Izumo, "Teamwork Holds Key to Organization Success," *Los Angeles Times,* 20 August 1996, D9; Daft, *Management,* 328–29; David, *Strategic Management,* 223.

16. John A. Byrne, "The Horizontal Corporation," *Business Week,* 20 December 1993, 76–81; "Is a Horizontal Organization for You?" *Fortune,* 3 April 1995, 96; Rahul Jacob, "The Struggle to Create an Organization for the 21st Century," *Fortune,* 3 April 1995, 90–96.

17. Steven Burke, "Acer Restructures into Six Divisions," *Computer Reseller News,* 13 July 1998, 10; Acer America Web site [accessed 20 July 2000] www.acer.com/aac/about/profile.htm.

18. Daft, *Management,* 328–29, 332; David, *Strategic Management,* 223; Bartol and Martin, *Management,* 376.

19. Dan Dimancescu and Kemp Dwenger, "Smoothing the Product Development Path," *Management Review,* 1 January 1996, 36.

20. Dimancescu and Dwenger, "Smoothing the Product Development Path."

21. Robbins, *Managing Today!* 209; Daft, *Management,* 333–36.

22. Daft, *Management,* 340–43; Robbins, *Managing Today!* 213–14.

23. Donna Fenn, "Managing Virtual Employees," *Inc.,* July 1996, 91.

24. Daft, *Management,* 340–43; Robbins, *Managing Today!,* 213–14.

25. "The Horizontal Organization," *Soundview Executive Book Summaries* 21, no. 3, (March 1999): 1–8.

26. "The Horizontal Organization."

27. "The Horizontal Organization."

28. Daft, *Management,* 352–53; Richards, *Strategic Management,* 217; Bartol and Martin, *Management,* 357–58.

29. Daft, *Management,* 338.

30. Stephen P. Robbins, *Essentials of Organizational Behavior,* 6th ed. (Upper Saddle River, N. J.: Prentice Hall, 2000), 105.

31. Daft, *Management,* 591; Robbins, *Managing Today!,* 295.

32. "Microsoft Teamwork," *Executive Excellence,* 6 July 1996, 6–7.

33. Jeffrey Pfeffer, "When It Comes to 'Best Practices'—Why Do Smart Organizations Occasionally Do Dumb Things?" *Organizational Dynamics,* 1 June 1996, 33; LaMar A. Trego,

"Reengineering Starts with a 'Clean Sheet of Paper,' " *Manage,* 1 July 1996, 17.

34. Daft, *Management,* 594–95; Robbins and De Cenzo, *Fundamentals of Management,* 336; Robbins, *Managing Today!* 309.

35. Pfeffer, "When It Comes to 'Best Practices.' "

36. Scott Kirsner, "Every Day, It's a New Place," *Fast Company,* April–May 1998, 132–34.

37. Daft, *Management,* 594; Robbins and De Cenzo, *Fundamentals of Management,* 336.

38. Jenny C. McCune, "On the Train Gang: In the New Flat Organizations, Employees Who Want to Be Competitive Must Be Versatile Enough to Perform a Variety of Tasks," *Management Review,* 1 October 1994, 57.

39. Daft, *Management,* 594; Robbins and De Cenzo, *Fundamentals of Management,* 338; Robbins, *Managing Today!* 310–11.

40. Seth Lubove, "Destroying the Old Hierarchies," *Forbes,* 3 June 1996, 62–64.

41. W. V. Bussmann, "Making a Difference at Chrysler," *Business Economics,* July 1998, 10–12.

42. Ellen Neuborne, "Companies Save, But Workers Pay," *USA Today,* 25 February 1997, B1; Daft, *Management,* 594; Robbins and De Cenzo, *Fundamentals of Management,* 338; Robbins, *Managing Today!* 310.

43. Richard Moderow, "Teamwork Is the Key to Cutting Costs," *Modern Healthcare,* 29 April 1996, 138.

44. Daft, *Management,* 594.

45. Robbins, *Essentials of Organizational Behavior,* 109.

46. Deborah L. Duarte and Nancy Tennant Snyder, *Mastering Virtual Teams* (San Francisco: Jossey-Bass Publishers, 1999), 23.

47. "Sharing Knowledge Through BP's Virtual Team Network," *Harvard Business Review,* September–October 1997, 152–53.

48. Daft, *Management,* 612–15.

49. Robbins, *Essentials of Organizational Behavior*, 98.

50. Ross Sherwood, "The Boss's Open Door Means More Time for Employees," *Reuters Business Report,* 30 September 1996.

51. Neuborne, "Companies Save, But Workers Pay," B2; Charles L. Parnell, "Teamwork: Not a New Idea, But It's Transforming the Workplace," *Vital Speeches of the Day,* 1 November 1996, 46.

52. Robbins and De Cenzo, *Fundamentals of Management,* 151.

53. Larry Cole and Michael Cole, "Why is the Teamwork Buzz Word Not Working?" *Communication World,* February/March 1999, 29; Patricia Buhler, "Managing in the 90s: Creating Flexibility in Today's Workplace," *Supervision,* January 1997, 24+; Allison W. Amason, Allen C. Hochwarter, Wayne A. Thompson, and Kenneth R. Harrison, "Conflict: An Important Dimension in Successful Management Teams," *Organizational Dynamics,* Autumn 1995, 20+.

54. "Team Players," *Executive Excellence,* May 1999, 18.

55. Robbins and De Cenzo, *Fundamentals of Management,* 334–35; Daft, *Management,* 602–03.

56. Robbins, *Managing Today!* 297–98; Daft, *Management,* 604–07.

57. Thomas K. Capozzoli, "Conflict Resolution—A Key Ingredient in Successful Teams," *Supervision,* November 1999, 14–16.

58. Daft, *Management,* 609–12.

59. Steven Crom and Herbert France, "Teamwork Brings Breakthrough Improvements in Quality and Climate," *Quality Progress,* March 1996, 39–41.

60. David, *Strategic Management,* 221.

61. Phyllis Gail Doloff, "Beyond the Org Chart," *Across the Board,* February 1999, 43–47.

62. Stephanie Armour, "Failure to Communicate Costly for Companies," *USA Today,* 30 September 1998, 1A.

## CHAPTER 8

1. Adapted from Michael O'Neill, "There's Something About Cisco," *Fortune,* 15 May 2000, 114–38; Karl Taro Greenfeld, "Do You Know Cisco?" *Time,* 17 January 2000, 72–74; Julie Pitta, "The Cisco Kid," *Forbes,* 10 January 2000, 108–10; Andy Reinhardt, "Meet Mr. Internet," *Business Week,* 13 September 1999, 129–40; Marguerite Reardon, "Sizzling Cisco," *Informationweek,* 28 February 2000, 46–61; Henry Goldblatt, "Cisco's Secrets," *Fortune,* 8 November 1999, 177–84; Andy Reinhardt, "John T. Chambers," *Business Week,* 27 September 1999, EB52; Glenn Drexhage, "How Cisco Bought It's Way to the Top," *Corporate Finance,* May 1999, 26–30; Jodi Mardesich, "Cisco's Plan to Pop Up in Your Home," *Fortune,* 1 February 1999, 119–20; Richard L. Brandt, "President and CEO of Cisco Systems: John Chambers—On the Future of Communications and the Failure of Deregulation," *Upside,* October 1998, 122–33; Andrew Kupfer, "The Real King of the Internet," *Fortune,* 7 September 1998, 84–93; Eric Neer, "Cisco," *Fortune,* 5 February 2001, 91–96; Edward Iwata, "Juniper Attacks Cisco With 'Smart Bomb' Accuracy." *USA Today,* 30 January 2001, 66-72.

2. Kim Komando, "Taking Control of Info Overload," *USA Today,* 16 June 1999, 6D.

3. Bill Gates, *Business @ the Speed of Thought* (New York: Warner Books, 1999), 3.

4. Larry Long and Nancy Long, *Computers,* 6th ed. (Upper Saddle River, N.J.: Prentice Hall, 1999), MIS 5.

5. Kathryn M. Bartol and David C. Martin, *Management* (New York: McGraw-Hill, 1991), 703–05.

6. Richard L. Daft, *Management,* 4th ed. (Fort Worth, Tex.: Dryden, 1997), 688.

7. Kayte VanScoy, "Get Inside Your Customers' Heads," *SmartBusinessMag.Com,* June 2000, 100–114.

8. John W. Verity, "Coaxing Meaning out of Raw Data," *Business Week,* 3 February 1997, 134.

9. Daft, *Management,* 686.

10. Daft, *Management,* 687.

11. Bartol and Martin, *Management,* 709–10.

12. David Morse, ed., *CyberDictionary* (Santa Monica, Calif.: Knowledge Exchange, 1996), 19.

13. Long and Long, *Computers,* 21–22.

14. Paul C. Judge, "Artificial Imagination," *Business Week,* 18 March 1996, 60.

15. John Woram, "Feature: PC: Talk to Me!—Voice Recognition is Starting to Make Some Noise," *Windows,* 1 November 1997, 208; Walter S. Mossberg, "Dragon Systems Take a Giant Step in Speech Recognition," *Wall Street Journal,* 12 June 1997, B1; Long and Long, *Computers,* 137.

16. Long and Long, *Computers,* CORE 18.

17. Mark Halper, "Bigiron.com: Why Merrill Lynch, J.C. Penney, Wells Fargo, and Others Turned Their Old Mainframe Computers into Hot Web Servers," *Forbes ASAP,* 2 June 1997, 38–39.

18. Long and Long, *Computers,* CORE 19.

19. "IBM's Powerful Supercomputer," *Wall Street Journal,* 29 June 2000, B8.

20. Gene Bylinksy, "The Digital Factory," *Fortune,* 14 November 1994, 92–110.

21. Timothy Trainor and Diane Krasnewich, *Computers!* (New York: McGraw-Hill, 1989), 90.

22. Laurie Flynn, "CD-ROMs: They're Not Just for Entertainment," *New York Times,* 24 April 1994, sec. f, 10; Nancy K. Herther, "CD-ROM at Ten Years: The Technology and the Industry Mature," *Online,* March/April 1995, 86–93.

23. Long and Long, *Computers,* CORE 117, 122.

24. Long and Long, *Computers,* CORE 161.

25. Scott Leibs, "Think Before You Link," *Industry Week,* 17 April 2000, 22–27.

26. Brent Schlender, "Damn the Torpedoes! Full Speed Ahead," *Fortune* (European Edition), 10 July 2000, 39–52.

27. G. Christian Hill, "First Voice, Now Data," *Wall Street Journal,* 20 September 1999, R4; Nicole Harris, "All Together Now," *Wall Street Journal,* 20 September 1999, R10; G. Christian Hill, "Siber-Talk," *Wall Street Journal,* 20 September 1999, R27.

28. Michael Krantz, "Wired for Speed," *Time,* 23 September 1996, 54–55; Michael Krantz, "The Biggest Thing Since Color?" *Time,* 12 August 1996, 42–43.

29. Richard Des Ruisseaux, "Tech," *Gannett News Service,* 30 March 2000, ARC.

30. Salina Khan, "Gadgets Help You Get Out of Line," *USA Today,* 20 December 1999, 3B.

31. Janet Guyon, "The World Is Your Office," *Fortune,* 12 June 2000, 227–34.

32. Samuel Greengard, "How Secure Is Your Data?" *Workforce,* 52–60; Nikhil Hutheesing and Philip E. Ross, "Hackerphobia," *Forbes,* 23 March 1998, 150–54.

33. Rob Kaiser, "FBI Hunts Hackers Who Hit Microsoft," *Chicago Tribune,* 28 October 2000, sec. 1, 1, 3.

34. Elisa Williams, "Workplace Web Cops on the Watch," *Chicago Tribune,* 1 June 1998, B1, B8.

35. Julie Deardorff, "With Voice Mail, You Never Know Who's Listening," *Chicago Tribune,* 6 July 1998, 1, 8.

36. John Galvin, "Cheating, Lying, Stealing," *SmartBusinessMag.Com,* June 2000, 86–99.

37. Ira Sager, Steve Hamm, Neil Gross, John Carey, and Robert D. Hof, "Cyber Crime," *Business Week,* 21 February 2000, 37–42.

38. Kevin Maney, "Tainted Love," *USA Today,* 5 May 2000, 1B–2B.

39. Sager et al., "Cyber Crime."

## CHAPTER 9

1. Lidia Kelly, "For Krispy Kreme, Doughnuts a Delicacy," *The Arizona Republic,* 20 June 2000, D1; Avital Louria Hahn, "Krispy Kreme IPO Brings Jelly-Filled to a Dot-Com World," *The Investment Dealers' Digest: IDD,* 17 January 2000, 9, 14; Karyn Strauss, "Looking to Raise Dough . . . The Public Way: Krispy Kreme Goes for IPO," *Nation's Restaurant News,* 3 January 2000, 26; Charles Fishman, "The King of Kreme," *Fast Company,* October 1999, 268–78; Scott McCormack, "Sweet Success," *Forbes,* 7 September 1998; Chuck Martin, "For the Love of a Good Doughnut: Krispy Kremes Gain Status Across the Nation," *Gannett News Service,* 10 September 1997; Fred Faust, "Doughnuts Holing on in Munch Crunch," *St. Louis Post-Dispatch,* 21 July 1997, 12; Paul Brown and Robert Siegel, "Krispy Kreme History," *All Things Considered,* National Public Radio, 17 July 1997.

2. Roberta A. Russell and Bernard W. Taylor III, *Operations Management: Focusing on Quality and Competitiveness,* 2d ed. (Upper Saddle River, N.J.: Prentice Hall, 1998), 21.

3. Justin Martin, "Are You As Good As You Think You Are?" *Fortune,* 30 September 1996, 143–44; "Creating Greater Customer Value May Require a Lot of Changes," *Organizational Dynamics,* Summer 1998, 26.

4. Diane Brady, Katie Kerwin, David Welch, Louise Lee, and Rob Hof, "Customizing for the Masses," *Business Week,* 20 March 2000, 130B–130F.

5. John Greenwald, "Cruise Lines Go Overboard," *Time,* 11 May 1998, 42–45.

6. Joseph G. Monks, *Operations Management, Theory and Problems* (New York: McGraw-Hill, 1987), 77–78.

7. Mark M. Davis, Nicholas J. Aquilano, and Richard B. Chase, *Fundamentals of Operations Management* (Boston: Irwin McGraw-Hill, 1999), 241–42.

8. Jae K. Shim and Joel G. Siegel, *Operations Management* (Hauppauge, N.Y.: Barron's Educational Series, 1999), 206.

9. Monks, *Operations Management, Theory and Problems,* 2–3.

10. Shim and Siegel, *Operations Management,* 206.

11. Monks, *Operations Management, Theory and Problems,* 125.

12. Davis, Aquilano, and Chase, *Fundamentals of Operations Management,* 254; Richard L. Daft, *Management,* 4th ed. (Fort Worth, Tex.: Dryden Press, 1997), 718.

13. Kathryn M. Bartol and David C. Martin, *Management* (New York: McGraw-Hill, 1991), 307–08.

14. Roger Crockett, "Chow (On) Line," *Business Week E.Biz,* 5 June 2000, EB 84–90.

15. Larry E. Long and Nancy Long, *Introduction to Computers and Information Systems,* 5th ed. (Upper Saddle River, N.J.: Prentice Hall, 1997), AT 84.

16. Stuart F. Brown, "Giving More Jobs to Electronic Eyes," *Fortune,* 16 February 1998, 104B–104D.

17. "IBM and Dassault Awarded Boeing CATIA Contract," *CAD/CAM Update,* 1 January 1997, 1–8.

18. Russell and Taylor III, *Operations Management,* 211

19. "CAD/CAM Industry Embracing Intranet-Based Technologies," *Computer Dealer News* 12 (28 November 1996): 21.

20. Drew Winter, "C3P: New Acronym Signals Big Change at Ford," *Ward's Auto World* 32 (1 August 1996): 34; Thomas Hoffman, "Ford to Cut Its Prototype Costs," *Computerworld,* 30 September 1996, 65; Drew Winter, "Massive Changes Coming in Computer Engineering," *Ward's Auto World* 32 (1 April 1996): 34.

21. Davis, Aquilano, and Chase, *Fundamentals of Operations Management,* 64; Russell and Taylor, *Operations Management,* 257–58.

22. Russell and Taylor, *Operations Management,* 255–56.

23. John H. Sheridan, "Agile Manufacturing: Stepping Beyond Lean Production," *Industry Week,* 19 April 1993, 30–46.

24. Brian McWilliams, "Re-engineering the Small Factory," *Inc. Technology,* 1 (1996): 44–5.

25. Neal M. Goldsmith and Ed Rosenfeld, "Shooting the Rapids—Business Process Reengineering Can Be a Wild Ride, But There Are a Number of Tools and Services Available to Help Companies Manage Change and Maximize Growth," *Information Week,* 25 November 1996, 65; John H. Sheridan, "Lessons from the Best," *Industry Week,* 19 February 1996, 16–17; Bartol and Martin, *Management,* 688.

26. Jon E. Hilsenrath, "Parts Shortages Hamper Electronics Makers Surging Demand Shows Flaw in Just-in-Time Chains," *Wall Street Journal,* 7 July 2000, B5.

27. Shim and Siegel, *Operations Management,* 326.

28. Russell and Taylor, *Operations Management,* 712–33.

29. Patricia W. Hamilton, "Getting a Grip on Inventory," *D&B Reports,* March–April 1994, 32.

30. Robert O. Knorr and John L. Neuman, "Quick Response Technology: The Key to Outstanding Growth," *Journal of Business Strategy,* September–October 1992, 63.

31. Russell and Taylor, *Operations Management,* 652–53.

32. Karl Ritzler, "A Mercedes Made from Scratch," *Atlanta Journal and Constitution,* 30 May 1997, S1.

33. Del Jones, "Training and Service at Top of Winners' List," *USA Today,* 17 October 1996, 5B.

34. John A. Byrne, "Never Mind the Buzzwords. Roll up Your Sleeves," *Business Week,* 22 January 1996, 84.

35. Davis, Aquilano, and Chase, *Fundamentals of Operations Management,* 177–79; Russell and Taylor, *Operations Management,* 131.

36. William M. Carley, "Charging Ahead: To Keep GE's Profits Rising, Welch Pushes Quality-Control Plan," *Wall Street Journal,* 13 January 1997, A1, A6.

37. Russell and Taylor, *Operations Management,* 131.

38. Hugh D. Menzies, "Global Guide: Quality Counts When Wooing Overseas Clients," *Your Company,* 1 June 1997, 64; Michael E. Raynor, "Worldwide Winners," *Total Quality Management,* July–August 1993, 43–48; Greg Bounds, Lyle Yorks, Mel Adams, and Gipsie Ranney, *Beyond Total Quality Management: Toward the Emerging Paradigm* (New York: McGraw-Hill, 1994), 212; Russell and Taylor, *Operations Management,* 115–16.

39. Ronald Henkoff, "Boeing's Big Problem," *Fortune,* 12 January 1998, 96–103; James Wallace, "How Boeing Blew It," *Sales and Marketing Management,* February 1998, 52–57; John Greenwald, "Is Boeing out of Its Spin?" *Time,* 13 July 1998, 67–69; John T. Landry, "Supply Chain Management: The Case for Alliances," *Harvard Business Review,* November–December 1998, 24–25.

40. Davis, Aquilano, and Chase, *Fundamentals of Operations Management,* 382.

41. Russell and Taylor, *Operations Management,* 440.

42. Landry, "Supply Chain Management."

43. Timothy M. Laseter, "Balanced Sourcing the Honda Way," *Strategy and Business,* Fourth Quarter 1998, 24–31.

44. George Taninecz, "Forging the Chain," *Industry Week,* 15 May 2000, 40–46.

45. David Woodruff, Ian Katz, and Keith Naughton, "VW's Factory of the Future," *Business Week,* 7 October 1996, 52, 56.

46. Saul Hansell, "Is This the Factory of the Future?" *New York Times,* 26 July 1998, sec. 3, 1, 12–13; Pete Engardio, "Souping Up the Supply Chain," *Business Week,* 31 August 1998, 110–12; John A. Byrne, "Management By Web," *Business Week,* 28 August 2000, 84–96.

47. Gene Bylinsky, "For Sale: Japanese Plants in the U.S." *Fortune,* 21 February 2000, 240B–240D.

48. Hansell, "Is This the Factory of the Future?"; Engardio, "Souping Up the Supply Chain."

49. Hansell, "Is This the Factory of the Future?"; Engardio, "Souping Up the Supply Chain."

50. Laurence Zuckerman, "The Jet Wars of the Future," *New York Times,* 9 July 1999, C1, C5.

## CHAPTER 10

1. Charles Fishman, "Moving Toward a Balanced Work Life," *Workforce,* March 2000, 38–42; Joanne Cole, "Case Study: SAS Institute Inc. Uses Sanity as Strategy," *HR Focus,* May 1999, 6; Charles Fishman, "Sanity Inc.," *Fast Company,* January 1999, 85–96.

2. Fishman, "Moving Toward a Balanced Work Life."

3. Stephanie Armour, "Workplace Hazard Gets Attention," *USA Today,* 5 May 1998, B1.

4. "Finding and Keeping Talent in the Internet Age," *Chief Executive,* February 2000, 32–34.

5. Michael A. Verespej, "Balancing Act," *Industry Week,* 15 May 2000, 81–85.

6. Dennis C. Kinlaw, "What Employees See Is What Organizations Get," *Management Solutions,* March 1988, 38–41.

7. John McMorrow, "Future Trends in Human Resources," *HR Focus,* September 1999, 8–9.

8. Robert B. Reich, "The Company of the Future," *Fast Company,* November 1998, 124–50.

9. Donald J. McNerney, "Creating a Motivated Workforce," *HR Focus* 73, 1 August 1996, 1+.

10. Frederick Herzberg, *Work and the Nature of Man* (New York: World, 1971).

11. Douglas McGregor, *The Human Side of Enterprise* (New York: McGraw-Hill, 1960).

12. Reich, "The Company of the Future."

13. Kelly Barron and Ann Marsch, "The Skills Gap," *Forbes,* 23 February 1998, 44–45; "Nine HR Challenges for 1999," *HR Focus,* December 1998, 1, 14–16.

14. U.S. Bureau of Labor Statistics, *Employment Statistics* [accessed 23 August 1999] www.bls.gov.

15. Aaron Bernstein, "We Want You to Stay. Really," *Business Week,* 22 June 1998, 67–72; Carol Kleiman, "The New Loyalty: A Work in Progress," *Chicago Tribune,* 15 August 1999, sec. 6, 1.

16. Barron and Marsch, "The Skills Gap."

17. Greg Jaffe and Douglas A. Blackmon, "Just in Time. When UPS Demanded Workers, Louisville Did the Delivering," *Wall Street Journal,* 24 April 1998, A1, A10; James Ott, "UPS Hub 2000 at Louisville Marks New Airport Era," 20 July 1998, 47+.

18. Jennifer Laabs, "Has Downsizing Missed Its Mark?" *Workforce,* April 1999, 31–38.

19. Aaron Bernstein, "We Want You to Stay. Really."

20. Jennifer Laabs, "The New Loyalty: Grasp It. Earn It. Keep It." *Workforce,* November 1998, 35–39.

21. Emily Thornton, "No Room at the Top," *Business Week,* 9 August 1999, 50; Michael A. Lev, "Lifetime Jobs May Be at Death's Door as Japan Tradition," *Chicago Tribune,* 11 October 1998, sec. 5, 1, 18.

22. John Greenwald, "Spinning Away," *Time,* 26 August 1996, 30–31.

23. Stephanie Armour, "Blame It on Downsizing, E-Mail, Laptops, and Dual-Career Families," *USA Today,* 13 March 1998, B1; Jennifer Laabs, "Workforce Overload," *Workforce,* January 1999, 30–37.

24. Michelle Conlin, Peter Coy, Ann Therese, and Gabrielle Saveri, "The Wild New Workforce," *Business Week,* 6 December 1999, 39–44.

25. Sue Shellenbarger, "More Executives Cite Need for Family Time as Reason for Quitting," *Wall Street Journal,* 11 March 1998, B1.

26. Richard L. Daft, *Management,* 4th ed. (Fort Worth, Tex.: Dryden Press, 1997), 771.

27. Stephanie Armour, "Workplace Demands Taking Up More Weekends," *USA Today,* 24 April 1998, B1; Laabs, "Workforce Overload."

28. Armour, "Workplace Demands Taking Up More Weekends."

29. Laabs, "Workforce Overload."

30. Michael A. Verespej, "Stressed Out," *Industry Week,* 21 February 2000, 30–34.

31. Verespej, "Balancing Act."

32. John W. Newstrom and Keith Davis, *Organizational Behavior: Human Behavior at Work,* 9th ed. (New York: McGraw-Hill, 1993), 345.

33. Jennifer Bresnehan, "The Elusive Muse," *CIO Enterprise,* 15 October 1997, 52; Kerry A. Dolan, "When Money Isn't Enough," *Forbes,* 18 November 1996, 164–70.

34. Toby B. Gooley, "A World of Difference," *Logistics Management and Distribution Report,* June 2000, 51–55; William H. Miller, "Beneath the Surface," *Industry Week,* 20 September 1999, 13–16.

35. Steven Greenhouse, "Foreign Workers at Highest Level in Seven Decades," *New York Times,* 4 September 2000, A1, A12.

36. "Work Force Facts," *Chicago Tribune,* 10 September 2000, sec. 6,1.

37. Nina Munk, "Finished at Forty," *Fortune,* 1 February 1999, 50–66.

38. Munk, "Finished at Forty."

39. Munk, "Finished at Forty."

40. Gooley, "A World of Difference."

41. Joan Crockett, "Winning Competitive Advantage Through a Diverse Workforce," *HR Focus,* May 1999, 9–10.

42. Joan Crockett, "Winning Competitive Advantage Through a Diverse Workforce."

43. "Is There Really Still A Gender Pay Gap?" *HR Focus,* June 2000, 3–4.

44. Linda Himelstein and Stephanie Forest, "Breaking Through," *Business Week,* 17 February 1997, 64; "Study Says U.S. Women Make Workplace Gains," *Reuters Business Report,* 2 January 1997; Martha Groves, "Women Still Bumping Up Against Glass Ceiling," *Los Angeles Times,* 26 May 1996, D1; Christopher Farrell, "Women in the Workplace: Is Parity Finally in Sight?" *Business Week,* 9 August 1999, 35.

45. Daft, *Management,* 462–63.

46. Joseph White and Carol Hymowitz, "Broken Glass: Watershed Generation of Women Executives Is Rising to the Top," *Wall Street Journal,* 10 February 1997, A1, 6; Andrea Adelson, "Casual, Worker-Friendly, and a Moneymaker, Too: At Patagonia, Glass Ceiling Is Sky-High," *New York Times,* 30 June 1996, sec. Earning It, 8; Joan S. Lublin, "Women at Top Still Are Distant from CEO Jobs," *Wall Street Journal,* 28 February 1996, B1, 12; "Firm's Diversity Efforts Even the Playing Field," *Personnel Journal,* January 1996, 56; Himelstein and Forest, "Breaking Through," 64–70; Groves, "Women Still Bumping Up Against Glass Ceiling," D1, 5; Farrell, "Women in the Workplace"; Reed Abelson, "A Push from the Top Shatters a Glass Ceiling," *New York Times,* 22 August 1999, Y21, Y23.

47. Michael Barrier, "Sexual Harassment," *Nation's Business,* December 1998, 15–19.

48. Marianne Lavelle, "The New Rules of Sexual Harassment," *U.S. News & World Report,* 6 July 1998, 30–31.

49. Mahlon Apgar IV, "The Alternative Workplace: Changing Where and How People Work," *Harvard Business Review,* May–June 1998, 121–36.

50. Genevieve Capowski, "The Joy of Flex," *Management Review,* March 1996, 13.

51. Charles Fishman, "Moving Toward a Balanced Work Life."

52. Charlene Marmer Solomon, "Flexibility Comes out of Flux," *Personnel Journal,* June 1996, 38–40.

53. Solomon, "Flexibility Comes Out of Flux."

54. Shari Caudron, "Workers' Ideas for Improving Alternative Work Situations," *Workforce,* December 1998, 42–46; Carol Leonetti Dannhauser, "Who's in the Home Office?," *American Demographics,* June 1999, 50–56.

55. Dannhauser, "Who's in the Home Office?"

56. Apgar, "The Alternative Workplace."

57. Apgar, "The Alternative Workplace."

58. Melanie Warner, "Working at Home—The Right Way to Be a Star in Your Bunny Slippers," *Fortune,* 3 March 1997, 166; Lin Grensing-Pophal, "Employing the Best People—From Afar," *Workforce,* March 1997, 30–32.

59. Kemba J. Dunham, "Telecommuters' Lament," *Wall Street Journal,* 31 October 2000, B1, B8.

60. Lisa Chadderdon, "Merrill Lynch Works—At Home," *Fast Company,* April–May 1998, 70–72.

61. Caudron, "Workers' Ideas for Improving Alternative Work Situations."

62. Caudron, "Workers' Ideas for Improving Alternative Work Situations."

63. Thomas A. Kochan and Harry C. Katz, *Collective Bargaining and Industrial Relations* (Homewood, Ill.: Irwin, 1988), 165.

64. Linda Grant, "How UPS Blew It," *Fortune,* 29 September 1997, 29–30; Shari Caudron, "Part-Timers Make Headline News—Here's the Real HR Story," *Workforce,* November 1997, 40–50.

65. Catherine Yang et al., "Low-Wage Lessons," *Business Week,* 11 November 1996, 108–10.

66. Martha Irvine, "Organizing Twentysomethings," *Los Angeles Times,* 7 September 1997, D5.

67. Kochan and Katz, *Collective Bargaining and Industrial Relations,* 173.

68. Michael A. Verespej, "What's Behind the Strife?" *Industry Week,* 1 February 1999, 58–62; Keith Bradsher, "General Motors and the U.A.W. Agree on End to Strike," *New York Times,* 29 July 1998, A1, C6.

69. *World Almanac and Book of Facts* (New York: Scripps Howard, 1989), 161.

70. Susan Carey, "United Grapples With Summer of Widespread Discontent," *Wall Street Journal,* 8 August 2000, A2; Laurence Zuckerman and Matthew L. Wald, "Crisis for Air Traffic System: More Passengers, More Delays," *New York Times,* 5 September 2000, A1, C12.

71. Stephanie Overman, "Unions: New Activism or Old Adversarial Approach?" *HR Focus,* May 1999, 7–8; Laurence Zuckerman, "Pilots Lose a Battle, Not the War," *New York Times,* 17 April 1999, B1, B14.

72. Eugene H. Methvin, "The Union Label: With the Level of Union Violence on the Rise, Congress Must, Again, Deal with the Courts," *National Review,* 29 September 1997, 47; Anya Sacharow, "Walking the Line in Detroit," *Newspapers,* 22 July 1996, 8–13.

73. Paul D. Staudohar, "Labor Relations in Basketball: The Lockout of 1998–99," *Monthly Labor Review,* April 1999, 3–9; Herman, *Collective Bargaining and Labor Relations,* 61; "NLRB Permits Replacements During Legal Lockout," *Personnel Journal,* January 1987, 14–15.

74. David Field, "Airline Chief Has Become Key Figure in Labor Dispute," *USA Today,* 6 March 1997, B1, B2; Donna Rosato, "American Airlines Pilots Ask to Extend Deadline for Talks," *USA Today,* 18 March 1997, 2B; David Field, "Clinton Unlikely to Act Unless Both Sides Ask," *USA Today,* 10 February 1997, 2A.

75. Glenn Burkins, "Labor-Union Membership Increases for Second Year in Row to 16.48 Million," *Wall Street Journal,* 20 January 2000, A2; Michael Barone, "The Unions Go Public," *U.S. News & World Report,* 4 October 1999, 30.

76. International Labour Organization, *World Labour Report,* 4 November 1997 [accessed 7 November 1997] www.ilo.org.

77. Lloyd G. Reynolds, Stanley H. Masters, and Colletta H. Moser, *Labor Economics and Labor Relations,* 11th ed. (Upper Saddle River, N.J.: Prentice Hall, 1998), 497; Indiana University News Bureau, "Trends in U.S. Labor Movement," *Futurist,* January–February 1996, 44; Barbara Presley Noble, "Reinventing Labor: An Interview with Union President Lynn Williams," *Harvard Business Review,* July–August 1993, 115–25.

78. Aaron Bernstein, "Sweeney's Blitz," *Business Week,* 17 February 1997, 56–62; Marc Levinson, "It's Hip to Be Union," *Newsweek,* 8 July 1996, 44–45; James Worsham, "Labor Comes Alive," *Nation's Business,* February 1996, 16–24; E. Edward Herman, *Collective Bargaining and Labor Relations,* 4th ed. (Upper Saddle River, N.J.: Prentice Hall, 1998); Michael Hickins, "Unions: New Activism or Old Adversarial Approach?" *HR Focus,* May 1999, 7–8.

## CHAPTER 11

1. Brenda Paik Sunoo, "Blending a Successful Workforce," *Workforce,* March 2000, 44–48; Karyn Strauss, "Perron: Jamba's Juiced for Growth, Plans IPO," *Nation's Restaurant News,* 24 January 2000, 1, 76; Karyn Strauss, "Report: Smoothie Indies Face Rocky Road as Chains Slurp Up Market Share," *Nation's Restaurant News,* 14 June 1999, 8, 138; "Best Healthy Choice Menu Selection: Jamba Juice: Jambola Bread is on the Rise," *Nation's Restaurant News,* 24 March 1999, 168; Michael Adams, "Kirk Perron: Jamba Juice," *Restaurant Business,* 15 March 1999, 38; Victor Wishna, "Leaving for Good," *Restaurant Business,* 1 May 2000, 64–74.

2. Joanne Cole, "Permatemps Pose New Challenges for HR," *HR Focus,* December 1999, 7–8; Sharon R. Cohany, "Workers in Alternative Employment Arrangements: A Second Look," *Monthly Labor Review,* November 1998, 3–21.

3. Felicia Jefferson and Don Bohl, "CBR Minisurvey: Part-Time and Temporary Employees Demand Better Pay and More Benefits," *Compensation and Benefits Review,* November–December 1998, 20–24.

4. "Microsoft Moves to Curb Use of Temporary Workers," *Wall Street Journal,* 3 July 2000, B2.

5. Steven Greenhouse, "Equal Work, Less-Equal Perks," *New York Times,* 30 March 1998, C1, C6; Aaron Bernstein, "When Is a Temp Not a Temp?" *Business Week,* 7 December 1998, 90–92.

6. William J. Stevenson, *Production Operations Management,* 6th ed. (Boston: Irwin McGraw-Hill, 1999), 698; Laurie Edwards, "When Outsourcing is Appropriate," *Wall Street and Technology,* July 1998, 96–98.

7. George Donnelly, "Recruiting, Retention, and Returns," *CFO Magazine,* March 2000 [accessed 10 April 2000] www.cfonet.com/html/Articles/CFO/2000/00MArecr.html.

8. Audrey Arthur, "How Much Should Employees Know?" *Black Enterprise,* October 1997, 56; Anthony Ramirez, "Name, Résumé, References. And How's Your Credit? *New York Times,* 31 August 1997, F8.

9. Jonathan Segal, "When Norman Bates and Baby Jane Act Out at Work," *HR Magazine* 41, 1 February 1996, 31; Jenny C. McCune, "Companies Grapple with Workplace Violence," *Management Review,* March 1994, 52–57.

10. Ellis Henican, "Nightmare at Saks Fifth Ave.," *Newsday,* 5 June 1996, A2.

11. "Substance Abuse in the Workplace," *HR Focus,* February 1997, 1, 41; Tyler D. Hartwell, Paul D. Steele, and Nathaniel F. Rodman, "Workplace Alcohol-Testing Programs: Prevalence and Trends," *Monthly Labor Review,* June 1998, 27–34.

12. Randall S. Schuler, *Managing Human Resources* (Cincinnati, Ohio: South-Western College Publishing, 1998), 386.

13. Katharine Mieszkowski, "Report from the Future," *Fast Company,* February–March 1998, 28–30.

14. Tonia L. Shakespeare, "High-Tech Training, Wal-Mart Style," *Black Enterprise,* July 1996, 54.

15. Michael Barrier, "Develop Workers—and Your Business," *Nation's Business,* December 1998, 25–27.

16. Kevin Dobbs, "Tires Plus Takes the Training High Road," *Training,* April 2000, 56–63.

17. Adolph Haasen and Gordon F. Shea, *A Better Place to Work* (New York: American Management Association, 1997), 19–20.

18. Bill Roberts, "://Training Via the Desktop://" *HR Magazine,* August 1998, 98–104.

19. Gina Imperato, "How to Give Good Feedback," *Fast Company,* September 1998, 144–56.

20. Kate Ludeman, "How to Conduct Self-Directed 360," *Training and Development,* July 2000, 44–47; Cassandra Hayes, "To Tell the Truth," *Black Enterprise,* December 1998, 55.

21. Imperato, "How to Give Good Feedback."

22. Bradely R. Schiller, *State Minimum Wage Laws: Youth Coverage and Impact* (Washington, D.C.: George Mason University, 1994).

23. Jeff Kersten, "Gain Sharing in College Station," *PM: Public Management,* May 1998, 19.

24. Ellen Neuborne, "Meeting Goals Just Got More Rewarding," *USA Today,* 15 October 1996, B1–B2.

25. Bobette M. Gustafson, "Skill-Based Pay Improves PFS Staff Recruitment, Retention, and Performance," *Healthcare Financial Management,* January 2000, 62–63; Rosalie Webster, "Both Sides of the Coin," *New Zealand Management,* November 1998, 122; Genevieve Capowski, "HR View Online," *HR Focus,* June 1998, 2.

26. Karen Jacobs, "The Broad View," *Wall Street Journal,* 10 April 1997, R10; Schuler, *Managing Human Resources,* 386.

27. Keith H. Hammonds, Wendy Zellner, and Richard Melcher, "Writing a New Social Contract," *Business Week,* 11 March 1996, 60; Don L. Boroughs, "The Bottom Line on Ethics," *U.S. News & World Report,* 20 March 1995, 63–65; Dawn Gunsch, "Benefits Leverage Hiring and Retention Efforts," *Personnel Journal,* November 1992, 91–92, 94–97.

28. Fiona Jebb, "Flex Appeal," *Management Today* (London), July 1998, 66–69; Milton Zall, "Implementing a Flexible Benefits Plan," *Fleet Equipment,* May 1999, B4–B8.

29. "Employees Prefer Finding Their Own Health Care Coverage," *Employee Benefit Plan Review,* March 2000, 49.

30. "Employers Pass Along More Health-Care Costs," *HR Focus,* May 2000, 12.

31. Jan Ziegler, "Why Work Where You Can't Get Coverage?" *Business and Health,* June 2000, 61–62.

32. Richard D. Pearce, "The Small Employer Retirement Plan Void," *Compensation and Benefits Management,* Winter 1999, 51–55.

33. Arleen Jacobius, "Retirement Programs Cover 70 Percent of Employees," *Pensions and Investments,* 31 May 1999, 25.

34. James H. Dulebohn, Brian Murray, and Minghe Sun, "Selection Among Employer-Sponsored Pension Plans: The Role of Individual Differences," *Personnel Psychology,* Summer 2000, 405–32.

35. George Van Dyke, "Examining Your 401k," *Business Credit,* January 2000, 59.

36. Dulebohn et al., "Selection Among Employer-Sponsored Pension Plans."

37. Michael Arndt, "Will United's Woes Spread?" *Business Week,* 13 November 2000, 180–92.

38. Floyd Norris, "Pilot Woes: Why Employee Ownership Didn't Help UAL," *New York Times,* 11 August 2000, C1; Michael Arndt, "The Industry Will Pay for United's Deal With Pilots," *Business Week,* 18 September 2000, 52.

39. Sara Nathan, "Stock Options Not Only for Top Dogs," *USA Today,* 23 July 1999, 3B.

40. Del Jones, "More Workers Get Options, Too," *USA Today,* 7 April 1999, 3B.

41. Gillian Flynn, "Employees Need an FMLA Brush-up," *Workforce* 76, no. 4 (April 1997): 101–104; Barbara Presley Noble, "At Work: We're Doing Just Fine, Thank You," *New York Times,* 20 March 1994, 25.

42. "Workplace Briefs," Gannett News Service, 24 April 1997; Julia Lawlor, "The Bottom Line," *Working Woman,* July–August 1996, 54–58, 74–76.

43. Stephanie Armour, "Employers Stepping Up in Elder Care," *USA Today,* 3 August 2000, 3B.

44. Sue Shellenbarger, "Employees Who Value Time as Much as Money Now Get Their Reward," *Wall Street Journal,* 22 September 1999, B1.

45. Del Jones, "Firms Take New Look at Sick Days," *USA Today,* 8 October 1996, 8B.

46. William Atkinson, "Wellness, Employee Assistance Programs: Investments, Not Costs," *Bobbin,* May 2000, 42–48.

47. Atkinson, "Wellness, Employee Assistance Programs."

48. Atkinson, "Wellness, Employee Assistance Programs"; Kevin Dobbs, Jack Gordon, and David Stamps, "EAPs Cheap But Popular Perk," *Training,* February 2000, 26.

49. "50 Benefits and Perks That Make Employees Want to Stay Forever," *HR Focus,* July 2000, S2–S3.

50. Edward Iwata, "Staff-Hungry Tech Firms Cast Exotic Lures," *USA Today,* 1 February 2000, B1.

51. Valerie L. Williams and Jennifer E. Sunderland, "New Pay Programs Boost Retention," *Workforce,* May 1999, 36–40.

52. "Well No, They Won't Go," *CA Magazine,* April 1999, 11.

53. "Well No, They Won't Go."

54. Rodney Ho, "AT&T's Offer of $10,000 May Test Entrepreneurship of Laid-Off Workers," *Wall Street Journal,* 12 March 1997; David Fischer and Kevin Whitelaw, "A New Way to Shine Up Corporate Profits," *U.S. News & World Report,* 15 April 1996, 55.

55. Gillian Flynn, "Why Rhino Won't Wait Until Tomorrow," *Personnel Journal,* July 1996, 36–39.

## CHAPTER 12

1. Jane Eisinger, "Capitalizing on Corporate Success," *Association Management,* February 2000, 47–49; Mike McNamee, "Isn't There More to Life Than Plastic?" *Business Week,* 22 November 1999, 173–76; Charles Fishman, "This is a Marketing Revolution," *Fast Company,* May 1999, 204–18; Leslie Goff, "Surviving the Data Minefield," *Computerworld,* 24 August 1998, 49–50.

2. "AMA Board Approves New Marketing Definition," *Marketing News,* 1 March 1985, 1.

3. Al Ries and Jack Trout, *The 22 Immutable Laws of Marketing* (New York: HarperCollins, 1994), 19–25.

4. Kevin Maney, "Consumers Latch onto Speedy Way to Get Gas," *USA Today,* 26 February 1998, 8B.

5. Fred Hapgood, "Death of the Salesman," *Inc. Tech,* no. 3 (1998): 95–98.

6. Hal Lancaster, "Managing Your Career: Giving Good Service, Never an Easy Task, Is Getting a Lot Harder," *Wall Street Journal,* 9 June 1998, B1.

7. Terry G. Vavra, "The Database Marketing Imperative," *Marketing Management* 2, no. 1 (1993): 47–57.

8. Suzanne Oliver, "Spoiled Rotten," *Forbes,* 15 July 1996, 70–73; "Skymall's Web Sales Take Flight as Shares Soar Nearly Threefold," *Wall Street Journal,* 29 December 1998, B9.

9. Peter Fingar, Harsha Kumar, and Tarun Sharma, Enterprise E-Commerce (Tampa, Fla.: Meghan-Kiffer Press, 2000), 24, 109.

10. Pierre M. Loewe and Mark S. Bonchek, "The Retail Revolution," *Management Review,* April 1999, 38–44.

11. Laurie Windham, *Dead Ahead* (New York: Allworth Press, 1999), 80–85.

12. Barbara Whitaker, "House Hunting with Cursor and Click," *New York Times,* 24 September 1998, D1, D5.

13. Janet Willen, "The Customer Is Wrong," *Business97,* October–November 1997, 40–42; William H. Davidow and Bro Uttal, *Total Customer Service: The Ultimate Weapon* (New York: Harper & Row, 1989), 8; Valarie A. Zeithaml, A. Parasuraman, and Leonard L. Berry, *Delivering Quality Service* (New York: Free Press, 1990), 9; George J. Castellese, "Customer Service . . . Building a Winning Team," *Supervision,* January 1995, 9–13; Erica G. Sorohan and Catherine M. Petrini, "Dumpsters, Ducks, and Customer Service," *Training and Development,* January 1995, 9.

14. Peter Burrows, "HP: No Longer Lost in Cyberspace?" *Business Week,* 31 May 1999, 124, 126.

15. Avery Comarow, "Broken? No Problem," *U.S. News & World Report,* 11 January 1999, 68–69.

16. Ronald B. Lieber, "Storytelling: A New Way to Get Close to Your Customer," *Fortune,* 3 February 1997, 102–10.

17. Steve Schriver, "Customer Loyalty: Going Going . . ." *American Demographics,* September 1997, 20–23.

18. Scott Woolley, "Get Lost, Buster," *Forbes,* 23 February 1998, 90; Jon Van, "$5 Question: When Does Not Calling Not Add Up?" *Chicago Tribune,* 8 April 1999, sec. 1, 1, 14.

19. Mary J. Cronin, *Doing More Business on the Internet* (New York: Van Nostrand Reinhold, 1995), 13.

20. Eryn Brown, Mary J. Cronin, Ann Harrington, and Jane Hodges, "9 Ways to Win on the Web," Fortune, 24 May 1999, 112–25.

21. Joshua Macht, "The New Market Research," *Inc.,* July 1998, 87–94.

22. Louisa Wah, "The Almighty Customer," *Management Review,* February 1999, 16–22.

23. Thomas A. Stewart, "A Satisfied Customer Isn't Enough," *Fortune,* 21 July 1997, 112–13.

24. David C. Edelman, "Satisfaction Is Nice, But Share Pays," *Marketing Management* 2, no. 1 (1993): 8–13.

25. Oren Harari, "Six Myths of Market Research," *Management Review,* April 1994, 48–51.

26. Robert Passikoff, "Loyal Opposition—The Limits of Customer Satisfaction," *Brandweek,* 3 March 1997, 17.

27. Pamela G. Hollies, "What's New in Market Research," *New York Times,* 15 June 1986, sec. 3, 19; Phyllis M. Thornton, "Linking Market Research to Strategic Planning," *Nursing Homes,* January–February 1995, 34–37; Harari, "Six Myths of Market Research."

28. Raymond R. Burke, "Virtual Shopping: Breakthrough in Marketing Research," *Harvard Business Review,* March–April 1996, 120–31.

29. Harry S. Dent Jr., "Individualized Marketing," *Small Business Reports,* April 1991, 36–45.

30. Janet Novack, "The Data Miners," *Forbes,* 12 February 1996, 96–97; Don Peppers and Martha Rogers, *Enterprise One to One* (New York: Doubleday, 1997), 120–21.

31. Wah, "The Almighty Customer"; James Lardner, "Your Every Command," *U.S. News & World Report,* 5 July 1999, 44–46.

32. Charles Fishman, "This is a Marketing Revolution," *Fast Company,* May 1999, 206–18.

33. William S. Hopkins and Britton Manasco, "The Coming Customer Free-For-All," *New York Times Supplement—Customer Relationships in a Wired World,* 14 February 2000, CU1–CU2.

34. Diane Brady, "Why Service Stinks," *Business Week,* 23 October 2000, 118–28.

35. Don Peppers, Martha Rogers, and Bob Dorf, "Is Your Company Ready for One-To-One Marketing?" *Harvard Business Review,* January–February 1999.

36. Owen Thomas, "Dell's Premier Pages," *Ecompany,* August 2000, 77; Brown et al., "9 Ways to Win on the Web."

37. Tom Content, "Nike Lets You Be a Shoemaker," *USA Today,* 22 November 1999, 14B.

38. James Lardner, "Your Every Command," *U.S. News & World Report,* 5 July 1999, 44–46.

39. Lardner, "Your Every Command."

40. Peppers and Rogers, *Enterprise One to One,* 145–46.

41. Malcolm H. B. McDonald, "Ten Barriers to Marketing Planning," *Journal of Product and Brand Management,* Fall 1992, 51–64.

42. Vanessa O'Connell, "Changing Tastes Dent Campbell's Canned-Soup Sales," *Wall Street Journal,* 28 April 1998, B1, B25.

43. Norihiko Shirouzu, "Japan's High-School Girls Excel in Art of Setting Trends," *Wall Street Journal,* 24 April 1998, B1, B7.

44. Leslie Kaufman, "Playing Catch-Up at the On-Line Mall," *New York Times,* 21 February 1999, sec. 3, 1, 6; Gary Samuels, "CD-ROMs First Big Victim," Forbes, 28 February 1994, 42–44; Richard A. Melcher, "Dusting Off the Britannica," *Business Week,* 20 October 1997, 143–146.

45. "Setting a Fast Pace for the Wireless Web," *Business Week,* 18 September 2000, 48.

46. Malcolm McDonald and John W. Leppard, *Marketing by Matrix* (Lincolnwood, Ill.: NTC, 1993), 10; H. Igor Ansoff, "Strategies for Diversification," *Harvard Business Review,* November–December 1957, 113–24; H. Igor Ansoff, *Corporate Strategy* (New York: McGraw-Hill, 1965).

47. Alex Taylor III, "How to Murder the Competition," *Fortune,* 22 February 1993, 87, 90.

48. Scott Hays, "Exceptional Customer Service Takes the 'Ritz' Touch," *Workforce,* January 1999, 99–102.

49. Ann Oldenburg, "Market Responds Slowly to a Growing Population," *USA Today,* 18 March 1998, 9D.

50. David Shani and Sujana Chalasani, "Exploring Niches Using Relationship Marketing," *Journal of Business and Industrial Marketing,* no. 4 (1993): 58–66.

51. Michael J. Weiss, *The Clustering of America* (New York: Harper & Row, 1988), 41.

52. Don Peppers and Martha Rogers, "One-to-One Business Travel," *Inside 1to1,* 17 September 1998 [via e-mail 16 September 1998].

53. Shani and Chalasani, "Exploring Niches Using Relationship Marketing."

54. Courtland L. Bovée, Michael J. Houston, and John V. Thill, *Marketing,* 2d ed. (New York: McGraw-Hill, 1994), 224.

55. Daniel Roth, "First: From Poster Boy to Whipping Boy," *Fortune,* 6 July 1998, 28–29.

56. Gary Armstrong and Philip Kotler, *Marketing an Introduction,* 5th ed. (Upper Saddle River, N.J.: Prentice Hall, 2000), 201–4.

57. Faye Brookman, "Brushing Up," *Supermarket Business,* February 1998, 57–62; Laurie Freeman, "Maintaining the Momentum," *Supermarket Business,* February 1999, 57–58.

58. Kotler, *Marketing Management,* 294–97.

## CHAPTER 13

1. Michael Schrage, "Martha Stewart: Living Well on the World Wide Web," *Adweek,* 14 February 2000, IQ18–IQ30; Diana Brady, "Martha Inc.: Inside the Growing Empire of America's Lifestyle Queen," *Business Week,* 17 January 2000, 63–72; Robert Barker, "How Tasty is Martha's IPO?" *Business Week,* 6 September 1999, 108; Andrew Wahl, "Home Economics," *Canadian Business,* 27 August 1999, 18; Don Hogsett, "Martha Cooks Up an IPO," *Home*

*Textiles Today,* 9 August 1999, 1, 21; Ann Smith, "A Living Brand," *Progressive Grocer,* November 1998, 21–22; Deborah Spence, "Marketing Martha By E-Mail," *Folio: The Magazine for Magazine Management,* 1 March 1998, 33.

2. Philip Kotler and Gary Armstrong, *Principles of Marketing,* 9th ed. (Upper Saddle River, N.J.: Prentice Hall, 2001), 296.

3. Gary Hamel, *Lessons in Leadership Lecture,* Northern Illinois University, 23 October 1997.

4. "Preparing for a Point to Point World," *Marketing Management* 3, no. 4 (Spring 1995): 30–40.

5. Al Ries and Jack Trout, "Focused in a Fuzzy World," *Rethinking the Future* (London: Nicholas Brealey Publishing, 1997), 183.

6. Bill Saporito, "Can Nike Get Unstuck?" *Time,* 30 March 1998, 48–53.

7. Michele Rosen, "Apple Escapes PC Market Crunch," *Forbes Digital Tool,* 15 April 1999 [accessed 16 June 1999] www.forbes.com/tool/html/99/apr/0415/mu2.htm.

8. John C. Dvorak, "Razor's with No Blades," *Forbes,* 18 October 1999, 168.

9. Marcia Mogelonsky, "Product Overload?" *American Demographics,* August 1998, 65–69.

10. Lisa Bannon, "Goodbye, Dolly: Mattel Tries to Adjust as 'Holiday Barbie' Leaves Under a Cloud," *Wall Street Journal,* 7 June 1999, A1, A8; Dana Canedy, "Beyond Barbie's Midlife Crisis," *New York Times,* 6 April 1999, C1, C8.

11. Jacob M. Schlesinger, "Firms Strive to Improve Basic Products," *Wall Street Journal,* 8 October 1985, B1.

12. "New Product Winners—And Losers," *In Business,* April 1985, 64.

13. Yumiko Ono, "Kraft Searches Its Cupboard for Old Brands to Remake," *Wall Street Journal,* 12 March 1996, B1, B4.

14. Tom Peters, "We Hold These Truths to Be Self-Evident," *Organizational Dynamics,* 1 June 1996, 27–32.

15. Tom Peters, *Lessons In Leadership Lecture.*

16. Bruce Horovitz and Melanie Wells, "Well-Known Products Try for Comeback," *USA Today,* 2 May 1995, B1.

17. Tim Stevens, "Lights, Camera, Innovation," *Industry Week,* 19 July 1999, 32–38.

18. Tim Stevens, "Idea Dollars," *Industry Week,* 16 February 1998, 47–49.

19. Tona Mack, "Let the Computer Do It," *Forbes,* 10 August 1987, 94.

20. *The New Economy Index* [accessed 13 April 2000] www.neweconomyindex.org/section1_page06.html.

21. Gary Armstrong and Philip Kotler, *Marketing an Introduction,* 5th ed. (Upper Saddle River, N.J.: Prentice Hall, 2000), 234.

22. Roberta Bernstein, "Food for Thought," *American Demographics,* May 2000, 39–42.

23. Armstrong and Kotler, *Marketing an Introduction,* 235.

24. Armstrong and Kotler, *Marketing an Introduction,* 206.

25. Bruce Horovitz, "Would You Like Fires with That Cappuccino?" *USA Today,* 22 September 2000, 1A.

26. Tim O'Brien, "Disneyland Paris Caters to European Tastes, Lowers Costs and Refines Service," *Amusement Business,* 5 May 1997, p. 18; "Disneyland Paris: How Beauty Became a Beast," *Reputation Management,* March–April 1995, 35–37.

27. Zachary Schiller, "Make It Simple," *Business Week,* 9 September 1996, 96–104; Katrina Brooker, "Can Procter & Gamble Change Its Culture, Protect Its Market Share, and Find the Next Tide?" *Fortune,* 26 April 1999, 146–52.

28. Tara Parket-Pope, "Custom-Made," *Wall Street Journal,* 26 September 1996, R22–R23.

29. Ernest Beck and Rekha Balu, "Europe Is Deaf to Snap! Crackle! Pop!" *Wall Street Journal,* 2 June 1998, B1, B12.

30. Thomas K. Grose, "Brand New Goods," *Time.com,* 1 November 1999 [accessed 17 February 2001] www.time.com/time/magazine/article/0,9171,33124-1,00.html.

31. Constance L. Hays, "No More Brand X," *New York Times,* 12 June 1998, C1, C4.

32. Kelly Barron, "The Cappuccino Conundrum," *Forbes,* 22 February 1999, 54–55.

33. Nina Munk, "Gap Gets It," *Fortune,* 3 August 1998, 68–82.

34. Diane Brady, "Why Tommy Hilfiger Is So Like, Um, 1998," *Business Week,* 24 April 2000, 55.

35. Melanie Wells, "Red Baron," *Forbes,* 3 July 2000, 151–60.

36. Jagdish N. Sheth and Rajendra S. Sisodia, "Feeling the Heat," *Marketing Management* 4, no. 2 (Fall 1995): 9–23.

37. Claudia H. Deutsch, "Will That Be Paper or Pixel?" *New York Times,* 4 August 2000, C1, C4.

38. David Leonhardt, "Cereal-Box Killers Are on the Loose," *Business Week,* 12 October 1998, 721.

39. Dean Takahashi, "Intel Steps Up Use of Price Cuts to Protect Its Turf and to Expand," *Wall Street Journal,* 9 June 1998, B6.

40. Terril Yue Jones, "Fearing the Old Shoddy Image," *Forbes,* 12 January 1998 [accessed 16 June 1999] www.forbes.com/forbes/98/0112/6101064a.htm.

41. Thomas T. Nagle, "Managing Price Competition," *Marketing Management,* 2, no. 1 (1993): 38–45; Sheth and Sisodia, "Feeling the Heat," 21.

42. Gurumurthy Kalyanaram and Ragu Gurumurthy, "Market Entry Strategies: Pioneers Versus Late Arrivals," *Strategy & Business,* Third quarter 1998 [accessed 16 June 1999] www.strategy-business.com.

43. Tim Klass, "Web Bookstores Discount Bestsellers," *Associated Press Online,* 17 May 1999 [accessed 21 May 1999] www.cbsmarketwatch.com.

44. Edwin McDowell, "Winging It, with Internet Fares," *New York Times,* 7 March 1999, sec. 3, 1, 10.

## CHAPTER 14

1. Barbara F. Thompson, "The Home Depot," *Library Journal,* 1 February 2000, 30; Bruce Upbin, "Profit in a Big Orange Box," *Forbes,* 24 January 2000, 122–27; Sara Rose, "Building a Powerhouse," *Money,* December 1999, 62–64; Julia King, "E-retailers Take Time to Nail Down Virtual Shelves, Service," *Computerworld,* 6 September 1999, 1, 99; Dan Hanover, "It's Not a Threat, Just a Promise," *Chain Store Age,* September 1999, 176; "Home Depot Tells Vendors to Stay Off the 'Net," *Industrial Distribution,* September 1999, 21, 28; Katrina Booker, "First: Awfully Nervous," *Fortune,* 16 August 1999, 28–29; Matthew Budman, "Built from Scratch: How a Couple of Regular Guys Grew the Home Depot from Nothing to $30 Billion," *Across the Board,* June 1999, 61; Roy S. Johnson, "Home Depot Renovates," *Fortune,* 23 November 1998, 200–204.

2. Neil Gross, "The Supply Chain: Leapfrogging a Few Links," *Business Week,* 22 June 1998, 140–42.

3. Lisa H. Harrington, "The New Warehousing," *Industry Week,* 20 July 1998, 52, 54, 57–58.

4. Saul Hensell, "Is This the Factory of the Future?" *New York Times,* 26 July 1998, sec. 3, 1, 12.

5. Lisa Chadderdon, "How Dell Sells on the Web," *Fast Company,* September 1998, 58, 60.

6. Gregory L. White, "GM Is Forming Unit to Buy Dealerships," *Wall Street Journal,* 24 September 1999, A3; Joann Muller, "Meet Your Local GM Dealer: GM," *Business Week,* 11 October 1999, 48.

7. Leslie Kaufman, "As Big Business, Wal-Mart Propels Changes Elsewhere," *New York Times,* 22 October 2000, 1, 24.

8. Philip Kotler and Gary Armstrong, *Principles of Marketing,* 9th ed. (Upper Saddle River, N.J.: Prentice Hall, 2001), 435.

9. "Hallmark, a New Name in Mass Retailing," *Supermarket Business,* March 1997, 84; Daniel Roth, "Card Sharks," *Forbes,* 7 October 1996, 14; Julie Rygh, "Hallmark Cards Find Success with New Expressions Brand," *Knight-Ridder/Tribune Business News,* 31 August 1997, 831B0958.

10. Warren Cohen, "Same Price.com," *U.S. News & World Report,* 25 May 1998, 59; Joseph Conlin, "The Art of the Dealer Meeting," *Sales and Marketing Management,* February 1997, 761.

11. Michael S. Katz and Jeffrey Rothfeder, "Crossing the Digital Divide," *Strategy & Business,* First Quarter 2000, 26–41; Anne Stuart, "Clicks & Bricks," *CIO,* 15 March 2000, 76–84.

12. "1997 Economic Census: Advance Summary Statistics for the United States 1997 NAICS Basis," U.S. Census Bureau, 16 March 1999 www.census.gov/epcd/wwww/advanc1ahtm [accessed 7 June 1999].

13. Marcia Stepanek, "Middlemen: Rebirth of the Salesman," *Business Week,* 22 June 1998, 146–47.

14. "1997 Economic Census," U.S. Census Bureau.

15. Linnea Anderson, "Industry Zone: Industry Snapshot: Retail & Wholesale," Hoover's Online[accessed 7 June 1999] www.hoovers.com/features/industry/retail.html

16. Anderson, "Industry Zone."

17. Bruce Horovitz, "Trend Shrinks Store Sizes to Save Money, Satisfy Customers," *USA Today,* 9 August 1999, B1.

18. William M. Bulkeley, "Category Killers Go From Lethal to Lame in the Space of a Decade," *Wall Street Journal,* 9 March 2000, A1, A8.

19. Paul Klebnikov, "Trouble in Toyland," *Forbes,* 1 June 1998, 56, 58, 60; I. Jeanne Dugan, "The Corporation: Strategies: Can Toys 'R' Us Get on Top of Its Game?" *Business Week,* 7 April 1997, 124.

20. Mike Troy, "Wal-Mart Supercenters: The Combo with the Midas Touch," *DSN Retailing Today,* 8 May 2000, 113–14; Wendy Zellner, "Look Out, Supermarkets—Wal-Mart Is Hungry," *Business Week,* 14 September 1998, 98, 100

21. William J. Holstein and Kerry Hannon, "They Drop Till You Shop," *U.S. News & World Report,* 21 July 1997, 51–52; Marci McDonald, "The Pall in the Mall," *U.S. News and World Report,* 18 October 1999, 64–67.

22. Holstein and Hannon, "They Drop Till You Shop."

23. Michelle Pacelle, "The Aging Shopping Mall Must Either Adapt or Die," *Wall Street Journal,* 16 April 1996, B1, B14.

24. Jennifer Steinhauer, "It's a Mall . . . It's an Airport," *New York Times,* 10 June 1998, B1, B4; Chris Woodyard, "Hamlets Feature Fewer Rivals, Higher Profits," *USA Today,* 3 February 1998, B1, B2.

25. Ginia Bellafante, "That's Retail-tainment!" *Time,* 7 December 1998, 64–65.

26. Julia King, "Retailers, Manufacturers Find Ways to Co-exist on Electronic Frontier," *Computerworld,* 17 May 1999 [accessed 21 May 1999] www.computerworld.com/home/print.nsf/all/990517a69e.

27. Philip Kotler, *Marketing Management,* 9th ed. (Upper Saddle River, N.J.: Prentice Hall, 1997), 567.

28. King, "Retailers, Manufacturers Find Ways to Co-exist."

29. Richard A. Feinberg, "Sobering Thoughts on Cybermalls," *Computerworld,* 14 April 1997, 35.

30. Susan Chandler, "Opening the Retail Gates for PCs," *Chicago Tribune,* 27 October 1999, B1, B2.

31. "Value of U.S. DM Driven Sales Compared to Total U.S. Sales," Direct Marketing Association [accessed 8 June 1999] www.thedma.org/services1/charts/dmsales_ussales.html.

32. Lorrie Grant, "Stores with Doors Not Passe," *USA Today,* 4 August 1999, 3B.

33. Grant, "Stores with Doors Not Passe."

34. Catherine Romano, "Telemarketing Grows Up," *Management Review,* June 1998, 31–34.

35. Nanette Byrnes, "Avon, The New Calling," *Business Week,* 18 September 2000, 136–40; Emily Nelson and Ann Zimmerman, "Avon Goes Store to Store," *Wall Street Journal,* 18 September 2000, B1, B4.

36. Joseph B. White, "What Works?" *Wall Street Journal,* 23 October 2000, R4.

37. Chris Woodyard and Lorrie Grant, "E-tailers Dash to Wild, Wild Web," *USA Today,* 13 January 1999, B1, B2.

38. Paul McDougall, "Dell Mounts Internet Push to Diversify Revenue," *Informationweek,* 10 April 2000, 32; Phil Waga, "Dell's Prowess on the Net," *Gannett News Service,* 23 November 1999, 11; Lisa Chadderdon, "How Dell Sells on the Web," *Fast Company,* September 1998, 58, 60; William J. Holstein, Susan Gregory Thomas, and Fred Vogelstein, "Click 'Til You Drop," *U.S. News & World Report,* 7 December 1998, 42–45.

39. Heather Page, "Open for Business," *Entrepreneur,* December 1997, 51–53.

40. Kelly J. Andrews, "Value-Added E-Commerce," *Entrepreneurial Edge,* 3 (1998), 62–64.

41. Jason Anders, "Yesterday's Darling," *Wall Street Journal,* 23 October 2000, R8.

42. Daniel S. Janal, "Net Profit Now," *Success,* July–August 1997, 57–63.

43. Tariq K. Muhammad, "Marketing Online," *Black Enterprise,* September 1996, 85–88.

44. Holstein, Thomas, and Vogelstein, "Click 'Til You Drop."

45. Patricia Gallup, "You, Me, and All Those Others Just Like Us," *Inc.,* 15 May 1998, 51–52; PC Connection Catalog, vol. 4, no. 6B, 1994, 2–3.

46. Lisa H. Harrington, "Coping with Adolescence," *Industry Week,* 19 October 1998, 110, 112, 114, 117; "Neiman Marcus Selects Circle as Global Logistics Supplier," Circle International, 21 April 1999 [accessed 8 June 1999] www.circleintl.com/news/releases/Neiman.html.

47. Ronald Henkoff, "Delivering the Goods," *Fortune,* 28 November 1994, 64–78.

48. Edward O. Welles, "Riding the High-Tech Highway," *Inc.,* March 1993, 72–85.

49. Colleen Gourley, "Retail Logistics in Cyberspace," *Distribution,* December 1996, 29; Dave Hirschman, "FedEx Starts Up Package Sorting System at Memphis Tenn. Airport," *Knight-Ridder/Tribune Business News,* 28 September 1997, 928B0953; "FedEx and Technology—Maintaining a Competitive Edge," *PresWIRE,* 2 December 1996.

50. Saul Hansell, "For Amazon, a Holiday Risk: Can It Sell Acres of Everything?" *New York Times,* 28 November 1999, sec. 3, 1, 15; Katrina Brooker, "Amazon vs. Everybody," *Fortune,* 8 November 1999, 120–28.

51. Steffano Korper and Juanita Ellis, *The E-Commerce Book: Building the E-Empire* (San Diego, Calif.: Academic Press, 2000), 71–72.

52. IBM e-Business Web site, [accessed 10 March 2000], www.ibm.com/e-business/info.

53. Marcia Stepanek, "Closed, Gone to the Net," *Business Week,* 7 June 1999, 113–14.

54. Barbara Boydston, "Ticket, Please," *Wall Street Journal,* 17 July 2000, R38, R42.

## CHAPTER 15

1. Floorgraphics Web site [accessed 9 August 2000] www. floorgraphics.com; John Grossman, "Upstarts: Nontraditional Ads," *Inc.,* March 2000, 23–26; David Wellman, "Floor 'Toons," *Supermarket Business,* 15 November 1999, 47; Skip Wollenberg, "Advertising Finds New Canvases," *Boulder News,* 1 June 1999 [accessed 8 April 2000] community.bouldernews.com/business/ 01bads.html; "Floor Show," *Dallas Morning News,* 4 September 1998, 11D.

2. Timothy E. Moore, "Subliminal Advertising: What You See Is What You Get," *Journal of Marketing,* Spring 1982, 38–47; Jack Haberstroh, "Can't Ignore Subliminal Ad Charges," *Advertising Age,* 17 September 1984, 3, 42, 44.

3. Chris Adams, "FDA Tells Glaxo to Halt Airing Flu Commercial," *Wall Street Journal,* 14 January 2000, B3.

4. Michele Marchetti, "What a Sales Call Costs," *Sales and Marketing Management,* September 2000, 80–82.

5. Direct Marketing Association Web site [accessed 23 November 1997] www.the-dma.org/services1/libres-home1b.shtml.

6. Gary Armstrong and Philip Kotler, *Marketing: An Introduction* (Upper Saddle River, N.J.: Prentice Hall, 2000), 409.

7. Beth Belton, "Technology is Changing Face of U.S. Sales Force," *USA Today,* 9 February 1999, 1A, 2A.

8. David Prater, "The Third Time's the Charm," *Sales and Marketing Management,* September 2000, 100–104; Armstrong and Kotler, *Marketing an Introduction,* 454.

9. "Rethinking the Sales Force," *Soundview Executive Book Summaries,* Pt. 3, vol. 21, no. 7 (July 1999): 1–8.

10. Dennis K. Berman, "From Cell Phones to Sell Phones," *Business Week,* 11 September 2000, 88–90.

11. Paul Duke Jr., and Ronald Alsop, "Advertisers Beginning to Play Off Worker Concern over Job Security," *Wall Street Journal,* 1 April 1988, A11; Ronald Alsop, "More Food Advertising Plays on Cancer and Cardiac Fears," *Wall Street Journal,* 8 October 1987, 33; George E. Belch and Michael A. Belch, *Introduction to Advertising and Promotion Management* (Homewood, Ill.: Irwin, 1990), 186.

12. Thomas R. King, "Pitches on Value Stick in Consumers' Minds," *Wall Street Journal,* 4 June 1990, B1.

13. Mark Hyman, "The Yin and Yang of the Tiger Effect," *Business Week,* 16 October 2000, 110.

14. Richard Sandomir, "Tiger Woods Signs Pact with American Express," *New York Times,* 20 May 1997, C1.

15. Weld Royal, "A Brand New Pitch," *Industry Week,* 6 March 2000, 41–42.

16. Janet Neiman, "The Trouble with Comparative Ads," *Adweek's Marketing Week,* 12 January 1987, 4–5; Joseph B. White, "Ford Decides to Fight Back in Truck Ads," *Wall Street Journal,* 28 February 1989, B1, B6.

17. Berman, "From Cell Phones to Sell Phones," 88–90.

18. "Direct Hit," *The Economist,* 9 January 1999, 55–57.

19. Sarah Lorge, "Banner Ads vs. E-Mail Marketing," *Sales and Marketing Management,* August 1999, 15.

20. Christine Blank, "Beating the Banner Ad," *American Demographics,* June 2000, 42–44.

21. Roger Reece, "The New Generation of Integrated Inbound/ Outbound Telemarketing Systems," *Telemarketing,* March 1995, 58–65; Malynda H. Madzel, "Outsourcing Telemarketing: Why It May Work for You," *Telemarketing,* March 1995, 48–49; "Despite Hangups, Telemarketing a Success," *Marketing News,* 27 March 1995, 19.

22. Bruce Horovitz, "Telemarketers on Hold," *USA Today,* 24 August 1999, 1A; Jerry Cerasale, "Pertinent New and Pending Legislation for Telephone Marketers," *Call Center Solutions,* November 1999, 104–7.

23. Bruce Haring, "Step Right Up for the Next Push in Remote Control," *USA Today,* 15 September 1999, 7D.

24. Nadya Labi, "Tae-Bo or Not Tae-Bo?" *Time,* 15 March 1999, 77.

25. Timothy R. Hawthorne, "Opening Doors to Retail Stores," *Direct Marketing,* January 1998, 48–51.

26. "Direct Marketing Industry Electronic Media Survey Results March 1999," Direct Marketing Association Web site [accessed 26 October 2000] www.the-dma.org/library/publications/ electronicmedia99.shtml.

27. Jennifer Gilbert, "Really Booming Net Grabs $3.6 Billion," *Advertising Age,* 5 June 2000, 44, 52.

28. Efraim Turban, Jae Lee, David King, and H. Michael Chung, *Electric Commerce a Managerial Perspective* (Upper Saddle River, N.J.: Prentice Hall, 2000), 120.

29. Rebecca Quick, "E-Tailers Say, 'Bah, Humbug!' to Lavish Ads," *Wall Street Journal,* 22 September 2000, B1, B4.

30. Jennifer Rewick, "Beyond Banners," *Wall Street Journal,* 23 October 2000, R38.

31. "Promotional Trends Survey Caps Two Decades," *Cox Direct,* 14 September 1998 [accessed 24 May 1999] www.justdelivered.com/itm/ pressreleases/pr-091498.htm.

32. "Coupons, Samples Drive Consumer Shopping Decisions," *Cox Direct,* 8 September 1998 [accessed 24 May 1999] www. justdelivered.com/itm/pressreleases/pr-090898-2.htm.

33. Paulette Thomas, "'e-Clicking' Coupons On-Line Has a Cost: Privacy," *Wall Street Journal,* 18 June 1998, B1, B8.

34. Micheline Maynard, "Ford Follows GM's Lead into Coupon Competition," *USA Today,* 24 April 1998, B1.

35. John Philip Jones, "The Double Jeopardy of Sales Promotions," *Harvard Business Review,* September–October 1990, 145–52; Laurie Petersen, "The Pavlovian Syndrome," *Adweek's Marketing Week,* 9 April 1990, P6–P7; "Coupons—Still the Shopper's Best Friend," *Progressive Grocer,* February 1995, SS11.

36. William M. Bulkeley, "Rebates' Secret Appeal to Manufacturers: Few Customers Actually Redeem Them," *Wall Street Journal,* 10 February 1998, B1, B8.

37. Lisa Z. Eccles, "Point of Purchase Advertising," *Advertising Age Supplement,* 26 September 1994, 1–6.

38. "Effective Sampling Strategies," *Sales Marketing Network* [accessed 7 November 2000] www.info-now.com/html/1022dir1.asp.

39. Mark Kleinman, "Olympics Beats Sponsor Goal By 50%," *Marketing,* 7 September 2000, 1.

40. Bob Tedeschi, "Running a Joint Promotion with Yahoo, Pepsi is in the Internet Generation," *New York Times,* 3 April 2000, C11.

41. Betsy Morris, "The Brand's the Thing," *Fortune,* 4 March 1996, 72–86.

42. Kate Bertrand, "Trade Shows Can Be Global Gateways," *Advertising Age's Business Marketing,* March 1995, 19–20; "Trade Shows: An Alternative Method of Selling," *Small Business Reports,* January 1985, 67.

43. Paul Holmes, "Public Relations," *Adweek's Marketing Week,* 11 September 1989, 234–35.

44. Kathryn Kranhold and Stephen Power, "Bridgestone Turns to Ketchum to Redo Image After Tire Recall," *Wall Street Journal,* 12 September 2000, A4.

45. Verne Gay, "Milk, the Magazine," *American Demographics,* February 2000, 32–33.

46. Armstrong and Kotler, *Marketing: An Introduction,* 405.

47. Wendy Zellner, "Southwest's New Direction," *Business Week,* 8 February 1999, 58–59; Jennifer Lawrence, "Integrated Mix Makes

Expansion Fly," *Advertising Age—Special Integrated Marketing Report,* 4 November 1993, S10–S12.

48. Janet Smith, "Integrated Marketing," *American Demographics,* November 1995, 62.

49. Mark Maremont, "How Gillette Brought Its Mach3 to Market," *Wall Street Journal,* 15 April 1998, B1, B4; Jeremy Kahn, "Gillette Loses Face," *Fortune,* 8 November 1999, 147–48.

50. David J. Morrow, "From Lab to Patient, by Way of Your Den," *New York Times,* 7 June 1998, sec. 3, 1, 10.

## CHAPTER 16

1. Arthur Schatzman, co-owner, Dental Limited, personal communication, December 2000.

2. Elizabeth MacDonald, "U.S. Accounting Board Faults Global Rules," *Wall Street Journal,* 18 October 1999, A1.

3. Jeffrey E. Garten, "Global Accounting Rules? Not So Fast," *Business Week,* 5 April 1999, 26; MacDonald, "U.S. Accounting Board Faults Global Rules."

4. John Von Brachel, "AICPA Chairman Lays the Foundation for the Future," *Journal of Accountancy,* November 1995, 64–67.

5. Tom Kennedy Smith, "The Changing Face of Accounting Services," Corporate Report—Minnesota, 1 August 1996, 61.

6. Melody Petersen, "Shortage of Accounting Students Raises Concern on Audit Quality," *New York Times,* 19 February 1999, C1, C3.

7. Richard Melcher, "Where Are the Accountants?" *Business Week,* 5 October 1998, 144–46.

8. Jennifer Reingold and Richard A. Melcher, "Then There Were Four," *Business Week,* 3 November 1997, 37; Sallie L. Gaines, "KPMG and Ernst Call Off Merger," *Chicago Tribune,* 14 February 1998, B1,B3.

9. Ralph Saul, "Keeping the Watchdog Healthy," *Financial Executive,* November–December 1995, 10–13; Melcher, "Where Are the Accountants?"

10. Daniel McGinn, "Sherlocks of Finance," *Newsweek,* 24 August 1998, 38–39.

11. Robert Stuart, "Accountants in Management—A Globally Changing Role," *CMA Magazine,* 1 February 1997, 5.

12. Jack L. Smith, Robert M. Keith, and William L. Stephens, *Accounting Principles,* 4th ed. (New York: McGraw-Hill, 1993), 16–17.

13. Stanley Zarowin, "The Future of Finance," *Journal of Accountancy,* August 1995, 47–49.

14. Frank Evans, "A Road Map to Your Financial Report," *Management Review,* October 1993, 39–47.

## CHAPTER 17

1. "Intuit, Metiom Plan Internet Marketplace for Small Businesses," *Wall Street Journal,* 11 September 2000, B8; Khanh T. L. Tran, "Intuit Beats Estimate for Quarter," *Wall Street Journal,* 24 May 2000, B6; Orla O'Sullivan, "Intuit's Opening Portals," *USBanker,* January 2000, 26; Glenn Coleman, "The Battle for Your Money," *Money,* December 1999, 134–40; Kathleen Murphy, "He Wants You to Pay Your Bills on the Web: An Interview with Intuit CEO Bill Harris," *Internet World,* 15 August 1999, 22–26; Tim McCollum, "End Your Internet Anxieties Now," *Nation's Business,* April 1999, 18–22; Steve Klinkerman, "The Perils of Progress," *Banking Strategies,* March–April 1999, 20–26; David Diamond, "Can Intuit Remake Itself on the Net?" *Upside,* September 1998, 96–100; Steve Hamm, "This Intuit Hunch May Pay Off," *Business Week,* 15 June 1998, 123; Edward W. Desmond, "Intuit Online," *Fortune,* 13 April 1998, 149–52; Eryn Brown, "Is Intuit Headed for a Meltdown?" *Fortune,* 18 August 1997, 200–202.

2. David H. Bangs Jr., "Financial Troubleshooting," *Soundview Executive Book Summaries* 15, no. 5 (May 1993).

3. Dean Foust, "The Check is in the E-Mail," *Business Week,* 30 October 2000, 120–22.

4. Bruce Horovitz and Chris Woodyard, "Quaker Oats' $1.4 Billion Washout," *USA Today,* 28 March 1997.

5. Mandy Andress, "Smart Is Not Enough: Cards Must Also Be Easy and Useful," *InfoWorld,* 16 October 2000, 94; Mary Shacklett, "American Express' Blue is Setting the Pace in U.S. Smart Card Market," *Credit Union Magazine,* September 2000, 16A–17A.

6. Beth Kwon, "Need Stamps, Stocks, Plane Tickets? Step Up to an ATM," *Newsweek,* 25 January 1999, 15; Kara K. Choquette, "Super ATMs Sell Lift Tickets, Exchange Currencies," *USA Today,* 19 January 1998, B1; Connie Guglielmo, "Here Come the Super-ATMs," *Fortune,* 14 October 1996, 232–34.

7. Thomas McCarroll, "No Checks. No Cash. No Fuss?" *Time,* 9 May 1994, 60–61.

8. Scott Woolley, "Virtual Banker," *Forbes,* 15 June 1998 [accessed 28 July 1999] www.forbes.com/forbes/98/0615/6112127a.htm; Dean Foust, "Will Online Banking Replace the ATM?" Yahoo! Internet Life, November 1998, 114–18.

9. "FDIC Statistics on Banking: Number of FDIC-Insured Commercial Banks, 1934 Through 1999," FDIC Databank [accessed 12 December 2000] www2.fdic.gov/hsob/SelectRpt.asp?EntryTyp510.

10. Stephan Labaton, "Accord Reached on Lifting Depression-Era Barriers Among Financial Industries," *New York Times,* 23 October 1999, A1, B4.

11. Patrick McGeehan, "Merrill Lynch Is Set to Move into Banking," *New York Times,* 26 January 2000, C1, C6.

12. Leah Nathans Spiro, "The Coca-Cola of Personal Finance," *Business Week,* 20 April 1998, 37–38; Joseph Nocera, "E-Banking Is Necessary—Banks Are Not," *Fortune,* 11 May 1998, 84–85; Glenn Coleman, "The Battle for Your Money," *Money,* December 1999, 134–40; Lorrie Grant, "Retail King Gets Thrifty Idea," *USA Today,* 30 June 1999, B1.

13. Sharon Nelton, "You Can Bank on the Personal Touch," *Nation's Business,* June 1999, 49–51.

14. "Important Banking Legislation," FDIC [accessed 28 July 1999] www.fdic.gov/publish/banklaws.html; "Interstate Branching," The Federal Reserve Board [accessed 23 July 1999] www.bog.frb.fed.us/generalinfo/isb.

15. Robert A. Rosenblatt, "Border Crossing," *Los Angeles Times,* 5 June 1994, D1, D4.

16. Jeffrey E. Garten, "The Fed Should Look Farther Than Its Own Backyard," *Business Week,* 31 August 1998, 18.

17. Laura Cohn, "Are T-Bills Y2K Insurance?" *Business Week,* 26 July 1999, 34.

## CHAPTER 18

1. Mike Hoffman, "Let's Get Physical," *Inc.,* 17 October 2000, 168–169; Louise Lee, "Tricks of E*Trade," *Business Week E.Biz,* 7 February 2000, EB18–EB31; Louise Lee, "Not Just Clicks Anymore," *Business Week,* 28 August 2000, 226–227; "The Story of E*Trade," E*Trade [accessed 28 April 1999] www.etrade.com; "More Secure Securities," E*Trade [accessed 28 April 1999] www.etrade.com; Kathleen Ohlson, "E*Trade Revenue Soars, Losses Continue," *Computerworld,* 20 April 1999 [accessed 28 April 1999] www. computerworld.com/home/news.nsf/all/9904202etrade; Saul Hansell, "Trading on E*Trade's Success," *New York Times,* 16 March 1999, C1, C11; Leah Nathans Spiro, "Will E*Trade Move Beyond E*Tragedy?" *Business Week,* 22 February 1999, 118; Sharon Machlis, "Glitch Snuffs Out Online Broker for Hours," *Computerworld,* 4 February 1999 [accessed 28 April 1999]

www.computerworld.com/home/news.nsf/ all/9902044etrade; Kimberly Weisul, "E*Trade Snafu Results in $4 Million Earnings Hit," *Investment Dealer's Digest,* 14 July 1997, 6–7; "E*Trade Solidifies Industry Leadership by Adding over 1,000,000 Net New Active Accounts in 12 months," E*Trade, 13 October 1999 [accessed 10 December 1999] www.etrade.com; Paul Beckett, "E*Trade Cases Net in Search of Alliances," *Wall Street Journal,* 20 March 2000, C1, C2.

2. "An Investor's Guide to Corporate Bonds: How Big Is the Market and Who Buys?" Bond Market Association [accessed 27 July 1999] www.investinginbonds.com/info/igcorp/big.htm.

3. David Rynecki, "CBOT Gazes into the Pit," *Fortune,* 15 May 2000, 279–94.

4. Harvey Shapiro, "You Gotta Have a Style," *Hemispheres,* July 1997, 53–55.

5. Martin L. Leibowitz and Stanley Kogelman, "Asset Allocation Under Shortfall Constraints," *Journal of Portfolio Management,* Winter 1991, 18–23.

6. Neil Weinberg, "The Big Board Comes Back from the Brink," *Forbes,* 13 November 2000, 274–81; New York Stock Exchange Web site [accessed 21 December 2000] www.nyse.com.

7. NASDAQ Web Site [accessed 20 December 2000] www. marketdata.nasdaq.com/asp/Sec1Summary.asp.

8. James K. Glassman, "Manager's Journal: Who Needs Stock Exchanges? Not Investors," *Wall Street Journal,* 8 May 2000, A42.

9. NASDAQ Web site [accessed 21 December 2000] www.nas-daq.com/about/nnm1.stm; American Stock Exchange Web site [accessed 21 December 2000] www.amex.com/about/amex_listus. stm; New York Stock Exchange Web site [accessed 21 December 2000] www.nyse.com/listed/listedr.html.

10. Greg Ip, "Big Board Overhauls Its Standards," *Wall Street Journal,* 5 June 1998, C1, C16.

11. Julie Bort, "Trading Places," *Computerworld,* 27 May 1996, 1051.

12. Fred Vogelstein, "A Virtual Stock Market," *U.S. News & World Report,* 26 April, 1999, 47–48.

13. Weinberg, "The Big Board Comes Back from the Brink."

14. Diana B. Henriques, "Stock Markets, Facing Threats, Pursue Changes," *New York Times on the Web,* 6 March 1999 [accessed 7 March 1999] www.nytimes.com/library/financial/030799market-changes.htm.

15. Mike McNamee and Paula Dwyer, "A Revolt at NASD?" *Business Week,* 2 August 1999, 70–71.

16. Weinberg, "The Big Board Comes Back from the Brink."

17. Michael Schroeder and Randall Smith, "Sweeping Change in Market Structure Sought," *Wall Street Journal,* 29 February 2000, C1.

18. Rynecki, "CBOT Gazes into the Pit."

19. David Barboza, "In Chicago's Trading Pits, This May Be the Final Generation," *New York Times,* 6 August 2000, sec. 3, 1, 12.

20. Lee Copeland, "After-Hours Trading," *Computerworld,* 27 March 2000, 57.

21. Copeland, "After-Hours Trading."

22. Rebecca Buckman, "Making the Trade: What Now?" *Wall Street Journal Online Investing,* 14 June 1999, R6.

23. Leah Nathans Spiro, "Bullish on the Internet," *Business Week,* 14 June 1999, 45–46.

24. Nanette Byrnes, "How Schwab Grabbed the Lion's Share," *Business Week,* 28 June 1998, 88.

25. John R. Dorfman, "Crash Courses," *Wall Street Journal,* 28 May 1996, R12–R13.

26. Katrina Brooker, "Could the Dow Become Extinct?" *Fortune,* 15 February 1999, 194–95; Anita Raghavan and Nancy Ann Jeffrey,

"What, How, Why—So What Is the Dow Jones Industrial Average, Anyway?" *Wall Street Journal,* 28 May 1996, R30; E. S. Browning, "New Economy Stocks Join Industrials," *Wall Street Journal,* 27 October 1999, C1, C15.

27. Jeffrey M. Laderman, "Why It's So Tough to Beat the S&P," *Business Week,* 24 March 1997, 82–83.

28. E. S. Browning, "Journal Goes 'Decimal' With Nasdaq Tables," *Wall Street Journal,* 2 August 2000, C1; "SEC Orders Decimal Stock Prices," *Chicago Tribune,* 29 January 2000, sec. 2, 2.

29. David Diamond, "The Web's Most Wanted," *Business 2.0,* August 1999, 120–28.

30. Thor Valdmanis and Tom Lowry, "Wall Street's New Breed Revives Inside Trading," *USA Today,* 4 November 1999, 1B.

31. Joseph Nocera, "No Whispering Allowed," *Money,* December 2000, 71–74; Heather Timmons, "The Full Disclosure Rule Could Mean More Secrets," *Business Week,* 9 October 2000, 198; Lee Clifford, "The SEC Wants to Open the Info Vault," *Fortune,* 13 November 2000, 434.

32. Amy Feldman, "The Seedy World of Online Stock Scams," *Money,* February 2000, 143–48.

33. Feldman, "The Seedy World of Online Stock Scams"; Aaron Lucchetti, "Some Web Sites Getting Tough on Stock Chat," *Wall Street Journal,* 28 May 1999, C1, C20; Rebecca Buckman, "NASD Maps War on Claims on Internet," *Wall Street Journal,* 24 March 1997, B98W.

## ILLUSTRATION AND TEXT CREDITS

### CHAPTER 1

**4** Exhibit 1.1, U.S. Department of Commerce, Bureau of Economic Analysis [accessed 24 September 1999], beadata.bea.doc.gov/bea/ dn2/gpoc.htm.

**5** Exhibit 1.2, Noshua Watson, "Scarce Labor: Then and Now," *Fortune,* 15 May 2000, 496.

**7** Exhibit 1.3, Adapted from Christopher Caggiano, "Will the Real Bootstrappers Please Stand Up?" *Inc.,* August 1995, 34; Mike Hofman, "Capitalism—A Bootstrappers' Hall of Fame," *Inc.,* August 1997, 54–57; 1999 Amazon.com Annual Report, Amazon Web site-Investor Relations [accessed 10 June 2000], www.amazon.com.

**10** Exhibit 1.4, Adapted from Chris Woodyard, "Firms Stretch Travel Dollars," USA Today, 16 March 1999, sec. B, 1–2. Ted Bridis and John R. Wilke, "Judge Orders Microsoft Broken in Two, Imposes Tough Restrictions on Practices," *Wall Street Journal,* 8 June 2000, A3, A12.

**14** Exhibit 1.6, Adapted from Budget of the United States Government Fiscal Year 2001, w3.access.gpo.gov/usbudget /index.html [accessed 21 April 2000].

**14** Exhibit 1.7, Adapted from Roger LeRoy Miller, *Economics Today and Tomorrow* (New York: McGraw-Hill, 1999), 354.

**17** Exhibit 1.8, Adapted from "100 Years of Innovation," *Business Week,* Summer 1999, 8+; Richard B. Brewer, "Is Biotech the Next High Tech?" *Forbes ASAP,* 31 May 1999, 60–62; *Inc. 20th Anniversary Issue,* 1999, 42–66; *Wall Street Journal Small Business,* 24 May 1999, R1–R30; Mark Borden, "Thinking About Tomorrow," *Fortune,* 22 November 1999, 170+.

### CHAPTER 2

**25** Exhibit 2.1, Adapted from Manuel G. Velasquez, *Business Ethics: Concepts and Cases* (Upper Saddle River, N.J.: Prentice Hall, 1998), 87; Joseph L. Badaracco, Jr., "Business Ethics: Four Spheres of Executive Responsibility," *California Management*

*Review,* Spring 1992, 64–79; Kenneth Blanchard and Norman Vincent Peale, *The Power of Ethical Management* (Reprint, 1989; New York: Fawcett Crest, 1991), 7–17; John R. Boatright, *Ethics and the Conduct of Business* (Upper Saddle River, N.J.: Prentice Hall, 1996), 35–39, 59–64, 79–86.

**26** Exhibit 2.2, Adapted from *The Institute of Electrical and Electronics Engineers,* [accessed 21 July 1999], ieeeusa.org/documents/career/career_library/ethics.html.

**30** Exhibit 2.3, Weld Royal, "Real Expectations," *Industry Week,* 4 September 2000, 32.

**37** Exhibit 2.5, Workplace Killers, USA Snapshot, *USA Today,* 28 September 1999, B1.

## CHAPTER 3

**44** Exhibit 3.1, "Going Global Has Its Barriers," *USA Today,* 3 May 2000, B1.

**47** Exhibit 3.2, Brian Zajac, "Spanning the World," *Forbes,* 26 July 1999, 202–206.

**49** Exhibit 3.3, adapted from U.S. Bureau of Economic Analysis Web site: Table 2—U.S. Trade in Goods, [accessed 15 May 2000], http://www.bea.doc.gov/bea/di/bopq/bop2-4.htm; Table 3—Private Service Transactions, [accessed 15 May 2000].

**50** Exhibit 3.4, James Cox, "Tariffs Shield Some U.S. Products," *USA Today,* 6 May 1999, 1B [graph source is Grant Jerding, *USA Today*].

## CHAPTER 4

**61** Exhibit 4.1, Small Business Answer Card 1998, Small Business Administration, Office of Advocacy, SBA Web site, [accessed 5 June 2000], www.sba.gov/ADVO/stats/answer.pdf.

**63** Exhibit 4.2, Adapted from Carrie Dolan, "Entrepreneurs Often Fail as Managers," *Wall Street Journal,* 15 May 1989, B1. Reprinted by permission of *The Wall Street Journal* © 1989 Dow Jones & Company, Inc. All rights reserved worldwide.

**65** Exhibit 4.3, Anne R. Carey and Grant Jerding, USA Snapshot, *USA Today,* 26 March 1998, B1.

**66** Exhibit 4.4, Adapted from Carol Lawson, "Life's Miraculous Transmissions," *New York Times,* 6 June 1996, B3; Nancy Rotenier, "La Tempesta," *Forbes,* 18 December 1995, 134–35; Anne Murphy, "Entrepreneur of the Year," *Inc.,* December 1995, 38–51; Christina F. Watts and Loyde Gite, "Emerging Entrepreneurs," *Black Enterprise,* November 1995, 100–110; Marc Ballon, "Pretzel Queen," *Forbes,* 13 March 1995, 112–13; Robert La Franco, "Beach Bum Makes Good," *Forbes,* 19 June 1995, 80–82; Carla Goodman, "Medical Garb With a Smile," *Nation's Business,* May 1999, 65–67.

**68** Exhibit 4.5, Adapted from Norman M. Scarborough and Thomas W. Zimmerer, *Effective Small Business Management,* (Upper Saddle River, N.J: Prentice Hall, 2000), 8–13.

**72** Exhibit 4.8, Adapted from Norman M. Scarborough and Thomas W. Zimmerer, *Effective Small Business Management* (Upper Saddle River, N.J.: Prentice Hall, 2000), 27–29.

## CHAPTER 5

**82** Exhibit 5.1, Adapted with the permission of Simon & Schuster, Inc. from the Macmillan college text, *The Legal Environment of Business,* 2nd ed., by Charles R. McGuire. Copyright © 1986, 1989 by Merrill Pubishing, an imprint of Macmillan College Publishing Company, Inc., 216.

**83** Exhibit 5.2, Adapted from "Business Enterprise," *Statistical Abstract of the United States, 1999,* 545.

## CHAPTER 6

**99** Exhibit 6.3, Adapted from Dell Computer homepage [accessed 15 June 1999] www.dell.com/corporate/vision/mission.htm.

**105** Exhibit 6.5, Adapted from and reprinted by permission of *Harvard Business Review,* an exhibit from "How to Choose a Leadership Pattern" by Robert Tannenbaum and Warren H. Schmidt, May–June 1973. Copyright © 1973 by the President and Fellows of Harvard College, all rights reserved.

**108** Exhibit 6.7, Adapted from Courtland Bovée et al. *Management* (New York: McGraw-Hill, 1993) 678.

**112** Exhibit 6.8, Stuart Crainer, "The 75 Greatest Management Decisions Ever Made," *Management Review,* November 1998, 17–23.

## CHAPTER 7

**122** Exhibit 7.4, Adapted from Steven Burke, "Acer Restructures into Six Divisions," *Computer Reseller News,* 13 July 1998, 10.

**128** Exhibit 7.6, Exhibit from *Management, Fourth Edition,* by Richard L. Daft, copyright © 1977 by Harcourt Inc., reproduced by permission of the publisher.

## CHAPTER 8

**144** Exhibit 8.6, Adapted from James A. O'Brian, *Introduction to Information Systems,* 7th ed. (Burr Ridge, Ill.: Irwin, 1994), 25.

**152** Exhibit 8.9, Adapted from Larry Long and Nancy Long, *Introduction to Computers and Information* Systems, 5th ed. (Upper Saddle River, N.J.: Prentice Hall, 1997), CORE 165–168.

**155** Exhibit 8.10, John Galvin, "Cheating, Lying, Stealing," *SmartBusinessMag.Com,* June 2000, 86–99.

## CHAPTER 9

**160** Exhibit 9.2, Adapted from Mark M. Davis, Nicholas J. Aquilano, and Richard B. Chase, *Fundamentals of Operations Management* (Boston: Irwin McGraw-Hill, 1999), 7.

**165** Exhibit 9.4, Adapted from Courtland L. Bovee, et al., *Management* (New York: McGraw-Hill, 1993), 648; Roberta S. Russell and Bernard W. Taylor III, *Operations Management: Focusing on Quality and Competitiveness,* 2d ed. (Upper Saddle River, N.J.: Prentice Hall, 1998), 294.

**166** Exhibit 9.5, Adapted from Gerald H. Graham, *The World of Business* (Reading, Mass.: Addison-Wesley, 1985), 1999.

**172** Exhibit 9.7, Adapted from National Institute of Standards and Technology, *National Quality Program, Award Criteria,* http://nist.gov/public_affairs/guide/qpage.htm [accessed 11 February 1998].

## CHAPTER 10

**183** Exhibit 10.3, Adapted from *Management,* 4th ed. by Richard L. Daft, copyright © 1997 by Harcourt Inc., reproduced by permission of the publisher.

**183** Exhibit 10.4, Douglas McGregor, *The Human Side of Enterprise* (New York: McGraw-Hill, 1960).

**192** Exhibit 10.5, From *USA Today* Snapshot, "9-to-5 Not for Everyone," *USA Today,* 13 October 1999, B1.

## CHAPTER 11

**205** Exhibit 11.4, USA Today Snapshot "Checking Out New Hires," *USA Today,* 18 May 2000, B1.

**213** Exhibit 11.6, USA Today Snapshot "Life Is Not Shabby at the Top," *USA Today,* 12 July 1999, B1.

## CHAPTER 12

**220** Exhibit 12.1, Gary Armstrong and Philip Kotler, *Marketing an Introduction,* 5th ed. (Upper Sadle River, N.J.: Prentice Hall, 2000), 5 (Figure 1.1—Core marketing concepts).

**222** Exhibit 12.3, Gary Armstrong and Philip Kotler, *Marketing an Introduction,* 5th ed. (Upper Saddle River, N.J.: Prentice Hall, 2000), 19.

**223** Exhibit 12.4, Adapted from Mary J. Cronin, *Doing More Business on the Internet* (New York: Van Nostrand Reinhold, 1995), 61.

**225** Exhibit 12.5, Joan O. Fredericks and James M. Salter, "Beyond Customer Satisfaction," *Management Review,* May 1995, 29.

**235** Exhibit 12.9, Gary Armstrong and Philip Kotler, *Marketing an Introduction,* 5th ed. (Upper Saddle River, N.J.: Prentice Hall, 2000), 201.

## CHAPTER 13

**242** Exhibit 13.1, Courtland Bovee, Michael Houston, and John V. Thill, *Marketing,* Second Edition (New York: McGraw-Hill, 1994), p. 240.

**243** Exhibit 13.2, Adapted from Charles D. Schewe, *Marketing Principles and Strategies* (New York: McGraw-Hill, 1987).

**247** Exhibit 13.4, Adapted from Charles D. Schewe, *Marketing Principles and Strategies* (New York: McGraw-Hill, 1987).

## CHAPTER 14

**260** Exhibit 14.1, Adapted from Philip Kotler, *Marketing Management,* 10th ed. (Upper Saddle River, N.J.: Prentice Hall, 2000), 491.

**264** Exhibit 14.3, Gary Armstrong and Philip Kotler, *Marketing an Introduction,* 5th ed. (Upper Saddle River, N.J.: Prentice Hall, 2000), 335.

**265** Exhibit 14.4, Adapted from Charles D. Schewe, *Marketing Principles and Strategies* (New York: McGraw-Hill, 1987), 294. Reprinted by permission of the publisher.

**271** Exhibit 14.6, USA Today Snapshot "What Lures Online Shoppers?" *USA Today,* 23 November 1999, B1.

## CHAPTER 15

**283** Exhibit 15.2, Adapted from Courtland L. Bovée and John V. Thill, *Marketing* (New York: McGraw-Hill, 1992), 590.

**288** Exhibit 15.3, "Leading National Advertisers," *Advertising Age,* 25 September 2000, S4.

**296** Exhibit 15.7, Adapted from O.C. Ferrell and Geoffrey Hirt, *Business in a Changing World,* 3d ed. (Boston, Mass., Irwin McGraw-Hill), 2000), 346.

## CHAPTER 16

**303** Exhibit 16.1, Adapted from Joyce Thomas, "The Future—It Is Us," *Journal of Accountancy,* December 1998, 23.

**304** Exhibit 16.2, Adapted from Gary Siegel and Bud Kulesza, "The Practice of Management Accounting," *Management Accounting,* April 1996, 20; "Up the Ladder of Success," *Journal of Accountancy,* November 2000, 24.

## CHAPTER 17

**328** Exhibit 17.5, Scott Woolley, "Virtual Banker," *Forbes,* 15 June 1998 [accessed 28 July 1999] http://www.forbes.com/forbes/98/0615/6112127a.htm; "Why Banks Don't Want to See You," *USA Today,* 17 February 1998, B1.

**331** Exhibit 17.6, "Money Stock and Debt Measures," Federal Reserve Release, 29 July 1999 [accessed 3 August 1999] http://www.bog.frb.fed.us/releases/H6/.

**333** Exhibit 17.8, Adapted from *Statistical Abstract of the United States* (Washington, D.C.: GPO, 1999), 521.

## CHAPTER 18

**346** Exhibit 18.3, Fred Vogelstein, "A Virtual Stock Market," *U.S. News and World Report,* 26 April 1999, 47–48; Exhibit is on page 48—Robert Kemp USN&WR.

**352** Exhibit 18.7, "How to Read the Monthly Performance Tables," *Wall Street Journal,* 5 June 2000, R2.

**353** Exhibit 18.8, Richard Korman, "Mining for Nuggets of Financial Data," *New York Times,* 21 June 1998, BU5.

**354** Exhibit 18.9, Amy Feldman, "The Seedy World of Online Stock Scams," *Money,* February 2000, 143–48.

## Chapter 10

page 178: SAS Institute, Inc.; page 187: Brian Coats Photography; page 194: Donna McWilliam/AP/Wide World Photos.

## Chapter 11

page 200: Amy C. Etra/PhotoEdit; page 207: Joseph Raymond.

## Chapter 12

page 218: LWA-Dann Tardif/Corbis/Stock Market.

## Chapter 13

page 240: Lynsey Addario/AP/Wide World Photos; page 246: Kyoko Hamada; page 249: David Kampfner/Liaison Agency, Inc.

## Chapter 14

page 258: Robert Holmgren Photography; page 269: Michael Newman/PhotoEdit; page 274: David Burnett/Contact Press Images Inc.

## Chapter 15

page 278: Bill Cramer Photography; page 282: Robin Nelson/Black Star; page 286: Karen Leitza/Karin Leitza.

## Chapter 16

page 300: Janice B. Terry Photography.

## Chapter 17

page 318: Robert Holmgren Photography; page 322: Robbie McClaran/Corbis/SABA Press Photos, Inc.

## Chapter 18

page 336: Ann Dowie/*New York Times* Pictures; page 340: BellSouth Corporation.